Proceedings of the
Sixth European Conference on
Computer Supported Cooperative Work

ECSCW '99

Proceedings of the
Sixth European Conference on
Computer Supported Cooperative Work
12–16 September 1999, Copenhagen, Denmark

Edited by

Susanne Bødker
University of Aarhus, Denmark

Morten Kyng
The Danish National Centre for IT Research, Denmark

and

Kjeld Schmidt
Technical University of Denmark, Denmark

Cover Design by Jette Guldfeldt, Graphix

KLUWER ACADEMIC PUBLISHERS
DORDRECHT / BOSTON / LONDON

Library of Congress Cataloging-in-Publication Data

ISBN 0-7923-5947-X

Published by Kluwer Academic Publishers,
P.O. Box 17, 3300 AA Dordrecht, The Netherlands.

Sold and distributed in North, Central and South America
by Kluwer Academic Publishers,
101 Philip Drive, Norwell, MA 02061, U.S.A.

In all other countries, sold and distributed
by Kluwer Academic Publishers,
P.O. Box 322, 3300 AH Dordrecht, The Netherlands.

Printed on acid-free paper

Printed in the Netherlands.

Table of Contents

From the Editors

This volume represents the proceedings of ECSCW'99, the 6th European Conference on Computer Supported Cooperative Work. The conference marks the 10 years' anniversary of ECSCW, an international forum for research activities from various technical and social disciplines. The conference alternates with the ACM international conference on CSCW to provide annually a principal point of focus for CSCW research.

The program of technical papers presented here is the result of a difficult review process. This year the conference received 94 submissions of very high quality from which the 23 papers making up the technical programme were selected. Both the number of submissions and the quality and diversity of the programme presented here are testimony to the health of the CSCW community. We are sure that you will enjoy the papers in this volume.

The technical papers in this volume are only one aspect of a diverse and dynamic event such as ECSCW. The technical paper program is complemented by tutorials, workshops, demonstrations and posters reflecting some of the most exciting and novel aspects of CSCW. These activities are essential to the success of the conference and the continued growth of the community. This conference could not have taken place without considerable enthusiasm, support and encouragement as well as sheer hard work. Many people have earned the thanks of those who attended and organized ECSCW'99. In particular, we would like to gratefully thank:

- All those who submitted to the conference. The standard was very high and reflects well on the research work in the community.
- All of those who contributed to the conference through workshops, tutorials, posters, demos, and paper presentations.
- All of those who contributed to the organization of the conference. Planning a major international conference is a complex endeavor and many people made significant contributions to realizing a successful conference.
- The Student Volunteers who work so tirelessly during the conference to ensure things run smoothly.
- Those members of the Conference and Program Committees who gave so freely of their time and energy to ensure that the conference was both smoothly run and of high technical quality. The many individuals we owe our thanks to are listed elsewhere in this volume.
- The many sponsors and supporters of ECSCW'99 for their contributions to the conference and to the CSCW community generally. Many of these people have been involved with the ECSCW conferences since the first conference 10 years ago.

We would also like to acknowledge the organizers of the ACM CSCW conference for the support and encouragement they extend to this conference. The close cooperation between ECSCW and the ACM CSCW conferences allows us to continue the growth of a truly international research community tackling the problems core to CSCW. Between both conferences we have been able to establish an annual international conference on CSCW for the last decade charting the development and maturity of the discipline. These proceedings represent the start of the next decade of international CSCW research and the further development of our research community. The future appears to hold considerable promise for us all.

Susanne Bødker, Morten Kyng, and Kjeld Schmidt

ECSCW'99 Conference Committee

Conference co-chairs:
Susanne Bødker, University of Aarhus, Denmark
Kjeld Schmidt, Technical University of Denmark

Program chair: Morten Kyng, The Danish National Centre for IT Research, Denmark

Proceedings chair: Kjeld Schmidt, Technical University of Denmark

Tutorials chair: Jakob Bardram, University of Aarhus, Denmark

Workshop chair: Peter Carstensen, Technical University of Denmark

Demonstrations chair: Preben Mogensen, University of Aarhus, Denmark

Video chair: Keld Bødker, Roskilde University, Denmark

Posters chair: Kim Halskov Madsen, University of Aarhus, Denmark

Student volunteer chair: Olav Bertelsen, University of Aarhus, Denmark

Doctoral colloquium chair: Liam Bannon, University of Limerick, Ireland

Technical support: Peter Berg, The Danish National Centre for IT Research

Local coordinator: Morten Hertzum, Risø National Laboratory, Denmark

Local arrangements: Morten Nielsen, Risø National Laboratory, Denmark

Liaisons

North America liaison: Saul Greenberg, University of Calgary, Canada

Australia liaison: Geraldine Fitzpatrick, University of Queensland, Australia

Japan liaison: Hideaki Kuzuoka, University of Tsukuba, Japan

China liaison: ZongKai Lin, Chinese Academy of Sciences, P. R. China

ECSCW'99 Program Committee

S. Bødker, M. Kyng, and K. Schmidt (eds.). *Proceedings of the Sixth European Conference on Computer-Supported Cooperative Work, 12-16 September 1999, Copenhagen, Denmark*
©1999 Kluwer Academic Publishers. Printed in the Netherlands

Taking the Work out of Workflow: Mechanisms for Document-Centered Collaboration

Anthony LaMarca, W. Keith Edwards, Paul Dourish, John Lamping, Ian Smith and Jim Thornton

Xerox Palo Alto Research Center, USA
lamarca@parc.xerox.com

Abstract: There are two aspects to technical support for collaborative activity; support for content work and support for coordination. The design of CSCW systems must typically address both of these, combining them in a collaborative application. This approach, however, suffers from a variety of well-known problems, not least the compatibility between collaborative and single-user applications, working styles and practices. In this paper, we describe an alternative approach that makes coordination and collaborative functionality an aspect of the collaborative artifact rather than a collaborative application. We present an infrastructure and a series of application examples to illustrate the idea of document-centered collaboration, in which coordination and collaboration are separated from and independent of applications.

Introduction

Most computer applications focus on the manipulation of content. They gather information from the user, record it, control access to it, organize it, act on it, and present it on demand. Content includes user-readable forms of information, such as is handled by a word processor, presentation package or software development environment, as well as internal machine-readable forms such as database records, index structures and object code formats.

Collaborative applications add a second concern to this focus on content: a concern with coordination. Schmidt and Bannon (1992) draw on the work of Anselm Strauss to argue that the central focus in CSCW is "articulation work"—the means by which people "divide, allocate, coordinate, schedule, mesh, interrelate, etc." their concerted activities.

Since CSCW systems must be able to deal with both content and coordination, a fundamental question for the development of CSCW technologies is the nature of the relationship between the two. It has been a troublesome one. Some CSCW applications have attempted to take on the entire problem single-handedly; this approach has led to the development of collaborative text editors, drawing tools, and so on. Other systems have focussed on the coordination aspects and left application development alone; this approach has led to the development of collaboration harnesses and run-time frameworks for transparent application sharing. Each of these approaches has problems, as we will discuss.

In this paper, we present a new approach to the relationship between the content and coordination facets of collaborative systems. In our approach, we focus on collaboration as a feature of the artifact rather than the application. In doing so, we free ourselves from a set of restrictions on the interoperability of content that come from an application focus. Our model adopts electronic documents as the primary means of content exchange. Electronic documents can be opened, read, manipulated, changed, clustered and sorted with a variety of familiar tools; but they also, critically, carry their semantics with them, rather than delegating them to an application.

Applications, Content, and Encodings

Applications manage content. They store, represent, render and manipulate content in a wide variety of formats.

Often, this content is encoded in application-specific ways, so that it can only be used or interpreted by specific applications imbued with the ability to understand the meaning of that particular encoding. The content types used by these applications may not be shareable with other applications, and indeed, they may not even be readily exposed to other applications at all. For example, a custom database application, such as an insurance claims processing tool, makes semantics assumptions about the validity of the information it will store and use. The data stored by this application will not be understandable by other applications. In fact, these other applications would likely be unable to even access the information, stored as it is in a custom database rather than a simple file.

In other words, applications contain encodings and representations of their content that are tailored to their specific needs, and the ability to interpret and manipulate these representations is encapsulated within the application itself. Although this approach is successful most of the time, it presents problem when we attempt to extend the functionality of the application into new areas.

Content and Coordination

On top of their concern with content, collaborative applications must also be concerned with support for the coordination of activities between individuals. A variety of mechanisms have been introduced to support coordination, such as the use of awareness within a shared workspace (Dourish and Bellotti, 1992) or the use of explicit representations of conversational action as a basis for managing patterns of interaction (Winograd and Flores, 1986). Support for coordination has been a primary research focus with CSCW. However, this has often been to the detriment of support for content in prototype collaborative tools; often, the latest research prototype shared text editor may well be shared, but isn't a very good text editor. The problem is how to combine application features—the interpretation and management of specialised content—with new features for collaboration and coordination.

There have been two common approaches to the relationship between content and coordination in shared applications. The first is to combine them in a single, monolithic application, in which the needs of collaboration can be fully integrated with the manipulation and presentation of content; the second is to use a collaboration harness to share single-user applications. Although the second approach has proved useful in specific scenarios, such as remote presentations, most deployed systems use the first approach.

Take a workflow application as an example. As discussed above, such an application will have an innate understanding both of the content and the process of the workflow. When a user updates one bit of content in the system—say, by digitally "signing" an expense request—the system notices this change in state and will move the process along to its next logical state. This change may involve displaying forms on other users' screens or in their work inboxes, removing documents from the queues of other participants, and so on. The workflow tool is able to do this because it is tightly integrated with the content it manages, can detect changes to that information (because changes come through the application itself), and can dynamically update the information on users' screens. The downside of this integration is that the workflow tool must take on all the responsibilities.

Document-Centered Collaboration

We have been exploring a new approach to the integration of content and coordination in collaborative systems. We call our approach *document-centered collaboration*. In our approach, we move coordination functionality out of the application and onto the documents themselves.

To achieve this, we exploit a novel document infrastructure which gives to *documents* the resources to maintain application integrity. As we will explain, in our infrastructure, all operations on a document, including reading, writing, moving, and deleting, can be observed by active code associated with the document. This active code can then take appropriate action, such as making notifications, performing the operation itself, or vetoing the operation. This ability to associate computation with content gives the ability to tightly bind application semantics in with the content that those semantics constrain. At the same time, by using active code to exploit knowledge about the external state of the world, documents can, in effect, become "situationally aware" and be responsive to changes in their use and in their users.

We believe that such a system can offer a novel approach to workflow, where the state of the workflow process is exposed as a set of documents that can be read, written, or operated on using standard, existing tools. Users need never directly see or use a workflow tool. Instead, computation attached to the documents enforces the coordination conventions of a workflow process, while still allowing the documents to be used in all the same ways as conventional electronic documents.

To enable the construction of these active documents, we have built a middleware layer that sits between ordinary applications and existing document repositories such as file systems. To general purpose applications, it can look like a file system, and to file systems, it can look like a general purpose application. The infrastructure can also maintain "extra" information about the documents that might not be provided by the underlying repository, and provides the ability to execute arbitrary code when documents are accessed. By sitting between files and the applications that use them, the infrastructure can add new capabilities to electronic documents, while allowing existing applications to continue to work with them.

We believe that this approach will have a number of tangible benefits. First, it does not force a choice between doing workflow and using a favorite set of document-based applications such as word processors and the like; workflow is brought to these applications, rather than creating standalone applications to do workflow. Coordination and the interpretation of content have been separated.

Second, we can still use all of the existing tools that are available for working with documents. Indeed, the ability to bind computation into document content can ensure that these general-purpose tools operate on our documents in semantically constrained ways that do not violate the requirements that workflow may place on them. Essentially, we enable the documents to be used in standard, general ways without corrupting workflow semantics; new, constrained functionality is layered on top of existing document functionality.

Third, for designers of workflow processes, we allow a rapid pace of development. A workflow process builder just has to write the pieces of computation that are attached to documents to implement the workflow process; not the surrounding tools and interfaces for mediating and visualizing the workflow process.

The work described here has been done in the context of the Placeless Documents Project at Xerox PARC (Dourish et al., 1999). Placeless Documents is an effort to build a "next generation" document management system that provides radical extensibility, as well as smooth integration with existing document repositories and tools. We shall describe the Placeless substrate on which our workflow experiments were founded, as well as investigate three separate collaborative applications we have built using our document-centered model.

Comparison with Existing Approaches

The relationship between content and coordination functionality is a fundamental issue in the design of CSCW systems. One approach has been to embed collaborative functionality in new tools. Users have been offered new sorts of drawing tools (e.g. Brinck and Hill, 1993), new sorts of spreadsheets (e.g. Palmer and Cormack, 1998), new sorts of presentation tools (e.g. Isaacs et al., 1994), etc., incorporating functionality for information sharing and collaboration. However, it has been regularly observed (e.g. Bullen and Bennett, 1990; Olson and Teasley, 1996) that the introduction of new tools for simple, everyday tasks has been a barrier to the introduction of collaborative tools. Even in the case of single-user systems, Johnson and Nardi (1996) attest to the inertia surrounding the adoption of new tools, even when the new applications are tailored to specific domain needs.

Another approach to this problem is the development of "collaboration-transparent" systems, and harnesses to make existing tools support collaborative functionality. Examples include Matrix (Jeffay et al., 1992), DistView (Prakash and Shim, 1994) and JAM (Begole et al., 1997) The collaboration transparent approach suffers from the problem that, since the applications are unchanged, their semantics cannot be revised to incorporate the needs and effects of collaborative use. However, it has the advantage that users can carry on using the tools with which they are familiar and in which they have an often significant investment.

Although collaboration transparency allows group members to carry on using existing single-user tools, another problem arises in that they may not all be using the *same* single-user tools. People use different incompatible software systems, and even incompatible versions of the same software system; and forcing people to upgrade their system to use your new collaborative system is no better than asking them to switch to a new word processor. What is more, if different group members like to use different word processors, then a collaboration-transparent approach will not be sufficient to let them work on a paper together.

Our approach is to focus not on *applications*, but on *artifacts*—in this case, documents. Our goal is to design a system in which one user can use Microsoft FrontPage on a PC, another can use Adobe PageMill on a Mac, while a third can uses Netscape Composer on a UNIX machine, and yet they can all three work seamlessly on the same web documents. We achieve collaboration by augmenting the documents themselves.

Coordination languages have been used to separate application functionality from that supporting collaboration, and so move coordination into the infrastructure Examples include Linda (Gelernter, 1985) in the domain of parallel systems and DCWPL (Cortes and Mishra, 1996) in the domain of collaborative ones. Our approach differs, though, in that our artifacts themselves take on an active role in managing coordination.

Perhaps the closest related approach is that of Olsen et al. (1998), who explore the use of collaboration and coordination through "surface representations." Like us, they want to move beyond the model in which each application encapsulates a fixed semantic interpretation of data that is kept separate from the actual document contents. Their approach is to abandon encoded semantics and, instead, to operate at the level of "human-consumable surface representations," or the simple perceptible graphical patterns in application displays. Our approach is similar in that we do not rely on semantics in the application, but different in that we move those semantics closer to the document itself rather than its representation.

Abbott and Sarin (1994) suggested that the next generation of workflow tools would be "simply another invisible capability that permeates all (or most) applications." By decoupling collaboration functionality from the application, and making it a middleware component, our approach has brought us closer to this model, as we will demonstrate.

We will begin by introducing the Placeless Documents system, a new infrastructure for document management which provides the basis for our approach. In the main body of the paper, we will introduce and illustrate the use of our approach by describing three example systems that have been built on top of Placeless Documents, and which serve to explain how the document-centered approach operates in practice. Finally, we will consider how this approach relates to current and potential future practice in the development of collaboration technologies.

The Placeless Documents Project

This section presents an overview of our system. We begin with a discussion of the basic facilities of the Placeless architecture, and look in particular at the mechanisms in Placeless that were necessary to build our document-centered view of workflow.

Overview of Placeless Documents

Traditional document management systems and filesystems present a hierarchical organization to their users: documents are contained in folders; folders can be nested within other folders. This structure, while easy to understand, is limiting. For example, should an Excel document for a project's budget be contained in the Excel folder, the budget folder, or the project's folder?

The goal of the Placeless Documents project is to build a more flexible system for organizing a document space. In the Placeless model, organization is based on *properties* that convey information about context of use: the document is a budget;

it's shared with my workgroup, and so on. Properties are *metadata* that can describe and annotate the document and can facilitate its use in various settings.

Active Properties

While many systems support the association of extensible metadata with files and documents, properties in Placeless can be *active* entities that can augment and extend the behavior of the documents they are attached to. That is, rather than being simple inert tags, extensionally used to describe *already-extant* states of the document, properties can also be live code fragments that can implement the user's *desired intentions* about the state of the document.

These active properties can affect the behavior of the document in multiple ways: they can add new operations to a document as well as govern how a document interacts with other documents and the document management system in which it exists. For example, in Placeless, active properties are used to implement access control, to handle reading and writing of document content from repositories (such properties are called "bit providers"), and to perform notifications of document changes to interested parties.

It is these active properties, particularly the bit providers, which provide the ability to associate computation with content. Since property code can perform arbitrary actions when it is invoked, properties can return results based on the context of their use, and the state of the document management system at the time they are invoked. Active properties are the heart of the Placeless Document System; we shall see how they are used to implement document-centered workflow in our particular examples.

Distribution and Compatibility

Placeless Documents was architected to be a robust distributed system. Our design allows users to access document collections across the network and, more importantly, to *serve* document collections where they see fit.

The attributes of the Placeless system described above—active properties and robust distribution—enable the construction of novel applications and document services. To be truly useful, however, the system must also work with *existing* document- and file-based applications. This is crucial to our desire to support workflow using arbitrary off-the-shelf applications. To this end, we architected a number of "shims" which map from existing document- and file-management interfaces and protocols into the concepts provided by Placeless. Examples of such shims might include file system interfaces, HTTP, FTP, IMAP and POP3 protocol interfaces, WebDAV, and so on. Existing applications "expect" to access files and electronic documents through these comment interfaces, and so Placeless provides these interfaces to its documents.

For example, we have built a Network File System (NFS) server layer atop Placeless. This layer lets existing applications—including such tools as Word and Powerpoint—which are only written to understand files, work with live Placeless documents. Existing applications do not have to change to work with Placeless, although there is a loss of power since many of the Placeless concepts do not find an easy expression in a more traditional file system model.

For the purposes of this paper, the Placeless infrastructure can be thought of as a middleware layer—essentially a multiplexor—capable of reusing or generating content from varied sources, creating a uniform notion of "documents" from that content, and then exposing the resulting documents via a multiplicity of interfaces. By exposing arbitrary entities as documents through the bit provider mechanism, and then making these documents widely available through arbitrary interfaces, we gain great leverage from existing tools and applications.

We have presented an architectural foundation that can allow computation to be tightly bound in with document content. The Placeless system can not only integrate existing sources of information from filesystems and web repositories, but can expose all of its documents through interfaces that make those documents accessible through existing applications. Now, we will present three experiments in workflow that we have built around the Placeless system. The systems described here provide a document-centered approach to workflow that allow their users to break away from closed, specialized applications, and bring the power of general-purpose computing tools to workflow processes.

A Simple Example: Travel Approval

The first and simplest of our applications is called *Maui* and manages a corporate travel approval process. The actual process description is simple: employees submit trip itineraries for approval, which requires consent from both the employee's manager and department head. It was our goal to allow employees to easily submit trip requests, check on trip status as well give managers an easy way to check for and access travel requests requiring their attention. The rest of this section describes how we implemented this in a document-centered style by building two new active properties on top of our flexible property-based document infrastructure.

User's View

In Maui, users can construct their itineraries any way they wish and are free to choose the application and document format of their choice. As an example a user might write a note in FrameMaker, or submit an Excel spreadsheet with detailed cost information, or simply scan in a paper copy of a conference invitation. This differs significantly from traditional workflow systems where relevant data must be manipulated with proprietary integrated tools.

To enter this new itinerary into the travel approval process, users open a standard document browser (like the Windows explorer) and drag the itinerary document onto the *trip status document*. The trip status document is special in that it serves as a central point of coordination for the approval process. Once an itinerary has been dragged onto the trip status document, the approval process in underway, and the employee's task is done, short of checking on the status of the trip. When a trip has been approved or denied by the relevant people, the employee is sent an email notification of the result.

As well as serving as a drop target for new trip itineraries, the trip status document contains content that summarizes the state of the user's travel plans. The content is in HTML format and contains a summary of all of the trips for which an employee has submitted requests (see Figure 1). In this way, an employee can run any application that understands HTML (such as Netscape, Word, or FrameMaker) and view this document to check on the status of their pending trips. The contents of the trip status document also help managers by giving them a list of the itineraries that require their attention. The trip status document serves as a nexus of coordination for those both taking trips and approving trips; and its content is dynamically updated as the states of the pending and processed travel approvals change.

The actual approval or denial of a trip is performed on the itinerary document itself. When a manager opens a travel itinerary that requires their vote they view the document as usual, but something else happens as well: they are presented with a Yes/No voting box, created by an active property, which allows them to decide to approve or deny the trip.

Note how the arrangement differs from classic workflow: users in our system never explicitly run any workflow software. In this case, a manager would open the document in whatever way they normally would to view or edit it, and the system augments their normal interaction to include access to the user interface components needed to drive the workflow process.

How It Works

Maui is made up of two new active properties. The first is the *StatusBitProvider*, which is attached to the trip status document. This property has two functions. First, it listens for drops of other documents and, when it receives them, starts those documents in the travel approval process. It does this by determining the user's manager and department head from organizational information stored in other documents that represent the users of the system (Edwards and LaMarca, 1999), and attaching copies of the second property, described below, to the dropped document. The dropped document becomes—in addition to whatever other roles it is performing—a trip request. Second, the StatusBitProvider serves up the HTML content which summarizes the state of the user's trips. This is

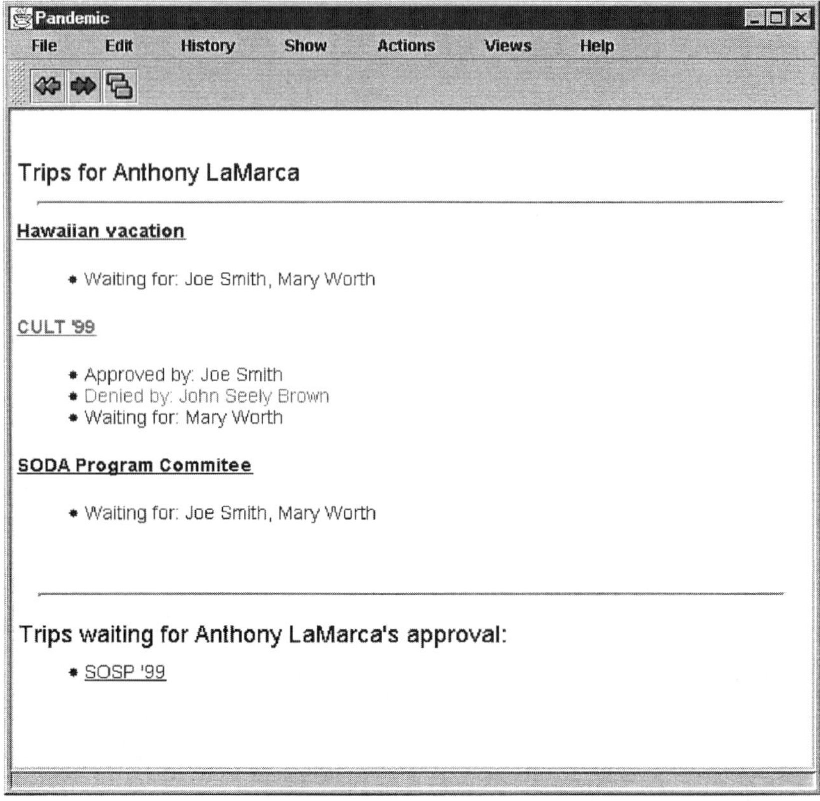

Figure 1: The Travel Status Document

largely a straightforward task of querying for travel documents and formatting the results in HTML; since the bit provider is invoked whenever content is required, it can dynamically generate new information based on the state of the world at the time it is invoked.

The second new property is the *Approve/DenyProperty*, which is what managers interact with when casting their votes on a trip. This property can determine if the user currently viewing the document it is attached to is a manager who's decision is needed for this particular travel request. When appropriate, the property can create and display a GUI component with a Yes/No button for voting. Clicking on one of these buttons will record the manager's vote on the document and send the employee notification if appropriate. Applications which are "Placeless-aware" can check for the existence of these components and display them alongside the document content. But the Approve/Deny property can also create a separate, stand-alone GUI control panel that would appear whenever a travel request is viewed by any application.

The knowledge and state of our travel approval process is distributed between these two properties. The status bit provider knows how to add and configure properties in order to turn an ordinary document into a pending itinerary, but does not understand how votes are applied. Any one instance of the Approve/Deny property knows about a single manager's vote, but knows nothing about how any other managers voted. In the next section we describe a more complex process, and we will see that the distribution of knowledge and state increases as more behaviors and users are included in the process.

Managing a Complex Process: Hiring Support

Here at our research lab we have a hiring process which involves a number of different steps and people. We chose to implement a hiring process application as our second document-centered workflow application as it potentially offers significant benefits to us and also tests our model of interaction.[1] As with the travel approval application, we have implemented this on top of Placeless Documents using properties to hold both the logic and state of the process; the collection of properties that comprise the hiring application is called *Carlos*.

The Hiring Process

An illustration of the hiring process in Carlos is shown in Figure 2. In this process, candidates submit their application in the form of a resume and a set of supporting documents such as articles and papers. Upon determining that the application is in order, reference letters are requested for the candidate. Once at least three letters have been received for the candidate, the materials are reviewed by the *screening committee*. It is the job of the screening committee to decide whether or not an interview should be scheduled. In Carlos, the screening committee can be of arbitrary size, but we designed our policy for a small group where every member votes. If an interview is approved, the candidate is contacted and a date is chosen for the interview through traditional administrative procedures. At this point, the candidate is brought in for the interview and the process moves into the general voting stage and all members of the lab are invited to submit a hiring proxy and vote on the candidate as described below. In Carlos, there are no rigid quantitative rules governing the number of votes that must be cast or what the rejection/acceptance thresholds are. Rather, votes and statistics accumulate for the review of the lab manager who makes the final hiring decision.

The User's View

In Carlos, users interact with a number of different document types throughout the hiring process. Some of these documents exist on a per-candidate basis and some

---

1. The process we describe is similar to, but not the same as the one we use in our lab. We have made changes to the process in order to both simplify and illustrate interesting things in the system.

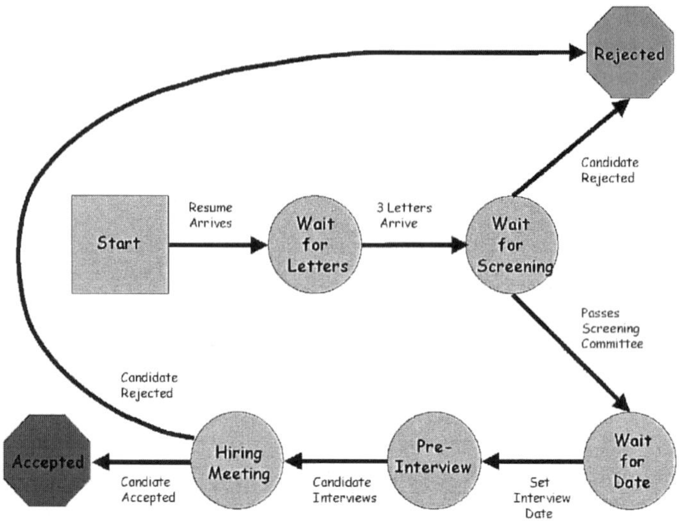

Figure 2: The Hiring Process

are shared. The most important shared document is the *hiring status* document which contains a live up-to-date summary of the status of all of the candidates in the system. A user, using any tool that understands HTML content, can open the status document and be apprised of where any candidate is in the process (See Figure 3). In this overview users can view candidate letters, jump to supporting documents, and see compilations of both screening and hiring votes that have been cast.

The status document also serves as the mechanism for adding new candidates to the system. A candidate can be entered into the hiring process by dragging a link to their resume onto the hiring status document. We again see the departure from traditional workflow: in Carlos resume documents can be composed in any application and can be saved in any format. This is especially useful in the hiring process where resumes and letters arrive in a number of different forms including PostScript, simple ASCII, and TIFF images from scanned paper documents.

Upon dragging a resume onto the status document, a new *candidate document* is created. This document serves three important functions. First, it contains HTML content that gives a detailed view of a candidate's status. The content is similar to that given in the hiring status document, but provides greater detail.

The candidate document also functions as the mechanism for adding reference letters and supporting documents for a candidate. When users drag documents onto a candidate document, they are presented with a choice of what type of document is being dropped (letter or supporting document); the system records their choice. Transitions between states in the hiring process take place automatically and user intervention is not required; upon dropping the third reference letter onto a candi-

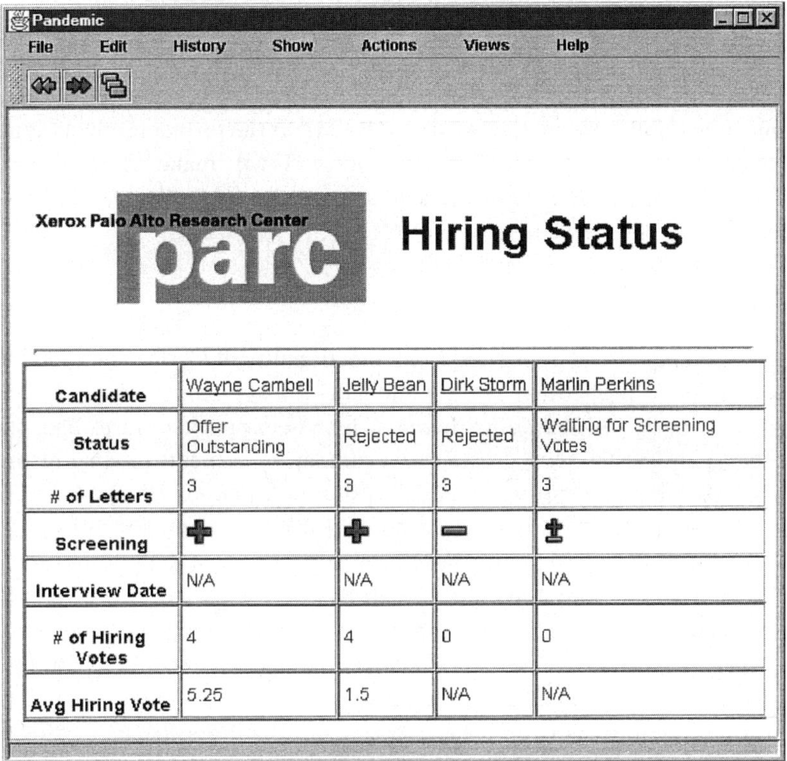

Candidate	Wayne Cambell	Jelly Bean	Dirk Storm	Marlin Perkins
Status	Offer Outstanding	Rejected	Rejected	Waiting for Screening Votes
# of Letters	3	3	3	3
Screening	+	+	—	±
Interview Date	N/A	N/A	N/A	N/A
# of Hiring Votes	4	4	0	0
Avg Hiring Vote	5.25	1.5	N/A	N/A

Figure 3: The Hiring Status Document

date, for instance, the candidate's status is automatically changed from "waiting for letters" to "requiring screening decision."

Finally, the candidate document is used to cast both screening and hiring votes in the system. In Carlos, a vote is not just a simple yes/no or a number. Rather, votes in our system have a quantitative portion plus a related document called the *proxy*. This gives users of our system considerably more flexibility to express what they are thinking and why they voted the way they did. To cast a vote for either screening or hiring, users compose their proxy however they desire and then drag this document onto the candidate. At this point, the user is presented with a small GUI to allow them to enter the quantitative portion of the vote. In the case of a screening vote, the quantitative portion is a simple yes or no, in the case of a hiring vote, candidates are judged on a scale from 1 to 7.

In our research lab, hiring votes are often cast in a number of ways. Roughly half the people in the lab attend a formal hiring meeting to discuss the candidate, some people send in email proxies, while others leave voice mail proxies. Due to its flexibility, our system can accommodate proxies in all of these forms. Email and voice mail are easy turned into documents and attached to the candidate document. Our digital video infrastructure makes it possible to record the entire hiring meeting and break it into different documents, each containing an individual's proxy.

Since Carlos is not a centralized application, but rather a set of coordinated properties, we make an effort to provide the user with as coherent an experience as possible. It is for this reason that we chose HTML as the format for the overall status and candidate documents. The hyperlinking in HTML makes it easy for users to smoothly move from the overall status to a single candidate's status and from there to one of the candidate's letters or proxies.

How It Works

Like our travel approval application, the functionality of Carlos is divided across a number of active properties. The functionality for the overall status document is provided by the *HiringStatusBitProvider* which both provides up-to-date status for all of the candidates and can create new candidate documents given a resume. The bulk of the logic for the hiring process lives in the *CandidateBitProvider*. Like the status bit provider, it knows how to produce HTML content describing the candidate's status. It also understands how to receive drops of supporting documents, reference letters and both screening and hiring votes. To do these things, it needs to understand the various states of the hiring process and how and when transitions take place. As an example, this property knows that if a candidate is in the "waiting for letters" state and has a third letter dropped on it, it should advance to the to "requiring screening decision" state. Finally, Carlos uses the *RelatedDocument-Property* which gives a document the ability to refer to another relevant document. Carlos adds this property to every supporting document, reference letter and proxy vote and configures it to point at the relevant candidate document. In this way, users can quickly jump across linked clusters of related documents.

Extending the Document Focus to Other Domains: Software Engineering

The final application we have built using our document-centered model is a tool to support the software development process, called *Shamus*. Software development, since it is such a fluid and often chaotic process, needs strong support from workflow tools. These tools try to provide clean task boundaries and separation of responsibilities that can enhance the software development process.

Software development *is* a collaborative process and has many of the same attributes of more "traditional" workflow processes: the task is shared by many people, all of whom have different, but perhaps overlapping, responsibilities for the result; the shared artifact (the code) moves from state to state as it progresses toward readiness.

One factor that complicates the software process greatly is the presence of multiple *versions* of the artifact—each developer may have his or her own copy of the software that differs from that of the others. This divergence is one of the things that distinguishes software development from more traditional workflow. In most workflow situations, there is *one* "version" of the artifact—either the travel is approved or it isn't; the candidate is being interviewed or not. The different participants in the workflow share what is a more-or-less fully consistent view of the state of the process. Contrast this to software where the developers have their own snapshots of the code state that may vary widely from one another.

We wanted to see if we could expand the reach of our document-centered model into the extremely fluid domain of software engineering. Our goals were two-fold. First, we wanted to support *awareness* of the overall state of the development process. Second, we wanted to support *automation* of the subtasks in the development process.

Providing a true and useful sense of awareness is typically a hard problem in collaborative development—I may know that you have a piece of code checked out, but I have no way of knowing at a finer granularity what you are doing with it, or even if you're actually changing it at all. Workflow systems are *designed* to provide awareness in the context of the task at hand: a manager is aware of the state of travel approvals in terms that "make sense" for the travel approval task, for example. Unfortunately, software engineers typically have only very coarse forms of machine-supported awareness available to them—only at the level of knowing who has an individual file checked out, for instance. We believed that we could support better facilities for fine-grained and task-focused awareness in our model.

We also wished to explore automation of the development process by embodying individual tasks as active properties attached to program content. These properties would serve to off-load some of the cumbersome chores of development, such as running tests, generating documentation, and ensuring that builds finish correctly.

Shamus provides a collection of properties to support the development process by enhancing awareness and automation. With its document-centered focus, it also brings with it the benefits that accrue in our other applications—the ability to use the tools at hand to operate on content, and the unification of disparate task models into a single document metaphor.

What Shamus Does

The Shamus "application" is actually a collection of properties attached to source code files. These properties control the behavior of the files, and ensure that they interact with one another to support the development process in a smooth way.

As mentioned, one of the common awareness problems in collaborative code development is knowing who is working in which source files. Typically the process of reconciling working versions is done when users "check in" the code to a centralized repository that represents the true view of the project.

Our desire was to lessen the potentially cumbersome and error-prone process of reconciling changes at check-in time by providing awareness of the changes others are making in the code base in real-time. The system shows details about where others are working in the code snapshots they have currently in use—regardless of whether this code has been checked in. The system also understands that users are working with program files and knows the basic structure of source code so it can provide awareness information in a way that is semantically meaningful for the task at hand. In our Java example, the system shows which methods in which classes have been changed by users. This form of awareness can allow users to know if they are working in a portion of the code that another user is—or has—worked in regardless of check-in status. The system doesn't prevent users from making overlapping changes—that is what the weightier check-in process is for—but it can provide information about what colleagues are doing.

Figure 4 shows an example of a Java source file being edited by a user. The display provides fine-grained information identifying areas that have been changed by other users, even though those changes may not have been checked in yet.

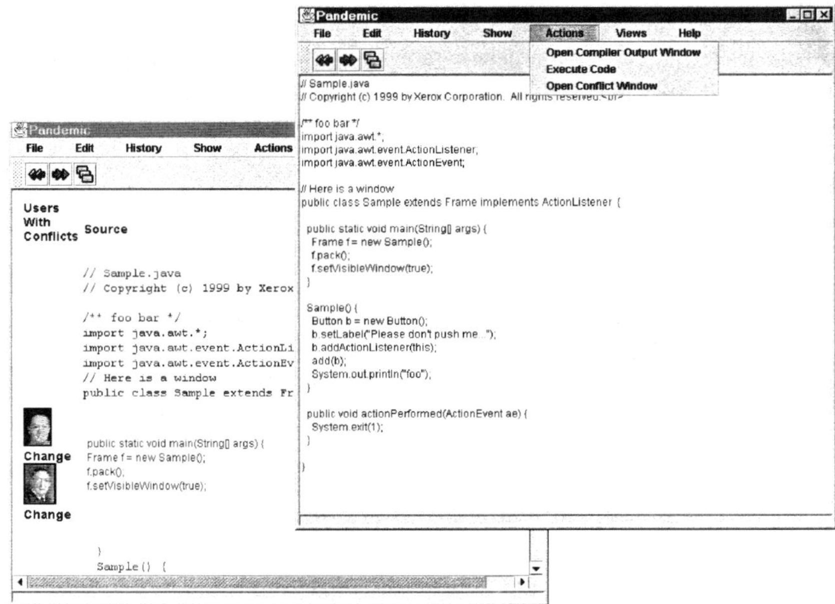

Figure 4: Shamus supports collaborative development

Shamus also supports the automation of common tasks in software development. Another set of active properties attached to source files can automatically compile and run the programs defined by the source files, and automatically generate documentation. Refer again to Figure 4. Shamus will automatically compile the program and generate documentation when the code is changed. The properties that comprise Shamus can generate new user interface components that will be presented to the user. Here we see a number of "views" that can display the up-to-date documentation for the currently-edited source file, and look at the state of a compilation of the file. An extra control is enabled if the code compiled without errors, allowing the user to easily run the application.

All of these tasks happen automatically without user intervention, and without requiring user attention to the results. These steps are typically a part of the build process that is automated by Makefiles or other build tools. Shamus allows new build tasks to be added incrementally and attached directly to code documents.

We should note that many of our developers work in integrated development environments (IDEs). While the properties that comprise Shamus cannot add new UI components to these applications, or change their innate controls for displaying code, they can still assist in the development process. For example, all of the developers can remain aware of what the IDE-using developer is doing, because the active properties that detect changes are still live and noticing updates to the document, even though it is being edited in an IDE. Second, the properties that provide new UI components for controlling Shamus and displaying conflicting updates can pop up as stand-alone windows next to the IDE's windows. And finally, the automation aspects of Shamus are still active, even though the user is running the IDE. Documentation and object files are being generated in the background, and the results of these operations are available as separate Placeless documents.

How Shamus Works

The awareness aspects of Shamus are driven through a property attached to code source files, called the *CodeAwarenessProperty*. This property awakens periodically and computes hash code signatures of the text of individual methods. These signatures are stored on the document as properties identifying the state of the content in terms of the source code structure.

With the signatures computed, the property performs a query to find all versions of the same source file that are in use by other Placeless Documents users. Since these documents also have the CodeAwarenessProperty attached to them, they will have up-to-date lists of their signatures attached to them as well. These signature lists can be compared to see if users are making potentially conflicting changes.

The CodeAwarenessProperty can provide a UI widget which presents these potential conflicts.

The automation tasks are implemented by a separate property, called the *CompilerProperty*. This property performs its tasks whenever new content is written, by invoking external tools to do their jobs. The CompilerProperty will run the *javac* compiler to compile Java code when needed, and the *javadoc* documentation generation system. The property captures the output of the external compilation process and creates a new Placeless document for it. The object files that result from compilation are imported into Placeless, as are the error and warning messages from the compiler. The javadoc-generated HTML documentation is also imported into Placeless.

These properties expose these derived documents as "views" of the original source, which are directly available from property-provided UI controls (they can, of course, also be accessed through a browser or via query from other applications). When the compilation executes successfully, the CompilerProperty also generates a "run" control that applications can use to invoke the code.

Our experiment with Shamus has convinced us that the facilities provided by the Placeless Documents system are applicable to a range of application domains. Shamus provides support for two of the most time-consuming tasks in collaborative development—coordination with peer developers, and automation of aspects of the build process. Shamus adds value to the development process while allowing users to use the tools they are comfortable with. It enhances the functionality of existing tools without getting in the way of commonly-used development processes.

Conclusions and Future Directions

Our work has examined a model of workflow which separates monolithic workflow applications into individual component behaviors which can be attached directly to the content which is at the heart of many work activities. By exposing the state of a workflow process as a document, we can leverage the wealth of general-purpose document management tools that already exist in our environments. Via the integration of computation and content, we hope to move closer to the model envisioned by Abbott and Sarin (1998) of workflow being an "invisible capability that permeates" *all* applications.

The ability to use these tools comes with a price, however—by using general-purpose tools we lose the tight semantic binding that specialized applications provide. Custom, stand-alone workflow tools can embody the semantics of the tasks they manage in ways that general-purpose tools cannot. This is a tension in our work: in the design of the workflow processes in our model, we must strike a balance between the use of general tools and the specific requirements of the task at hand. Managing this balance effectively is a direction for future research.

In addition to the pragmatic benefits of allowing standard tools to integrate with workflow practice in a novel way, our model of active content also can be used to provide more fluid expressions of workflow tasks. For example, a single piece of content can participate in multiple workflows via a "layering" of active properties. New behaviors can easily be added to documents without disrupting the behaviors already in place.

While our primary focus has been on enabling the types of tasks that workflow applications have typically managed, we believe that our infrastructure has implications and uses for other types of tasks as well. The software engineering example presented in this paper is one of these—it represents a class of task that, while collaborative, is very different from the rigorously structured and "globally consistent" views that traditional workflow processes enhance. The same active property mechanisms that support workflow can be used by this task to great benefit, though. We believe that the foundation provided by the Placeless Documents infrastructure can support the construction of "applications"—or more accurately, clusters of active property sets—for a range of document organization, management, and use tasks.

The systems described in this paper have been implemented atop the Placeless Document system. While Placeless itself is approximately 100,000 lines of Java code, the amount of code needed to implement the active properties we use is quite small—on the order of 300 lines of code each. We believe that Placeless provides an excellent substrate for constructing and experimenting with new document services and tools, as it allows easy development of behavior in a piecemeal fashion.

This paper is primarily an exposition of the "systems" aspects of Placeless and how they can be applied to novel applications; indeed, our original motivation for doing this work was to see if the facilities provided by Placeless could be applied to a demanding domain such as workflow. We believe that the primary value of this work is in the collection of systems concepts that allow the construction of new forms of document-based interaction, more than any particular expressions of these systems concepts in actual workflow examples. Our desire is to put forward a novel model of workflow and a description of the infrastructure that would be required to support this model.

We are currently investigating new applications for Placeless, including electronic mail, general-purpose organizational tools, and new "vertical" application domains including more workflow examples. We plan to continue to refine and extend our infrastructure throughout the next year based on the lessons we learn from these applications.

Acknowledgments

The Placeless Documents project at PARC is a large effort that has benefited from the involvement and support of many people. In particular, we'd like to thank Karin Petersen and Douglas B. Terry, both of whom contributed to the Placeless design and implementation, but were not directly involved in the workflow applications described here.

References

Abbott, K. and Sarin, S. (1994). Experiences with Workflow Management: Issues for the Next Generation. Proc. ACM Conf. Computer-Supported Cooperative Work CSCW'94 (Chapel Hill, NC). New York: ACM.

Begole, ., Struble, C., and Smith, R. (1997). Transparent Sharing of Java Applets: A Replicated Approach. Proc. ACM Symp. User Interface Software and Techology UIST'97 (Banff, Alberta). New York: ACM.

Brinck, T. and Hill, R. (1993). Building Shared Graphical Editors Using the Abstraction-Link-View Architecture. Proc. European Conf. Computer-Supported Cooperative Work ECSCW'93 (Milano, Italy). Dordrecht: Kluwer.

Bullen, C. and Bennett, J. (1990). Learning from Users' Experiences with Groupware. Proc. ACM Conf. Computer-Supported Cooperative Work CSCW'90 (Los Angeles, CA). New York: ACM.

Cortes, M. and Mishra, P. (1996). DCWPL: A Programming Langauge for Describing Collaborative Work. Proc. ACM Conf. Computer-Supported Cooperative Work CSCW'96 (Boston, MA). New York: ACM.

Dourish, P. and Bellotti, V. (1992). Awareness and Coordination in Shared Workspaces. Proc. ACM Conf. Computer-Supported Cooperative Work CSCW'92 (Toronto, Ontario). New York: ACM.

Dourish, P., Edwards, K., LaMarca, A., Lamping, J., Petersen, K., Salisbury, M., Terry, D. and Thonton, J. (1999). "Extending Document Management Systems with Active Properties." Submitted, *Transactions on Information Systems.*

Edwards, K., LaMarca, A. (1999). "Balancing Generality and Specificity in Document Management Systems." Submitted, Interact'99.

Gelernter, D. (1985). Generative Communication in Linda. ACM Trans. Programming Lanaguages and Systems, 7(1), 80-112.

Grudin, J. (1988). Why Groupware Applications Fail: Problems in the Design and Evaluation of Organizational Interfaces. Proc. ACM Conf. Computer-Supported Cooperative Work CSCW'88 (Portland, OR). New York: ACM.

Isaacs, E., Morris, T. and Rodriguez, T. (1994). A Forum for Supporting Interactive Presentations to Distributed Audiences. Proc. ACM Conf. Computer-Supported Cooperative Work CSCW'94 (Chapel Hill, NC). New York: ACM.

Jeffay, K., Lin, J., Menges, J., Smith, F. and Smith, J. (1992). Architecture of the Artifact-Based Collaboration System Matrix. Proc. ACM Conf. Computer-Supported Cooperative Work CSCW'92 (Toronto, Ontario). New York: ACM.

Johnson, J. and Nardi, B. (1996). Creating Presentation Slides: A Study of User preferences for Task-Specific versus Generic Application Software. ACM Trans. Computer-Human Interaction, 3(1), 38-65.

Olsen, D., Hudson, S., Phelps, M., Heiner, J., and Verratti, T. (1998). Ubiquitous Collaboration via Surface Representations. Proc. ACM. Conf. Computer-Supported Cooperative Work CSCW'98 (Seattle, WA). New York: ACM.

Olson, J. and Teasley, S. (1996). Groupware in the Wild: Lessons Learned from a Year of Virtual Collocation. Proc. ACM Conf. Computer-Supported Cooperative Work CSCW'96 (Boston, MA). New York: ACM.

Palmer, C. and Cormack, G. (1998). Operation Transforms for a Distributed Shared Spreadsheet. Proc. ACM Conf. Computer-Supported Cooperative Work CSCW'98 (Seattle, WA). New York: ACM.

Prakash, A. and Shim, H. (1994). DistView: Support for Building Efficient Collaborative Applications using Replicated Objects. Proc. ACM Conf. Computer-Supported Cooperative Work CSCW'94 (Chapel Hill, NC). New York: ACM.

Schmidt, K. and Bannon, L. (1992). Taking CSCW Seriously: Supporting Articulation Work. Computer-Supported Cooperative Work, 1(1-2), 7-40.

Winograd, T. and Flores, F. (1986). Understanding Computers and Cognition: A new foundation for design. Norwood, NJ: Ablex.

S. Bødker, M. Kyng, and K. Schmidt (eds.). *Proceedings of the Sixth European Conference on Computer-Supported Cooperative Work, 12-16 September 1999, Copenhagen, Denmark*
©1999 Kluwer Academic Publishers. Printed in the Netherlands

The *Manufaktur*:
Supporting Work Practice in (Landscape) Architecture

Monika Büscher[1], Preben Mogensen[2], Dan Shapiro[1], Ina Wagner[3]

1 Lancaster University, 2 Århus University, 3 Vienna Technical University

{m.buscher, d.shapiro}@lancaster.ac.uk p.mogensen@daimi.aau.dk i.wagner@email.tuwien.ac.at

Abstract. We describe fieldwork with (landscape) architects in which we identify key features of their work settings. We analyse the ways in which materials, many of them graphic and visual, are assembled, arranged and manipulated as an integral aspect of their work. We describe an early prototype of a 3D environment to provide a digitally-enhanced work setting, the organisation of which will emerge from use by practitioners.

Picture a practice of architects in their design studio. There are several interconnected largish rooms, each with two or three desks, each of these with a workstation. Some desks are sparse and tidy, perhaps with a single printed plan. Others are a seeming jumble of disparate materials – plans, sketches, notes, photographs, documents, books, samples, etc. On a large display table there is a more 'staged' setting of material on show – inspirational objects, art and design books and magazines open at particular pages, drawings of a recent project. On another table is a large physical model of a current project – a cinema complex – and lying next to it an endoscope with which internal views can be obtained. On shelves are models from other projects and on one wall a library of reference materials. The walls too are used as an exhibition space and decorated with plans and photographs of previous work.

Most of the desks are occupied and often work proceeds quietly with little movement, to be interrupted by bursts of activity. This reflects the character of the architects' work. On the one hand it involves a smaller number of quite large projects, each of which lasts for months if not years. On the other hand the office puts in many tenders for competitions for which a design proposal has to be prepared quickly under high pressure. Communication with external consultants is interwoven with planning in an ongoing process. These interactions take place in different forms: asking for ad-hoc advice on the phone, exchanging faxes and files, or meetings.

Our other user partners are a practice of landscape architects. Their offices are very similar in their mix of tools, materials and activities, though the practice has fewer people and the space is more compressed. There is a more continuous movement of people around the space, combining and recombining in different patterns and with a steady flow of conversation. This also reflects the character of the work. In comparison with the architects, the landscape architects typically work on a larger number of simultaneous projects which are smaller in scale and shorter in duration (though sometimes with a long hiatus during which work is suspended). There is correspondingly a less stable division of labour and more frenetic switching between jobs.

How – if at all – should this work be provided with better computer support? In part, of course, that is a matter of providing better versions of the computer-based tools which are already in daily use: specific tools such as CAD packages and graphics tablets, and general tools such as spreadsheets, email, browsers, printers. But it is also a matter of trying through computer support to enhance the *environment* within which work can take place, and which is different than just the sum of these tools.

Fuzzy concepts and rich visions: the *Gasometer Study*

We have therefore been studying the character of this work environment, and we have given particular attention to how it is constituted by the *deployment of the materials* that are in use. One example undertaken by the one of our user partners is the *Gasometer Study*, which is an urban planning study that covers a large, partly derelict area bordering the highway to Vienna Airport, including four huge and striking brick-built gasometers dating from the end of the last century. It is connected to a series of architecturally prestigious revitalisation projects, among them the conversion into apartments of the gasometers themselves, an entertainment centre (*Pleasure Dome,* another of the office's projects), and the extension of a metro line into the area. Two people from the architectural practice are collaborating on this project with an external consultant, under the direction of the principal architect. Their approach to urban planning is to create a relational field with places of different qualities, and to define a set of principles on which further building projects will be based, rather than planning the area in detail. While the relational field is created by combining different methods (grid, vistas, zoning), the spatial qualities are largely described through *metaphors* and *images*.

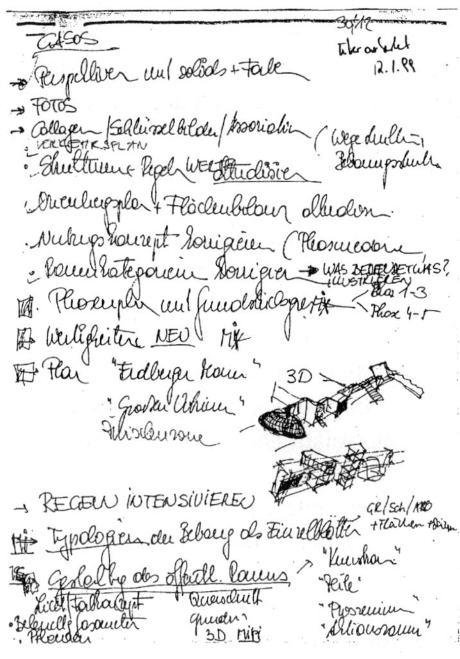

The planning process is guided by a series of 'concept sheets' produced by the principal architect, usually in intense conversations with other members of the team. These sheets are not just lists of what to do and what to clarify, but complex visualisations of methods and open questions. They often include small sketches, arrows, references to material to look for, or people to contact. Sometimes they appear on photocopies of a plan or a sketch. This concept sheet (left; one of almost 20) specifies some of the main elements of the planning process – methods, spatial categories, and representational techniques. It was produced in the very first planning session and has since been annotated from time to time.

The team's task is to translate these concept sheets into a design which will be described through a variety of representations – different types of plans, a model, text, photographs, association images. A crucial aspect of this work is to be able to work with 'fuzzy concepts' and to maintain things at different stages of incompletion. In the following transcript the principal architect is discussing how to represent the separation of and fluent transitions between residential and industrial/trade areas:

"… there are a number of things we can indicate in this area, there is this wall which can be animated, developed, similar to the wall in *Austria Email* (a previous project), where we also have such an in-between zone, where these areas for trades, meeting places, greenhouses, …, here one should draft a structure, as a placeholder for what might be there, a phase-plan, this is also something which we still need to, this story with this in-between space, we could mark this symbolically in the plan …" (13/1/99).

This passage shows how topics are addressed and 'encircled', often taking the team through the entire area or object being planned, since each topic has ramifications for others. While some aspects are discussed in detail and fixed, others are left entirely open. The conversations unfold through addressing particular issues, trying to clarify the facts, generating and testing preliminary ideas or solutions, and deciding how to proceed further. The openness of this process is captured by the notion of *a placeholder for what might be there* (Tellioglu et al., 1998). It stands for something that is in formation and may only be defined on a conceptual and metaphorical level. Placeholders may range from very small things (e.g. a missing parameter in a product specification) to large ones (the detailed design of the in-between space mentioned in the excerpt).

Talking through a topic is intermingled with the handling of a variety of materials – plans, drawings, sketches, faxes, letters, images, photographs. Their assemblage is expressive of the way the design problem is addressed and solved. One of the first steps taken in the *Gasometer Study* was to structure the whole  area by constructing a series of visual lines representing vistas and openings from different places to particular points or places beyond. This also creates a particular silhouette as seen from a distance. From these visual relations a 'grid' or 'relational field' is constructed which can be filled with places of different qualities (Lainer & Wagner, 1998). For developing this structure a series of photographs was taken from different viewpoints (above). While working on the area plan, the architects use them as visual instantiations of the lines to be constructed:

"... on the first day, when you look from Baumgasse, you see how the gasometers disappear under the Tangente (a main highway), and then appear again, the whole air space, and then there near the *Arena*, this box covers them again. You can see this in the section plan, how dominant this is, ... , these are the 'visual relations'" (15/12/98).

Fitting this structure onto the existing one of buildings and roads requires a high level of fuzziness. Details have to be ignored in order to highlight the main structural qualities of the design, as in this excerpt where the two junior architects are discussing how to visualise structure:

"... maybe in this case it is better to leave out these differences of structure, and just to highlight the paths, to do this a bit differently, in a much more abstract way, not like the one I just started to draft, these zones, this doesn't tell us much" (24/11/98).

A central task in this project is to define places within this structured urban space with specific spatial categories and qualities – among others 'activity space', 'art space', 'row', 'display case', 'bridge as skywalk'. Much time is spent within the team clarifying these concepts which are encircled by using metaphors, producing sketches, and searching for association images. Going back to the conversation about in-between spaces, this time between *Pleasure Dome* and *Gasometer*:

"... this cross-section through the 'art space' on the one hand means that there is this wall of the *Pleasure Dome* which is defined as a wall which is drenched with colour and light and has a certain visual transparency, and on the other hand the base of the gasometers, which are covered with green plants and represent a harsh image of nature. Then the question is, what do we do with this in-between space ... we might emphasise this transition zone of the base, that we say, there is this dip where nature transgresses into the space of the road, there are stones and light, that we point to this base... and then these entrances and drives, ... this dreary sequence, that we amplify this." (13/1/99)

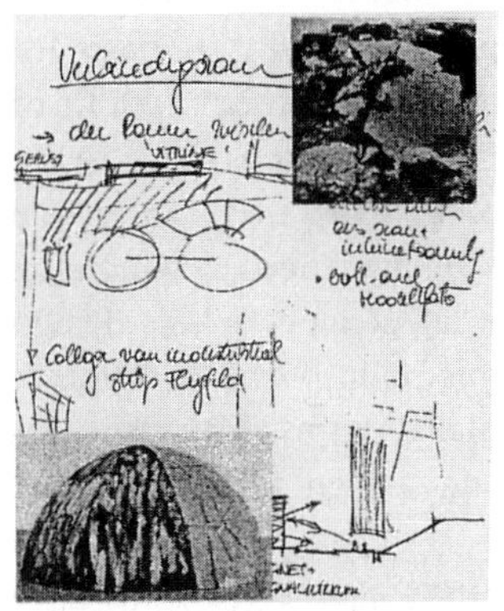

The language here differs from that required for technical detail. Qualities such as 'art space' with its transparent walls filled with light and colour, the 'harsh nature' of the *Gasometer* base, and the 'dreary sequence' of driveways require the construction of rich narratives which others can grasp. Some of these images and metaphors were taken from previous work, others from memories of sites and paintings, such as a 'hill' painting by Mario Merz or an installation by Lois Weinberger "who works with the principle of denaturation, ... he just left strips within the asphalt for wedges and plants, which create an interesting structure" (13/1/99). These images are merged with a sketch for communicating the idea of 'Verbindungsraum'.

Another example of spatial qualities is 'the Display Case', with a variety of meanings which are expressed in images (such as this sketch from a previous project and a screen façade by Oskar Nitzchké from the 1930s). As an 'osmotic wall' it may

mediate between inside and outside, between public space and entertainment and consumption space. It may be walked through as a 'space for movement', or be used as an 'exhibition space' (Lainer & Wagner, 1998). Sketches and stories are created around each of these themes or qualities, and the growing, metamorphosing idea of each is represented in the material that is collected and produced, including the talk around it. This is a good example of Mitchell's (1994) observation that although an image (or idea) may be 'abstract', "language, narrative, and discourse can never – should never – be excluded from it" (p. 226). In this sense, visualisations are used for bringing the narrative element in a concept to the fore (Büscher et al., 1999).

A recurrent theme of the design sessions is what to make visible and how.

Plans of different types are defined, some of them part of the standard repertoire of architects, others innovative and, again, difficult to envision and implement. Examples are 'image plans' (a collage of photographs, sketches, and association images on a plan), schematic plans (sketches which explain a theme or principle), or abstract 3D visualizations of layers, cuttings, and openings. 'Shadow plans' are another example, a series of pictures of the physical model with the light coming from different angles. These attractive images of volumes, light and shaded areas serve multiple functions. As a basis for defining heights, cuttings, edges (open/closed, soft/hard), transparency, width of roads, open spaces, etc., they are essential for formulating the 'rules' to be observed by building projects in this area. On the other hand they enrich the imagination space both of the design team itself and of the audiences to which the project will be presented. Although not all the material created in the design process will be published, it is hard to distinguish at this point between different uses and audiences. All of the representational material will be used by the team itself – creating a representation always means taking a step forward in the common understanding of the design.

In a highly conceptual project as the *Gasometer Study* a problem is how to maintain a connection between the rich context of a given urban area, and the host of structuring principles and spatial categories that form the core of the design. The physical layout of the office and its use as an exhibition space help in this. Although projects are allocated to specific rooms, the space is open and only lightly and flexibly regionalized. The office provides practitioners both with specific affordances for carrying out their activities, and with a particular perspective on their work. It is an ideal place for co-located work and dense interactions. However, this way of preserving context has its limitations. Project material, unless visibly placed on the desk, tends to get 'lost' in the maze of tasks and parameters to consider simultaneously. Just moving a concept sheet, a sketch, an association image, or text into a pile of documents makes it invisible, filing it may mean never retrieving it again.

This lack of presence of context creates real problems in the actual process of producing plans. Drafting is an absorbing activity, with its own logic, involving trained visual conventions to be observed, as well as a certain level of detail and precision. Also, some plans may be huge, difficult to handle on a computer screen, impossible to compress into an A3 format, full of inaccuracies, difficult and time consuming to correct, etc. All this is not conducive to a conceptual,

metaphorical approach to designing, for which one needs to emphasise principles and qualities in an open way. Much of the time of the junior architects is spent on drafting plans. This creates a mental and practical distance from the context, which comes alive through telling stories, looking at images, encircling with metaphors. This is why time has to be spent on comparing and modifying the plans that are produced for a first project presentation, to reconstruct their context and reconnect each of them to it.

Different participants need different kinds of context. From the point of view of the principal architect (who manages at least 6-10 projects of various kinds in parallel), the context of the *Gasometer Project* is represented by a limited set of visual reminders. On his desk he has artfully arranged these reminders, most of them his own concept sheets, together with sketches, post-its of different colours, images. The pictorial character of these reminders is crucial. They are of a type that one can 'fly through', take in 'at a glance', and 'recognise immediately'. These selected reminders of the context of a project which is one of many (see left) are different in kind from the detailed view needed for completing particular design tasks.

Many matters which are consequential for understanding work practices and the working environment can be drawn from this extended example. A key perception, for our purposes, is to do with the ways in which materials are selected, assembled, arranged and handled. What emerges is that manipulating the presence and absence of materials and bringing them into dynamic spatial relations in which they can confront each other are not just a context or prerequisite for doing the work; rather, they are an integral part of accomplishing the work itself. *To manipulate the context is to do the work.* Typically, what is important is not just to create or change a document or other materials, but to do so in the presence of and in relation to others.

That is the case for most forms of work and certainly, we would suggest, for all forms of office work. But it is intensified and given a particular character by the *graphical and visual* features of many of the materials used by architects and landscape architects: plans, sketches, diagrams, photographs, scale models, samples of materials, catalogues, etc. etc. The presence, placing and inter-relationship of these materials – sometimes precise and detailed, sometimes placeholders and metaphors – underpin the passage from possibility to actuality which is the work of design.

These are processes that repeat themselves at different levels of detail and over different temporal scales. In the Gasometer example, much of the purpose was to create, develop and maintain a high-level urban planning concept that will itself inform a range of other detailed projects. The arrangement of materials therefore inhabits the temporal 'longue durée', as a means through which the underlying concepts can be kept present and active over the lifetime and the diversity of the urban plan. As we shall see later, other contexts are far more immediate and short term.

Collections and handovers: *Central Square*

From time to time in the design process documentation is produced which has a different status in that it is explicitly intended to capture or summarise the point that a project or part of a project has reached. This often happens when negotiation needs to take place or agreement needs to be obtained from outside parties. Such materials have been referred to in studies of science as 'punctualisations' (Law 1992). One role of such documentation 'packages' is to serve as a resource around which different perspectives can be explored (as 'boundary objects', Star & Griesemer 1989) in discussions with clients or partners in the design process. Another is to act as a 'recruitment device' (Latour 1990) which will carry persuasive force. Often, agreement relies on the support of other parties (e.g. planning authorities, public consultations, or council decisions) which are themselves complex organisations or institutions. If so, such packages can be handed over and used by partners to gather support within their own ranks and to return to the (landscape) architects at a later stage to commission the continuation of work. Projects can stretch over long periods of time, sometimes years, and some of the 'punctualisation packages' return after many months of internal negotiations elsewhere.

The landscape architects have a three-year contract with the Metropolitan Borough Council of 'AMBC' to undertake all landscape architecture projects as they arise. There are altogether 20 different projects associated with this contract and, at present, the landscape architects spend the majority of their time working on various stages of these. *'Central Square'* – the main square in front of the town hall in AMBC – is one of the most important.

After some negotiation, a layout plan for the design of *Central Square* was agreed with the client. The start date for the implementation of this scheme is only a few months away and the next item on the overall schedule for the project is the specification of paving, planting, lighting, and seating. These details have been under consideration since the beginning of the project. *Central* Square is one amongst many projects in the overall scheme of regeneration in AMBC, and continuity of materials is one aspect of the overall design. Moreover, the actual look and feel of such materials is entwined with the conceptual design. This 'stage' in the design process thus does not constitute a discrete 'step' within the flow of a sequential 'design process'. Rather, it can be described as a shift of focus in the development of the field of artefacts, interaction and communication in and through which the work of designing is achieved – and which is now being brought to a particular 'punctualisation'.

Specifying materials for *Central Square*

The landscape architects have arranged a meeting with the client where preferred options for materials can be discussed and decided on. Samples of candidate materials have been ordered over the past few months. Now it is a question of considering the options in earnest and putting together a 'package' to take to the meeting. Steve, one of the junior landscape architects involved in the design for *Central Square,* has annotated a copy of a part of the current layout plan with ideas and open questions (below). Lynn, a senior landscape architect who spends 3 days a week working from home and two days in the office, is in today. Steve and Lynn take some paving samples and lay them out on the floor. The design of the square is divided into two main areas – a large semi-circle in front of the town

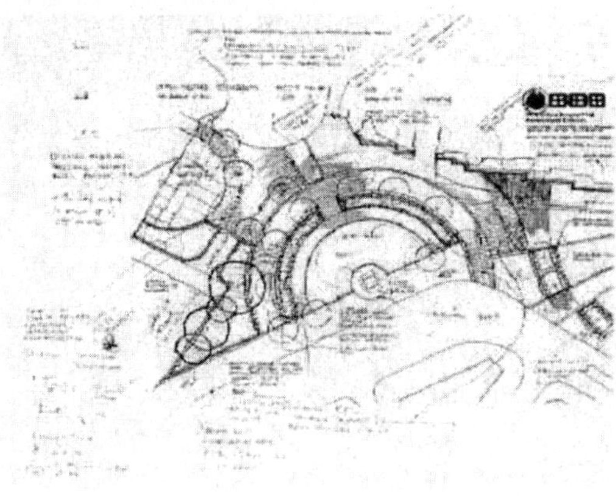

hall, and a smaller circle to the side of the town hall with a statue of Queen Victoria. In both areas light coloured paving fills the circles while darker and smaller paving blocks define lines fanning out from the town hall steps and at various radii of the circles.

Two fairly firm decisions about materials have already been made: the lines will be defined by small blueish blocks (*Brindle*®), and larger, sandy coloured Yorkstone blocks will be laid in the semi-circle in front of the town hall. These Yorkstone blocks cannot be used in the smaller semi-circle around the statue of Queen Victoria because they are too big for the radii. A smaller stone which is similar in texture and appearance has to be found. There is a paving stone that would meet

these requirements (*Tegula*®), but it has been used widely within AMBC and so would not convey the sense that this space is something 'special'. Both Steve and Lynn remember having seen stones that might have all the desired qualities. They turn to the manufacturer's brochures on the shelves. Steve finds a suitable example first:[1]

S: Here we go Lynn (Perfecta), three hundred by two hundred ((handing her product information brochure)), look at that photograph.

L: Yeah

S: They're a bit dead on texture, …

L: Mhm.

S: … aren't they.

L: mhm. And they don't have – what I like about this ((pointing to paving stones laid out on the floor)) kind of system is that you get that randomness. ((gesture))

S: Mhm.

L: You get the courses ((gesture depicted on the right)), constant courses, but within that course …

S: Different sizes, yeah.

L: … you get different sizes, and that just makes it that bit

---

1   Transcripts are given in simplified and non-technical form.

> more lively. ((leafs through brochure)) You see they've got their own version of ...
> S: Tegula.
> L: Yeah.

Gestures and talk translate or formulate (Lynch 1990) the main design concept of 'fluidity' as 'courses' that structure the design of the whole of the square and associate it with 'randomness' and 'liveliness'. Here, the arrangement of resources 'tells the story' of the process of making decisions, about the options considered, final choices, and  discarded alternatives. A similar procedure is repeated for many of the elements that need to be specified (other surfaces, seating, planting, lighting). Steve produces the materials sheets over the next few days, and Lynn updates the layout plan in the light of their discussions. Steve and Lynn then take these documents and an assortment of samples to the meeting with the client.

In generating a package to present to the client, the architects also *configure a context* for the design task. After completing the package, a copy is filed away together with some of the resources used in its production in the 'job file(s)'. Other elements of the context are returned to their original locations (e.g. books to the library, brochures to the shelves), some are collected in personal spaces (personal files, boxes, or just in a pile on one's desk), yet others are discarded (e.g. quick 'doodles' or sketches, hand-written notes). However, the relations between different elements of the context established during the course of unfolding work are dissolved. On returning to a project after a potentially very long period of dormancy, there is a lack of information about *how* this particular package is tied into the context of the work as a whole. Even though the punctualisation was itself designed to produce and to convey a context, its own working context would be quite difficult for the landscape architects to recover.

Choreographies of design

In our previous examples we have discussed the use of materials for individual projects, and to do that we had to abstract work on each project out of the general flow. But in everyday work projects are *intermingled*, not neatly separated, and to understand and support this it is necessary to follow the complex mappings and interweavings of materials, projects and people over time. We will illustrate this by following in bare outline a sequence of activities which unfolds over about 40 minutes. On this particular typical working day, 4 landscape architects are present in the office and they do significant work on 7 different projects, while several more are touched on. These include the redesign of two industrial sites, one local and one in London; three parks, all in the local region; and several invitations to tender for new jobs.

An ex-industrial and now heavily overgrown site in London, *'Southsite'*, is to be regenerated and converted into a park. Based on an ordinary map, a sketch layout, some sections, and an analysis drawing had been produced some time ago, and Will, the senior landscape architect, has these on his desk in front of him. The project is on the verge of being given the go-ahead, for which more precise drawings will be required, and Will therefore commissioned a survey of the site, which he has just received. It is on his desk on top of the other material. There are deficiencies in the survey and Will speaks to the surveyor on the phone to explain these and ask for a corrected version – Will promises to obtain and send him a benchmark height so that he can do so, even though that should really be the surveyor's job. Will finishes the telephone call and turns his attention to an invitation for a bid for a project in Wales, which he places on top of all the *Southsite* materials.

Diane stops on the way past his desk, hands him a letter and a brochure sent by civil engineers introducing their services: "These were in Lynn's tray" [downstairs]. Will looks at them briefly, then places them in Lynn's in-tray next to his desk. He turns around further and asks if Diane is on track with getting together the drawings for another project – *'Northsite'*. She hesitates. Will stresses that the deadline is fixed and suggests that perhaps Victor could produce the site location plan, while Lynn works up and amends the already existing detail drawings, so that Diane could focus on the layout. In order for this division of labour to work, Diane needs to compress and then email the detail drawings by modem to Lynn at home. Diane gets onto this task, while Will walks across to Victor and Steve. Victor agrees to take care of the site location for Diane. Diane stopping past has provided Will the occasion to monitor progress and priorities, without being excessively intrusive or 'managerial'. A negotiated reordering of the local and remote sharing of work activities results.

Victor and Steve have meanwhile been working on another project, *'NewPark'*, that concerns the design of secure sports facilities for different areas of a park. One aspect is the design and specification of fencing for an area with a high risk of vandalism. The client's engineers had asked for repeated upgrading. Now, several months on, the clients realise that this has taken the costings far higher than the budget originally agreed, and there are some awkward discussions with the client about whose fault this is and how to resolve it.

Victor took over the job from Mark, who left SGS after completing his final exams several months ago. Six weeks ago, Victor was sent off at very short notice to participate in an 8-week ecology project in Nigeria, which has torn a hole in the division of labour in the office. Victor is now back for one week to prepare for and take his final professional qualification exams. Before Victor left for Nigeria he produced an overview plan and specification of all the fencing around the secure area and then handed this job over to Steve. He briefed Steve by 'talking him through' the file and the status of the project. In the course of this briefing meeting he added post-it notes to all the documents that were particularly relevant to the fencing around the secure area.

Steve and Will had held a previous meeting with the client at which they agreed to produce alternative specifications to reduce the cost. They are due to discuss this at another meeting with the client tomorrow. After Victor agreed to Will's request to help Diane with the *Northsite* preparations, Victor and Will discuss when to meet to talk through Victor's pending exam. Will then says (à propos *NewPark*), "it'd be good if you could go to this meeting, if only for diplomacy." Will moves closer to Victor's drawing board, pulls a photograph of the secure pavilion area towards him. Victor slides another photograph next to it. They go on to discuss, with reference to the plans and pictures in front of them, ways of reusing some of the existing fencing materials, but repositioned and repainted in a much less insensitive and aggressive manner. Hence Victor, who is back for a week, is drawn into the preparation for this meeting, leaving a rather muddied allocation of responsibilities between Victor, Steve and Will – albeit a productive one, in that it draws in additional expertise. Victor goes off to a meeting about the Nigeria project, and Steve goes on to work through all the *NewPark* documents.

What emerges from this apparently mundane sequence is how matters which are highly consequential for the work – negotiating and modifying the contents of a project, reordering a division of labour, communicating and briefing, sharing and managing the work, deciding on priorities, maintaining an external focus on the client, coping with contingencies, making handovers, assembling activities into coherent collections, and much more – find reflection in the working materials, and are achieved through the intricate 'choreography', the rapidly-switching assembly, which is enacted among people, projects and materials as work unfolds. All of them are productively and purposively organised in space and time by the participants so as to facilitate the flow of work. This involves multiple overlaps; serendipitous connections, overhearings and overseeings; and the exercise of various sensitivities by the participants to each other's situations and activities.

Taken together, the fieldwork examples have, among other things, illustrated three different perspectives on the ways in which materials are assembled and deployed to constitute work settings. First, to provide long-term, deeply-informing contexts of an underlying conceptual character, as in the Gasometer Study. Second, the working up of punctualisations – sets of documentation for particular handovers at particular points in time – and their background, as in the materials for 'Central Square'. And third, the rapid-fire choreography of ongoing work, with its continuous flow of people, materials and projects. Of course, these are ideal-typical distinctions, and most examples in the real world will have a mixed character. We can also see that the use of materials has both a 'synchronic' or static aspect, arising from a particular arrangement, and a 'diachronic' or animated aspect, arising from their movement and sequential display. The latter comes closer to a narrative of the work, in which stories can be woven and demonstrated about a project, its possibilities and its progress – for the benefit of the members of the practice themselves, and also for other audiences.

A 3D *Manufaktur* Space

A key aspect of the support that a work setting for architecture and landscape architecture must provide is support for the assembly, arrangement and manipulation of materials, as well as for acting on them with appropriate tools. But why should this be a *digitally-enhanced* work setting? If there is a justification for this, it is that it may permit some limitations of the physical work setting to be partially overcome. Specifically, a digitally-enhanced work setting:

- may overcome some of the boundedness of physical space. Materials and participants may be brought in from other places.
- may overcome some of the inflexibility of physical space and the 'mass' of objects in it. Physical spaces (desks, walls, rooms) are finite and costly; digital spaces are not, or not in the same ways. Physical objects can only be in one space and one arrangement at a time, digital objects can occupy many. In physical work settings, one arrangement in a space (a layer) obliterates others, creating an 'archaeology' of working materials; in an electronic space, arrangements need only be layered if that is specifically desired.
- can contain active objects as well as passive ones. A document may, for example, exhibit a behaviour as it approaches a deadline. A collection of materials can be animated in a presentation. Materials can be linked to each other, and one can update as another is changed. The relationships connecting a set of materials – their grouping or arrangement – can be stored. Materials can be selected or found by interrogating their properties and contents.

Of course these benefits do not come free, and any digitally-enhanced work setting will also have limitations and deficiencies compared to a physical one.

We have been experimenting with a computer-based work setting which supports and, in a cautious sense, replicates this environment. This has been conceived around the metaphor of '*Manufaktur*' ('craft workshop'). The *Manufaktur* is a 3D workspace which will support the configuring of multi-media documents to specific *views* of a project, including the possibility of 'pre-fabricating' such views for recurrent tasks. It will contain a series of desktop applications, some of which are underlying services (exploring & navigating technologies, linking facilities, support for sharing and awareness, document management, etc.). Specific applications will be developed in support of needs such as creating and displaying narratives, organising, and component design.

Up to now, the potential of electronic technologies to support the visualisation of information in three dimensions has been approached from three main perspectives (see Mariani 1998 Ch. 1). First, approaches that utilise the properties of 'information objects' and define rules for their distribution in space. These include 'Benediktine' Cyberspace (Benedikt 1991) and approaches that add to this statistical clustering and proximity measures – VIBE (Olsen 1993), BEAD (Chalmers 1992), and Q-PIT (Mariani 1998 Ch. 7), see also Benford et al. (1996). Second, visualisations of hypermedia-link based systems (Card 1991, Stenius et al. 1998). Third, human-centred approaches that explore the possibilities for the development of tools and techniques to allow people to structure and display information in electronic spaces flexibly. So far, the work undertaken in this area is mainly conceptual (Gray 1990, Benford & Snowdon 1997). Our work in some ways combines linking with a human-centred approach, but it is deeply grounded in the specifics of (landscape) architectural practice. Rather than attempting to structure the information field through the use of automated mechanisms, we are experimenting with the potential of providing an environment and some tools and techniques to organise and access different views onto the information. This approach takes into account the flexible and situated use of information resources.

We have seen the importance of selecting and relating materials. In a setting such as this, what kind of machine can there be for determining which materials are relevant and how they should be arranged? None, we propose. The members of the community of practice engaged in the work are the authority that decides how materials should be arranged. The purpose of the presence and arrangement of materials is to support context, awareness and action, but these are situated and relative. The same thing can be the work object for one activity, background material or context for another activity, and would be an irrelevant distraction for a third – all in ways which change on a moment-to-moment basis. *The presence and arrangement of materials is therefore not something which can be automatically generated, but must emerge from the flow of the work itself*, in the kinds of ways described in our fieldwork examples.

The *Manufaktur* is a workspace in several senses. First, it facilitates the (3D) *spatial arrangement* of objects, similar to the spatial arrangements of models, books, drawings, pictures, etc. in any (landscape) architectural office. In this sense, we envision the *Manufaktur* as a 3D environment, with an abstract and unbounded space, which can be furnished with various objects for particular projects and/or activities. Second, it provides space in the sense of supporting the *context* of the project or task specific assemblage of multi-media documents, their purposeful arrangements, and links between them. From this perspective, the *Manufaktur* is *document-based*. Third, it provides shared space between people. When we speak of the arrangement of objects etc. we really speak of *references* to objects which physically may be stored anywhere within a local area network (and potentially on a wide area network too). Somewhat similar to the sharing of physical office space, the *Manufaktur* allows, for example, all the members of an office to work in the same unbounded space, in a distributed manner.

Below is a partly fabricated screen dump from a first and very crude prototype of the *Manufaktur*, which has only been in development for 6 months. The picture (minus the icons and the task bar) is a screen dump from the prototype running as an application. That screen dump has been used as wallpaper to show the vision of having *Manufaktur* running as a kind of 'desktop' (e.g. using Active Desktop).

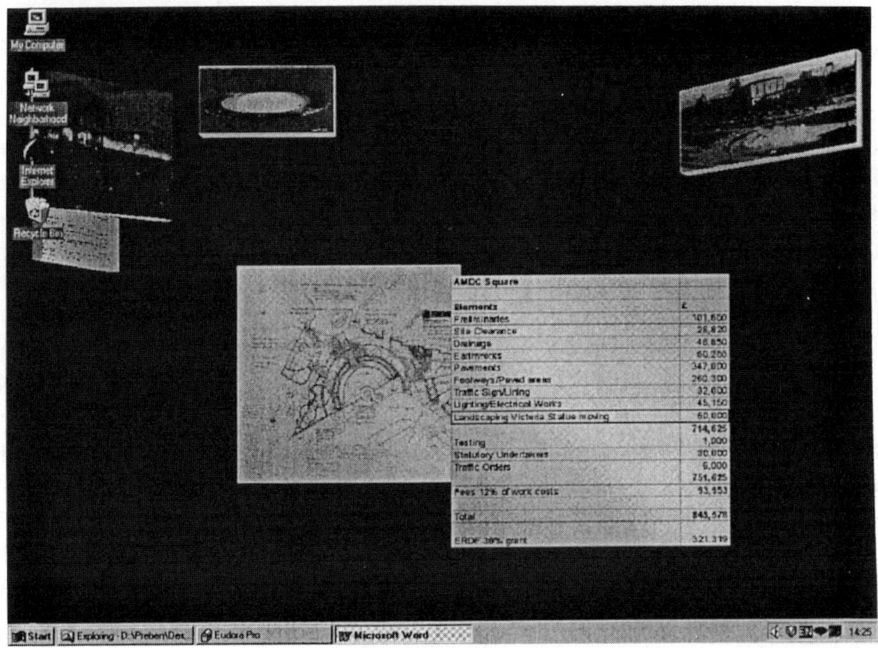

Double clicking any of the documents will launch the proper application with that document, on the active 3D 'desktop', and changes to it will be updated on the 'desktop' in near real time. The objects can be moved, rotated, etc. The prototype is developed in C++, using COM/ActiveX technology for integrating the documents, and DirectX v.6.0 for rendering them in the 3D environment.

Objects in the *Manufaktur*

Objects in this 3D space (as can be seen in this simple visualisation) can be moved around in different ways. They can be pulled to the front, where they are most clearly visible, or pushed further back. They can be turned so that one can see their spine (which can be given a semantic, e.g. with the thickness of an object indicating the number or size of documents in them, and the spine colour indicating an affiliation), or their back (which may be used e.g. for displaying a table of contents or relationships to other documents). Placing objects at an angle adds a perspectival dimension.

Several different types of objects can populate the space:

- 'Live' documents of various kinds (Word, Excel, CAD drawings etc.) residing in 3D rendered OLE/ActiveX containers. An example of such a 3D rendered OLE container could be a Microsoft Word document rendered on to one of the sides of a 3D box. The document is 'live' in the sense that what is rendered onto the 3D object is the current display from the document's host applications, and updates are received as the document changes (OLE linking) – double clicking an object opens it within its host applications.

- (3D) models of parks, buildings, towns, etc. The (3D) models may, for example, be artefacts used in a project such as models of a building, urban area, landscape site, or entire counties. The models can be scaled, moved, turned, flipped, animated, etc. as any other object. They therefore lend themselves to several uses: as a reference point 'up in the corner' that one might take down and explore if appropriate, as models to 'walk into' or change, or as one big and 'fixed' object that is used for defining the topography of the space (e.g. a wireline of a site gradually filled with documents as the project progresses).

- 'Implantations' – objects or devices that support the customising of a space to changing uses, for example, to create spatial partitions or for imprinting specifically expressive codes (Lainer & Wagner, 1998). An example may be the use of walls for providing a sense of size, location, or direction, or semi-transparent objects such as boxes, cylinders, spheres, etc. to define specific areas. Another example is applying 'spotlighting' of a specific colour to a certain area within the 3D space, to indicate some particular status of the documents placed in that area. Thus topographical features may (but do not have to) be added to decorate or aid the 'intelligibility' of the space – the system treats them just like any other object.

- Special applications such as 'The Wunderkammer', a collectively used multimedia archive for inspirational objects (images, sound, video), a collection support, and a view generator which is currently being developed in parallel with the Manufaktur (Büscher et al., 1999).

A 3D environment not only makes it possible to have many windows open at the same time, but it also, by spatial proximity, allows to indicate the (changing) relevance of a document for work-in-progress. This means that there are in effect different 'levels of openness' of a document, which can still be identified from far away. We see this as a possibility for supporting the kind of fluent relationships between fuzziness and precision described in our field work – "to zoom into a detail and out to see the whole" – and to simultaneously hold present a large number of parameters and their relationships.

At the beginning of an activity, this workspace is almost empty. People create their workspace as activities evolve. It could be handed over or inherited as others start working on the same or a similar project or activity. There might also be a case for having 'pre-fabricated' views for certain types of projects or activities.

Groupings

Even smaller projects rapidly involve hundreds of documents. One way of structuring these documents, besides visual appearance and spatial placement, is the notion of groupings. A grouping is comparable to a folder in a file system, except that here we only speak of *references* to objects. So any object may appear in as many groups as one wishes. One example of a grouping would be clustering together all material that describes and details a specific spatial quality, such as 'bridge as skywalk'. We are still in the early days of the prototype, and need to experiment with the exact appearance and functionality of groups. Obviously, we will have to support such features as naming, saving, re-finding, moving (both of objects in and out of groups, and of groups with or without 'content').

Views

Any given arrangement of objects, including position, lighting, shading, transparency, references etc. we call a 'view'. A view can be named and saved. One can, thus, shift between views (e.g. representing the context of different projects) or have several views open at the same time (in panes, in separate windows, or in principle on separate screens). Because, as mentioned before, we only store references and do so in a separate, shared database, one can open one's 'own' views or those of other colleagues. Naturally there are some privacy issues involved here, as there would be if parts of views were made publicly available to other contractors in the project or, potentially, to the public at large. At the moment, we focus on supporting cooperation between colleagues in an office.

Links

All the above are means to support the establishment and use of context when working on projects. They do so by providing means of arranging objects. But having them co-present is not the only form of supporting context and expressing relationships between parts of documents. Consider, for example, the work involved in producing a CAD drawing of a building. Here there are relationships between, say, the drawing and several initial sketches of the concept guiding it, between corridors and specifications for the widths, between doors and fire regulations, between a room and various suggestions for furnishing it, between a wall and potential materials for it, etc. All these relationships are hard to express by means of spatial arrangement alone, and if attempted would often produce unwanted clutter. Therefore we also operate with the notion of *links*. The support of linking is obtained through integration with the DEVISE, Hypervise hypermedia system (Grønbæk et al. 1993, Grønbæk & Mogensen 1997). The basic idea in Hypervise is to support a browsable network of references, stored in a separate hypermedia database, between various kinds of "documents", called *components*. Components may be of all sorts, for example text documents, movies, WWW pages, spreadsheets, CAD drawings, etc. all being viewed and edited within their respective host applications. Links are from parts of one document (selection of text, selection of cells, object in a CAD drawing, sequence of frames in a movie, etc.) to parts of another. A link can be followed both 'forward' and 'backward' (in contrast to e.g. HTML links) and can have as many endpoints as one wants. Following a link could, for example, result in a text file being opened in a word processor on, say, page 27, a spreadsheet being opened using its respective host application with certain cells selected, and a CAD drawing with a particular object highlighted. All the links are stored in a database separate from the documents being inter-linked allowing for sharing of various collections of links as well as various link browsers. These links are robust over, for example, the relocation of folders or files containing their targets.

The features and philosophy of Hypervise links are extensively described elsewhere, but for us an important aspect of its philosophy which *Manufaktur* shares is that its patterns *emerge from work practices themselves* as they unfold, not from any attempt to apply 'intelligence' to the automatic formation of the population of *Manufaktur* objects, or their configuration.

Using the *Manufaktur*

The current *Manufaktur* prototype is too early to be trialled in serious use in working architecture or landscape architecture settings – at the time of writing it has only been in development for 6 months. However, our user partners have been deeply involved in its development and an interim experiment which we have carried out is to prototype the *Manufaktur* in a manual version, creating a view of the *Gasometer Study* with paper documents on a large pinwall, and discussing with our user partners how they would envisage using the electronic environment. The documents related to a particular theme were clustered together into groups. It was a great advantage to be able to see (at least parts of) all these documents simultaneously, rather than having to leaf through piles to find them. The spatial arrangement was also very helpful in 'framing' documents with different kinds of relationship to each other, in ways that could be easily changed. It is possible to move them around, e.g. to highlight a central part, to move closer for accentuating a conceptual relationship. A stronger and more content oriented frame would be provided by a 3D model or map of the gasometer area itself within which documents could be arranged. The arrangement not only provided a good overview, but was also a good pointer to things that were missing, providing a strong 're-cognition' effect for material that got lost. The spatial arrangement of fields and documents also has narrative properties and 'tells the story' (or history) of the project. Although it was rather close to the ways material is arranged for project presentations to outside audiences, it also proved highly useful for ongoing work.

Throughout the paper we described our fieldwork examples in ways which, we hope, make it easy to conceive scenarios in which equivalent work is done with the added resource of the *Manufaktur*. It is easy to picture the advantages, such as the capacity to save and retrieve views, to work with remote people and materials, to work with multiple arrangements of materials, to work with active materials. One of the main challenges which successful use would have to face, however, is the integration of electronic and physical work settings. This is partly a practical and technical matter, to do with such things as making it as convenient as possible to scan and to print material, to use graphics tablets, etc., to do with display technology, to do with the bandwidth available between offices and into the home. It is partly a 'historical' matter, to do with the developing availability of catalogues, regulations, standards, archives, images, etc. online. But it is more importantly a matter of what is a 'comfortable' medium for different kinds of work, and of the various trade-offs between 'physical' and 'digital' advantages. The time horizon for the development is around three years, so we anticipate that an environment which works adequately on, say, a 20" monitor will work very well on a 30" flat screen, and better still, eventually, in a true 3D environment.

Summary and conclusions

We have described some of the key features of the work settings of architects and landscape architects. We highlighted in particular the ways in which diverse materials are assembled, arranged, manipulated and displayed in their workspaces – around their desks, rooms, furniture and equipment. Much of this material, naturally, is graphical and visual in character. Some of it is precise and detailed but much of it is conceptual, metaphorical and in formation. It forms a context for their work but, more than this, we show that organising their materials importantly *constitutes* their work.

We have developed an early prototype of a 3D computer-based environment, the *Manufaktur*, to support these work settings. It enables practitioners to place, orient and move materials, and themselves, in three dimensions, analogously to their use of physical space. The aim is to take up the advantages of electronically-mediated spaces and materials while minimising their disadvantages. It enables them to work on materials in the space with their usual software tools, to 'furnish' it with a topography, and to share it with others. Another cornerstone of the environment is the provision of Hypervise hypermedia links, so that meaningful connections between materials can also be maintained without requiring their visible presence. In both *Manufaktur* and Hypervise, the organisation of materials, spaces and links emerges from the work of practitioners themselves. It is intended that the *Manufaktur* and the physical work space will be combined by practitioners in use to form a digitally-enhanced work setting.

40

Acknowledgements

We are especially grateful to the members of our user partners, Architekturbüro Rüdiger Lainer (A) and SGS Environment (UK). They have been deeply involved in the fieldwork, development, conceptualisation and design of the *Manufaktur*. We are very grateful for the contributions of other members of our research teams, and of the other partners in EU ESPRIT LTR Project 31870 'DESARTE - The Design of Artefacts and Spaces', funded by the European Commission. Earlier work on landscape architecture was funded by the UK Economic and Social Research Council.

References

Benford, S. Ingram, R., & Bowers. J. (1996). Building virtual cities: Applying urban planning principles to the design of virtual environments. *Proc. ACM Conference on Virtual Reality Software and Technology* (VRST'96), Hong Kong, July, New York NY: ACM.

Benford, S., & Snowdon, D. (1997). Informing the design of collaborative environments, in *Proceedings. GROUP'97* (Phoenix, Arizona, Nov.16-19, 1997), New York NY: ACM.

Card, S.A., Robertson, G. & Mackinlay, J. (1991). The Information Visualiser and Information Workspace. *Proc. CHI'91,* New York NY: ACM, pp. 181-188.

Chalmers, M. and Chitson, P. 1992. Bead: Explorations in Information Visualisation. In *Proc. SIGIR'92*, published as a special issue of SIGIR forum, ACM Press, pp. 330-337, June 1992.

Colebourne, A., Mariani, J. & Rodden, T. (1996) Q-PIT: A Populated Information Terrain, in G. Grinstein & R. Erbacher (eds) *Visual Data Exploration and Analysis III*, pp. 12 - 22.

Gray, P.D., Waite, K.W., & Draper, S.W. (1990) Do-It-Yourself Iconic Displays. *Human-Computer Interaction – INTERACT '90*, D. Diaper et al (Eds.), Elsevier Science (N Holland), pp. 639-644.

Grønbæk, K., & Mogensen, P. (1997). Informing General Product Development through Cooperative Design in Specific work domains. *CSCW: The Journal of Collaborative Computing*, **6**, 275-304.

Grønbæk, K., Kyng, M., & Mogensen, P. (1993). CSCW Challenges: Cooperative Design in Engineering Projects. *Communications of the ACM*, **36**(6), 67-77.

Lainer, R. & Wagner, I. (1998). Connecting Qualities of Social Use with Spatial Qualities. Cooperative Buildings - Integrating Information, Organization, and Architecture. *Proc. CoBuild'98*. Eds Streitz, N. et al., Springer: Heidelberg, pp. 191-203.

Latour, B., Drawing Things Together, in *Representation in Scientific Practice*, M. Lynch and S. Woolgar, Editors. 1990, Kluwer: Amsterdam. p. 19-68.

Law, J., Notes on the Theory of Actor-Network: ordering, strategy, and heterogeneity. *Systems Practice*, 1992. **5** (4): p. 379-393.

Mariani, J. (1998). Chs. 1 & 7 in *eSCAPE Deliverable 3.1* Lancaster University. ISBN: 1-862220-052-1 (available from: http://escape.lancs.ac.uk)

Mitchell, W.J.T., 1994. Picture Theory. Essays on Verbal and Visual Representation. Chicago, The University of Chicago Press.

Büscher, M., Kompast, P., Lainer, R. & Wagner, I. (1999). Space for Inspiration: Ethnography and User Involvement in Designing the Wunderkammer. Proc. Workshop on Ethnographic Studies in Real and Virtual Environments, Edinburgh, Jan 24-26.

Olsen, K.A., Korfhage, R, Sochats, K., Spring, M. & Williams, J. (1993). Visualisation of a Document Collection: The VIBE System, in: *Information Processing and Management*, **29**: 1, pp. 69-81.

Star, S.L. & Griesemer, J. (1989) Institutional Ecology, 'Translations' and Boundary Objects. *Social Studies of Science*, **19**: pp. 387-420.

Stenius, M., Frecon, E., Fahlen, L., Simsarian, K. Bino (1998). Ch. 5: The Web Planetarium Prototype – Visualising the Structure of the Web. In *eSCAPE Deliverable 3.1* (available as above).

Tellioglu H., Wagner I. & Lainer R (1998). Open Design Methodologies. Exploring architectural practice for systems design. Proc. PDC'98, Seattle, November 12-14.

S. Bødker, M. Kyng, and K. Schmidt (eds.). *Proceedings of the Sixth European Conference on Computer-Supported Cooperative Work, 12-16 September 1999, Copenhagen, Denmark*
©1999 Kluwer Academic Publishers. Printed in the Netherlands

Six Roles of Documents in Professionals' Work

Morten Hertzum
Centre for Human-Machine Interaction, Risø National Laboratory, Denmark

Documents are used extensively by professionals in their execution of their own work and to share information with others. Professionals use and manage their documents in ways that are woven into their work activities and leave most of the context unsaid because the documents are understood as belonging to a certain ongoing activity. Contrary to this, organisations have a strong interest in storing information in less person-dependent ways than simply relying on their employees' memory and personal files. To support document management effectively we need to balance the individual professionals' focus on their current activities against the long-term interests of the organisation, and we need a fuller understanding of the affordances and constraints of documents. This study identifies six roles documents play in professionals' work, namely that documents serve: (1) as personal work files, (2) as reminders of things to do, (3) to share information with some yet withhold it from others, (4) to convey meaning, (5) to generate new meaning, and (6) to mediate contacts among people. Painstakingly standardised and very time-consuming methods are required for documents to convey meaning but such efforts are rarely considered worthwhile compared to relying on other document roles or rework.

1. Introduction

Documents are used extensively by professionals in their execution of their own work and as a means of sharing information with others. The ways professionals use and manage documents for their own purposes are woven into their work activities and have been studied by researchers interested in how people organise their individual information spaces (e.g., Malone, 1983). However, most work is co-operative and furthermore organisations have a large interest in storing information in less person-dependent ways than simply relying on the memory and personal files of their employees. The use of documents for information sharing has for example been studied by Bannon & Bødker (1997), Harper & Sellen (1995), and Star & Griesemer (1989), but at least with respect to paper documents little research has looked systematically at their role in organisations (Sellen & Harper, 1997). During the past 30 years computers have been assigned a key role in various efforts to support document management, but these efforts have time and time again failed to produce the expected results. It seems as if the role of documents in professionals' work has yet to be properly understood.

This study identifies six roles documents play in professionals' work. Professionals are subject specialists characterised by putting to work their intellectual skill learned in systematic education and through experience, and they are to a large extent paid to organise their own work, make sense of things, and pass judgements. The starting point in identifying the six document roles has been that documents are part of the context in which they are produced. This introduces a crucial distinction between subsequent use of the documents in this context and (re)use of them in other contexts (see Figure 1). The former use of documents include such situations as documents written for personal use or use within a project group, whereas the latter is exceedingly common in settings where the involved professionals are geographically dispersed or involved in projects that outlast their own involvement in them.

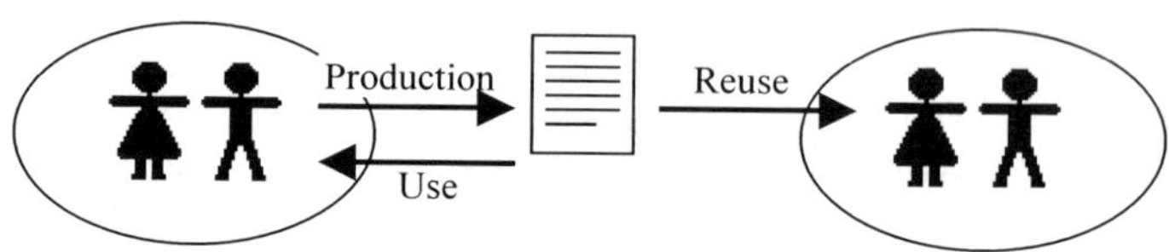

Figure 1. The general setting for production, use, and reuse of documents.

Document archives, whether personal or corporate, may serve many purposes, including accountability, operational continuity, planning, legal evidence, disaster recovery, research, and corporate history. Two types of document value can be distinguished in this connection. The evidential value of a document is its value in providing evidence of an organisation's structure, procedures, transactions and the like, whereas the informational value of a document is the value of its contents for reference, contemplation, and research (Bikson & Frinking, 1993). This study is concerned with the informational value of documents. Their evidential value is however important too, as illustrated by the central role of documents in proving ownership of ideas in patent applications.

It has been estimated that professionals spend 25% of their time distributing, filing, and retrieving documents (Gordon, 1997). This study is intended to expand our understanding of *document management* and inform the design of systems that support this pervasive activity. The study also aims at contributing to the elaboration of the concept of *common information spaces* (CISs) as developed by Bannon & Bødker (1997), Bannon & Schmidt (1989), Schmidt & Bannon (1992). The CIS concept has mostly been discussed in connection with co-located, co-present persons such as air traffic controllers, but it is also intended to inform discussions of situations where people are distributed in time and space. This study investigates the work involved in creating and maintaining CISs and people's inclination to do it.

The next section outlines how documents enter into professionals' work at three levels, which differ markedly with respect to intensity, principles for organising the documents, and intentions of information sharing. This section also gives an introduction to the concept of common information spaces. Section 3 is about how the context, frozenness, and permanence of documents affect their ability to communicate meaning. Section 4 discusses how the document roles directed toward the professionals' individual information spaces and those directed toward information sharing can be brought together in the design of document management systems. Section 5 concludes the paper by summarising the six roles of documents in professionals' work. Please note that I make no claims as to the exhaustiveness of the six roles.

2. Individual and common information spaces

Several studies have found that professionals interact with three levels of information in their files (e.g., Cole, 1982; Hertzum, 1993): *Action information* which includes documents readily at hand and often piled up on the desk, *personal work files* which are within reach but usually put on shelves or held in other conventional filing devices, and *archive storage* which comprises information stored away from the office. Action information is to a large extent arranged on the basis of spatial clues, which require frequent interaction to stay functional. Personal work files are loosely systematised, and though some people maintain personal indexes to aid retrieval many people rely on their memory of the documents' location. Personal work files exist primarily to provide the individual professional with convenient access to the material, not to make it available to others. With respect to archive storage, Cole (1982) notes that the information items are rarely dealt with and when they are it is almost exclusively through extensive category structures. The change from a spatial, loosely systematised, memory-based organisation to category structures as the documents move from 'action' to 'archive' fundamentally changes the nature of the activities carried out to manage the documents. This change is also one from an individual to a common information space.

2.1 Individual information spaces

Professionals know the documents they keep in their offices, hence retrieval of these documents means re-locating them. The documents are typically organised according to their relation to the professionals' past and present work, so retrieval essentially means recalling this relation. Many professionals utilise this known-universe situation to emphasise retrieval over filing in that they minimise the up-front time spent on filing and base their ability to locate their documents on their memory of the relation between their documents and their work activities. These professionals are willing to spend more time on retrieval since retrieval is immediately valuable – it seems more worth the effort to spend five minutes retrieving a document than to spend five minutes filing it. Other professionals prefer to spend up-front time on filing to keep their items organised and reduce retrieval costs (Berlin et al., 1993). These professionals maintain orderly offices to make the known universe more efficient, and they may extend it with category structures that provide access to documents through for example authors, projects, or keywords.

Jahoda et al. (1966) found that 46 (61%) of their respondents maintained a personal index with category structures that provided access to their documents through one or more access points. The respondents reported a number of shortcomings of these personal indexes, the three major ones being: too time-consuming to prepare, inconsistencies in indexing, and not enough access points. These shortcomings reflect difficulties creating and maintaining the necessary category structures within the available time limits. Case (1991) found that 12 (60%) of his respondents maintained some kind of card file to index their documents, but very few of these indexes were like library catalogues in their purpose or exhaustiveness. The indexes included, for example, only the documents relevant to a project currently underway. Several of the respondents had tried to develop an index for their entire document collection but gradually abandoned the attempt. Similarly, Hertzum (1993) found that attempts to inventory everything or just papers from periodicals were not carried through or not considered at all. The respondents were somewhat frustrated about the ad hoc way many of their documents were organised but either overall structures were considered inappropriate or the overhead involved in creating and maintaining them was considered too big.

Rather than category structures consisting of document attributes such as author and subject, Kwasnik (1991) found that the factors people take into account in classifying their documents consist to a very important degree of situational factors such as the use to which the document is to be put. This reflects the short term, personal, and work-oriented motivation that underlies the organisation of professionals' individual information spaces. Probably, the most far-reaching of the situational factors is that much of the information on people's desks is there to remind them to do something, not just to be available when they look for it. This way the documents on the desk are action information in a sense beyond being drawn upon as information sources in the course of the professional's activities: They play an active role in the management of the professional's work. The profound differences between category structures and the ways professionals organise their documents can be vividly illustrated by examples of organising principles used in individual information spaces:

- Keeping the material for this week's classes on the floor, where it would be impossible to overlook (Case, 1991).
- The top document in a pile, i.e. the immediately visible one, has a special status as pile representative (Hertzum, 1993).
- 'On the top shelf are books that are very seldom used' (Kwasnik, 1991).

Most documents are written on a computer but to a considerable extent computers are just used to produce documents, not to file them. The electronic version is stored for later elaboration, correction, and reuse but the authoritative copy is the paper copy on the shelves. One reason for this is that professionals often find it desirable to store their own documents together with documents available in paper copy only, for instance to collect correspondence pertaining to a project in one folder. Barreau (1995) and Barreau & Nardi (1995) find that people's behaviour in organising their electronic documents is consistent with the behaviour observed in organising physical offices. Thus, people prefer filing by location because it supports finding as well as serves a crucial reminding function, and they file documents according to the dictates and vagaries of their work because in the end carefully architected logical schemes do not yield enough value. It is however unknown whether the observed commonalities reflect genuine preferences of the studied people or stem from the desktop metaphor of the studied systems, a metaphor which relies heavily on a direct mapping to physical offices (Fertig et al., 1996).

2.2 Common information spaces

A key capability of documents is to facilitate the sharing of information among professionals who are not present at the same time or in the same place. Whereas oral communication is ephemeral and requires that the actors are co-present, the permanent nature of documents suggests that if professionals document their work in writing then organisations will retain the professionals' knowledge when the professionals retire, move to other jobs, or otherwise leave the organisation. However, empirical studies indicate that people tend to look for a person to ask rather than a document to read (Carstensen, 1997; Pinelli et al., 1993). It is often claimed, or tacitly assumed, that this state of affairs is the result of unsatisfactory documentation and that there is an urgent need for better documentation and, consequently, for improving the tools and practices used in documenting work (see, for example, Blair, 1996). In many cases these arguments convey the impression that good documentation will make organisations far less dependent on the memory and continued presence of their employees. In this study we stress the context-dependent nature of written as well as oral communication, and how the frozenness of documents makes the context inherently underspecified.

Central to document sharing is the creation and maintenance of an archive or a database containing the shared information items. While archives and shared databases are effective at making documents accessible within a community or organisation it is crucial to note that shared access to documents does not imply that the meaning and implications of these documents are available in any complete or unambiguous way. Schmidt & Bannon (1992) emphasise that co-operative work 'requires the active construction by the participants of a common information space where the meanings of the shared objects are debated and resolved, at least locally and temporarily.' To share an information space involves that the local actors interpret the shared information items – make sense of them. The sum of the information items and the locally constructed, shared agreement about their meaning is termed a common information space or CIS (Bannon & Bødker, 1997; Bannon & Schmidt, 1989; Schmidt & Bannon, 1992). CISs come into existence only when a shared agreement can be reached, which is surely not always the case, and they cover just the points where the actors' individual perspectives come together. In the most coherent exposition of the CIS concept to date, Bannon & Bødker (1997) stress that CISs are not confined to situations where people are co-located and co-present, it also includes situations where people are working separately and the main connection between them is a shared database:

> Most discussions of shared spaces in CSCW have tended to confine themselves to situations in 'real-time', or near real-time. Our conceptualization of CISs however extends to situations where information is entered into a database at one point in time and subsequently accessed by others, perhaps months or even years later. In what sense can we characterize this situation as a CIS? In our view, the reason is because both the producer and the receiver consciously make an effort to understand each other's context – of production and use, so that even though the efforts may be distributed over time and space, there is a form of communication, of "putting in common", going on in such activity.

Situations where people are co-present, co-located, and working together differ quite a lot from those where CISs are distributed in time and space. This span of the CIS concept is one of its attractions but also necessitates studies of CISs in a range of contexts to prevent the concept from becoming biased toward some situations and consequently describe others inaccurately. Tightly coupled co-operation such as air traffic control and loosely coupled co-operation such as communicating through documents in a shared database can be seen as extremes with respect to the nature of the CIS.

A major difference between tightly and loosely coupled co-operation is that in loosely coupled co-operation people must more explicitly attempt to include aspects of the context with the information items in an effort to ensure that in a future use situation others will be able to deduce their intended meaning. Bannon & Bødker (1997) use the term *packaging* to denote this effort to put information items in common, i.e. to extend the stored items with some explanation of their context. Conversely, the reader's effort to recreate the context and get the intent of the message is denoted *unpacking*. This effort is as demanding and partial as the one that goes into packaging. Thus, packaging and unpacking are meant 'to draw attention to the myriad of ways in which people struggle to make sense of each other' (Bannon & Bødker, 1997) – they do not imply a smooth, perfect process.

2.3 Professionals' inclination to package and unpack

Several studies report considerable disuse or underutilisation of archived documents (e.g., Harper & Sellen, 1995; Kidd, 1994; Mintzberg, 1975). This may be due to practical circumstances such as lack of critical mass or slow retrieval facilities but other, more principal causes may also enter into it. Nardi & Barreau (1997) argue that old information is not, in general, useful information and ask what someone would do with all the old information even if they could find it quickly and easily. While they acknowledge that there are situations where old information is essential they argue that large-scale archiving is often promoted without a clear notion of what it should achieve. The lack of clarity regarding the purpose of such archives arises chiefly from vague relations to the primary work performed in the organisations. As long as the document archive is an appendix to the primary work, rather than a contributing part of it, many people will experience it as more or less pointless (Waters & Nagelhout, 1995).

Packaging also requires that the professionals suspend their normal way of looking at and working with their documents to take an outsider's look at them. This is, however, difficult because the individual professional has an inherently incomplete sense of whether his/her documents will eventually be of interest to someone else and, if so, to whom and in what context. Furthermore this outsider's look is to some extent even unpleasant for the professional. It becomes unpleasant because activities such as selecting keywords and setting the security level of a document form a detached view, which does not adequately reflect the professionals' own understanding of their documents or forces the professionals to state things, such as the importance of a document, on which they are not yet sure. Neither of these circumstances provide professionals with a strong inclination to carefully package their documents, rather the combination of these circumstances tends to create a situation where packaging is perceived as a tedious, low-priority task.

In summary, two roles of documents can be identified in the professionals' individual information spaces. Documents serve as *personal work files* to provide the professionals with easy access to the documents they need in their current work. The essential aspect of this role of the professionals' documents is that the documents are collected by an individual professional and organised according to their relationship to this professional's primary work. Strict category structures are not required, and apparently seldom used, to organise documents in this role. As a consequence shared access to personal files must normally be facilitated by the professional collecting and maintaining the file because only this professional knows its organisation and contents. Moreover, a request for a document may involve querying not only the files but also their collector's expertise (Blomberg et al., 1996).

Documents also serve as *reminders of things to do*. Here the essential aspect is that documents play an active role in the professionals' management of their work tasks – the documents are not just passively available. Malone (1983) makes this point succinctly clear when he notes that 'a primary reason for placing tasks on the desktop in the first place is so that intentional search does not have to be relied upon.' Documents generally fulfil this role through their spatial location and visibility, rather than through their contents or an elaborate indexing scheme. This is evident in the organisation of individual professionals' offices and in the co-ordination of co-operative work, for instance when the documents pertaining to a task follow the person currently responsible for the task. In general, documents used in co-ordinating co-operative work serve to remind the involved actors of the co-ordination mechanisms that structure their work and the ways in which they are supposed to do or document their work (Schmidt & Simone, 1996).

In relation to professionals' use of document archives to share information across time and space boundaries the role of documents is less clear. On the one hand documents are an inadequate carrier of meaning in that packaging and unpacking are required but cannot make the full context available to the reader. On the other hand it is often claimed that documents are underutilised in that better documentation and more time spent reading documents should be a cost-effective strategy. For example, Repo (1987) reports that a group of energy researchers saved an average of just under $1300 for every report they read. These savings are the estimated value of avoiding repeated investigations, but it is not clear whether the acquired information was extracted directly from the reports or, for example, provided by persons whom the reader contacted as a result of reading the reports. To better understand the roles that documents play in professionals' information sharing the next section introduces the notion that documents contain multiple 'voices'.

3. Text and context

Human communication is often conceptualised in terms of the transmission of information. This transmission model involves the encoding of an idea into a signal by a sender, the transmission of this signal to a receiver, and the decoding of the signal into a message by the receiver (Wertsch, 1993). In their account of how documents can mediate common information spaces Bannon & Bødker (1997) suggest a very similar conceptualisation: The writer must package the information in documents which are then transferred to the reader who must unpack them to make sense of them. This view of communication is problematic because it tends to imply that documents have a single correct interpretation, which it is the reader's task to extract. While it is true that the wording of a document is frozen at the time the author completes it, the meaning of the document is not frozen. Documents are monologic conversations in the sense that the writer remains unaware of the concrete questions and intentions that cause subsequent readers to examine a document, but in terms of their meaning documents are dialogic.

3.1 The Multivoicedness of documents

The dialogical nature of spoken as well as written utterances has been studied by Bakhtin (1981, 1986), a Soviet philosopher and semiotician. Dialogicality, the basic theoretical construct in Bakhtin's approach, concerns how one speaker's concrete utterances are a compound of her/his own voice and the voices of others. As Bakhtin (1986) says, 'the utterance is filled with dialogic overtones.' These overtones are carried by the speaker's utterance but they need in no way be related to the speaker's voice, i.e. to what the speaker is trying to communicate. For example, one professional's argumentation may gain additional credibility from being phrased in ways that carry well-esteemed scientific overtones, while another professional's argumentation may be blurred by his inadvertent use of a phrase that conveys the voice of a recent episode in a comedy series. Wertsch (1993) summarises Bakhtin's ideas about dialogicality:

> A shorthand way of formulating Bakhtin's ideas about dialogicality for a sociocultural approach to mind is to pose a fundamental Bakhtinian question about forms of semiotic mediation: "Who is doing the talking?" From a Bakhtinian perspective, the answer will always be: "At least two voices."

The concept of dialogicality brings it to the fore that the context of an utterance is not a largely passive background against which the utterance is made. On the contrary, the context is actively present in the individual utterance as overtones of the speaker's voice.

In the case of clinic records, Garfinkel (1967) has studied how such records intertwine (1) a voice reporting who did what to the patients with (2) another voice whereby clinics demonstrate that they have honoured claims for adequate medical care. This involves a delicate balance between detail and intentional ambiguity. On the one hand, the records serve as an essential tool for the clinic personnel in their day-to-day work. On the other hand, for the records to make sense the reader must be able to correctly interpret the utterances and omissions made with regard to the possibility that the records may have to portray the transactions with patients as having been in accordance with accepted medico-legal practice. That is, to make use of the records the reader must be able to tell who is speaking, and this requires detailed knowledge of the domain and of established local practices, i.e. of the context. By intertwining these two voices the clinic records allow for the appropriate use of informational materials by competent readers, and competent readers only, both in normal day-to-day practice and in unknown, future situations. Clement & Wagner (1995) give a similar account of how information is shared with some and at the same time deliberately withheld from others.

Wertsch (1993) distinguishes between the use of documents to convey meaning adequately and to generate new meaning. For a document to *convey meaning* the reader must be familiar with the context of the writer and thus able to distinguish the voice of the writer from the overtones induced by the context. Such agreement on the code used in preparing the document and that used in interpreting it presupposes some kind of standardisation of the employed language. This is clearly illustrated in Harper & Sellen's study of the International Monetary Fund. Harper & Sellen (1995) found that data in the statistical database were shared by a number of people because all data in this database were known to be derived from standard methods. As a consequence it sometimes took years for figures to be approved and added to the database, and there were numerous omissions in it since data were left out if they required any judgement to determine vagueness or inconsistency. Thus, data that did not adhere to the no-judgement rule governing the statistical database were not added to it, and the effort required to determine whether data items belonged in the database was by no means trivial – it could extend over several years. In contrast, collaboratively written reports were not shared, though facilities to do so were available. When economists were working on their own data, the data were unsuited for sharing and general use because they had not yet been through the social processes of validation and assessment. When the data had been through these processes, only the authors of the report were able to know when the data were usable, since only the authors could tell judgement from hard fact. Thus, the reports were of limited value to others because the data in them were either of unknown validity or inseparable from the judgements that interpreted them.

Harper & Sellen (1995) find that information items have to be packaged according to painstakingly standardised methods for people to consider them reusable, otherwise documents are considered useful to their authors only. The standardised methods are required to enable the words of a document to provide a passive link between the writer and the reader. Latour (1986) terms documents with this characteristic immutable mobiles to emphasise that they can be transported over long distances and convey unchanging information. In the absence of painstakingly standardised methods it becomes crucial to distinguish between the wording of documents and their meaning, but this distinction is often blurred. For example, Levy (1994) argues that documents are both fixed and fluid but he restricts his discussion to the wording of the documents and seems to assume that the meaning remains fixed as long as the wording is not changed.

When documents serve to *generate new meaning* there is an inherent tension between the writer's world and the reader's world. This tension indicates that the document functions as a 'thinking device' rather than a passive link between the writer and the reader (Wertsch, 1993). In reading a document this way the reader brings a question or incoherence to the document and listens for a voice that will contribute to make coherent sense of his/her world. This involves that the reader enters into a dialogue with the text. On the one hand this dialogue can take many directions since documents are heterogeneous objects and readers have varying interests, on the other hand the wording of the document is frozen and severely bounds the possible dialogues. In this role documents are what Star & Griesemer (1989) term boundary objects, that is objects that are both adaptable to different viewpoints and robust enough to maintain identity across them.

Extensive use of condensed forms of communication, which leave most of the context unsaid because the document will be understood by the primary readers as belonging to a certain ongoing activity, preserves resources during document production but reduces the ability of documents to maintain identity across contexts. To make documents understandable to people who are not familiar with the context the condensed forms of communication must be elaborated, often to the exasperation of the primary readers who can see the elaboration as redundant (Brown & Duguid, 1996). When professionals are in a hurry or simply absorbed in their day-to-day work they are likely to document their work to support their own sense-making process; they are much less inclined to spend time expanding their writings into documents understandable to unknown future readers.

3.2 Document reuse versus depth of understanding

A radical way to circumvent the limitations of documents with respect to conveying information is to abandon information sharing altogether and do the work anew. Reading often gets a frustrating experience, which does not seem worth the effort because the professional is left in doubt about some aspects of the document or discovers that it only partially provides the needed information. Doing the work anew may be more work but it is experienced as more satisfying because the professional is in control and gets the understanding of the topic that comes out of doing the work herself/himself.

In connection with systems development Naur (1985) explicitly argues that it should be seriously considered to build new versions of existing applications from scratch if the upgrade is to be made by persons who have not been deeply involved in the writing of the current version. 'Such a procedure is more likely to produce a viable program than program revival, and at no higher, and possibly lower, cost' (Naur, 1985). Reuse is of questionable value in these cases because the program code and documentation cannot provide the necessary understanding of the system. Naur describes systems design as a process of theory building, a theory being an all-compassing, coherent understanding of the way a selected part of the real world is handled in a specific computer system. This theory is neither contained in the program code nor in the documentation but built gradually by the developer through his/her active involvement with the program code, the documentation, and their relation to selected aspects of the real world. A person having the theory is able to tell whether and how potential modifications of the system can be implemented as new elements fitting coherently into the structure and idea of the system, whereas a person who is not in possession of the theory is unable to preserve its coherence in face of modifications.

A very similar account of professionals' sense-making is given by Perby (1987) who studied meteorologists making local weather forecasts in an airport. The meteorologists maintained that taking over ready-made forecasts would degrade the quality of their briefing of the pilots since the process of making the forecasts was necessary in building the inner weather picture that provided the foundation of their work. What the meteorologists defended was an active assimilation of the continuous stream of information about various, evolving weather elements instead of passively receiving a lot of data. The crucial quality of this active assimilation was that it guaranteed a certain depth in the individual meteorologist's interpretation of the information. Again, doing the work anew has advantages over reusing documents produced by others – in a sense the choice between rework and document reuse resembles the choice between project-based and lecture-based teaching.

It seems that many efforts to emphasise documentation and document management have seriously overestimated the ability of documents to convey meaning or underestimated the amount of work required to package and unpack information contained in documents. The apparently ever-increasing storage capacity of computers has made it feasible to store literally every document, email, fax, letter, memo, minute, note, report etc. produced or received in an organisation. Such an archive would provide access to the text of the documents, but many archives have been influenced by a much more far-reaching idea of a vast information repository giving everyone within the organisation immediate access to the accumulated knowledge of past and present employees (see Ackerman, 1996). This amounts to considering filing documents an alternative to being informed by them (Kidd, 1994). The result is systems that are capable of storing masses of documents but largely fail to support professionals in reaching the understanding they need to perform their work. These systems focus on preserving a record of the professionals' past activities and thereby give priority to the evidential value of the documents as opposed to their informational value.

It seems warranted to suggest a stronger focus on the informational value, in terms of document management systems that aim more directly at the professionals' present activities.

In between reuse and rework professionals rely on oral communication with informed colleagues, though this involves both interrupting them in their work and succeeding in presenting the question in a way that triggers their attention and gets them constructively involved. While the wording of documents is frozen and thus does not adapt to the readers, oral communication affords mutuality and enables the actors to adjust to each other. Questions often lead to queries about the situation that gave rise to the question to provide the person being asked with a more solid basis for interpreting and answering the question. In the course of the conversation the person asking a question may encounter that it misses the real problem and rephrase it or ask additional questions. Also, the person asking the question will be interested in some background information about the experiences that gave rise to the answer in order to assess its reliability. Thus, neither the question nor the answer exists beforehand, both are products of the communication process. A number of studies have found that personal contacts are an essential source of information, which is often preferred to seeking written information (e.g., Pinelli et al., 1993).

While some of the persons professionals contact are part of their personal network documents play an important role in *mediating contacts among people* who do not know each other beforehand. This sixth role of documents emphasises that an important aspect of a document is to record that the author is a potential source of information about the document subject (Hertzum, 1993). Since documents often report from co-operative projects other people apart from the author(s) may also know something about the subject. Therefore information about where a document has been used is also of potential value – who participated in the project where the document was created, who were the document circulated to upon completion, etc. In paper archives some of this information is often stored haphazardly, for example information about who initially received a copy of a document may be handwritten on the cover page in the form of an instruction to the secretary who did the copying and mailing. In electronic archives such information must be explicitly captured to remain available. Another implication for document management systems is that they should provide users with an easy way to obtain current contact information for authors and other people mentioned in the documents, as opposed to contact information that was valid at the time the document was created.

In summary, the analysis has identified four roles documents play in professionals' information sharing. Documents serve to *share information with some yet withhold it from others*. These politics of sharing and withholding become necessary because the permanence of documents means that the writer cannot know who will later obtain a document and what they will want to use it for. Thus, the very ability of documents to support information sharing makes it necessary for writers to take precautions against unintended sharing. This role of documents is not restricted to situations where documents may later be used as evidence about a course of events but has to be considered whenever ownership of information is important to a professional's position, power, or privileges.

Documents prepared according to painstakingly standardised methods can also serve to *convey meaning*. Standardised methods are required to reduce the multivoicedness of a document to a level sufficiently low to allow reading without continuously engaging in interpretation to establish the meaning of the document. While conveying meaning adequately is the ultimate type of information sharing the most important message regarding this document role is that documents rarely play it. Writers refrain from the required standardisation to avoid being overloaded, and readers may find that documents do not apply uninterpreted anyway because the world has changed since the document was written. In this sense documents change by virtue of staying the same while time passes and situations change.

Documents that fail to convey meaning often serve to *generate new meaning*. However, such documents may mistakenly be believed to convey meaning because interpretation and personal judgement are so integral to professional work that they easily go unnoticed. When documents serve to generate new meaning the reader unpacks the document to make sense of it in her/his own context. The basic condition necessitating this unpacking is that the meaning of a document is 'hiding in the light' of its words. While the text of a document is tangible, sharable, and obviously visible its informational contents has to be brought out through the reader's active building of an understanding not conveyed in the text.

Writers have to significantly prune their dialogue with their readers to fit it into documents and this pruning leaves only weak traces of what the writers could have stated but did not. To circumvent this limitation documents frequently serve to *mediate contacts among people*. In this role a document is not read to provide the reader with the needed information directly but to determine whether the document can be used as a directory of people who may possess the needed information.

4. A Janus-faced approach to document management

While several of the six document roles complement each other and can be supported side by side, there seems to be a conflict between individual and common information spaces. From the individual professionals' perspective the document management that goes on in their offices is part of their primary work and hardly experienced as a separate activity, whereas the document management involved in putting documents in common is often experienced as a low-priority appendix to their work. Contrary to this, corporate efforts to improve document management practices have often included strong requests to abolish personal collections, which are seen as a threat to the authority and up-to-dateness of the shared archive. These two perspectives on document management are to a certain extent mutually exclusive in that adopting one perspective tends to make people blind toward the other.

Memex (Bush, 1945) and Dynabook (Kay & Goldberg, 1977) are seminal examples of visions about how computers could support individuals' document management. These systems present the collection as a browsable 'landscape' of inter-linked multimedia documents, but they also take the user to be an independent actor, i.e. not embedded in an organisational setting. Numerous commercial systems have attempted to canonise an organisational view on document management (Hertzum, 1995). These systems have introduced archiving requirements that are dependent upon the active co-operation of the professionals but have failed to provide any support for the professionals' personal document management.

It seems that most work in this area has focused on either the personal or the organisational part of document management. This study hypothesises that it should be a central consideration in the design of document management systems to strike the balance between supporting the individual professional in managing his/her personal documents and supporting information sharing among professionals. To achieve this it is suggested that systems be conceived of as two separate but interfaced parts: one directed toward the individual professional, the other toward the needs of the organisation. The interface between the two parts specifies what the individual professional must put in common and how this 'up-loading' is done as well as what the professional can 'down-load' from the corporate part of the system. Such a design brings personal and organisational document management together but maintains a boundary between them, a property with at least two advantages: (1) By accentuating that document management has two faces the boundary helps avoid designs that neglect the differences between them or are unduly biased toward one or the other. (2) Since the information that must be up-loaded is singled out the professionals will know when they use the system for their own benefit and when they fulfil their obligation toward the organisation.

One way to conceptualise an archive is as a number of intertwined, personal threads, each thread being the chronologically ordered sequence of documents written or received by an individual professional. This emphasises the personalised nature of the information and the possibilities for using documents to mediate contacts among professionals. The threads can be visualised as personal timelines where documents or clusters of documents constitute events in the person's corporate history (see Lansdale & Edmonds, 1992; Plaisant et al., 1996).

Such a visualisation retains some context in the sense that documents appear close to other roughly simultaneous events such as other documents or calendar notes. This enables document retrieval via searches for the context in which a document has been used. An additional feature of timelines is an element of automated document management in that old documents are gradually moved out of the user's immediate view as time passes (Fertig et al., 1996). Timelines belong in the personal part of a document management system because the only thing that adds useful structure to the chronological sequence of events is the searcher's memory of the temporal relationships between past events. Information sharing requires a different visualisation of the system, one that focuses on providing searchers with an impression of what they can expect to find.

Document management must strike a balance where it inflicts minimal inconvenience on the individual professional and yet ensures the quality of the shared archive. To keep packaging manageable and avoid information overload on the part of the receivers it is probably reasonable to package selected documents only. It is, in other words, counterproductive to aim at a level of documentation that makes everything that has been done once available for reuse. In connection with the production of documents – a pervasive activity in the environments of most professionals – it may even be beneficial to opt for reuse of fragments of document text rather than for preservation and reuse of experience, insights, and other kinds of information. Carefully made documents often contain well-structured explanations of complex concepts or meticulously thought-through formulations of critical issues such as contractual terms and legal obligations. Blomberg et al. (1996) describe how the personal files of an attorney in a large law firm were used in this way, i.e. as templates for new documents, by himself and his colleagues. Shared access to the documents was provided through personal contact to the attorney who also contributed comments on the specific qualities of the documents. Thus document fragments were frequently reused but their meaning was established through discussion among colleagues, not through strict, corporate-wide category structures. This may indicate that document management systems should supplement the facilities that take a whole document as the entity with facilities for handling document fragments (Levy, 1993). However, document fragments are exactly like whole documents in that they too have multiple voices unless made according to painstakingly standardised methods, and therefore reuse of document fragments is subject to essentially the same obstacles as reuse of whole documents.

5. Conclusion

Professionals have made extensive use of documents for centuries but the role of documents in professionals' work is still not well understood, as evidenced by the meagre results of the past 30 years of work on providing effective computer support for document management. This study has investigated the ways professionals use and manage documents with special emphasis on the interactions between the use of documents in the individual professionals' execution of their current activities and the use of documents for information sharing among professionals who are separated in time or space. This investigation has identified six roles documents play in professionals' work:

- *As personal work files.* Documents serve in this role to be readily available to the individual professional and through her/him to colleagues within the organisation. Generally, such documents are organised according to their relation to the professional's work, rather than according to category structures.

- *As reminders of things to do.* Through their spatial organisation documents in this role serve a crucial function in the professional's management of his/her work activities. Also, such documents are kept visible to cue the professionals back into a line of thinking they have been engaged in but not yet finished.

- *To share information with some, yet withhold it from others.* Access to information may affect the distribution of power and privileges in an organisation. As a precaution against unintended sharing many documents are intentionally ambiguous and thereby understandable to competent readers only.

- *To convey meaning.* Painstakingly standardised methods are required to reduce the multivoicedness of a document sufficiently for it to convey meaning. In practice, this substantial effort is rarely considered worth it compared to doing the work anew or relying on people's ability to actively build a coherent interpretation of the document – i.e. generate new meaning.

- *To generate new meaning.* Rather than relying on the writer to produce a document that can be moved to other contexts and provide unchanged information, it is usually left to the reader to reinterpret the document in her/his own context. In this role, what the writer provides is a thinking device to be used by readers in their making sense of their world.

- *To mediate contacts among people.* Since documents are a restricted form of communication and reading is a quite slow process, readers frequently use interesting documents as pointers to people. This way documents serve to direct readers in their search for people with specific competencies.

Organisations have an obvious interest in storing information in less person-dependent ways than simply relying on the memory and personal files of their employees. However, using written documentation to store and share information involves two time-consuming activities, packaging and unpacking, and seems to result in a reduced depth of understanding compared to doing the work oneself. Furthermore, the sole purpose of packaging is to support sharing; for those involved first hand packaging is superfluous and in fact tends to interfere with efficient execution of their ongoing work. As a result packaging and unpacking shall be applied selectively, that is in situations where actual time savings are achieved and these time savings outweigh the costs in terms of reduced depth of understanding.

This study hypothesises that document management systems should avoid canonising either the professionals' individual information spaces or the use of documents to support the creation and maintenance of common information spaces. Both perspectives seem necessary to understand the dynamics of document management and to strike a balance that avoids overloading the professionals in their current work and yet achieves effective information sharing. However, the relative importance of the six document roles depends on the concrete circumstances and must thus be established through analysis of the work domain. Science differs from engineering, safety-critical domains from transaction-processing ones, bureaucratic institutions from entrepreneurship etc., and this calls for future work into the concrete implications of the document roles in different domains of professional work.

Acknowledgements

This work was supported by a grant from the Danish National Research Foundation. The major part of this study was done while I was at the University of Limerick in the context of the EU Training & Mobility of Researchers project COTCOS. My stay there was co-funded by a grant from Christian and Ottilia Brorson's trust for the endowment of young scientists. I wish to thank the people in the Interaction Design Centre, University of Limerick, for their support.

References

Ackerman, M. S. (1996): 'Definitional and contextual issues in organizational and group memories', *Information Technology & People*, 9, 1, pp. 10-24.

Bakhtin, M. M. (1981): *The dialogic imagination: four essays by M. M. Bakhtin* (edited by M. Holquist), University of Texas Press, Austin.

Bakhtin, M. M. (1986): *Speech genres and other late essays* (edited by C. Emerson and M. Holquist), University of Texas Press, Austin.

Bannon, L. and Bødker, S. (1997): 'Constructing common information spaces', in J. Hughes, T. Rodden, W. Prinz and K. Schmidt (eds.): *ECSCW'97: Proceedings of the 5th European Conference on CSCW*, Kluver, Dordrecht.

Bannon, L. and Schmidt, K. (1989): 'CSCW: four characters in search of a context', in: *EC-CSCW'89: Proceedings of the First European Conference on CSCW*. Reprinted in J. M. Bowers and S. D. Benford (eds.): *Studies in Computer Supported Cooperative Work: Theory, Practice and Design*, North-Holland, Amsterdam, 1991, pp. 3-16.

Barreau, D. K. (1995): 'Context as a factor in personal information management systems', *Journal of the American Society for Information Science*, 46, 5, pp. 327-339.

Barreau, D. and Nardi, B. A. (1995): 'Finding and reminding', *ACM SIGCHI Bulletin*, 27, 3, pp. 39-43.

Berlin, L. M., Jeffries, R., O'Day, V. L., Paepcke, A. and Wharton, C. (1993): 'Where did you put it? Issues in the design and use of a group memory', in: *Proceedings of the ACM/IFIP INTERCHI'93 Conference*, ACM Press, New York, pp. 23-30.

Bikson, T. K. and Frinking, E. J. (1993): *Preserving the present: Toward viable electronic records*, Sdu Publishers, The Hague.

Blair, D. C. (1996): 'STAIRS redux: Thoughts on the STAIRS evaluation, ten years after', *Journal of the American Society for Information Science*, 47, 1, pp. 4-22.

Blomberg, J., Suchman, L. and Trigg, R. H. (1996): 'Reflections on a work-oriented design project', *Human-Computer Interaction*, 11, pp. 237-265.

Brown, J. S. and Duguid, P. (1996): 'The social life of documents', *First Monday*, 1, 1, http://www.firstmonday.dk/issues/issue1/documents/index.html.

Bush, V. (1945): 'As we may think', *Atlantic Monthly*, 176, 1, pp. 101-108.

Carstensen, P. H. (1997): 'Towards information exploration support for engineering designers', in S. Ganesan (ed.): *Advances in Concurrent Engineering - CE97*, Technomic, Lancaster, Pennsylvania, pp. 26-33.

Case, D. O. (1991): 'Conceptual organization and retrieval of text by historians: The role of memory and metaphor', *Journal of the American Society for Information Science*, 42, 9, pp. 657-668.

Clement, A. and Wagner, I. (1995): 'Fragmented exchange: Disarticulation and the need for regionalized communication spaces', in H. Marmolin, Y. Sundblad and K. Schmidt (eds.): *ECSCW'95: Proceedings of the 4th European Conference on CSCW*, Kluwer, Dordrecht, pp. 33-49.

Cole, I. (1982): 'Human aspects of office filing: Implications for the electronic office', in: *Proceedings of the Human Factors Society 26th Annual Meeting*, Human Factors Society, Santa Monica, pp. 59-63.

Fertig, S., Freeman, E. and Gelernter, D. (1996): '"Finding and reminding" reconsidered', *ACM SIGCHI Bulletin*, 28, 1, pp. 66-69.

Garfinkel, H. (1967): '"Good" organizational reasons for "bad" clinic records', in H. Garfinkel: *Studies in Ethnomethodology*, Prentice Hall, Englewood Cliffs, NJ, pp. 186-207.

Gordon, M. D. (1997): 'It's 10 a.m. Do you know where your documents are? The nature and scope of information retrieval problems in business', *Information Processing & Management*, 33, 1, pp. 107-121.

Harper, R. and Sellen, A. (1995): 'Collaborative tools and the practicalities of professional work at the International Monetary Fund', in: *Proceedings of the ACM CHI'95 Conference.* ACM Press, New York, pp. 122-129.

Hertzum, M. (1993): 'Information retrieval in a work setting: A case study of the documentation part of chemists' work', in J. P. Bansler, K. Bødker, F. Kensing, J. Nørbjerg and J. Pries-Heje (eds.): *Proceedings of the 16th IRIS. Information Systems Research Seminar in Scandinavia*, DIKU report 93/16, University of Copenhagen, Copenhagen, pp. 786-798.

Hertzum, M. (1995): 'Computer support for document management in the Danish central government', *Information Infrastructure and Policy*, 4, 2, pp. 107-129.

Jahoda, G., Hutchins, R. D. and Galford, R. R. (1966): 'Characteristics and use of personal indexes maintained by scientists and engineers in one university', *American Documentation*, 17, 2, pp. 71-75.

Kay, A. and Goldberg, A. (1977): 'Personal dynamic media', *IEEE Computer*, 10, 3, pp. 31-41.

Kidd, A. (1994): 'The marks are on the knowledge worker', in: *Proceedings of the ACM CHI'94 Conference*, ACM Press, New York, pp. 186-191.

Kwasnik, B. H. (1991): 'The importance of factors that are not document attributes in the organisation of personal documents', *Journal of Documentation*, 47, 4, pp. 389-398.

Lansdale, M. and Edmonds, E. (1992): 'Using memory for events in the design of personal filing systems', *International Journal of Man-Machine Studies*, 36, pp. 97-126.

Latour, B. (1986): 'Visualization and cognition: Thinking with eyes and hands', *Knowledge and Society: Studies in the Sociology of Culture Past and Present*, 6, pp. 1-40.

Levy, D. M. (1993): 'Document reuse and document systems', *Electronic Publishing*, 6, 4, pp. 339-348.

Levy, D. M. (1994): 'Fixed or fluid? Document stability and new media', in: *ECHT'94: Proceedings of the European Conference on Hypertext*, ACM Press, New York, pp. 24-31.

Malone, T. W. (1983): 'How do people organize their desks? Implications for the design of office information systems', *ACM Transactions on Office Information Systems*, 1, 1, pp. 99-112.

Mintzberg, H. (1975): 'The manager's job: Folklore and fact', *Harvard Business Review*, 53, 4, pp. 49-61.

Nardi, B. A. and Barreau, D. (1997): '"Finding and reminding" revisited: Appropriate metaphors for file organization at the desktop', *ACM SIGCHI Bulletin*, 29, 1, pp. 76-78.

Naur, P. (1985): 'Programming as theory building', *Microprocessing & Microprogramming*, 15, 5, pp. 253-261.

Perby, M.-L. (1987): 'Computerization and the skill in local weather forecasting', in G. Bjerknes, P. Ehn and M. Kyng (eds.): *Computers and Democracy*, Avebury, Aldershot, pp. 213-229.

Pinelli, T. E., Bishop, A. P., Barclay, R. O. and Kennedy, J. M. (1993): 'The information-seeking behavior of engineers', in A. Kent and C. M. Hall (eds.): *Encyclopedia of Library and Information Science*, vol. 52, supplement 15, Marcel Dekker, New York, pp. 167-201.

Plaisant, C., Milash, B., Rose, A., Widoff, S. and Shneiderman, B. (1996): 'Lifelines: Visualizing personal histories', in: *Proceedings of the ACM CHI'96 Conference*, ACM Press, New York, pp. 221-227.

Repo, A. J. (1987): 'Economics of information', in M. E. Williams (ed.): *Annual Review of Information Science and Technology*, vol. 22, Elsevier Science Publishers, Amsterdam, pp. 3-36.

Schmidt, K. and Bannon, L. (1992): 'Taking CSCW seriously - Supporting articulation work', *Computer Supported Cooperative Work (CSCW)*, 1, pp. 7-40.

Schmidt, K. and Simone, C. (1996): 'Coordination mechanisms: Towards a conceptual foundation of CSCW system design', *Computer Supported Cooperative Work: The Journal of Collaborative Computing*, 5, pp. 155-200.

Sellen, A. and Harper, R. (1997): 'Paper as an analytic resource for the design of new technologies', in: *Proceedings of the ACM CHI'97 Conference*, ACM Press, New York.

Star, S. L. and Griesemer, J. R. (1989): 'Institutional ecology, 'translations' and boundary objects: Amateurs and professionals in Berkeley's Museum of Vertebrate Zoology, 1907-39', *Social Studies of Science*, 19, pp. 387-420.

Waters, P. M. H. and Nagelhout, H. (1995): 'Revolution in records: A strategy for information resources management and records management', *American Archivist*, 58, 1, pp. 74-83.

Wertsch, J. V. (1993): *Voices of the mind*, Harvard University Press, Cambridge, MA.

S. Bødker, M. Kyng, and K. Schmidt (eds.). *Proceedings of the Sixth European Conference on Computer-Supported Cooperative Work, 12-16 September 1999, Copenhagen, Denmark*
©1999 Kluwer Academic Publishers. Printed in the Netherlands

61

AREA: A Cross-Application Notification Service for Groupware

Ludwin Fuchs
Boeing Mathematics & Computing Technology, USA
email: ludwin.fuchs@boeing.com

Abstract: This paper presents AREA, an integrated synchronous and asynchronous notification service for awareness information. AREA uses a semantic model of the client applications to support cross-application awareness. The service is based on the dichotomy of interest and privacy. Notifications of user activities are a function of relevance in the current work situation and the privacy requirements of the involved users. The paper motivates the AREA framework and discusses the system in terms of its formal modeling capabilities and its operational aspects. This is followed by practical implementation considerations addressing the role of AREA as a groupware infrastructure. Finally, a prototype groupware application is presented, which uses the AREA service to support user awareness.

Introduction

The Nineties have seen an important paradigm shift in the usage of computer technology: Systems are no longer exclusively seen as number crunchers helping us to solve difficult problems. Instead, driven by the enormous growth in network bandwidth and the ubiquity of the Internet, the computer evolves more and more into an inhabited information space, in which we interact with other people.

One of the most obvious manifestations of this is denoted by the term *awareness*: the ability of the technology to expose the activities of the people in the electronic space. In collaborative environments the role of awareness for coordinating work activities has been shown in numerous studies (see e.g. Heath and Luff, 1992, Rogers, 1993). But support for awareness is not just important in the work environment. An obvious proof to this is the commercial thrust, which has been initiated more recently by the need for awareness on the Internet. An example is ICQ, an Internet buddy list application, which has led the 1998 shareware download surveys for months with more than 10 Million estimated users online.

This paper focuses on collaborative environments as constituted by a shared information space and a variety of independent tools being used individually as well as jointly among the group members. The paper proposes treating awareness as a global, i.e. application independent requirement in such an environment.

Based on these considerations the paper presents AREA, an integrated synchronous and asynchronous notification service for awareness information. AREA supports cross-application awareness using a model of the clients' semantics to capture the awareness-related operational aspects of the applications. The model explicitly addresses the potential for conflicts of awareness and privacy: Notifications of user activities are a function of relevance in the current work situation and the privacy requirements of the involved users.

The emphasis of the paper is to motivate the AREA framework and to discuss the system in terms of its formal modeling capabilities and its operational aspects. This is followed by practical implementation considerations about the role of AREA as a groupware infrastructure. Finally, a prototype groupware application is presented, which uses the AREA service to support user awareness.

Design Issues

Supporting group awareness creates difficult design problems for developers of distributed collaborative applications, problems with both technical and organizational dimensions.

Technically, the developer is faced with the heterogeneity of applications. Groupware can only be commonly characterized by the weak incentive to support collaboration between a number of users. Workflow systems, shared design tools, email, collaborative web applications, and document management systems all are first class groupware systems. These technologies lack a common base that could be abstracted out to form the core of a formal model of groupware and eventually inform the design of awareness support. Supporting awareness in a shared text editor is a fundamentally different problem than supporting awareness in a persistent discussion space such as Lotus Domino.

A further challenge is introduced by the global nature of the awareness problem: collaborative environments consist of a multitude of tools and applications. Performing a collaborative task rarely is a continuous and concerted activity and almost never maps to a single technology that could support it.

Instead, working together is opportunistic: users frequently switch between a number of tools running in parallel and also the shared information crosses the boundaries of applications. Collaborating requires working in synchronous and asynchronous mode, frequently switching between modes, or even working in both modes at the same time. We talk on the phone while we browse our email or look up information in a shared discussion database. Writing a shared document involves working at different times on individual parts followed by meetings to discuss and merge them together. Supporting awareness thus becomes a global issue. What we really need is an integrated view on the activities in the work environment as a whole, covering many applications, rather than just one. Even if we have a good formal model of a particular groupware application domain, the provision of awareness will be restricted to the boundaries of a single tool and lack the global perspective.

Global awareness support is not only difficult to achieve architecturally, it also introduces new problems: If information about user activities is collected and disseminated in the whole work environment, it is likely to overload the user with irrelevant and out-of-context notifications. To prevent this, users need a way to define their information needs in terms of the work they are performing. The same event can be highly important for one user and completely uninteresting for another user in the same situation. Similarly, an event may be important for a user in some situation and irrelevant for the same user in another.

Supporting individual awareness leads to a number of socio-technical conflicts. These result from two constellations of conflicting goals between the individual user and other users or the group as a whole: (1) the user's demand for privacy creates a conflict with other users' or the group's demand for awareness and (2) the user's goal to reduce information overload clashes with other users' or the group's goal to establish common reference.

The first issue also has organizational and legal dimensions: in many countries data protection laws restrict the organizational usage of personal data such as awareness information. The second issue is particularly important in the group context. Only if awareness of activities provides a common reference to all members of the group can it be a vehicle for coordination in a team environment. For example, a design team working on a model of a particular section of an airplane often faces many interdependencies between the individual sub-parts. Changing one part can violate constraints imposed by another part maintained by other group members. When a designer changes a part of his model it is critical that these changes are reliably visible to the other group members in order to minimize disruption caused by conflicting changes.

If users can individually tailor awareness notifications, others can no longer be certain that their actions are perceived by the group as a whole, i.e. the activities no longer form a common reference in the group. Technology intended to support awareness needs to address this fundamental tradeoff.

Awareness Frameworks

The inherent complexity of supporting awareness as outlined in the last chapter has fueled the development of awareness frameworks that provide a simplified model of collaboration for particular application domains. They offer basic mechanisms that can be used by systems designers in order to make the actions in the environment visible to others. The following section provides a brief review of various awareness frameworks.

A number of approaches address synchronous collaboration. Gutwin et al. (1996) describe a shared editing environment providing awareness based on multi-user GUI mechanisms. The system offers a number of awareness widgets showing the current focus of others in the application using distortion techniques. Activities close to the user's own focus are visible whereas those parts of the document with no ongoing activities are only visible in a global minimized layout view. Thus the authors show that an overview in its physical sense can support user awareness. The design of such multi-user interface components can be largely supported by toolkits such as GroupKit (Roseman and Greenberg, 1992) or Habanero (Chabert et al., 1998). More recently, Smith and O'Brian have proposed a similar GUI-oriented approach for awareness in 3D virtual environments (Smith and O'Brian, 1998).

While the user interface approach provides useful mechanisms for developing synchronous relaxed WYSIWIS applications, it doesn't address awareness as a groupware infrastructure issue. This is one of the goals of the Notification Service Transport Protocol (NSTP, see Patterson et al., 1996), an application independent notification protocol for synchronous groupware. NSTP is based on a client-server model, where the server maintains a number of places managing the shared state. Clients can enter any number of places. They can manipulate the shared state and receive automatic notifications whenever state changes occur in the places they have entered. NSTP is a lean framework strictly focusing on efficiency. Consequently, it is free of any assumptions concerning the application's semantics. Another synchronous application-independent notification service similar to NSTP is Corona (Shim et al., 1997). Unlike NSTP, Corona provides a persistent data store for the shared state and adds more flexibility for updating the shared state.

All awareness architectures discussed so far focus on synchronous groupware. Among the asynchronous models, GroupDesk, a shared workspace prototype, implements awareness using relationships between artifacts in the work environment to notify users about activities (Fuchs et al., 1995). The asynchronous behavior in the GroupDesk awareness model results from distributing events between the artifacts and storing them persistently. Notifications are triggered as soon as interested users access the artifacts. The usage of object relations has been adapted in the Aether model to support asynchronous awareness in 3D populated information spaces (see Sandor et al., 1997). A further asynchronous awareness model is implemented in the Interlocus prototype (Nomura et al., 1998). Interlocus monitors individual user activities and creates snapshots of the objects when the user makes changes. Awareness is provided by intelligently merging individual snapshots and providing chronological views on the documents in the workspace.

The AREA Awareness Model

In the following sections the AREA awareness model is introduced. Similar to NSTP, AREA is an attempt to provide an awareness infrastructure component for collaborative environments. In contrast to NSTP, AREA is not only an application development environment but may also be used by preexisting groupware tools. Similar to GroupDesk, AREA implements situation-oriented awareness based on relevance relationships among the shared objects. Unlike GroupDesk, AREA offers an open service interface enabling multiple applications to specify event distribution, user-defined interest and privacy specifications, as well as awareness-related group facilitation mechanisms.

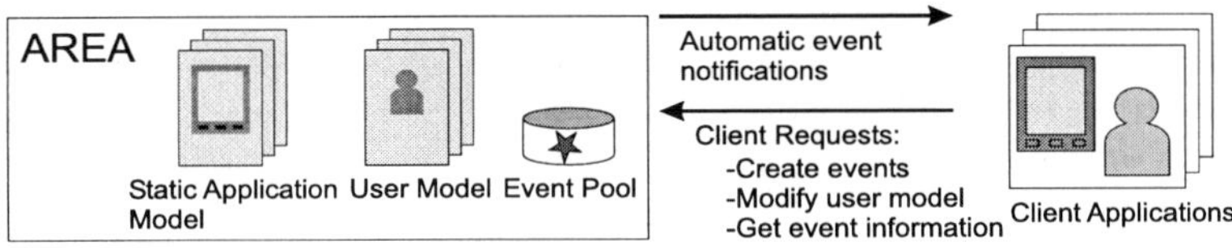

Figure 1: Client-server communication in AREA

AREA applies a client-server architecture, where the server manages the shared state and clients receive automatic event notifications. The shared state consists of a static description of the application semantics, a dynamic user model[1], and a persistent event pool. Client applications can issue requests to create events or to access the user model. Create-event requests cause the server to add a new event to the event pool and issue notifications to other clients.

AREA uses the semantic model of the applications and the user models to determine which clients receive an event notification. This decision is based on the principle of mutual exclusion of awareness and privacy in the following way: a user A can be aware about the actions of another user B if A's user model specifies interest in the action and there are no conflicting privacy requirements of B that prevent the notification.

---

[1] Note that the notion of a user model in AREA does not mean the system is making inferences based on user actions at the application's GUI, as it is usually the case in adaptive systems. The model is solely updated based on explicit requests issued by the application.

Approach

AREA supports awareness by providing notifications about *activities* performed by users in any of the client applications. AREA captures activities in terms of *events*. As users perform activities in the collaborative environment, the system creates new events describing these activities. For each new event AREA determines all users who will be notified about the event by evaluating all user profiles according to their interest specifications and matching them against the privacy requirements of the performing actor. This is illustrated in Figure 2:

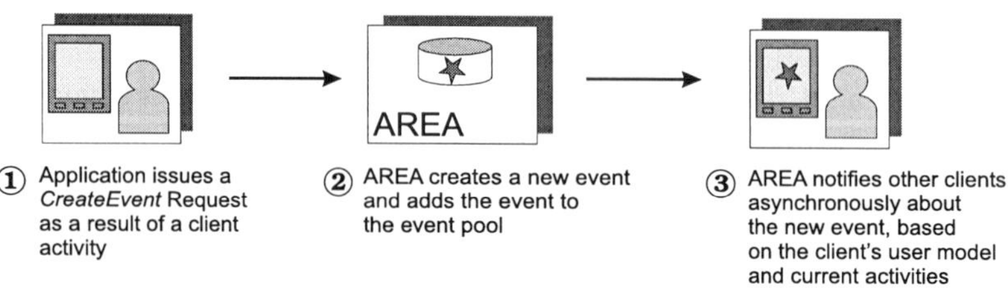

(1) Application issues a *CreateEvent* Request as a result of a client activity

(2) AREA creates a new event and adds the event to the event pool

(3) AREA notifies other clients asynchronously about the new event, based on the client's user model and current activities

Figure 2: Event notification in AREA

The notions of interest and privacy are at the core of the AREA awareness framework. Both terms can be defined very specifically or may be kept very general. An actor's interest can cover a broad range of situations common to the kind of work she performs. It can specify a higher degree of importance for more special situations or it may completely exclude events for some situations.

The Application Model

The awareness framework in AREA is based on four basic model components: actors, relations, events, and artifacts. The following paragraphs describe each of these components and discuss how they can be used to describe the application semantics.

Actors

Actors denote users of the client applications. An actor is usually a real person working in the environment but any actively performing entity can be registered as an actor in AREA, e.g. a software agent. Actors are equipped with a profile describing their interest in the actions of others as well as their privacy requirements.

Artifacts

Each action in AREA involves an actor and an artifact, which is the object of the action. In document management systems artifacts typically consist of documents, discussion items, or folder hierarchies. In a technical design application for building airplanes they might consist of drawings, geometric objects, or more abstract entities like constraints that need to be met. Artifacts may have a long lasting life cycle (e.g. a jointly produced research paper) or they may exist only for a brief time period, such as a telepointer in a multi-user brainstorming tool.

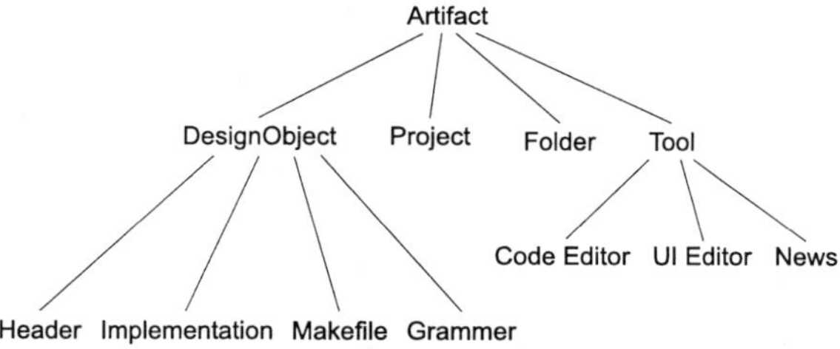

Figure 3: A simple artifact class hierarchy for a software development application

Artifacts belong to classes. The system defines a class hierarchy, which is shared among all applications using the system. Figure 3 gives an example of a class hierarchy for artifacts that might appear in a software design environment. Note that the primary criterion of introducing a class in the hierarchy is not sharing but rather whether the usage of the artifact is worth being aware of. Thus, although a news reader rarely is used collaboratively it can be interesting for group members to be aware that another is reading news and hence shouldn't be disturbed.

Applications may extend the class hierarchy with their own specific classes or they may reuse existing classes. For example, a shared drawing application could add its own artifact classes for application specific items, such as the various drawing tools and filters but it can reuse the classes for JPEG- and GIF-images, already defined by another application.

In this way, the class hierarchy maintained in AREA forms a unified set of classes for all artifacts in the work environment that are suitable candidates to be aware of. Note that AREA does not actually maintain instances of the artifact classes. The class hierarchy in AREA is only an abstraction for the application entities for the purpose of describing awareness behavior. AREA only maintains artifact references (e.g. as attributes of events). The actual instances only exist in the applications and will almost certainly belong to a completely different application-internal class hierarchy. The application may not even be object-oriented at all.

Events

Events formally describe actions performed on an artifact. Each event has at least 3 attributes: the actor responsible for the event, the corresponding artifact reference, and a time stamp. Similar to the artifacts, events are structured in a class hierarchy that defines the semantics of the events. An application can define

68

new event classes. A new class inherits the attributes of its parent class and may
add additional attributes.

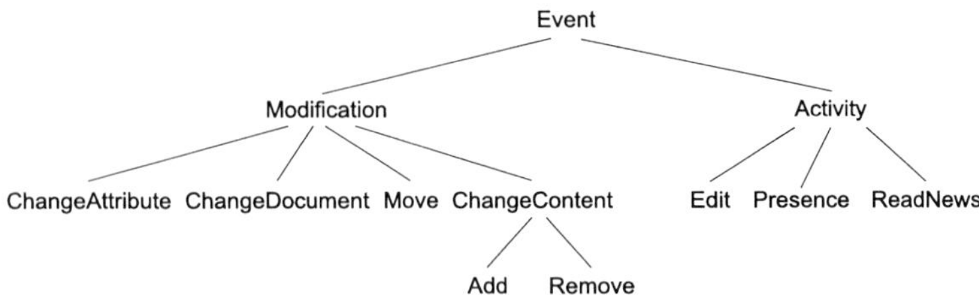

Figure 4: An example for an event class hierarchy

Figure 4 shows an example of a suitable class hierarchy for events, which users
might want to be aware of in the design environment example. Note that not all
events can occur on all artifacts. For example, *ChangeContent* events can only be
created by compound objects like folders. AREA keeps a mapping between event
classes and the artifact classes, which can create these events.

Formally, events in AREA denote state changes and thus do not have a
temporal duration. But the system defines a specific class of events that can be
used to describe actions covering a continuous time span. These are called *activity
events*. Activity events consist of a *begin-event* and a matching *end-event* marking
the time frame of the user activity. In AREA the term "being active" implies that
the system has created a begin-event but not yet received a request for an end-
event. AREA tracks begin-events in an activity list and uses this information to
determine if actors should be notified synchronously.

Relations

AREA uses relations to describe collaborative interdependencies in the
application domain. Relations are always *1:n* and can only exist between artifacts.
In contrast to artifacts and events, AREA does not define an extensible class
hierarchy for relations. An application can only define relation instances, which
may be assigned to one or more of the following predefined groups of relations:
components, *compositions*, and *situations*.

A component defines a part-of relationship between two artifacts. A
composition usually is the inverse relation of a component and yields the
aggregate for a given part. A formal requirement in AREA is that for each
component there exists at least one composition, which is denoted as the inverse
of the component. Note that different component relations can be assigned the
same inverse relation.

Situations are relationships between artifacts expressing relevance in terms of
collaboration. For a given artifact a particular situation defines all other artifacts
that share a common awareness-relevant relationship with this object. Thus, the

set of situations for an artifact should be defined such that it makes sense to be aware of events of this artifact whenever the user accesses another artifact belonging to the situation.

Relation	If available for an artifact it yields...	Is defined for...	Relation groups
Identity	...the same artifact	...all artifacts	Component, Composition, Situation
ContainedIn	...all superior folders	...all artifacts	Composition, Situation
Contains	...the content artifacts	...folder artifacts	Component
Dependents	...the design artifacts with a software dependency	...implementations	Situation

Table 1: Some example relations

Table 1 shows an example of 4 relations, which could be used in the software environment example. The *Identity* relation is defined as component, composition, and situation simultaneously (since each artifact is a part as well as a composition of itself). All relations except the *Contains* relation are defined as situations, since each defines a useful awareness situation for the notification of events.

The User Model

Having introduced the four basic components of AREA, we can now turn to the user model and the operational aspects. A user model consists of a list of interest specifications and a list of privacy requirements. Interest specifications have four parts:

- *The event description* specifies the actions the user wants to be aware of. It consists of a predicate over the set of available event classes and attributes.
- *The scope* defines the space of artifacts for which the description is valid. This in turn involves a predicate expression over the artifact class hierarchy and a component relation. The predicate is evaluated against the artifact raising a new event. The role of the component is to enable indirect specifications, e.g. for all artifacts in a container. This introduces additional flexibility for defining interest descriptions.
- *The situation* defines when notifications about the events shall be issued to the actor. They only consist of a situation relation.
- *The intensity* consists of a discrete value that will be interpreted by the application to determine how a notification should be performed at the GUI.

The following figure shows an example of two interest descriptions:

Event description	Scope	Situation	Intensity
e.class < ChangeEvent	a.class < Folder	Identity	1
	Contains		
e.class < ActivityEvent AND e.actor = "John Smith"	a= "GMD-Folder"	Immediately	3
	Identity		

Figure 5: Two example interest descriptions in a user profile

The first description defines interest in all change-events.[2] The scope of the first description has been specified indirectly: it covers the content of any folders. A notification of a matching event occurs when the user accesses the artifact creating the event (since the situation is the Identity relation). The value of the notification intensity is 1, i.e. the event notification should be performed in the lowest intensity. The second interest description defines interest in the activities of user John Smith. The scope of this description only covers one particular artifact "GMD-Folder". The situation *Immediately* is a predefined symbolic situation relation. If it is used in an interest description, a notification takes place immediately or as soon as the actor enters the environment.

Event Notification

The sum of all interest descriptions in all user models drives the event notification in AREA. Figure 6 illustrates the notification algorithm:

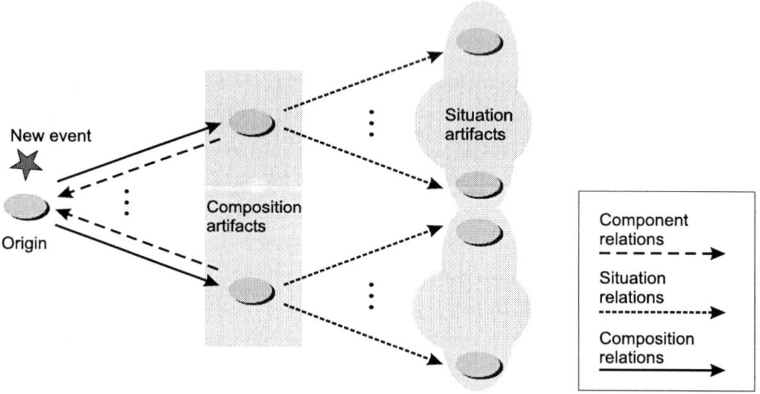

Figure 6: Determining the notification situations for new events

---

[2] The operator < yields the value *true*, if the left operand is a base class of the right operand. *e* and *a* are keywords that are matched against the new event and the artifact creating the event, respectively.

When an application sends a create-event command AREA adds a new event instance of the requested class to the event pool and fills in the values of the attributes. At the minimum these consist of the reference of the affected artifact (subsequently called origin), the actor, and a time stamp.

The next step consists of determining the set of matching user profiles, whose scope covers the origin. These are determined by examining all composition artifacts of which the origin is a component. A user profile is valid if the following conditions are met: (1) the event description matches the new event, (2) the predicate expression in the scope-component evaluates to true, and (3) the component-relation in the scope-specification is the inverse of the current composition.

With this, each of the composition artifacts to which the origin belongs can be associated with a list of matching interest descriptions. These interest descriptions determine the actual situation artifacts that upon access will trigger a notification of the new event. They are determined by applying the situation relations in the remaining interest descriptions on each composition artifact.

The final result of this approach is a list of situation artifacts, each of which is associated with one or more actors to notify and a corresponding maximum intensity value for the notification. At this point a synchronous event notification takes place for all actors who are listed as being active on one of the situation artifacts in AREA's activity list. For all other actors AREA saves the result of the event distribution and notifies them asynchronously as soon as they perform an activity on one of the situation artifacts.

Privacy

In order to motivate the privacy strategy of AREA it is important to review the situation-oriented awareness framework presented so far. AREA restricts awareness about the actions performed on a particular artifact to the set of awareness situations available for the artifact's class in the static application model. At runtime such a situation applies if an actor accesses one of the artifacts constituting the situation. In a reasonable implementation, situations will most often comply with the formal organization of work in terms of access and group collaboration.

As an example, consider an application such as a shared drawing tool in which documents can be organized in projects: a useful user model could specify notifications about changes of drawings when the user is active in a project containing the drawing. The situation "when active in a project containing the drawing" implies that the user needs to have access to the project in order to see what happens with the drawing contained therein and is thus compliant with the work organization.

However, AREA also allows the definition of situations that aren't compliant to the information access restrictions in the work setting. As an example consider a document management application. Here it could be useful to have a *RelatedDocument* situation: when accessing a particular document this situation notifies about events of other documents sharing some properties in terms of content. These documents would not necessarily have to be located in the same place. In fact, they could exist completely outside of the document space accessible to the user.

Thus a reasonable strategy to enforce privacy in AREA can be obtained by restricting the set of users that may receive events for a given situation. Since it is very common that users are willing to expose their activities to others, if they have access to the corresponding work artifacts, this strategy requires users only to deal with notification situations that cross the border of shared access.

Formally, a privacy specification in AREA looks similar to an interest description: It consists of an event description, a scope, and a situation, with each of these components having analogous meaning. The event description defines for which actions a user wants to define privacy, the scope defines the artifact space on which the specification applies, and the situation-relation denotes the particular awareness situation that shall be restricted for other actors. Instead of an intensity value, the fourth component of privacy specifications defines an admission list of actors, listing those that are granted the right to receive the specified event.

The event notification accounts for privacy specifications in the following way: For each new event AREA determines the set of privacy descriptions defined for the responsible actor in the scope of the origin. Formally, this is similar to the first step in the evaluation of the interest profiles. For each composition artifact there is now a list of matching interest descriptions as well as a list of matching privacy descriptions. These privacy descriptions can then be grouped according to the situation they apply to. If no privacy descriptions exist for a particular situation, all actors receive the event notification according to their interest specification. If a privacy description does exist for a particular situation, only those actors listed on the admission list can receive notifications.

Global User Models

AREA does not directly include groups as components of the awareness framework. Nevertheless, the model does support a group-oriented notion of awareness: A set of global user models can be used to enforce the existence of interest and privacy specifications for individual actors. Formally, global user models have the same characteristics as the standard models, except that they apply for each actor in the environment.

Using global user models an application can enforce the visibility of events for each actor and hence create a common reference for those actions. In contrast, global privacy descriptions make sure that nobody in the system can receive notifications about the specified events in the corresponding situation. In this way, legal and organization-wide regulations in terms of privacy can be enforced. Note that global user profiles cannot be used to prevent an actor from enhancing his privacy.

How does this help to establish group policies? The key to achieve this is to make use of the flexible scoping of the global user models. Coordination of group activities in collaborative environments always involves managing common artifacts. By defining global user models scoped to these shared artifacts it is possible to establish group policies for awareness notifications.

AREA as an Awareness Infrastructure

So far, AREA is described as a formal framework for asynchronously managing event notifications in a collaborative object space. The framework uses a semantic model of the application to allow event notifications in application-relevant work situations. While many aspects of the application model can be defined statically, others require close collaboration of the application and AREA at runtime. The following sections concentrate on the role of AREA as a groupware infrastructure component.

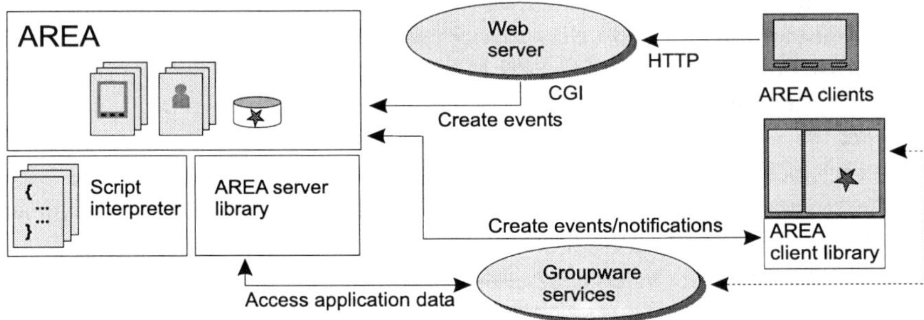

Figure 7: Architecture alternatives for clients using AREA

Figure 7 shows various options for client-server communication using AREA. On the client side there are two alternatives to access the service: using a client library or using a HTTP/CGI interface. Only clients using the library are capable of receiving event notifications. Obviously, this is only possible for newly developed applications, where the source code is available, or in applications capable of extending their functionality using dynamic link libraries. Besides creating events and receiving event notifications, the client library provides access to the details of the static application model and the user models as well as a query interface to the event database. This information needs to be accessed by the client in order to interpret event notifications triggered by the server.

Clients using the HTTP interface can only create events. Although restricted in functionality this interface offers a perspective to add a range of standard applications as clients of AREA. A prerequisite for using this alternative is the availability of a scripting component, or a macro processor capable of issuing HTTP requests. However, many office productivity tools include such an interface. In this way, AREA can support awareness about activities, such as reading email or working with a word processor.

On the server side AREA provides two alternatives for defining the static application model: using a script interpreter and using a server-side library. The server side library contains stubs, which can be used to generate portions of the static application model. A common use of the library is to access the server component of groupware applications or general infrastructure services such as a directory service. In this way, portions of the application model can be generated.

In addition to the server-library, the application model can also be described in a scripting language. The language is particularly useful to define class-level attributes, e.g. event life cycle and persistency properties as well as user-friendly naming for the model components. The dual approach of scripting and using a library offers additional flexibility to define the dynamic portions of the model components: the scripting language offers a construct to call function stubs that are defined using the library, thus providing means to extend the functionality of the scripting component. Since the evaluation of relations and the computation of event attributes are performed on the server side, accessing client side functionality plays a critical role in the event distribution.

User Interface issues

AREA abstracts from the actual application's semantics. Consequently, the system doesn't make assumptions concerning the user interface. A notification in AREA means the application receives a description of the new event and the corresponding intensity value. It is completely in the application's responsibility how to display the event at the user interface. An application may choose among a variety of different user interface techniques, e.g. sound, symbol animations, color annotations, or standard techniques such as dialog boxes, whichever technique fits the application's user interface metaphor and meaning of the intensity.

Cross-Application Awareness

AREA is a cross-application awareness service. To a user working in application A the system can provide notifications about activities of another user working in a distinct application B. Obviously, this requires the notifying application to be capable of interpreting events in the domain of B. This requirement is addressed in AREA by giving clients access to the complete static application model. The class hierarchies for events and artifacts contain user-friendly naming support, such that an application can display meaningful event information about any event.

An Example Application

The following sections describe PoliAwaC, an application of AREA in a document management groupware application. The application has been implemented in the POLITeam[3] project developing groupware technology for a German federal ministry distributed between Bonn and the new German capital, Berlin (see e.g. Prinz et al., 1998).

POLIAwaC extends an existing document management system (Digital's LinkWorks) with an Interface providing synchronous and asynchronous awareness. The system uses AREA for the management and notification of events generated by the core document management server and office tools used to manipulate the documents. The following description concentrates on the application model of POLIAwaC in AREA and discusses the resulting support for awareness in terms of the available notification situations. The details of the system and the user interface mechanisms are described by Sohlenkamp (1998) and Mark et al. (1997)

The application model

The following figure provides an overview of the static application model of POLIAwaC as it is defined in AREA:

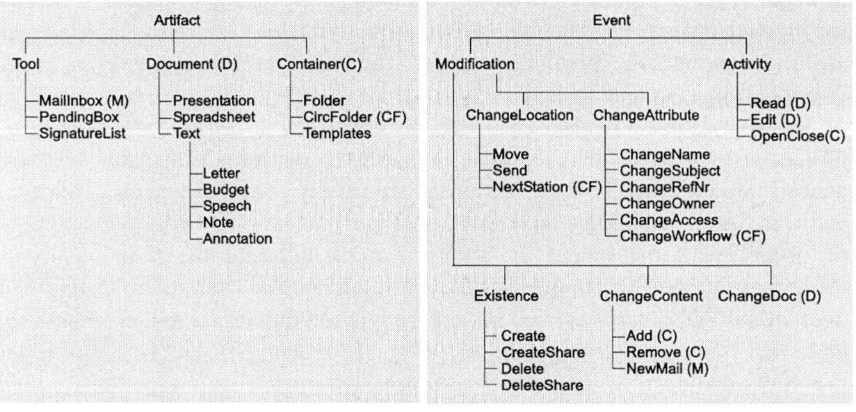

Figure 8: The class hierarchies for artifacts and events in POLIAwaC

---

[3] POLIAwaC = POLITeam Awareness Client.

The left side of Figure 8 shows the artifact class hierarchy. Since POLIAwaC is a document-sharing environment for an administration, the most important artifacts are the different types of text documents. The other classes represent the tools and shared container that are available in POLIAwaC. The class *CircFolder* denotes a special folder offering some basic document routing capabilities.

The right side of Figure 8 illustrates the event class hierarchy. POLIAwaC defines three classes of activity events: Opening and closing folders and editing and reading documents. All other events are modification events, i.e. events describing discrete state changes. The abbreviations behind class names correspond to some of the artifact classes on the left. If present, they indicate that an instance of this event class can only be created by artifacts of the corresponding artifact class. Otherwise, any artifact can use the event class.

The following table lists some of the relations defined in POLIAwaC:

Relation	If available for an artifact it yields...	Is defined for...	Relation groups
Identity	...the same artifact	...all artifacts	Component, Composition, Situation
Immediately	N/A (symbolic relation)	...all artifacts	Situation
ContainedIn	...all superior folders	...all artifacts	Composition, Situation
Contains	...the content artifacts	...folder	Component
SameProcess	...all artifacts with the same reference number	...all documents	Situation
Workflow	...all documents belonging to the same workflow	...all documents	Situation

Table 2 : Some example relations in POLIAwaC

The table lists the most commonly used relations in POLIAwaC. Similar to the example in Table 1 the system defines a *ContainedIn*-relation, which can be used for indirect interest descriptions. Among the situations, *SameProcess* yields all artifacts with the same reference number[4]. The *SameWorkflow* situation covers all documents in a circulation folder.

The application model allows users to create very specific (e.g. "notify all ChangeDoc-events of text 'report99' immediately with high intensity") or very general interest descriptions (e.g. "notify all activity events of objects when I am active in the corresponding workspace with low intensity"). POLIAwaC enhances the usability of the model by allowing users to share the functionality of predefined interest descriptions and by using a wizard interface to define new ones. Also, POLIAwaC applies several simplifications in the model to ease the definition process, e.g. the predicates in the scope specification are simplified to match only single artifact classes or instances.

The facilities for defining privacy have been hidden completely from the user.

---

[4] Reference numbers are used throughout the application in order to assign documents to a particular process.

For each artifact, event notifications are restricted to those users having access to the artifact. Technically, this is achieved by automatically defining privacy descriptions for those situation relations that are not compliant to the formal work organization. This applies only to two relations: *Immediately* and *SameProcess*.[5] This strategy emphasizes the need-to-know principle for the dissemination of awareness information while at the same time reducing the cognitive complexity of interest specifications. It also guarantees that the privacy of awareness information is compliant with the degree of information sharing, i.e. private spaces are also private in terms of awareness information.

Notification mechanisms

Figure 9 shows the application's main window. The client uses the standard desktop metaphor. The document hierarchy and the contents of opened containers are displayed in different windows. Users have the possibility to define different views on objects regarding sorting criteria and iconic or textual display, thus allowing for individual working styles.

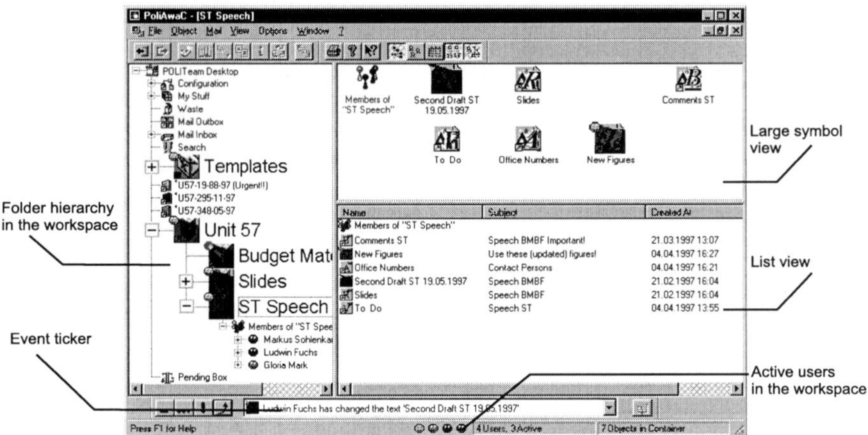

Figure 9: The main application window of POLIAwaC

The notification techniques employed in POLIAwaC depend on the class of event and the event intensity. Four different intensity levels are defined in POLIawaC with the respective UI techniques being more disruptive as the intensity increases.

In the lowest intensity, events are displayed using symbol embellishments for activity events and color overlays for change events. In the next higher intensity level, POLIAwaC uses icon enlargements, which are particularly useful to signal

---

[5] Artifacts can belong to the same process without being accessible in a common folder or workspace.

past and ongoing activities in the folder hierarchy shown in the tree view on the left side of the main application window. Events in the third intensity level are displayed as a message in an event ticker at the bottom of the main window. The ticker widget can be used to browse through the list of recent events. Events with the highest intensity value are displayed in a modal dialogue box, which has to be acknowledged by the user. Thus the low intensity levels cause events to be perceivable using peripheral vision while the higher levels force users to focus on the information presentation explicitly.

Conclusions

The experience with POLIAwaC has shown that AREA provides a very powerful tool for adding awareness support to a groupware environment. Unlike alternative notification services such as NSTP, AREA requires an extensive model of the application domain to be supplied. The POLIAwaC example has shown that with a relatively lean domain model the usefulness of awareness notifications can be enhanced substantially. Nevertheless, the creation of this model is a significant overhead in using the service. The following benefits justify these additional costs:

First, having an integrated domain model is a prerequisite for cross-application notification. Applications can only exchange and present events that are occurring in another application in a meaningful way, if they have access to a semantic model of the events.

Second, the application model offers a homogeneous interface to specify work-oriented support for awareness. Events can be notified according to individual and group interest profiles such that notifications occur at the right time, i.e. synchronously, if the user happens to be in the right situation at the time the event occurs, or asynchronously, as soon as the user enters the appropriate notification situation.

Third, the availability of the application model frees client applications from having to deal with the complexity of notifying events in the appropriate situation and enforcing privacy constraints. By maintaining a unified application model AREA provides a single interface to the applications as well as to the user for the delegation of this complexity.

Privacy is considered as an integral requirement for providing awareness in a groupware setting. The notification service takes a 0-1 approach to deal with conflicts resulting from incompatible privacy and interest specifications in the user models. Event notifications only take place, if there is no conflicting privacy profile. This strategy is clear and simple and guarantees that organizational and legal restrictions as well as local group policies can be applied. However, this approach may not be flexible enough for some applications in which a continuous degradation of the awareness notification is desired in response to enhanced privacy demands.

As an application independent groupware service AREA requires the application to supply the user model. AREA only provides an interface for specifying interest and privacy. In the POLIAwaC example a dual approach was taken: the client provides a dedicated user interface to specify interest profiles but privacy profiles are defined automatically, hidden from the user. In general, using AREA requires deciding who is responsible for setting the awareness parameters. The experience with POLIAwaC indicates that it may be desirable to provide more support on the side of the service for this. For example, it could be helpful to have an independent tool to define general group- and work-oriented awareness strategies. For example, instead of the need-to-know strategy for privacy taken by POLIAwaC it might be desirable to realize a reciprocity-based privacy strategy. Identifying suitable strategies for privacy and interest and making them available in AREA requires further research.

What are the technical limitations of the AREA awareness model? The system is restricted to notify discrete events rather than provide awareness using continuous media streams. Also, the event distribution mechanism can be computationally demanding, depending on the underlying application model. The biggest impact results from the evaluation of relations. As a consequence, AREA is not suited to disseminate synchronous, time critical events typically found in synchronous 3D environments. However, situation oriented event notification has the potential of being a useful strategy for synchronous application sharing (e.g. to support relaxed WYSIWIS). Determining the borderline of applicability for synchronous shared applications remains to be investigated.

Acknowledgements

The research described in this paper has been performed when I was working at the German National Research Institute for Information Technology (GMD-FIT). I want to thank all the members of the POLITeam project for their great support. Also I want to thank Steve Poltrock at Boeing and the reviewers of the ECSCW '99 program committee for their comments.

References

Chabert, A., Grossman, E., Jackson, L., Pietrowicz, S., and Seguin, C. (1998): "Java Object-Sharing in Habanero", *Communications of the ACM*, Vol. 41, No. 6, pp. 69-76.

Fuchs, L., Pankoke-Babatz, U., and Prinz, W. (1995): "Supporting Cooperative Awareness with Local Event Mechanisms: The GroupDesk System", in *Proceedings of the European Conference on Computer Supported Cooperative Work (ECSCW'95)*, Stockholm, pp. 247-262.

Gutwin, C., Roseman, M., and Greenberg, S. (1996): "A Usability Study of Awareness Widgets in a Shared Workspace Groupware System", in *Proceedings of the Conference of Computer Supported Cooperative Work (CSCW'96)*, Boston, MA, ACM Press, pp. 259-267.

Heath, C., and Luff, P. (1992): "Collaboration and control: crisis management and multimedia technology in London underground control rooms", *Computer Supported Cooperative Work*, Vol. 1, No. 1-2.

Mark, G., Fuchs, L., and Sohlenkamp, M. (1997): "Supporting Groupware Conventions through Contextual Awareness", in *Proceedings of the Fifth European Conference on Computer Supported Cooperative Work (ECSCW'97)*, Lancaster, UK, Kluwer Academic Publishers, pp. 253-268.

Nomura, T., Hayashi, K., Hazama, T., and Gudmundson, S. (1998): "Interlocus: Workspace Configuration Mechanisms for Activity Awareness", in *Proceedings of the International Conference on Computer Supported Cooperative Work (CSCW '98)*, Seattle, WA, ACM Press, pp. 19-28.

Patterson, J. F., Day, M., and Kucan, J. (1996): "Notification Servers for Synchronous Groupware", in *Proceedings of the Conference of Computer Supported Cooperative Work (CSCW'96)*, Boston, MA, ACM Press, pp. 122-129.

Prinz, W., Mark, G., and Pankoke-Babatz, U. (1998): "Designing Groupware for Congruency in Use", in *Proceedings of the International Conference on Computer Supported Cooperative Work (CSCW '98)*, Seattle, WA, ACM Press, pp. 373-382.

Rogers, Y. (1993): "Coordinating Computer-Mediated Work", *Computer Supported Cooperative Work*, Vol. 1, pp. 295-315.

Roseman, M., and Greenberg, S. (1992): "GroupKit: A Groupware Toolkit for Building Real-Time Conferencing Applications", in *Proceedings of the Conference on Computer Supported Cooperative Work (CSCW '92)*, Toronto, Canada, ACM Press, pp. 43-50.

Sandor, O., Bogdan, C., and Bowers, J. (1997): "Aether: An Awareness Engine for CSCW", in *Proceedings of the Fifth European Conference on Computer Supported Cooperative Work (ECSCW'97)*, Lancaster, UK, Kluwer Academic Publishers, pp. 221-236.

Shim, H. S., Hall, R. W., Prakash, A., and Jahanian, F. (1997): "Providing Flexible Services for Managing Shared State in Collaborative Systems", in *Proceedings of the Fifth European Conference on Computer Supported Cooperative Work (ECSCW'97)*, Lancaster, UK, Kluwer Academic Publishers, pp. 237-252.

Smith, G., and O'Brian, J. (1998): "Re-Coupling Tailored User Interfaces", in *Proceedings of the International Conference on Computer Supported Cooperative Work (CSCW '98)*, Seattle, WA, ACM Press, pp. 237-246.

Sohlenkamp, M. (1998): *Supporting Group Awareness in Multi-User Environments through Perceptualization*, dissertation thesis, University Paderborn, Institute of Computer Science, Paderborn, Germany. Also available at http://orgwis.gmd.de/projects/POLITeam/poliawac-/ms-diss.

S. Bødker, M. Kyng, and K. Schmidt (eds.). *Proceedings of the Sixth European Conference on Computer-Supported Cooperative Work, 12-16 September 1999, Copenhagen, Denmark*
©1999 Kluwer Academic Publishers. Printed in the Netherlands

Moving Out of the Meeting Room
Exploring support for mobile meetings

Jens Bergqvist, Per Dahlberg and Fredrik Ljungberg
Viktoria Institute, Gothenburg, Sweden

Steinar Kristoffersen
Norwegian Computing Centre, Oslo, Norway

"The structuring properties of the interaction order in real-time settings such as meetings have enormous (and as yet largely ignored) consequences for the overall structuring of organizations. Caught in a meeting and connected through a series of interactions across time and space are the people, ideas, decisions, and outcomes that *make* the organization."

(Boden 1994, p. 106)

Recent research in CSCW shows that people become mobile in order to meet. Such meetings take place everywhere. Therefore, they are difficult to conduct using traditional meeting support. In this paper, we empirically examine mobility in face-to-face meetings. The objective is to characterise such encounters and suggest meeting support beyond the meeting room. We have identified four dimensions of such mobile meetings: establishing meetings, multiple threads, briefings, and technology. The implications from this study complement existing research with guidelines for mobile meetings.

1 Introduction

Within the field of CSCW considerable attention has been paid to information technology (IT) support for meetings. One strand of this research has focused on meetings between co-located people. Research efforts in this category involves technological contributions, e.g., the design of meeting rooms (Nunamaker *et al.* 1991), roomware (Streitz *et al.* 1997), advanced meeting technologies (Elrod *et al.* 1992), and software applications (Pedersen *et al.* 1993), but also empirical contributions, e.g., studies of the ways in which people make meetings happen (Mantei 1989; Moran *et al.* 1996). Clearly, these contributions have been very important to the field.

One issue that has not been so much addressed in the research on meeting support is mobility. In fact, mobility has until recently been largely overlooked in the CSCW literature (Luff and Heath 1998). Some recent empirical accounts on the topic have shown that people are often mobile to meet each other and solve problems (Bellotti and Bly 1996; Kristoffersen and Rodden 1996). Such meetings can occur in many different places, which makes them difficult to assist by means of traditional meeting support (e.g., electronic whiteboards), which tend to be static and tied to dedicated places. By meeting support we understand any IT designed to assist collaboration between people who have "come together" to deal with work-related issues (see, Nunamaker *et al.* 1992). Related to but yet different is support for informal communication, which seeks to assist unarranged, unscheduled, and less goal-oriented engagements with random participants (Fish *et al.* 1990; Kraut *et al.* 1990). The empirical research on informal communication has involved studies of interaction between co-located people (Whittaker *et al.* 1994), however the technological contributions have exclusively supported remote interaction (Fish *et al.* 1993).

The objective of our research is to explore meeting support beyond the context of the meeting room, i.e., assist people who come together in face-to-face meetings in other places. The purpose of the study reported in this paper is to begin to investigate work in real settings in a systematic way, with a particular objective to inform the design of such meeting support. The study explores the work of staff at the central IT department of the city of Gothenburg, Sweden. By reporting the fieldwork and elicit implications for the design of support for mobile meetings, we seek to add to and extend the emerging CSCW literature that investigates mobility for the purpose of design.

We start the paper by summarising the research on meeting support and mobility (Section 2), and describe the research context of the study (Section 3). In section 4, we report the results of the empirical study, and in section 5 we discuss the findings in relation to existing research, and the implications the results may have for design. In section 6, we conclude the paper.

2   Related work

There are two areas of related work to the research presented in this paper. These are the CSCW research on meeting support and mobility.

One strand of research on meeting support for co-located people has focused on equipping meeting rooms with IT support (Nunamaker *et al.* 1991). These rooms often involve expensive and special-purpose hardware, which makes them static and tied to dedicated places. Related to this research is what recently has been called roomware, i.e., the combination of information devices and physical objects in a room, e.g., walls, chairs and tables (Streitz *et al.* 1997). The research on roomware tends to go beyond the context of the meeting.[1] Research on meeting support also explores advanced hardware technologies, e.g., electronic whiteboards (Elrod *et al.* 1992), and software applications with which these could be equipped, e.g., the Tivoli application (e.g., Pedersen *et al.* 1993). Software for meeting support running on light weight technologies like PDAs (Personal Digital Assistant) has been explored as well (Myers *et al.* 1998). Research also investigates the integration of meetings along the dimensions of time and space (Inoue *et al.* 1997), as well the integration of meetings and other group activities (Mark *et al.* 1995). Another strand of research conducts empirical studies of meetings. The studies evaluate meeting support and inform design (e.g., Mantei 1989; Olson *et al.* 1992).

Most research on mobility can be characterised as empirical studies (but see Kristoffersen and Ljungberg (1998) for an exception). Most of these concern mobility as a *consequence* of an interest in another topic, e.g., informal workplace communication (Whittaker *et al.* 1994), the effects of video technology in banking (Kristoffersen and Rodden 1996), co-operation and IT use in a dispersed design team (Bellotti and Bly 1996), and the practice of photocopier technicians (Orr 1991). As far as we are aware, Luff and Heath (Luff and Heath 1998) is the only contribution in CSCW that explicitly investigates mobility for the purpose of design. Luff and Heath reconsider three empirical studies from the point of view of mobility. The focus is not personal mobility only, but also the mobility of artefacts, called micro mobility. The analysis involves three cases with three different focuses on mobility. These are micro mobility in medical consultation, remote mobility at a construction site, and remote and local mobility in the London Underground.

In this paper, we seek to bring together meeting support and mobility, and in doing so, address an issue that has not been previously explored: meeting support for mobile settings.

3 Research site and method

The research was conducted at an IT company owned by the local government of Gothenburg, Sweden. The company has a wide range of responsibilities. The most important are: consultation, design, installation and support of software,

---

[1] See for example the conference on "Cooperative Buildings" (Streitz *et al.* 1998) and the panel on "Roomware for cooperative buildings" at the CSCW'98 conference.

installation and support of hardware, and maintenance of the local government's servers. The clients are distributed all over the city. The company employs 300 personnel, and the annual turnover is approximately 280 million SEK (approximately $30 million).

The department we investigated has about 25 employees. The main task is to design, install, and support Lotus Notes applications and databases. Many employees both work as project leaders and developers. The manager of the department (Bonnie[2]) has her own office. Everybody else either shares office or works in the office landscape.

We spent approximately 70 man-hours doing close participant observations (or, shadowing), i.e., following every single move of a particular person. Everybody was aware of the research and its purpose, and field notes were taken continually. The analysis of the empirical data aims to "make sense of massive amounts of data, reduce the volume of information, identify significant patterns, and construct a framework for communicating the essence of what the data reveal" (Patton 1990, p. 371-372). Having transcribed the field notes, we started the coding of the empirical data. This meant going through the data carefully, making notes and labelling data that seemed to capture underlying patterns. In the analysis, we used pseudo HTML to tag the field data, e.g., meetings in the office, and Perl scripts for processing it, e.g., meetings in the office following a formal meeting. Gradually, the coding process became a matter of interpretation, i.e., "attach significance to what was found..." (Patton 1990, p. 423).

4 Results

In this section, we summarise the results of the empirical study. The analysis is based on the 88 face-to-face meetings we observed. These meetings took place away from the desktop for at least one of the participants (thus, they were considered mobile), and they were clearly related to work. We excluded traditional meetings, e.g., the weekly group meeting.

In table 1, we summarise the meetings observed according to where they took place (away, home and elsewhere) and whether or not IT was involved (IT involved and no IT involved). Home means that the meeting took place in the office of the person shadowed, i.e., someone else (one or more) had been mobile to establish the meeting. Away means that the meeting took place in the office of someone else, i.e., (at least) the person shadowed had been mobile to establish the meeting. Elsewhere means that the meeting did not take place in an office but somewhere else, i.e., all people involved had been mobile to establish the meeting.

As we can see in the table, the number of meetings were quite equally divided

---

[2] The names of the people investigated have been changed for anonymity.

between the three categories (28, 24 and 36). Of the 88 meetings, 52 took place in offices, and 36 elsewhere. We can also observe that most of the meetings did not involve IT (74 of 88).

Place	IT involved	No IT involved	Total	%
Away	4	24	28	32%
Home	3	21	24	27%
Elsewhere	7	29	36	41%
	14	74	88	100%

Table 1. Summary of the meetings observed.

The purpose of the analysis is to serve as a source from which we can elicit implications for the design of meeting support for mobile workers who engage in face-to-face meetings. We identify four important aspects of the ways in which such meetings take place. These are:

- establishing meetings,
- multiple threads,
- briefings, and
- technology.

4.1 Establishing meetings

The focus of the analysis is meetings in mobile settings, i.e., meetings that take place away from the desktop of at least one participant. This means that all meetings we report here were preceded by at least one person being mobile. In most cases (52 of 88), the person who wanted to establish the meeting simply walks to the office of the person with whom she wants to interact. When arriving there, one of the persons would typically indicate the presence of herself or the other party (one or several). For example, the arriving person could ask "Do you have a minute?" or "Have you read the email I sent you this morning?".

However, this does not always happen. For example, consider the excerpt below. Previous to this situation, Ursula and Bonnie have been discussing a contract.

> [Bonnie is engaged in a meeting with Henry in her office.] Ursula enters the office. She says nothing but leaves a document on top of Bonnie's keyboard. Bonnie and Henry continue to talk as if nothing had happened. [...] Henry leaves. Ursula returns and points at the document she left earlier...

What seems to happen in this situation is that neither Henry, Bonnie nor Ursula think it would be appropriate to interrupt the ongoing meeting. Bonnie and Henry just continue their conversation, and in doing so, they indicate to each other, and Ursula that it makes sense to continue the meeting. Because Ursula says nothing, but leaves immediately after having placed the document on the keyboard, she seems to agree. Accordingly, for all three people involved, it seems to make sense not to establish a new conversation when Ursula shows up, and therefore a new meeting does not happen. We made several similar observations during the study.

Of the 88 meetings, 36 took place elsewhere, i.e., in another place than the office of a person involved. One reason why is that the person who wants to establish the meeting encounters the person(s) with whom she wants to interact on the way to her office. For example:

> [Bonnie and Ursula have previous today been discussing a contract] Bonnie reads the contract. After a while, she walks towards the door of the office "to check something with Ursula." But Ursula is just passing by in the hallway. [...] A new discussion follows.

In other cases, the person who wants to establish the meeting does not find the person with whom she wants to interact with (typically: she is out of the office). She continues to seek for her and finds her somewhere else. For example:

> Arriving at his desktop after the lunch break, Errol finds a PostIt note on his desktop written by Amanda. Amanda writes that she wants to talk to him. Errol walks away towards Amanda's office, but she's not there. Errol finds her in the printer room from which they head towards Amanda's office.

Quite frequently, meeting participants want to invite more people in to the discussion. To do so, they could go to the person (one or several) in question, asking her to join the meeting. For example:

> Annie and Errol are discussing the X SOFTWARE[3] application when they realise that they need to invite Ursula into the discussion. Therefore, they simply walk away towards Ursula's office. ...

Sometimes this kind of mobility does not aim at a particular person, but a role. For example:

> Errol and Annie are engaged in a meeting. They discuss the software licenses of X SOFTWARE [a Lotus Notes based system]. Errol says: "It's funny that X SOFTWARE is include in the Y SOFTWARE[4] package, yet it seems to require new licenses." In order to find out they need to talk to "somebody who knows." However, "since the boss is gone, it may be the best thing to do to talk to Ursula." They decide to go see her.

In this situation, Errol and Annie seem to want to talk to anybody who can help them solve the problem ("somebody who knows"). It seems as if they would have asked the boss if she had been there. However, since she is not available at the moment, they decide to see someone else who could help (i.e., Ursula).

4.2 Multiple threads

The meetings typically involve discussions on many different topics. Topics are introduced, suspended, replaced and resumed, and while some are picked up in several meetings others just seem to fade away. Such micro discussions and the ways in which they occur, have been called threads. Because meetings tend to

---

[3] The name of the software package has been changed for anonymity.

[4] The name of the software package has been changed for anonymity.

involve many threads, which are not introduced, dealt with and completed in a sequential manner, we will describe the structure of the meetings in terms of multiple threads.

Threads that have been dealt with in previous meetings are sometimes just picked up in later meetings. This would typically happen in meetings with the manager. New threads in a meeting seem to be picked up in many different ways. For example, one person could associate a topic with something that another person said, e.g., "By the way, I also …". However, threads do no just pop up, but are introduced and resumed in an intelligible way. In some cases, the topic would be obvious, e.g., someone reporting that she has done what was agreed on in a previous meeting, while in other cases it would have to be explained, e.g., when someone in a discussion says "This reminds me of…" and introduce a new thread. If someone picks up a thread that does not make sense, then the other people would typically make this obvious. They would do so by hinting that an explanation is expected.

To illustrate the structure of threads during and between meetings, let us briefly describe a typical situation for Bonnie (the manager).

[Bonnie is in her office]. Ursula enters the office with a contract. Ursula wants Bonnie to go over it before filing it in the Lotus Notes system. […] Ursula leaves the room […]

[Bonnie and Ursula have previous today been discussing a contract] Bonnie reads the contract. After a while, she walks towards the door of the office "to check something with Ursula." But Ursula is just passing by in the hallway. […] A new discussion follows.

Henry enters the office and explains that he cannot attend a meeting: "Can anyone else attend?" Bonnie calls Ian [on the phone] to check what the meeting is about... Henry leaves the office during the call. […]

During the conversation [the call] Ursula paces back and forth across the room. She leaves after a minute or two. [...] Bonnie returns to reading the contract.

Ursula returns. Bonnie briefs her about the telephone conversation. They start a long discussion on the issue of software ownership. […]

Larry arrives. He picks up the discussion about laptop computers [..]

Henry enters. He wants to discuss a pricing issue […]

Ursula enters the office. She says nothing but leaves a document on top of Bonnie's keyboard. Bonnie and Henry continue to talk as if nothing had happened. […] …Henry leaves.

Ursula returns and points to the document she left earlier. […]

As we can see, the meetings in Bonnie's office involve several threads. When Ursula first enters the office, she introduces a new thread, the contract. The contract is temporarily suspended when the meeting is over and Ursula leaves the room. Later, Bonnie resumes the contract when inviting Ursula into the office. Then the contract is suspended again. However, it is picked up again when Henry leaves the office and Ursula returns. It is interesting to notice that the contract lasts for several meetings (with several other threads).

4.3 Briefings

Much time during the meetings is spent describing things to each other. Some of these briefings concern what people have done in the past, while others concern what they plan to do in the future.

Briefings about the future could be information about, for instance, a future project or a customer visit. One example is when Amanda informs Errol about the new file structure for the web site.

> Amanda [a Lotus Notes administrator] enters Errol's office. She describes to Errol that the file structure of the web server is messy. One reason, she explains, is that "it was not designed for so many documents." [...] She continues: "It was designed by company X and Paul." Amanda explains that a new server is going to be purchased, and that Chrystal has designed a new structure."

In this situation, Amanda briefs Errol about things that do not concern him primarily, but which are good-to-know. It is interesting to notice that the briefing involves past events as well as future plans.

Briefings about the past can be follow ups on tasks that have been discussed previously. We also observed the ways in which people brief each other for the purpose of making sense of past events. Previous to the excerpt below, the servers at the company had crashed. This was noticed by the employees.

> The systems administrator shows up in the corridor. He is in a hurry. When passing by the door to Bonnie's office, he exclaims "Somebody has dropped a plate on a fuse! The server of our company and the tramway had a power failure!"

Here, the systems administrator explains to Bonnie why the servers are down, thus he gives reasons for why the servers had dived.

Briefings could also be people describing what they plan to do. Consider the following example:

> Ursula enters Bonnie's office. She brings with her a contract. She says she wants Bonnie to go over it before filing it in the Lotus Notes system. Ursula explains to Bonnie that "the contract partner will probably visit them this evening." [...] Bonnie explains that she "can't access some objects in the project data base from home." She also says that she's "going to convert the document verbal description of the business plan to a word processing file." In addition, she describes that she "plans to work at home tonight," and that she will contact Ursula if she makes any updates.

In this situation, we can observe at least two briefings which seem to play major roles in the interaction. First, Ursula describes to Bonnie that the contract partner will make a visit later. Second, Bonnie says she plans to work at home tonight, but that she will contact Ursula if she makes any updates.

There are also briefings that appear serve the purpose of giving order. For example, consider the following excerpt.

> Ursula's cellular phone rings. In the subsequent conversation, she makes an offer [it's a client]: "we can do this... we can do that." She informs the caller about costs and what is included: "education and support." She also says that "Annie will be responsible." When the phone call is finished, Ursula walks to Annie's office. She tells Annie about the call, and the task. She

also describes that it could be good to make some cost calculations. Ursula leaves.

Here, Ursula in a descriptive manner explains to Annie what has been said during a phone call with a client. She also describes a task and what ought to be done. Clearly, she does not simply describe the call and the task to Annie, but requests her to assume the responsibility. Since Annie does not express another stand point, she seems to accept the request. We made other similar observations about people briefing each others about what ought to be done in the future.

4.4   Technology

Of the 88 meetings observed 14 involves the use of IT. On these occasions, IT either serves as a resource for face-to-face interaction, or as a means for interaction with remote people.

When people enrol IT (e.g., a PC) in a face-to-face meeting, they typically re-arrange the way in which the interaction takes place. In a sense, what often happens is the opposite to the micro-mobility observed in the studies by Luff and Heath (Luff and Heath 1998, p. 306), i.e., "the way in which an artefact can be mobilised and manipulated for various purposes around a relatively circumscribed, or at hand, domain." According to our observations, it is not the artefacts (IT) that are "mobilised and manipulated," but rather the participants of the meetings (Luff and Heath made similar observations). What typically happens is that people want to check something on the computer network. Therefore, they move to a PC at hand which one of them starts to operate. The other participants would stand behind the operator, glancing over her shoulder.

The way in which the meeting takes place when the PC is enrolled differs significantly from the way it took place previously. When the PC is used, only one person can be in control, if many people are involved it can be difficult for everybody to see what happens on the screen, eye-contact is lost when everybody looks in the same direction, and so on. However, these were the premises on which the PC could be involved in the face-to-face interaction. It is striking how this differs from Luff and Heath's (Luff and Heath 1998) description of the ways in which medical records were used in medical consultations.

We also made observations of how IT was used in meetings for interaction with remote people. The IT that people use in these situations is the cellular phone. What typically would happen when someone in a meeting starts to use a cellular phone, is that the meeting is suspended (compare: threads). Everybody but the person using the phone is quiet. It seems as if they just listen and wait for the call to end.

Making a phone call would typically be a consequence of an emerging need for external contact defined by the meeting participants, e.g., that something needs to be sorted out and a phone call is made accordingly: "Let's call her and find out." Consider the following excerpt from a meeting.

> Errol explains that it's not obvious who is going to join the project. "Susan and myself know something about the technological issues," he explains. But they would also like to see some more people involved. [...] Susan picks up the phone to give Bonnie (the manager) a ring "to find out."

As mentioned previously, instead of making a phone call, the entire meeting sometimes moves to persons who needs to be enrolled into the conversation.

Upon finishing the phone call, the caller would typically explain to the other meeting participants what the other party said (in a sense, recapitulate the conversation).

We also observed meetings where a participant received a call. What typically happens then is that the receiver explains to the other meeting participants who was calling, e.g., by saying "Hi Mr X!", but also for the caller that she was in a meeting, e.g., "I'm in a meeting...". For example:

> Steve's cellular phone rings. He answers. "Hi there... I'm in a meeting with Bonnie." [...] Upon finishing the call, he explains: "It was Amanda."

5 Discussion

The meetings we investigated seem to share features with informal communication and meetings, as described in the CSCW literature. However, as we shall see in the discussion below, there are also important differences. To emphasise these, and highlight in what ways our observations can be distinguished from previous contributions in the field, we introduce the concept of mobile meeting.

5.1 Mobile meetings

Interaction takes place in meetings, but meetings are not simply interaction. Meetings are deliberate efforts to establish organisational order and bring about work. Meetings bracket out people, places, and agendas in such a way that it becomes clear who are the appropriate participants, which topics may be raised, etc. One objective of this paper is to bring the social accomplishments of this bracketing to the fore, and sensitise designers to the practical requirements of attending such meetings. Within a CSCW context, the purpose thereby is to improve technological support for achieving mobile meetings.

A meeting may comprise of formal or informal arrangements for turn-taking, participation and sticking to the agenda. The typical meeting (see, Jay 1993) takes place in a meeting room. It fulfils a specific function, it is scheduled and organised according to an agenda, it is usually attended to by an invited group of people, and it often takes place regularly. Formal meetings are usually understood as officially convened, with fixed membership and agendas. They often occur regularly and have a directed and restricted set of turn-taking mechanisms, which are managed by a chairperson. Informal meetings, on the other hand, are generally task or decision-oriented. They are clearly distinguished from informal communication, as understood by Kraut *et al.* (Kraut *et al.* 1990), by being convened, albeit often verbally. Informal communication is often positioned as the opposite to meetings. Informal communication is usually not planned or used to articulate formal functions. It can take place anywhere and involve random participants. It may be seen a social event rather than a meeting, nevertheless, it may of course relate to work in other ways.

The issue of participation is crucial. An organisationally defined group attends to a typical meeting. Attendees to mobile meetings were, on the other hand, all closely engaged in the activities of concern to the meeting (compare: establishing meetings). Moreover, we observed that people even left mobile meetings when they did not concern them any longer, which may be considered inappropriate behaviour in typical meetings.[5] Informal communication, on the other hand, has an open set of participants.

Informal meetings are generally unrecorded, or even explicitly off-the-record (Boden 1994). This is in contrast to mobile meetings, which are often concerned with allocating responsibilities and action points which are recorded, or need to be recounted for an external purpose later (compare: briefings).

Informal meetings, albeit not having a designated chair, usually have a *de facto* responsibility assigned to the most senior person (Boden 1994). The activity of chairing, moreover, is often territorial, inasmuch as the meeting often takes place in the office of the person who takes on the role as chair. According to our observations, mobile meetings often (in our case: 73%) take place away from the office of the initiator, and they tend to be less territorial. In contrast to typical meetings, which are tied to a few dedicated places, mobile meetings and informal communication could take place in almost any places.

We claim that mobile meetings may be informal as well as formal and that they are, indeed, proper meetings, with a expected and accountable set of participants and agenda that needs to be followed - clearly, from our excerpts, alien issues are often simply ignored.

5.2 Establishing mobile meetings

Mobile meetings are established through deliberate efforts involving *physically seeking out* and *negotiating* with potential participants, *bracketing* the subsequent communication and *agreeing on topics*

Some meeting support systems treat the convening and establishing of meetings as detached from the meetings themselves. They usually support requests for participation, and may distribute documents. Some systems also

---

[5] As Boden (Boden 1994, p. 87) puts it: "...participation by particular organisational members is expected and accountable."

maintain the shared calendars of participants (Ephrati *et al.* 1994). These designs, therefore, assume that people will be at their workstations well before the meetings, with time set aside to prepare and articulate competing organisational chores.

The main implication of our fieldwork is to support locating people, physically as well as virtually, in a highly mobile environment. Supporting negotiation of meetings is a tempting enterprise, but one that we believe may be too obstinate given the formalising nature of technology (see, Kristoffersen and Ljungberg 1999). Leaving the entire process of establishing meetings (locating and establishing) to social protocols, on the other hand, may be too defensive.

Hence, a promising principle for establishing mobile meetings could be affording awareness of the activities (Dourish and Bly 1992) and position of potential participants. Maintaining and managing this type of state information should be a low-overhead activity (Grudin 1994). For the mobile user, calm information appliances (Norman 1998), may support this functionality. Position may be either absolute or relative to other users. Absolute position shows, for instance, at which office a person is located. ParcTab is one system that provides this kind of support (Want *et al.* 1995). However, we find that the relative positioning is equally exciting. Relative positioning is based on proximity, one example of which is the Hummingbird system (Holmquist *et al.* 1998). Hummingbirds give notice when users are nearby.

Establishing meetings is cumbersome (Ephrati *et al.* 1994). Even with simple technologies, such as the telephone, as many as 60% of all calls fail to connect with their intended recipient (Rice and Shook 1990; Whittaker *et al.* 1994). We think that one important lesson to be learned for CSCW is that this is part-and-parcel of organisational life. One novel implication of this paper is that members of organisations conspicuously use mobile meetings as a feature to resolve this problem. Perhaps this is one good explanation of why we found no mobile meetings that were pre-arranged using IT (in contrast to (Fish *et al.* 1993)).

Boden (Boden 1994) claims that meetings cannot start without having a critical mass of members in attendance. We argue that mobile meetings are one way of reaching critical mass, since they take place with fewer participants, topics are dynamically adjusted to the availability of participants, and it may be suspended and resumed when appropriate. The threshold is lower indeed, since one person with a mission seems to be able to pull off a mobile meeting almost regardless.

5.3 Multiple threads

Mobile meetings involve multiple topics. *Threads* relate to topics, and may be seen as their enactment. Mobile meetings have many topics, but usually only one active thread at any time. Threads are not always completed within a meeting, and the pertaining contributions do not always occur sequentially. Threads are, moreover, sometimes moved between meetings, thus, they tend to be suspended and resumed.

McDaniel *et al.* (McDaniel *et al.* 1996, p. 41) define a thread as "…a stream of conversation in which successive contributions continue a topic, following an initial contribution which introduces a new topic." Whittaker *et al.* (Whittaker *et al.* 1994) on the other hand, reported that informal communication tend to be one long session, that is suspended and resumed over time. We found that threads in mobile meetings do not consist of *sequential* (uninterrupted) contributions, they are not always introduced explicitly, and they can be involved in several meetings.

Considering threads instead of topics as the atomic unit of meetings opens up a new design space, inasmuch as they lend themselves more easily to representations comprising, for instance, participants, documents and place. Thus, a system could conceivably always show the closest thread on top of the mobile user's display. Threads are, in contradistinction to topics, bracketed in actual time and space. In the meetings, threads were shifted frequently and effortlessly. New IT should not make switching more difficult.

5.4 Briefings

Mobile meetings serve as important ways for people to brief each other about past and future events. Because the attendees typically are closely engaged in the activities of concern, briefings are likely to be important for everybody involved.

The PC could be a useful tool for briefings. For example, a project member could perhaps more effectively brief someone else when accessing to the common information space of the project. However, not even a laptop PC seems light weight enough for mobile meetings. Therefore, we suggest the use of calm, ubiquitous devices equipped with features for replication and browsing.

5.5 Technology

Technology in mobile meetings either serves as a resource for face-to-face interaction, or as a means to carry out interaction with remote people. Technology is only used when absolutely needed, and it often makes people rearrange the ways in which they interact, e.g., by trying to use individual IT like the PC as if it was a group technology. When people use the cellular phone in meetings, they typically explain the use context; that they are in a meeting, who the other party is, etc.

Luff and Heath (Luff and Heath 1998) coined micro mobility to describe the ways in which technology (objects-in-interaction) should serve as a flexible resource in interaction. They also reported how people rearrange interaction to cope with technology that does not have this property. Overall, our findings of technology in co-present interaction echo those of Luff and Heath. However, one novel observation seems to be the ways in which people explain context - who is calling, where they are, etc. - when using technology for remote interaction (cellular phone) within the context of mobile meetings.

Clearly, if technology is to serve as a flexible and augmenting resource in mobile meetings, people need to be able to "mobilise and manipulate" it according the emergent needs of the group.[6] One approach would be to make technology group aware, i.e., make it possible to accommodate it to group use. However, this way of integrating functionality into artefacts may make them capable of doing many things, but non of them particularly well (Norman 1998). Another approach would be to design dedicated information appliances for groups (Norman 1998). It is interesting to notice that this suggestion is quite the opposite of what often is argued in the meeting support literature, namely that group support needs to be accompanied with support for the individual (e.g., to protect privacy).

5.6   Design in progress

Based on the empirical study, and the implications derived from the results, we are currently developing a series of applications for mobile meetings. The applications are programmed in C and run on the Palm III platform. The Palm III is the most widely used portable device. In a sense, it could also be described as micro mobile. Let us briefly introduce two applications that are being developed.

The Dynamic to do list runs on a Palm III equipped with a radio transceiver (originally developed for the IPAD project at the Viktoria Institute, see (Holmquist *et al.* 1998)). The device scans the environment and give priority to the items of the user's to do list based on the proximity of others. This may support the establishing of mobile meetings, and briefings. We plan to experiment with the same technique on threads.

Figure 1. The dynamic to do list runs on a Palm III equipped with a radio transceiver.

---

6 Streitz and associates at GMD early articulated the need to integrate "traditional" support for face-to-face interaction with other types of meetings (same time other place, different time same place, different time different place). These ideas have been explored in, among others, the DOLPHIN project (e.g., Streitz *et al.* 1994).

The portable project database replicates selected items from a Lotus Notes project database. The idea is to provide users with easy access to information that is potentially relevant in a mobile situation, e.g., to brief someone about the progress of a project.

We plan to evaluate the applications in the organisation investigated in the study.

6 Conclusions

In this paper we have introduced the concept of mobile meeting. We have argued that mobile meetings are different from meetings already discussed in the literature and supported by CSCW systems, among others, by having: a managed set of records and responsibilities, a dynamic agenda which is closely aligned with current topics, and an open yet not arbitrary set of participants. In contrast to informal communication, on the other hand, mobile meetings are clearly bracketed from other organisational activities.

We have introduced four important dimensions of mobile meetings, each of which has design implications for CSCW.

- First, mobile meetings are established through deliberate efforts involving physically seeking out and negotiating with potential participants. CSCW design should take locating participants into account, but perhaps not attempt to support negotiation.

- Second, mobile meetings involve multiple topics, which are enacted by threads. Threads lend themselves more easily (than topics) to representations comprising participants, documents and place. However, it is important that new IT does not make switching between threads more difficult.

- Third, mobile meetings serve as important ways for people to brief each other about past and future events. Support for briefing could be calm and ubiquitous devices equipped with features for replication and browsing of information spaces.

- Fourth, technology in mobile meetings either serves as a resource for face-to-face interaction, or as a means to carry out interaction with remote people. Technology support is currently limited, and should to a larger extent support situated sharing and micro-mobility.

We are currently designing models and prototyping meeting support based on these recommendations. We believe that mobile meetings represent an emerging organisational feature of which the series of interactions across time and space are the people, ideas, decisions, and outcomes really *make* organisations.

7 Acknowledgement

This research is a part of the Mobile Informatics programme, which is funded by the Swedish Information Technology research Institute (SITI).

We would also like to thank our industrial partner Linq Systems AB and the research site company.

8 References

Bellotti, V. and S. Bly (1996). "Walking away from the desktop computer: Distributed collaboration and mobility in a product design team," In *Proceedings of ACM 1996 Conference on Computer Supported Cooperative Work*, edited by K. Ehrlich and C. Schmandt, ACM Press, pp. 209-218.

Boden, D. (1994). *The business of talk. Organizations in action.* Cambridge, Polity Press.

Dourish, P. and S. Bly (1992). "Portholes: Supporting Awareness in a Distributed Work Group," In *Proceedings of ACM 1992 Conference on Human Factors in Computing Systems*, ACM Press, pp. 541-547.

Elrod, S., *et al.* (1992). "Liveboard: A Large Interactive Display Supporting Group Meetings, Presentations and Remote Collaboration," In *Proceedings of ACM 1992 Conference on Human Factors in Computing Systems*, ACM Press, pp. 599-607.

Ephrati, E., G. Zlotkin and J. Rosenschein (1994). "Meet your destiny: A non-manipulable meeting scheduler," In *Proceedings of ACM 1994 Conference on Computer Supported Cooperative Work*, edited by T. W. Malone, ACM Press, pp. 359-371.

Fish, R., R. Kraut, R. Root and R. Rice (1993). "Video as a technology for informal communication." *Communications of the ACM* Vol 36,No 1, pp. 48-61.

Fish, R. S., R. E. Kraut and B. L. Chalfonte (1990). "The VideoWindow system in informal communications," In *Proceedings of ACM 1990 Conference on Computer-Supported Cooperative Work*, edited by T. K. Bikson, ACM Press, pp. 1-11.

Grudin, J. (1994). "Groupware and social dynamics: Eight challenges for developers." *Communications of the ACM* Vol 37,No 1, pp. 93-105.

Holmquist, L.-E., a. Joakim Wigström and J. Falk (1998). "The Hummingbird: Mobile Support for Group Awareness," Demonstration at *ACM 1998 Conference on Computer Supported Cooperative Work.*

Inoue, T., K.-i. Okada and Y. Matsushita (1997). "Integration of face-to-face and video-mediated meetings: HERMES," In *Proceedings of International Conference on Supporting Group Work*, ACM Press, pp.

Jay, A. (1993). How to run a meeting. In *Readings in Groupware and Computer-Supported Cooperative Work: Assisting human to human collaboration.* R. Baecker. San Francisco, CA, Morgan Kaufmann Publishers Inc: pp. 130-144.

Kraut, R., R. Fish, R. Root and B. Chalfonte (1990). Informal communication in organizations: Form, function and technology. In *Readings in Groupware and Computer-Supported Cooperative Work: Assisting human to human collaboration.* R. Baecker. San Francisco, CA, Morgan Kaufmann Publishers Inc: pp. 287-314.

Kristoffersen, S. and F. Ljungberg (1998). "MobiCom: Networking dispersed groups." *Interacting with Computers* Vol 10, pp. 45-65.

Kristoffersen, S. and F. Ljungberg (1999). "An Empirical Study of How People Establish Interaction: Implications for CSCW Session Management Models," To appear in *Proceedings of ACM 1999 Conference on Human Factors in Computing System*, Pittsburgh, ACM Press.

Kristoffersen, S. and T. Rodden (1996). "Working by Walking Around. Requirements of flexible interaction management in video-supported collaborative work," In *Proceedings of Human Computer Interaction*, edited by B. Spence and R. Winder, Springer Verlag.

Luff, P. and C. Heath (1998). "Mobility in Collaboration," In *Proceedings of ACM 1998 Conference on Computer Supported Cooperative Work*, edited by S. Poltrock and J. Grudin, ACM Press, pp. 305-314.

Mantei, M. (1989). Observation of executives using a computer supported meeting environment. In *Readings in Groupware and Computer-Supported Cooperative Work: Assisting human to human collaboration*. R. Baecker. San Francisco, CA., Morgan Kaufmann Publishers Inc.: pp. 695 - 708.

Mark, G., J. Haake and N. Streitz (1995). "The use of hypermedia in group problem solving: An evaluation of the DOLPHIN electronic meeting room environment," In *Proceedings of The Fourth European Conference on Computer-Supported Cooperative Work*, edited by H. Marmolin, Y. Sundblad and K. Schmidt, Kluwer Academic Publishers, pp. 197-213.

McDaniel, S., G. Olson and J. Magee (1996). "Indentifying and analyzing multiple threads in computer-miedated and face-to-face conversations," In *Proceedings of ACM 1996 Conference on Computer Supported Cooperative Work*, edited by K. Ehrlich and C. Schmandt, ACM Press, pp. 39-47.

Moran, T. P., P. Chiu, S. Harrison, G. Kurtenbach, S. Minneman and W. v. Melle (1996). "Evolutionary engagement in an ongoing collaborative work process: A case study," In *Proceedings of ACM 1996 Conference on Computer Supported Cooperative Work*, edited by K. Ehrlich and C. Schmandt, ACM Press, pp. 150-159.

Myers, B. A., H. Stiel and R. Gargiulo (1998). "Collaboration using multiple PDAs connected to a PC," In *Proceedings of ACM 1998 Conference on Computer Supported Cooperative Work*, edited by S. Poltrock and J. Grudin, ACM Press, pp. 285-294.

Norman, D. (1998). *The invisible computer*. Cambridge, MA., MIT Press.

Nunamaker, J., A. Dennis, J. Valacich, D. Vogel and J. George (1991). "Electronic meeting systems to support group work." *Communications of the ACM* Vol 34,No 7, pp. 40-61.

Nunamaker, J. F., J. F. George, J. S. Valacich, A. R. Davis and D. R. Vigel (1992). Electronic meeting systems to support information systems analysis and design. In *Challenges and strategies for research in systems development*. W. W. Cotterman and J. A. Senn. New York, John Wiley: pp. .

Olson, J. M., G. M. Olson, M. Storrosten and M. Charter (1992). "How a group-editor changes the character of a design meeting as well as its outcome," In *Proceedings of ACM 1992 Conference on Computer-Supported Cooperative Work*, edited by M. Mantei and R. Baecker, ACM Press, pp. 91-98.

Orr, J. E. (1991). Talking about machines. An ethnography of a modern job. Xerox PARC, Report: SSL-9107.

Patton, M. Q. (1990). *Qualitative Evaluation and Research Methods*. New York, Sage.

Pedersen, E. R., K. McCall, T. P. Moran and F. G. Halasz (1993). "Tivoli: an electronic whiteboard for informal workgroup meetings," In *Proceedings of ACM 1993 Conference on Human Factors in Computing Systems*, ACM Press, pp. 391-398.

Rice, R. and D. E. Shook (1990). Voice messaging, coordination and communication. In *Intellectual teamwork: Social and technical foundations of cooperative work*. J. Galegher, R. Kraut and C. Egido. Hillsdale, New Jersey, Lawrence Erlbaum: pp. 327-350.

Streitz, N., J. Geissler, J. Haake and J. Hol (1994). "DOLPHIN: Integrated meeting support accross local and remote desktop environments and LiveBoards," In *Proceedings of ACM 1994 Conference on Computer Supported Cooperative Work*, edited by T. W. Malone, ACM Press, pp. 345-358.

Streitz, N., S. Konomi and H. Burkardt, Eds. (1998). Cooperative buildings. Integrating information, organization and architecture. Darmstadt, Springer Verlag.

Streitz, N. A., P. Rexroth and T. Holmer (1997). "Does "roomware" matter? In vestigating the role of personal and public information devices and their combination in meeting room collaboration," In *Proceedings of The Fifth European Conference on Computer-Supported Cooperative Work*, edited by J. Hughes, W. Prinz, T. Rodden and K. Schmidt, Kluwer Academic Publishers, pp. 297-312.

Want, R., B. N. Schilit, N. I. Adams, R. Gold, K. Petersen, D. Goldberg, J. R. Ellis and M. Weiser (1995). The PARCTAB Ubiquitous Computing Experiment. Xerox PARC, Report: CSL-95-1.

Whittaker, S., D. Frohlich and O. Daly-Jones (1994). "Informal workplace communication: What is it like and how might we support it?," In *Proceedings of ACM 1994 Conference on Human Factors in Computing Systems*, edited by B. Adelsom, S. Dumais and H. Olson, ACM Press, pp. 131-137.

S. Bødker, M. Kyng, and K. Schmidt (eds.). *Proceedings of the Sixth European Conference on Computer-Supported Cooperative Work, 12-16 September 1999, Copenhagen, Denmark*
© 1999 Kluwer Academic Publishers. Printed in the Netherlands   99

Activity Awareness: A Framework for Sharing Knowledge of People, Projects, and Places

Koichi Hayashi[1], Tan Hazama[1], Takahiko Nomura[2], Toshifumi Yamada[1], and Stephan Gudmundson[3]
[1]IT Business Development Dept., Fuji Xerox, Kanagawa, Japan
[2]Knowledge Design Initiative, Fuji Xerox, Tokyo, Japan
[3]Dept. of Computer Science, University of British Columbia, Vancouver, Canada
hayashi.koichi@fujixerox.co.jp, Takahiko.Nomura@fujixerox.co.jp,
hazama.tan@fujixerox.co.jp, Toshifumi.Yamada@fujixerox.co.jp,
stephang@netinfo.ubc.ca

Abstract. In this paper we describe the concept of *activity awareness,* which gives workers indications of what is happening and what has happened recently in collaborative activities. The key feature of activity awareness is the use of individual workspaces, as opposed to shared workspaces. We introduce an activity representation that can be extracted from workers' individual workspaces. By using extracted activity information, it extends the scope of awareness from tight collaboration within a shared workspace to more loose collaboration. It enables workers to be aware of the latest information created within other members' individual environments and of the progress made by loosely connected groups. We introduce three *awareness nodes: people, projects,* and *places.* In our model, individual activities interact at these awareness nodes. Our current implementation adopts a temporally threaded workspace model for representing individual activities and introduces an *awareness presentation schema* for representing the three awareness nodes. The temporally threaded workspace model captures a worker's activity as a sequence of changes to the information space of the individual's workspace. An awareness presentation schema generates web pages to show awareness information about the monitored activities.

Introduction

The recent revolutionary changes to information infrastructures have increased knowledge workers' opportunities to work collaboratively with people outside of their immediate workgroup. To perform jobs, workers can share and exchange information with others within the Internet and Intranet. The information accessed through the network reflects the activities of colleagues in companies, and friends in research institutes. Furthermore, changes to the information are available immediately. However, it is not easy for workers to know what is happening and what has happened recently in related activities from information on the network. Preparation of information to deliver or publish is often so time-consuming that emails can become infrequent and web pages can become obsolete. A Workflow system provides status information only on predefined tasks.

Shared workspace systems are one of the most promising approaches for keeping groups distributed over space to focus on a collaboration (Dourish and Bellotti, 1992; Tolone et al., 1995; Roseman and Greenberg, 1996). A shared workspace is a virtual place (on the network) where workers can perform collaborative work. Changes caused by any events, even including ad-hoc actions, within a space are immediately visible to other group members. Furthermore, workspace awareness has made these spaces more usable (Gutwin and Greenberg, 1997). Workspace awareness provides workers with a perspective on the current state of the collaborative work. It can help group members by succinctly presenting the state of a concurrent activity, hinting at upcoming events, and indicating when to communicate with others.

Employing the metaphor of a physical place or room for shared workspaces has both advantages and disadvantages. It provides users with an intuitive scope of communication and information sharing, but it limits the scope of awareness to explicit and intentional collaboration. This limitation negatively impacts workspace awareness in two ways.

First, awareness of the latest information of other group members is often not provided. Recent progress of technology enables workers to store all of the information for performing their job locally. They work in their individual environments and use the shared workspace only to exchange completed documents. Since the latest (and often most important) information remains inside the individual's environment, shared workspaces do not provide awareness of the most recent changes to the information.

Second, shared workspaces do not support awareness of related activities for dynamic collaboration structures. When a worker does her individual work, even though the task initially may seem simple and isolated, it often ends up affecting several other activities in the organization, formally or informally, closely or loosely. For example, suppose a worker wishes to publish experimental data on a web page. During preparation of the page, she might need to collaborate closely with research colleagues to complete the data and with her supervisor to formally report progress within a shared workspace. When publishing the page, she might informally coordinate with the owner of a web site publishing similar information. She might maintain loose contact with sales staff who use her data in their sales proposals. For providing necessary awareness among this sort of concurrent and dynamic collaboration, the requirement of defining a workspace for information exchange before starting collaboration becomes unrealistic.

We believe that workspace awareness is essential to support dynamic collaboration, but that the scope of the awareness should not be as limited as in a shared workspace. To extend the scope of workspace awareness, we have proposed the concept of *activity awareness* and developed a prototype system called *Interlocus* (Nomura et al., 1998). The distinctive feature of activity awareness is that it provides awareness of a set of interrelated activities, each of which is executed within an individual workspace.

Activity awareness requires a framework comprised of an *individual activity representation* and a *dynamic awareness scope* to provide awareness without employing shared workspaces. It enables the generation of a *collective activity perspective* and *asynchronous progress notifications* as awareness functions to solve the problems identified above. The individual activity representation defines a computer-manageable object corresponding to an individual activity. In this model we use the word *activity* to mean a human process of a worker to achieve some specific goal (e.g. writing a specific report). Generally, each worker will execute more than one activity. Dynamic awareness scope determines the scope of awareness as a set of individual activities related to a collaborative activity. This set of activities may change dynamically as the collaboration proceeds. An individual activity may be included in more than one awareness scope, allowing an individual activity to affect several collaborative activities. The collective activity perspective provides awareness of the most recent information in the individual activities involved within the collaborative work. Asynchronous progress notification provides awareness of changes to loosely connected activities.

In this paper we introduce *awareness nodes*, which provide perspectives on collaborative activities. We have introduced them to address limitations found through the usage of Interlocus, which is the first implementation of activity awareness. Interlocus adopts the *temporally threaded workspace* model (Hayashi et al., 1998) for supporting awareness based on individual activities and uses *workspace configuration* mechanisms to provide awareness. An Interlocus workspace is an environment in which individual workers can their own activities. In other words, it provides an individual view of an activity. The workspace configuration mechanisms add information about related activities into the individual view. In usage, we observed that this approach does not adequately represent the relationships between activities. To provide viewer-independent viewpoints for activity structures, we introduce three awareness nodes: *people, projects, and places.*

In the following sections, we first review related work about awareness on shared workspaces. Next, we illustrate experiences with the first implementation of activity awareness based on workspace configuration. We then introduce the three nodes of activity awareness. We also describe awareness presentation schema, which is the current implementation of awareness nodes. We then discuss the characteristics of activity awareness compared with previous work and show the possibility of the further extension of the activity awareness. Finally, we mention future work and give conclusions.

Related Work

Since awareness is the essential function for collaborating in a workspace, leading researchers in this field have been investigating awareness. Gutwin and Greenberg coined the term "workspace awareness" and pointed out that shared workspace systems should include this feature (Gutwin and Greenberg, 1997). Fuchs classifies modes of workspace awareness into four categories: synchronous-coupled, asynchronous-coupled, synchronous-uncoupled, and asynchronous-uncoupled (Fuchs et al., 1995). The synchronous mode provides awareness of what is happening currently; the asynchronous mode shows what has happened since the last visit. The coupled mode focuses on the actual scope of work; the uncoupled mode focuses on something important or of interest to the user.

The shared workspace approach is most effective when a coupled mode of awareness is required. The TeamRooms system (Gutwin et al., 1996) supports the synchronous-coupled mode of awareness. It provides shared workspaces, in which users can collaborate with certain tools, and supports awareness within the workspaces by tracking each member's telepointer and scrollbar. The BSCW system (Hortstmann and Bentley, 1997), which provides shared workspaces entirely in the WWW, supports the asynchronous-coupled mode of workspace awareness. A BSCW workspace maintains a set of documents and records actions performed against the documents in the space. BSCW records what has happened lately in each document space, as well as the current status of the space. Although the shared workspaces implemented by these systems provide intuitive information about others' actions in the collaboration, the scope of awareness is limited to events that occur within the shared workspace. Therefore users cannot see the latest information on individual workspaces or the progress of other shared workspaces.

The uncoupled mode of awareness is an extension for supporting dynamic information exchanges between workspaces. GroupDesk (Fuchs et al., 1995) is a shared workspace system that further offers the functionality of event notification between workspaces. It distributes local events via structural, operational, and semantic relations among actors and artifact-objects. A user receives an event if it matches an interest context, which is used to indicate what events interest the user. PoliAwaC (Mark et al., 1997) allows users to attach awareness profiles to shared objects. The awareness profile indicates what types of events should be presented to the user. Using awareness profiles, each user can obtain a personalized view that indicates what changes have been made to the specified objects and in which workspace these changes occurred. Although the event distribution approach adopted in these systems is an effective way for extending the scope of awareness to outside workspaces, it requires users to predefine structured relationships, to specify shared objects, or to specify necessary events. These requirements make it difficult to apply the idea to individual workspaces, because it is difficult to predict which documents in others' workspaces will become important.

We think the essence of workspace awareness is notifying members in a collaboration of unpredictable events. An individual workspace is the place where each user is doing the most creative and flexible activities. Our approach delivers awareness information between activities, which are executed in individual workspaces, to extend the scopes of awareness beyond that of shared workspaces.

Activity Awareness with Workspace Configuration

In this section we briefly describes Interlocus, which is the first prototype system to provide activity awareness, and describe our experiences from a trial with the system. Out of the observations, we identify the limitations of the awareness mechanisms and derive the requirements for additional awareness functionality.

Design and Implementation of Interlocus

Interlocus adopts the *temporally threaded workspace* model (Hayashi et al., 1998) for providing an awareness framework based on individual activities, and introduces *workspace configuration mechanisms* (Nomura et al., 1998) to provide awareness functions.

Activity Model

The temporally threaded workspace model provides a way to extract activity from an individual workspace as a computer-manageable information structure.

In this model we use the word *activity* to mean a human process of a worker to achieve some specific goal (e.g. writing a specific report). We do not deal with activity classes (e.g. writing reports). Generally, each worker will execute more than one activity. This model provides a workspace for each activity of each worker. A workspace has two roles: to function as an environment for maintaining the set of information necessary for performing an activity; and to

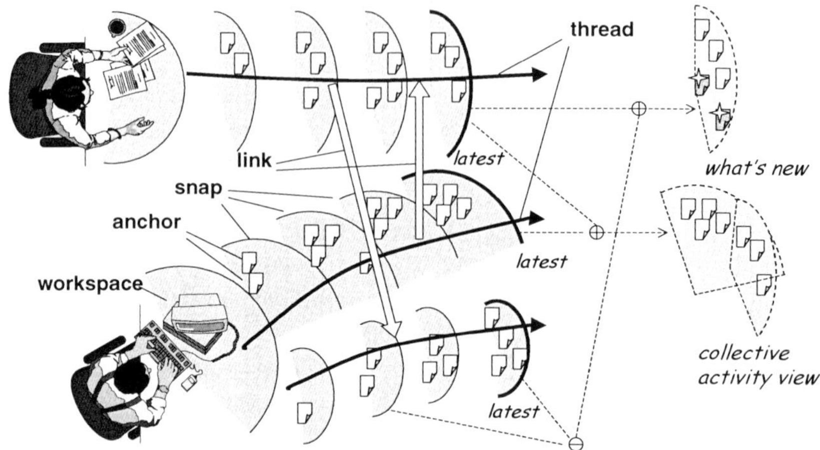

Figure 1. Temporally Threaded Workspaces and Workspace Configuration

record the process of the activity. Since the information in a workspace represents the present focus of the worker, it changes according to the progress of the associated activity. The temporally threaded workspace model represents an activity as a chronological thread of snapshots of the information in a workspace.

Conceptually, a workspace may be a physical desktop or a room, which maintains necessary paper documents and memos for performing a specific activity. In the conventional information system, a workspace may be implemented as a computer desktop or a folder, which maintains necessary electronic documents and applications.

Interlocus Workspaces

Interlocus is a server/client system implemented in Java. Interlocus server maintains activity objects, which is based on the temporally threaded workspace model, and manages documents, which are referenced from workspaces. The Interlocus client provides a two-dimensional workspace, which is a worker's environment employing the desktop metaphor. A user organizes the set of documents and tools used for carrying out an activity (Figure 1).

Based on the temporally threaded workspace model, Interlocus adopts individual activity representation, which is comprised of threads, snaps, and anchors. A thread is a recorded sequence of changes to information on the user's graphical workspace. A thread is defined as a set of *snaps* bound with their creation times. A snap(shot) represents the state of an activity at a given time. Snaps are used for both current and recorded workspace states.

A snap holds a set of document and tools placed on the graphical workspace. A snap is defined as a set of *anchors* bound with positions. An anchor is a spatial element on the graphical workspace that references a document or a tool relevant to the activity. There are two types of anchors: icons and regions. An icon shows

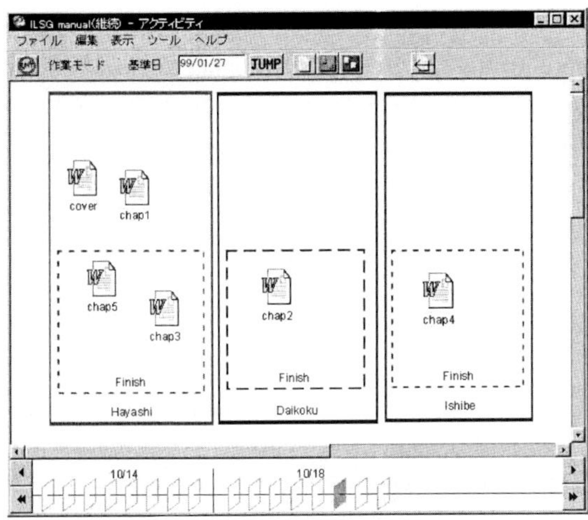

Figure 2. Example of Interlocus Workspace (Making Manual)

an image to reference documents or programs. A region shows a wider image that fills a region in which icons can be placed. A user can represent the state of an activity by placing document icons in appropriate regions of the workspace.

An Interlocus workspace is an environment on which users can carry out the associated activity and access past states of the activity. A workspace consists of the *spatial frame* and the *time line frame* (Figure 2). The spatial frame displays anchors on a two-dimensional desktop metaphor. Usually it shows the latest snap of a workspace to represent the worker's present state in the associated activity. In the spatial frame, a user can execute operations on anchors or documents to carry out an activity.

The time line frame presents the snaps comprising the chronological thread. A thread enables workers to restart at a past stage of the activity, to reuse documents from past activities, and to see the progress of others' activities. By selecting one of the snap symbols, the spatial view displays the state corresponding to the selected snap. With a selected snap a user can create another thread to restart the activity from the past state.

Construction of Thread Structure

Based on the temporally threaded workspace model, Interlocus has mechanisms for structuring threads as workers proceed in their activities. Each worker has more than one workspace, each of which is used for a specific activity. The mechanism that records snaps grows a thread. Snaps are both explicitly and implicitly recorded. In the trial use, they were recorded when creating a thread, saving a snap, closing a workspace, deleting an anchor, importing an anchor, and saving a document version.

In this model, an awareness scope is defined as a set of related threads.

Interlocus has two types of relationships among threads: document sharing between snaps in multiple threads and *links* connected between threads. Document sharing occurs when one copies or moves anchors from one workspace to another. Links are defined both implicitly and explicitly. The implicit definition mechanism is invoked when one executes specific operations. For example, operations for copying documents or starting new thread with a past snap implicitly define links. These links are used to determine the scope of awareness.

Awareness Functions

To provide awareness functions, *collective activity perspective* and *asynchronous progress notification*, Interlocus provides functions based on workspace configuration mechanisms. The mechanisms generate a virtual snap by applying set operators to related snaps, which are sets of anchors.

To present a summary of activities related to a collaborative activity, Interlocus provides *collective activity view* function. This function provides a synthesized view of the collaborative activity, in place of a shared workspace. Thus, collaborative activities are not represented directly by Interlocus, but are synthesized dynamically from their component individual activities. The scope of awareness is the set of workspace threads connected by links to the user's thread. The synthesis function is simply the union of the latest snap of each linked workspace thread. Since the anchors are taken directly from others' individual workspaces, one always receives the most current information in others' activities. Note that workspace thread binds only one worker as the owner, who can edit the workspace and thus further the thread. Therefore one cannot move or delete anchors collected from others' workspaces.

To notify people of progress in related activities asynchronously, Interlocus provides the *what's new* function. This function shows the changes to the workspace since the user last visited it. The scope of awareness of this function is the set of workspaces connected by links to the user's thread. For each referenced workspace, this function subtracts the last snap that the user accessed from the current snap in the thread. These anchors are then overlaid into the user's workspace. The overlaid anchors are for display only, and are not considered as part of the snap during other workspace configuration operations. Since a user can define links to any threads that they can access, she can get awareness on loosely related activities from her workspace.

Requirements through Usage

To evaluate the temporally threaded workspace and workspace configuration mechanisms, we performed short-term Interlocus trials in daily work situations. Four workers used Interlocus for two months. One uses Interlocus for every

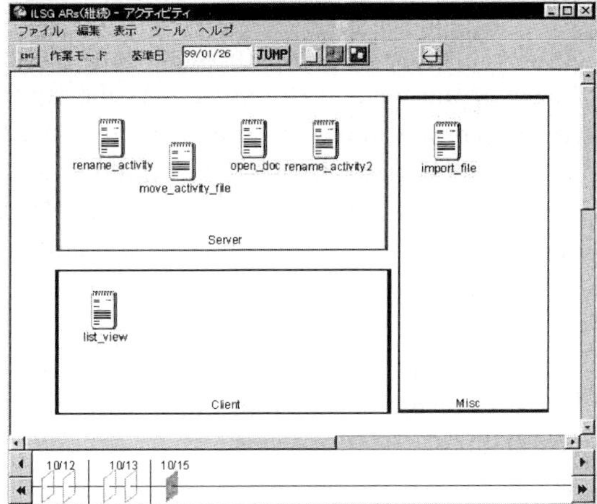

Figure 3. Example of Interlocus Workspace (Exchanging Action Requests)

activity to which Interlocus can be applied, while the others use Interlocus for collaborative activities only.

Individual Activity Monitoring

We observed that the temporally threaded workspace model recorded the worker's activities as designed. This model was designed to monitor the threads that have the following characteristics.

- Threads are separately extracted with different set of core documents.
- A thread grows snaps as the associated activity proceeds.
- Threads related to each other to form larger collaborative activities.

Throughout the trial, Interlocus recorded forty-one activities. We observed that each worker executes several activities, each of which is related to a different document set. Ten activities were short term and very simple activities that had less than five snaps. Almost all of them were the preparation of one or two documents, and were completed within a day. Thirteen activities that lasted over a week (five days) recorded more than ten snaps. Most of these activities included more than five documents. Except for a few personal notes, almost all of the recorded activities affected collaborative work (involved exchanging documents with others). For example, an idea memo created in an activity for preparation of discussion was used in the discussion meeting and then reused in another activity for writing a technical report.

Use of Collaboration Features

We observed two cases that used the collaboration features of Interlocus. Both cases were related to the implementation of a prototype system. One is a set of activities for making a users' manual and the other is a set of activities for exchanging action requests. For the manual, we observed collaboration that assigns each member a specific role. One person supervised the whole process, and the others prepared the parts of the manual. The supervisor established a workspace with a region for each writer of the manual (Figure 2). As the figure shows, each writer produces the assigned part and moves it to their regions when completed. By placing document icons in appropriate regions, the whole process of making the manual proceeds. The workspace configuration mechanism was useful to gather portions of the manual from each writer's workspace. For sharing action requests, collaboration in equal roles was observed. The test users and developers reported action requests using a workspace with a region for each module of the system (Figure 3). The developer for each module collected the requests and fixed the problems. The workspace configuration mechanism was useful to obtain new action requests from others' workspaces.

Requirements from Usage

From this experience, we obtained several requirements for improving the collaborative features of Interlocus. We describe key requirements below. In particular, our observations of collective activities have motivated the development of a model of awareness nodes, as described in upcoming sections.

- Interlocus should be integrated with other collaboration tools, specifically email systems. Interlocus successfully captured activities in which a user made documents as products of work. However, it could not monitor many activities related to writing emails. It is important to include such simple personal activities since they often fall into larger collaborative activities.
- Perspectives on collective activities should be provided. We observed that the workspace configuration mechanism lacks the capability to show the relationships between activities. A workspace is an environment for each worker to execute an activity. In other words, it provides an individual view of an activity. The configuration mechanisms work to add information to the individual view of each worker. To help understand the state of collaboration, we should present the overall progress of the collaborative activity at a glance. For example, to understand how the progress of the group members affects the supervisor's workspace, it is not enough to see the recent changes in the workspaces of each member.
- Alternatives to the spatial view are needed. When using the workspace configuration mechanisms, the limitation of the spatial representation is clear. The amount of information, like action requests, rapidly increases and becomes impractical for display.
- A means to edit others' workspaces is needed. Since an individual workspace belongs to a specific worker, we have not allowed other members to alter the states of an individual's workspace. However, this restriction sometimes frustrates workers. We should relax this restriction or introduce some editing protocol.

Awareness Nodes for Activity Awareness

The key feature of our concept of activity awareness is that it uses individual workspaces to capture individual activities and to present awareness information. The experience described in the previous section shows that an individual workspace is useful for capturing activities, but not adequate for presenting awareness information. In this section, we introduce three viewpoints to provide three different categories of awareness: awareness of others, organizational awareness, and workspace awareness. The existing awareness functions, collective activity perspective and asynchronous progress notification, may be used in combination with these viewpoints. Within our definition of activity, a human process of a worker to achieve a specific goal, the types of awareness correspond to three types of nodes where a set of activities can interact: people, projects, and places (Figure 4).

Awareness of others

Awareness of others is an indication of what people are doing. Each worker performs several activities, each of which has a different goal, such as writing a paper on a specific theme or making on a specific business plan. People are the nodes where activities are created and from which activities grow.

Awareness of activities from the viewpoint of people enables us to understand what our colleagues are doing. Passive-monitoring mechanisms provide this type of awareness. Since the activities to be recorded are varied, from personal work to collaborative work, from routine work to ad-hoc work, from trivial to long-term assignments, a collaborative tool must be flexible enough to support this variety of tasks in order to provide awareness of others. Our approach, extracting activity information from individual workspaces, is suitable for this purpose.

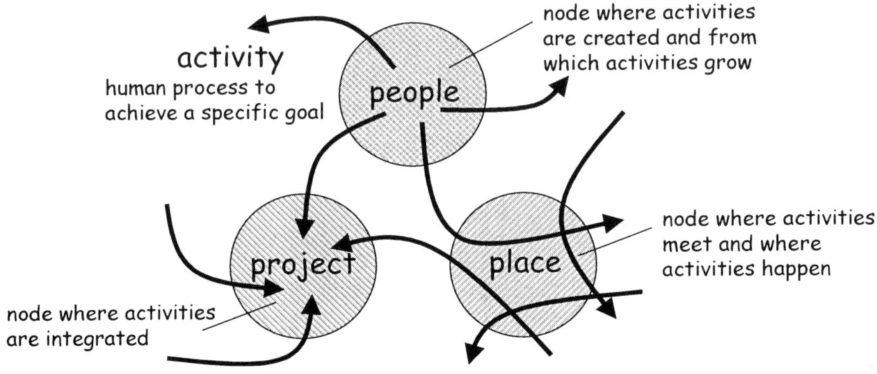

Figure 4. Awareness Nodes

Organizational Awareness

Organizational awareness is an indication of what the organization has effected. A worker in an organization often performs an activity that is a part of a higher level activity. For example, when writing a document collaboratively, the results of activity for preparing each section are used by an upper level activity for making a whole document. Projects are the nodes where activities are integrated.

The manual composition activities in the previous section are examples of this type of collaboration. Each activity involved in the collaboration has specific goal, such as preparing a section, preparing figures, and composing the manual. Workers exchange information with each other according to a predefined structure. For this situation, the awareness mechanism must indicate how each activity contributes to the collaborative activity, according to the project structure.

Awareness of activities from the viewpoint of a project node enables us to understand what groups or companies are currently producing. The definition of a *project* must be useful in a conventional organization and in a virtual corporation or an ad-hoc task force.

Workspace Awareness

Workspace awareness is indication of what is happening and has happened recently in a place. A worker may join a network community and collaborate with members, who do not belong to the same project, do not share common goals, or perhaps do not even know each other. For example, in our daily life we exchange information about problems with a common information system in this style. Unlike projects, individual activities in this type of collaboration may not be part of a predefined activity structure. Places are the nodes where activities meet and where activities happen.

The action request activities in the previous section have the characteristics of this type of collaboration. Developers and test users share the action request information through the collective view. A developer for each part gathers necessary action requests from anonymous users' workspaces. Since this specific example was a short-term collaboration involving only a small number of activities, we were able to organize these activities with a single goal oriented activity structure. However, we may want to extend this collaboration to form a larger community and to exchange ideas for future functions. For this purpose, the awareness must help users to define shared themes or interests in the activities in a community.

Awareness of activities from the viewpoint of a place node enables us to understand past and current events in meeting rooms or workshops. The definition of place must cover virtual workspaces like electronic chat rooms and message boards as well as physical meeting spaces.

Implementation of Awareness Nodes

In this section, we present the current implementation of awareness nodes. We adopt the temporally threaded workspace for representing activities. In addition to the workspace configuration mechanisms presented earlier, we introduce *awareness presentation schema,* which is a mechanism to generate *awareness pages* representing the three awareness nodes.

Extensions to Interlocus

Awareness pages have two roles. First, they show the recent state of each node, even to non-Interlocus-users. Second, they can provide starting points for Interlocus users to search for activities related to their own. In the experimental system for awareness pages, we developed two additional components for Interlocus: Activity Store and Awareness Page Composer. Interlocus captures individual activities, which contain the set of information needed to generate the awareness pages. The Activity Store stores monitored activity objects as XML documents. By synthesizing the XML documents corresponding to the activities, the Awareness Page Composer generates HTML awareness pages and stores them on the WWW server. People can then see these awareness pages with standard WWW browsers.

To extract the information necessary for generating awareness nodes, we have extended the original activity representation of the temporally threaded workspace by introducing region structure and anchor comments. Region structure is a way to define logical structure within workspace snaps. In the original model, a region is just a type of anchor. Placing icons on some region may have certain semantics for people, but not for the Interlocus system. The region structure enables users to describe the state of documents to Interlocus; this information can be used by the Awareness Page Composer to extract only relevant information from activities. The anchor comments field of anchor allows users to attach information to a document-referencing anchor. By using comments, the user can indicate the reason for an action or requirements of the document that he processed.

Awareness Presentation Schema

An awareness presentation schema is a procedure for composing awareness pages corresponding to people, project, and place nodes. We have not yet developed a common language to describe these different types of schema. We are currently investigating what information should be presented for each type of awareness page.

Figure 5: People Awareness Page

People Awareness Schema

A people awareness schema summarizes activities performed by a given individual. To determine the scope of awareness, this schema requires users to identify the person of interest. The scope of composition is then all of the activities owned by the specified person. Through a people awareness page, one can access documents created as products of a given person's current activity. To prevent exposing private information to the Intranet or Internet, awareness pages include only activities that the originator marked as "public".

Figure 5 shows an example of a people awareness page that presents a summary of the activities performed by Hayashi. This page contains *personal profile*, *what's new*, and *activity list*. *Personal profile* presents the name and affiliation of the person. *What's new* presents recent events, using information extracted from the activity representation. It shows recently created activities and recently created, revised, or removed documents (anchors). The document list indicates the region of the activity in which the document is located. The list of revised documents also presents document version information. Users can access documents via hyperlinks attached to the document names in the list. The activity list shows the lists of live and paused activities. The live activity list contains activities that have recently recorded new workspace snaps. The name of a live activity is shown with the date of the latest snap. Activities move to the paused activity list when they remain unchanged for a determined period of time and disappear from the lists altogether if they remain unchanged after another period of time.

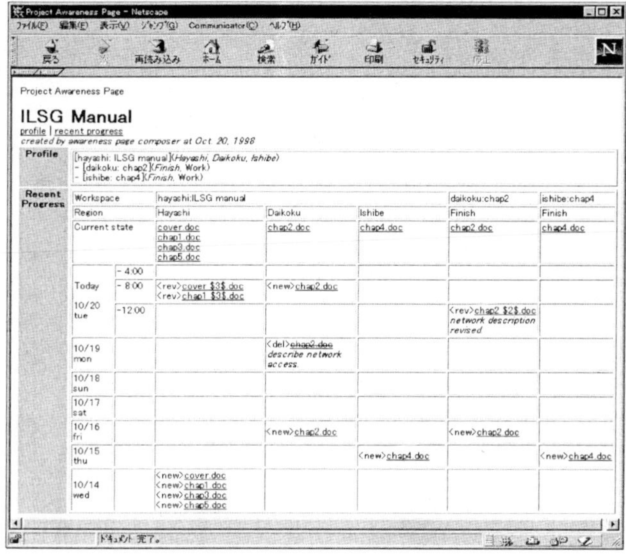

Figure 6: Project Awareness Page

Project Awareness Schema

A project awareness schema summarizes activities that are components of a given project. To determine the scope of activities, this schema requires users to specify a linked structure for the project. With this structure a user also specifies which regions within the workspaces are to be presented in the awareness page.

Figure 6 shows an example of a project awareness page that presents a summary of activities that are integrated into Hayashi's "ILSG manual", which is a supervisory activity for preparing a manual consisting of a cover page and five chapters. This page contains *project profile* and *recent progress. Project profile* presents hierarchical structure whose root is the "ILSG manual" activity. It has subordinate activities: Daikoku's "chap2" and Ishibe's "chap4". Following the activity name are the names of the regions placed in each workspace. A region name shown in italic fonts indicates that the project awareness schema monitors the region. Note that a user may define a structure of arbitrary depth. *Recent progress* presents recent events that have occurred in the monitored regions of each workspace. For example, the document "chap2.doc", which is revision 1 of chapter 2, appears in the "Finish" region in Daikoku's "chap2" workspace on Oct 16. Hayashi puts "chap2.doc" into the "Daikoku" region once, but the next week he adds a comment ("describe network access") to the anchor and removes it from the region. Daikoku revises the document and puts revision 2 of "chap2" into the "Finish" region with the comment "network description revised". In this way, this page summarizes the collective activities of two roles, supervisor and writer, and triggers actions for each role.

Profile		region		workspace
	Requests	Server, Client, Misc		ILSG ARs
	Actions	Fixed, Accept		IL Develop

Document List		document	date	region	comments
	Requests	default icon.txt	10/14	[yamada:ILSG ARs](Client)	notice
		new document.txt	10/14	[yamada:ILSG ARs](Server)	ASAP
		list view.txt	10/14	[hayashi:ILSG ARs](Client)	
		anchor menu.txt	10/13	[yamada:ILSG ARs](Server)	idea
		scroll.txt	10/13	[yamada:ILSG ARs](Client)	
		open doc.txt	10/13	[hayashi:ILSG ARs](Server)	FATAL
		rename confirm.txt	10/13	[hayashi:ILSG ARs](Server)	
		import file.txt	10/12	[hayashi:ILSG ARs](Misc)	idea
		rename activity.txt	10/12	[hayashi:ILSG ARs](Server)	FATAL
		move activity file.txt	10/12	[hayashi:ILSG ARs](Server)	
	Actions	rename activity.txt	10/15	[daikoku:IL Develop](Accept)	CANNOT FIX
		new document.txt	10/14	[daikoku:IL Develop](Fixed)	
		open doc.txt	10/14	[daikoku:IL Develop](Fixed)	
		rename confirm.txt	10/14	[daikoku:IL Develop](Accept)	
		default icon.txt	10/14	[ishibe:IL Develop](Fixed)	thanks
		list view.txt	10/14	[ishibe:IL Develop](Accept)	next version
		import file.txt	10/13	[daikoku:IL Develop](Accept)	next version
		anchor menu.txt	10/13	[daikoku:IL Develop](Fixed)	
		move activity file.txt	10/13	[daikoku:IL Develop](Accept)	next version
		scroll.txt	10/13	[ishibe:IL Develop](Accept)	

Other Region	Region	workspace
	(Fatal)	[hazama:ILSG ARs]
	(Reject)	[daikoku:IL Develop] [ishibe:IL Develop]

Figure 7: Place Awareness Page

Place Awareness Schema

A place awareness schema summarizes activities that interact at a place. To determine the scope of activities, the user specifies a set of region conditions. This schema then locates all activities whose workspace includes the regions indicated. This mechanism can be used to dynamically form structures among activities and allow users to refine region structures for more effective information exchange within a community.

Figure 7 shows an example of a place awareness page that presents a summary of activities that are related to action requests for a system. This page contains *place profile*, *document list*, and *other regions*. *Place profile* lists the set of region conditions used to select regions for inclusion on the page. In this page, there are two of region conditions: "Requests" and "Actions". "Requests" specifies the regions "Server", "Client", and "Misc" in the "ILSG ARs" activity. "Actions" specifies the regions "Fixed" or "Accept" in the "IL Develop" activity. The *document list* enumerates all documents placed in the identified regions. In the example, the page lists documents collected from the regions in "Request" and "Actions". Each document list item gives the name of the document, when it was placed in the region, the name of the anchor's workspace, and any attached comments. *Other regions* shows the other regions included in the workspaces in this place. This list can provide candidate regions for refining the scope of the place.

DISCUSSION

Awareness Category based on Activity Model

In this paper we presented categories of activity awareness based on our activity model. Awareness is one of the most important concepts when designing CSCW systems. So far, several leading researches have proposed categories of awareness. Fuchs classified awareness into four categories: synchronous-coupled, asynchronous-coupled, synchronous-uncoupled, and asynchronous-uncoupled (Fuchs et al., 1995). Gutwin and Greenberg introduced workspace awareness, and identified the following types of awareness information: presence, location, activity level, actions, intentions, changes, objects, extents, abilities, influence, and expectations (Gutwin and Greenberg, 1997). Rodden proposed a classification of awareness based on the dynamic pattern of the interrelationship between each user's presence position (Rodden, 1996), and defined a protocol for user awareness via WWW clients to promote cooperative information sharing (Palfreyman and Rodden, 1996).

The distinctive feature of our model is that it bases awareness on activities, not people. We have defined awareness in terms of information flow among activities. In this sense, the awareness node "people" is unique to our work. Awareness nodes for projects and places correspond roughly to the coupled and uncoupled awareness characterizations introduced by Fuchs.

We have defined an activity as a structured collection of information (i.e. anchors and regions). However, BSCW (Bentley et al., 1997) takes another approach to providing activity awareness. This system provides information about other activities by listing events that have occurred on shared objects in shared workspaces. PoliAwaC (Mark et al., 1997) also handles awareness through events on shared objects. In general, the event approach is advantageous when one can predetermine the core objects used in collaboration. In contrast, our approach works well when workers cannot predefine the structure of the collaboration. Thus, these two approaches are complimentary.

Loose Constraint for Workspace Use

In our model, we have carefully avoided imposing rigid restriction on workers' ways of using workspaces since each individual workspace belongs to the user. However, for making awareness pages to present relevant information succinctly, users have to adopt a common set of regions. While the description of the projects and places are given outside the activities, workers define regions in a workspace to suit the activity. Therefore, it would be difficult to coordinate region names among related activities when the range of collaboration becomes large. However, we are optimistic that the natural structure of activities will influence their

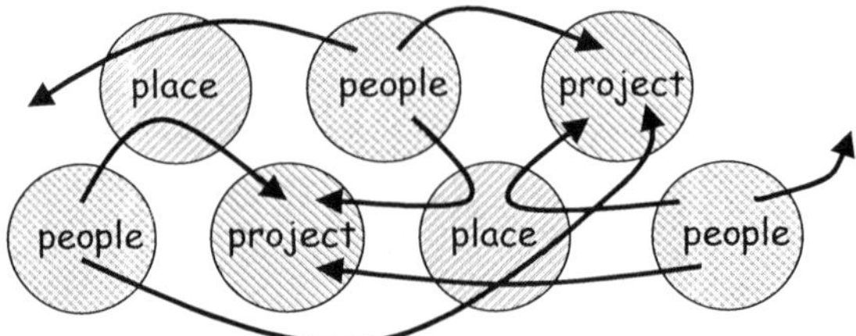

Figure 8. Awareness Node Network

description by users. Furthermore, we hope that users will change the way they structure their workspaces as they observe how the structure is used in awareness pages.

So far we have not introduced a predefined structure to control information flow among activities. Our model only uses relationships that can be defined by creating simple structural links, sharing documents among activities, and sharing region structures among activities. For enhancing project awareness nodes, it would be useful to introduce some predefined structure for distributing information, such as the semantic net adopted in GroupDesk (Fuchs et al., 1995) or workflow features.

Activity Oriented Perspectives and Analysis

An activity is an invisible human process. What we have proposed in our work is a way to extract human activity as a computer-manageable information structure without forcing workers to explicitly describe their activity states or to follow a predefined procedure. The discussion of activity awareness in this paper would be a starting point for investigating a larger theory of collaboration based on individual activities. Starting with our individual activity representation, we can derive a model of collaboration as a form of information exchange among activities. Such formalization could analyze the collaborations within an organization.

Furthermore, we can extend the model to consider the combination of the awareness nodes of people, projects, and places. Combinations of these nodes could produce higher level units, providing a complete understanding of an activity within the organization. Since our three awareness nodes are theoretical extremes derived analytically from the characteristics of activities, we would expect to find various mixed forms in practice. Further, they form an organization-wide network structure that is connected with shared activities (Figure 8). Representation of such a structure would provide perspectives on how organizations are really operating and help in decision making. As (Haeckel and Nolan, 1993) stated, "When information from previously unrelated source is structured in a meaningful way, human beings become capable of thinking thoughts that were previously unthinkable."

FUTURE WORK

To make activity awareness a realistic solution for supporting various forms of collaboration, we have to further investigate mechanisms for monitoring and presenting individual activities.

Although the temporally threaded workspace model does not limit the kind of information managed, the current Interlocus implementation monitors only the small range of activities that use conventional document files. To monitor a wider range of activities, we should integrate our system with other collaboration tools, such as email or workflow systems. We may further extend the system to handle multi-media documents to record the state of physical workspaces.

For providing users with sufficient awareness about activities, we must improve the current implementation in several ways. We have to introduce graphical representations that succinctly show how collaboration proceeds. We will also investigate a common language to determine scope, to extract information, and to present the awareness information.

Conclusion

As network technology accelerates innovation in social and corporate information infrastructures, the ability to collaborate with others via a shared information space becomes vital for knowledge workers. Activities, which are the source of change for information spaces, can provide a useful viewpoint for exchanging and sharing information with distant colleagues. In this paper we describe the concept of *activity awareness*, which gives workers indications of what is happening and what has happened recently in related activities. The key feature of activity awareness is that it is based upon individual, rather than shared, activities. To help collaborative work, activity awareness provides perspectives on *people, projects,* and *places*, which are nodes where activities can interact. Our current implementation adopts a temporally threaded workspace model for representing individual activities and introduces *awareness presentation schema*, which generate web pages to present the three different awareness nodes. We require further investigation on how the activities should be presented in the people, project, and place pages.

Acknowledgments

We would like to thank a number of colleagues in Fuji Xerox for their fruitful discussion. In particular, we thank Mitsuhiro Ishibe and Yuji Daikoku for their contributions to this work. I wish to thank anonymous reviewers for their many useful suggestions.

References

Bentley, R., Appelt, W., Busbach, U., Hinrichs, E., Kerr, D., Sikkel, K., Trevor, J. and Woetzel, G. (1997): 'Basic Support for Cooperative Work on the World Wide Web', *International Journal of Human-Computer Studies: Special Issue on Innovative Applications of the World Wide Web*, Academic Press, Cambridge, Vol. 46, No. 6, June 1997, Pages 827-846.

Dourish, P. and Bellotti, V. (1992): 'Awareness and Coordination in Shared Workspaces', *Proceedings of CSCW'92*, ACM Press, Toronto, November 1992, pp. 107-114.

Fuchs, L., Pankoke-Babatz, U., and Prinz, W. (1995): 'Supporting Cooperative Awareness with Local Event Mechanisms: The GroupDesk System', *Proceedings of ECSCW'95*, Kluwer Academic Publishers, Stockholm, September 1995, pp. 247-262.

Greenberg, S. and Gutwin, C. (1998): 'From Technically Possible to Socially Natural Groupware', *Proceedings of the 9th NEC Research Symposium: The Human-centric Multimedia Community*, Nara, August-September 1998.

Gutwin, C. and Greenberg, S. (1997): 'Workspace Awareness', *CHI 97 Workshop on Awareness in Collaborative Systems*, http://www.cpsc.ucalgary.ca/projects/grouplab/papers/1997/97-StudyingAwareness.CHIWorkshop/gutwin.html, Atlanta, March 1997.

Gutwin, C., Roseman, M., and Greenberg, S. (1996): 'A Usability Study of Awareness Widgets in a Shared Workspace Groupware System', *Proceedings of CSCW'96*, ACM Press, Boston, November 1996, pp. 258-267.

Haeckel, S and Nolan, R. (1993): 'Managing by Wire', *Harvard Business Review*, Harvard Business School Publishing, September-October 1993, pp122-132.

Hayashi, K., Nomura, T., Hazama, T., Takeoka, M., Hashimoto, S., and Gudmundson, S. (1998): 'Temporally Threaded Workspace: A Model for Providing Activity-based Perspectives on Document Spaces', *Proceedings of HyperText'98*, ACM Press, Pittsburgh, May 1998, pp.87-96.

Hayashi, K. and Tamaru, E. (1999): 'Information Management Strategies Using a Spatial-Temporal Activity Structure', *Proceedings of CHI'99*, ACM Press, Pittsburgh, May 1999 (to appear).

Horstmann, T. and Bentley, R. (1997): 'Distributed authoring on the Web with the BSCW shared workspace system', *ACM StandardView*, ACM Press, Vol. 5, No. 1, March 1997, pp.9-16.

Mark, G., Fuchs, L., and Sohlenkamp, M. (1997): 'Supporting Groupware Conventions through Contextual Awareness', *Proceedings of ECSCW'97*, Kluwer Academic Publishers, Lancaster, September 1997, pp253-268.

Nomura, T., Hayashi, K., Hazama, T., and Gudmundson, S. (1998): 'Interlocus: Workspace Configuration Mechanisms for Activity Awareness', *Proceedings of CSCW'98*, ACM Press, November 1998, pp. 19-28.

Palfreyman, K. and Rodden, T. (1996): 'A Protocol for User Awareness on the World Wide Web', *Proceedings of CSCW'96*, ACM Press, Boston, November 1996, pp.130-139.

Rodden, T. (1996): 'Populating the Application: A Model of Awareness for Cooperative Applications', *Proceedings of CSCW'96*, ACM Press, Boston, November 1996, pp.87-96.

Roseman, M. and Greenberg, S. (1996): 'TeamRooms: Network Places for Collaboration', *Proceedings of CSCW'96*, ACM Press, Boston, November 1996, pp.325-333.

Tolone, W., Kaplan, S., and Fitzpatrick, G. (1995): 'Specifying Dynamic Support for Collaborative Work within WORLDS', *Proceedings of COOCS'95*, ACM Press, 1995, pp.55-65.

S. Bødker, M. Kyng, and K. Schmidt (eds.). *Proceedings of the Sixth European Conference on Computer-Supported Cooperative Work, 12-16 September 1999, Copenhagen, Denmark*
©1999 Kluwer Academic Publishers. Printed in the Netherlands

The Properties of Mixed Reality Boundaries

Boriana Koleva, Steve Benford and Chris Greenhalgh
The University of Nottingham, Nottingham NG7 2RD, UK
{bnk,sdb,cmg}@cs.nott.ac.uk

Abstract: Mixed reality boundaries establish transparent windows between physical and virtual spaces. We introduce a set of properties that allow such boundaries to be configured to support different styles of co-operative activity. These properties are grouped into three categories: permeability (properties of visibility, audibility and solidity); situation (properties of location, alignment, mobility and segmentation); and dynamics (properties of lifetime and configurability). We discuss how each of these properties can be technically realised. We also introduce the meta-properties of symmetry and representation. We then describe and compare two contrasting demonstrations, a performance and an office-door, that rely on different property configurations.

Introduction - approaches to shared mixed reality

There has been a growing interest in techniques for combining real and virtual environments to create *mixed realities* – spatial environments where participants can interact with physical and digital information in an integrated way (Milgram & Kishino, 1994). Mixed realities may be shared, enabling people who are distributed across multiple physical and virtual spaces to communicate with one another. A variety of approaches to creating a shared mixed reality have been demonstrated, including augmented reality, augmented virtuality, tangible bits and mixed reality boundaries.

Augmented reality involves overlaying and registering digital information (e.g., text and graphics) onto a real world scene in such a way that the digital information appears to be attached to physical objects, even as they move about.

The physical scene might be the local environment, with the digital information being introduced via a see-through head-mounted display. Alternatively, it might be remote, being viewed on a video display that is then enhanced with digital information. Early examples of collaborative augmented reality include the *Shared Space* system (Billinghurst et al, 1996), in which users share virtual objects across a physical table top and *Studierstube* (Schmalstieg et al, 1996), in which virtual objects are also displayed in a physical space between multiple users. Both of these systems utilise see-through head-mounted displays. Systems based on video views of remote scenes are inherently sharable as the video display is usually located in a shared physical space.

In contrast, *augmented virtuality* (Milgram & Kishino, 1994) takes a virtual world as its starting point and then embeds representations of physical objects within this. These might take the form of textured video views, for example views of participants' faces on their avatars as in the *Freewalk* system (Nakanishi et al, 1996), or views of remote physical locations as in the 3-D media-space interface of (Reynard et al, 1998). Alternatively, telemetry data captured by remote physical sensors might be visualised using graphics, text and audio.

The approach of *tangible bits* (Ishii & Ullmer, 1997) involves the use of graspable physical objects called phicons to interact with digital information, for example moving physical models across a table top in order to access a digital map that is projected onto it. This may be coupled with the use of ambient display media such as sound, light and airflow to provide more peripheral awareness of background information, for example, showing the volume of network traffic as reflections of water ripples on the ceiling.

The approach of *mixed reality boundaries* involves joining together distinct virtual and physical spaces by creating a transparent boundary between them (Benford et al, 1996). With this approach, the spaces are not overlaid, but instead are distinct but adjacent. The occupants of the shared physical space can see into the next-door virtual space and can communicate with its occupants (e.g. avatars within a collaborative virtual environment). In turn, the occupants of the virtual space can see back into the physical space. A distinguishing feature of this approach is that it places equal weight on physical and virtual environments, considering how each can be accessed from the other. It also offers the potential to use multiple mixed reality boundaries to join together many physical and virtual spaces into a larger mixed reality environment in the same way that everyday boundaries such as doors, walls and windows are used to structure physical buildings.

Our paper is concerned with this last approach. Its departure point is the idea of a simple mixed reality boundary as described in (Benford et al, 1996). Figure 1 shows how such a boundary can be established. On the left of the figure is a physical environment into which are projected graphics and audio from the virtual environment on the right. In turn, a video camera and microphone capture video and audio from the physical environment and this is transmitted back to the virtual environment over a computer network. The live video image is then displayed as a dynamic texture map within the virtual environment. The result is the creation of a transparent bi-directional window between the physical and virtual environments. This approach was demonstrated through an application called the Internet Foyer, in which a visualisation of an organisation's home pages on the World Wide Web, complete with representations of their visitors (a virtual foyer), was joined to its physical foyer using a mixed reality boundary.

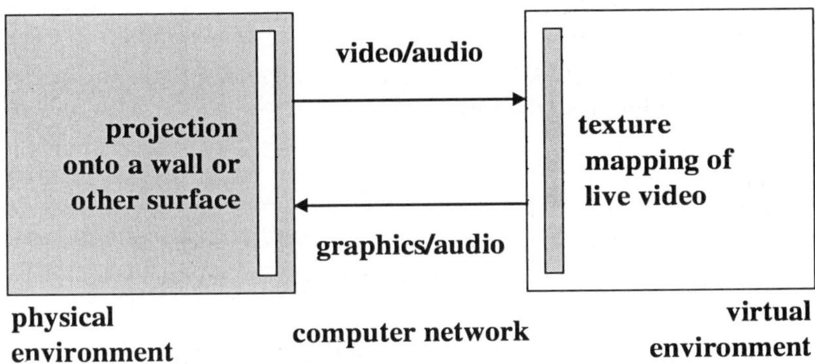

Figure 1: a simple mixed reality boundary

This paper further develops this approach by identifying a set of properties that can be associated with mixed reality boundaries. These properties are intended to support the design of mixed reality boundaries for a broad range of potential collaborative applications. Applications as diverse as distributed meetings, performances, media-spaces, document editing and 3-D design will have varying requirements for managing awareness and privacy; for positioning a boundary and aligning it to different participants; and for scheduling its appearance. The set of boundary properties is also intended to provide an analytic framework for reasoning about how different boundary configurations (e.g., based on different combinations of projection and camera technologies) might afford different styles of co-operative activity.

The following section introduces our boundary properties and explores their technical realisation. We then present two contrasting demonstrations of how these properties can be configured to support different co-operative activities. The first is a distributed performance between a poet in a virtual world and an audience in a physical theatre. The second involves the use of a persistent boundary to allow remote visitors to "drop in" to an office over a network. We offer a property by property comparison of their design and conclude by considering how this work can draw on and contribute to related research areas such as tangible interfaces (Ishii & Ullmer, 1997) and co-operative buildings (Streitz, 1998).

Boundary Properties

We now introduce the fundamental properties of mixed reality boundaries, examining the utility of each and considering how each might be technically realised. Our choice of properties has been influenced by analogies with the real-world boundaries that partition physical space and also by our previous work on developing boundaries within virtual space (Benford et al, 1997a). Our proposed properties are grouped into three general categories: *permeability*, properties that define how information passes through a boundary; *situation*, the spatial properties of the boundary; and *dynamics*, the temporal properties of the boundary. We also introduce the meta-properties of *symmetry* and *representation* that apply to the other properties.

Permeability

Permeability describes how the boundary affects sensory information passing between the linked spaces. We break down permeability into visibility, audibility and solidity, based on the three primary types of information that can pass through the boundary. Our discussion focuses on vision, sound and touch because most current interfaces between the physical and the virtual are based on a combination of these. However, we note that smell and taste information might also be "transmitted" through mixed reality boundaries in the future.

Visibility – considers what visual information is permitted through the boundary and consists of two components: visual resolution and field of view. Visual resolution concerns the amount of visual information obtained through the boundary and is affected by factors such as the resolution of capture and display technologies and graphical level of detail. Field of view describes the volume of the connected space that is made visible through the boundary and is determined by factors such as the field of view/projection of (physical and virtual) cameras and projectors.

Audibility – considers what audio information is permitted through the boundary and is determined by factors such as the positioning and sensitivity of microphones as well as sampling rates.

Drawing on previous work on virtual boundaries and crowd representations (Benford et al, 1997a), we propose that visibility and audibility can be further described in terms of the combination of four effects:

- *attenuation* – for example, reducing video resolution or audio volume;
- *amplification* – for example, projecting audio in the manner of a public address system;
- *transformation* – for example, distorting audio and video to establish anonymity; and
- *aggregation* – summarising what lies beyond the boundary. For example, showing only the number of remote participants instead of each individual.

Solidity – refers to the ability to traverse the boundary. This includes metaphorically extending a limb through the boundary to manipulate or feel a remote object; pushing an object through the boundary so that it becomes available on the other side; and stepping through the boundary and assuming control of an avatar or physical proxy on the other side. Strictly speaking, this last case establishes a second mobile boundary between the spaces (see below) as the participant may not actually leave their local physical space behind. However, metaphorically, there is a sense of stepping through the boundary.

Traversal from the physical to the virtual can be realised using 3-D interaction devices and tracking technologies to manipulate virtual objects that appear on a projected display or to track local physical objects and update their virtual counterparts. Allowing the user to sense virtual objects is achieved through haptic devices such as those described by Fogg et al (1998) and Colwell et al (1998). Traversal from the virtual to the physical involves remote control of physical proxies such as mobile cameras and robots as in the *GestureCam* system (Kuzuoka et al, 1995). Digital documents can be pushed through the boundary by projecting them onto a desktop in the manner of the *Digital Desk* (Wellner, 1993) or by placing them directly on the boundary itself in the style of Clearboard (Ishii & Kobayishi, 1992).

The potential for combining different visibility and audibility effects with varying degrees of solidity allows the definition of a wide range of boundary types. These include analogies of familiar everyday physical boundaries such as windows, walls, curtains, fences, one-way mirrors and even lines on the ground, as well as new kinds of boundary that have no common physical counterpart. Furthermore, a systematic exploration of all possible combinations of visibility, audibility and solidity might identify the fundamental building materials that can be used to join together physical and virtual spaces.

Situation

Situation concerns the spatial relationships between the mixed reality boundary, the physical and virtual spaces that it connects and the participants and objects that these contain. This includes the location of the boundary, whether this location is fixed and whether the boundary is segmented. Between them, these properties determine the spatial understanding that the participants in one space have of the connected space.

Location – describes the placement of the boundary within the connected spaces. A vertical location involving projection onto a physical wall or screen or texturing onto a virtual wall or screen will establish the boundary as a window between the two spaces. Given a large enough display, the remote space might even be presented as a direct extension of the local space. A horizontal location involving projection onto a physical or virtual desk or board will establish the boundary as a shared drawing surface. The use of ambient display media as proposed in (Ishii & Ullmer, 1997), could establish a more peripheral connection between the spaces.

Alignment – concerns the orientation of the boundary with respect to the different participants and objects and may establish different possibilities for turn taking and access to other participants. For example, the triangular alignment of figure 2 allows a physical performer to simultaneously address a physical and a virtual audience while allowing the two audiences to address one another.

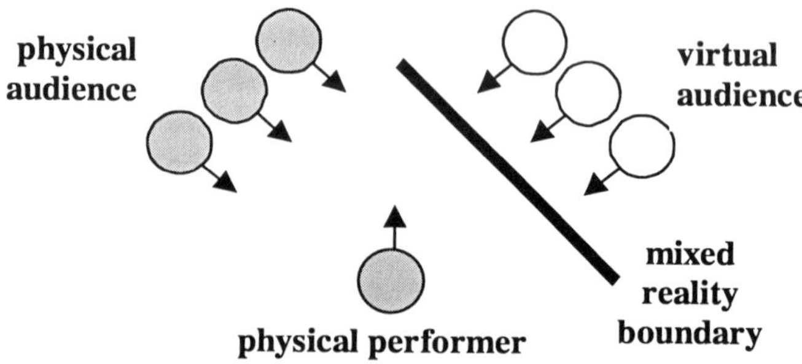

Figure 2: a triangular boundary alignment

Mobility – describes whether the boundary assumes a static situation, thus offering connection between two fixed sections of the linked spaces, or whether the boundary can join different parts of the spaces over time. A mobile boundary is one that the participants can steer through the linked spaces or which follows a pre-programmed trajectory. In practical terms, mobility requires that the boundary components (e.g., physical or virtual cameras and microphones) can themselves be moved. There can be various restrictions on the movement of the boundary. For example, participants may only be able to rotate the boundary around a fixed point without translating its position.

Segmentation - a boundary can be segmented in terms of its properties and spatial location. The former refers to when a boundary is made up of one or more segments with distinct property sets. A spatially segmented boundary, on the other hand, links the two spaces through multiple non-adjacent segments (these can themselves be property segmented).

So far in our discussion of the situation properties we have assumed that the spatial co-ordinate system of one space is related to that of the other in a spatially consistent way. More specifically, that the connected spaces provide to some extent a unified frame of reference across which position, distance, orientation and perspective are consistent. However, there are two problems in establishing detailed spatial consistency. First, the use of a single fixed camera (physical or virtual) on any side will only provide an accurate perspective from one viewing position. A participant may move along the boundary or change their viewing angle, but will still retain the same view of the connected space. The use of multiple cameras, mobile cameras and even stereo cameras may overcome this problem to some degree, but only for one participant at a time. Second, it may be necessary to locate audio information in a spatially consistent manner. This may require the use of multiple or mobile microphones and spatialised audio rendering.

The issue of spatial consistency is a very important one as it affects the level of detail to which participants on opposite sides can establish mutual orientation, a reciprocity of perspective and can use spatial language and gesture.

Combining these situation properties with the permeability properties described previously, defines the regions of each space that are public (i.e., accessible from the connected space) versus those that remain private to each space (i.e., are out of camera shot or microphone range).

Dynamics

Dynamics concern the temporal properties of the boundary, including its lifetime and its degree of configurability.

Lifetime – refers to when and for how long the boundary is in existence. Boundaries may be scheduled to appear at specific, even periodic, times to support the pre-planned nature of many activities (e.g., performances and meetings) or may be created on the fly. The potential duration of a boundary can be considered in the light of previous research into media spaces that distinguished different services ranging from persistent "office share" connections through to short-term "glance" facilities lasting for just a few seconds (Gaver et al, 1992).

Configurability – describes how dynamically the various boundary properties can be changed. Permeability might be adjusted in order to reflect changing privacy requirements. Configuring situation involves being able to move cameras and projectors and re-positioning furniture and other aspects of the connected spaces, for example in order to accommodate new participants. Finally, dynamic properties such as lifetime might also be directly configurable.

So far, we have established the fundamental boundary properties of permeability, situation and dynamics. We now discuss the two meta-properties of symmetry and representation that relate to each of these.

Symmetry

Symmetry refers to the extent that the properties of a mixed reality boundary are configured to be the same on both of its sides (i.e., from the physical to the virtual and vice versa). A degree of asymmetry may often be imposed as a result of the technologies used (e.g., where cameras and projectors differ in the their field of view). In other cases, it may be desirable to deliberately create asymmetric boundaries in order to meet a specific communication need (e.g., using a one way boundary to unobtrusively observe activity). Mixed reality boundaries may be asymmetric with respect to permeability, situation and dynamics.

Asymmetry introduces an additional dimension to the configurability of boundaries. We propose that participants should be able to configure their own side of the boundary and also set limits on the potential configuration of the other side as it affects them. For example, a participant may wish to set an upper limit on what the other side can see of them. To generalise, each control for configuring a boundary property might combine the ability to set the property in one direction and limit the property in the reverse direction.

Representation

Mixed reality boundaries are potentially complex technologies that may take many different forms. We argue that, in order to successfully use a boundary, participants will need to understand both the current and potential settings of its properties. In other words, the properties of mixed reality boundaries should be made visible (and possibly audible), be it explicitly through controls and labels, or implicitly through metaphor, interior design or architecture. Considering permeability, a boundary should indicate the current and potential settings for visibility, audibility and solidity at each side. Considering situation, the separation of public from private space should be clearly marked so that participants know how to position themselves in order to communicate or avoid those on the other side. For example, the view frustra of physical and virtual cameras could be made explicitly visible by marking them on the floor. Considering dynamics, participants might be notified in advance when a boundary is going to appear or disappear so as they may adjust their behaviour and/or appearance appropriately.

This concludes our introduction to the properties of mixed reality boundaries. The following section presents two examples of how these properties might be configured to meet different application requirements.

Demonstrations

We present two demonstrations of mixed reality boundaries that rely on different configurations of boundary properties to support different activities:
- a performance in which a performer on a virtual stage engages an audience in a physical theatre through a mixed reality boundary;
- an "office door" that establishes an open connection between a public virtual world and a private physical office. This necessitates the management of virtual visitors in relation to local physical activity, especially with regard to shifting privacy requirements.

For each demonstration we state its goals, describe its design and offer some initial reflections. We then compare the two in terms of the property configurations of their boundaries.

First Demonstration – a Mixed Reality Performance

Our performance demonstrator extends our previous experience of staging a poetry performance simultaneously in physical and virtual theatres as reported in (Benford et al, 1997b). This previous attempt involved poets performing in a conventional physical theatre and at the same time, appearing as avatars on a virtual stage in front of an on-line audience in a virtual environment. A view of the virtual environment was then projected as a back-drop to the physical stage. A key observation from this previous performance is that the event became fragmented into two parts – a conventional performance and a social-chat virtual environment. We have argued in (Benford et al, 1997b) that the nature of the projection of the virtual space into the theatre may have been a key factor in these problems. In particular:

- the projection created a one way boundary between the two spaces – the physical audience and performer could see their virtual counterparts, but not vice versa;
- for aesthetic reasons, the projection was rendered from a moving viewpoint. Consequently, there was no stable spatial relationship between the two spaces and it would been difficult for the participants in the physical theatre to establish any consistent reference or orientation to those in the virtual theatre.

The current demonstrator has therefore focused on the issue of whether effective social engagement can be established between real and virtual theatres. In this case, the performer (a poet) appeared on a virtual stage and attempted to engage the attention of an audience who were located in a remote physical theatre. The poet attempted to persuade the audience to join in the performance by answering questions, standing up and chanting as part of an improvised poem – essentially a test of whether they could exert sufficient social pressure on the audience. A key design goal was therefore that the boundary should be as invisible as possible, especially to the audience. Specific differences to the previous performance were that:

- the physical and virtual worlds were linked through a mixed reality boundary that allowed the audience to see and hear the virtual poet and vice versa;
- the boundary had a fixed spatial location with the intention that the virtual stage would appear to the audience as a conventional physical stage would;
- the poet was physically separated from the audience and was immersed in the CVE using a head-mounted display. As a result, the only option for communicating with the audience was via the mixed reality boundary.

Technical Realisation of the Performance

Figure 3 summarises the realisation of the performance.

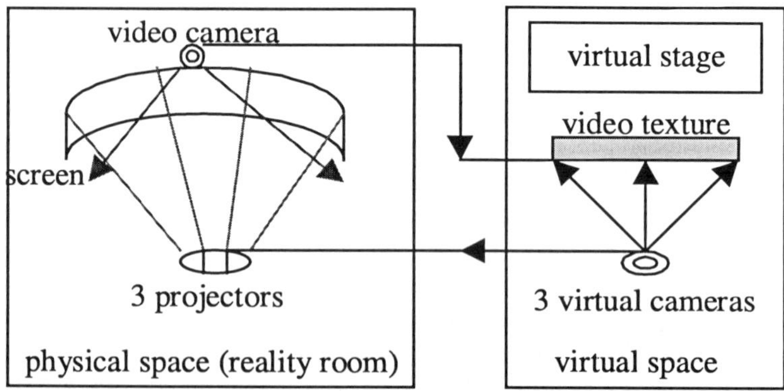

Figure 3: the design of the mixed reality performance

The physical audience were located in a Reality Room, a facility that allows the output of a high-performance computer (Silicon Graphics Infinite Reality Engine) to be projected onto a wide angle curved screen (using three separate projectors whose output is blended together). The poet was located in a separate physical room and used an Eyegen 3 head-mounted display to become immersed in the virtual and appear on the stage. Their view included a video texture looking back out into the audience space taken from a video camera mounted at the top and centre of the projection screen. Note that the video texture was transparent from the other side and did not interfere with the virtual cameras. A separate analogue circuit provided an audio link between the two spaces. By positioning a microphone in the audience space at the focal point of the curved screen we could easily pick up any noise made by the physical audience, a useful additional feature of placing a curved screen in a shared space. Finally, in order to introduce an extra element to the performance, an additional virtual actor was able to enter the virtual stage using a workstation that was located in the audience space.

Experience from the Performance

Our initial performance lasted for half an hour and involved one of the poets from the previous performance (Dave "Stickman" Higgins). The stage and poet's avatar were designed by the artist Derek Richards who also joined in the end of the performance as a supplementary actor. The performance began with the virtual poet entering from the wings and improvising a poem while the audience watched. After five minutes the poet directly addressed the audience for the first time, requesting that they stand up and asking them a series of questions. After picking on several other individuals in the audience, he then persuaded them all to rise and to clap and chant along with the poem. Figure 4 is taken from the audience space and shows the poet avatar on the virtual stage addressing an audience member.

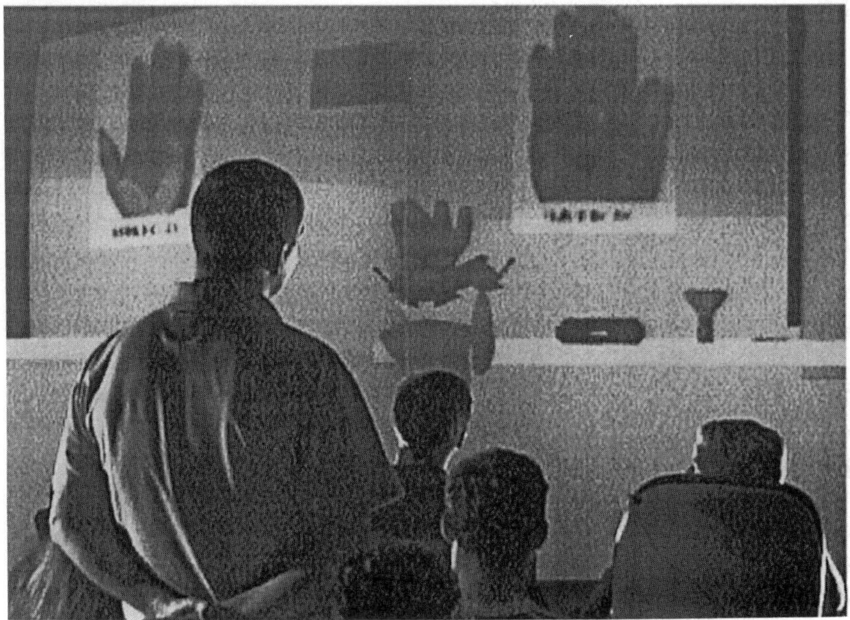

Figure 4: the poet interrogates an audience member

This initial test suggested to us that the poet was able to engage the audience to some degree. They did respond to his requests, although on some occasions (e.g., on first asking them all to stand up) this took several attempts, emphasising the importance of visibility through the boundary (it was clear that he could see when they had not responded to his request). The resolution of the textured video made it impossible for the poet to pick out details such as facial expression, but he was able to pick out gross physical features such as clothing and to spot large gestures. There were several problems with the performance, especially with the poet becoming disorientated. However, we argue that this simple test demonstrated a level of engagement between the real and virtual that was not achieved in our earlier performance.

In some ways, these observations reflect the current successful use of virtual actors to engage physical audiences through large screens at entertainment events and installations, see for example, (SimGraphics, 1999). However, in these events the human actor typically adopts an out of body view and sees the remote audience on a separate video monitor. Our experiment involved full-immersion with a textured video view of the remote audience being presented as a window in the virtual world.

Second Demonstration – the "Office Door"

In contrast to the previous demonstrator that focused on a specific event, the "office door" demonstrator explores how a mixed reality boundary might be configured to establish a persistent connection between a physical and virtual space. The aim of the demonstrator is to connect a private physical office to a public virtual corridor to enable remote visitors to drop by over a computer network. This has been inspired by previous work on media-spaces that introduced the ideas of "glancing" into remote offices and establishing long-term "office-share" relationships (Gaver et al, 1992). However, in this case, one of the connected spaces is a collaborative virtual environment. An important aspect of this demonstrator is that, in contrast to the performance, it raises the issues of dynamically managing and representing availability and privacy when using mixed reality boundaries.

Technical realisation of the office door

To create the office door boundary, we have projected a view of a virtual corridor onto the wall of a private office. At the same time, we have texture mapped the reverse video view of the office into the virtual corridor. By using a workstation on their desk, the occupant of the office can also step into the corridor, taking on the form of an avatar. Thus, the physical side of the boundary is not solid. Two potential views of the corridor are therefore available to the occupants, a permanent view looking out of their office (wall projection) and sometimes a mobile view from within the virtual corridor (using a workstation).

We have extended the basic mixed reality boundary design to offer varying degrees of visibility and audibility. On the virtual side, the volume of audio from the physical can be adjusted as can the resolution of video (down to no audibility or visibility). On the physical side, audio volume can also be adjusted as can the level of detail of the graphical view of the virtual corridor. For the latter, the current demonstrator supports four levels of detail: no visual information, an aggregate count of how many people are beyond the boundary, indication of the positions of these people (they are represented as simple blocks) and finally a full view of individual avatars. These levels of audibility and visibility are directly configurable at each side of the boundary through a series of interface controls that also indicate their current settings. Specifically:

- each side of the boundary provides a control for setting and indicating the visibility of the other side. A parallel control is provided for audibility.
- each side of the boundary provides a separate control for limiting the maximum visibility of this side to the other. Using this control, participants can set an upper limit on how visible they wish to be, including reducing their visibility to zero. A parallel control is provided for audio.

By using these controls, participants can dynamically negotiate degrees of privacy. It is important to note that levels of visibility and audibility need not be symmetric across the boundary.

Figure 5 offers a screenshot of these controls as seen from the virtual corridor. The two sliders at the side of the video texture set the desired audibility and visibility of the other side. The two sliders above the texture limit the ability of the other side to see and hear this side. We can see two avatars in the virtual corridor looking into the physical office and one person looking back at them. The part of the corridor that is visible from the physical office is shaded a different colour to the part that is not (although this is difficult to see in the greyscale image).

Figure 5: Controls for visibility and audibility

Experience of the Office Door

We installed the office door boundary in two offices within our laboratory, one that was shared by four researchers and a second that was the private office of our laboratory manager. The boundary was established as an open-connection between these spaces and the virtual corridor. It was also used during regular weekly laboratory meetings. The latter involved three or four members of the laboratory attending these meetings remotely and appearing in the virtual corridor, with the remaining participants (between five and eight) being physically present in the office. For the shared office, the boundary was placed diagonally across a corner of the room so that the participants could arrange themselves in a circle when seated. For the private office, it was placed at the end of an existing meeting table.

Our initial reflections have raised a number of issues for further exploration. First, although virtual visitors appeared visually on a large projection and could be heard as soon as they spoke, the silent nature of movement in the virtual corridor was potentially disconcerting for those in the physical space. Sensing presence and movement near the boundary and indicating these through additional audio cues may prove useful, especially on the virtual side of the boundary. Second, several different avatars were tested for the virtual visitors. Those featuring a live video face seemed best suited to this particular application, perhaps because they offered a degree of symmetry in terms of providing a reverse video view back into their user's own physical space. In particular, they would make it possible for occupants of a physical office to tell when several remote users people were looking at them through a single shared avatar. Third, the circular arrangement of participants worked adequately for the laboratory meetings. Participants in the virtual space claimed that, at least some of the time, they could tell when they were being looked at and could identify individuals in the physical space (although, unlike the performance, the participants knew each other well). We suspect that swapping turns across the boundary as opposed to our usual progression around the circle may have promoted communication between the physical and virtual spaces.

Comparison and Discussion

We conclude our presentation of the two boundary demonstrations by directly comparing and discussing their properties. Our aim is to show how their different configurations reflect their intended uses. Table 1 summarises this comparison.

We begin with permeability. Visibility and audibility were fixed for the performance boundary with the aim of achieving the best possible visual and audio experience for both sides. In contrast, they were defined to be dynamically configurable for the office door boundary, allowing the participants to select a configuration best suited to their current requirements for awareness and privacy. In terms of solidity, both demonstrators allow one person to metaphorically step through the boundary from the physical to the virtual by controlling an avatar. In both cases, the boundaries were solid from the virtual to physical, due to a lack of locally available tele-presence technology (e.g., remote controlled robots).

There were also differences between the two boundaries in terms of their situation properties, especially alignment and location. With the performance, the aim was to link the whole physical room with all of its audience members to the virtual stage, making the two spaces appear to be direct extensions of each other. In other words, the boundary was intended to be as transparent as possible. This was facilitated by the use of a wide screen projection facility housed in a purpose built room. Indeed, a key element of the performance was the moment of surprise when it was revealed that the performer could actually see the audience through the projection screen! In contrast, an important aspect of the office door alignment was the desire to deliberately keep one area of the office out of view of the boundary so as to retain a private area. The office door alignment was also limited by the physical shapes of the existing offices. This severely constrained the location of screens and projectors.

Property	Performance		Office door	
	Virtual	Physical	Virtual	Physical
Visual resolution	Video resolution 120 x 120 pixels	Projector resolution 3556 x 1024 pixels	Configurable video resolution from 120 x 120 to 0 x 0 pixels	Configurable graphical level of detail (4 levels)
Field of view	60°	175°	60°	65°
Audibility	Amplified		Variable – volume can be adjusted at both sides	
Solidity	Solid	one person can step through	Solid	one person can step through
Location	Vertical - establishes boundary as window	Vertical - establishes boundary as extension of space	Vertical - establishes boundary as window	
Alignment	Facing seats	Facing stage	Into part of office	Onto corridor
Mobility	Static		Static	
Segmentation	Property segmented		Not segmented	
Lifetime	Half hour		Persistent	
Configurability	None		Visibility, audibility	

Table 1: summary of boundary properties of the office door and the performance

The performance boundary raises an additional issue, that of property segmentation. As the table shows, there is a difference between the field of view offered by the projection (175 degrees) and by the video texture (60 degrees). In effect, this created a property segmented boundary consisting of a central segment which was roughly symmetrical with respect to visibility and audibility and two outer segments that were asymmetric (the audience could see the performer, but there was no reverse video texture by which the performer could see them). This segmentation was an accidental side-effect of the locally available camera and projection technologies. However, it could have had significant effects on social interaction, as it created areas of the boundary that were in effect one-way mirrors. We anticipate that such situations might arise regularly where boundaries exploit existing local facilities. Furthermore, we propose that our boundary properties provide a useful analytic framework for predicting when such accidental effects are likely to occur.

A key difference between the two boundaries concerns their dynamics. In the case of the performance, the boundary was created at a specific time for a pre-planned event, it had a set duration and its properties remained static throughout its lifetime. The office door boundary, on the other hand, had an open-ended lifetime. The connection of a public space to a private space in which different activities could occur (including private consultations), necessitated the dynamically configurable nature of the boundary as was realised through the controls mentioned above.

Considering their symmetry, the performance boundary was intended to be symmetrical and any asymmetries were side effects of the technologies that were used. In contrast, the potential for asymmetry was deliberately designed into the office door. For example, the occupant of the office might have closed down their side of the boundary during a private meeting while retaining a view into the virtual corridor to see if any potential visitors were waiting.

Issues of representation of properties were particularly significant with the office door due to its configurability (i.e., it was necessary to convey the current and potential state of both sides of the boundary) and also due to the need to mark the distinction between public and private space. In contrast, the intended transparency of the performance boundary led to its properties not being directly represented.

Finally, considering spatial consistency, there was slight vertical misalignment at the virtual side of the boundary in both demonstrators. This is due to the video camera being located at the top of the projection screen for the performance and at the bottom for the office door as opposed to at its vertical midpoint.

Positioning the camera at the vertical midpoint behind the projection would have been ideal, but would have required a special screen that was transparent from the rear. In both cases, the correct alignment was achieved at the virtual side because the video texture was defined to be a one sided polygon through which the virtual camera could see.

In summary, we have presented two contrasting demonstrations of mixed reality boundaries that exploit different configurations of boundary properties in order to achieve their goals. The performance seeks to establish from scratch a boundary that is invisible to its users and that exists for a fixed period of time. In contrast, the office door requires that the boundary be integrated in an existing working environment and so must be visible, understandable and configurable. A further key point concerns the way in which purely technological factors (such as differences in the field of view of available cameras and projection equipment) can result in accidental asymmetries and segmentation of boundaries. We argue that our notion of boundary properties provides a framework for understanding when these might occur and how they might affect participants.

This concludes our analysis of mixed reality boundary examples in terms of properties. In the next section we generalise the idea of boundaries and use it to briefly discuss other CSCW systems

Summary and Future Work

This paper has extended the basic idea of mixed reality boundaries by identifying the properties that such boundaries might have. These include properties affecting their *permeability* (visibility, audibility and solidity); properties affecting their spatial *situation* (location, alignment, mobility and segmentation); and properties affecting their temporal *dynamics* (lifetime and configurability). The central argument of this paper has been that through appropriate configuration and analysis of these properties, mixed reality boundaries might support a diverse range of applications. To support this argument, we have described and compared two contrasting demonstrators: the performance and the office-door. We conclude by raising issues for further work.

Implementing the full-range of boundary properties

Creating non-solid boundaries is currently difficult. Traversal from the virtual to the physical requires a greater integration with work on robotics and especially tele-operated physical proxies. In turn, traversal from the physical to the virtual might exploit non-solid projection surfaces that would require a participant to physically step through them in order to gain access to the virtual world beyond. In this way, a participant would leave behind their local physical environment as they stepped into the remote virtual environment. We are currently experimenting with this idea with the UK theatre company Blast Theory who have been experimenting with projecting images into a vertical curtain of water.

We believe that the technique of directly representing boundary properties, especially field of view, is an important one. Future work might consider how this could be achieved more subtly through furniture design, interior design and architecture. For example, the design of carpets, rugs and tables might encourage participants to align themselves appropriately to a boundary. We propose that similar techniques could be used by other applications that make use of cameras.

The idea of mobile mixed reality boundaries is currently unexplored. This raises issues of steering boundaries, integration with mobile cameras and the representation of mobile field of view and other situation properties.

Applying the boundary approach to other areas of CSCW

We propose that we can extend the approach of boundaries to cover not only CSCW systems that link the physical and the virtual, but also CSCW systems that connect two remote physical spaces or two synthetic environments. For example, videoconferencing, media-space and tele-presence applications can be seen as creating boundaries with particular property configurations between remote physical spaces. Could we use our framework of properties as a means of designing and analysing a wider range of CSCW applications? For example, previous work on using multiple video views in media-spaces identified problems in working with fragmented views of a remote scene (Gaver et al, 1993). Could this and other examples, be described in terms of our boundary properties of segmentation and location and the issue of achieving spatial consistency?

Adopting a still broader perspective, shared mixed reality is a topic of growing research interest, with some of the most radical recent developments being made in areas such as tangible interfaces and co-operative buildings. We propose that the approach of mixed reality boundaries can both draw on and contribute to this work. First, ubiquitous computing and tangible interfaces provide techniques for introducing digital information into local physical environments. These might be used to create more accessible mixed reality boundaries. Conversely, work on mixed reality boundaries suggests a greater consideration of how physical environments appear from the perspective of remote and digital environments (e.g., that of networked participants). Second, early work on co-operative buildings has explored how displays and computing facilities might be integrated with furniture, interior design and architecture. As noted above, mixed reality boundaries require the same consideration. Conversely, our approach of directly representing boundary properties within the connected spaces is relevant to the design of co-operative buildings.

In summary, the past few years have seen the development of new ideas for situating the digital in the physical. Our work on mixed reality boundaries is intended to balance this trend by also considering how the physical can be situated in the digital and by developing new techniques for joining the two domains of physical space and digital space on an equal footing.

Acknowledgements

This work has been carried out in the European Union (EU) funded *eRENA* project (ESPRIT IV I^3 programme) and the EPSRC funded *Multimedia Networking for Inhabited Television* project (Multimedia Networked Applications programme). We gratefully acknowledge the EU and the EPSRC for their support.

References

Benford, S. D., Greenhalgh, C. M. and Lloyd, D.(1997a): "Crowded Collaborative Environments", *Proc. CHI'97*, ACM Press, pp. 59-66

Benford, S. D., Greenhalgh, C. M., Snowdon, D. N. and Bullock, A. N.(1997b): "Staging a Public Poetry Performance in a Collaborative Virtual Environment", *Proc. ECSCW'97*, Kluwer

Benford, S., Brown, C., Reynard, G. and Greenhalgh, C. (1996): "Shared Spaces: Transportation, Artificiality and Spatiality", *Proc. CSCW'96*, ACM Press, pp. 77-85

Billinghurst, M., Weghorst, S., Furness III, T. (1996): "Shared Space: An Augmented Reality Interface for Computer Supported Collaborative Work", *Proc. Workshop on Collaborative Virtual Environments (CVE'96)*, The University of Nottingham, Nottingham, UK.

Colwell, C., Petrie, H., Kornbrot, D., Hardwick, A. and Furner, S. (1998): "Haptic Virtual Reality for Blind Computer Users", *Third Annual ACM Conference on Assistive Technologies (ASSETS 98)*, ACM Press, pp. 92-99

Fogg, B., Cutler, L., Arnold, P. and Eisbach, C. (1998): "HandJive: Device for Interpersonal Haptic Entertainment", *Proc. CHI'98*, ACM Press, pp. 57-64

Gaver, W., Moran, T., MacLean, A.,Lovstrand, L., Dourish,P., Carter, K. and Buxton W. (1992): "Realising a Video Environment: EuroPARC's RAVE System", *Proc. CHI'92*, ACM Press, pp. 27-35

Gaver, W., Sellen, A., Heath, C. and Luff, P. (1993): One is not enough: multiple views in a media space, Proc. InterCHI'93, Amsterdam, 1993, ACM Press.

Ishii, H. and Kobayishi, M. (1992): "Integration of Inter-Personal Space and Shared Workspace: ClearBoard Design and Experiments", *Proc. CSCW'92*, ACM Press, pp. 33-42

Ishii, H. and Ullmer, B. (1997): "Tangible bits: Towards Seemless Interfaces between People, Bits and Atoms", *Proc, CHI'97*, ACM Press, pp. 234-241

Kuzuoka, H., Ishimoda, G. and Nishimura, T. (1995): "Can the GestureCam be a surrogate?", *Proc. ECSCW'95*, Kluwer, pp. 181-196

Milgram, P. and Kishino, F. (1994): "A Taxonomy of Mixed Reality Visual Displays", *IEICE Trans. Information Systems*, Vol E77-D, No 12, December 1994.

Nakanishi, H., Yoshida, C., Nishimura, T. and Ishida, T. (1996): "Freewalk: Supporting Causal Meetings in a Netwrok", *Proc. ACM Conference on Computer Supported Cooperative Work (CSCW'96)*, Boston, pp. 308-314, ACM Press, Vol 16-20.

Reynard, G., Benford, S., and Greenhalgh, C. (1998): "Awareness Driven Video Quality of Service in Collaborative Virtual Environments", *Proc CHI'98*, ACM Press, pp. 464-471

Schmalstieg, D., Fuhrmann, A., Szalavari, Z. and Gervautz, M. (1996): "Studierstube - An Environment for Collaboration in Augmented Reality", *Proc. Workshop on Collaborative Virtual Environments (CVE'96)*, The University of Nottingham, Nottingham, UK.

SimGraphics Vactors (1999): http:/www.simg.com/vactorlbe.html (web page as of January 1999)

Streitz, N. (Ed) (1998): *Proc. International Workshop on Cooperative Buildings (CoBuild'98)*, Springer, Germany, February 1998.

Wellner, P., (1993): "Interacting with Paper on the DigitalDesk", *Communications of the ACM*, Vol. 36, No 7, July 1993, pp. 87-96

S. Bødker, M. Kyng, and K. Schmidt (eds.). *Proceedings of the Sixth European Conference on Computer-Supported Cooperative Work, 12-16 September 1999, Copenhagen, Denmark*
©1999 Kluwer Academic Publishers. Printed in the Netherlands

The Adoption and Use of 'BABBLE': A Field Study of Chat in the Workplace

Erin Bradner
University of California at Irvine, USA
ebradner@ics.uci.edu

Wendy A. Kellogg, Thomas Erickson
IBM T.J. Watson Research Center, USA
wkellogg@us.ibm.com, snowfall@acm.org

Abstract. One way to gain a principled understanding of computer-mediated communication (CMC) use in the wild is to consider the properties of the communication medium, the usage practices, and the social context in which practices are situated. We describe the adoption and use of a novel, chat-like system called BABBLE. Drawing on interviews and conversation logs from a 6-month field study of six different groups at IBM Corporation (USA), we examine the ways in which the technical properties of the system enable particular types of communicative practices such as waylaying and unobtrusive broadcast. We then consider how these practices influence (positively or negatively) the adoption trajectories of the six deployments.

Introduction

The CSCW and related literatures are well populated with empirical studies of groupware adoption (e.g., Ehrlich, 1987; Grudin & Palen, 1995; Orlikowski, 1992). In particular, social factors impacting the adoption and use of computer-mediated communication (CMC) technologies in the workplace have been studied for over a decade (e.g., Ehrlich 1987; Markus & Connolly, 1990; Sproull & Kiesler, 1991). These studies reveal ways in which behavior and social conventions affect adoption, a common conclusion being that understanding adoption requires careful examination of the interactions between technological features and the social context of use. As Ehrlich (1987) put it: "planning for successful [CMC] adoption requires knowledge of individual and organizational communication patterns and the relationship between those patterns and particular communication systems solutions." Yet specific examples of communication patterns and the interactions between patterns and features of CMC technology are largely absent from the literature, as are conceptual tools for detecting and describing such interactions. One contribution of this paper is to address this absence by closely examining the how features of a newly deployed system supported particular communicative practices and thus stimulated, or suppressed, its adoption. A second contribution is to investigate the use of chat in the workplace. While many studies examine chat (e.g., MUDs and MOOs) in academic and social settings (e.g., Correll 1995; O'Day *et al.,* 1996; Turkle, 1995) and email in organizations (e.g., Sproull & Kiesler 1991), few look at the use of chat in business settings (see Churchill & Bly, 1999; Kovalainen *et al.,* 1998).

In this paper we present a field study of the adoption and use of a system called "BABBLE" by six groups in a large U.S. corporation. We begin with background: the deployment process, field study, and system interface. Next, we examine how communicative practices arise from interactions among the technical properties of the system and the social characteristics of the groups, and how they stimulated or suppressed adoption. Finally we discuss critical mass, social affordances and interaction ecologies, concepts which, we believe, can provide a basis for a better understanding of adoption.

The BABBLE Deployment and Field Studies

Site Selection and Deployment

Six groups at the IBM T. J. Watson Research Center were studied, including a Software Engineering, Staff, and Human Resources group, a professional and a social cohort, and "the BABBLE Lab" group (which developed the system). Group size ranged from 5 to 175 people. The Software Engineering, Staff, and Human Resources groups were collocated (i.e., had adjacent offices) and organizationally bound (i.e., members belonged to the same department). Cohorts were geographically distributed but shared professional or social interests. The BABBLE lab's members were co-located and organizationally bound. (See Table I).

Groups were recruited via in-house demonstrations. Each received a separate discussion server. The client software included on-line help, but barring rare interactions between the authors and individual users, no formal training or usage guidelines were provided. BABBLE use was entirely discretionary.

Field Work and Data Collection

Prior to deployment, the first author observed the physical distribution of offices and conducted unstructured interviews investigating group work practices (e.g., delegation of work) and culture (e.g., perceptions of information sharing). After deployment, additional interviews were conducted at approximately four-week intervals. Throughout deployment, at frequent, unscheduled times, live BABBLE discussions were observed. Most observations and interviews were conducted over approximately a twelve-week period during the summer of 1998, with additional interviews in December, 1998. The BABBLE system automatically archived all conversations (with the exception of private chats).

Table I summarizes the deployments. 'Adoption status' reflects the subjective opinion of the workgroup members themselves. 'Use' shows the number of months of logs for each group.

BABBLE Deployment Summary					
Group Name	**Group Purpose**	**N**	**Local:Remote**	**Use (mos.)**	**Adoption Status**
BABBLE Lab	Software Design	12	10:2	18	Adoption
Software Engineering	Software Engineering	6	6:0	6	Adoption
Human Resources	Personnel Mgmt.	10	8:2 (adjacent offices)	3	Non-adoption
Staff	Staff	5	5:0	2	Non-adoption
Social Cohort	Summer Interns	175 12*	Non-collocated	3	Adoption
Professional (HCI) Cohort	HCI Researchers	28 8*	Non-collocated	3	Adoption

* Indicates the number of cohort members who actually used the system.

Table I: Deployment Summary

The BABBLE Environment

In this section we describe the interface and functionality of the BABBLE environment, and provide an example of use by one group of long term users.

142

The BABBLE Interface

BABBLE is a chat-like communication tool in which typed messages are transmitted across a TCP/IP network, stored on a server and displayed to each client. BABBLE allows its users to engage in synchronous or asynchrovnous textual conversations, and provides visual feedback regarding who has recently participated in a conversation (see Erickson *et al.*, 1999).

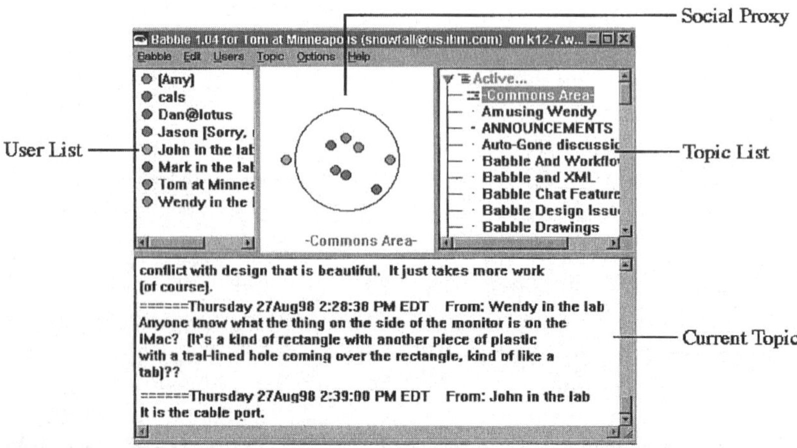

Figure 1: The BABBLE Interface

The panes of the BABBLE window (Figure 1) display the following information: a list of all connected users; the social proxy (a minimalist graphical representation of user activity); a list of topics (user-defined conversation areas); the current topic (i.e., text of the conversation). Messages appear in the order posted.

Three features of BABBLE distinguish it from other chat systems. First, BABBLE conversations are persistent: the conversations stay on the server permanently, thus permitting asynchronous conversations and activities. A user who is not on-line when a comment is made can see it later, and can scroll back through the entire history of a conversation. Second, a minimalist graphical representation called a social proxy is used to provide information about who is currently present in the conversation. The proxy uses a large circle to represent the conversation, and colored dots (a.k.a. "marbles") to represent individuals. A marble inside the circle represents a user who is 'in' the displayed conversation; a marble outside the circle is in some other conversation. When a user interacts with BABBLE — either by posting a message, or simply by scrolling or clicking on the interface — her marble rapidly moves towards the center of the circle; with inactivity the marble will slowly drift out to the inner edge of the circle. In Figure 1, five participants have recently 'spoken' or 'listened,' two have been idle, and one is in a different conversation. The third distinguishing feature of BABBLE is that it lacks technical mechanisms for enforcing behavior. Originally intended for small workgroups, it provides no technical means for 'kicking' people off, creating private topics, etc. With the exception of private, one-to-one chats, all BABBLE conversations were visible to everyone in a deployment group. Although various usage conventions have arisen, all negotiation and enforcement of such conventions is social.

An Example of BABBLE Usage

As the longest running BABBLE, the Lab BABBLE (Table I) provides a glimpse of how a successfully adopted BABBLE might evolve. It has grown steadily as measured by the amount of information and number of topics it houses, and the number and variety of communicative practices its inhabitants use.

Overall, the Lab BABBLE can be characterized as a core of synchronous activity surrounded by a constellation of asynchronous conversations. At the center of activity is the Commons Area, a place where collocated and remote members share news, engage in banter, get help, and 'hang out.' Analysis of Commons Area conversation over two-weeks showed a more synchronous temporal rhythm than other topics, and a mix of work and social talk. Approximately 50% of messages are social, including greetings, chit-chat, general announcements, and non-work questions; over half (65%) of these were posted by remote users (at home, traveling, etc.). Other topics tend to be used asynchronously (hours or days often separate comments) and largely, though not exclusively, for work-oriented discussion or information sharing. Of fifty-nine other topics: 8 are non-work related (e.g., Dilbert Trivia, Bad Jokes), 8 are group maintenance topics (e.g., Announcements), and the remaining 43 are project or topic related.

Communicative Practices in BABBLE

In this section we look at four communicative practices that emerged among the six BABBLE deployments. We describe each practice, and discuss how it arises from the technical properties of the BABBLE system and the social properties of the user groups. In the subsequent section we describe the influence that these communicative practices had on the success or failure of the adoption of BABBLE.

Waylay

BABBLE enables its users to lie in wait for, or "waylay" their coworkers. In terms of simple behaviors, it is possible to log into BABBLE, wait for signs that a particular person is around, and then open a communication channel with that person. More specifically, five properties of the BABBLE system enable waylaying:

1. BABBLE displays a list of participants (and updates when newcomers arrive)
2. BABBLE identifies every participant by name
3. BABBLE allows the name of the topic each user is reading to be displayed
4. BABBLE maintains an open communication channel among users once a user has logged in or once a private chat is initiated
5. BABBLE shows visually whether a person has recently read or written to a topic or has recently changed their state of activity.

Properties 1, 2 and 3 enable a user to determine the arrival, identity and current location of a user. Property 5 shows when a user is actively attending to the conversation topic in which she is located. In particular, at the moment the person being sought logs on or interacts with the interface after being idle, her 'marble' moves abruptly to the center of the circle, a movement that easily attracts attention. Thus, property 5 shows that the person being sought is attending and able to see a request for attention from the person doing the seeking. Property 4 allows the user to engage the attention of another user by addressing a comment directly to that user within the conversation in which she is currently active, or by opening a private chat window onto her screen. In addition, the person being sought becomes socially accountable to the person doing the seeking, because the person being sought *knows that the person seeking her knows* that she is paying attention to BABBLE (property 5), and has seen the request (property 4).

Just because BABBLE makes waylay technically possible is not proof that it occurs. However, our data show that waylay does occur, and that it differs depending on context. Two types of waylay are evident in our interviews. One type can be construed as an act of expertise selection (McDonald & Ackerman, 1998); for example, users might open a private chat window on an expert's screen and leave it open until the expert responds. This type of waylay is similar to 'camping on' a telephone extension or video connection (Fish *et al.*, 1993). A summer intern explains how he used waylay to get answers to programming questions:

> "Most of the people who are on now aren't programmers so I barely ever ask [programming questions]. When Eugene comes on, I ask him because he's a Java programmer." – Intern

Another type of waylay occurs when a manager uses BABBLE to assign work to a subordinate. Managers often walk a fine line between what they see as necessary socializing (such as inquiring how someone is 'doing' before making a work request) and the desire to be productive. A manager explains this tradeoff:

> "When I go to [my assistant], because you have to have a proper human interchange when you do that, usually I have to start with a little chat first... 'how is everything? Good.' And then you get to: 'Could you do this for me?' But Babble has the potential for cutting off some of the extraneous noise that maybe you don't want. So there is a balance between 'how's everything going?' and getting on to the next task. – Human Resources Manager

In addition to the technical properties of the BABBLE interface that enable waylay, the existence of social relationships between user dyads (information seeker and expert, manager and subordinate) make waylay a socially viable interaction.

Unobtrusive Broadcast

Another type of communicative practice is what we call "unobtrusive broadcast" of information. Unobtrusive broadcast stands in marked contrast to waylay; users reported that they often used BABBLE over other forms of communication because it enabled them to request or share information *without* interrupting others.

An example of a question and answer exchange from the Software Engineering group (Figure 2) illustrates unobtrusive broadcast.

==Thursday 6Aug98 11:40AM From: Peter

Is there a problem with marvin? I am trying to run textract on Dhaka and even though I have exported DICTPATH I am getting a LEX: No POE DICTPATH error.

==Thursday 6Aug98 11:41AM From: Megan

Not that I know of. Perhaps it's your /tmp directory that is too full. Try emptying it

==Thursday 6Aug98 11:57AM From: Peter

Responding to: <<Perhaps it's you /tmp directory that is too full>>

Yes, that was it. Thanks...

==Thursday 6Aug98 12:11PM From: Megan

It's the beauty of BAI - it fills the /tmp directory with garbage and eventually it can't do so anymore. No msg, no warning, it took Karen forever to figure this one out!

Figure 2: Unobtrusive broadcast in the Software Engineering Group

This excerpt shows a question broadcast to the Software Engineering group. In it, Peter, a relatively new member, posts a question in the Commons Area regarding an error message he encountered while using an unfamiliar system. Shortly after his post, Megan responds with a solution (later attributing it to Karen). In follow up interviews, these participants explained that the origin of the problem was obscure and the solution was extremely non-intuitive. Peter explained that BABBLE allowed him to get the help he needed while not overburdening his more senior colleagues.

There are a number of technical properties of the BABBLE system that support unobtrusive broadcast:

    1. BABBLE maintains an open communication channel among users

    2. BABBLE is persistent (e.g., it stores messages indefinitely)

    3. BABBLE concatenates and displays a topic's messages within a single window

    4. All messages are displayed in the order in which they are generated.

Property 1 enables synchronous, distance communication among users. Property 2 enables asynchronous communication such that messages (e.g., questions) posted when a user is absent, or not attending, can be read and responded to at any time (presumably when it is convenient for the respondent to do so). Property 3 enables messages to be broadcast and easily read — since all a topic's messages are in a single window, users do not open separate windows to read each message. Property 4 guarantees that answers appear after questions, so that all users can easily tell that a question has been answered simply by scanning the display. This in turn helps avoid duplicating answers and permits users to build upon each other's work, for example, elaborating a previous answer or suggesting alternatives (cf. Ackerman & Palen, 1996).

Users appreciated the unobtrusiveness supported by these properties. When asked how BABBLE was used, a software engineer responded:

> "[BABBLE] is used to ask a question of everybody if somebody needs something, not even very urgently, but it is a very unobtrusive way of asking everyone for help. It is very fast and gives immediate response [from other people] without being intrusive." – Software Engineer

With regard to choosing BABBLE over a face-to-face interaction with a specific colleague, another software engineer commented:

> "Karen doesn't like to be disturbed in her office, when you knock on her door and ask her a question. She does not get disturbed at all when you post it on Babble." – Software Engineer

With regard to choosing BABBLE over email, a staffer explained:

> "When you have a little question and you send it out [using email] to four different people and then over a period of time you get four different answers back, you are wasting three people's time there. If you try to let them know that somebody already answered you, you are making more unnecessary email. I would rather use Babble." – Staffer

These, and other comments from interviews, suggest that BABBLE was well liked because it minimized disruption to colleagues when information was being sought, and avoided "wasting people's time." Users also felt that BABBLE lessened the perceived assertiveness of question asking. The alternatives — yelling down the hall, knocking on doors, or sending broadcast email, were viewed as inappropriate, potentially disturbing, and a nuisance, respectively.

Staying 'In the Loop'

When BABBLE is used for questions and answers, not only do all users know a question has been answered, they also know who asked the question, who responded, and what the answer was. To the extent that BABBLE users share the same work context, such exchanges also provide a basis for inferring how a project is progressing, who is working on what, and so on. Thus, a side effect of public information broadcast is passive information sharing and an increased awareness of the activity of others that is idiomatically called being 'in the loop.'

The same properties of BABBLE that support unobtrusive broadcast also support activities such as 'talking out loud' and peripheral monitoring. An excerpt of conversation among members of the Software Engineering team (Figure 3) provides examples of 'talking out loud' (lines 1-6), monitoring by the group manager (lines 8-10), and 'overhearing' by a coworker (lines 13-15). The excerpt reveals how the BABBLE system's time-stamping and speaker identification support the practice of peripheral monitoring. Reading the text in Figure 3, we learn what Paul has been working on for two days (a software release) and that he had problems with a file (the `op_tools` file). From these posts the manager, George, concludes that Paul is making progress and asks him to provide a solution to a looming problem (how to build RTPS), which Paul does (use release numbers to track changes). Approximately two hours later, Karen 'overhears' the conversation and objects. Because discussion between Paul and George is available to Karen, she is informed of and, more to the point, involved in a decision that concerns her.

<table>
<tr><td>1.</td><td>=======Monday 31Aug98 4:04:14 AM EDT   From: Paul in France</td></tr>
<tr><td>2.</td><td>Friday afternoon, before i left work, i completed a build of the system....</td></tr>
<tr><td>3.</td><td>=======Monday 31Aug98 8:35:57 AM EDT   From: Paul in France</td></tr>
<tr><td>4.</td><td>Peter is the person assigned here in Lyon to study Silvercom and see what they have...</td></tr>
<tr><td>5.</td><td>=======Monday 31Aug98 11:28:19 AM EDT   From: Paul in France</td></tr>
<tr><td>6.</td><td>i've built op_tools several times now with different options and after fooling with...</td></tr>
<tr><td>7.</td><td>=======Monday 31Aug98 11:37:05 AM EDT   From: George</td></tr>
<tr><td>8.</td><td>Paul,</td></tr>
<tr><td>9.</td><td>It sounds as if you're making progress. One thing I've not heard much about yet (perhaps it's in the part of Babble I haven't read yet) is details about how we're going to use RTPS. What mechanisms are you building to make it "as easy as bbvc" for us?</td></tr>
<tr><td>10.</td><td>If I've missed discussions of this stuff, please give me pointers.</td></tr>
<tr><td>11.</td><td>=======Monday 31Aug98 11:44:09 AM EDT   From: Paul in Lyon</td></tr>
<tr><td>12.</td><td>at this point, separation will have to be done by different release numbers for different changes, and it is up to us to negotiate which things appear in the next release. anything not specifically accepted for the next release of the product has to be done as part of a "research-only" release and integrated back in manually if that status changes later.</td></tr>
<tr><td>13.</td><td>=======Monday 31Aug98 1:56:38 PM EDT   From: Karen</td></tr>
<tr><td>14.</td><td>Responding to: <<integrated back in manually>></td></tr>
<tr><td>15.</td><td>Excuse me, but I somehow thought manual integration and acute versionitis were supposed to be only one-time occurrences, after the initial switch-over.</td></tr>
</table>

Figure 3: Examples of Talking Out Loud and Peripheral Monitoring

These sorts of practices provide a way for group members to share information, both synchronously and asynchronously, while placing minimal demands on coworkers. Furthermore, 'talking out loud' frees the speaker of the burden of deciding who needs to be kept informed.

> "I think the main advantage to Babble as opposed to voice mail or email is being able to keep track of a whole set of discussions so other people also know what is going on. One of the best features ... is being able to keep other people abreast of what is going on without sending email. Or without having to call. Or getting up out of my chair [laugh]." – Software Engineer

Interview data show that the desire to 'talk out loud' about projects and to peripherally monitor others' work activity motivated BABBLE use in all groups.

These behaviors help users stay apprised of news, the status of each other's projects and changes in the work environment. Because BABBLE also supports unobtrusive broadcast, it makes 'being kept in the loop' less onerous.

Our analysis of peripheral monitoring in BABBLE recalls several studies of information flow that reveal communicative practices used to synchronize activities and integrate information in the workplace (e.g., Heath & Luff, 1991; Watts *et al.,* 1996). These studies focus on auditory and gestural communication surrounding event-driven collaboration, such as real-time coordination of London's underground trains and space shuttle mission control. Although BABBLE communication is less temporally interdependent and more asynchronous than in these event-driven contexts, we also observed a dual role of workplace communication. Like train controllers who speak out loud in the control room and mission controllers who use open voice channels, BABBLE users broadcast messages both to communicate their activities and to allow other group members to observe the consequences of their own actions (see Watts *et al.*, 1996).

Discussion Sanctuary

BABBLE provides secure communication and access control. A firewall restricts access to IBM users, and separate servers for each group ensure that users access only their own BABBLE. Server access requires only the appropriate client, so a group regulates access by controlling distribution of its client.

Interview data show that the technical properties of secure communication and access control promoted the feeling that BABBLE was a 'safe' place to talk. Informants stressed that restricting access to 'members only' promoted informal conversation, a free-flowing exchange of ideas, and social banter.

> "I think [BABBLE is] less formal. I treat it less formal. I wouldn't write mail about someone else's bug unless I check very very carefully that it is indeed in their code. ... It's funny but it's OK to write things [in BABBLE] that are not 100% finished... not that thought through... half-baked ideas are OK. Somehow it's much more like conversation." – Software Engineer

Users also said that they were less careful about the mechanical aspects of writing using BABBLE (e.g., as compared to email) because they knew that BABBLE discussion was confined to the group. For example:

> "When you are in Babble it seems like a more relaxed atmosphere and you don't have to watch your spelling, you don't have to have your sentence structure perfect and all that. [In email] you feel like everything has to be correct." – Recruiter

That BABBLE provides a safe sanctuary becomes quite evident when members perceive that quality being threatened. This occurred in the Software Engineering group when a client joined BABBLE. Several core members voiced strong concerns that the client's presence threatened the integrity of their BABBLE, for example:

> "Peter asked the person in Lyon to be on all the time. So I think to myself, 'is she listening to every word?' Once you start being very careful [about what you say] then you start to lose something essential to the discussion." – Software Engineer

These concerns are serious because BABBLE's access control is all or none: once 'outsiders' are allowed in, they can see everything. Conversely, because BABBLE makes user actions visible via the social proxy, and provides ways of finding out who has been in a topic, 'outsider' behavior can be monitored.

To summarize, we have examined four communicative practices: waylay, unobtrusive broadcast, staying 'in the loop' (including 'talking out loud' and peripheral monitoring), and discussion sanctuary. These practices emerge from the technical features of the BABBLE environment and the social dynamics and practices of each workgroup. They provide grounding for understanding the patterns of adoption and non-adoption that we observed, to which we now turn.

The Adoption of BABBLE

In this section we look at the adoption (or lack thereof) of the various BABBLE deployments. We analyze adoption in terms of the communicative practices BABBLE supports, and the ways in which those communicative practices support or conflict with the social dynamics and work practices of the groups.

The First Month

Initial use does not necessarily mean that a system will be adopted: all six BABBLEs had significant use in the first four weeks (Figures 4 and 5), especially in total postings (Figure 6). Only after 4-6 weeks is there any evidence of adoption failure.

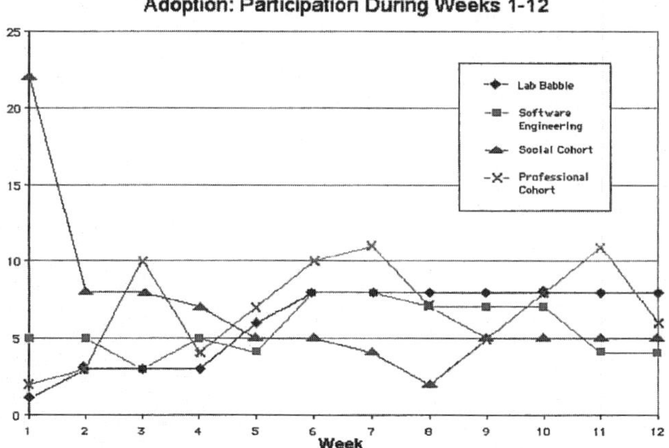

Figure 4: Number of Users Who Posted in BABBLE (Adopters)

Logs showed that BABBLE was used for both private and group conversations. We put conversation into four categories: interactive discussion, announcements,

150

requests for information, and dedicated topics. Interactive discussion included greetings, shop talk, and social chit-chat; it was subdivided into social and work-related discussion. Announcements covered meetings, out-of-office messages, and workplace news (social or work related). Requests for information included technical assistance, business-related and social inquiries (and responses). Dedicated Topics included asynchronous interaction associated with a project or topic area (Adams *et al.*, 1999). Figure 6 summarizes the first four weeks of use.

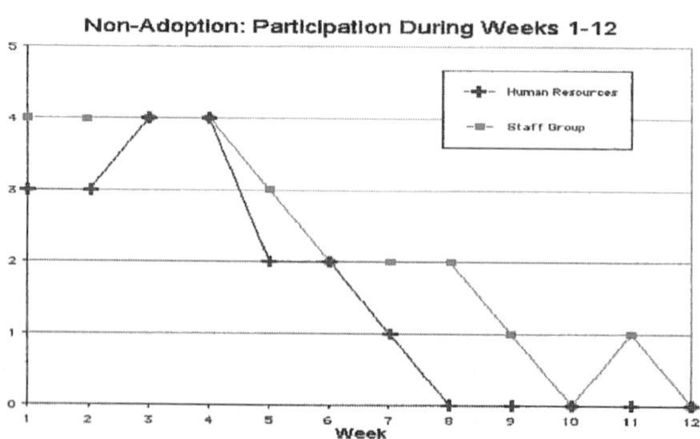

Figure 5: Number of Users Who Posted in BABBLE (Non-Adopters)

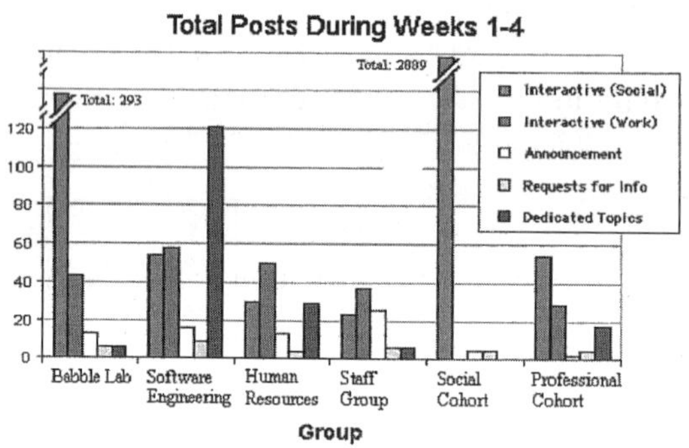

Figure 6: Total posts in the first 30 days of use, broken down by category.

Although one might expect groups using the same software within the same organization to exhibit somewhat similar behavior during the first month of use, Figure 6 shows varied usage patterns among the six groups. Interactive social discussion dominates in three groups, whereas use of dedicated topics dominates the Software Engineering group. The Human Resources and Staff groups show a slight dominance of interactive work discussion with relatively little social discussion. In short, although participation is relatively high for all groups during the first month (Figures 4, 5), the content varies considerably during this time (Figure 6), indicating that differences among groups in social dynamics and work practices affect the earliest stages of use. This suggests that groups appropriate new technology differently; understanding the relationship between group dynamics and adoption is the topic of the next section.

The Communicative Practices and Adoption Relationship is Complex

How might we understand an initial burst of usage followed by failure (or not) of adoption? Our data suggest that one answer lies in looking closely at the communicative practices that BABBLE supports. Communicative practices affect adoption by making certain social behaviors more pronounced. If BABBLE enables a practice that is not desired by some group members, or that produces consequences some members dislike, adoption may fail.

Waylay is a good illustration of the relationship between communicative practices and adoption. As noted elsewhere (Ackerman & Palen, 1996), electronic waylay for the purposes of soliciting technical assistance appears to reinforce ongoing use of chat as a distributed help environment. Our data bear this out: high levels of work-related interaction (Figure 6) can be associated with successful adoption in the Software Engineering group (Figure 4).

However, when waylay is or can potentially be used to assign work, it inhibits use. Interview data strongly indicate that the fear of waylay was a strong deterrent to use among the members of one group. After an initial period of several weeks during which most of the group was using BABBLE, the group failed to adopt. One member of this group reported that he and his colleagues were hesitant to log in to BABBLE because it made them too accessible. He explained that he and his coworkers feared that their increased accessibility might enable their manager to rope them into additional projects. In effect, the increased accessibility created by participation in BABBLE threatened their autonomy. Our informant described the fear of waylay below:

> "I'm [near] Mike [the manager] and Susan isn't that far away. When random [unassigned] work comes in, it sticks to us. Babble means that everyone is immediately accessible, so people who aren't geographically near Mike [the manager] are thinking that this accessibility is a down side [to BABBLE]." – Staffer

Although the use of chat to waylay subordinates for the purposes of assigning work is a blessing for managers because it reduces the social overhead required to engage a subordinate (discussed above), it may be considered a curse by workers. Thus, the communicative practice of waylay reinforces or inhibits adoption among different sub-groups within an organization.

Similarly, the use of BABBLE to maintain a closed discussion sanctuary encouraged use in the case of the BABBLE Lab and Software Engineering group (Figure 6). BABBLE encouraged free exchange of ideas, uninhibited brainstorming and casual chit-chat in these groups. At the same time, by using BABBLE to create and protect a discussion sanctuary, groups could hobble growth of participation. For example, usage logs and interviews indicate a "cliquish" behavior among the social cohort (i.e., the summer interns). In this deployment, access to BABBLE was extended to the entire population of summer interns. However, within a week of deployment a small faction of eight people established a sanctuary for their 'BABBLE club' excluding all others. The initial spike followed by flat line at five users in the usage graph (Figure 4) bears this out. In an interview, an intern revealed that uninvited users were deliberately alienated through vituperative comments:

> "… a couple of the other people decided that they were going to have a Babble "club" for the cool Babble people. So people kept [deliberately] getting into arguments the first couple of days about all different things. They were just trying to get rid of some people." – Intern

In summary, our examination of the differential adoption of Babble has revealed a number of issues. First, early usage, even if it is fairly extensive, does not necessarily mean a system will be adopted. Indeed, our data suggest that at least in some cases, initial usage leads to the evolution of communicative practices which, as they play out in the work situation, may have consequences that are not be desired by the group, thus leading to rejection. Furthermore, even when a system is adopted, it is important to ask by whom it is adopted and to what ends: adoption of a CMC system by a group, or portion of a group, is a more gradual and complex process than simply speaking of adoption suggests.

Discussion: Concepts for Understanding Adoption

Although this study sheds some light on adoption, clearly a more principled understanding is needed. In this section we discuss three concepts — critical mass, social affordances and interaction ecologies — that we have found useful in trying to understand adoption, and that we believe could benefit from further elaboration.

Critical Mass

Adoption is often thought to require a critical mass of users. While generally true, the adoption patterns we observed suggest a need to elaborate this relationship. For example, the Human Resources BABBLE seemed to us to be "fragile," for lack of a better term. Fragility can be framed as an issue of critical mass (Grudin, 1988; Markus, 1990), and indeed this BABBLE seemed barely to have a critical mass. With ten potential users, less than five posted in any given week (Figure 5). One or two people, by dropping out, might cause the deployment to fail. As we examined the nature of the messages in this BABBLE we noticed that with certain communicative practices, (e.g., information exchange), it was the composition of participants rather than the number of people involved in the practice, that reinforced use. For example:

"Linda and I were very productively able to use Babble for some very specific things. So the critical mass there is two. For very hard and fast stuff. For a repository of information on something as important as BOV, it has to be the whole group." – Recruiter

Certain communicative practices, then, may require as few as two users to legitimate and sustain use of a groupware system. In much the same way that interface features (e.g., meeting reminders in shared calendars) provide individual benefit and may attract a critical mass of users (Grudin & Palen, 1995) productive communicative behaviors practiced among user dyads may reinforce adoption.

Furthermore, BABBLE's adoption patterns support the notion that use is an interactive phenomenon where payoffs to (a subset of) adopters may depend on the behavior of both adopters and non-adopters (Markus & Connolly, 1990). Consider a scenario where as the number of adopters increases, payoffs to non-adopters decrease, and payoffs to adopters increase. This situation exists when group members use BABBLE to keep each other 'in the loop.' If a preponderance of members are using BABBLE in this way, then non-adopters will be 'out of the loop' if they don't adopt. Since non-adopters are presumably motivated to stay 'in the loop,' it would seem that this practice would inevitably lead to adoption. But this is not necessarily the case. Assume that a group uses only one (electronic) medium at a time to 'keep in the loop', and that maintaining 'the loop' requires that all members have access to the same information. Then, from the perspective of any member, adoption payoffs exist under two conditions: when the entire group is using Babble to broadcast information, or when no one is using it (i.e., all use another medium). Critical mass in this scenario is an all-or-none phenomenon. Thus ironically, the communicative practice of 'staying in the loop' creates a condition where partial adoption is conceivably worse than no adoption! In effect, the critical mass for BABBLE depends on which communicative practices are enacted within a given group.

Social Affordances

We have discussed the ways in which the technical properties of the BABBLE interface enable certain types of communicative practices among its users. We believe there could be great value in framing this sort of relationship more precisely. One approach to this is to draw on the notion of affordances. Originally proposed by J.J. Gibson (1979), "affordance" refers to the relationship between an object's physical properties and characteristics of an agent that enable particular interactions between agent and object. Thus, a door knob affords grasping and turning to a normally-abled human, but not to one with severe arthritis or to one lacking an opposable thumb. The term affordance was appropriated by Norman (1988) and Gaver (1991) as a conceptual tool for discussing the design of interactive systems. It has proven useful for understanding how design and perception impact technology use, and it could be useful in explaining groupware adoption.

Our working definition of a social affordance[1] is *the relationship between the properties of an object and the social characteristics of a group that enable particular kinds of interaction among members of that group*. For example, consider a door that opens out into a busy hallway. If a person opens the door quickly, it may strike someone entering from the other direction. One possible solution is to put a glass window in the door. The glass window addresses the problem at two levels. At the level of individual perception, the glass makes a person on the other side visible (i.e., the window affords seeing through it to a sighted person). At the social level, since people are socialized to not strike others with doors, they will refrain from doing so if given the chance. Furthermore, not only can the potential door opener see through the window, but the person on the other side can see as well, and thus there is shared knowledge of the situation (e.g., 'I know that you know that I know'). As a consequence, the door opener will be held accountable for her actions. This accountability, which arises from the optical properties of glass, human perceptual abilities, and the social rules of the culture, is an example of what we call a social affordance.

To apply this to the case of BABBLE, let's consider waylay through the lens of social affordances. Instances of the communicative practice of waylay — watching for a person to be active and then opening a communication channel with them — were observed in many groups. However, the existence of waylay does not mean that it is welcomed, necessarily results in helpful interactions, or is viable over the long term. For example, remote users in one group feared that their manager would use BABBLE to waylay them and delegate work to them, and hence avoided using BABBLE. Thus, although BABBLE supported the communicative practice of waylay, waylay was not socially afforded because of the social characteristics of the group. This stands in contrast to other groups in which waylaying was a regular and recognized feature of group interaction, and members might issues invitations to waylay, like 'catch me when I'm on BABBLE and we'll chat about it.' In these cases, waylay is socially afforded by the interaction of BABBLE'S functionality and group characteristics such as stronger social ties, generalized reciprocity, and perhaps by shared understandings of the limits of what may be asked in a waylay.

This discussion highlights one other useful feature of the concept of social affordances: the notion that an affordance is bound up with perception. In Gibson's original work, affordances were important because agents were seen to perceive objects (e.g. the doorknob) in terms of affordances, that is, in terms of potential interactions (grasping and turning). In our appropriation of the term, we

---

[1]   First used but not defined in (Ackerman & Palen, 1996)

suggest that as a group gains experience with a system, it comes to understand, collectively, how to appropriately apply the system to its own ends. That is, BABBLE's social affordances are the set of recurring communicative practices that a particular user group has come to recognize as appropriate and legitimate. While the concept requires more elaboration, particularly via application to a variety of cases, we believe that it may offer a principled way to discuss adoption.

An Ecology of Communicative Practices

Based on our observations of the different BABBLEs our intuition is that some deployments have, for lack of a better word, a sort of 'life' to them. That is, some instances of BABBLE seem alive and healthy; others seem alive but fragile; and others dead or dying. As we watched groups' reactions to BABBLE, our notion of 'aliveness' began to draw on an ecological metaphor. We began to think of the various BABBLEs as ecosystems populated by communicative practices requiring the input of energy from human participants to be sustained.

For example, compared to the Human Resources BABBLE, the Lab BABBLE is a very 'healthy' interaction ecology that is characterized by a great diversity of communicative practices (species). One common practice in the Lab BABBLE is the "Morning Greeting:" members of the lab often log in to BABBLE, say 'Good Morning' to one another and then engage in social chat about the weather, etc. Another practice is "Announcements:" lab members use BABBLE to announce impromptu meetings and issue reminders about events.

Looking closely at these practices, their relationships to one another and to the group engaging in them we notice three things. First, the way in which people engage in a communicative practice differs from practice to practice. Two people can indeed sustain the Good Morning activity, if they both 'speak.' However, even though a larger number of people is required to sustain Announcements, all that is necessary is that one person 'speak' and others 'notice' the announcements often enough to make use of them. Thus, different 'species' of communicative activities not only require a different number and different composition of participants, they require different types of participation. Second, it appears that some communicative practices are stronger attractors to participation than others. For example, it is our sense that although people make the effort to log on to BABBLE to read announcements (thereby 'staying in the loop'); they do not usually log on to BABBLE expressly to say 'good morning.' But, once connected for some practical reason, they are happy to participate in the 'good morning' practice. Third, we found that both dependencies and interdependencies of practices exist. Certain communicative practices, such as 'talking out loud' and peripheral monitoring, are interdependent: they reinforce one another. Others are dependent: although the 'announcements' practice reinforces the 'good morning' practice, the reverse is not true. If for some reason the announcements activity ceased, the 'good morning' activity might suffer, but the inverse is not likely.

While viewing CMC systems as ecologies of communicative practices is currently closer to metaphor than it is to a crisp conceptual framework, the work of Pirolli and his colleagues on information foraging (e.g., Pirolli & Card, 1995) demonstrates that ecology offers useful models that can be applied to other ends. It remains to be seen whether the adoption of CMC systems might be usefully modeled in this fashion.

Conclusions

We are not the first to report that local culture impacts groupware adoption. Orlikowski's (1992) and Bowers' (1994) studies are just two that draw similar conclusions. We have, however, approached adoption in a more systematic way by conducting a longitudinal study of several groups within the same organization.

Discussing controversy that arose surrounding the adoption of a CMC system, Bowers (1994) observed: "...several members felt that sending messages to a computer conference was a dangerous thing to do." Our study helps to answer questions such as: 'What *specific* features of a software interface (could) make it dangerous to use?' and 'Which social practices give rise to the perception of danger?' More generally, we have demonstrated how specific technical properties of a novel CMC system interact with the social characteristics of groups to enable a variety of communicative practices. These practices, depending on the ends to which they are put and their social context, in turn impact adoption.

We have also suggested a number of concepts that may be useful in future analyses of adoption. The concept of social affordances offers a way of getting a handle on the interplay between a communicative practice and the social characteristics of the users group, particularly with respect to practices that the group recognizes as legitimate. We believe that the notion of critical mass requires further elaboration, since our observations indicate that the number and roles of users necessary to sustain a communicative practice differ from one practice to another. One possible elaboration involves the concept of an ecology of communicative practices, a way of framing the complex dependencies and interdependencies among various communicative practices.

Our study's focus on chat is timely. Recent reports suggest that many US and European organizations are presently looking towards technologies based on chat to support distance collaboration in organizations (McGrath, 1999; Wojcik *et al.*, 1999). Yet most research in this area focuses on user modifiable virtual worlds (Doppke, 1998), virtual communities (e.g., McGrath, 1999; Wojcik *et al.*, 1999) or virtual, 3D environments (Greenhalgh & Benford, 1995). By closely examining the uses of chat in the workplace, this study may assist others in understanding the technical and social possibilities that chat offers for collaboration.

Acknowledgements

This research was conducted while the first author was a summer intern at the IBM T.J. Watson Research Center in 1998. This research has been partly supported by grants from the CISE/ISS/CSS Division of the U.S. National Science Foundation, and the NSF Industry/University Cooperative Research Center on Information Technology and Organizations (CRITO) of the University of California, Irvine. We thank Mark Ackerman, Amy Bruckman, Jason Ellis, Jonathan Grudin, Christine Halverson, and three anonymous reviewers for comments. Thanks to Teresa Wilkeson at UCI; and to the Social Computing and Niche Networking groups at Watson, particularly Cal Swart for critical work in the deployment of the BABBLES, and David N. Smith, Mark Laff, and Amy Katriel, the BABBLE programmers.

References

Ackerman, M. and Palen, L. (1996). "The Zephyr help instance: Promoting ongoing activity in a CSCW system," *Proceedings of CHI '96*. ACM, New York, pp. 263- 275.

Adams, L., Toomey, L., and Churchill, E. (1999). "Distributed research teams: Meeting asynchronously in virtual space," *Proceedings of the 32nd Hawaii International Conference on System Sciences (HICSS'99)*, IEEE.

Bowers, J. (1994). "The work to make a network work: Studying CSCW in action," *Proceedings of CSCW'94, Conference on Computer Supported Cooperative Work*, pp. 287-297.

Churchill, E.F. and Bly, S. (1999). "Virtual environments at work: Ongoing use of MUDs in the workplace," *Proceedings of WACC'99*, February 22-25, 1999, San Francisco, CA.

Correll, S. (1995). "The ethnography of an electronic bar," *Journal of Contemporary Ethnography*, vol. 24, no. 3, pp. 270-298.

Doppke, J., Heimbinger, D., Wolf, A. (1998). "Software process modeling and execution within virtual environments," *ACM Transactions on Software Engineering and Methodology*, vol. 7, no. 1, January 1998, pp. 1-40.

Ehrlich, S.E. (1987). "Strategies for encouraging successful adoption of office communication systems," *ACM Transactions on Office Information Systems*, vol. 5, pp. 340-357.

Erickson, T., Smith, D.N., Kellogg, W.A., Laff, M.R., Richards, J.T. , and Bradner, E. (1999). "Socially translucent systems: Social proxies, persistent conversation, and the design of 'BABBLE'," *Proceedings of CHI '99* (Pittsburgh, PA May 15-20), ACM, New York.

Fish, R., Kraut, R. E., Root, R., Rice, R. (1993). "Video as a technology for informal communication," *Communications of the ACM*, vol. 36, no.1, January 1993, pp. 48-61.

Gaver, W. (1991). "Technology affordances," *Proceedings of CHI 1991* (New Orleans, Louisiana, April 28-May 2, 1991) ACM, New York, pp. 79-84.

Gibson, J. J. (1979). *The Ecological Approach to Visual Perception*. New York, NY: Houghton Mifflin.

Greenhalgh, C. and Benford S. (1995). "Massive: A virtual reality system for tele-conferencing," *ACM Transactions on Computer Human Interfaces*, vol. 2, no. 3, pp. 239-261.

Grudin, J. (1988). "Why CSCW applications fail: Problems in the design and evaluation of organizational interfaces," *Proceedings of the Conference on Computer-Supported Cooperative Work (CSCW '88)*, Portland OR, pp. 85-93.

Grudin, J. & Palen, L.: (1995) "Why Groupware Succeeds: Discretion or Mandate?," *Proceedings of ECSCW'95, European Conference on Computer Supported Cooperative Work (ECSCW '95)*, pp. 263-278.

Heath, C. and Luff, P. (1991). "Collaborative Activity and Technological Design: Task Coordination in London Underground Control Rooms," *Proceedings of ECSCW'92, European Conference on Computer Supported Cooperative Work*, pp. 65-80.

Kovalainen, M., Robinson, M., Auramäki, E. (1998). "Diaries at work," *Proceedings of CSCW '92* (Seattle, WA), November 14-18. ACM, New York, pp. 49-58.

Markus, M. L. (1990). "Toward a 'critical mass' theory of interactive media," In J. Fulk and C. W. Steinfield (eds.), *Perspectives on Organizations and New Information Technology*. Newbury Park, CA: Sage Publications.

Markus, M. L. and Connolly, T. (1990). "Why CSCW applications fail: Problems in the adoption of interdependent work tools," *Proceedings of ACM CSCW'90 Conference*, pp. 371-380.

McDonald, D., and Ackerman, M. (1998). "Just talk to me: A field study of expertise location," *Proceedings of CSCW '92* (Seattle, WA), November 14-18, ACM, New York, pp. 315-324.

McGrath, A. (1999). "The Forum: Helping people who cannot be together, work together," *SIGGROUP Bulletin*, vol. 19 no. 1, ACM, New York.

Norman, D. (1988). *The Psychology of Everyday Things*. New York: Basic Books.

O'Day, V.L., Bobrow, D.G., and Shirley, M. (1996). "The social-technical design circle. In ," M.S. Ackerman (ed.), *Proceedings of the ACM 1996 Conference on Computer Supported Cooperative Work*, pp. 160-169.

Orlikowski, W. (1992). "Learning from Notes: Organizational issues in groupware implementation," *Proceedings of CSCW'92, Conference on Computer Supported Cooperative Work*, pp. 362-369.

Pirolli, P. and Card, S.K. (1995). "Information foraging in information access environments," *Proceedings of the Conference on Human Factors in Computing, CHI '95*, (Denver, CO), ACM Press, pp. 51-58.

Sproull, L. and Kiesler, S. (1991). *Connections: New Ways of Working in the Networked Organization*. Cambridge, MA: MIT Press.

Turkle, S. (1995). *Life on the Screen: Identity in the Age of the Internet*. New York, NY: Simon & Schuster.

Watts, J., Woods, D., Corban, J., Patterson, E. Kerr, R., Hicks L.C.(1996). "Voice Loops as Cooperative Aids in Space Shuttle Mission Control," *Proceedings of CSCW'96, Conference on Computer Supported Cooperative Work*, pp. 48-56.

Wojcik, R., Fuchs, L., Poltrock S. (1999). "Business value of 3D collaborative virtual environments," *SIGGROUP Bulletin*, Vol. 19, No. 1, ACM, New York.

S. Bødker, M. Kyng, and K. Schmidt (eds.). *Proceedings of the Sixth European Conference on Computer-Supported Cooperative Work, 12-16 September 1999, Copenhagen, Denmark*
©1999 Kluwer Academic Publishers. Printed in the Netherlands   159

Meeting at the Desktop: An Empirical Study of Virtually Collocated Teams

Gloria Mark[1], Jonathan Grudin[2], Steven E. Poltrock[3]
GMD-FIT[1], Germany, Microsoft Research[2], USA, The Boeing Company[3], USA
gloria.mark@gmd.de, jgrudin@microsoft.com, steven.poltrock@boeing.com

Abstract: Corporate mergers, global markets, reduced willingness to relocate, and the increased need to reorganize and respond dynamically – we are entering an era of distributed organizations and groups. New technologies are needed that enable distributed teams to work as though virtually collocated. This case study examines how one such technology, desktop conferencing with application sharing, is used routinely by four groups within a major company. We discuss differing and evolving patterns of use. A range of difficulties arising from impoverished communication are documented. Success factors are identified, focusing on the use of technology facilitation and meeting facilitation. We conclude by describing benefits possible with this merger of communication and application sharing, as well as the challenges of organizational change that may be needed to achieve the benefits.

> D to main site: Does anyone in this room understand what he's saying?
> Remote site: I do
> D: You're not in this room
> Remote site: I'm in the global room

1. Introduction

Two categories of group-support technology are merging: communication technologies and information sharing technologies. Communication technologies such as telephones and email are conduits through which human discourse passes, often ephemerally, the lasting trace being the impression on the receiver. Information sharing technologies represent, structure and store information, such as documents and databases. These technologies have been used relatively independently and studied in isolation.

The distinction between communicating and sharing information is not perfect, but it is important. While most communication is unstructured and ephemeral, email has some structure and may be archived. While limited computational analysis of email content is possible, email is usually treated as ephemeral because communication is the intent. (Similarly, a telephone conversation can be recorded, but few are.)

Communication technologies often support group members working at the same time, synchronous activity. In contrast, persistent information sharing technologies usually support asynchronous activity. Again, the division is imperfect: electronic and voice mail operate somewhat asynchronously; a projection system supports sharing persistent information in real time. But the distinction is significant – most email is used once; persistent objects are reused.

Of course, work requires both communication and information sharing. When one is absent, frustration is common. The inability to share data often hinders people limited to communication technology. We accepted it out of necessity with the telephone for decades, but fax spread quickly: a communication device serving an information-sharing need. Similarly, videoconference participants may hold documents up to the camera in vain efforts to have them viewed by remote participants. Email was used solely for communication, but once email attachments (supporting information sharing) came into wide use, they quickly became indispensable. The Boeing Company recently shifted 100,000+ employees to a standard email platform: the need to share attachments was a key motive for this massive effort.

Robinson (1991) noted that computer systems had not adequately merged information sharing and communication channels to support discussing shared information. Fax and attachments are useful but relatively crude enhancements. Two more powerful syntheses have emerged, first in research laboratories and now in workplaces:

i) Semi-structured documents, such as Lotus Notes, add communication features to asynchronous information sharing capabilities.
ii) Desktop conferencing, such as NetMeeting, adds data or application sharing to real-time communication systems.

Studies of semi-structured documents in work settings have been reported (e.g., Orlikowski, 1992). We present an early ethnographic study of sustained use of the second of these powerful new group support tools, desktop conferencing.

1.1 Virtually collocated teams

Desktop conferencing can act as a key enabler of geographically distributed teams, allowing team members to communicate and share information as though they are collocated. Economic globalization and competition drive the formation of geographically distributed teams that span different sites within the same company and sometimes cross corporate boundaries. Researchers have investigated virtually collocated teams from the perspectives of identity formation (Wiesenfeld et al., 1998), effects of cultural diversity (DeSanctis and Poole, 1997) and trust (see Jarvenpaa and Leidner, 1998, for a review). The teams studied previously were generally supported by a mix of email, telephone, and document exchange (e.g. Sproull and Kiesler, 1991; Zack, 1993). Ackerman et al. (1997) investigated the effects of a continuous audio-only media space.

Studies of desktop conferencing have focused primarily on how it affects the task performance of small ad hoc groups. For example, Whittaker et al. (1993) found a shared workspace beneficial for tasks with graphical information and demanding text-based tasks. Other studies report similar positive results (e.g. Minneman and Bly, 1991). These studies suggest benefits from desktop conferencing technology, but we cannot safely generalize from ad hoc groups to teams with long-term agendas (McGrath, 1984).

The key issues when studying technology use in business settings are adoption patterns, impacts on performance and process, problems created by the technology, and innovative solutions. We sought to understand how teams adopt and use desktop conferencing in their work setting. Do teams with different histories and long-term agendas experience different patterns? What problems do teams experience while collaborating through desktop conferencing, and how do they circumvent them? How can systems be better designed and used?

1.2 Background and setting

We studied four geographically distributed teams in The Boeing Company. All four teams had existed for six months or longer when the study began, and they all had recently begun using desktop conferencing technology combined with telephone conference calls to support their meetings.

Boeing has a history of using communication technologies to support geographically distributed teamwork. Video conferencing suites in different cities have supported distributed project team meetings since the 1970s. Mergers with Rockwell North American and McDonnell Douglas in 1996 have led to rapid growth of distributed collaborations. These mergers approximately doubled the number of employees and radically changed their geographic distribution. Previously, about 80% were distributed around the greater Seattle area. Most employees could attend meetings at any other site by driving less than 90 minutes. After the merger, only about 40% of the approximately 235,000 employees worked and lived in the greater Seattle area; others are distributed across the United States, with large concentrations in southern California, St. Louis, Missouri, and Wichita, Kansas.

The merger minimally affected many projects and programs, which continued working with existing staff, suppliers, and partners. Some teams and organizations, however, quickly needed to find ways of working with people at other locations, in some cases with people they had never met. For example, prior to the merger, executive meetings were held face-to-face at corporate headquarters, but following the merger the travel and time costs of collocated meetings were prohibitive. Many distributed teams were created to define how the newly merged company would operate and how enterprise services would integrate. Existing enterprise-wide teams were expanded to include members from other locations. Distributed design teams worked on the same section of an airplane. Effective virtual collocation has become a necessity.

2. The case studies

2.1 The technology used

All four teams used Microsoft NetMeeting[1] (henceforth **NM**) client software that manages desktop conferencing sessions of up to 32 participants. NM enables any participant to share any PC application object (e.g., PowerPoint slides) with all the other participants simultaneously. A participant can also allow others to interact with the application, such as editing portions of a document. NM includes a multi-user whiteboard, chat, and a file-transfer feature. A desktop conferencing service includes a directory of NM users, a server for scheduling and hosting meetings, and instructions on effective use of these technologies.

Although NM has audio and video features, these were not used. Instead, all the teams communicated in meetings via telephone conference calls by connecting to a teleconference bridge. Speakerphones were used in the conference rooms, and in cubicles, handsets or headsets were generally used.

Although NM is designed for desktop use, some participants gathered in a conference room, where a shared PC or a laptop connected to a projector enabled everyone to see. Some conference rooms had large interactive displays (SMART Boards[2]) with touch screens.

2.2 Research Methodology

Four teams were chosen that met the following criteria: they were willing to be observed, were geographically distributed, had long-term objectives, and used desktop conferencing technology. The investigation was ethnographic: the behavior of team members was observed in their work context. One author attended meetings "silently"[3] and took notes. Recording was not permitted. Groups were observed for 3 months, and meetings took place weekly (for one

---

[1] NetMeeting ™ 1998, The Microsoft Corporation

[2] SMART Board™, SMART Technologies Inc.

[3] At the beginning of each meeting the observer always announced her presence to the group.

group, bi-monthly). Some members of two teams met face-to-face in a conference room while others participated from remote sites; for these meetings the observer sat in the conference room. The other two teams met from their offices; like all other participants, the observer remained at her desk and connected to the meeting through the telephone and NM channels (Figures 1a and 1b).

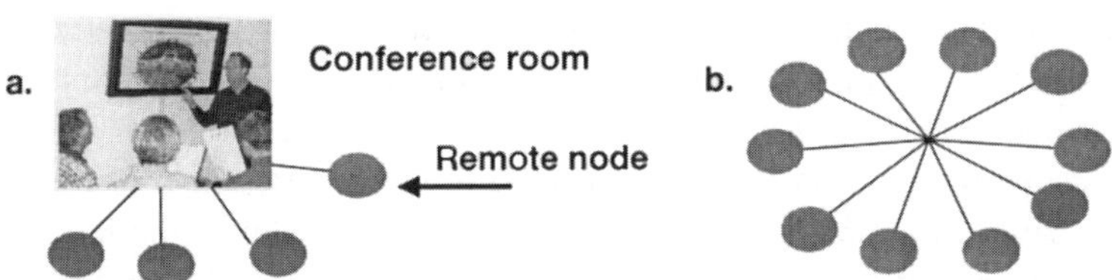

Fig. 1. Two meeting configurations: a) conference room with remote sites, b) all remote sites

After each meeting a questionnaire was distributed by email to all participants, asking questions related to ease of using the technology, social aspects of participation, and satisfaction with the meeting. Supplementary materials were collected, such as meeting agendas, minutes, and chat windows used during the sessions. In-depth interviews were also conducted with 19 selected members of the groups, lasting around 45-60 minutes each. Using content analysis, classes of problems and solutions could be identified.

2.3 The Cases

The four teams had commonalties but different goals. All teams had long-term agendas influenced by their funding, mandate, or organization, and spanned geographical and organizational boundaries within Boeing. The teams met regularly using NM and audioconferencing. Between meetings, communication was by email supplemented with occasional telephone calls. Most participants had met some key members in face-to-face meetings. Three teams were formed eight to nine months before the study began. A fourth, the Scientific team, had existed for five years, evolving, and expanding its membership.

2.3.1 The Scientific Team: Volunteers teaming for innovative solutions

The Scientific Team began as a small face-to-face staff meeting in Bellevue[4] for a project concerned with monitoring drilling processes. As participation expanded to include members from other sites, the team shifted the meetings to open discussion and information exchange in their technical domain. The team's success at applying science to solve real manufacturing problems became widely recognized in the company. Attendance increased, with people commuting as much as an hour each way to attend. Following the merger, people from several distant locations asked to participate by audioconference (telephone conference

---

[4] A location in the greater Seattle area

call), with presentation materials delivered prior to each meeting. The significant challenges of supporting remote participation led the team leaders to consider ending or curtailing the meetings. The adoption of NM reversed this: among the first teams in Boeing to use NM, its members were enthusiastic about its value.

From 8 to 16 members met face-to-face weekly in a conference room in Bellevue and one to three members attended from sites in Wichita, St. Louis, California, and Philadelphia (figure 1a). Members from other Seattle area sites drove to the meeting or connected remotely from their offices. Team membership was interdisciplinary: physicists and mathematicians at the main site met with machinists, engineers, and shop-floor people at the remote sites. The entire group had met only once face-to-face, in a workshop. Their three-hour meetings consisted of presentations, often showing scientific data, followed by up to two hours of open discussion where drilling problems were discussed.

The Scientific team was unusually successful in its operation, developing solutions for many problems faced by the other three teams. Their success may be partly due to the prior experience that most members had working together as they progressed from face-to-face to audioconferencing to NM use.

2.3.2 The Technical Working Group: Open participation throughout the company

The meetings of the Technical Working Group were open to anyone in the company. This unusual format was well suited to their goal of establishing best practices in their technical domain: the team could benefit from expertise at any geographic site, and employees throughout the company could benefit through participation, sharing their practices and asking questions to improve them. This increased efficiency; formerly, members had to acquire expertise themselves on a topic in order to present it. The group met through audioconferences (telephone conference calls) for several months before they began using NM.

Many members were highly specialized database management professionals. About 12-15 people attended the bi-monthly meetings, usually including the leader and nine core group members. The leader was in California; core members were located in different places, including St. Louis, Philadelphia, Huntsville, and greater Seattle, one person per site (figure 1b). Although the team leader received frequent requests to meet face-to-face, the core group members of the Technical Working Group had only met face-to-face twice. The 90-minute meetings usually consisted of a presentation of about 45 minutes followed by open discussion.

2.3.3 A Virtual Staff: Distributed colleagues with a mobile manager

A vice president responsible for information systems offered Bill a position as chief architect. For personal reasons Bill was "willing to do everything in his power" to remain in St. Louis. The vice president agreed to let Bill pioneer new technology for long distance collaboration; Bill and his staff became NM "guinea pigs." Eight were collocated in Bellevue. Bill, his administrative assistant, and a support company liaison were in St. Louis, and one staff member, Aaron, was in

California (figure 1a).

The team met weekly for 90 minutes. The main goal was information exchange and team building. NM was mainly used to display the agenda; a few meetings included short presentations by Bellevue or St. Louis members. The last half-hour of each meeting was open discussion in a round-robin format. About every two months Bill traveled to Bellevue to meet those members face-to-face; Aaron traveled about once every three months. As part of the agreement, Bill offered to pay for travel of anyone on the staff if they wanted to meet with him. The office assistant in St. Louis had never met the staff members in Bellevue.

2.3.4 The Best-Practice Team: Combining forces country-wide

The Best-Practice Team was charged to define the best practice for designing aerospace products. It was initiated by a vice president after several technical workshops and began weekly project activities using NM three months before this study began. The team consisted of 20 managers representing all geographical areas of the company. Although one member called the meeting "semi-mandatory," only about eight attended each meeting, all from their offices (figure 1b). The team had met face-to-face about six times at various locations.

The Best-Practice Team was the least interactive in meetings, of the four teams observed in this study. The team leader presented a list of action items and only permitted reports on their status. The little open discussion that occurred was limited to the last part of meetings in round-robin style.

2.4 Technology adoption

In three of the four cases, team leaders introduced NM. The Scientific and Best-Practice team leaders learned about NM from Boeing researchers and Bill, the Staff leader, discovered NM while searching on his own for a technology to suit his needs. The Technical Working Group had sought a better solution than audioconferencing. Soon after one member suggested NM, it was adopted by about half of the core team members, including the team leader.

Remote members of the Scientific and Staff teams were much slower to follow the main site in adopting NM. Some Scientific Team sites and several members of the Technical Working Group and Best-Practice Team participated only by audioconference during this study. Delays in adopting NM were due to:
1. Participation on some teams was voluntary and part-time; managers were reluctant to approve purchasing computers to run NM. Different sites often had different types of computers, operating systems, and support organizations.
2. Many members reported that because team participation was a part-time activity, they acted slowly to get the equipment, download the software, or in one case, obtain a special firewall-spanning account.
3. One member reported that others at his site discouraged him from using NM by saying that a lot of time would be wasted getting it synchronized.

4. Members at some sites reported having no one to consult about the technology.
5. M, the leader of Best Practice, believed that his team members were resistant to NM as they had been to other unfamiliar applications in the past. M felt that peer pressure was needed to influence adoption. In a virtually collocated team, peer pressure and other influence must work from a distance.

3 Results and Discussion

In addition to the 3 months of observation, note-taking, and materials collection, 158 questionnaires were received from team members following meetings: 73 from the Scientific Team, 38 from the Technical Working Group, 19 from the Staff, and 26 from the Best Practice Team. Members reported medium high satisfaction with the quality of documents, quality of meeting, use of time, and their participation, with no group differences (4.8 averaged across satisfaction questions, on a scale of 1 to 6, strongly disagree to strongly agree). The use of NM was felt to be worthwhile.

The meetings did not flow without problems, which particularly affected the three younger groups. The next sections describe these, categorized into problems with technology, with coordinating interaction, and with maintaining engagement. The subsequent sections describe technology facilitation and meeting facilitation methods that the Scientific Team developed to overcome such problems, and how a parallel communication channel (NM chat) was employed by members of the Technical Working Group to reduce interaction difficulty. The results conclude with advantages provided by application sharing.

3.1 Problems with technology: The role of a driver

In most meetings one person, a "technology driver," established the NM session, helped others join, and used NM to share an application (such as a presentation or agenda) that was passively viewed by other meeting participants. The technology driver was crucial to the smooth flow of a meeting; inexperience with the technology impeded the entire group. The three younger groups did not carefully consider the role of a technology driver, and they consistently wasted time setting up the technology and repeatedly encountered problems using it.

For example, the Staff meeting often required 15 minutes to begin, a substantial loss of time for the 10 members present. The role of technology driver was assigned to two administrative assistants, but they were not suited for this role and it was several months before they felt comfortable with the technology.

The Technical Working Group often seemed confused setting up NM, usually getting underway about 10 minutes late. Once it took them 30 minutes:

User 1:   (after 30 minutes) we start over too many times. this can hinder getting anything done. I hope this one sticks.
User 2:   Are we in control? Who's in control? I seem to have lost some degree of control.

This team negotiated the technology driver role in an ad-hoc fashion. In the following private chat discussion conducted during a meeting (and later shared with us), two users discuss the poor use of the technology and resolve that one of them will assume control in the next meeting:

User 3 (to User 1): Yours [driving the technology] was better...

User 1 (to User 3): Understand, but [User 4] offered to drive so until there are major problems, let [User 4] drive. Can you drive next meeting?

The Best-Practice Team used the technology more smoothly, but its use was limited. One member described how NM could be used to write collaboratively or to help the group arrive at a consensus on the action items or group mission. Another member said that the group would benefit more if it used the technology to create a product (e.g., a document). But the leader imposed a restrictive meeting format (only item status was to be reported), so there was little occasion for the group to explore the use of the whiteboard or other functionality.

The Staff and Technical Working Group also made limited use of the technology. The Staff wrote a document collaboratively, but only one person typed. In one meeting a remote participant put an important email message on the screen. This confused Aaron, another remote participant, proving that not all users understood the application sharing capability. (In another meeting Aaron shared his calendar, although this seemed unintentional.) On one occasion the Technical Working Group used a shared Notepad to list proposals, but did not again share any application except PowerPoint in the period of observation.

Another problem was that participants did not consider the configuration of other sites. One member noted that people are accustomed to viewing material on high-resolution screens at a distance of 45 centimeters, but details may not be visible for those in conference rooms viewing a projected image from five meters.

To avoid delaying meetings, the technology driver must be proficient in using NM, the hardware, the operating system, and all applications used in the meeting. Additionally, the driver must consider how to match the applications to the group's purpose. The role is quite public; one Staff member complained that the use of the technology reveals a lot about you to the team if you are not competent with it – if you make spelling errors, cannot type, or cannot locate a file.

3.2 Problems coordinating interaction

Remote member: I hear the voice, but there is a vacancy for the whole human being.

Interacting through NM adversely affected performance by making it difficult to coordinate participation, identify remote speakers, and know who was present.

As suggested in previous studies of audio communication (e.g. Short et al. 1976), uncertainty about turn-taking often disrupted the communication flow, especially during presentations and open discussions in the Technical Working Group and Staff meetings. Interaction was hardest for remote site members; they often reported not knowing when to interject. One described the awkwardness of the give and take: *"are they pausing for a comma, or for a period?"*

Coordinating interaction poses a different problem for these distributed teams than for ad-hoc groups previously studied. The interviews indicated a profound problem in understanding the expressions of others. Members felt they lacked enough knowledge of others' intent to make sense of their on-line behavior. Their difficulty was reflected in a response near the scale midpoint to the following questionnaire item (no difference across groups):

| I could always tell how other people were reacting to the things I or others said | 3.6 |

Teams are struggling to develop group processes, such as impression management (Schein 1990) and team identity (Wiesenfeld et al. 1998), and the limited social cues in audio channels make these difficult. Face-to-face meetings, when they occurred, helped the team members later make sense of on-line behavior. Face-to-face Staff and Best-Practice Team meetings were observed to be characterized by considerable side discussion, story-telling, and interjections, which rarely occurred in their NM meetings. Members reported:

> Face-to-face is much better. You can see expression and feel more of a team. Especially when people don't speak...With NM it is an abstract group, for example when do you interrupt?

> I get extra feedback of the body language of a person. Having met that person, I have that in the back of my mind [during NM use]. Without it, something is missing.

> Reflective looks means they are thinking. Silence on the line doesn't. People may say things sarcastically, but the expression on-line is confused. Many signals that you have face-to-face are lost.

> You have to interact with this person. Your stereotype of the person doesn't work on the program, the person works on the program.

> [A Scientific Team member]: It's really important to meet face-to-face to be comfortable. To know if this is an open or formal person. It does change the interaction, and the comfort level is high in this group.

The desire for a visual image of remote participants was shown in amusing ways. The Staff leader placed Dilbert cartoons on his monitor with their names.

A major problem with mediated interaction is not knowing who is present at remote sites. In NM, a window that lists participants in the session is generally soon covered and indicates only one person per office or conference room. And those who are listed may be multi-tasking (discussed later) or may have left their offices. Uncertainty is revealed by frequent inquiries into the presence of others:

> Cathy: I'm Cathy, I work at ----, my area is data exchange.
>   [long pause]
> Cathy: Is everyone still there?
>   [a few say yes]
> Cathy : Because I didn't hear the background noises and didn't know if everyone is still there.

Similar events occurred in the Best-Practice Team, where it was often unclear who was speaking and whence they spoke. Members often tried to clarify this, or the leader identified the person. In Staff meetings, after a period of silence from a remote site, someone sometimes checked attendance:

St. Louis, still there?
We're still there. [Note the irony.]

These observations were also consistent with the low response to the question:

It was clear who was present and who left remote sites	
Scientific Team	3.3
Technical Working Group	3.7
Staff	4.3
Best Practice Team	3.3

The higher Staff response could be due to the occasional attendance-checking. Also, with only two remote sites, remote members' behaviors were evident.

Not knowing who was present was also a problem identified in Ackerman et al. (1997). The group in their study developed norms to make public who was present. Whereas their group included fewer participants interacting continually, the meetings in this study had more members (some who had never met face-to-face), were of a formal nature, and were discontinuous. Thus, it appears that in this study, a nonuniform set of conditions inhibited the development of clear identities, for norms to be established.

To a lesser extent, people complained they could not identify who was speaking, or the speaker's organizational home. Even though written guidelines advised announcing one's name prior to speaking, this was seldom observed. This was mainly a problem in the Technical Working Group since the meeting was open and non-core members participated. A typical interchange was:

Leader: Did everyone have a chance to review the charter?
R: no
Leader: Who is this?

Fortunately, the same people usually spoke at the meetings, typically the leader and a few core group members, and their voices became familiar. Participants did not consider speaker identity a major problem (no group differences):

It was easy to identify who was speaking	4.4

3.3 Problems of low involvement due to multi-tasking

Many people reported performing other tasks during meetings. Multi-tasking has both costs and benefits. Most considered this a big advantage – one can attend more meetings and accomplish other work. Remote members of the Technical Working Group and Best-Practice Teams reported the most multi-tasking. This is not surprising: their 8-20 remote site participants were much less salient than the handful in the other two teams.

Some members described multi-tasking as a distraction and detriment. One Best-Practice Team member reported often reading email or talking with other people in his room, but he acknowledged that it reduced his commitment to the group. Usually members muted their telephones while multi-tasking but often forgot to turn off the mute function before speaking, which disrupted meetings:

Leader:	Sue, anything else?
	[long pause]
Dick:	Sue left us awhile back.
	[further pause]
Sue:	No, I haven't. My mute button was on. [Sue then explains that she put 2 URLs in the chat window. The leader replies that he does not have NM in front of him so he cannot see the chat window].

During one Best-Practice Team meeting, frustration was strongly expressed:

Mark:	Dan, that's your action item.
Dan:	Sorry, I didn't catch that.
Mark:	Jack, what's your comment? [long pause] Jack, are you there?
Jack:	I had my mute button on.
Mark:	Next is the rotocraft area, but he is not here.
Rob:	We need communication. 80 hours is not the problem. I waste 80 hours talking on the telephone. It requires a tremendous amount of extra effort to clearly communicate. When someone says we're having a telecon, then we need to be on the telecon.... People need to be on the telecon. We need a schedule.
Joe:	We all sit here and what are we doing? Is everyone trying to be on these telecons?......We have to decide on issues that we feel are important. Things can be done but we need to talk to each other and use these telecons.
Mark:	Thank you, Joe. [Mark moved on to the next action item]

These comments illustrate a difficulty that teams face in forming commitments: counteracting a lack of engagement, which can be exacerbated by multi-tasking.

3.4 Overcoming technology use problems: technology facilitation

Because the Scientific Team had struggled when using telephone conference calls, its leader created a new *technology facilitator* role, expanding the role of technology driver. This person was responsible for all aspects of technology use: establishing a connection, trouble-shooting, and controlling the presentation. This helped make their meetings strikingly more effective.

First, meetings almost always started promptly. Once when a server failed, the facilitator told the remote participants how to dial into another conference server, solving the problem quickly. Second, the facilitator monitored whether people at the main site were being heard, and brought in an additional clip-on microphone for someone who spoke softly. The facilitator even drove the technology when a remote member gave a presentation, by gesturing with a pointer on the display or zooming to a shared image as the speaker described it. He explained his role:

Every node [site] needs a technical facilitator. The main goal is he must make sure how the details are implemented. The medium must be as transparent as possible. This minimizes the effect on the meeting. To be successful, everyone must be on the same page. The goal is that when the meeting starts, the same page should appear. I try to be in synch with the presenter. I try to be on the same mental page, the view that the presenter wants to give to the virtual group. For example, if the presenter wants to zoom in, I hear the word zoom, and zoom in.

In contrast to the Staff, Scientific Team speakers used the touchscreen SMART Board effectively when explaining data on the display. For example, when explaining visual images to remote sites: "machines which have a crush-grind operation" [back and forth motion] or "initially you want to push as hard as you can, then slowly." Yet speakers at the main site also used hand gestures, as when indicating specific drilling operations, which remote people could not see.

The Scientific Team responded most favorably about technology driving:

The control of the data on the display was smoothly managed:	
Scientific Team	4.8
Technical Working Group	3.9
Staff	4.2
Best Practice Team	4.3

3.5 Overcoming interaction problems through meeting facilitation

In the early stages of the Scientific Team, the leader was also the facilitator, but he discovered that it was too stressful to facilitate the meeting, take minutes, and answer questions. He created a new role in the group, a *virtual meeting facilitator,* who acted as a "bridge" to involve the remote sites in the meeting: *"The conceptual framework is that we are the central site with nodes."* This reflected his awareness of the need to integrate the remote sites into the meeting.

The role of this facilitator, Al, was multivariate; he addressed many of the interaction problems observed in other groups. First, he established who was present at each site. Roll call protocols were very informal in the other groups. As with face-to-face group facilitation, he kept order by introducing agenda items and by beginning and adjourning meetings. He continually confirmed that remote sites could see the display, and addressed uncertainty of attendance by continually checking with remote sites, for example:

Al:	St. Louis had to leave?
Remote:	No, we're still here.
Al:	Who's there?
Remote:	Just me.
Al:	Is Canoga Park there?

He was also concerned that all speakers were identified, especially at remote sites, and made sure that everyone was heard.

Al: You have to speak up. Why don't you move over here closer to the mike?

Being a technical expert, he also clarified points for all by repeating them, or summarized or rephrased someone's explanation.

Al: Jeff this is Al. What is the Y axis?
Al: He is basically saying......

In his nontraditional function as facilitator, Al also coordinated speaking turns by recognizing body language in the conference room (e.g. when someone sat forward or raised a hand) or by hearing an utterance on-line. For example, Nick at the main site asked a question, and then was interrupted by Jim at a remote site.

Al asked Jim to hold on, explaining that Nick just asked a question. He then asked Nick to move closer to the microphone, believing that the remote site did not hear the question. When Nick was finished, Al asked Jim to ask his question again.

Al worked hard to involve remote members in the discussion by asking specific individuals to make sure their questions were answered, referring to people when he believed that they were interested in a topic, or calling on specific people who might have the expertise to answer a question:

> Al: This is for John and Matt in St. Louis. One of our meeting goals is to find ways for our modeling efforts to be useful for you and how we might collaborate together. I'd like to hear what interests you have in this data. I need your feedback so we can be responsive to your needs.
>
> Al: Does St. Louis have a comment on that? [He explains that someone in St. Louis is working on that problem].

In addition, Al encouraged questions at certain points in the presentation, explained to remote participants what was happening at the main site, such as when silences occurred, and kept order during discussions by calling on people.

The facilitator described a difference in problem-solving perspectives. This is a very heterogeneous group, with machinists, scientists, customers, people with different priorities, knowledge, patience levels, and so forth. Al worked to draw out and consider these conflicting perspectives, to get everyone "thinking on the same page," and to balance the discussion to suit all parties' interests, important for the technical exchange. Meeting people face-to-face had value for him:

> It helps to know what they mean when they ask a question. Otherwise it's like getting a written question. For example, knowing their background: Jeff in drilling, Matt in statistics, Hal in vibrations.

The effect of the meeting facilitator appears in the questionnaire data (fig. 2). The Scientific Team and the Staff both had a main node and remote nodes (fig. 1a). But questions about remote interactions produced different responses. Remote Staff sites had far more difficulty identifying and understanding who was speaking and knowing each others' reactions, and reported that interruptions interfered with the meeting. The data must be viewed with caution, since the Staff responses are from only two remote sites. Still, this suggests the value of distributed meeting facilitation to identify who is speaking, explain comments for the benefit of remote sites, and facilitate turn-taking in speaking.

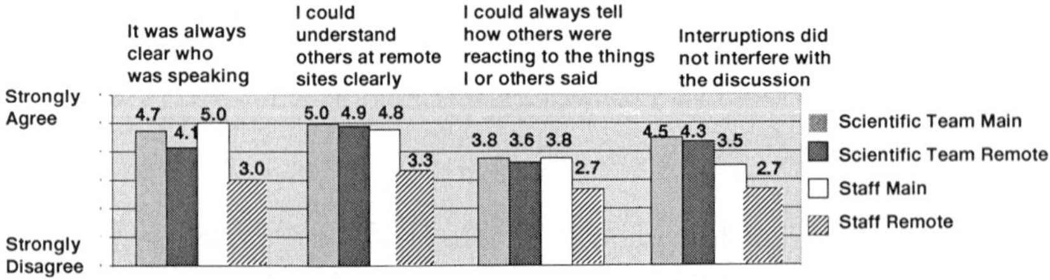

Fig. 2. Questionnaire responses about interaction: Scientific Team and Staff, main and remote sites

3.6 Easing interaction problems with an additional channel: chat

Only the Technical Working Group used NM's chat functionality. It was initiated and sustained by one member, who had used chat in other conferencing systems.

In contrast to the formal content of the meetings, the chat window was used to communicate a range of information, from private jokes to elaboration on meeting content. The principal user, who saved all public chat windows, found them very useful and entertaining, but above all claimed that it helped group members bond. In the first 5-10 minutes of a meeting, the chat was used for greetings, but also to affirm that everyone who wanted to attend this open meeting was connected properly. The chat window was also used to track attendance and any problems, especially if someone was not connected via audio:

> User 6: AOK now
> User 1: telecon number is 742-3000 password 6342#
> User 2: Diane, are you on the telecon?
> User 3: I'm on the telecon.

This checking was relatively constant; for example, in one meeting, it appeared in the chat window 16 minutes, 19 minutes and 45 minutes into a meeting. In another meeting, User 1 gave the telephone number and password three times in the chat window during the first 17 minutes.

Some found the chat window to be a useful back channel. For example, if a Web page or phone number was needed, one person sought the information as the meeting continued and placed it in the chat window. One member saved chat windows to retrieve contact names. He kept meeting minutes and supplemented them with information from the chat window. He felt that all chat should be public due to its potential contribution to the minutes. The chat window was also used to give advice on technology problems without disrupting the meeting:

> User 4: I'm having trouble seeing the whole screen.
> User 2: Scroll your mouse to the border and it should move your screen viewpoint.

Especially important, the chat window is used during the meeting for side discussions and private conversations (the following later shared with us):

> User 3 (to User 5): This last point is what I am afraid of by the web publishing flash heads.
> User 5 (to User 3): I looked away. What was the last point? (the funky sales data?)

Thus, chat can have value for distributed teams: without disrupting the meeting, it can confirm attendance and connections, be used to gather information, solve usage problems, and enable frequent side conversations.

3.7 Moving beyond audioconferencing: being on the same page

The Scientific Team leader reported that when the meeting relied on telephone conference calls, he almost disbanded it due to his frustration over the considerable preparation time. Compared to face-to-face meetings, 50% more time was needed to fax information. Last minute changes were not faxed, and members missed up-to-date changes in experimental results, which could be critical data for materials scientists. Often the meeting stopped to fax information.

Application sharing enabled access to last minute changes, in color with high resolution, such as a microphotograph of a metal cut "just off the press." Fax quality could not compare. The cursor could be used as a shared reference, focusing attention across sites on the same point in an image. This was especially important for detailed scientific diagrams and microphotographs.

Before NM use, the Technical Working Group had also briefly used audioconferencing only. They tried to synchronize the shared information by announcing web URLs over the telephone, but when 12-15 people tried to type a URL, everyone had to wait (a member noted) for one person's "fumble fingers." Sometimes the group gave up and distributed the URL via email. This group also saw the value of application sharing.

Similarly, members in the Best-Practice Team who connected only by telephone had trouble keeping up with the 35-40 action items per meeting viewed by others on the Web, and could not see other documents accessed by the group.

Teams reported that application sharing contributed more than live video, which many members had used. One reported that video "gave a picture of the group that was interesting, but it had no value" because it could not show data. The Scientific Team leader agreed; they had sometimes met in video studios, but these were expensive and hard to schedule, and they abandoned the use of video.

Thus, for distributed team meetings, application sharing provides a real advantage. It enables smooth coordination when changing document views. The shared cursor directs all members' attention to the same point, particularly useful with detailed diagrams. Advantages of shared references have been reported by Stefik et al. (1987) for face-to-face groups; we find that a shared reference also markedly improves the efficiency of virtually collocated team meetings.

3.8 The effect of application sharing: more distributed participation

Adding application sharing also changed the team's distribution. The Scientific Team's meticulous attendance records show that attendance increased from a median of 12 during face-to-face meetings to a median of 21 with audioconferencing. A few participants joined from greater distances and more also attended at the Bellevue main site (median of 18, see figure 4).

Adding NM with application sharing increased participation to a median of 23. However, face-to-face attendance at the main site dropped (figure 4). Median attendance dropped from 18 to 8 over the next 12 months: team members at sites in greater Seattle (up to an hour away) began attending from their offices. Figure 5 shows the number of sites during each technology phase: one for face-to-face meetings, three for audioconferences, and seven after 12 months of NM use. The data thus show that adding application sharing coincided with a marked decrease in travel by members in greater Seattle to attend the face-to-face meetings.

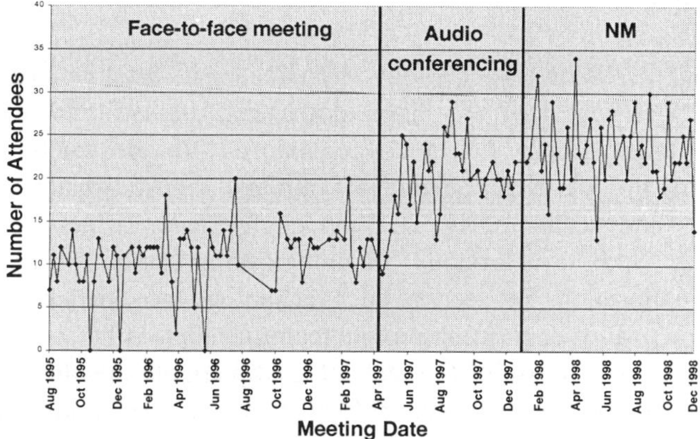

Fig. 3. Scientific Team attendance during technology phases

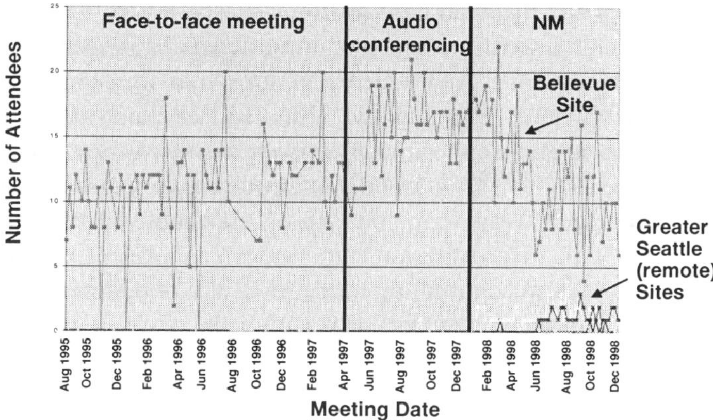

Fig. 4. Change in attendance distribution in greater Seattle by site

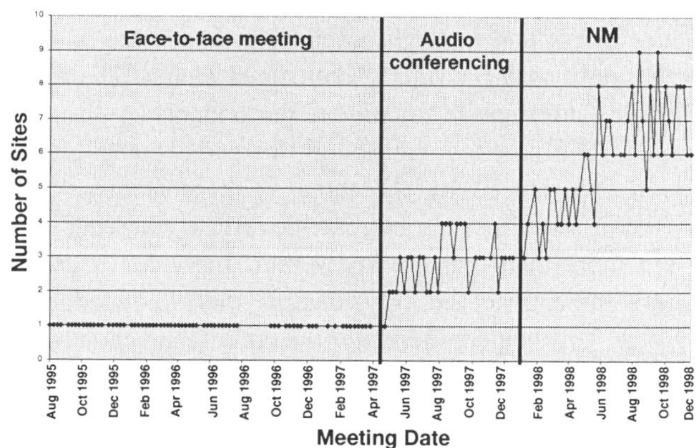

Fig. 5. Total sites for Scientific Team during technology phases

4. Conclusions

We have crossed a divide. Technology has made it feasible for many organizations to rely on geographically distributed teams, but distributed meetings are relatively inefficient. Email, fax, and telephone do not adequately support such teams: consider the successful Scientific Team that almost disbanded due to the limitations of these technologies. Desktop conferencing, which combines information-sharing with synchronous communication, holds promise for supporting virtual collocation. Yet users of such technology face challenges.

To start with, the goal of connecting remote team members is hard to achieve. Impediments to adoption and use of the technology by remote members include having no one to consult about the technology at a site, the relative lack of importance of remote teams in the eyes of managers and participants, and local discouragement. It is a Herculean task to overcome these from a distance.

In addition, as with face-to-face groups, teams with long-term agendas must consider how to develop and maintain appropriate social behaviors, such as trust and cohesion. When interviewed, members of these teams expressed concerns over how they could develop trust. Audio media are known to offer limited social cues for expression (Short et al., 1976), and we observed that it also affects team-building; team members complained *"with NM it is an abstract group"* and *"NM makes us one step removed, so it's a feeling of being on the periphery."* The challenge of team-building is further compounded by the double-edged nature of multi-tasking, which offers advantages yet can hinder engagement and reduce commitment to the group. Also contributing to the difficulty of building cohesion is that teams may have to overcome not only geographical distance, but also organizational boundaries and cultures, and even language codes, as had occurred in these groups through corporate mergers. Handy (1995) says that trust requires touch, but it is difficult to guarantee that dynamically changing teams will have adequate face-to-face interaction-and what is 'adequate' is not yet known.

To counteract these difficulties, the scientific team, perhaps through their maturity and experience of passing through other technology phases, developed new roles that offered solutions for virtually collocated teams. The technology facilitator enhanced display information for remote participants by gesturing with the cursor and zooming. The meeting facilitator overcame many problems in coordinating interaction experienced by the three younger teams. Aware that remote participants find it hard to interject, he governed speaking turns. He identified speakers, but more than that, he knew their individual expertise and directed questions and comments accordingly, making their knowledge and role more evident to the group. This helped to counter the complaint echoed by several that *"...anything we've learned – the job description, the work role – comes from personal face-to-face interaction. With NM we would not have gotten this information..."*. The meeting facilitator continually identified who was present at remote sites, another valuable contribution. NM might be enhanced to make members' status continually visible during the meeting in a nondisruptive way: who is present and who has left the meeting temporarily, or permanently.

The teams we observed were at relatively early phases of technology adoption. They maintained much the same meeting behaviors of face-to-face meetings, but introducing a new technology affects existing processes. Remote participants reported difficulty in contributing, not knowing when to interrupt, feeling left out. As reported by Isaacs et al. (1995), presenters can be unnerved by the lack of engagement of remote participants. Chat was used by one group to recreate social interactions absent in formal remote meetings. To gain greater advantage from new technologies, virtually collocated teams must reflect on their goals and how to restructure their activities to achieve them. Only one team had developed facilitation roles that greatly enhanced the contribution of remote members.

Distributed teams benefit from adding application sharing to audioconferencing. The value of shared reference and views cannot be understated; getting top quality materials "off the press" does not compare to faxes, even apart from the work of faxing materials (or sending email) to 15-20 participants. The use of application sharing by the scientific team coincided with a marked decline of traveling, suggesting that members felt that application sharing, but not audio conferencing alone, is sufficient for good distant participation in meetings. Competent facilitators and a history of face-to-face interaction may also have eased their transition to virtually collocated meetings.

No team in this study worked full time on a shared set of deliverables. Members of a team that communicated continuously via audio developed norms to move easily in and out of group participation (Ackerman et al., 1997). Remote team members are not part of the continuity of each others' work. We do not suggest continuous communication for all teams and tasks, but our results confirm the need for a seamless transition between remote and collocated activities for diverse distributed teams. This could be achieved through support for informal interaction (Whittaker et al., 1997) together with formal meetings. In this way, technology can become well integrated with virtually collocated teamwork.

The participant who insisted "I'm in the global room" expressed succinctly the changing nature of interaction. We see a new metaphor: a computer as a window onto a global meeting room where information can be displayed by anyone in the team and seen anywhere. This metaphor reflects new kinds of flexibility, where anyone in a company can participate in a Technical Working Group meeting, and where the team leader relocates across the country and remains leader of the group. To the mobile officeless Staff leader, the technology enables impromptu information sharing, holding a meeting "with whomever, and wherever he is."

Acknowledgements

This research has been partly supported by grants from the CISE/ISS/CSS Division of the U.S. National Science Foundation and the NSF Industry/University Cooperative Research Center on

178

Information Technology and Organizations (CRITO) of the University of California, Irvine. We would like to thank Don Sandstrom, Rich Harkness, George Engelbeck, Pam Drew, Kjeld Schmidt, Mike Stowe, Barry Fox, Frank Wrabel, Sarah Greene and especially the team members.

References

Ackerman, M. S., Hindus, D., Mainwaring, S. D., and Starr, B. (1997): "Hanging on the 'wire: A field study of an audio-only media space", *ACM Trans. on Computer-Human Interaction*, vol. 4, no. 1, pp. 39-66.

DeSanctis, G. and Poole, M.S. (1997): "Transitions in teamwork in new organizational forms", *Advances in Group Processes*, 14, Greenwich, CT: JAI Press, Inc, pp. 157-176.

Handy, C. (1995): "Trust and the virtual organization", *Harvard Business Review*, vol. 73, no. 3, pp. 40-50.

Isaacs, E.A., Morris, T., Rodriguez, T.K. and Tang, J.C. (1995): "A comparison of face-to-face and distributed presentations", *Proceedings CHI'95*, Denver, ACM Press, pp. 354-361.

Jarvenpaa, S. L. and Leidner, D. E. (1998): "Communication and trust in global virtual teams", *Journal of Computer-Mediated Communication*, vol. 3, no. 4, http://www.ascusc.org/jcmc/.

McGrath, J. E. (1984): *Groups: Interaction and Performance*, Englewood Cliffs, N.J.: Prentice-Hall.

Minneman, S. L. and Bly, S. A. (1991): "Managing à trois: a study of a multi-user drawing tool in distributed design work", *Proceedings CHI'91*, New Orleans, ACM Press, pp. 217-224.

Orlikowski, W. (1992): "Learning from Notes: Organizational issues in groupware implementation", *Proceedings CSCW'92*, Toronto, ACM Press, pp. 362-369.

Robinson, M. (1991): "Double level languages and co-operative working". *AI & Society*, vol. 5, pp. 34-60.

Schein, E. H. (1990): *Organizational Culture and Leadership*, San Francisco: Jossey-Bass.

Short, J., Williams, E. and Christie, B. (1976): *The Social Psychology of Telecommunications*, London: John Wiley & Sons.

Sproull, L. and Kiesler, S. (1991): *Connections: New Ways of Working in the Networked Organization*. Cambridge, MA: MIT Press.

Stefik, M., Foster, G., Bobrow, D., Kahn, K., Lanning, S., Suchman, L. (1987): "Beyond the Chalkboard: Computer Support for Collaboration and Problem Solving in Meetings", *Communications of the ACM*, vol. 30, no. 1, pp. 32-47.

Whittaker, S., Swanson, J., Kucan, J., and Sidner, C. (1997): "TeleNotes: Managing lightweight interactions in the desktop", *ACM Trans. on Computer-Human Interaction*, vol. 4, no. 2, pp. 137-168.

Whittaker, S., Geelhoed, E. and Robinson, E. (1993): "Shared workspaces: how do they work and when are they useful?", *International Journal of Man-Machine Studies*, vol. 39, pp. 813-842.

Wiesenfeld, B. M., Raghuram, S. and Garud, R. (1998): "Communication patterns as determinants of organizational identification in a virtual organization", *Journal of Computer-Mediated Communication*, vol. 3, no. 4, http://www.ascusc.org/jcmc/.

Zack, M. H. (1993): "Interactivity and communication mode choice in ongoing management groups", *Information Systems Research*, vol. 4, no. 3, pp. 207-239.

S. Bødker, M. Kyng, and K. Schmidt (eds.). *Proceedings of the Sixth European Conference on Computer-Supported Cooperative Work, 12-16 September 1999, Copenhagen, Denmark*
©1999 Kluwer Academic Publishers. Printed in the Netherlands

Broadcasting On-Line Social Interaction as Inhabited Television

Steve Benford, Chris Greenhalgh and Mike Craven
The University of Nottingham, Nottingham, UK
{sdb, cmg, mpc} @cs.nott.ac.uk

Graham Walker, Tim Regan and Jason Morphett
BT Laboratories, Martlesham Heath, UK
{graham.walker, tim.regan, jason.morphett}@bt-sys.bt.co.uk

John Wyver
Illuminations Television, London, UK
john@illumin.co.uk

John Bowers
Royal Institute of Technology (KTH), Stockholm, Sweden
bowers@nada.kth.se

Abstract. Inhabited TV combines collaborative virtual environments (CVEs) with broadcast TV so that on-line audiences can participate in TV shows within shared virtual worlds. Three early experiments with inhabited TV raised fundamental questions concerning the extent to which it is possible to establish fast-pace social interaction within a CVE and produce a coherent and engaging broadcast of this action. This paper presents a fourth more recent experiment, *Out of This World*, that directly addressed these questions. We describe how the formulation of inhabited TV design principles, combined with the use of dedicated production software, for constraining and directing participants' actions and for controlling virtual cameras, enabled us to create a fast-moving and coherent show. We conclude that our experiments to date demonstrate the technical feasibility of inhabited TV, but that greater attention needs to be paid to developing appropriate formats and content for this new medium before it becomes truly engaging. We also suggest that our real time production and camera software may be useful in other areas of CSCW.

Introduction

Inhabited TV combines collaborative virtual environments (CVEs) and broadcast TV to create a new medium for entertainment and social communication. The defining feature of this medium is that an on-line audience can socially participate in a TV show that is staged within a shared virtual world. The producer defines a framework, but it is audience interaction and participation that brings it to life. A broadcast stream is then mixed from the action within the virtual world and transmitted to a conventional viewing audience, either as a live event or sometime later as edited highlights.

Inhabited TV is motivated by the belief that TV and CVEs can benefit from one another. On the one hand, TV may benefit from access to the on-line communities that are enabled by CVEs as these may provide new forms of content, an important commercial issue with the arrival of digital TV. Furthermore, inhabited TV extends interactive TV to include social interaction among participants, new forms of control over narrative structure (e.g. navigation within a virtual world) and interaction with content (e.g. direct manipulation of props). On the other hand, TV may be a powerful driving force for the commercial uptake of CVEs and the development of richer on-line experiences than are provided by current chat environments.

Inhabited TV also raises new issues for CSCW in general. First, it focuses on the production and management of fast-pace on-line social interaction that follows a pre-scripted structure. Second, it raises the question of how social interaction can be captured and broadcast in a way that external viewers find engaging.

The following section introduces the idea of layered participation as a mechanism for describing inhabited TV applications. We then discuss the key challenges that were raised by three early experiments in inhabited TV, namely the difficulty of producing fast-pace and coherent social interaction within a CVE and of producing a coherent and recognisable broadcast of this action. Following this we describe a fourth experiment called *Out of This World* (*OOTW*) that addressed these challenges. We focus on the use of dedicated production software to configure the temporal structure of the show, to constrain participants' actions and to support real-time control of virtual cameras. Finally, we reflect on the experience of *OOTW,* drawing on responses from its audiences.

Layered participation in inhabited TV

Inhabited TV can be described in terms of four layers of participation. Each layer corresponds to a distinct responsibility within the show and to a distinct combination of interface and network technologies to access the shared virtual world and its contents.

Performers – the innermost layer, typically have the fullest involvement in the show requiring the greatest commitment and the richest forms of expression. In turn, this may require the support of relatively powerful equipment such as immersive peripherals, high performance workstations and high-speed networks. Performers represent core content and typically have global visibility in terms of being seen by the other layers. As each performer's data has to be broadcast to all other participants, the number of performers will be limited by available network bandwidth and processing power.

Inhabitants – the next layer describes the inhabitants, on-line members of the public who navigate through the virtual world, interact with its contents, are represented by avatars and communicate with one another. Inhabitants may have various kinds of involvement in a show including being an on-line audience (e.g. spectators at an event or a 'studio' audience), contributing content through some collective action or socially watching the show in each other's company. Inhabitants typically use commonly available equipment. Currently this would be a commodity PC with an Internet connection, although in the future this may evolve towards a set-top box with access to a broadband public network.

Viewers – the third layer describes the viewers who experience the show via broadcast or interactive TV. Viewers typically have only very limited possibilities for navigation and interaction. In the simplest case, they will be traditional TV viewers, i.e., the recipients of a broadcast mix that has been produced on their behalf and that can be received on a conventional TV set. However, interactive TV might offer them some additional possibilities such as choosing from among different perspectives or voting as part of large-scale audience feedback. In general, viewers are not visible within the content of the show (other than through abstractions of voting and similar feedback mechanisms). However, they may still be socially active via off-line feedback and discussion mechanisms.

Producers – the final layer of participation describes the producers of an inhabited TV show. In this case, production spans all aspects of technical support and 'behind the scenes' activity. Examples include, directors, operators of the virtual cameras that capture views of the virtual world and software and hardware support. The producers may often be invisible to the other layers, although there may be exceptions, such as making virtual camera people directly visible to performers so that they can target their actions for viewers to see.

Early experiences with inhabited television

Between 1996 and 1997 we were involved in staging three public experiments with inhabited TV in order to test its feasibility and to frame key research issues.

The NOWninety6 poetry performance was staged using the MASSIVE-2 CVE (Benford, Greenhalgh, Snowdon and Bullock, 1997). The performers (poets) and viewers were co-located in a physical theatre so that each performer appeared simultaneously on a physical stage and on a corresponding virtual stage in the virtual world. A broadcast stream was mixed down in real time from the viewpoint of a virtual camera-operator, an example of a producer. This was projected into the theatre alongside each poet for the viewers to see. Ten members of the public at a time could enter the virtual world as inhabitants using workstations that were located in a nearby café bar. These inhabitants could move about, experience the poetry and could communicate with one another using real-time audio. The event lasted for one evening and approximately 200 people were in attendance. Sixty experienced the virtual world in cycles of 10 at a time, with the remainder watching the broadcast in the theatre.

The Mirror in the first quarter of 1997 involved public access to a series of six virtual worlds on the Internet (Walker, 1997; McGrath, 1998). The experiment ran in parallel to the BBC television series *The Net* and the content of the conventional TV programmes provided inspiration for the design of the virtual worlds. Edited highlights from the virtual worlds were shown on subsequent TV shows. The virtual worlds included interactive collaborative games and tricks (such as a virtual rocket launcher and bouncy castle) and an art gallery where inhabitants could display their own VRML 2.0 creations. Special events were also held within *The Mirror*, including debates (e.g., between the science-fiction author Douglas Adams and Peter Cochrane, Head of Research at BT) and an end of the world party. The inhabitants accessed *The Mirror* from their homes or workplaces over the Internet using Sony's Community Place software (Lea, 1997). This allowed for text and graphical communication between inhabitants and performers. Over 2300 people registered to become citizens of *The Mirror* and received a CD-ROM containing the browser software and VRML2.0 content.

Heaven and Hell – Live was an hour-long game show that was staged inside a CVE and simultaneously broadcast live on the UK's TV Channel 4 in August 1997. In other words, access by inhabitants and broadcasters to viewers happened simultaneously, with the latter seeing the activities of the former. The performers consisted of a host and two contestants (celebrities on UK TV) as well as three 'reporters' who provided additional commentary. The performers were physically located in an inhabited TV studio along with the production team that was responsible for creating the live TV broadcast. This studio combined a local network of PCs, a TV outside broadcast unit and an Internet connection. The production team included a director, vision mixer, sound mixer and production assistant. They had access to six virtual cameras within the world, taken from the viewpoints of the host, contestants and reporters, with the latter responding to instructions from the director. As with *The Mirror*, the inhabitants accessed the shared virtual world from their using the Community Place software. They could also be viewers if they had a TV set in the room alongside their PC.

Games within *Heaven and Hell – Live* included a participatory treasure hunt, a quiz and a gambling game. The intention was that the inhabitants would assist or hinder the performers in these games. Communication within the virtual world (i.e. among performers and inhabitants) was via text and graphics. In addition, a live audio stream containing spoken communication between the performers was added to the final TV broadcast. The program was broadcast in August 1997 in a late-night slot. The on-line audience of inhabitants peaked at 135. The viewing audience was estimated at 200,000.

Lessons from these early experiments

The lessons learned from these early experiments can be grouped under two headings: problems with establishing coherent social interaction within a CVE and problems with producing a coherent broadcast output from a CVE. These lessons were distilled from the opinions of the inhabitants and viewers themselves as voiced over email for *The Mirror* and *Heaven and Hell – Live* and at a post-performance debate for the *NOWninety6 Poetry Performance*.

Establishing coherent social interaction within a CVE – one of the goals of inhabited TV is that viewers will become more involved in a TV show by becoming inhabitants – they will become socially active and will contribute to a show. However, our early experiences suggest that it is difficult to engage the public in a coherent, real-time and fast-pace narrative within a CVE.

It was difficult to establish a productive engagement between the inhabitants and the performers. At one extreme, the inhabitants were unable to get a word in edgeways as the performers dominated the interaction (Heaven and Hell – Live). At the other, the inhabitants spent all of their time chatting to one another and ignored the performers (NOWninety6).

It was difficult for inhabitants to achieve precise and co-ordinated movement within a CVE. A conventional studio-based TV show often requires participants to move to precise locations at particular instants (e.g. standing on a mark so as to be in camera shot) and for several participants to move in a co-ordinated way.

The difference in pace between CVEs and broadcast TV was problematic. Conventional live TV shows are scripted, highly structured and have a fast pace that involves precise (i.e. to the second) timings for events. In contrast, current CVEs have a much slower pace, due to delays in interaction (e.g. navigation) and network delays. This is especially true where text communication is used.

Producing a coherent broadcast output from a CVE – the second general issue raised by our early experiments concerned the quality of the broadcast output that was created from the action within the CVE. This was especially evident in *Heaven and Hell – Live* due to the rigorous demands of producing an hour-long live broadcast on national TV. The key problem here was with camera control. Camerawork is an essential part of conventional TV production. There are various forms of camera (e.g. boom and track mounted or handheld) and dedicated mixing facilities for editing a single broadcast stream from multiple cameras. In contrast, the development of CVE interfaces has focused on controlling an individual participant's view of the world, but has not considered how social action can best be captured and displayed to external viewers.

In summary, early experiments in inhabited TV demonstrated the difficulty of establishing fast-pace, structured interaction between performers and inhabitants within a CVE and also of producing a coherent and entertaining broadcast mix of this action for external viewers. We next present a fourth more recent experiment that was intended to address these problems.

A fourth experiment – *Out of this World*

Out of this World (*OOTW*) was a public experiment with inhabited TV that was staged in front of a live theatre audience. The event was part of *ISEA: Revolution*, a programme of exhibitions and cultural events that ran alongside the *9th International Symposium on Electronic Art (ISEA'98)* held in the UK in September 1998. There were four public performances of *OOTW* in the Green Room theatre in Manchester over the weekend of the 5th and 6th of September. These were preceded by two days of construction, testing and rehearsal.

OOTW was implemented using the MASSIVE-2 system, the same system that had supported the *NOWninety6* experiment described above. Useful features of MASSIVE-2 for *OOTW* included: support for up to fifteen mutually aware participants; streamed audio and video; immersive and desktop interfaces; and realising simple collaboration mechanisms using third party objects (Benford and Greenhalgh,1997) as described later.

Like *Heaven and Hell – Live, OOTW* was a gameshow. This choice allowed a direct comparison to be made between the two experiments. Given the observations above, the design of *OOTW* was motivated by two key questions:
• could we involve members of the public in a fast-moving TV show within a collaborative virtual environment? In particular, could we clearly engage the inhabitants with the performers and with one another, could they keep up with the action, and would they enjoy the experience?
• could we produce a coherent broadcast from the CVE? Would the broadcast be recognisable as a form of TV and would it be entertaining?

The remainder of this section provides a brief overview of *OOTW* in terms of layers of participation and the structure and content of the show.

Layered participation in *OOTW*

We begin by describing how our layers of participation were realised in *OOTW*.

The inhabitants

OOTW adopted a 'cheesy' outer space theme. The inhabitants were divided into two teams, aliens and robots, who had to race across a doomed space station in order to reach the one remaining escape craft. On their way they had to compete in a series of interactive games and collaborative tasks in order to score points. The final game was a race in which these points were converted into a head-start for the leading team. The two teams each consisted of four inhabitants, members of the public who had been selected from the theatre audience. Every participant in the show could speak over a live audio channel. The teams were separated into women (aliens) versus men (robots) so that viewers would be able to more easily associate the voices that they heard with the avatars that they saw on the screen, although this turned out to be controversial decision as we shall see below. The team members were given cartoon-like avatars that could be distinguished by a visible number on their backs and fronts. A speech bubble would appear above their heads whenever they were transmitting audio. The inhabitants used standard PCs with joysticks and combined headphone/microphone sets. They were located behind the scenes, out of sight of the viewers in the theatre.

The performers

The teams were guided by two performers: an actor and an actress, who played the role of team captains. The role of the captains was to encourage the teams to take part, to act as foci for the games and to improvise around the inhabitants' dialogue. The performers used immersive virtual reality equipment (left of figure 1), including Polhemus magnetic sensors to track the positions of their head and both hands which were then represented on their avatars in order to give them a greater expressive ability than the inhabitants. Unlike the *NOWninety6* poetry performance, the performers were fully immersed (i.e. were wearing a head-mounted display). They were also given a virtual 'light stick' that they could activate by pressing a button on a hand-held flying-mouse and which allowed them to point at objects, locations and participants in the virtual world.

Figure 1: The performer equipment (left) and location next to the screen in the theatre (right).

Although logically they would have been out of sight of any viewer at home, the performers were actually physically located in the theatre space so that the viewers could see them working with the immersive technology (right of figure 1). This compromise was designed to enhance the viewers' understanding of the concept of inhabited TV and to create a staging appropriate to a theatre space.

The show was hosted by a third performer who appeared in the form of a live video face that was texture mapped onto a large mobile virtual screen within the world. This screen could rotate around to show the game scoreboard.

The viewers were seated in a conventional theatre facing a large screen onto which the broadcast output was projected. The two performers were physically located on either side of this screen. For most of the time the viewers did not directly interact with the content of the show and as such resembled a traditional TV audience. However, they were provided with an opportunity for mass-interaction towards the end of the show. This involved them choosing the best losing team member through a mechanism called Wobblespace that was inspired by the CINEMATRIX interactive entertainment system (CINEMATRIX, 1998). Each member of the audience was asked to vigorously wave one of four coloured cards in order to express their vote. The overall level of activity of each colour was automatically detected from a video image of the audience and the resulting scores were passed to the CVE software. The audience was encouraged to test this voting mechanism by playing a game of 'Pong' in the pre-show warm-up in the style of a previous CINEMATRIX demonstration at SIGGRAPH. The warm up also involved a brief explanation of the concepts behind *OOTW*. Finally, after the show, the viewers were invited to stay behind and provide us with feedback.

The production team

OOTW involved an invisible but essential production team who were responsible for managing the CVE software and for producing the broadcast. Four virtual camera-people were present in the world, although they were not visibly embodied. Using purpose built interfaces (see below), they were able to capture the action from various perspectives. Video and audio output from their computers was then fed into a conventional TV mixing desk where it was mixed by a professional TV director and her assistant. The resulting video mix was sent to the projector in the theatre. In addition, a world manager was able to control the virtual world software, including activating virtual objects and constraining the actions of the participants (see below). The left of figure 2 shows the director and her assistant at the mixing desk. The four camera monitors with feeds from the virtual cameras can be seen on the far left. To the right of these is the current transmission monitor (showing the actual broadcast) and a monitor for previewing video material (the face of the host, the title sequences or other videotape inserts). The right of figure 2 shows the four virtual camera operators at their machines (physically located just behind the director).

Figure 2: The director and her assistant (left) and the camera operators (right).

The structure and content of *OOTW*

We now move on to consider the structure and content of the show. *OOTW* involved a journey through five arenas that were joined together into a linear structure by a series of virtual travellators. Each arena involved the two teams in a different task as follows:

Arena 1: introductions – an overview of the show from the host followed by introductory statements from the captains and individual team members (figure 3).

Arena 2: flipping frogs – a collaborative action game in which the teams had to flip space-frogs onto spiky hats worn by their team leaders. Flipping was achieved by closely approaching a frog, causing it to jump away in the opposite direction. The teams had to impale the most frogs to win the game (figure 4).

Arena 3: falling fish – the team members had to harvest space-fish by collaboratively lifting their team leader up into the air and moving them about so that the leader could knock the fish from the ceiling by swiping them with their hands. The team leader was on a platform whose height varied according to the number of team members that were inside it and whose position was the average of its current members. The team members therefore collectively steered the platform and the team leader could only reach the fish when all four team members were inside. The team that harvested the most fish won the game. The platform is an example of a third party object in MASSIVE-2 that combines a group membership mechanism with a dynamically computed aggregate group representation (Benford and Greenhalgh, 1997).

Arena 4: culture quiz – a quiz where the host asked the questions and the team members conferred to agree an answer that was then relayed through the captains. Each team had to answer questions about the opposing culture (i.e. robots about aliens and aliens about robots). A point was scored for each correct answer, resulting in the captain being raised up through a hoop that would start spinning, accompanied by a fanfare.

Arena 5: space-car race, wobblespace and the end of the world – the final game was a race in which the teams had to steer a space-car along a twisted course in order to knock down a series of cones (figure 5).The space-car was steered in an identical way to the platform from the falling-fish game, i.e. the team members controlled it through their collective movement. The team with the most points from the first three games was given a head start. The first team to cross the finish line won the show and was transferred to the space-craft ready for their escape. The losing team members were then asked to state a case for why they should be saved. Following this, the distant viewers voted for the best loser using Wobblespace and this loser was then transferred to the ship. The climax of the show was then the ship departing and the space-station imploding.

While journeying along the travellators between each arena, the teams (and hence viewers) were shown a pre-prepared video of the next game that appeared as a video–texture on the host's virtual screen. At the start and finish of each arena the host would encourage the team captains and team members to comment on their play up to that point. As a final detail, in addition to various sampled sound effects, synthesised sound was played to convey a sense of the environment of each of the arenas (e.g. mutated watery sounds during falling fish), the motion of the travellator, the take-off of the space-craft and the space-station imploding.

Figure 3: the alien team.

Figure 4: the alien captain.

Figure 5: racing space cars.

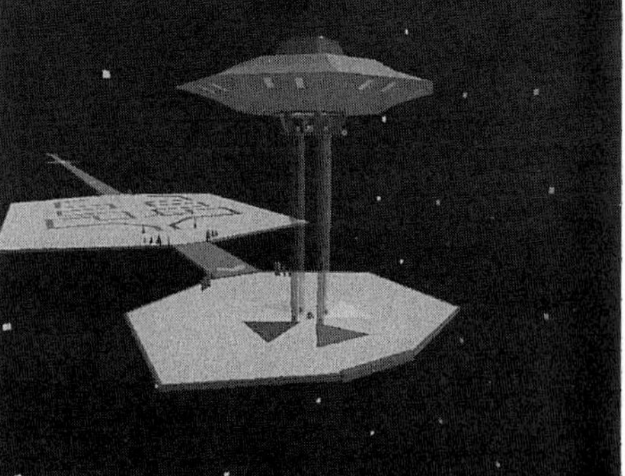

Figure 6: the space station.

Given this general introduction to *OOTW*, the following section now focuses on the steps taken to address the lessons of previous experiences.

Design principles and production software for *OOTW*

OOTW addressed the lessons from previous experiences through two innovations. First, we introduced a set of design principles, intended to increase the coherence of the show in terms of its visual appearance, social interaction and narrative structure. Second, we developed a suite of production software to support the temporal structuring of the show, the application of constraints on participants' actions and the control of virtual cameras.

Show design principles

In a direct response to our previous experiences with inhabited TV, especially with *Heaven and Hell – Live,* the structure and content of *OOTW* was designed according to several key principles. These were intended to maximise the coherence of the interaction within the world and of the broadcast output and to establish a clear engagement between the participants, especially between the performers and inhabitants. Briefly stated, these principles were:

Simplicity of concept and representation – the games should be as simple as possible in terms of concept, interaction required and graphical representation. Emphasis was to be placed on interaction mechanisms rather than on graphical richness. In fact, the graphical designer was introduced at a relatively late stage once the entire show had been protoyped.

Clear roles for participants – the roles of the inhabitants and performers should be clearly defined and the outcome of each game should depend upon both (no-one should be relegated to the role of observer or mere 'helper').

Co-operation – the games must require co-operation, both between inhabitants and between inhabitants and the performers.

Interaction through proximity – we favoured indirect interaction with objects (e.g. having objects that react to the proximity or movements of participants) rather than direct manipulation of objects (e.g. selecting them with a mouse). This principle ensured that participants only had to learn to perform two tasks: moving about the world and speaking into a microphone. It also encouraged participants to engage in the highly visible and relatively interesting activity of moving about and required them to get close to the objects of interest as opposed to standing back and picking them off from a distance. In this way, it was intended that the composition of camera shots depicting close action could be facilitated.

Action at ground level – we generally restricted participants' movements to be at ground level. This was intended to simplify their movement as well as enhance camera work. For example, camera operators should be able to more easily locate participants than if they were distributed throughout 3D space. Furthermore, the vertical dimension would be free for pulling back and up to get overview shots.

190

Production software

We developed dedicated production software to support *OOTW*. This consisted of an event structuring notation, participant constraints, a real-time management interface and a virtual camera interface.

Event structuring notation, participant constraints and management interface

All CVE platforms allow designers to specify the spatial structure of a shared virtual environment, at least in terms of its geometry and in more advanced systems, in terms of higher-level structures such as regions, locales and third party objects. In order to support inhabited TV applications, we extended the MASSIVE-2 platform to also support the definition of the temporal structure of an event in a CVE in terms of a series of phases. For each phase, the designer could configure a number of properties including:

- a name for the phase.
- objects that would be active during the phase.
- trajectories for these objects during the phase.
- hierarchical groupings of objects so that they could be attached to one another during this phase. For example, attaching a 'costume' to one of the participants.
- audio levels and extents (as defined by audio nimbus in MASSIVE-2) for specific participants.
- whether this was a roll-over phase, in which case the next phase would automatically be activated after a specified time interval.
- default positions for the virtual cameras.
- constraints on participants' movements. Each participant could be placed inside a bounding box outside of which they could not move during this phase. This box might be small enough that they could only turn on the spot or could be large enough for them to be able to explore a large area. The bounding box could have its own animated trajectory enabling participants to be gradually pulled along to a new destination during the phase, over a specified time period.

The phases and their properties were specified in a configuration file that was then loaded into MASSIVE-2. The structure of *OOTW* consisted of over fifty phases which spanned movement on the travellators, dialogue at the exit and entry points to the arenas and the structure of the games themselves. These fifty phases occurred in a forty-five minute show. Examples of the use of phase properties included moving the participants to start and end positions in each arena; moving them along travellators; attaching the team leaders to objects such as the spiky hats in the frog game; and activating objects such as the spinning rings in the quiz.

A dedicated world management interface was developed to support a member of the production team in dynamically triggering different phases as the show progressed. The phases were presented as a list and any phase could be selected by name, causing the whole show to jump to that phase. By following a script (and taking cues from the gameshow host), the world manager could push the show along, moving participants to their correct positions and initialising objects. In this way the show could be made to run to a strictly timed schedule and participants could be brought together into a structured arrangement at key moments before being released again into more exploratory activity.

This ability to dynamically apply constraints to participants was therefore intended to support the orchestration of co-ordinated movements and crowd control (avoiding inhabitants becoming lost or running away) and to increase the pace of the show by enforcing time limits and by rapidly shuttling participants to new locations. In addition, the use of constrained positioning meant that potential camera shots could be established in advance and that directors and camera operators could plan for them accordingly (see below).

Phases were also used to represent branching points in the narrative, for example, choosing the next action according to which team had won a particular game. The manager could also choose to return to previous phases or to miss out phases. Finally, several contingency phases were specified in the expectation that participant's equipment might fail. For example, there were alternative versions of the falling-fish game in which the team leader could reach the fish if only three, two or even one team member was in the platform.

Virtual camera control interface

The second component of our production software supported the control of virtual cameras. In *Heaven and Hell – Live*, the virtual cameras had used standard participant navigation controls to move through the virtual space. As noted above, this led to difficulties with following the action, getting lost and having a camera's view obscured by passing inhabitants. For *OOTW*, we developed a new virtual camera control interface that was dedicated to the task of capturing the action in a CVE from a third party perspective. At the heart of our approach was the idea of *object centred navigation* that we had first tried at the *NOWninety6* poetry performance. This involves locking a virtual camera onto a specific focus or target and then controlling it in such a way that the target is not lost from view and can be framed appropriately, for example, zooming in or pulling back to show its relationships to other targets. Our design was also intended to facilitate artistically engaging camera work, involving the kinds of long sweeps, zooms and tracking shots that can be seen in expensive movies and computer animations.

OOTW introduced a wide range of potential targets including scenery, individual participants and the teams. We addressed three major considerations in designing a virtual camera interface to cope with this level of complexity:

Target selection – we provided three ways of specifying the current target of a virtual camera. First, the operator could jump to pre-set fixed points in the virtual environment. These were selected from a list in the camera interface and included key locations, defined separately for each phase of the show at configuration time, as well as locations that had been previously marked by the operator. Second, the operator could choose to track a single participant or a group of participants (e.g. one of the teams), again by selecting them from a list in the camera interface. The camera would then dynamically adjust its position to follow the target as it moved. For groups, it would take the average position of the group's members. Third, more conventional free form flying was also provided of the type that would normally be associated with an inhabitant interface.

Relative viewing control – we then enabled the camera operator to move the camera relative to the target. The operator could use independent sliders in the interface to control the yaw, elevation, distance and vertical offset of the camera relative to the target (the position of the camera in relation to the target was described using spherical polar co-ordinates). These controls allowed the camera operator significant control over the framing of the target within the shot.

Temporal control – although the target was selected directly and interactively, the relative viewing controls could be applied with three different timings. With real-time control the camera would move as each slider was moved. This was subject to a controllable damping coefficient so that the operator could trade off responsiveness for speed of movement. With just-in-time control the operator could disconnect the sliders from the camera, use several different sliders to adjust different relative viewing parameters and then apply the changes as a single atomic operation. With pre-programmed control, the operator could define and store sets of viewpoint parameters. Selecting a set of parameters would trigger a smoothly interpolated movement to the specified position. In addition, in both the just-in-time and pre-programmed modes, the operator could build up a sequence of camera moves to be triggered one after the other and then step through this sequence using a single interface button.

As noted above, *OOTW* employed four virtual cameras whose operators were given different roles by the director (e.g. following different participants or capturing a bird's-eye view). The camera operators and director were also on a live talk-back system so that they could communicate freely during the show.

Reflection on *OOTW*

We now present an initial assessment of the extent to which the two goals described above (involving the public in a fast-moving enjoyable show in which they were engaged with the performers; and producing a coherent and entertaining broadcast output) were met by *OOTW*. This assessment is based on post-event discussions with the viewing audiences, feedback from the performers, inhabitants and production team and opinions from press reviews. Notes were taken during the audience discussions and these were supplemented with various personal reflections via email immediately after the event and at post-event meetings. In addition, one of us conducted an ethnographic field study of the production work during and around the shows, which has also influenced the reflections here. In what follows, we synthesise our reflections and, where relevant, illustrate them with quotes from audience members and inhabitants.

Did we produce coherent, fast-pace interaction within a CVE?

Our overall sense is that we succeeded in staging a gameshow in a CVE where members of the public interacted with actors around a loosely structured script. Unlike *Heaven and Hell – Live*, the inhabitants were clearly central components of the show. The pace of the action was rapid, at least when compared to our previous experiences with CVEs. The games were mostly playable and generally recognisable in form, with the possible exception of the frogs game that confused some teams and was harder to follow as an observer.

> The frogs were too complicated. [audience]

> I couldn't understand the frogs. I couldn't see what my team were doing. [inhabitant]

Did we produce a coherent and entertaining broadcast output?

We believe that the broadcast was coherent and recognisable as TV, again to a level that we hadn't achieved with previous experiments. Indeed, as we shall see below, viewers' reactions to the piece mostly focused on the content of the show and seemed to take it as read that this was a form of television—the technology was mostly transparent.

We attribute the difference in pace and coherence between *OOTW* and our previous experiments to a combination of the production software and the design principles described above. In particular, the ability to constrain and move participants through a series of fine-grained phases using the management interface allowed us to push the action along and sustain the overall pace of the show, particularly when combined with the use of real-time audio among the inhabitants. The success of the event structuring notation and management interface in this respect is probably the most positive outcome of *OOTW* and signifies an important direction for the development of inhabited TV technology. The virtual camera control interface also allowed us to produce a relatively coherent broadcast, although this was a qualified success as problems remained in capturing key moments of collaborative activity such as a dialogue between two participants or key interactions with a game object.

It must be noted, though, that sustaining the 'pace' of *OOTW* was only in part a matter of how the event notation, management and camera control interfaces had been technically designed. It is also to do with how these can be used to support the cooperative work of TV production. For example, some audience members found the pace of editing in the first two shows excessively fast:

> Cutting caused me problems of attention. The shifting point of view, the sounds, people talking. It all builds up cumulatively to make it difficult to follow.

Overnight, in response to remarks like this and her own unease, the director slowed the pace of editing for the later shows and this kind of critical comment was not heard again. From the point of view of evaluating the technologies developed for *OOTW*, this is pleasing. Not only is it possible to create a coherent and appropriately paced show, there is enough scope for skilled directors to experiment with different styles (including styles which turn out to be 'too fast'). Pace and coherence are not mechanically determined but technically supported and creatively produced. Our technologies and the *OOTW* design principles allowed, we believe, an appropriate mix of new technology and the expression of established broadcasting skills.

In contrast, although applause and laughter could be heard frequently in all performances, the content of *OOTW* attracted considerable criticism in subsequent discussion with the audience as the following paragraphs now describe.

Lack of empathy with the show and its characters

Several viewers commented that they did not warm to the show or feel empathy with its characters. Major contributing factors to this seem to be the lack of expressive capability of the avatars and the low quality of the audio.

> I had problems identifying with an avatar. It's the expressions and gestures which are missing. [audience]

> One of the problems is identification. We miss what we're familiar with. We need other strategies for this without texture-mapped video on faces. When they win, maybe they should show more eccentric behaviour. Something to bring them closer. [audience]

> I was straining to hear what people were saying so I didn't want to make a lot of noise. [audience]

> I couldn't identify all the time with the robots. I was ready to but the cutting prevented it. [audience member after early show, see also discussion of editing tempo above]

While this lack of empathy was generally reported, some audience members were uneasy about the use of Wobblespace to vote for a survivor:

> I felt somewhat uncomfortable about consigning someone to oblivion. [audience member]

to which an inhabitant replied:

> I was a robot in the first show. Just to assure you I wasn't sad when I was decimated.

With the exception of adding some gestural capability to the team leaders through the use of immersive interfaces, issues to do with creating empathic avatars were not directly addressed by *OOTW*. Furthermore, applying our game design principles may have resulted in a more sparse, albeit coherent landscape that contributed to the feeling of emptiness.

Lack of legend and the importance of community

A further subtle factor in this lack of empathy may have been a lack of legend. Our actress commented that her character lacked a sense of history. There was no established background to the show – why were the participants on this space station? How long had they been there? What had happened previously? This lack of a shared history made it difficult to establish an interesting dialogue between the performers and inhabitants or to improvise interesting content around the framework of the show. Our impression is that a common reaction among participants was to resort to stereotypes to fill this void, in this case based on the gender division between the teams. In one show, most notably, two of the women volunteers in the aliens team spoke throughout in high pitched pastiches of girls' voices and 'ham' acted a weak-female sterotype. Resorting to such stereotypes was a major concern with *OOTW* for some of the show's viewers.

> I thought it was sexist the way there were two sexes.

Thus, although *OOTW* did succeed in establishing engagement between the performers and inhabitants through the collaborative nature of its games, the resulting relationship wasn't especially interesting, entertaining, or, for some highly critical viewers, politically acceptable.

Future inhabited TV should invest greater effort into developing interesting characters and narratives. This might be achieved through the more central involvement of authors, scriptwriters and producers early on in the development process. However, it might also emerge naturally from long-term on-line communities; a strength of CVE technology. In many ways, the latter approach was successfully demonstrated in *The Mirror* (Walker, 1997), where a sense of community was established over six inhabited TV shows.

Format

Our choice of a gameshow was repeatedly highlighted as an issue in the post-show discussions. This raises the further question as to the extent to which inhabited TV should mimic existing TV formats versus the extent to which it should introduce new formats and narrative structures.

> I had difficulties with you copying a gameshow as it is such an established format.

> Why do a gameshow at all? It's something with a narrow age-range appeal. You should do something more imaginative.

Another audience member asked:

> Did you think of something which stepped outside of TV conventions?

and once the motivation for a conventional format was explained ("if we couldn't get a highly structured form of TV right then we really would have trouble") he retorted:

> Okay so you wanted to do something conventional but you could've looked at other conventions. Pantomime conventions. Physical theatre conventions.

Clearly, for this audience member, there was something disappointing about using virtual reality technology for reproducing such "closed" (in his terms) conventions as a TV gameshow:

> A paradox for a technology that promises openness.

Although we would justify the choice of the gameshow for *OOTW* in terms of enabling a direct comparison with *Heaven and Hell – Live* amongst other reasons, we strongly agree with those who questioned the gameshow format and existing TV formats in general. A key step for inhabited TV is to develop alternative narrative forms that exploit its novel characteristics, especially combining on-line communities, real-time narrative and broadcast TV.

We therefore argue that *OOTW* partially addressed the issues of coherence and pace raised by earlier experiments. In particular, our production software allowed us to script and direct a framework within which the public and our actors could engage one another. However, the content of *OOTW* was more problematic and content should be a major focus of future work. We summarise with the following quote from a review in the London Times:

> At this stage Inhabited Television is merely an interesting diversion hinting at greater things. One suspects it will be some time, and several more surreal previews, before the system can generate material strong enough for television. (Times, 1998)

or as an audience member put it:

> The subject matter was simplistic but the technology was interesting.

Summary and future work

Inhabited TV aims to create a new entertainment and communications medium by combining traditional TV with CVEs so that the public can become on-line participants within TV shows. Our paper began by summarising three early experiments, *NOWninety6, The Mirror* and *Heaven and Hell – Live!,* that demonstrated the problems of creating a basic coherent inhabited TV show and helped define the technical research framework for subsequent work. Problem areas included: engagement between performers and inhabitants; achieving precise and co-ordinated movement; the pace of CVEs versus broadcast TV; and control of virtual cameras.

We then described a fourth experiment, *Out of This World,* that was conceived to address some of these problems. *OOTW* aimed to create an inhabited TV show where interaction within the CVE and the broadcast output were both coherent and entertaining and where the show exploited a real engagement between inhabitants and performers. The key technical innovation in *OOTW* was the development of dedicated production software to support event structuring and management, and the control of virtual cameras. This was combined with a set of design guidelines for the show. We have argued that this software played a major role in enabling us to create a fast-pace and coherent inhabited TV show for the first time. However, there were still many problems with *OOTW*, both in terms of the earlier issues that it did not address but also in terms of its content. The second major lesson from *OOTW* is that greater attention needs to be paid to creating new formats for inhabited TV, ideally ones that combine community and broadcasting.

The lessons from *OOTW* may be relevant to other areas of CSCW. *First*, the idea of scripting the temporal structure of a collaborative activity and then dynamically managing it, including constraining participants' actions, is a powerful one. On-line meetings and events of all kinds could be supported through the involvement of production teams using dedicated production software. In our recommendation of this, it should not be thought that constraining participants' actions *necessarily* involves any (ethically) objectionable loss of liberty though this might occur to some readers. Our experience in *OOTW* is not that inhabitants complained of being (e.g.) tied to the groundplane but that they were grateful for the simplicity and easy learnability of the interaction techniques. In short, constraints can be enabling too (a point sometimes not fully appreciated in the debates about 'formalisms' in CSCW).

Second, the idea of deliberately capturing and making collaborative activity visible and engaging to others might also have a broader applicability, for example in other areas of entertainment or in education and training. *Third*, our notion of object-centred navigation (here exemplified in the camera control interface) may offer a novel and generally applicable alternative to conventional 6DOF navigation in virtual worlds.

We are currently planning our next experiments in inhabited TV. Although at an early stage, our strategy is to first establish a CVE community and then to use this as a source of inspiration, legend, characters, plots and designs for a series of broadcasts. As part of this we will concentrate on refining the basic layered participation model of inhabited TV. We aim to provide mechanisms for feedback between layers and to enable participants to make transitions between layers (e.g. so that interesting characters can emerge from the on-line community to become core broadcast content). Given the current capabilities of our CVE platforms, this may initially exploit two distinct systems, a graphics and text CVE that can support a large community of users over the public Internet and a media-rich CVE with further extended production software to support fast-pace action for broadcasting. Future technical development will focus on merging these facilities into a single system so that a large public community can be placed alongside broadcast content with real-time feedback between the two. It will also focus on extending production software, especially scripting and directing facilities. We hope that it will then be possible to create innovative and engaging inhabited TV.

198

Acknowledgements

We acknowledge the support of the European Community for the *eRENA* project under the ESPRIT IV *Intelligent Information Interfaces* (I3) programme and also the EPSRC for the *Multimedia Networking for Inhabited Television* project under the *Multimedia Networking Applications* programme. Additional support for *Out of this World* was provided by FACT and North West Arts.

The Mirror was a collaborative project with Sony and the BBC, whilst *Heaven and Hell – Live* involved Sony and Channel 4. We gratefully acknowledge the involvement of many colleagues in those organisations, and also the contributions of numerous others at BT Labs, Nottingham University, Illuminations and the Royal Institute of Technology.

References

Barrus, J. and Anderson, D. (1996): 'Locales and Beacons.' Proc. *1996 IEEE Virtual Reality Annual International Symposium (VRAIS'96)*, San Jose, US, Kluwer.

Benford, S. D., Greenhalgh, C. M., Snowdon, D. N, and Bullock A.N. (1997): 'Staging a Poetry Performance in a Collaborative Virtual Environment', *ECSCW'97*, Lancaster, UK, Kluwer.

Benford, S. D. and Greenhalgh, C. M. (1997): Introducing Third party Objects into the Spatial Model of Interaction, Proc. *ECSCW'97*,189-204, Lancaster, UK, Kluwer.

Capin, T. K., Pandzic, I. S., Noser, H., Magnenat-Thalmann, N., Thalmann, D. (1997): 'Virtual Human Representation and Communication in VLNet Networked Virtual Environments', *IEEE Computer Graphics and Applications*, IEEE Press.

CINEMATRIX (1998): http://www.cinematrix.com/

Damer, B. (1997): 'Demonstration and Guided Tours of Virtual Worlds on the Internet', Proc. *CHI'97*(demonstrations), Atlanta, US, ACM Press.

Greenhalgh, C. and Benford, S. (1995): 'MASSIVE: A Virtual Reality System for Tele-conferencing', *ACM Transactions on Computer Human Interaction*, 2 (3), pp. 239-261.

Lea, R., Honda, Y. And Matsuda, K. (1997): 'Virtual Society: Collaboration in 3D Spaces on the Internet', *Computer Supported Co-operative Work: The Journal of Collaborative Computing*, 6, 227-250, Kluwer.

McGrath, A., Oldroyd, A. and Walker. G. (1998), 'The Mirror: reflections on inhabited TV', Proc. *CSCW'98 Video programme*, Seattle, ACM Press.

The Times (1998): 'TV from another planet: something virtually different', *The Times Interface Section*, October 7th 1998.

Walker, G. R. (1997): 'The Mirror - reflections on Inhabited TV', *British Telecommunications Engineering Journal*, 16 (1), pp. 29-38,1997.

S. Bødker, M. Kyng, and K. Schmidt (eds.). *Proceedings of the Sixth European Conference on Computer-Supported Cooperative Work, 12-16 September 1999, Copenhagen, Denmark*
©1999 Kluwer Academic Publishers. Printed in the Netherlands

A Groupware's Life

Volkmar Pipek and Volker Wulf
ProSEC, Department of Computer Science III, University of Bonn, Germany,
{pipek, volker}@cs.uni-bonn.de

The paper describes a long-term study of a groupware application which covers the complete lifecycle from the groupware's introduction to its removal. During that time our field of application offered the opportunity to gain deep insights into personal, organizational and technical aspects of the groupware's usage. We focus on the late phases of a groupware's life, i.e. on the new aspect of groupware removal and the resulting requirements for groupware platforms. Additionally we contribute to the current discussion on organizational change processes which are initiated by the introduction of groupware.

Introduction

Groupware is more and more applied in different types of organizations. As a consequence of practical experience, the CSCW community has become increasingly aware of the intertwined relationship between groupware usage and the structure and culture of organizations (cf. Button and Sharrock 1997). The introduction of groupware is often related to processes of organizational change. From an economist's point of view the introduction and the change process can be measured by evaluating whether they improve the given work processes, increase the quality of the output or offer new options of future development. But looking at the case studies presented in the literature, we find success stories as well as major failures even when introducing the same kind of applications (cf. Lloyd and Whitehead 1996). The different experiences indicate that the way groupware is introduced and maintained in organizations is a crucial success factor. Describing our experiences in the POLITeam project, we discuss how those organizational change processes can be stimulated. These processes lead to a beneficial assimilation of groupware technology in organizations. We also report on possible problems and obstacles for those processes.

Since groupware technology is rather new there are only few studies which have followed the organizational adaptation of these technologies over several years (cf. Orlikowski 1996, Karsten and Jones 1998). Such studies are important to judge on the role groupware can play in organizations Our study offered the opportunity to cover a complete lifecycle of a groupware application, from its introduction to its removal. Especially the removal phase with its problems has not yet been observed in field studies elsewhere and induced new requirements for groupware platforms.

We will first describe the research setting and methods. Then we take a closer look at the core work processes in our application field. Using the groupware lifecycle phases as a structure, we then describe the major experiences in the application field and finally analyze and discuss the results.

Research Setting and Method

The case study took place in the government of a Northern German state in the context of the POLITeam project (cf. Figure 1). In this contribution we focus on work processes connecting the State Chancellery (SC) (located in the state's capital)of that state and the State Representative Body (SRB) in the federal capital Bonn with the Bundesrat (The second chamber of the German parliament representing the different states).

In the SRB about 30 people were occupied representing the interest of their state within the process of federal legislation. The SRB belongs to the State Chancellery. Within the State Chancellery one organizational unit (a head and three employees) is responsible for the coordination of the different state ministries within the process of political decision finding. The SRB is responsible for transferring documents and distributing information between the state government and the

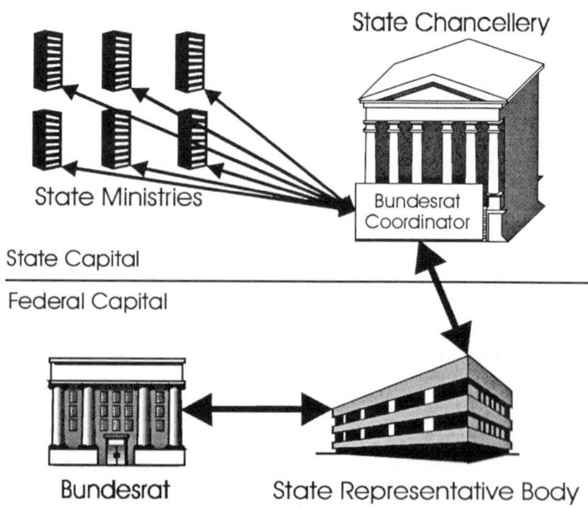

Figure 1. Organizations and Information Flow

Bundesrat. A detailed description of the related work processes will be given later.

Before the beginning of the POLITeam-project, employees of the state government were only partly equipped with computers. Network-PCs were mainly used by typists and secretaries. Thus, the SRB had no IT-department on its own, the IT-department associated with the SRB belonged to the State Chancellery in the state's capital, 700 kilometers away. When problems occurred they asked the IT-support of another state's Representative Body in the same building.

A groupware application based on LINKWORKS™ by Digital was introduced in the government administration of the state and its SRB in the federal capital Bonn. The functionality of the system offered support for shared workspaces, electronic circulation folders, e-mail including electronic document transport and related basic awareness services. The groupware based on a client/server architecture. An application programming interface allowed extensions of the groupware system.

The POLITeam project was a cooperative software development project in which the applying organizations required technical support for distributed cooperation. We developed the groupware application evolutionary according to the users' requirements. After the project was established in summer 1994, it started with a series of semi-structured interviews with nearly all potential users to learn about their work practice. The interviews resulted in textual scenarios describing typical work processes. Following this we tailored the LINKWORKS application according to the requirements found, and presented it to the users of the different organizational units in training workshops. By the end of 1994 the system was introduced. During the introduction phase users have been supported with daily site visits. Over the following four years of usage project members visited the different sites twice a month for a full day to provide individual support by visiting every user briefly. A telephone hotline was offered to the users. When necessary, we facilitated discussion groups in workshops where mainly organizational problems were discussed. Once a year we conducted interviews with selected users to ask about training and support, individual and collaborative work with the system, cooperation and usage of information, search facilities, awareness of others and conventions. The results presented in this paper are based on a collection of transcripts from user interviews, site visits, telephone hotline calls, and group discussions. Concerning POLITeam in the state government the authors were engaged in different roles: interviewer, facilitator of discussion groups and provider of system support.

Most of the published POLITeam papers, which are related to organizational aspects (eg. Mambrey et al 1996, Mark et al. 1997, Wulf 1997, Prinz et al. 1998), draw their cases from another application field: a federal ministry. As the industrial partner of the POLITeam consortium guided the project in the state government, originally less scientific attention was paid there.

Preparing a session of the Bundesrat

We will now describe the main work processes of the SRB in the federal capital as they were given in the beginning of the project. These processes represent the core activity of the organization. Other activities, as for example the organization of representational events or the writing of press releases, later also involved groupware usage (e.g. collaborative text writing), but will not be discussed here.

The main task of a SRB is the management of the information flow between the federal and the state capital concerning the legislation procedure in the Bundesrat. The Bundesrat meets every three weeks to discuss and vote on an agenda of about 80 different issues. The SRB and specific sections of the State Chancellery and the state ministries cooperate in determining the state's vote on each of those issues. As the state was governed by a coalition of two parties which were opposing each other on the federal level, the decision concerning the state's vote on an issue in the Bundesrat occasionally required complex negotiations. In that work context, we distinguish four different, but closely connected work processes.

The first work process we have named *Issue Distribution* is the distribution of information materials from the Bundesrat to the appropriate sections of the state government. The treatment of an issue began with printing the federal government's proposal in the print shop of the Bundesrat. It was sent via a courier service to the SRB. After the registrar had taken out some copies for internal use, the remaining ones had been sent by another courier to the State Chancellery. There, some more copies were taken out and sent via courier to the state's ministry of internal affairs. From there, couriers brought the documents to all other ministries involved in that issue. The document transport took three days. Any other transport of documents between the Bundesrat and the state government was going a similar way.

The second work process prepares the negotiation processes which leads to the state's vote. This one we call *Vote Preparation* (cf. Figure 2). Two weeks before the meeting of the Bundesrat its different commissions (e.g. commission for internal affairs) meet to discuss and vote on the different issues of the next agenda. An issue is typically worked on in several commissions. The state is represented in each commission by one employee of the SRB who typically is the head of the corresponding section in the SRB. After the meetings of the commissions a personal protocol including main discussion points and results of test voting was hand-written by each section head. They gave it to a secretary for typing, followed by further correcting and re-typing until the result was satisfactory. Then it was sent by fax to the corresponding state ministry. Besides, a secretary of the Bundesrat wrote an official protocol about each of the commissions' meetings and sent the paper document via the SRB to the corresponding state ministries. Within the commissions each state ministry acts independently by means of the corresponding section of the SRB. To coordinate the different ministries' activites, which concern one issue of the agenda, the SRB had invented a coordination mechanism (cf. Schmidt and Simone 1996) based on a form sheet. It worked as follows:

For each issue one section of the SRB took the main responsibility (Issue leadership). The issue leader created a hand-written form sheet for each issue he was responsible for. He marked the issue and gave a rough political judgement. He added the result of the test voting in the commission of the Bundesrat, for which he was responsible. He wrote down the names of other sections of the SRB, whose commissions were also dealing with that issue leaving space for those sections to add comments and their commission's test vote. That "form sheet" was

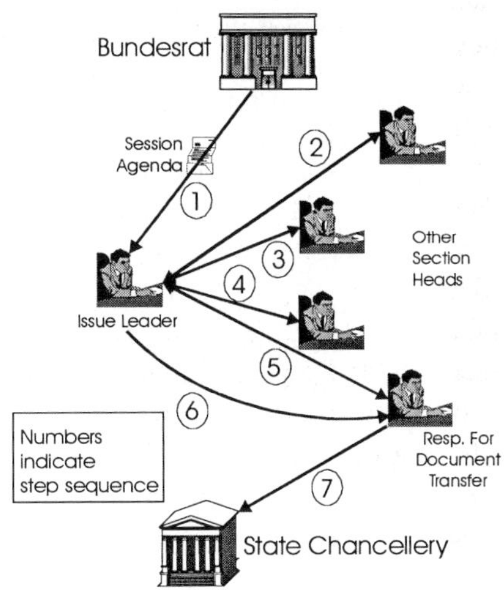

Figure 2. Vote Preparation Process

typed and printed by a secretary, and re-checked by the issue leader. Then he carried it to the heads of the other sections involved to get their test vote results and further comments were integrated into the paper. With the section heads being absent quite often, this could take several attempts in each section. Finally, all the form sheets were given to one section head who was responsible for collecting them and transferred by fax to the section of the State Chancellery which was responsible for the coordination of the state's activities in the Bundesrat. The deadline for the arrival of the papers alway was the Tuesday of the week before the meeting of the Bundesrat, which frequently led to high time pressure in completing the papers. The Chancellery used the form sheets to get a survey on the political process so far and to recognize inconsistent activities of the different ministries.

The third work process (*Vote Negotiation*) mainly took place in the State Chancellery. The state's vote now was negotiated at government level. Having identified possible conflicts between different ministries, the employees of the State Chancellery contacted the conflicting ministries, identified the political dissent and tried to find a compromise. Inside each ministry, there was a section responsible for the coordination of the Bundesrat activities. To coordinate the negotiation process, those sections again had to contact sections responsible for certain special issues. The negotiations continued for the following days. In the State Chancellery the negotiation results were summarized for the state cabinet, which decided how to act on each agenda issue in a meeting three days before the session of the Bundesrat. The options have been to agree, to disagree, to abstain or to suggest a modification of the given issue proposal. The results were transmitted via fax to the SRB where they were used to prepare the Bundesrat session (negotiation with other states, additional test votes, etc.). If the cabinet decided to propose a modification concerning one of the issues on the agenda, it had to reach the Bundesrat two days before the meeting. These modification proposals have been formulated in one of the ministries, sent to the SRB to check formal correctness, approved by the State Chancellery and finally sent to the Bundesrat through the SRB by courier. This process had to be carried out within one day. During that phase the documents usually have been sent by fax, which led to frequent text retyping.

The forth process we call *Session Preparation.* The day before the meeting of the Bundesrat the modification proposals of the other states have been sent via the SRB to the State Chancellery and the ministries. The state government had to make up its mind on how to react upon the proposed modifications until the next morning . This means, that coordination task suffered from extreme time pressure as well.

The lifecycle of the POLITeam groupware

The term lifecycle is often related to an acknowledged model distinguishing more or less distinct phases, e.g. product lifecycle models in marketing (Kotler 1980) or the software lifecycle in software engineering (Sommerville 1989). We do not rely on such a model, because neither is there a model representing a groupware lifecycle, nor is there enough empirical basis to build one.

We only roughly distinguish the phases introduction, use and removal. The introduction phase covers the installation of the new technical tools, related qualification processes, analyses of the work processes, identification of processes which should be improved with the help of the new tools, etc. During the use phase the adaptation of the new technical infrastructure by the organization takes place. Technical fine-tuning, adjustment to new external developments, discovering and implementing organizational innovations, and minor qualification measures for new users are typical activities here. The removal phase begins with the decision to remove the groupware infrastructure or to change to another groupware product.

Our project started in late 1994. The introduction began in December 1994 and can - for the SRB - be considered as completed in March 1995. The subsequent use phase ended in September 1998, where the decision for the removal had been fixed. The groupware application had been de-installed by December 1998. We will now describe important organizational changes within these phases.

Introduction Phase

The SRB in Bonn got equipped with the hard- and software by the end of

1994. Due to problems with the hardware infrastructure the corresponding unit of the State Chancellery got equipped more than a year later.

As a result of the initial interviews and analyses two major problems became apparent:

- The transport of paper documents from the Bundesrat via the SRB to the state government was very time consuming.
- The typing of protocols and other documents by the secretaries was a bottleneck for the SRB's activities. As all the sections worked in the same rhythm, it created peaks in the work load of the secretaries causing a significant prolongation of processing time. Additionally, the quality of typing was judged to be rather bad.

The groupware application has been deployed among the secretaries, the registrar and those sections which wanted to be equipped with computer support. There was no organizational pressure on the staff members to participate in the introduction of IT. As the Bundesrat already provided most of its documents electronically via a X.400 message transfer system, we equipped the groupware with a X.400 interface at the registrar's workplace, which accelerated the reception of documents considerably.

We started to deploy the LINKWORKS and MICROSOFT OFFICE applications by means of a one day workshop where participants could explore system functionality guided by a trainer. The trainer focused on presenting the functionality he judged as being most important for supporting the work processes identified before. After the training, the systems were directly installed on the desks of the users. During the first week, members of the project team were permanently present in the SRB to answer questions and support system usage. Additionally, a hotline has been established during working hours and task-oriented handbooks have been provided for the users.

Use Phase

After the introduction project members visited the users about every second week. Users got additional training, got the possibility to ask about new functions and got support in solving technical problems. Moreover, it turned out that these visits were major occasions to coordinate cooperative work and to develop process innovations.

Task Shifts

The first effect of the groupware assimilation was a dramatic decrease of the workload for the typists. The users equipped with a computer started writing their texts on their own or gave them to the typists only for typing drafts and entered corrections on their own PC. Although most staff members were not able to type very fast, the elimination of correction-retyping-cycles and the faster document transport shortened the time for text production significantly. We started with three full positions in the typing pool. After one and a half year of groupware usage, only one part-time position remained. Since typists left the SRB rather often due to bad payment, the decline of the typists' workload did not lead to active discharges. Positions which became vacant were not filled in again but were moved to other sections of the SRB. Similar effects have been observed in other application fields of POLITeam (cf. Wulf 1997).

Even the intense support offered by the project members was not enough. During everyday work many questions - mainly concerning the OFFICE products – occurred where immediate help was needed. Slowly one staff member, who showed more knowledge and interest for computer usage than others, took over the role of a local computer expert. Soon after the introduction his increasing workload concerning computer support impaired his regular work too much. It took a longer discussion with the organization's head until he finally got compensated by adding half a position of a secretary to his section.

Process Innovations

The work processes Issue Distribution, Vote Negotiation and Session Preparation within the SRB improved in two ways. First, since the process of document production was conducted by the users themselves, process speed as well as the quality of outputs improved (the latter due to less misunderstandings). Second, the use of electronic documents offered faster document transport and easier handling (e.g. copying) of document distribution. Especially the Issue Distribution process underwent slow but constant change over the four years since more and more external sources and documents were made electronically available by the cooperating organizations.

The work process Vote Preparation underwent more significant changes (cf. Figure 3). It also improved with the benefits described above, but the main improvement came with the parallelization of a sequential process part. Neither the project members, who have conducted the interviews with the users before introducing the system, nor the users themselves,

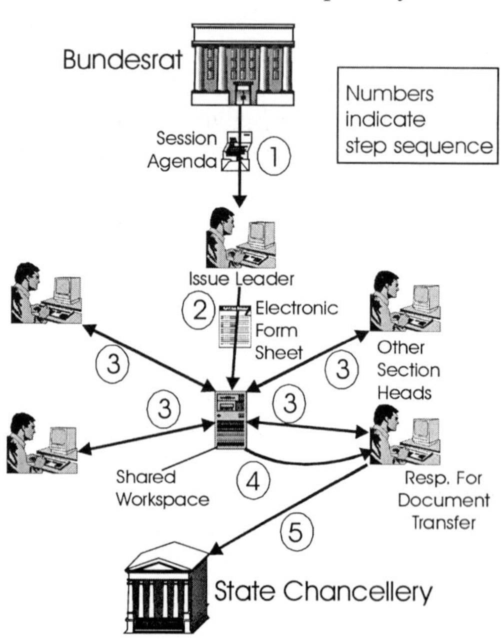

Figure 3: Vote Preperation revised

having been taught about the functionality of the application, directly recognized that potential for process innovation. During a site visit several months after the introduction, a project member and a section head discussed rather accidentally the stack of "form sheets" (see description of the Vote Preparation process) on the head's desk. They noticed that the process of filling out the "form sheets" could be supported by the object sharing feature of the groupware application. They involved other section managers to form an electronically supported procedure.

In that procedure the document template of the form sheet is stored in a public folder. The issue leader can copy it from there and fill it out for this issue of the agenda stating the commission's test voting results and further comments. Then a link to the document is sent via e-mail to all the other section managers being involved in that issue. The recipients can enter the vote of their section whenever they like. Because of the document-sharing, it is not necessary to maintain a temporal order, except that it is not possible for two users to have access to the same document at exactly the same time. After all sections, which had to contribute to an issue, had entered their votes and comments, the issue leader sent a link to the completed form sheet via e-mail to the section head responsible for transferring the documents to the State Chancellery. So, the shared workspace of the LinkWorks system allowed to overcome the sequential order to fill in votes immanent in the paper based version.

Groupware Distribution within the Organisation

At first, only those users who voluntarily agreed on groupware usage have been involved into the introduction process. The improvement of the Vote Preparation process described above boosted groupware usage among the section heads significantly. When the reorganized process had been implemented, the available workstations had to be redistributed among staff members according to the needs of that process innovation. The other staff members then got equipped by and by, according to the tight IT budget of the SRB.

Not all users who had the groupware installed actually used it. One of the section heads let the (remaining) secretary still type the forms for the Vote Preparation process for him and made her handling the data exchange. Since she only had a part-time position that slowed the process down. It took more than two years until he finally used the computer by himself. The head of the SRB was another example for a very reluctant attitude towards groupware usage. The major motivation for her to finally participate had not been to improve the work processes, but because she felt that a new field of activity had risen in "her" organization she was not involved in. Thus, other than peer pressure (cf. Grudin and Palen 1995), the desire to follow up what ones subordinates are doing can play a role in groupware adaptation.

Social Aspects

The organizational changes also altered social aspects of work life. While the local expert in our example agreed to his new role, the typists did not welcome the task shifts. Due to that development the last remaining typist regarded her position as endangered. To make herself indispensable she began storing macros and document templates outside the groupware application in local directories. That caused breakdowns in collaboration when she was on vacation, and endangered system security when computer viruses spread around and only the server had been cleaned assuming that this would cover all infected files.

Other effects came from the improvement in the Vote Preparation process. Usually, when the section heads went around to collect the votes, they talked to each other about private as well as business issues. This has been a valuable occasion for informal communication. Although there were still opportunities for floor talks, some staff members missed those occasions.

Removal Phase

Near the end of the project, the situation in the application field did get complicated. The state's government had changed, so that there was quite some fluctuation among staff members. In the State Chancellery the members of the IT department developed plans for a new unified groupware application for all state government authorities. The SRB still favored LinkWorks as their infrastructure, which resulted in an intra-organizational conflict. Additionally, the groupware system with its handling and interface, and even more the underlying hardware infrastructure, had grown out of date.

In that situation the head of the SRB, the State Chancellery and its IT department failed to agree upon a joint strategy to maintain or further develop the groupware infrastructure. Approaching the end of the project, in October 1998 the IT department of the Chancellery decided to change to another groupware platform, because it already relied on the network products of this specific groupware's manufacturer. It soon became clear that it would take some months until the infrastructure change was possible. It was considered as being too dangerous to rely on an unsupported groupware infrastructure, and so the SRB decided to work with a temporary solution, based on the existing hardware as stand-alone-PCs. The option to map the shared workspaces of the groupware to the shared directory service of the operating system was rejected. Parts of the network hardware had been de-installed, and it was considered too difficult to establish necessary conventions (e.g. that computers offering shared directories should be always online) and the access rights seemed to be too complicated to be handled by ordinary users.

We now describe some issues concerning the groupware deinstallation process and the new work situation in the application field.

Technical Issues

The biggest technical problem to solve was to assure availability of the documents stored in the groupware server's database and file system. A project member wrote a program based on the groupware's application programming interface to export the documents, but due to different naming conventions between the groupware (long filenames) and the operating system (filenames restricted to eight characters) this turned out to be a very time-consuming process. The users had to rename files with long names before a project member exported them. In case they had not prepared the export well, he had to rename them individually. After all, documents are now stored on the PC of their creators.

Difficulties with Metaphor Transfer

Several problems occurred concerning application usage. The groupware worked with office metaphors like "desk", "cabinet", "folder" or "document". Some users were not able to abstract from these container metaphors and had significant difficulties using ordinary directories as a means for structuring their documents. Navigation in directories was also considered as being more difficult. The groupware also knew the concept of "document patterns" to be reused e.g. for standard letters. With opening those patterns, the pattern was first copied, than the copy has been opened. With the ordinary file system it was now possible to overwrite a pattern accidentally with an instance of it.

Communication and Collaboration Breakdowns

The PC at the registrar still serves as the X.400-Gateway of the organization. But since the groupware's messaging system is missing now, all information has to be printed before it can be passed on to the relevant sections. This took considerably more time, and the gateway became a bottleneck for inter-organizational communication. The section for European politics for instance had established an intensive document exchange with colleagues from the Representative Bodies of other German states which she now was not able to sustain. Other staff members returned to the former practice of faxing documents. They heavily complained about busy lines and clumsy handling of documents. With the lacking document sharing functionality the need for text retyping occurred again, but now with significant less support by typists. Collaborative text production survived somehow; some users were now using floppy disks for document transfer, which proved to be a continuous source of mistakes and misunderstandings.

The Breakdown of Process Innovations

Since the groupware's messaging service was not available anymore, in almost all of the four processes the procedures changed drastically. The Vote Preparation process is now mainly paper based again. The issue leader creates the form sheet on his PC, prints out a sufficient number of copies and distributes them to the other sections. When the sheets return, she types the remarks of all of his colleagues into the final version, prints it and passes it on. This causes an extra burden upon those section heads who have many issue leaderships.

Since all extra-organizational electronic documents had to be printed now, the staff member at the X.400-Gateway was not able to handle the full workload anymore. Information flows had to prioritized, and finally the only process which remained at least in parts supported by electronic document transport was the Issue Distribution, since the incoming papers from the Bundesrat still are forwarded to the State Chancellery. In all other processes, documents are now transferred via fax again.

Results and Related Work

Referring to the experiences made we now point out issues we consider important for discussing the relation between groupware and organizational change. We also relate our findings to the ongoing discussions concerning organizational change.

The other topic we discuss are the experiences which relate to groupware removal, which up to now has not been discussed in the CSCW community. We show which problems we have to face there and what new requirements for groupware platforms arise.

Introduction Phase

The main lesson learnt from the introduction phase is the need to prepare users for active participation in the introduction process. Ploeger (1996) reports of a failed introduction project due to lacking user involvement. Summing up the results of 24 Lotus Notes case studies, Whitehead (1996) points out the importance of user involvement in applying tailoring or (re)developing groupware. This point is supported by a large body of work in the CSCW literature (cf. Schmidt 1991, Okamura et al. 1994, Bardram 1996, Hepsoe 1997). The focus and the extent of user involvement vary largely within the different case studies. One can distinguish between direct and indirect involvement. Turrel (1996) presents a rather indirect mode of involvement with the help of user forums where representatives of different organizational units meet to select new fields of application, to drive joint application development and to monitor the progress of certain applications. Within each single organizational unit involved, promoters have been selected to push the application of Lotus Notes. Nevertheless, the selection of fields of groupware application often happened top-down without involving the end users. This strategy caused severe problems, because "... the gap between the way people work and the way they are supposed to work is just too great and the system fails" (Turrel 1996, p. 43).

Our experiences indicate that there is a strong need to directly involve all potential users of groupware especially concerning three issues: First, for choosing and reorganizing the work processes to support, participation is necessary since only the users know how they really work. Second, user participation is needed to configure and further develop the groupware's functionality reliably. Although the electronic circulation folders feature the groupware offered was judged as "interesting" on the management level, the majority of users never felt a need for that since processes had been simple enough to maintain an overview. And third, user participation was crucial for sustaining a high level of interest in the ongoing change process. Even after their working hours, staff members of the SRB voluntarily participated in the evaluation of three research prototypes based on LinkWorks and suggested new modes to apply the groupware system. The employees have been prepared and motivated for participation throughout the first workshops and initial interviews. Workshops, interviews and site visits also provided social platforms where new ideas have been generated and continuous reflection on the way the organization worked has been stimulated.

Use Phase

Our findings confirm the importance of observing and stimulating organizational change processes accompanying groupware introduction. An integrated and evolutionary view on technological and organizational change leads to a more theoretical discussion. So we relate our findings to Orlikowski and Hofmann's (1997) "Improvisational Model of Change Management". Additionally, we discuss appropriate manners to handle productivity gains and inter-individually different views on "successful" groupware introduction.

Supporting Organizational Change with Persistence

In the CSCW literature, there are only few long term studies describing how the adaptation of groupware changed over time. Orlikowski (1996) gives an interesting example on how a Lotus Notes application evolved in the customer support department of a software company over time. She analyses that this evolution had not been fully planned in advance but was the result of emergent and opportunistic changes. Considering their experiences Ciborra (1996) speaks in this sense about the "drifting of groupware technology". Karsten and Jones (1998) report in their 3-year-study of a consulting company on how groupware usage differed in quality as well as quantity depending on economic conditions, management styles and role shifts. The greatest extent of collaboration has been achieved at the end of the study period in a situation of an advantageous constellation of those parameters.

In POLITeam similar observations have been made. For instance, first the available groupware workstations have been distributed according to tasks (the typists, the registrar) and interests (other users). Work processes improved by faster document transport and newly evolving collaboration patterns evolved concerning text production. After the electronic form sheet for the Vote

Preparation had been invented, the tight budget did not allow the purchase of additional hardware, and so the existing computers had to be redistributed according to the requirements of the process innovation. Throughout the following two years little by little other users have been (re-)integrated into the groupware network and a sustainable culture of collaboration evolved.

In the beginning the major obstacles were knowledge and perspective gaps between users and designers (Mambrey and Pipek 1999). Users did not know about the options groupware systems offered, and designers were not confident with the work processes and the organizational culture. Although the members of the project team conducted extensive interviews with almost all users of the SRB, they did not realize the application of the shared workspace to improve the Vote Preparation. Additionally, new cooperation partners may get access to the application and the organization's task can change over time (cf. Philipps 1996, Orlikowski 1996). Since not everything can be foreseen or analyzed, the adaptation of groupware has to be seen as an evolutionary process, which has from an action research point of view implications for training, system support and software adaptation.

Integrated View on Organizational and Technological Development

In the literature one can roughly distinguish between two different approaches on how to introduce groupware. The first one, which we have named "technology first", focuses on the new technological options groupware offers. The decision makers in the organization - often from IT departments - decide to employ the groupware technology mainly to gain experiences with a technology which is regarded as being important for the organization's development. An example for this approach is the adaptation of electronic calendars in two major computer companies (cf. Grudin and Palen 1995; Palen 1997).

In the second "organization first" approach, organizational goals are dominant. Groupware technology is introduced to support organizational goals with adequate information and collaboration structures. An example is presented by Turrell (1996). He describes how groupware has been used following the decision to reorganize a multinational company around profit centers.

Our project had a "technology first" perspective. The initiative was taken by the middle management a to learn about groupware technology. In the beginning of the project organizational change was not intended by the promoters.

Our experience indicates that for the introduction of groupware an *integrated* view on organizational and technological development is helpful. Technology-induced task shifts and new emergent collaboration patterns change work culture and qualification requirements. On the one hand, organizational structures have to be adapted to reflect these developments. On the other hand, organizational changes may require modifications of the technical infrastructure and its configuration.

Supporting these findings are the cases of the invention of the new Vote

Preparation process (organization adapts to technology); the redistribution of PCs among section heads following that invention (technology adapts to organization); or the task shifts following the easier text production and the need for computer support (organization adapts to technology). Another example for "technology adapts to organization" emerged from the handling of document sharing. Sharing started when the document's owner sent a link to the document to another user and could only be ended by the recipient. With the invention of the Vote Preparation process, that behavior became unacceptable for the section head responsible for the document transfer to the State Chancellery. He was worried that other section heads might change the form sheet document after the deadline set for completion. The program had to be extended to allow document owners to end document sharing.

Lacking attention towards organizational and educational problems can lead to severe problems in "technology first" projects (e. g. Rogers 1994). Examples from our context are lacking attention to task shifts, e.g. the management's denial to provide a UNIX course for the local expert, and the events that led to the groupware's removal. So options for organizational development should be considered from the very beginning of any groupware introduction. On the technical side, the groupware applications should offer the highest degree of technical flexibility possible, e.g. through tailoring functionality.

Consensual Handling of Gains in Productivity

Successful adaptation of groupware tends to increase the productivity of labor. This may endanger jobs as long as there is no increase in an organization's output. As successful groupware adaptation requires the direct involvement of users, the paradoxical situation might arise that users are required to participate in the elimination of their own jobs. In the POLITeam project, insecure job perspectives and lacking trust led to organizational complications when the remaining secretary tried to secure her position by storing macros and document templates outside the groupware on her PC. So when establishing a groupware project it is important to actively address this issue. A contractual framework on how to handle gains in productivity is a way to cope with that problem.

Different Perspectives on the Outcome of Organizational Change

Improvements could be seen concerning the speed of the work processes and the quality of their outcomes. Two patterns led to these changes: parallelization and document transport acceleration. All processes have been boosted by the opportunity to transport documents electronically. The parallelization of the Vote Preparation process saved two days of work according to a staff member. Part of the time saved was used to extend negotiations on some Bundesrat issues. This could have been considered a quality gain in the outcome of the process. But it has quite contrary been considered as an unnecessary complication by some users. Similarly, a section head doubted the usefulness of enabling all users involved in

Vote Preparation to directly access the Webserver of the Bundesrat, which provided relevant documents for all issues. He expected the decision finding to be more difficult when all ministries had access to all issues. In his eyes the existing time pressure eased decision making considerably. Additionally, intense Webserver usage would endanger his and the SRB's position as "information gateway" considerably. So, judgements on the quality of groupware-induced work process changes are far from equivocal. Even in cases where improvements are obvious, these improvement may be judged differently by the different actors (cf. Bowers 1994). This fact supports the argument of Blythin et al. (1997) that contrary to earlier expectations (e. g. Grudin 1988) successes or failures of groupware adaptations are difficult to measure. Additionally, this finding pleads for a pluralistic interpretation of Button and Sharrock (1997) who asked the CSCW community to "...develop measures to the value of proposed systems for organizations and users that trades on the entwined relationship between technology and organization" (p. 14). According to our experiences, such measures will not be valid in a universal sense but strongly biased by the role played by those who define them.

Organizational Change revisited

Orlikowski and Hofmann (1997) suggested a weak categorization of technology-induced change processes which could help in change management. Categories are whether a change has been anticipated or not and whether it is planned and introduced purposefully or not. "Anticipated changes" are those which have been anticipated and planned and introduced purposefully. "Opportunity-based" changes occur unanticipated but are then planned and transposed in an organized way. "Emergent changes" refer to changes which are unanticipated and emerge in a more chaotic way. This "Improvisational Model of Change Management" is based upon two assumptions. The first assumption is that "changes associated with technology implementations constitute an ongoing process rather than an event with an end point after which the organization can expect to return to a reasonably steady state." The second is that "... all ... organizational changes ... cannot, by definition, be anticipated ahead of time."
The model is confirmed by our experiences in its assumptions as well as in its categories. The first assumption was underlined by the changes the work practice in the SRB underwent. The process innovation in the Vote Preparation process serves as an example for the second assumption. In POLITeam we found anticipated changes in the acceleration of document transport and the task shift concerning text creation. The process improvement of the Vote Preparation is a case of an opportunity-based change, because it occurred unanticipated, but was planned and introduced purposefully afterwards. An emergent change showed in the emergence of collaborative document production, which has been unanticipated and unplanned.
But our findings also show that for the goal of the change management model

to help to "effectively respond to change" (Orlikowski and Hofmann 1997, p.14) that categorization might not be differentiated sufficiently. The shift concerning typing tasks, which moved from the typists to the section heads, who produced the texts now by themselves, was clearly anticipated and planned. But the full extent of work shift could not be anticipated for two reasons. First, it was impossible to estimate how much of the work load would shift from the typists to the section heads, because the writers didn't know by themselves, how much work would be acceptable to them. In fact, there have been huge individual differences concerning this. Second, the extent of the work shift that occurred was dependent on the time saving resulting from the improvement of the Vote Preparation process, which was an unanticipated change.

Removal Phase

Groupware removal is an issue not yet covered in field studies. In our case the removal mainly resulted from management failures, but the technical infrastructure has also been outdated. The desire to have a uniform, organization-wide infrastructure, the urge to unite different organizations' infrastructures, being discontent with the vendor's service or with the product itself might be other reasons that cause an organization to change its groupware infrastructure. Supporting the deinstallation process is a yet not considered requirement for groupware products.

Support for Groupware Deinstallation

Clearly, the documents stored in the groupware system have to be made available for the users appropriately. The export of documents out of the groupware with its client/server architecture into structures of the underlying operating system should be automated by the groupware as far as possible. This should include document export to all users which had read access to a document and automated copying of the workspace structures to (shared) directory structures. Additionally, the organizational structures (workflows, roles, workspace structures, etc.) mapped in the groupware system should be exportable as text or graphics for documentation and conservation. Findings from the tailorability discussion indicate, that users want new program versions to be equipped with the screen design and menu structures they are already used to (cf. Mackay 1990). Presumably informal knowledge like group conventions (document naming, storing strategies) or individual habits will have to be newly developed with the introduction of the new groupware platform. Support for usage documentation could ease the transition.

For the technical aspects it would also be helpful if an interoperability standard would evolve, similar to the one of the Workflow Management Coalition maintains for workflow management systems. Since groupware products are more flexible in its different functionalities this standard would have to be extensible.

Sustainability of new Patterns of Collaboration

Surprisingly collaboration patterns sustained even when the infrastructure which enabled them was taken away. Users now operated with floppy disks to transport documents. In the new Vote Preparation process the pattern of parallelization has sustained even though the process now is mainly paper-based again. Although our application field was comparatively collaboration-friendly even before POLITeam, these developments show that groupware can strengthen collaboration in organizations and have an impact on organizational culture even beyond its physical presence. This finding is similar to the observations of Karsten and Jones (1998).

Intertwined Relationship between Technology and Organization

How intertwined technological and organizational issues really are can be studied to its full extend when observing the removal of the technology. In our case the interorganizational communication was narrowed significantly and shifted to older media (fax), leading also to qualitative loss. The staff members had serious problems to readapt to the old procedures, and several breakdowns have been observed. Especially the typist had to face an unmanageable workload. Just as the introduction, the removal of groupware has to be seen as an evolutionary process. Organization-internal and -external expectations concerning process speed and quality have risen during groupware usage, but those standards could not be matched anymore. These experiences also support our pleading for an integrated view towards technological and organizational development.

Conclusion

The introduction of a groupware application into an organization is often related to processes of organizational change. In fact, the intertwined relationship between technological and organizational issues makes appropriately facilitated organizational change processes a crucial factor for the successful assimilation of groupware technology. Describing and discussing some experiences from our four-year-study of an application field of the POLITeam project as well as experiences from related studies we traced the question, how organizational change and technology introduction influence each other and what obstacles to establish collaboration there might be.

We found that users should be motivated and instructed for participation from the very beginning of groupware introduction. They have the knowledge which is necessary to find out what work processes will especially benefit from groupware support. It is also important to maintain an integrated view towards technological and organizational development especially regarding organizational and educational measures. A consensual handling of productivity gains is needed to ensure user participation throughout the lifecycle of the groupware. The fact, that even obvious process improvements might be judged differently by different users which might be a possible source of conflict and distrust, adds to the problem.

Relating our experiences to Orlikowski's and Hofmann's Improvisational Model of Change we found it would have been well applicable in our case though it might have to be refined to appropriately serve its goals.

Since our study gave us the opportunity to cover the complete lifecycle of a groupware application, we also took a closer look on the process of groupware removal at the end of the lifecycle. Additional requirements arose from our observations such as technical support for deinstallation. Surprisingly, we found that collaboration patterns, initiated during the groupware usage phase, now tend to sustain even without the underlying groupware technology.

Surely the re-introduction of another groupware platform into that application field is something to observe. If we can rely on the personal relations established to key users over the four years, we will report on this ongoing process. So watch for 'A Groupware's Life: The sequel'.

Acknowledgements

We would like to thank our colleagues Torsten Engelskirchen, Helge Kahler and Bianca Schröter for their work in the application field and their comments on earlier versions of the paper. Four anonymous reviewers provided us with valuable input to improve the paper. The POLITeam project was supported by the German Ministry for Education and Research (Research Grant Nr. 01 IT 402B/2).

References

Bardram, J. E.: Organizational Prototyping: Adapting CSCW Application in Organizations, in: Skandinavian Journal of Information Systems, No. 1, 1996, pp. 69 - 88

Blythin, S.; Hughes, J.A.; Kristoffersen, S.; Rodden, T.; Rouncefield, M.: Recognizing success and failure: Evaluating Groupware in a Commercial Context; in: Proc. of the SIGGROUP Conference on supporting group work (SIGGROUP'97), ACM Press, New York, 1997

Bowers, J.: The work to make a network work; in: Proc. of the Conference on Computer Supported Cooperative Work (CSCW'94), ACM Press, New York, 1994; pp. 287-298

Button, G.; Sharrok, W.: The production of Order and the Order of production, in: Proc. of the European Conference on Computer Supported Cooperative Work (ECSCW'97), Kluwer Academic Publ., Dordrecht 1997

Ciborra, C. (ed.): Groupware & Teamwork, J. Wiley & Sons; Chichester 1996

Grudin, J.: Why CSCW applications fail: Problems in the design and evaluation of organizational interfaces, in: Proc. of the Int. Conference on Computer Supported Cooperative Work (CSCW'88), ACM Press, New York, USA, 1988

Grudin, J.; Palen, L.: Why groupware succeeds: Discretion or Mandate? in: Proc. of the European Conference on Computer Supported Cooperative Work (ECSCW'95), Kluwer Academic Publ., Dordrecht 1995, pp. 263-278

Karsten, H.; Jones, M.: "The long and winding road: Collaorative IT and organisational change"; in: Int. Conference on Computer Supported Work (CSCW'98); pp. 29-38; ACM Press; Seattle, WA, USA; 1998.

Kotler, P.: Marketing Management: Analysis, Planning and Control, Prentice-Hall, Ingelwood Cliffs, NJ, USA, 1980

Lloyd, P.; Whitehead, R. (eds.): Transforming Organizations through Groupware, Springer, London et al. 1996

Mackay, Wendy E.: Users and customizable Software: A Co-Adaptive Phenomenon, PhD-Theses, MIT, Boston (MA) 1990

Mambrey, P.; Mark, G.; Pankoke-Babatz, U.: "Integrating User Advocacy into Participatory Design: The Designer's Perspective"; in: Blomberg, J.; Kensing, F.; Dykstra-Erickson, E.A. (Ed.): Participatory Design Conference; pp. 251-259; CPSR; Cambridge, MA, USA; 1996.

Mambrey, P.; Pipek, V.: "Enhancing Participatory Design by Multiple Communication Channels"; in: Bullinger, H.-J. (ed.): Proceedings of the Int. Conference on Human-Computer-Interaction (HCI'99), Lawrence Erlbaum, 1999 (in press)

Mark, G.; Fuchs, L.; Sohlenkamp, M.: "Supporting Groupware Conventions through Contextual Awareness"; in: Hughes, J. A.; Prinz, W.; Rodden, T.; Schmidt, K. (Ed.): 5th European Conf. on CSCW (ECSCW'97); pp. 253-268; Kluwer; 1997.

Orlikowski, W. J.: Evolving with Notes: Organizational change around groupware technology, in: Ciborra, C.: Groupware & Teamwork, J. Wiley, Chichester et al. 1996, pp. 23 - 60

Orlikowski, W. J.; Hofman, J. D.: "An Improvisational Model for Change Management: The Case of Groupware Technologies"; in: Sloan Management Review (Winter 1997); pp. 11-21; 1997.

Palen, L.: Groupware Adoption & Adaptation: Studies on Successful Use, in: SIGGROUP Bulletin, Vol. 18, No. 3, 1997, pp. 51 - 55

Phillipps, R. W.: Am Bank: Managing Client Relationships, in: Lloyd, P.; Whitehead, R.: Transforming Organizations through Groupware, Springer, London et al. 1996, pp. 46 - 54

Ploeger, E.: Ambouw BV: Stalled Pilot at Dutch Wholesaler, in: Lloyd, P.; Whitehead, R.: Transforming Organizations through Groupware, Springer, London et al. 1996, pp. 55 - 62

Rogers, Y.: Exploring Obstacles: Integrating CSCW in Evolving Organizations, in: Proceedings of the Confe-rence on Computer-Supported Cooperative Work (CSCW'94), ACM-Press: New York, 1994, pp. 67 - 78

Prinz, Wolfgang; Mark, Gloria; Pankoke-Babatz, Uta: "Designing Groupware for Congruency in Use"; in: Int. Conference on Computer Supported Cooperative Work (CSCW'98); pp. 373-382; ACM Press; Seattle, WA, USA; 1998.

Schmidt, K.; Simone, C.: Coordination mechanisms: Towards a conceptual foundation of CSCW systems design, in: Int. Journal on CSCW, Vol. 5, Iss. 2-3, 1996, pp. 155-200

Sommerville, I.: Software Engineering, Addison-Wesley, Wokingham, UK, 1989

Turrell, M.: ABB Asea Brown Boveri: Supporting the multi-cultural Multinational, in: Llyod, P.; Whitehead, R.: Transforming Organizations through Groupware, Springer, London et al. 1996, pp. 39 - 45

Whitehead, R.: Making use of the case studies, in: Lloyd, P.; Whitehead, R.: Transforming Organizations through Groupware, Springer, London et al. 1996, pp. 11 - 22

Wijn, W.: GM Europe: World's Largest User of Notes, in: Lloyd, P.: Transforming Organizations through Groupware, Springer, London et al. 1996, pp. 95 - 100

Wulf, V.: Storing and Retrieving Documents in a Shared Workspace: Experiences from the Political Administration. In: Howard, S.; Hammond, J.; Lindgaard, G. (eds): Human Computer Interaction: INTERACT 97, Chapman & Hall, S. 469-476, 1997

S. Bødker, M. Kyng, and K. Schmidt (eds.). *Proceedings of the Sixth European Conference on Computer-Supported Cooperative Work, 12-16 September 1999, Copenhagen, Denmark*
©1999 Kluwer Academic Publishers. Printed in the Netherlands

The Network Communities of SeniorNet

Elizabeth D. Mynatt[1], Annette Adler[2], Mizuko Ito[3], Charlotte Linde[3], and Vicki L. O'Day[4]

[1]Georgia Institute of Technology, USA
mynatt@cc.gatech.edu

[2]Xerox Palo Alto Research Center, USA
adler@parc.xerox.com

[3]Institute for Research on Learning, USA
mito@itofisher.com
charlotte_linde@irl.org

[4]University of California, Santa Cruz, USA
oday@calterra.com

Abstract: With the explosion of participation on the Internet, there is increasing interest and speculation in extending its uses to support diverse online communities, and particular interest in using the Internet to combat loneliness and isolation amongst senior citizens. For the past year, we have been investigating SeniorNet (SN), a 12 year old organization that attempts to bring seniors together via computer networking technologies. We found a rich tapestry of human relationships supported by various technical and social underpinnings. In this paper, we delve into the richness of an active community and describe the intertwining technical and social factors that make it valuable and useful for its members. An underlying question in these discussions is "If network communities have to be principally created and maintained by their members (as we posit), then how do designers help without getting in the way?"

220

Introduction

With the explosion of participation on the Internet, there is increasing interest and speculation in extending its uses to support diverse online communities (Hagel, 1997; Kiesler, 1997; Rheingold, 1993; Schuler, 1996). As a new communication medium that could potentially reach into many homes it seems a likely tool for connecting people, combating isolation and loneliness. One obvious target population for such endeavors is senior citizens, as they are entering a new stage of their life with retirement and are increasingly likely to be geographically separated from family. But senior citizens are typically thought of as technology naive, and even adverse to computer use, preferring traditional methods for their communication needs.

For the past year, we have been investigating SeniorNet (SN), a 12 year old organization that attempts to bring seniors together via computer networking technologies. A typical SN site has chat rooms and news group-like areas, called roundtables on the WWW and forums on AOL[1] on a host of topics. SN first started with Delphi in 1986. Currently they have nearly 20,000 members comprising thriving online communities on both America Online (AOL) and the World Wide Web.

In 1998 (Mynatt, 1998), we presented our observations on network communities. As researchers, designers, and users of MUDs and media space technologies, we pointed to the constellation of technical affordances and social requirements that comprise a network community. In our framework, we explored three design dimensions of network communities: supporting the rhythms of an online community, nurturing community development, and managing the real and virtual worlds. Following this work, we wanted to look at a new network community in detail. This motivation led us to our current investigation of SeniorNet.

We found a rich tapestry of human relationships supported by various technical and social underpinnings. Instead of exhaustively listing the ways that SN satisfies the conditions of a network community, in this paper, we point to the characteristics that we believe are particularly salient for the research community. One contribution of this work is that we delve into the richness of a active community and describe the intertwining technical and social factors that make it valuable and useful for its members. An underlying question in these discussions is *"What is the role of design in creating a network community?"* This question is timely as more and more businesses wish to use net communities both internally for their staff as well as externally for their customers. Many internet entrepreneurs see community

---

1. For the remainder of this paper, we will refer to both roundtables and forums as roundtables.

as the hook for their commercial web sites, while the population of the Net, their potential clientele, is rapidly expanding and diversifying.

We first provide an overview of the history and current organization of SeniorNet and describe our one-year case study. We then focus our discussions on three main observations of SeniorNet's network communities:

- Network communities exhibit a complex collage of interaction styles and rhythms. This richness enables the depth of expression needed to nurture multi-layered relationships (a key component of a community). In our previous work, we examined the rich interaction modalities available in media spaces with audio and video connections, graphical MUDs[2] as well as programmable text-based MUDs. The building blocks for interaction in SN's network communities appear to be much more limited. Yet, we observed how SN members use various technical and social mechanisms combined with the basic building blocks of roundtables, email, and chat to create a necessary and sufficient set of interaction modalities to support community.

- One defining notion of network communities is of boundaries, the ability to sense a "groupness" about the members. This groupness is defined by identities and shared practices that have been created and nurtured over time. By "seeding" new sites (e.g. the recent Web site) with members of the community, SN has been able to transplant itself several times. The "groupness" of SN includes multiple roles and modes of participation that support a variety of needs within the community (e.g. hosts) and stages of participation (e.g. learner, new member, old timer) Although one obvious boundary to SeniorNet is that membership is limited to people over 50 years of age, this boundary is more opportunistic than defining. The community spans much more than "senior-like" identities and practices. This insight is important to those who want to start network communities defined by a demographic groups.

- In contrast to the hype surrounding the promise of anonymity on the Internet, SN is strikingly grounded in the real world, while still embracing the charm of fantasy in the virtual realm. SN members connect their virtual interactions to their "real," physical lives in many ways, strengthening the SN community. One perceived advantage to this virtual-real connection that may be surprising is it contributes to a sense of safety and trust. This observation is in sharp contrast to ensuring safety through

---

2. MUDs are computationally-based environments that provide access to a persistent, online "world."

anonymity. Although SN is strongly grounded in the real world, the members also embrace the fun of virtual fantasy with online birthday parties and shared cups of tea.

In each section, we reflect on the role of design in creating network communities. If network communities have to be principally created and maintained by their members (as we posit), then how do designers help without getting in the way? As the majority of our research has been principally focused on net communities in the workplace (including educational settings), our discussions revolve around common themes such as peer sharing, informal learning and multilayered relationships that are important for all network communities. By examining this successful community, we both contribute to the growing consensus (e.g. Kollack 1996) about how net communities operate, as well as offer insights in how to sustain a long-term community and nurture a particular set of practices. One benefit of examining a net community in such rich detail is that this richness nurtures a designer's evolving intuition in addition to marking general design guidelines.

The SeniorNet community does not fall into a neat classification as a recreational community or a work community or an educational community. All of these endeavors are practiced on a daily basis. SeniorNet members *work* to accomplish their goals in a purposeful and meaningful fashion. These goals include planning gatherings, collecting diverse views on a topic, and attending to the needs of a particular member. As Internet access grows, we have the opportunity to understand collaborative practices outside of traditional work settings. As a long-standing community, SeniorNet is an excellent example of this growing form of computer-supported, cooperative work.

The SeniorNet Project

The SeniorNet organization was founded 12 years ago to help seniors gain access to computing technology. SeniorNet supports robust network communities on the Web and on America On-Line (AOL), and it sponsors over a hundred volunteer-staffed "Learning Centers" throughout the United States, where seniors can take computer classes on a variety of subjects, including how to buy a computer, how to use financial software, and how to get online.

A SeniorNet online site provides a multitude of communication affordances. Most prominently are the roundtables on a multitude of topics ranging from book clubs to WWII memories, including a Cafe for casual socializing as well as roundtables to support grieving. Both sites offer simple, real-time chat capabilities. Participants can register themselves with a user name, a password and other self descriptions, with optional pointers to a homepages. Non-registered people can still post as guests although they cannot use chat. As we will discuss later, both members and non-members lurk as well.

For the past year, we have been engaged in an ethnographic study of SeniorNet. We are interested in the issue of broad access to computing. We chose to study SeniorNet as a case of long-lived, successful computer access among a population which is not commonly thought to be adept at learning new technologies. The themes of our research have centered on understanding the social and technical features that support access and help people become fluent in online participation.

As SeniorNet is a distributed enterprise with activity in different online and physical locations, we carried out observations and interviews in a variety of sites, to develop a better sense of SeniorNet's membership and practices than any particular location could provide. We interviewed SeniorNet staff members, observed four classes at three Learning Centers, observed online activity in discussion roundtables both on the Web and AOL over a period of months, participated in chat regularly on the Web for a week, interviewed 20 members drawn from both network communities, and interviewed 9 students from two of the classes we had observed. We also posted questions and research themes on an online roundtable created for us by the SeniorNet staff, to generate discussion among members on topics of interest to the project.

We have research findings in several areas, including access issues, network communities, online fieldwork practices, and learning to become a Net participant. In this paper, we focus on the combinations of social practices and technological affordances that have supported these long-standing network communities.

Rhythm and Other Communication Patterns

In (Mynatt 1998), we discussed the importance of predictable rhythms in supporting social interaction in network communities. Our observations suggest that communities are more enduring when people know when and how they can find others online and can structure their participation to match. Learning to sync up to the prevailing style is part of becoming a member of the group.

Generally a network community does not have *one* prevailing rhythm, but instead is made up of a myriad of communication possibilities and social practices, each with a distinctive rhythm. From daily interactions that build into social routines, these patterns of interaction are the basis for rich, multi-layered relationships in network communities.

Predictable Rhythms

One clear observation of SN is that it relies on many *predictable* rhythms. Predictability is necessary to support a feeling of connection (Kiesler 1997). A change in the predictable rhythm might mean a temporary technical problem or it might mean that someone is experiencing social problems—either way, participants notice changes in the pattern and can often account for them. These observable patterns lead to a more robust sense of community where people can work through occasional glitches. The technology must be reliable enough for these rhythms to develop, but then, when the patterns are in place, technical problems can often be understood and tolerated. For example, inhabitants would remark that the chat server was down even if it appeared to be up and empty, if this happened at a peak time when regulars should be present.

The same effect holds for a change in personal rhythm, such as when a regular poster temporarily disappears. When these situations occur, others notice, and they may monitor the absence or check up on the missing person through other means. For example, the overall mood of the "Living with Cancer" roundtable on AOL is one of an intimate support group with a small number of regular members. Absences and reappearances of regular members were often noted since an absence may indicate surgery or illness. For example, one person posts "Wondered where you were! Glad you're fixed up and back with us now" [3], or another posts "Sue, I'm so glad you're all right. I was worried about you". Lapses in postings are also noted, for example: "I miss all of you... where did you go" (Amenta), during a one day lapse in postings. Similarly, John notes a four day lapse: "Where did everyone go? No postings since the 14th."

Range of Communication Affordances Needed

The SeniorNet case reveals a wide range of interactional rhythms across the different arenas for participation. Chat rooms feel different than discussion roundtables, of course, but also each individual discussion roundtable has its own conventional pace and style. Participants have their favorite places to be, and no one interacts in all of the possible settings. But many participants have several favorite places, and they adjust to the rhythms of different groups as they move among them.

SeniorNet roundtables vary in topic (books, religion, health issues, history and policy, social chat), tone (intimate, informational, joking), frequency and volume of postings (from tens of messages each day to gaps of several days between single

---

3. In this paper, we have attempted to contact everyone whom we have interviewed, or whose on-line posts we have used, to give them the option of using real screen names or pseudonyms when quoted. When we have been unable to contact people, we have quoted their material with pseudonyms or no names.

messages), and media used (text, color, graphics). Together, these differences contribute to a high level of expressiveness and a distinctive character for each group. For example, the SeniorNet Cafe on the Web is a high-volume, chatty place, with approximately several hundred messages a day where posters go to see and be seen. It is a kind of centrally-located watering-hole for SeniorNet on the Web. By contrast, the AlAnon group on AOL is a place for relatives of alcoholics to gather and share long stories and mutual encouragement; the postings here are often separated by many hours or days, and the tone is both serious and supportive.

This range of communication choices is useful in supporting the diverse needs of a community. It seems to us that one reason SeniorNet flourishes is that people can bring many facets of themselves to light—they can involve their "whole selves" in the SeniorNet community if they wish. It is not just a place for talking about professional or intellectual interests, hobbies, family crises, or physical ailments, or for talking in the daytime or in the middle of the night, or for quick chat or long, thoughtful debate—it can be all of these. People seem to draw on what they need and want at different times and diverse members can choose among the various options. Such a range of expressiveness helps people get to know others whom they are not interacting with face-to-face. The online technologies do not mimic face-to-face interaction at all, but they are rich enough to allow people to say different things differently.

Range is also important to support change within the community. SN oldtimers often mentioned that their needs and thus their participation had changed over the years. A likely path is starting with a light-weight roundtable such as the Cafe, dabbling with chat for a bit and then, in turn, concentrating on different roundtables. One AOL participant describes her path:

"I have been a member of the Seniornet community for 7 years. Many of those I originally met here are still active members. At first, it was the community center (chatroom) that interested me. It seemed to me magical to be able to chat with people across the nation, and indeed become quite close to them. I feel like it is a cocktail party with a variety of topics going on, and light social chitchat....After a year or two, I found the forum more interesting....primarily because topics of more depth could be discussed, and it permitted time for reflection. I now participate in half-a-dozen of the message areas and rarely go into the chatroom."

Two Modalities, Multiple Practices

The SN members have taken up the two principal communication modalities, roundtables and chat, and created a rich a diverse set of shared practices. Within roundtables, we first noticed that people frequently made "off topic" remarks, with the tacit approval of their fellow community members. Initially, it seemed to us that virtually nothing could be considered off topic—personal greetings showed up in the book group, and complaints about junk phone calls showed up in the technical support group (and were followed up by constructive suggestions). But as we looked more carefully, it was clear that the practices of each group do steer people to certain forms of expression more than others. For example, both the SeniorNet chat room and the SeniorNet Cafe on the Web are lively social gatherings where light-hearted talk prevails. Few people discuss serious or troubling issues there, and one member commented that she goes to a particular roundtable to "dump" when upset, rather than the Cafe, though she is a well-known "regular" in the Cafe.

Participants develop a sense of what is appropriate in each setting, according to its rhythm and other features. Although there are only two public SeniorNet chat rooms, one for the Web and one for AOL, they feel different at different times of day. In the evenings a large and cheerful group gathers to talk, and in the mornings a smaller, much quieter crowd appears. People either sort themselves into different temporal groups according to their own preferred social styles or they adapt to the patterns in effect at different times. An AOL chatter described the chat crowds this way:

> *"I've discovered that, like on America OnLine Senior Chat, there are certain people that usually go on at certain times. There's a morning group, an afternoon group, and then an evening group. And they're all entirely different, for the most part, different people, and they have different interests. The evening people are, the late evening people, are very much into Singles' kinds of things and flirting on the Net, and that. And a little bit of whatever. And that's not true so much of the morning. The morning people are a different group. You very seldom have a group come on at six o'clock in the morning and say, "Let's all jump in the hot tub." Whereas that's a very common practice at, say, twelve o'clock at night. And I'm not a hot tub type person, so I don't, so I prefer the morning crew. Not that I have anything against their fantasies, but that's, it's just not mine."*

The differences between the Cafe and AlAnon or between morning chat and evening chat do not stem from any official rules, nor do they emerge from technology differences. The character of each place is developed through its own particular social patterns and conventions. Sometimes these conventions are implicit, as in the example of the Cafe regular going elsewhere to tell SeniorNetters about her troubles, and sometimes they are explicit. For example, some groups agree that graphics should not be used in their postings, because not everyone has the right software or modem speed to be able to see them. There are roundtables dedicated to sharing graphics, for those who can see and use them.

Technology Affordances

Though technology cannot account for all the differences in social rhythm, it does have a strong impact on expressiveness. Some modalities, such as chat, require participants to be co-present, and others, such as roundtables, allow participants to be far apart in time as well as space. The use of color in text is heavily used in Web messages, and it was quickly appropriated by AOL members when it became available to them part-way through our study.

Color interacts in an interesting way with the high volume and multi-threading of some groups. Some members use the technology affordance of a virtual "notepad," that they keep open for note-taking while reading a stream of messages. Then they post a bundled response with specific replies embedded within. Color is often used here to distinguish the embedded messages in a bundled note.

In a sense, the particular technologies available for network communities are not the most important—the human infrastructure is far more crucial. There are examples of long-lived network communities built on very impoverished technologies. But even if members would make do with whatever building blocks they found (if they were sufficiently motivated and other community support mechanisms were present), it isn't enough to offer a random or impoverished collection of blocks. The need for a coherent set of building blocks was apparent when the SeniorNet Web site opened without a chat capability, though it did have many discussion roundtables. Until it was added, members reported that they went elsewhere on the Web to chat. Perhaps they needed and wanted chat because they knew it was out there somewhere, or perhaps they needed something lightweight and immediate to complement the more persistent conversations available in roundtables.

One technology affordance still lacking from SN is mechanisms for background awareness. Lurking is an acceptable practice on roundtables and is often cited as a way to get a feel for the community as well as a strategy for managing time online (read more than write). But members comment of sometimes feeling disconnected in areas where they lurk as well as awkward when trying to break into a conversation. Background awareness of lurkers might help people make the jump from lurker to participant.

Design Implications

To design technology for a network community with rhythm in mind means offering diverse communication possibilities that can be used alongside one another or together. These modalities must also be presented in a way to allow appropriation and shaping by community members. This range is needed for a number of reasons: First, the range supports the inherent diversity in the community. Providing a spectrum of topics, interaction styles and rhythms allows a larger population of people to find the right match for their interests, personality, level of technical expertise and availability of time. Diversity makes the community interesting and a place of continual learning. Without supporting this diversity, the community will be too narrowly focused and will likely not thrive for any substantial period of time. Second, this range allows individual members to share parts of their whole identity in different forums. This flexibility encourages members to "try out" ways of participating, as well as providing a tractable way for members to share their various interests, concerns and personalities. Third, members can move through different stages of participation without dropping out of the community. We saw numerous examples of members keeping their connection with SeniorNet while partaking in different activities during their tenure.

Movement from one modality or style to another must be straightforward and fluid to allow people to shift their attention and participation easily. Common interfaces and quick short-cuts between related forums allow members to easily shift between their areas of interest. While the various modalities support different modes of participation, they must still be part of one "place." Although SN members participate in numerous forums, they still referred to "going to SeniorNet."

While the SN community makes great use out of one technical building block, forums, there are other technical requirements. As was discussed, the members needed a realtime chat capability to support primarily light-hearted conversation amongst temporally-based groups. The SN study points to a positive model for the role of lurkers where lurking is an encouraged and acceptable practice. Nevertheless interfaces that support the shift from lurker to writer are needed. For example, visibility of lurkers in real-time chat could help people initiate conversations. In forums, "footprints" of readers could increase community awareness of silent members and the patterns of communication amongst the whole community. Finally, the technology must be reliable enough to support the development of predictable rhythms.

Groupness and Community Development

Communities of any kind are characterized by affinity and shared practices that create meaningful context and define the boundaries of the group (Kiesler 1997, Rheingold 1993). Our early work suggested that their cohesion was the result of a shared history, multilayered relations and contexts and a sense of "locality." In the case of SeniorNet, the sense of locality and cohesion of the community is maintained through the enabling networking technologies, as well as a rich history, dedicated members, age cohort affiliation, and a shared set of social conventions.

History and Change

SeniorNet provides a particularly rich case study of a network community not only because of it's robust and diverse social life, but also because of its history, which spans over ten years and three different online sites.

The SeniorNet community is the result of a long series of developments and the hard work of dedicated members and staff through the years. Like other "intentional" communities, SeniorNet had a founding ethos and an ongoing mission "to provide older adults education for and access to computer technology to enhance their lives and enable them to share their knowledge and wisdom." SN grew from a concept funded by an initial research grant in 1986, to a small social group on Delphi, to larger and more diverse communities on AOL and the web, Throughout its history, core members and volunteers have maintained social and cultural continuity of the group, as well as created openings for new members to find a voice and develop new directions.

In the shift from Delphi to AOL in 1991, most of the 3-400 members were transplanted, so the community was essentially reproduced wholesale in a new technical infrastructure. These established members took ownership of this new space and formed a durable core identity as the community grew through its affiliation with AOL to the current numbers of over 5000 participants. When the web site debuted in 1997, some members from the AOL group were asked to "seed" the new site and were instrumental in transplanting the ethos of SeniorNet in the founding of an almost entirely new group.

While SeniorNet has been remarkably successful in maintaining continuity in the various dimensions of community through its many permutations, the character of the community has also gone through many inevitable changes, as the group has grown, computer networking has become more mainstream, and through oldtimers changed their relationship with the community. In the early years of SeniorNet, the relative rarity of computer networking in general, and among seniors in particular, contributed to a sense of wonderment and a pioneering spirit among early members. As one early member recalls, ."...for us, at the beginning, it was so strange and so wonderful! Here we are!"

As the community has expanded, some oldtimers have continued to be active, helping to seed the new permutations of the community, and taking a leadership role. Other oldtimers have moved to a more peripheral role in the community, preferring to maintain the numerous close ties that were developed in their early involvement, rather than continue to widen their participation in the community.

Ways to Participate

The history of the SeniorNet community is one of a small cohort of computer-using pioneers transforming itself into a group of thousands, differentiated into many different sub-communities. In the initial days, it was possible for an active member to keep track of most of the postings on a site, and thus "know" all other active participants. Currently, only the most dedicated of members can even hope to keep up with the volume of postings community-wide, and almost all members choose certain aspects of either the web or AOL to frequent regularly.

As SeniorNet has grown and become more differentiated, different modes of participation have emerged. These distinctions are familiar to network communities in general: hosts and sysops, moderators, regulars, newbies, and lurkers. These categories allow for a diversity of ways of participating and also support learning by providing openings for newcomers to lurk, enter, and engage with the group. Each sub-community we observed, including chat and different roundtables on the Web and AOL, has a core set of regulars. However, we also noticed in each group that newcomers are welcomed with warmth, and on the web, hosts will welcome any new poster that they see with a personal email that gives information on how to navigate the site. In chat, a new "face" is welcomed with warm hellos and introductions all around. While lurking is awkward in chat, there does seem to be tolerance for lurking in the roundtables. We saw that when former lurkers post for the first time, they are usually greeted with encouragement rather than ignored or chastised for their earlier silence.

A posting in the AOL Newcomers Forum sums up the SeniorNet ethos for extending a welcome to newcomers:

> *"SeniorNet is made up of people of your age group and there are many nice people here. Be nice to them and they'll be nice to you. There's always someone here that is willing to help with puter and other problems. If you're new to puters I would suggest you just lurk (hang around observing) in different places till you get a feel for the tone of the area you're in. Then when you find an area you like and feel secure in-----participate. Be sure to read the items on the first page upon entering SeniorNet---it explains our whole thing.(newcomer)"*

Identity

In addition to a unique history, mission, and organizational structure that has defined the norms and boundaries of the SeniorNet communities, SeniorNetters also share an affiliation based on their inclusion in an "over 50" age cohort. Formal membership in the SeniorNet organization is based on this age criteria. And while there are no formal age defined boundaries to participation in the online sites (nobody is officially barred from participation, including under 50 researchers), there is a shared understanding that the community is meant for people age 50 and above. This age-based social boundary is clearly operative in the community: there are discussion topics related to aging and historically specific experiences such as reflections on WWII. Further, social practices in the community are related to the social norms of this generation. In particular, the community is characterized by what we came to call *civility*, a sense of courtesy and social protocol that differentiated SeniorNet from the interactional practices of most other Internet communities.

The age-defined group boundary seems, at first blush, to be the most defining feature of the community, and the one most easily at hand when considering how membership is constructed. This age-based identity, however, like any other social category that is not necessarily of an individual's choosing, is cause for contestation, resistance, and appropriation. The boundary of "over 50" obscures an incredible diversity of experience and social locations, not to mention over 40 years in age range, a much larger range than any other age cohort (children, teens, twenty somethings, thirty somethings, boomers, etc.).

Participants in SeniorNet include people who are working full time, part time, or completely retired, who may be travelling to obscure parts of the world or largely homebound, who may be taking care of children, grandchildren, or their own aging parents. Feminists have mulled over the complexities of what it might mean to demand solidarity based on the shared category of "women," as it obscures the diversities of women's experiences across different cultures, races, and classes (hooks 1997, Butler 1990). Similarly, the category of "senior" can be considered a particular kind of social production that at once is a source of solidarity and shared identity, and something to be resisted as a "box" that incompletely defines the self.

In the two roundtables that we started on the AOL and the Web to discuss our research, we had a number of lively conversations on the category of "senior," that informed our understanding of the complex identities participants bring to this community. On one hand, we received a handful of challenges to our research because there are no seniors on our research team. Could we really understand what it meant to be a senior on SeniorNet? Clearly, in this context, the category did matter in some important ways. When we opened up the topic of senior identity as an explicit discussion item on the roundtables, lively exchanges ensued. Many participants pointed out the many positive dimensions associated with their age—wisdom, knowledge and comfort with self, having a good time. But most of the responses in some way worked to contest and complicate any simple notion that we might have had of the category of "senior." The following excerpt summarizes the sense that "seniorness" is an occasion for affinity, but is, at the same time, not exhaustive of a person's identity:

> *"Like attracts like...seniors attract seniors. That is not to say I don't mingle or socialize with younger people, I do..However my comfort zone is with people I can relate to and with...Some of the youth of today do not understand us. They categorize us in one lump image. Not so, and we as seniors know it. Each day is the day I again start to live..."*

SeniorNet is thus a new kind of organization and community that works both to sharpen this age-based identity and muddy its definition. Computer networking has enabled a new form of "locality" to be produced that is roughly defined by age cohort rather than spatial boundary. But just as co-location says little in itself about what a certain group of people might share, "seniors" as a category is an organizationally useful distinction, but one that is not personally or socially encompassing. SeniorNet has provided one of the most successful online spaces for those of an age cohort to explore both their similarities and differences and most importantly, to define a community that is not reducible to their age-based affiliation.

Civility

Once within the boundary of this new territory, what is interesting is less how people do or don't affiliate, construct or deconstruct the category of "senior," but rather what it is that they do find meaningful and rewarding within this shared social space. SeniorNet casts a wide net with its age-based boundary, and a diversity of topics, styles, and personalities co-exist in this community of communities. Despite this diversity, there is a diffuse but pervasive ethos of SeniorNet, which we have come to characterize as "civility," a sense not only of courtesy and manners, but also an ethic of care, friendliness, and support.

In interviews, SeniorNetters repeatedly commented on the warmth and friendliness of the community as something that differentiated SeniorNet from other net communities, and as a reason for their participation and comfort with the community.

This quality of the community has already been alluded to in the discussion of how newcomers are welcomed. In the roundtables in general, off topic comments are treated warmly. In the technical help areas, even very beginner or vague questions are treated with courtesy and warrant thoughtful responses. Throughout the roundtables, but in illness, bereavement, and support areas in particular, the amount of supportive sentiment is overwhelming, expressed through ongoing "hugs," warm wishes, and demonstrations of concern.

Like any community, SeniorNet is not without its occasional conflicts, personality clashes, and flame wars. These conflicts can, however, actually be evidence of the pervasiveness of the ethos of civility, by demonstrating the response to a breech in social etiquette. Posts that are perceived as impolite or argumentative are not considered appropriate. A guest user looking for typical net debates received these responses:

> *This is an interesting group. linked into it via www.hotsheet.com for the first time to see if there were others who, when they were little and saw an airplane, waved at it and screamed, "hi, lindy!" been browsing for the past hour and began to wonder why there's no diversity of opinion. is it because no one seems willing to stir up a little controversy (or maybe a big one)? (Guest User)*

> *Fred - Welcome to the RoundTables. If you think there is no diversity of opinion expressed in the RoundTables, you just haven't been to the right folders. We do argue about religion and we do argue about politics - albeit in a friendly adult manner, seldom with any recriminations. .... (Beth)*

> *FRED I'm laughing at you because you've missed some of the best fights...albeit polite ones. They are to be found in the nostics folder in the liberal folder..my own area for swinging at windmills and the feminist and mens lounge..the lifestyles folder is a good place to get bashed for one reason or another if you are a male..nicely of course. I'm a political liberal and an athiest. want to have a swing at me. Glad to meet up with another lively gadfly.....(Violet)*

Design Implications

SeniorNet demonstrates how a demographic group can be used to define a boundary for a network community. At the same time, the case demonstrates how a demographic category does not encompass the identity of a community. SeniorNet has grown into a community by accommodating not only a diversity of participants but a diversity of content and modalities, enabling people to pursue avenues both related and unrelated to a "senior" identity. Thus these notions of range of modalities and diversity of content discussed in the previous section still emerge as requirements even when a collection of people with common characteristics are drawn to a networked place.

The SN study provides a clear example of "seeding" a net community with a particular set of characteristics and practices. When it is necessary to migrate or expand a community, calling upon senior members to lead by example helps ensure continuity of the community.

While research has shown that the medium of internet communication encourages certain personality traits and practices (Kiesler 1997), such as flaming, the SN community provides a clear counter-example to the assumption that networked interaction must conform to the norm.

Real/Virtual

Network communities are conglomerates of people, practices, and places that are computationally, physically and otherwise embodied. A myriad of technical and social structures and conventions are required to manage the linkages and disjunctures between computational and "real" elements. For example, representations of people and objects in online environments often draw upon pre-existing social conventions. Additionally, events in the physical space, ranging from dinner to a family crisis, may have repercussions in the online space. Actions or practices in the real world, such as introducing yourself or participating in a cocktail party, may have new mechanisms (both technical and social) when adopted to an online space.

In short, there can be numerous links between the real and virtual realms. One hypothesis is that some successful online communities *require* strong and numerous links between the social spaces of the virtual space and the physical space. Amid ongoing debate regarding the value of online participation with respect to the quality of life in one's physically local social set (Kraut et al 1998), our observations of SN demonstrate the feasibly of integrating real life with virtual interactions such that real life referents form the dominant context of their community.

Grounded in Reality

Interactions in SN are integrated with the real-world lives of its members in multiple ways. These connections range from annual face-to-face gatherings to coordinating daily interactions.

We were impressed with the importance of face-to-face interactions amongst a number of the SN members. Some examples are:

- Annual national and regional conferences sponsored by SeniorNet,
- Arranging opportunities to travel together such as booking a block of rooms on a cruise to Alaska,
- Visits to SN members who live in different cities, and
- Informal lunches with members who live in the same area.

One characteristic of the SN population is that many of them have both the time and the ability to get out of the house, if not to travel extensively, at least to attend regional gatherings. In addition to scheduled gatherings and informal social events, a face-to-face encounter can make the support and concern of the online community tangible:

> *"The event (or series thereof) that created an almost unbreakable bond between me and the Seniornet Community was a period which brought with it the end of my mother's life after a*

long illness. It may be important as Seniornet history since I'm sure that many of us at that time (and now) were living in that critical space where we were dealing with children, grands, and aging parent or parents. Most of us had seen the death of loved ones, but were just learning to share that pain with others. ..... And, on the day of her funeral, one couple from Seniornet was standing beside me as an unofficial representative of the group, and we'd made the transition from virtual to real."

Still, many SN members do not frequent face-to-face gatherings as they may be homebound due to infirmity, illness, or caring for a parent or spouse, or they may live in a remote location. Some SN members who are home-bound still find ways to connect, for example with daily phone calls. Others report that SN provides a social outlet even if they do not see each other face-to-face.

Face-to-face encounters are just one way that virtual interactions on SN are connected to the physically-grounded real lives of its members. Other examples are:

- Many people include their real names with their posts, although they may also use a fun nickname/handle as well.

- Couples may use a joint account together. In these cases, SN seems to be part of their lives as a couple. We learned about Alice due to her virtual birthday party on AOL. Although Alice is a long-time participant, she never posts. Her husband, Ken, who is her caretaker, posts updates about their lives and her condition, and he prints out the messages for her to read.

- Interactions in SN are organized around real-life rhythms. For example, the regular evening chatters know that they should wait until after dinner time for most of the crowd to show up.

Reality, Not Just a Feature

The connection between virtual interactions and the real, physical world is more than just a curious characteristic of the SN community. It is key to what makes SN tick, what makes it worthwhile for many of its members.

One of the reasons SN members prefer SN to the other offerings of the Internet and AOL is that they report that they feel more "safe," safe from predatory, deceptive or offensive behavior. In contrast to other virtual sites that try to create a sense of safety via anonymity, SN members share enough personal information so that they no longer feel like strangers to each other on the Internet but they "feel like people like me." One possibility is that the existing social norm of introducing oneself, saying where you're from and a little bit about you is extremely important to follow even, or especially, in virtual interactions. We do not mean to imply that this practice of sharing real-world information is done in a naive or risky manner.

For example, members are instructed to not post their phone numbers and an authorized user (e.g. a host) will remove a phone number from a posting.

In addition to real life practices influencing life in SN, SN also becomes an integral part of real life events. Again, members stress that it is this connection that makes SN special. When Gerine's husband had a heart attack while traveling in Atlanta, she was online with SN when her son called her with the news. She tells one of her online "sisters" Helena the news and rushes to catch a plane to Atlanta:

> *"and I'm standing right in the middle of the Intensive Care Unit floor, and the phone rang. It's Helena: is everything all right? What can we do? The phone rings again: it's John from Maryland. And then, a third time, Bill: do you need anything? Do you need money? Do you want me to come down and be with you? Neither of my kids called, but those SeniorNet friends called. That's caring. When he got home, there were 75 emails waiting for him."*

SeniorNet's mission statement includes "to enhance their lives and enable them to share their knowledge and wisdom." The sharing of life experiences is an important component in the relationships of SN members. When one person writes of a painful, possibly ongoing, issue in their life, not only do other people express their sympathy and support, but some can also write that happened to me too. It is difficult to imagine that this sharing of experience and lessons learned would work without the overall real-world grounding of the community.

Virtual Fun Too

SN is not simply an online place that simply replicates real-world interactions. SNetters still enjoy the freedom of virtual play in the SN Cafe, at online parties, and other online events. This mixture of real-life concerns with the charms of virtual play is wonderful to experience.

Design Implications

Understanding the role of design in integrating real-world components into a virtual space is a challenge. More and more evidence seems to point to the benefits of connecting the real and virtual realms. What these connections are varies from community to community. Safety concerns for children are different than those for adults. Workplace groups using media spaces with audio and video connections have different needs than recreational groups that use primarily textual communications. The key message here is that designers should not discount the value of real-world connections and should provide multiple paths for information to flow between the two realms. Additionally, practices from representing oneself to assigning rights and responsibilities can fruitfully spring from existing real-world norms.

Concluding Thoughts

SeniorNet is an active community that combines work, learning and play. Our hope is that the details of this study will fuel the intuitions of designers and members of network communities. General observations from this study include:

- Primitive building blocks can be the foundation for community interaction if members can appropriate these tools, technical infrastructure supports predictable rhythms, and these blocks are designed together to create a sense of common place.

- Common Internet customs do not have to be the norm. In SeniorNet lurking is an accepted and encouraged practice. Civility reigns in contrast to flaming and other antagonistic behaviors. Members refer to their community as a place that is "right for them" in contrast to the rest of the Internet as a foreign and unfriendly experience.

- Longevity of a community requires providing a range of ways for members to participate in order to support diversity within the community as well as encourage participation over time. Migration and other major shifts in the community require leadership by example from senior members to maintain the community's practices and characteristics.

- Connections with the "real world" can be the backbone of a community while still partaking in the advantages of virtual interaction.

Acknowledgments

This research has been funded by the National Science Foundation under Grant SBR-9712414. We are grateful to the SeniorNet staff who supported us in this project, especially Marcie Schwarz and Ann Wrixon, and to all of the SeniorNet members who generously shared their network communities and classes with us. We appreciate the contributions of our Advisory Board members, Claude Fischer, Malcolm McCullough, Sim Sitkin, and Terry Winograd, and our Xerox PARC colleagues Paul Dourish and Steve Harrison. And we thank Luna Ito-Fisher, who joined our project at its midpoint, for her cooperation and charm during our meetings.

References

Butler, Judith. 1990. Gender Trouble: Feminism and the Subversion of Identity. New York: Routledge.

Hagel, J. and Armstrong, A. G. (1997). *Net Gain: Expanding Markets Through Virtual Communities*. Harvard Business School Press. Cambridge.

hooks, bell. 1997. "Sisterhood: Political Solidarity between Women." In Diana Tietjens Meyers Ed., *Feminist Social Thought: A Reader*. New York: Routledge, pp. 484-500.

Kiesler, S. (1997) *Culture of the Internet*. Lawrence Erlbaum Associates.

Kollock, P. (1996) Design Principles for Online Communities" in *Harvard Conference on the Internet and Society* also published in *PC Update,* 15(5): 58-60, June 1998.

Kraut, R. Patterson, M. Lundmard, V. Kiesler, S., Mukophadhyay,T & Scherlis, W. (1998). "Internet paradox: A social technology that reduces social involvement and psychological well-being?" *American Psychologist*, Vol. 53, No. 9, 10171031.

Kraut, R. E., Scherlis, W., Patterson, M., Kiesler, S. & Mukhopadhyay,T. (1998). "Implications of the Internet Paradox research," in *Communications of the ACM*, 41(12), 21-22.

Mynatt, E.D., Adler, A., Ito, M., and O'Day, V.L. (1998). Network Communities: Something Old, Something, New, Something Borrowed... *In Computer Supported Cooperative Work, Interaction and Collaboration in MUDs,* Vol. 7, Number 1/2, 123-156.

Schuler, D. and Stone, T. (1996) *New Community Networks: Wired for Change*. Addison Wesley.

Sproull, L, and Kiesler, S. (1995). *Connections: New Ways of Working in Networked Organizations*. MIT Press.

Rheingold, H. (1993) *The Virtual Community: Homesteading on the Electronic Frontier*. Addison Wesley Publishing Company.

S. Bødker, M. Kyng, and K. Schmidt (eds.). *Proceedings of the Sixth European Conference on Computer-Supported Cooperative Work, 12-16 September 1999, Copenhagen, Denmark*
©1999 Kluwer Academic Publishers. Printed in the Netherlands

GestureLaser and GestureLaser Car
Development of an Embodied Space to Support Remote Instruction

Keiichi Yamazaki,   Akiko Yamazaki
Department of Liberal Arts, Saitama University, Japan
yamakei@sacs.sv.saitama-u.ac.jp, RXU04370@nifty.ne.jp

Hideaki Kuzuoka,   Shinya Oyama
Institute of Engineering Mechanics and Systems
{kuzuoka | oyama}@esys.tsukuba.ac.jp

Hiroshi Kato,   Hideyuki Suzuki
C&C Media Research Laboratories, NEC Corporation, Japan
{kato | hideyuki_suzuki}@ccm.cl.nec.co.jp

Hiroyuki Miki
Media Laboratories, Oki Electric Industry Co. Ltd., Japan
miki455@oki.co.jp

Abstract. When designing systems that support remote instruction on physical tasks in the real world, one must consider four requirements: 1) participants must be able to take appropriate positions, 2) they must be able to see and show gestures, 3) they must be able to organize the arrangement of bodies and tools and gestural expression sequentially and interactively 4) the instructor must be able to give instructions to more than one operator at a time. GestureLaser and GestureLaser Car are systems we have developed in an attempt to satisfy these requirements. GestureLaser is a remote controlled laser pointer that allows an instructor to show gestural expressions referring to real world objects from a distance. GestureLaser Car is a remote controlled vehicle on which the GestureLaser can be mounted. Experiments with this combination indicate that it satisfies the four requirements reasonably well and can be used effectively to give remote instruction. Following the comparison of the GestureLaser system with existing systems, some implications to the design of embodied spaces are described.

Introduction

We propose a new system, the 'GestureLaser system', which allows us to instruct multiple operators at a remote site. The goal of this system is to facilitate remote instruction on physical tasks in the real world, such as repair and maintenance of mechanical devices, laboratory classes, medical treatment, etc. At the same time, we want to clarify the requirements and problems in the design of remote instruction systems for multiple operators in the real world.

In this paper, we consider the basic elements required to support instruction on physical tasks in the real world by reviewing conversational analysis and ethnomethodological studies of work places. We then introduce GestureLaser and GestureLaser Car. Based on observation of remote collaboration experiments, we show that GestureLaser and GestureLaser Car are effective in supporting remote instruction on physical tasks in the real world. By comparing GestureLaser system with other systems that have been proposed up to now, we clarify factors that should be considered when designing a system that supports collaborations by multiple operators in the real world.

Collaboration in the Real World

Most current groupware uses fixed computers and fixed TV monitors to mediate communication. This means that shared objects have to appear on such monitors. In other words, the work area is confined to what can be captured by a stationary camera, and displayed on a flat screen. Other shared objects are usually limited to computer data such as drawings and texts, which are stored in a common database.

On the other hand, there are many tasks that require operators to share physical objects and their disposition in the real world. In fact most of our tasks such as laboratory classes, machinery assembly, furniture repair, etc., require us to collaborate using the human body and physical tools. In this paper, we consider a system that can support an instructor to direct multiple operators at remote sites, as required in remote medicine, remote education and so on.

What, then, is necessary to support remote instruction on physical tasks in the real world? In order to get an answer to this question, we would like to review some ethnomethodological studies.

Conversational analysis and ethnomethodological studies of workplaces (Heritage, 1997; Goodwin, 1994) are strongly interested in problems of instruction and collaborative work in the real world. Their main interest is to explain how participants organize human actions interactively and sequentially. For example, when B answers A' s question, B displays how B understood A's question. Through this sequential understanding mechanism, conversation is organized interactively and sequentially (Heritage, 1997).

According to Heath these mechanisms are also relevant in bodily interaction. Heath says that "The emergent and sequential organization of interaction is also relevant to how we might consider the contextual or in situ significance of visual conduct and the physical properties of human environment" (Heath, 1997).

For example, A says to B 'take this' and at the same time points to an object (perhaps a book on the table). A's pointing connects with A's utterance 'take this'. At the same time pointing is organized not only by A's utterance but also by B's utterance and bodily movements. A's pointing is done at the time and space when and where B can see A's pointing to the book. When B sees A's pointing to the book, B turns his body to the direction of the book and says 'okay'. B's body movement and utterance display his understanding of A's utterance and gesture. After that A draws away A's hand which pointed to the book. By withdrawing the hand, A displays A's understanding of B's understanding to all participants, including B (Goodwin, 1994; Goodwin, 1998). Gestures, including pointing, are connected with utterances. They are performed and monitored in an arrangement of bodies and tools. In collaborative work, participants maintain and reorganize arrangements of bodies and tools interactively to monitor their pointing and other work (Kendon, 1990).

According to Goodwin (Goodwin, 1994), when instruction is given face-to-face, operators move their bodies into appropriate positions, which allow them to see the shared artifact. The instructor likewise moves in such a way that his view of the shared object is not obstructed by the operators and makes sure that the operators are watching his/her gestures while they are given instructions. The operators in turn express their understanding using words and gestures while they are performing their tasks. During such sequences an instructor and operators not only use words, but also gestures, and body arrangement. It should be noted that body arrangement is not static, but changes dynamically during collaboration.

These resources can be monitored naturally when participants are talking face-to-face. When they have to collaborate via video-mediated communication systems, however, such resources easily become disembodied (Heath et al., 1991).

In order to alleviate this problem, we must design new video-mediated communication systems that can embody participants behavior (Kato et al., 1997). How is it possible to embody participant's interactions via video communication? Based on the above mentioned ethnomethodological studies and our own studies on video mediated communication, we formulate the following four requirements for a system intended to support remote instruction in the real world.

(1) *Arrangement of bodies and tools requirement*: The arrangement of bodies and tools should be appropriate for monitoring other participants behavior for both instructor and operator. In particular, (i) the operator should be able to see where the instructor is pointing; (ii) the instructor should be able to see that the

operator is orienting himself/herself towards the indicated object as well as the pointer, when he/she observing the instructor's pointing; (iii) the instructor should be able to reassure the operator by words and actions that the instructor is aware of the operator's orientation.

(2) ***Gestural expression requirement***: The instructor must be able to use freely not only verbal expressions, but also body movements and bodily expressions (gestures).

(3) ***Sequential organization requirement***: Sequential and interactive organization of the arrangement of bodies and tools and gestural expression must be possible.

(4) ***Multiple operators requirement***: All the above should work even when several operators are present.

We named virtual spaces that satisfy these requirements "embodied spaces". By satisfying these requirements, we believe, a system can embody the behavior of the participants.

We used these four requirements to design a video mediated system and developed our own embodied space system which we call GestureLaser system. We have conducted some experiments with the system.

The analysis of the experiments shown in this paper aims not just to show the effectiveness of our system. By developing a system and conducting experiments with it, we want to find out what kind of resources participants use and how they organize their bodies for participation in interaction in this particular video mediated communication system (Heath et al., 1992; Heath et al., 1995; Dourish et al., 1992; Nardi et al., 1993). By doing so we will be able to compare our system with other systems and design an improved system.

GestureLaser and GestureLaser Car

Laser Pointers are convenient devices and quite popular tools for presentations at scientific conferences. A speaker can precisely indicate positions and spaces to a large audience. Sometimes he/she can show motions and directions by its movement. Although these expressions are not as good as real hand gestures, when used with verbal explanations, a laser spot can communicate a variety of meanings. Since the laser emitter is very small nowadays, a system can be implemented small and light enough so that it can be mounted on a mobile mechanism and thus permits a large work area. Based on these ideas, we have developed a remotely controlled laser pointing system named GestureLaser and GestureLaser Car.

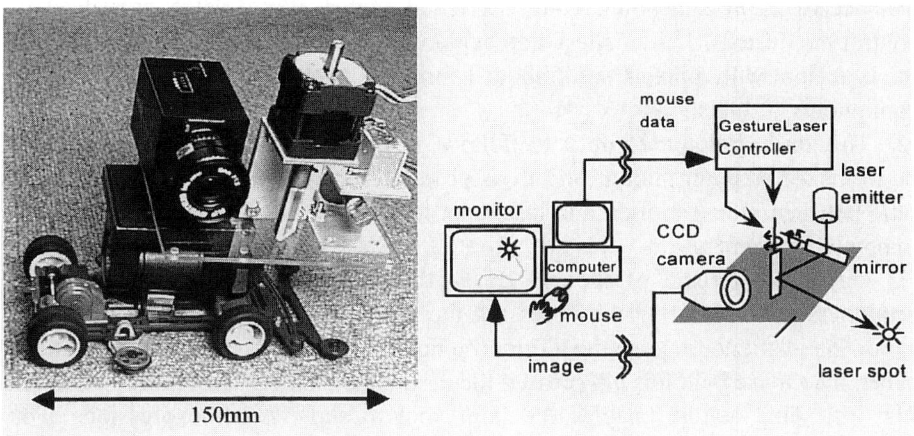

Figure 1. GestureLaser and GestureLaser Car.   Figure 2. Overview of GestureLaser system.

GestureLaser

The GestureLaser is a remote controlled laser spot actuator developed by the authors (Kuzuoka et al., 1998). GestureLaser reflects the laser emitter's ray off two orthogonal mirrors into the workspace.

One of the authors had previously developed a system for support of remote collaboration called GestureCam (Kuzouka et al., 1994). This system consisted of a camera and laser pointer mounted on a remote controlled manipulator with three degrees of freedom of movement. Since camera and laser pointer were mounted on the same manipulator, the pointer could not be moved independent of the camera. Although the instructor could move the laser spot, because of technical limitations, this could not be done with the precision and ease of GestureLaser, while the quality of the camera picture also deteriorated.

In contrast to this, GestureLaser's pointer is independent of the camera, so that the instructor can move the pointer even while the camera remains fixed (Fig.1, Fig.2). Because of this, the instructor is able to transmit a variety of expressions through movements of the laser pointer.

We give a short description of the main characteristics of the GestureLaser System.

(1) The laser spot can be moved like a mouse cursor. The instructor controls the location of the laser spot with a mouse. Input from the mouse is sent through the instructor's computer to the GestureLaser Controller, where it is translated into mirror movement. As shown in Fig. 2, the instructor can monitor the position of the laser spot as well as objects and operators on an image from a CCD camera. It is thus possible for the instructor to treat the laser spot as if it were a mouse cursor (Fig. 3a). In this way, the instructor can show various expressions such as rotation and direction by a movement of the laser spot. To allow precise pointing even at a

244

distance of 2-3m a stepping motor (Oriental Motor: PMC33BHV2) is used to control the mirrors. The smallest step angle is 0.036°, which allows movement of the laser spot with a precision of about 1 mm at a distance 2 m, making it appear continuous.

(2) The laser pointer is able to follow fast movements. By using a high performance stepping motor, and by appropriately adjusting the correspondence ratio between mouse motion and laser spot motion, we were able to avoid delays in pointer movement.

(3) One characteristic of the system is that the instructor can increase the brightness of the laser spot by pressing the left mouse button to give emphasis. When the instructor presses the left mouse button, the laser spot becomes brighter. When the mouse button is not pressed the laser spot is dim, but remains visible (cf. Fig. 3b). This feature enables the laser spot to show richer expressions. For example, the instructor can emphasize an expression by making the laser spot blink by repeatedly pressing the left mouse button.

(4) One important aspect of GestureLaser is the fact that it is light and portable. It can easily be mounted on a transport device that moves it into appropriate positions.

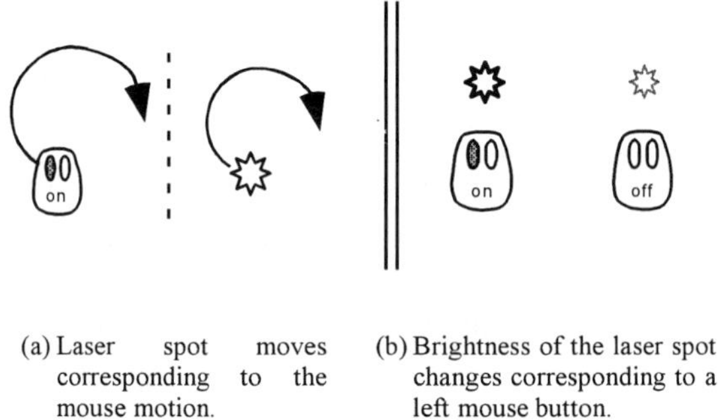

(a) Laser spot moves corresponding to the mouse motion.

(b) Brightness of the laser spot changes corresponding to a left mouse button.

Figure3. Control of a laser spot.

GestureLaser Car

By conducting numerous preliminary experiments we realized that in order to actually use the GestureLaser for instruction in the real world, it is necessary to solve the following problems. (1) Sometimes certain areas cannot be viewed by the camera either because they are hidden behind objects or because of a restricted field of vision. (2) It may be impossible to point at a desired location because the laser beam is obstructed by objects or operators.

When we tried to use GestureLaser in the real world we thus ran into problems, because the instructor could not see the object of instruction sufficiently well or because the operator could not see the laser spot. We therefore decided to take advantage of GestureLaser's lightness and portability and constructed a system where it can be moved by remote control. More specifically, we mounted GestureLaser on a four-wheeled conveyance, which we call GestureLaser Car. This car can move horizontally on rails, controlled by the instructor's keyboard. Fig.4 gives an idea of the working space. A rail, comprising a straight part and rounded corners at the ends with an overall length of 140 cm is installed at a height of approximately 150 cm. It thus becomes possible to change the position and angle of the GestureLaser. Operators work and receive instructions in front of the rail, while the instructor can watch them on his monitor and give instructions.

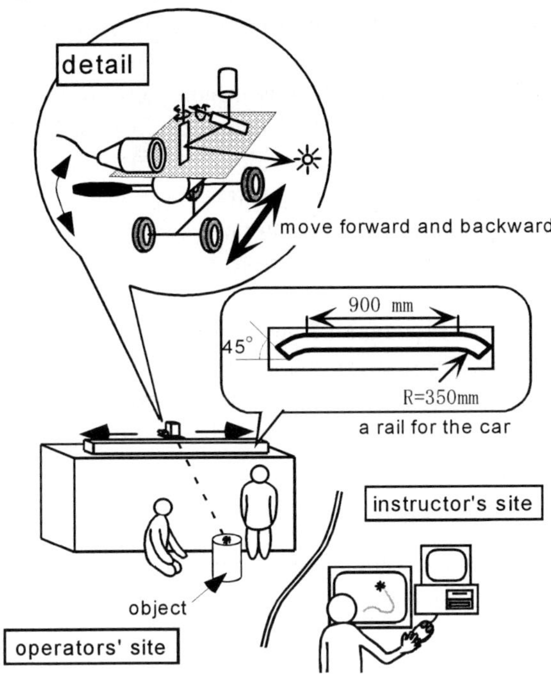

Figure 4. GestureLaser Car and experimental environment.

Experiments

We performed experiments to see how subjects performed under remote instruction in the real, three-dimensional world using a GestureLaser and a GestureLaser Car.

Experimental Tasks

As instructors we used 2 students who had practiced the basic use of the setup to some extent. The 7 students who worked as operators had no prior knowledge of the tasks required.

There were two kinds of tasks. Task 1 was the installation of a PCI board in a PCI slot of a personal computer. Task 2 was the assembly of furniture. Task 1 was performed twice with one instructor and one operator (one-on-one) and three sessions were conducted. Task 2 was performed in a one-on-one session as well as in two sessions with two operators (one-on-two). For each session the combination of instructor and operator was changed. Instructor and operators were placed in separate rooms, but allowed to communicate freely through a sound system. The instructor could thus accompany pointing with verbal instruction. Each session took about 30 to 40 minutes. Several VCRs were used to record participants' activities and recorded videos were used for later analysis.

In the following we would like to demonstrate how instructors and operators communicated during remote instructions on physical tasks in the real world. We perform a detailed analysis of video data from instruction as it occurred during our experiments.

First, we analyze the arrangement of bodies and tools when the GestureLaser system was used. Second, gestural expressions with a remote controlled laser spot are analyzed. Finally, using a transcript, we analyze how interaction was sequentially organized between the instructor and the multiple operators.

Analysis of Experiments (1) — Arrangement of Bodies and Tools —

We first asked in which position the instructor and operators gave and listened to directions and performed tasks. We also analyzed under which circumstances the instructor moved the GestureLaser Car.

The Basic Arrangement

Fig. 5 shows an example of the position of operator and instructor during experiments. The GestureLaser is off to the side behind the operator while the object of instruction is in front.

It is thus not only possible for the operator to see the laser pointer and the indicated object, the arrangement of bodies and tools also allows the instructor to recognize that the operator is looking at the object. It is realized because pointing is projected directly onto an object where it can be seen by a camera.

This natural body arrangement is not realized with existing video mediated communication systems, where it is thus often not easy to determine "what a co-participant is referring to" (Hindmarsh, 1998).

Figure 5. Basic arrangement. The instructor (upper right) and the operator (lower left).

Movement of GestureLaser Car

The instructor moved the GestureLaser Car when he was trying to capture an object outside of the camera's angle of vision or when it was impossible to point at an object with the laser, because the operator was in the way.

In the example shown in Fig. 6, the instructor began instruction only after having moved the laser on its conveyance into a position that avoided the operator and made pointing possible.

By moving the GestureLaser the instructor was able to see objects in a large region of three dimensional space and point at these objects with the laser. The operators, on the other hand, also moved when the GestureLaser moved and a new spot was indicated, in order to better be able to see the laser beam and the object pointed at, creating again the previously mentioned basic arrangement. In this way the GestureLaser Car mounted GestureLaser was able to satisfy the 'arrangement of bodies and tools' requirement.

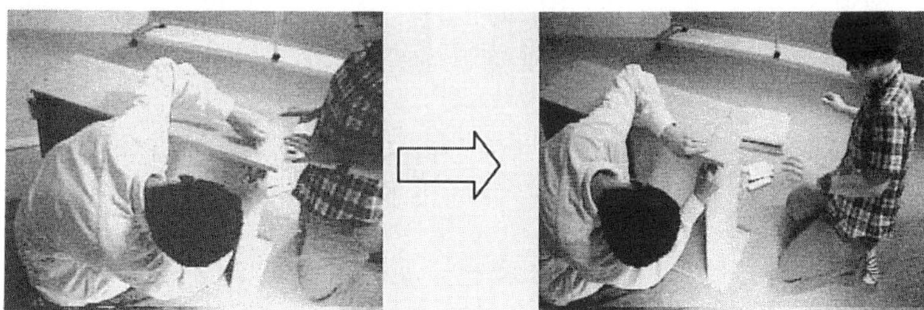

Figure 6. Movement of GestureLaser Car to change angle.

Analysis of Experiments (2) — Expressions with a Laser Spot —

The GestureLaser is designed not only to accurately indicate a location in the real world, but also to convey instructions by blinking and movement controlled by a mouse.

By studying the scenes occurring during actual experiments one realizes that there are numerous cases where the dynamic features of the laser pointer, motion and blinking, are employed. There are also cases where motion and blinking are used at the same time. We call the expressions made possible by use of these dynamic features of the laser 'gestural expressions'.

Use of GestureLaser's gestural expressions can be roughly divided into two categories: Instances where the instructor is using motion of the laser or blinking to achieve movement of the object or operators, and instances where the instructor is trying to indicate an object or a particular property of the object by tracing with the laser spot or by blinking.

Directing Motion

i) Using pointer movement

In Fig. 7 the operator was being asked to turn the object, which had been placed parallel to the angle of the camera, sideways. The instructor indicated this by moving the laser spot in an arc on the floor, as shown by the arrow in the picture. The concrete indication of the direction of rotation facilitated the operator's comprehension of the instructor's intent, and easily accomplished its aim. We also observed cases where the laser moved around at a spot visible to the operator to tell the operator to do something there.

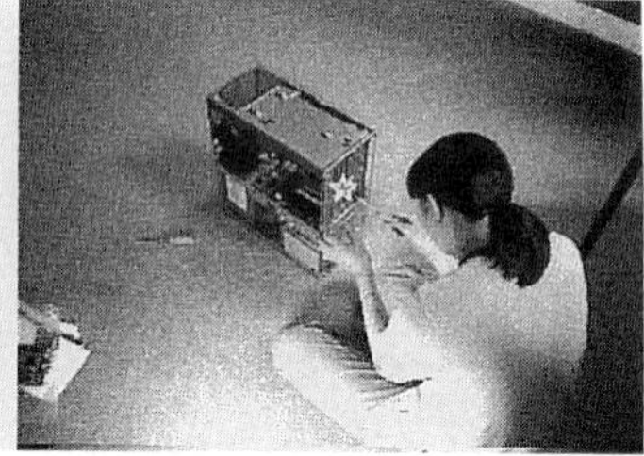

Figure 7. Requesting rotation.   Figure 8. Use of blinking.

ii) Use of blinking

Tasks involving movement of the object are not limited to moving the object up, left, etc., but also include things like pushing buttons, making a hole, and screwing in a screw. Indicating such actions through laser motion only is difficult. In these cases blinking was used. Fig. 8 shows an example where blinking was used to indicate when a screw was to be turned.

iii) Use of blinking and motion at the same time

When the object is to be moved, the direction may be up, down, left, or right.

However, if the instructor simply moves the pointer in the desired direction, the problem is how to return it to its initial position if the gesture must be repeated. The operator will also observe the return movement and may get confused. Consequently, except in the case of rotation, there were cases where the intended direction of movement was not communicated well. In these cases it helped, when the instructor indicated the starting point of the movement by blinking before moving the pointer.

Indicating Objects

Indicating objects in the real world does not simply mean placing the pointer precisely on a certain spot. The same spot on an object may have different aspects depending on how it is perceived: there may be an indentation, or a long groove, or the spot may be part of a surface, all at once. In everyday situations we use gestures such as waving our hands, etc., and utter demonstratives such as 'this' or 'that one', while tracing the shape of it, or pointing repeatedly while moving our finger, when referring to an object. With GestureLaser the instructors referred to the various objects in the workspace during instruction with demonstratives, while tracing the object with movements of the laser spot or making it blink at a certain point. Instructions making use of this capacity of the GestureLaser were well understood by operators.

i) Indicating a line by tracing

In Fig. 9 the laser spot is moved in the direction of the arrow following a groove in the board. The instructor traces the groove many times while giving verbal explanations.

ii) Indicating a surface by tracing

Fig. 10 shows an example where the same method of tracing is used to indicate a surface. The instructor shows that he is referring to this surface by moving the laser spot around on it while saying 'This side of the board...'

Figure 9. Following a groove.   Figure10. Indicating a surface.

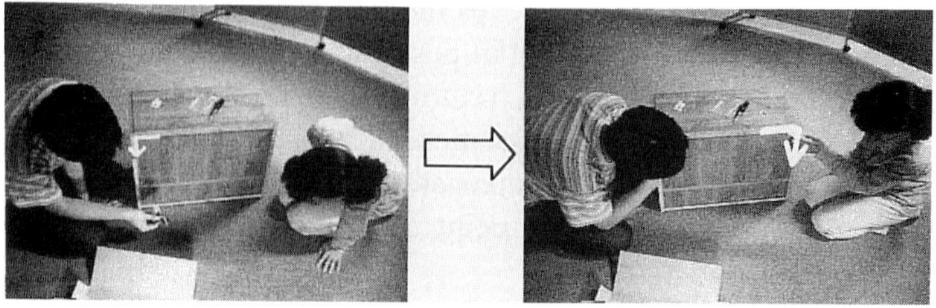

Figure 11. Tracing the left corner.   Figure 12. Then the right corner.

iii) Reference to an object by tracing of its shape

The instructors were able to refer to objects or tools of a certain shape by tracing and by drawing the shape with the laser spot. In Fig. 11 and Fig. 12 one can see how this was done by tracing, but there were also cases where the instructor drew the shape of a tool, that was not at hand, on the floor to help the operators search for it.

iv) Indicating small objects

Small objects, such as screws, were indicated by blinking. There were also cases where a small object was indicated by tracing with the pointer around it.

Analysis of Experiments (3) —Interaction with Multiple Operators—

Here we would like to consider an example of instruction with more than one operator in somewhat more detail. In particular we are interested in how the operators indicate their understanding of the instructor's gestural expressions, and how in turn the instructor recognizes this.

Fig. 13 shows an exchange between an instructor and two operators. The physical setting of the scene is shown in Fig.11 and Fig.12. In this scene, the instructor was trying to instruct the operators as to where a small triangular pieces were to be attached. At (1) in the transcript the instructor, while saying "here", pointed at the upper left corner of the object with the laser spot. However, at this very moment only O2 was watching the spot and O1 who was bending his body toward the other side of the cupboard is not ready to see the spot. Soon the instructor restarted his instruction. At (2) in the transcript the instructor pointed at the same corner of the cupboard again with the word 'here'. Immediate after this restarted instruction, O1 set his body toward the laser spot. By his body movement O1's recipiency was socially indicated and thus a shared space where instruction could be done was mutually constructed. However, the instructor moved the laser spot from left to right and began tracing the right corner with the word "here"(3). It is presumed that this was because the laser spot was blocked by the head of O1 who moved his body.

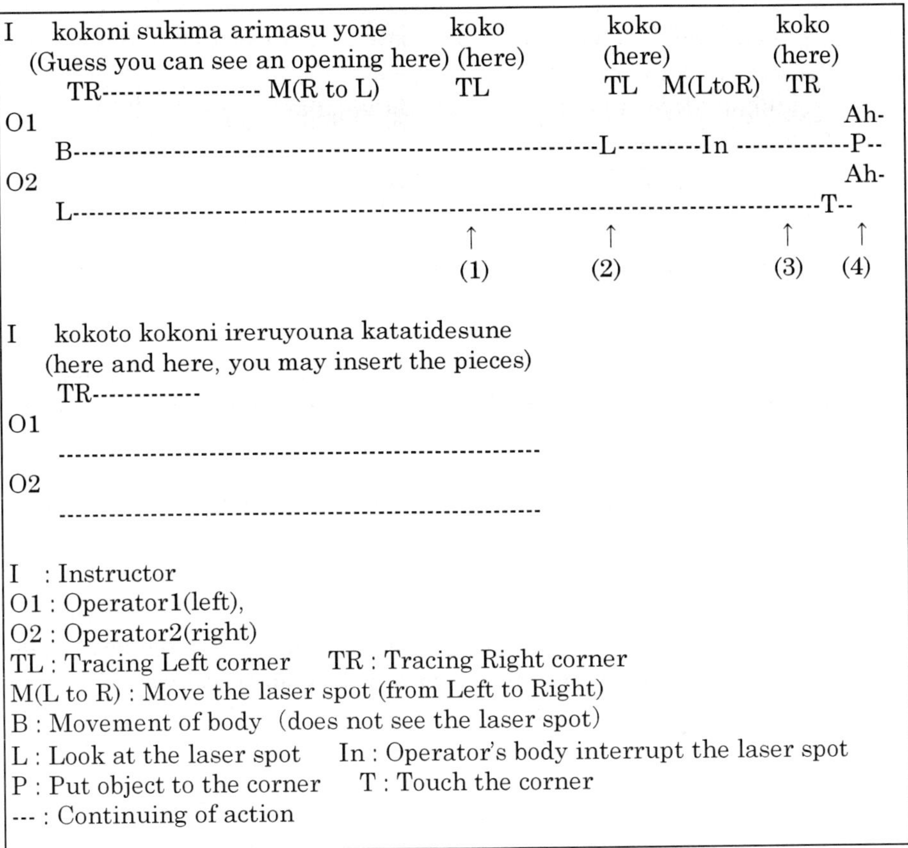

Figure 13. Transcript.

Right after that both of the operators said 'ah' (4) simultaneously, indicating that they had understood the instruction. This indication of understanding was followed by the instructor's quickly uttered summary, i. e., "here and here, you may insert the pieces" and he traced the right corner again, which displayed the instructor's understanding that the operators had understood his instruction.

As shown at (1), (2), and (3) in transcript 1, the instructor's instruction used movement of the laser spot accompanied by verbal expressions. Then, the operators' understanding was shown by moving their hands to the indicated places (as shown at (4) in the transcript). Furthermore, the instructor's understanding of the operators' understanding was expressed by tracing the corner again with verbal expressions (as shown at (5) in the transcript). Thus motion of the laser spot was one of the important resources to mediate interaction and reciprocal understanding between the instructor and the operators.

When guiding the work of more than one operator performing a task in the real world under everyday circumstances, it often happens that instructions are not directed at all operators at once. Instead 'individual instruction' is used to make operators perform different subtasks at the same time. GestureLaser allows the instructor to direct each operator to perform an independent task or to make operators perform different tasks at the same time. There were several instances of this in our experiments.

Evaluation of the Experiments

The analysis of the experiments in which GestureLaser Car was used shows that the system satisfies the four requirements set out for support of remote collaboration in the real world.

In particular, the 'arrangement of bodies and tools' requirement is satisfied, as indicated in Analysis of Experiments (1) because of GestureLaser's wide range and the mobility contributed by GestureLaser Car.

Analysis of Experiments (2) shows that GestureLaser with GestureLaser Car also meets the 'gesture expression' requirement through a variety of gestural expressions using movement and blinking.

One may think that GestureLaser is inferior to other remote collaboration systems in that it has only the laser spot to express actions and reference. However, when one looks at the actual experiments, one sees that the instructors were able to use their knowledge of particular aspects of the work object (a corner, point, side, or surface, a distinctive shape or property) to create effective gestural expressions with the limited repertoire of laser spot movements and blinking. A line can be indicated by 'following' it with the laser spot, a surface by 'circular movement' of the spot, a point of interest by 'keeping steady and blinking'.

The 'multiple operators' requirement is fulfilled because GestureLaser and GestureLaser Car are able to point at each operator in his/her work area. In order to give different instructions to individual operators, it must be possible for the instructor to give instructions to each operator in the space where s/he is working (his/her work area) and the instructor and each operator together must be able to observe how the instructions are given. This must furthermore be transparent to the other operators. If this is not the case, discrepancies in the process of instruction will occur. As shown in Analysis of Experiments (3), GestureLaser solves this problem.

Also this analysis showed that the GestureLaser system could support sequential organization requirement. By controlling a laser spot with a mouse the instructor could show gestures directly on each object. The instructor could also observe the operators' activities and orientation. Furthermore, by moving the laser spot in response to the operators' behaviors, the instructor could sequentially show understanding, approval, or disapproval regarding the operators' actions.

In this way GestureLaser is able to seamlessly fuse actions occurring in the world of the computer (mouse moves) and work in the real world, using the practice and knowledge of body movements and body language as a guide, and is thus able to support work in the real world.

Comparison with Other Systems

Although we could show some advantages of the GestureLaser, it also has some limitations. In this section, by comparing the GestureLaser with existing systems, we try to describe some factors that we must pay attention, when we design improved systems.

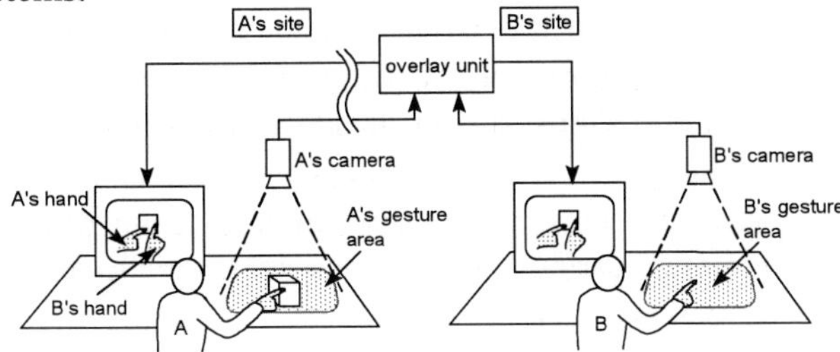

Figure 14. TeamWorkStation type configuration.

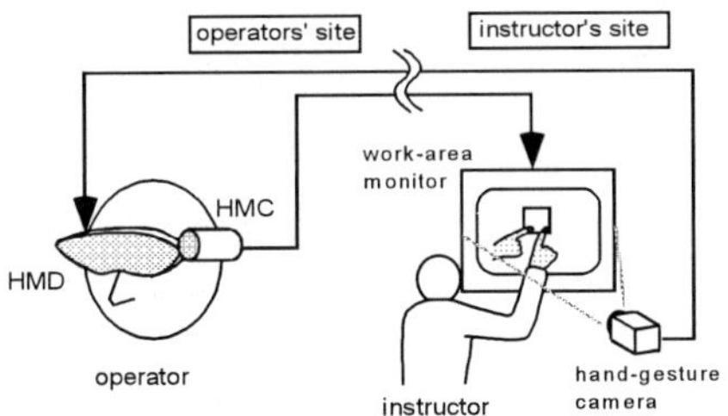

Figure 15. Remote instruction system using HMD + Head Mounted Camera.

At first, we briefly explain some existing remote collaboration systems that enabled the use of gestures. VideoDraw (Tang et al., 1990) and TeamWorkStation (Ishii et al., 1991) (Fig.14) are pioneering systems that overlay participants' hand images over shared desktop surfaces. ClearBoard (Ishii et al., 1992) is an improved system that additionally overlays participants' upper body images over the shared drawing surfaces and effectively supports eye contact and gaze awareness. Double DigitalDesk uses a unique mechanism to overlay hand images (Wellner, 1993). A video projector and a camera is mounted above each desk. The camera grabs images from its local desktop and the projector projects down the image from a remote desktop. In this way, artifacts and hand gestures on the local desk are projected onto a remote desk and vice versa. Finally, some systems used combinations of Head Mounted Display (HMD) and Head Mounted Camera

254

(similar to Fig. 15) to give remote instructions (Kraut et al., 1996; Kuzuoka, 1992).

In the following, GestureLaser and the above mentioned systems are compared in terms of expressiveness of gestures, visibility of gestures, width of work area, possible number of participants, and safety.

Expressiveness

When a person wants to express complicated three-dimensional motions or hand posture, a mere laser spot is not good enough. In such cases, to use real hand images like previously mentioned existing systems may be better. As mentioned in the following chapter, however, there are some problems to use such technologies for remote instruction on physical tasks in the real world.

Also, as already described in this paper, it should be remembered that assistance of verbal expressions and context of interaction make an instructor possible to communicate various expressions by moving and changing the brightness of a laser spot.

Visibility of Gestures

In order to support remote instruction of real world tasks, it is necessary that a system can show gestural expressions so that operators can easily recognize them.

Although VideoDraw and ClearBoard basically allow participants to do their tasks only on desktops, when a technique like TeamWorkStation is employed, it is possible to give remote instructions on real world tasks. Since objects are specified on a monitor, however, a worker has to find the real physical object in the real environment. When there are similar objects close to an intended object, it is hard to determine the correct one (Kuzuoka et al., 1995).

Systems using video projection work well as long as the work area is flat, as is the case with DigitalDesk, but when they are to be used for instruction in using machinery, problems arise. The reasons for this have to do with the fact that normal projectors are not very bright, which requires the workspace to be relatively dark. When the workspace is bigger than a table surface, when the work objects are widely distributed in space, or when they have complicated shapes, it becomes difficult to use projection. There are 3 reasons for this: 1) the projected image blurs when it is not in the focus area, 2) when the projection surface is not almost perpendicular to the direction of projection, the image will get distorted, 3) when operators enter between the projector and the object, shadows will appear.

In the case of the GestureLaser, since only a laser spot is projected, problem 1 and 2 are alleviated. Also GestureLaser Car alleviates problem 3 since it can change the position of the GestureLaser when an operator obstructs the laser beam. If a small, light weight and bright video projector is developed in the future, however, some problems of the video projector can be alleviated by mounting it on a mechanical rover.

HMD + Head Mounted Camera may be the best way to show an operator hand gestures because hand images appears right in front of an operator's eyes. Based on our experiences, however, many operators complained that such hand images obstructed their view.

Work Area

The extent of work areas of systems other than HMD + Head Mounted Camera are limited because cameras and displays are settled in fixed positions. HMD + Head Mounted Camera, on the other hand, can turn any space into a shared work area as long as a worker can look at it. Because of the narrow field of vision and low resolution of cameras and HMDs, however, visibility of most of the HMDs is much lower than that of the naked eye.

In the case of GestureLaser, because it was designed light and small, the work area could be enlarged by using GestureLaser Car. The current implementation, however, allows the system to move only along rails and it cannot point at an object from behind. Currently, we are planning to mount the system on a movable robot like the PRoP (Paulos et al., 1998).

Support of Collaborative Work with More than One Operator

When it comes to complicated tasks such as assembly, repair, emergency medicine, etc., it will often be the case that several operators are needed. The system must therefore provide effective support for instruction in such situations as well.

In HMD systems, even if all operators are equipped the same way, each operator's angle of view will be different and thus the pointing device can be overlaid on only one view at a time. Of course one might attempt to give each operator a camera and the instructor a monitor for each operator, but then the task of mapping each operator's position and viewpoint in the work space becomes a burden for the instructor.

As for video projection systems, the problem of obstruction by operators becomes all the more severe as the number of operators increases.

GestureLaser, on the other hand, can point directly at objects independent of the operator's angle of view, and can give precise instructions to several operators at the same time. There remains of course the problem of obstruction, but this can be alleviated by switching to GestureLaser Car.

Safety

One of the big problems of using a laser pointer is that it is dangerous if a strong laser beam gets directly into an eye. Although, our laser emitter is not strong and we have never experienced such an accident, we have to consider using a low power laser or normal light beam.

HMD also has some problems. Since it limits the field of vision and the resolution of a worker's sight, it can be dangerous for him/her to walk around.

Summary of Comparison

In summary, GestureLaser system can simultaneously support four aspects (expressiveness, visibility, work area, number of operators) reasonably well. Therefore, in order to support remote instruction on physical tasks in the real world with multiple operators, the GestureLaser system has advantages over other systems.

We also realize, however, that there are many other kinds of remote collaboration for which the GestureLaser may not be the best solution. Number of participants, kinds of tasks, and physical and social environment of tasks change the utility of a systems. For example, for a task that requires only one operator, HMD may be better than the GestureLaser. On the other hand, for desktop tasks, Double DigitalDesk maybe the best. The purpose of this paper is not to claim that the current GestureLaser is the best system for all the situations but to clarify factors that should be considered and functions to be improved when designing a system. Thus this comparison is important to design a next system. So far, we are planning to add a laser drawing function to improve expressiveness and mounting the GestureLaser on a mobile robot to further enlarge the work area. We also have to think seriously about increasing the safety of the system.

Conclusions and Implications

In this paper, we have shown that GestureLaser and GestureLaser Car can reasonably satisfy the requirements for support of remote instruction on physical tasks in the real world. We do not mean to claim that the system we designed is more effective for various tasks across various settings compared to existing systems. But by observing the interaction of participants while they were using the system, we tried to clarify how participants use their bodies and the tools afforded by the system for achieving their tasks. Understanding of these processes is essential for designing and elaborating systems for remote instruction in the real world, such as remote education, tele-medicine and so on.

We were able to delineate some implications to the design of embodied spaces, i.e. virtual environments that can embody participants' behavior. The main point is that the system should not support gestures as individual iconic expressions (Luff, 1999). That is when a remote collaboration system is designed, it is important not only to enable the system to show gestural expressions well, but also to consider how such expressions can be used as parts of the resources of sequentially organized interactions. To allow efficient use of these resources, the system must be designed in such a way that participants can use gestures and arrange and orient their bodies without time delay, and such resources must be simultaneously observable.

With GestureLaser, since it allows the instructor to project a laser spot directly onto an object, operators can monitor gestural expressions easily. Furthermore, because the camera is placed so that the laser spot and operators can be monitored simultaneously, an instructor can observe operators' actions and orientations in response to instructions. Furthermore, by employing a mouse to control the position of the laser spot, an instructor can use various gestural expressions with minimum time delay. These sequential gestures also help the instructor to show understanding, approval, and disapproval to operators.

Although GestureLaser cannot show gestural expressions as clearly as real hands, we realized that it is important not only to improve the expressiveness of the laser spot itself, but also to consider how the system can support participants to use and monitor various resources sequentially.

In addition to GestureLaser, we have developed and studied other embodied space systems, which support other kinds of collaboration (Kuzuoka, 1992; Kuzuoka et al., 1994; Kato et al., 1997; Kuzuoka et al., 1999). By continuing improvements and experiments in various kinds of remote instruction situations, we hope to build more effective systems and elucidate the mechanism of collaboration in the real world.

Acknowledgements

We would like to thank Prof. P. Luff and Prof. C. Goodwin for many suggestions to our study. This research was supported by NEC, Oki Electric Co. Ltd., Oriental Motor Inc., VBL budget from the Ministry of Education, and Telecommunications Advancement Organization of Japan.

References

Dourish, P.,Adler, A., Belloti V. and A. Henderson (1992): 'Your Place or Mine? Learning   from Long-Term Use of Video Communication', EuroPARK Technical Report EPC-1994-105, Rank Xerox EuroPARK, UK., 1992.

Goodwin, C., (1994): 'Professional vision', American Anthropologist 96: (1996), pp.606-33.

Goodwin, C. (1998): 'Pointing as Situated Practice', presented at the Max Planck Workshop on Pointing Gestures.

Heath, C., and Luff, P. (1991): 'Disembodied Conduct: Communication through video in a multi-media environment', Proc. of CHI'91, 1991, New Orleans, pp. 99-103.

Heath, C., and Luff, P. (1992): 'Media Space and Communicative Asymmetries: Preliminary Observation of Video-Mediated Interaction', Human Computer Interaction, 7(3), pp.315-346.

Heath, C., Luff, P., and Sellen, A. (1995): "Reconsidering the Virtual Workplace: Flexible Support for Collaborative Activity", Proc. of ECSCW'95, 1995, pp. 83-99.

Heath, C. (1997): 'The Analysis of Activities in Face to Face Interaction Using Video', David Silveraman (ed.) Qualitive Sociology, London: Sage, 1997, pp-183-200.

Heritage, J. (1997): 'Conversational Analysis and Institutional Talk', David Silveraman (ed.), Qualitive Sociology,London:Sage, 1997, pp.161-182.

Hindmarsh, J., Fraser, M., Heath, C., Benford, S., and Greenhalgh, C (1998): 'Fragmented Interaction: Establishing mutual orientation in virtual environments', Proc. CSCW'98, 1998, pp. 217-226.

Ishii, H., Miyake, N. (1991): 'Toward an Open Shared Workspace: Computer and Video Fusion Approach of TeamworkStation', Communications of the ACM, Vol.34, No.12, 1991, pp.37-50.

Ishii, H., Kobayashi, M. (1992): 'ClearBoard: A Seamless Medium for Shared Drawing and Conversation with Eye Contact', Proc. CHI'92, 1992, 525-532.

Kato, H., Yamazaki, K., Suzuki, H., Kuzuoka, H., Miki, H., Yamazaki, A. (1997): 'Designing a Video-Mediated Collaboration System Based on a Body Metaphor', Proc. of CSCL'97 (Toronto Canada), 1997, pp. 142-149.

Kendon, A. (1990): 'Conducting Interaction: Patterns of Behavior in Focused Encounters', Cambridge Univ. Press.

Kraut, R., Miller, D., and Siegel, J. (1996): 'Collaboration in Performance of Physical Tasks: Effects on Outcomesand Communication', Proc. of CSCW'96, 1996, pp. 57-66.

Kuzuoka, H. (1992): 'Spatial Workspace Collaboration: A SharedView Video Supported System for Remote Collaboration Capability', Proc. of CHI'92, May 1992, pp.533-540.

Kuzuoka, H., Kosuge, T., and Tanaka, M. (1994): 'GestureCam: A Video Communication System for Sympathetic Remote Collaboration', Proc. of CSCW'94, October 1994, pp.35-43.

Kuzuoka, H., Ishimoda, G., Nishimura, Y., Suzuki, R. and Kondo, K., (1995): 'Can the GestureCam be a Surrogate?', Proc. of ECSCW'95, 1995, pp.181-196.

Kuzuoka, H., Oyama, S., Yamazaki, K., Yamazaki, A., Kato, H., Suzuki, H., and Miki, H. (1998): 'GestureLaser: Supporting Hand Gestures in Remote Instruction', Video Program of CSCW'98, 1998.

Kuzuoka, H., Yamashita, J., Yamazaki, K., Yamazaki, A. (1999): 'Agora: A Remote Collaboration System that Enables Mutual Monitoring', Late-breaking Results of CHI'99, 1999.

Luff, P. (1999): Dr. Paul Luff's personal comments in his email.

Nardi, B., Schwarz, H., Kuchinsky, A., Leichner, R., Whittaker, S., and Sclabasi, R. (1993): 'Turning Away from Talking Heads: The Use of Video-as-Data in Neurosurgery', Proc. of INTERCHI'93, 1993, pp.327-334.

Paulos, E. and Canny, J. (1998): 'PRoP: Personal Roving Presence', Proc. Of CHI'98, 1998, pp.296 - 303.

Tang, J., Minneman, S. (1990): 'VideoDraw A Video Interface for Collaborative Drawing', Proc. of CHI'90, 1990, pp.313-320.

Wellner, P. (1993): 'Interacting with the Paper on the DigitalDesk',Communications of the ACM , Vol. 36, No. 7, 1993, pp.87-96.

S. Bødker, M. Kyng, and K. Schmidt (eds.). *Proceedings of the Sixth European Conference on Computer-Supported Cooperative Work, 12-16 September 1999, Copenhagen, Denmark*
©1999 Kluwer Academic Publishers. Printed in the Netherlands

Exploring Support for Knowledge Management in Mobile Work

Henrik Fagrell, Fredrik Ljungberg
Viktoria Institute, Gothenburg, Sweden

Steinar Kristoffersen
Norwegian Computing Centre, Oslo, Norway

This paper reports fieldwork from the electrical utilities industry, examining the suitability of current knowledge management perspectives to the day-to-day work of mobile staff. Reporting the results of the empirical study, we make a distinction between four aspects of local and mobile "knowledge management" as it took place in the mobile work setting: *sharing*, i.e., several parties exchange knowledge; *indexing*, i.e., one party explains to another what knowledge to retrieve; *diagnosing*, i.e., two parties make sense of how to interpret a situation, and; *foreseeing*, i.e., one party (or more) uses knowledge to project the future. We compare and contrast the empirical findings with current knowledge management perspectives, and outline an initial sketch of a framework for "practical knowledge management."

1   Introduction

Organisational memory and knowledge management have inspired important debates within the field of CSCW (e.g., Randall *et al.* 1996; Bannon and Kuutti 1996). This paper reports from an empirical study where these two issues were examined in the day to day work of mobile service engineers. The study also explored the concept of local knowledge since its importance has been much recognised in the field (see, e.g., Rouncefield *et al.* 1994; Randall *et al.* 1996). Local knowledge has mainly been conceived as specific to place and procedures and the ways in which it appears in mobile work settings have not been investigated. Moreover, there has been a tendency, within CSCW, to localise activities to an individual user, and thereby missing to enhance the flexible and unexpected collaboration that often emerges out of a mobile work situation (cf., Luff and Heath 1998).

To collect empirical data we observed (Hammersley and Atkinson 1993) and interviewed the mobile staff (Patton 1990). The study lasted for about five months with an average intensity of two days per week. Large parts of the empirical material was transcribed and analysed according to the principles of grounded theory (Glaser and Strauss 1967).

Our analysis provides a critique that challenges some of the current conceptions of knowledge management, but at the same time gives opportunity for new mobile applications. We suggest a conceptual framework based on how knowledge sharing mechanisms map into action. Our point is that knowledge management in mobile settings is *social* and *dynamic*. It is this *social* mapping process that deserves our attention, although it may not in itself be suitable for computerisation.

The structure of this paper is as follows: Section 2 outlines the related work and is followed by the research background and setting. Section 4 presents an analysis of the fieldwork. Section 5 discusses the results, the related research and derives design implications. Section 6 concludes the paper.

2 Related Work

Organisational memory is an established theme in CSCW. Research contributions on the topic involve empirical studies, systems design, as well as conceptual debates. Organisational memory systems are typically based on hypermedia that links different sources of information, e.g., records. Recently, the notion knowledge management has been introduced into the CSCW field (cf., Greif 1998). It seems to have much in common with organisational memory. However, an emphasis on *managing large repositories of information* with information retrieval and artificial intelligence techniques can be noted (see, Abecker *et al.* 1998; O'Leary 1998).

One of the first organisational memory systems described in the literature was gIBIS (Conklin and Begeman 1988). The aim of gIBIS was to make decision processes explicit by capturing the argumentation.[1] Another system is "TeamBuilder," of which the objectives is to support team members in identifying expertise and collaborate more effectively (Karduck 1994). "Answer Garden"

---

[1] The gIBIS is now a commercial product called QuestMap (http://www.gdss.com/OM.htm).

aims to help organisations to capture and enable retrieval of experiences made by their employees (Ackerman 1994). In "Answer Garden 2," there are also features for finding and interacting with experts directly (Ackerman and McDonald 1996).[2]

Under the knowledge management label, Terveen *et al.* (1993) report from a project of creating a "living design" for software developers. The system provides access to, and updating features of design-relevant information. More recently Edwards and Mahling (1997) explored design implications for knowledge management in the legal domain. In addition to their advice about putting knowledge "chunks" into organisational context, they suggest that roles should be assigned for assuring relevance, accuracy, and periodically review the material (similarly to library work).

Empirical studies on knowledge management have aimed at eliciting design implications, e.g., by analysing the work of a telephone hotline group (e.g., Ackerman and Halverson 1998) and expertise location in a software development company (McDonald and Ackerman 1998). Studies have also evaluated organisational memory systems in use (e.g., Ackerman and McDonald 1996).

The conception of an organisational memory has been criticised for diverging from remembering, as it actually takes place in organisations (Randall *et al.* 1996; Bannon and Kuutti 1996). A similar position is taken by Kovalainen *et al.* (1998) who sees organisational memory as an "artefact mediated process." Many ideas on the topic derive from the decision-making perspective on organisations. This perspective has been heavily criticised by, among others; March (1991) who argues that this is simply not the way things happen in organisations. Another issue is the uneasy relation between learning and memory. As Weick (1979) puts it: "to organise[3] is to reduce variety and remember but to learn is to keep variety and to forget." This type of learning, however, is of a different character then the less ambitious learning-by-doing that is mainly considered in this paper. Orr (1996) describes an example of this sort of learning where the staff of mobile photocopier repairmen uses stories to assistant the communities learning. To further explore this, we turned towards the concept *local knowledge.*

Geertz (1983, p. 167) views local knowledge from the perspective of "to-know-a-city-is-to-know-its-streets." Here, local knowledge could be similar in many different geographically dispersed workplaces, but *it is created through local experiences* and *used locally* by a limited group of people that are working more or less together. In CSCW, local knowledge has been described as: knowledge of the particularities (Rouncefield *et al.* 1994), what makes work run

---

[2] Systems that link users with similar interests are also known under the label 'recommender systems' (see Foner 1997, Kautz *et al.* 1997).

[3] Weick (1979) make a difference between organisation and organising arguing that the noun form encourages us to see the phenomenon as a static thing, whereas the verb encourages us to see the phenomenon as a dynamic process. This is similar to the suggestion by Randall *et al.* (1996) to shift from using noun memory to the verb remembering.

smoothly (Randall *et al.* 1995), to know who knows what, who is busy, who is worth asking about "x" (Bowers *et al.* 1996).

The focus of this paper is the mobile work setting. Recently, it has been argued that there is a need to explore how mobility takes place in collaboration (Luff and Heath 1998). "Walking away from the desktop" means new problems and possibilities (Bellotti and Bly 1996). Luff and Heath (1998) identify three types of mobility: *micro mobility*, *local mobility* and *remote mobility*. Micro mobility is the way in which the artefact may by mobilised and manipulated for various purposes around a relatively circumscribed, or "at hand" domain. Local mobility is more scattered, for instance, walking between rooms, floors and buildings at a local site, e.g., that of product designers at a consulting firm (Bellotti and Bly 1996), personnel at London underground (Luff and Heath 1998), bank officers at a customer service centre (Kristoffersen and Rodden 1996). Remote mobility is when remote users interact with each other using technology, e.g., construction foremen visiting work teams. The case study of dispersed and mobile IT support staff, described in Kristoffersen and Ljungberg (1998), involves both remote and local mobility.

3   Research background

Göteborg Energi (GE) is a publicly owned Swedish energy provider with approximately 900 employees and 3,000 million SEK (approx. 333 million *euro*) in yearly revenue. Every year GE provides just over 4,700 GWh electricity, 3,600 GWh district heating and 700 GWh of natural gas. Their 350,000 customers can be anything from a single flat to heavy industrial production facilities or sports stadiums.

A couple of years ago the Swedish electricity monopoly was disbanded and the market de-regulated. GE suddenly had to cope with more than a hundred suppliers instead of one and more competitors in the provider layer. As a consequence of this, the company had to undergo substantial organisational changes and become more customer-oriented than before, in order to answer to the competition and keep their advantage and market share.

3.1   Large scale introduction of GIS

GE is currently engaged in significant IT investment as a way of transforming the company. The old mainframe-based systems are being replaced with a client-server solution and much paperwork is computerised. One of the investments has been to computerise maps of the electricity network. This activity is finished and many kinds of information have been integrated with a Geographical Information System (GIS). One example of this is that 15,000 cable boxes, i.e., the connecting nodes for houses and streetlights, are represented in the graphical view of the map. Additionally, information is provided about the cable box's components and to which customer's it is serving.

The GIS is accessible on the companies 850 networked PCs. The next step is to make it accessible for the 300 employees that do a majority of their work away from a networked stationary PC. The idea is to equip GE's 200 vehicles so that the GIS can also be accessed from the vehicles. The expected benefit of the mobile system is that less driving back and forth would be required to get information, e.g., maps, from stationary computers.

We followed a pilot project to evaluate the types of techniques under actual work conditions. A car was equipped with a laptop with network access via the Global System for Mobile communication (GSM)[4]. The laptop was connected to a colour printed making it possible to download maps and print them in the car.[5]

3.2   The local service station and roles

GE has several local service stations and they are responsible for a limited geographical area in which they are located. The responsibilities are for *installations, maintenance* and *error repairs*. The work assignments are generally distributed from the central administration office, but lately the stations' personnel have been allowed to initiate customer relations, which is a big change. They are also to a great extent autonomous at an operational level. There are three major roles at the station, namely electricians, planners and administrators.

Electricians work in pairs, mainly for security reasons, but also so that skills in both high and low voltage are represented. The work pairs get their assignments from the planner, but they often do the final co-ordination with the customers themselves. The work in the field generally involves planned work, i.e., installations and maintenance, but also emergencies, e.g., power failure, which has to be taken care of immediately. Almost all of the electricians at GE are on a rolling timetable for 24-hour on-call duty. In these situations they may have to operate beyond their ordinary geographical areas. The electricians have cellular phones and pagers as standard equipment.

The planner schedules assignments by allocating resources, such as personnel, raw material and vehicles. An important issue for the planner is to manage co-ordination with contract entrepreneurs that could be large construction companies or a one-man firm with a bulldozer. It is also the planner's responsibility to make security certificates of finished jobs and inform customers and neighbours of potential disturbances. The planner has an office in the main building with a phone and a networked computer. However, the planner uses his cellular phone

---

[4] More information about GSM can be found at the GSM association (http://www.gsm.org/).

[5] To solve the problem of low bandwidth over GSM the server computer had software, which used data compression techniques and with the ability to store frequently displayed graphics on the client computer instead of repeatedly downloading them.

very much since most of his working time is spent in the field. Constant communication is vital because of the need continually to change priorities. As a planner put it:

> We think we have control of the situation. We have projects and deadlines. But we never do one job at a time. We have five or six assignments simultaneously. And then new customers call and want the electricity connected to their houses. No matter how much work we have, we must do it within two days.

Planners administrate complexity, and try to control resources that are constantly changing.

The administrators work in the main building. One of them does accounting, communication with the central office and takes care of the customer telephone calls. The other one mainly creates prospects for future installations in the area, e.g., new housing and industries.

The first thing that happens (about 7 am) on a workday is that most employees at the station meet, having an informal coffee break. They talk about the work and how it should progress during the week. Afterwards, assignments are divided among the work pairs (of electricians). The planner and the work pairs negotiate the division of work and decide how to proceed. When this is done, the cars are loaded with appropriate equipment. After this the pairs go to the customers that are at several geographical locations. If the schedule is not rearranged, they will return to the service station during the day. They will normally spend the afternoon doing some more work in the field, followed by paper work back at the office.[6] More time is spent in the field on bigger assignment on projects and maintenance. Figure 1 gives an overview of the staffs geographic distribution and roles.

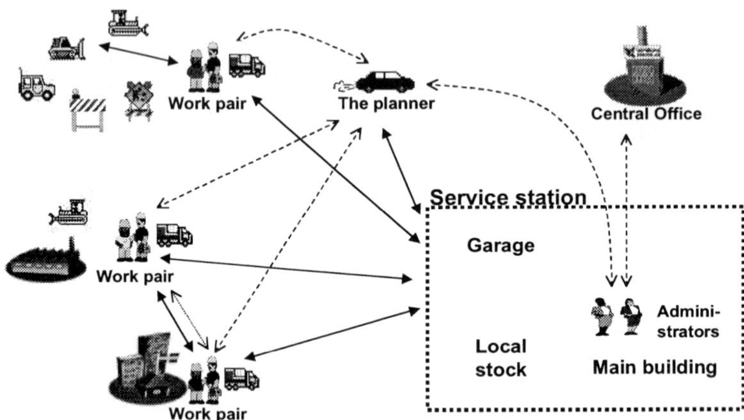

Figure 1: The communication flow (dotted arrows) and the mobility of the workforce.

---

[6] Other systems, e.g. billing and order, where accessible, but not used in the mobile environment during the time of our study.

Our observations consisted of following the electricians and the planner at the station, in the vehicles and in the field (see figure 1).

4 Results

Reporting the results of the empirical study, we make a distinction between four aspects of local and mobile "knowledge management" as it took place in the mobile work setting investigated. These are:

- *Sharing*: Several parties exchange knowledge.
- *Indexing*: One party explains to another which knowledge to retrieve.
- *Diagnosing*: Two parties make sense of a situation, i.e., how it should be interpreted.
- *Foreseeing*: One party (or more) uses knowledge to project the future.

Let us now consider these types in more detail.

4.1 Sharing

We found three types of sharing, namely ephemeral, persistent and stories. The one categorised as *ephemeral* took place at the daily coffee meeting. When people meet they discuss their work. This is where they get updated and informed. The following paragraph is an example of an event that was repeated every morning with only small variances.

> The planner comes in and pulls out his agenda and starts to discuss some reorganisations of today's work. He throws out a couple of questions of what the work pairs are doing this day and how long they think that it will take.

The planner tries to see if there is anyone that can reschedule today's program if something urgent comes up. Since this is a collective effort, the electricians gain knowledge of what their colleagues are doing. In many other studies the "talking out loud" and "overhearing" has been identified to give colleagues peripheral awareness what is going on and inviting the to give feedback (e.g., Heath and Luff, 1991). This mainly occurs during the morning meeting, but it was also observed at other places around the station. It makes it possible for the planner to call the correct work pair if a reorganisation is necessary. It is also useful for the electricians since they become aware of their colleagues' whereabouts in case they need to ask someone. If the planner calls them with a question or assignment they cannot answer, they may know whom else to recommend.

If someone knows something that concerns everyone, it is often brought up on the morning meeting, as the following example shows.

> George says so everyone can hear: "There may be a need for more personnel at Tuve. I was there yesterday ... it seemed like there was a lot of things that they would like us to do." [The others were listening and some nodded in agreement]. The planner takes a note and says that he is going to call them [the customer].

This helps the planner to plan ahead and it notifies the other electricians to prepare for what they might be doing next.

The formalised organisational sharing functions are to a great extent embedded in documents (forms and maps) that electricians fill in during and after assignments. We call this *persistent* sharing. These would then be sent to other organisational units, e.g., map surveyors and customer billing.

One example of how people share persistent knowledge was a *filer* the electricians used when they were on duty (during nights and weekends). When on duty, the electricians may have to visit sites where they rarely go, or have not been before. This could be problematic. For example, it could be difficult to remember details from time to time. It could also be difficult to get hold of people for assistance. To cope with the problem, the electricians have developed a (paper) *filer*. The *filer* is indexed by street address and contains information about local conditions of specific places. Some illustrative examples of entries from the *filer* are:

- *Karl Gustav's street 22-30: "The cable box is behind the basement door in the backyard of Engelbrekt's street 45."*
- *Erik Dahlberg's stairs: "Call the janitor on 111 22 33 to get the key to entrance 5. In case of no answer call the FM housing centre on 111 44 33."*
- *Viktor Rydberg's street 42: "The box is in the heating room. The key is in the cupboard and its got a wood piece on the ring."*

The content of the *filer* is designed to provide information that is relevant for on-call duty work. It bridges some of the representational shortcomings of the maps, e.g., location of keys and doors. The electricians who are on-call duty update the *filer* when they encounter something they find worthwhile noting. Several electricians have referred to the *filer* as being useful.

A way of sharing how to deal with problems that occur on a regular, but unplanned basis is to tell *stories* of previous problems and their solutions. These stories are told in order to transfer knowledge in the work group. They were told in any place when the work pace was low. Telling these stories was a way of producing, maintaining and communicating knowledge. They also form "traces" of the community's common experience and knowledge that had been built up over time. The stories often have a specific topic, e.g., the following one that is about finding a place.

> A little chat on how much the landscape had changed during over the years leads into a story about "the old days." Roy started telling a story about how he had problems in finding a certain work site in the sixties. This was when a big suburb was being built. The story circles around problems of finding a site and that the map was wrong. When driving around in the woods without being able to find the construction site, Roy finds that his car is running out of petrol. Just as the car starts to cough, he sees a petrol station downhill and manages to get the car to roll down. When refuelling the car he looks around. And there... he sees the small gap between the trees that lead to the construction site where he is supposed to do his job.

We heard several version of this story. The story is not exactly about diagnosis and specific problems solving, as discussed by Orr (1991, p. 160). It is an allusion for how to find places. The literal places or situation that story refers to is not of current interest; it is from the sixties! However, some hints may still be useful, e.g., a small road often leads to a construction site and there may be settlements nearby a petrol station.

Another topic for the story telling is how customers may be taken care of. It can for example be frustrating when the customers are not really prepared. Here is an illustrative example:

> We got the place were there was this guy who was stressed up beyond belief, he just could not talk... [laugh] So we helped him out. I mean we could not just leave and there is always something we could do... I gave Dennis [planner] a call, but he was not answering – I knew he shouldn't but anyway...

It is the planner's job to take care of these situations. However, this is sometimes prohibited by a high workload, and the electricians may have to solve it themselves. They have to negotiate with the customer and come up with a solution. Moreover, the attitude of the stories is to relieve some pressure from the planner (and for the customer too).

4.2 Indexing

One way in which knowledge management takes place in the mobile setting is what could be called "indexing." For example, when people explain to someone else "how to find a particular place," they would typically relate to recognisable physical objects, e.g., "do you remember where we did this and that work two years ago." Whether or not the other party (one or several) knows a particular object becomes obvious in the conversation. For example, "You mean where...?! Yes, I know where it is...," would be a typical example of someone recognising a "sign," while simply being quiet would indicate the opposite.

Let us now consider an example of how people use this kind of knowledge.

> The planner receives a call to his cellular phone (while driving). It's from a construction site where they "want service now." The planner says that he is going to "fix it." Then he hangs up and makes a phone call. "Jonsson?... could you go to 'project Hjalmar'? They need 'construction electricity' [preliminary connection used by construction firms]... Can you fix it immediately? They know that you're going there.. the same place as the last time." He hangs up.

The task in question was quite small, and the planner just wanted to get it out of the way. The planner knows that the electricians are away on maintenance work that is not time-critical. Therefore, he could tell the client that the two electricians will show up. The planner also knows that the electricians he calls have been doing work there before, and they know exactly where it is; thus, they are the best-fit work pair at this point.

4.3 Diagnosing

"Diagnosing" is related to "indexing." In "diagnosing" one or more people collaboratively seek to make sense of a situation. One example of is when electricians encounter a cable that is not on the map. If it is not determinable whether or not the voltage is up, the cable has to be "shot," i.e., putting it out of operation forever. This could mean for example that a housing area looses electricity, but it is, of course, better then that someone gets injured. This is, however, a decision that the electricians would collectively take with the planner as a last-way-out-solution.

A more interesting thing is that maps cannot be strictly followed since minor inaccuracies are very common. The following paragraph is an illustrative example of an error in the map is "diagnosed."

> A work pair was going to connect power to new houses. At the site the map did not seem to fit the landscape. Chris and Bernie started turning and shuffling the map back and forward while discussing intensively. After a few minutes Chris says that the construction firm may have built an extra lane of houses that we do not to have on the map. This turned out to be correct and the work could continue, now with additionally six houses to connect power to.

In this case Chris suggested "there is an extra lane of houses," and since Bernie seemed to agree, this was the way in which they made sense of the situation.

One of the reasons maps do not match the landscape is that landscapes change. Moreover, the surveyors and the electricians do not always agree on the updates of the maps, which results in compromises. Confusion may occur, but the electricians can still make sense of the map since they know about these circumstances. Another difficulty is that other companies have equipment in the ground (telecom cables and water pipes). Even if this information is shared among the companies there is always be the risk that the maps differ.

4.4 Foreseeing

"Foreseeing" is using knowledge to make suggestions about the future. Let us consider one example. When the electricians are at a specific place they would typically project beyond the task at hand. For example:

> John says to the civil engineer at when they have finished a job: I can see that you are going to call us later this week to get those poles moved over there... I can call my boss and see if we could do it right away? The civil engineer gladly accepts the offer.

Here, John knows that there will be a need to "get those poles moved over there" in the near future, and for that reason, he could provide the client with a good offer. He uses his knowledge to "foresee" how things will proceed. It is tightly coupled to the circumstances that are unveiled for the electrician at a specific place and the local knowledge of what possible action to take.

4.5   Practical knowledge management: an initial sketch

Based on the empirical observations, we have started to develop a framework of "practical knowledge management." The objective is to join the debate of knowledge management in a constructive way, that is to say make suggestions that may be helpful in practice.

We start by examining the relations between the *sharing mechanisms* and their utilisation. We are fully aware of the fact that these relationships may not be clear-cut. Nevertheless, there seems to be connections between the mapping

- from ephemeral into indexing,
- from persistent into diagnosing, and
- from stories into foreseeing.

One example of how ephemeral sharing maps into indexing is when the re-organisation of personnel relies on the plans of the day as stated at the daily morning meeting. For example, a morning meeting we observed involved a discussion about "how much personal a particular assignment will need." Later during the day, we observed how Chris called Ronnie (the planner), requesting more people.

> Chris: "We need more people here. Roy said that they had it slow today. Should I call him and ask them to come?" He hands up and calls Roy.

In this situation, Chris explains for Ronnie that Roy had told him previously that he and his peers will not have a very high workload this particular day. When Chris finds out he needs more people, he (seemingly) therefore makes the suggestion (for Ronnie) to call Roy, and in doing so, he explicitly refers to what Roy has told him. Thus, ephemeral sharing was mapped into indexing.

Persistent sharing mechanisms, such as maps and documents, were used for diagnosing. Most often, diagnosing took place in the field where the local conditions of the place could be matched with the records. The *filer* for instance, is an obvious support in some diagnosing processes.

The administrators have got a lot of persistent record at the office. When they are in contact with the electricians it is most often some information at the office that is needed, e.g., customers address or telephone numbers.

Stories contain a more abstract type of knowledge. The stories map into actions of foreseeing and diagnoses. Not only situations, problems and solutions are communicated in the stories, but also opportunities for giving better service.

A system based on these categories could support improvisation and help the electricians to gain an overview of the customer's needs and available resources. It could also be useful in some cases of minor emergencies for on-call duty. Bigger assignments, on the other hand, could still be centrally co-ordinated.

5 Discussion

Knowledge management and *organisational memory* have inspired important debates within CSCW. Often these are contrasted with reference to *local knowledge*. Bringing these perspectives together, we have proposed new categories of "practical knowledge management" that cover the layered abstraction and creative mapping of local knowledge to new places and procedures. Exploring knowledge management in the day to day work of electricians, we found four important ways in which it took place. To summarise:

- Sharing, i.e., the exchange of knowledge between parties.
- Indexing, i.e., one party explains to another what knowledge to retrieve.
- Diagnosing, i.e., two parties make sense of a situation, i.e., how it should be interpreted.
- Foreseeing, i.e., one party (or more) uses knowledge to project the future.

For each of these we would like to compare and contrast some central views of organisational memory and knowledge management literature:

- Making the argumentation explicit

Central to the argumentation of organisational memory is the notion of *rationale*, i.e., that supplying the motivation and structure of the "memory creation process" (Conklin and Begeman 1988; Yakemovic and Conklin 1990). It follows from this focus that an organisational memory system should try to make the *decision processes explicit* by capturing all essential aspects. In a sense, everything relevant should be saved and made available to anyone who might need it.

- Finding and interacting with experts

Another important objective of organisational memory is to support team members in finding and interacting with experts, and to accomplish such work more effectively (Ackerman and McDonald 1996; Karduck 1994).

- Putting knowledge in chunks

In knowledge management, the central objective is often to capture, organise and share the knowledge of employees for the achievement of a common, strategic goal. This objective necessitates breaking up knowledge in manageable chunks of various types, for instance, administrative data, facts and figures about the operations, declarative knowledge, procedural knowledge, and analytic knowledge (Edwards and Mahling 1997).

- The roles of knowledge

In knowledge management it is also suggested that roles should be assigned for assuring relevance, accuracy, and periodically review of material. It is also suggested that various techniques from automated retrieval reasoning are central to this kind of learning organisation.

We will not, in the paper, argue against the central tenets of these two related disciplines. We think, however, that the picture emerging from the following comments may be one on the basis of which some design implications may be drawn.

5.1 Sharing

In our case, mechanisms were implemented in attempts to persistently share knowledge through artefacts. On the other hand, we also found ephemeral sharing that was generated for a purpose and for dedicated receivers (explicitly seeking it). In this respects our findings are much closely aligned with those of Bannon and Kuutti (1996), Randall *et al.* (1996), and Anderson and Sharrock (1993), who claim that knowledge is actively constructed for the individual in a particular context. We think that the shear volume of relevant information that conceivably could be captured in this case is prohibitive of the former approach.

Organisational memory has to assume that people are willing to be experts for "unknown others," thus taking on additional work by explicating and storing experiences in a common information space. A related assumption is that users of these systems will actually trust that they contain reliable, updated information. We did not observe knowledge explicating and storing activities that were external to work itself, i.e., at least not in a formal way. Thus, the practical use of knowledge as the manipulation of "knowledge chunks" does not agree with our observations. One central design implication would be to avoid redundant work imposed by explicating knowledge creating chunks as well as allowing users to partake in designating experts. The role of experts is one of several roles that were not explicit in the organisation. It seem hard to see what could be gained by forcing the organisation to allocate and manage roles such as "gatekeepers" and "knowledge librarians" (Edwards and Mahling 1997).

5.2 Indexing

In traditional organisational memory, "knowledge" is usually structured by a theory of argumentation. For some aspects of knowledge, in our case, such as rules and formal procedures, this is certainly an appropriate approach. Also, when the solution space may be anticipated, i.e., when and if the problem relate to a specific geographical location only. We found in other instances, that people organise information in an individual and situated fashion. Thus, one design implication could be to allow personal, rather than general mark-up, indexing and organisation of the data captured.

It is often rightly assumed that people could be helped by experts (or rather get assistance) in solving problems. However, knowing who the expert is for the particular problem at hand, does not seem to be a matter of formal roles. We found that people often rely on informal, individual networks in combination with open requests. Knowing who should have been asked may not be known until after the problem is solved. Put simply, *knowing who* is sometimes a major part *knowing what.*

The ways in which we observed people collaboratively indexing knowledge, imply that it is a complex phenomenon, which is related to action rather than representation, and thus, cannot easily be broken down into general chunks. This also shows that all members of an organisation could serve as "experts," "gatekeepers," "knowledge librarians," etc., depending on the situation.

5.3 Diagnosing

Many organisational memory systems, such as Answer Garden, require that the requesters of knowledge know, in advance, how to formulate a question. This is often possible when the problem space is limited, for instance when it is (yet) an instance of a problem with new parameters (call the janitor first – what is the telephone number?). We found, however, that in many instances this is undertaken as a collaborative task, during which the problem-solving process is already ongoing. It is a known phenomenon in information retrieval that to express an interest in a formulised query is difficult (see, Marchionini 1995). This could mean that the organisational memory system should not be conceived separately from the task-support for these users. As Anderson and Sharrock (1993, p. 149) puts it: "patterns of knowledge and patterns of action define each other." These ideas are not so far from the work on "living design" (Terveen *et al.* 1993) and social activity indicators (Ackerman and Starr 1995).

Diagnosing was a truly collaborative effort that seldom was preceded by one person explicitly trying to find and interact with an expert. It would be necessary to engage assistance in implementing and evaluating solutions as well as giving advice on a more abstract level.

5.4 Foreseeing

Traditionally, organisational memory has been concerned with the past. The majority of requests documented in our case similarly tries to resolve a current problem using previous experiences. We also found, however, some instances of future projections and business planning on the basis of situated problem solving. This could means that knowledge management should be seen in connection with a relaxed workflow design. Foreseeing is about creating possibilities for action and thus making a business opportunity for the people present in the situation. Thus, it is not always necessary to find experts that fit the "problem," but rather to define a problem that may be solved by the experts that are already engaged.

6 Conclusion

This paper adds to the existing body of empirical work in CSCW by dealing with a novel class of work, namely mobile service work. Our empirical results provide a sound grounding for further design and evaluation of distributed support for practical knowledge management in a mobile setting. The analysis challenges some conceptual underpinnings of work in both sides, but, at the same time, this critique opens windows of opportunities for implementers of CSCW systems in what seems to be, for researchers and consultants alike, a very compelling domain.

Acknowledgement

This research is a part of the Mobile Informatics programme that is funded by the Swedish Information Technology research Institute (SITI).

We would like to thank our colleagues at the Viktoria Institute, especially Magnus Bergquist and Peter Ljungstrand. Finally, thanks to Wayne Lutters for a thoughtful review.

7 References

Abecker, A., A. Bernardi, K. Hinkelmann, O. Kühn, and M. Sintek (1998) "Towards a Technology for Organizational Memories," *IEEE Intelligent Systems*, 1998, 13 (3) pp. 40-48.

Ackerman M.S. and B. Starr (1995) "Social Activity Indicators for Groupware," In *Proceedings of the 8th ACM symposium on User interface and software technology.* pp. 159-168. Pittsburgh, PA: ACM Press.

Ackerman M.S. and C. Halverson (1998) "Considering an organization's memory," In *Proceedings of ACM 1998 Conference on Computer Supported Cooperative Work.* pp. 39-48. Seattle, WA: ACM Press.

Ackerman, M.S. (1994) "Augmenting the organizational memory: a field study of answer garden," In *Proceedings of ACM 1994 Conference on Computer Supported Cooperative Work.* pp. 243-252. Chapel Hill, NC: ACM Press.

Ackerman, M.S. and D.W. McDonald (1996) "Answer Garden 2: Merging organizational memory with collaborative help," In *Proceedings of ACM 1996 Conference on Computer Supported Cooperative Work.* pp. 97-105, Cambridge, MA. ACM Press.

Anderson, R. and W. Sharock. (1993) "Can Organisations Afford Knowledge?" *Computer Supported Cooperative Work*, 1993, 1 (3) pp. 123-142.

Bannon, L.J. and K. Kuutti (1996) "Shifting Perspectives on Organizational Memory: From Storage to Active Remembering," In *Proceedings of the 29th Hawaii Conference on System Sciences. Vol. IV.* pp. 156-167. Los Alamitos. IEEE Computer Society Press.

Bellotti, V. and S. Bly (1996), "Walking away from the desktop computer distributed collaboration and mobility in a product design team," In *Proceedings of ACM 1996 Conference on Computer Supported Cooperative Work.* pp. 209-218, Cambridge, MA: ACM Press.

Bowers, J., J. O'Brien and J. Pycock (1996) "Practically accomplishing immersion: cooperation in and for virtual environments," In *Proceedings of ACM 1996 Conference on Computer-Supported Cooperative Work.* pp. 380-389, Cambridge, MA: ACM Press.

Conklin, J. and M.L. Begeman (1988) "gIBIS: a hypertext tool for exploratory policy discussion," In *Proceedings of ACM 1988 Conference on Computer Supported Cooperative Work.* pp. 140-152. Portland, OR: ACM Press.

Edwards, D.L. and D.E. Mahling (1997) "Toward knowledge management systems in the legal domain," In *Proceedings of the international ACM SIGGROUP conference on Supporting group work: the integration challenge.* pp. 158-166, Phoenix, AZ: ACM Press.

Foner, L. (1997) "Yenta: A Multi-Agent, Referral Based Matchmaking System," In *Proceedings of the first international conference on Autonomous agent*s. pp 301-307, Marina del Rey, CA: ACM Press.

Geertz, C. (1983) *Local Knowledge: Further Essays in Interpretive Anthropology,* New York: Basic Books.

Glaser, B. and A. Strauss (1967) *The Discovery of Grounded Theory.* Chicago: Aldine.

Greif, I. (1998) "Everyone is talking about knowledge management, " In *Proceedings of ACM 1998 Conference on Computer Supported Cooperative Work.* pp. 405-406. Seattle, WA: ACM Press.

Hammersley, M., and P. Atkinson (1993) *Ethnography. Principles and practice,* Second edition, London: Routledge.

Heath C. and P. Luff (1991) "Collaborative Activity and Technological Design: Task Coordination in London Underground Control Rooms," In *Proceedings of the Second European Conference on Computer-Supported Co-operative Work.* pp. 15-22. Amsterdam, The Netherlands: Kluwer Academic Publishers.

Karduck, A. (1994) "TeamBuilder: a CSCW tool for identifying experts and team formation," *Computer Communications,* 1994, 17 (11) pp. 77-87.

Kautz, H., B. Selman and M. Shah (1997) "Referral Web: combining social networks and collaborative filtering," *Communications of the ACM,* 1997, 40 (3) pp. 63-65.

Kovalainen, M., M. Robinson and E. Auramäki (1998) "Diaries at work," In *Proceedings of ACM 1998 Conference on Computer Supported Cooperative Work.* pp. 49-58. Seattle, WA: ACM Press.

Kristoffersen, S. and F. Ljungberg (1998) "MobiCom: Networking dispersed groups," *Interacting with Computers,* 1998, 10 (1) pp. 45-65.

Kristoffersen, S. and T. Rodden (1996) "Working by Walking Around. Requirements of flexible interaction management in video-supported collaborative work," In *Proceedings of Human Computer Interaction.* pp. 315-329. London, UK: Springer-Verlag.

Luff, P. and C. Heath (1998) "Mobility in Collaboration," In *Proceedings of ACM 1998 Conference on Computer Supported Cooperative Work.* pp. 305-314. Seattle, WA: ACM Press.

March, J.G. (1991) "How Decisions Happen in Organizations," *Human-Computer Interaction,* 1991, 6, pp. 95-117.

Marchionini, G. (1995) *Information Seeking in Electronic Environments.* Cambridge Series on Human-Computer Interaction. Cambridge University Press.

McDonald, D.W. and M.S. Ackerman (1998) "Just talk to me: a field study of expertise location," In *Proceedings of ACM 1998 Conference on Computer Supported Cooperative Work.* pp. 39-48. Seattle, WA: ACM Press.

O'Leary, D.E. (1998) "Enterprise knowledge management," *IEEE Computer,* 1998, 31 (3) pp. 54–61.

Orr, J. (1996). *Talking about machines: An ethnography of a modern job.* Ithaca, NY: ILR Press, an imprint of Cornell University Press.

Patton, M.Q. (1990) *Qualitative Evaluation and Research Methods.* New York: Sage.

Randall, D., J. O'Brien, M. Rouncefield and J.A. Hughes (1996) "Organisational Memory and CSCW: Supporting the 'Mavis Phenomenon'," In *Proceedings of the 6th Australian Conference on Computer-Human Interaction.* Hamilton, New Zealand: IEEE Computer Society.

Randall, D., M. Rouncefield and J.A. Hughes (1995) "Chalk and Cheese: BPR and ethnomethodologically informed ethnography in CSCW," In *Proceedings of the Fourth European Conference on Computer-Supported Cooperative Work.* pp. 325-340. Stockholm, Sweden: Kluwer Academic Publishers.

Rouncefield, M., J.A. Hughes, T. Rodden and S. Viller (1994) "Working with 'constant interruption': CSCW and the Small Office," In *Proceedings of ACM 1994 Conference on Computer Supported Cooperative Work.* pp. 275-286. Chapel Hill, NC: ACM Press.

Terveen, L.G., P.G. Selfridge and M.D. Long (1993) "From 'folklore' to 'living design memory'," In *ACM 1993 Conference proceedings on Human factors in computing systems.* pp. 15-22. Amsterdam, The Netherlands: ACM Press.

Weick, K.E. (1979) *The social psychology of organising.* Second Edition. McGraw-Hill: New York.

Yakemovic, K.C.B., and E.J. Conklin (1990) "Report on a development project use of an issue-based information system," In *Proceedings of ACM 1990 Conference on Computer Supported Cooperative Work.* pp. 105-118. Los Angeles, CA: ACM Press.

S. Bødker, M. Kyng, and K. Schmidt (eds.). *Proceedings of the Sixth European Conference on Computer-Supported Cooperative Work, 12-16 September 1999, Copenhagen, Denmark*
©1999 Kluwer Academic Publishers. Printed in the Netherlands

Dynamics in Wastewater Treatment:
A Framework for Understanding Formal Constructs in Complex Technical Settings

Olav W. Bertelsen & Christina Nielsen
Department of Computer Science, Aarhus University, Denmark.
olavb@daimi.au.dk, sorsha@daimi.au.dk

Abstract. Based on the study of unskilled work in a Danish wastewater treatment plant, the problem of formalisation of work is discussed and extended to technical processes. Five symmetrical levels of dynamics in complex technical work arrangements are proposed as a tool for understanding the limits of formalisation and for designing formal constructs in such settings. The analysis is based on concepts of heterogeneity, granularity of goals and motives, and process and structure.

Introduction

An inevitable problem in the design of CSCW systems is that work is not standing still. Rather, work settings are dynamic: routines evolve over time and unusual situations force deviations from the routine. For this reason, purely formal constructs and descriptions of work have proven inadequate when designing effective, real world CSCW systems.

Suchman and Wynn (1984) set off the debate about the role of formalism in CSCW, and their empirical studies clearly illustrated that there is more to office work than formalised, or formalizable, procedures. Heath and Luff (1992) continue this in their study of work in line control rooms on the London Underground, showing that even seemingly specialised routine tasks rely on peripheral awareness and the participation of others. Thus, impossible to subsume under formal constructs. Bowers et al.'s (1995) study of workflow systems in the printing industry demonstrates their inability to encompass and support the actual course of work. Such systems structure work from without, emphasising inter-organisational accountability rather than the smooth execution of the work. Thus, the CSCW community has succeeded in questioning our ability to completely formalise CSCW.

However, as Schmidt (1997) correctly points out, concentrating only on the non-formalisable parts of work ignores the situations in which formalisation can be a resource and an important tool in cooperative work. He suggests that formal constructs, including written procedures, schemes, charts, workflow systems, and other artefacts, are important artefacts that support CSCW. This is particularly true in the case of complex manufacturing or process plants, where formal constructs, like blueprints or the physical plant itself, are fundamental features. Accordingly, Robinson (1989) argues that CSCW applications must support two levels of interaction, the formal and the cultural. Applications that support one at the expense of the other tend to fail.

Wastewater treatment plants are highly-distributed technical settings. Unlike office-work, the plant operates continuously, independently of the people employed there. Unlike control rooms, risk factors are minimal, since most of the work done at a wastewater plant is not time-critical. In addition, formalisation in wastewater treatment plants both intervenes with the technical aspects of the plant and of the work. Thus a wastewater treatment plant presents a technically and procedurally complex system that differs from the work settings typically found in the CSCW-literature. It is our claim that investigating into the limits of formalisation and the design of formal constructs in the wastewater treatment setting will present findings that add to the previous work of formalisation within CSCW.

This paper reports on our study of a modern wastewater treatment plant in Denmark. The following section describes the plant and its operation and sets the scope for our case study. We then look at different theoretical frameworks that offer ways of analysing the type of work that is wastewater treatment. The next section provides a framework for identifying levels of dynamics in wastewater treatment, based on the theoretical frameworks discussed. With this, we identify five symmetrical levels of dynamics in the case of wastewater treatment plants, on one hand questioning the general formalisability of technical arrangements, on the other hand pointing to a framework for understanding the limits of formalisation in CSCW-design.

A study of wastewater treatment

The case study is part of a long-term research cooperation in the areas of HCI and CSCW involving Danfoss and the Computer Science Department at Aarhus University as well as several other partners. The purpose is to explore the theoretical notion and practical design of common information spaces. The project has focussed on field studies of three wastewater plants, conducted by researchers from the participating organisations. This paper reports on our observations of work at one of the plants. We selected 6 days, within a 5-month period, to follow workers through their entire daily routine. Different researchers followed different workers, using hand-held video cameras to capture the events. We later analysed the video, with special emphasis on the daily work practice, use of artefacts, and how workers dealt with the disruptions. We selected groups of clips to present to the plant employees during feedback sessions and user workshops. We also compared the work practices at this site with data collected by other project researchers at the other wastewater treatment plants.

The wastewater treatment plant

We conducted a study of a modern wastewater treatment plant in Denmark, paying particular attention to how formalisation and flexibility exist in the work practices, and how it affects the coordination of work. The purification process at the plant includes mechanical, chemical and biological phases. The resulting segmented sludge is used to produce gas, which produces enough electricity to run the plant. The remainder is pressed and taken away to an incinerator plant. The plant was one of the first to implement automatic process optimisation for the removal of nitrogen. The automation has been possible due to the development of new sensor technology, which allow for on-line measuring and control of the primary parameters of operation. Not surprisingly, the process optimisation has radically decreased the use of chemicals. The plant has an estimated capacity of 220.000 person equivalents. However, it is constantly running at 110 - 150% over capacity because the plant has not been able to expand to match the increase in the city's production of wastewater.

The work

The wastewater treatment plant employs a total of 8 people. The two managers are responsible for the overall management of the plant. The remaining six employees work in pairs, with the following areas of responsibility:

- chemical test lab, receiving the sludge-trucks, preliminary sorting area, sand trap
- outside plant areas, putrefaction tanks, sludge tanks, gas-turbine building, control room
- sludge press

The three pairs of workers are each responsible for tasks associated with a specific part of the treatment process. Individual workers may temporarily take on other tasks, as when someone is ill, but the overall division labour is quite stable.

Within the bounds of the set of work tasks, individuals are free to 'juggle' the tasks as the situation demands. An important goal of this organisation of the work is to keep the relevant part of the plant in a condition that will allow the underlying purification process to run effectively, even when the worker responsible is home on nights or weekends. For example, the worker in charge of the lab spends two to three hours every morning collecting water samples and sludge and then analysing the quality of the water at different stages of the purification process. The worker in charge of the gas turbine area checks each of the different machines and collects the read-outs of how much gas has been produced during the last 24 hours. The plant manager's area of responsibility is wider, but the tasks are of the same nature. He starts every morning at his computer, getting an overview of the status of the plant by looking at his customised graphs and the lists of alarms.

Although each worker's daily routine of checking and maintenance is highly standardised, there is also a high degree of unpredictability at the plant. The majority of alarms received at the wastewater treatment plant are warnings, such as when the water level is at the maximum limit for a tank. Some alarms call for (relatively) immediate action, while others may be addressed over a period of days. Sometimes the worker can handle it himself, other times an outside specialist must be called. If the alarm is due to machine failure, several workers may completely break off their daily routine and enter into a cooperative problem-solving effort. Workers and managers specifically pay attention to warning alarms and physical signs of problems, since it is much more desirable to prevent rather than recover from machine breakdowns.

The wastewater plant is continuously engaged in a number of experiments to optimise the purification process, to produce cleaner water and decreased costs. Experimentation usually involves introducing new technology or work practices which may provoke unanticipated events and effects on everyday work. Outside visitors, such as school classes, also disrupt the normal routine, even though the visits are carefully planned and executed.

In general, the daily work routine has a dynamic structure. The workers need a deep understanding of the assignments and the plant itself in order to perform their tasks without continuously having to reinvent their work practices. This enables them to place equipment in the area for later use, and allows them to redefine the order of tasks in order to cope with the numerous events that cannot possibly be anticipated.

Perspectives on wastewater treatment work

In the standard engineering literature wastewater treatment is described as a fixed series of well-defined components (e.g. Droste 1997). This analytic perspective is in marked contrast to the plant manager's perspective. He sees things as a result of a historical process, from the first basins built to a prediction as to where a new set of tanks will be added. The former view is static and formal; the latter is dynamic and situated in the current context.

The discrepancy between the static engineering view and the manager's historical conception is no coincidence but rather a result of different needs. The engineer focuses on optimal constellations of technical components, using the fixation of as many variables as possible as an important tool. The wastewater plant manager "lives" in the plant for a longer period. For him the engineer's plan is a starting point, what Star (1986) calls a border condition, among many others, against which running the plant is realised.

Process and structure

Both the systematic, static view and the historic, dynamic view are needed to understand and design technical systems; neither can be abandoned. Thus we need a conceptual framework that can deal with these simultaneously, and the dialectics between structure and process.

In analytical philosophy, process means mere movement, 'a sequence of events' (Blackburn, 1994). In dialectical materialism, process includes the sense of transformation of the given (Israel 1979). With this background, Mathiassen (1981) introduces and utilises an analysis of process and structure as a framework for understanding the development of computerised work arrangements. A model with structure in focus sets limits for sub-processes within the structure, but at the same time super-processes may change the structure. Structure is in this context denote the qualities we perceive as solid or stable but which are changeable. In the same way, a model with process in focus is changing subsumed structures at the same time, as it is itself structured by super-structures.

Mathiassen argues that the choice of whether to focus on structure or process depends on how well-known a situation is with respect to the object of activity, the means for realising the object, the constraints on the object, and the outcome of different actions, or to which degree a situation is *established* or *emergent*. Andersen et al. (1990), also reflect this relationship with regards to system development. In highly established routine situations, a high degree of formalisation is possible because both the problem and the working practice to solve it are known. In problem solving situations where the working practice is unknown, the degree of formalisation is completely dependent on the situation's emergent nature. In problem setting situation, which are highly emergent, formalisation will be counter-productive because neither problem nor means of solving it are known. The degree of uncertainty in a work situation is particularly interesting because its analysis is fundamental to understanding the (cooperative) work practices build around them.

Human activity and the dynamics of collaborative work

The three levels of uncertainty by Andersen et al. (1990) has some similarity with the hierarchical structure of human activity identified by activity theory (e.g. Engeström, 1987). Where Andersen et al. define levels of uncertainty according to goals and means being known or unknown, activity theory structures human acts according to their motivation and automaticity. Human activity is seen to be mediated by artefacts in a dialectical process of continuos and reflective recreation. Human activity is situated and can only be analysed in its social, historical and technical context. The basic unit of analysis is the connected structure of subject, object, instruments, based in socio cultural context — the activity system. At the topmost level of its hierarchical structure *activity* is motivated, directed to fulfil a need. Activity is realised through conscious *actions* directed to relevant goals. In turn, actions are realised through unconscious operations triggered by the structure of the activity and conditions in the environment.

Within this hierarchical structure, Raithel (1996) propose, a framework for understanding collaborative work, identifying three levels of collaboration: co-ordination, co-operation and co-construction. At the co-ordination level, collaboration is an integral part of routine work: the participants act according to scripted roles, defined by explicit written rules, the division of labour, traditions and tacit knowledge. At the co-operation level, collaboration is directed to a known object (or goal) shared by the actors, but the means are not shared or even known to all the actors. Thus, actors continuously modify actions based on intermediate results, adapting to others' actions and conceptualising their own actions in the process of realising the object. At the co-construction level new motives are created. Neither the object of work nor the means of obtaining it are fixed or shared between all actors. Instead they continuously re-negotiated and re-conceptualised throughout the process to create a commonly shared set of objects and rules. This framework has been used in studies of court cases (Engeström et al. 1991), and in studies of the dynamics of collaboration in hospital settings (Bardram 1998). It can be understood as an elaboration of the uncertainty framework referred to above, pointing to the construction of goals and motives as central aspects of the dynamics of collaboration.

At the wastewater treatment plant, situations connected to breakdowns of machines are examples of co-operation. The breakdown changes collaboration from co-ordination to co-operation. Co-construction rarely occurs at the wastewater treatment plant but may be prompted by external factors like new technology, new environmental legislation or critical changes in the quantity and quality of wastewater from industry and the city. In such cases co-construction primarily involves the manager and people at the city wastewater office.

Identifying dynamics

As wastewater treatment is a dynamic setting with processes at many levels, from water flow to transformative changes of the overall purpose and structure of the plant, it is necessary to develop a detailed analysis of these dynamics. In identifying the dynamics in the wastewater treatment plant we have constructed the following checklist. The checklist is based on the concepts introduced above, and is suggested as a general tool for the analysis of complex technical work arrangements.

- Identify contextual units
- Consider granularity of goals and motives
- Identify processes
- Link processes with the structuring of contextual units
- Identify modes of formalisation
- Identify types of technical structuring

Identifying contextual units

Contextual units are units of the setting that make sense according to specific situations, tasks or purpose; heterogeneous and overlapping. According to Star (1989), boundary objects are objects used by different parties in different localities; robust enough to maintain identity across heterogeneous use, but plastic enough to adapt to the constraints and needs of the different parties working with them. Components of the wastewater treatment plant are boundary objects in the sense that are parts of overlapping contextual units. However, the interpretability is in general somewhat limited. As part of the daily round of one of the workers, a specific gas motor is looked at and listened to, thus part of the contextual unit of the daily round. However, the same motor constitutes it own isolated contextual unit in situations when it is taken down for repair. Further, the motor is part of the subpart of the plant transforming gas in the sludge into electricity. This gas production is a contextual unit from one perspective, but at the same time an important indicator of the load of the whole plant. Another example: the managers office is the centre and symbol of management and general monitoring of the plant, but it is also where one of the unskilled workers daily enters results from the laboratory tests into the process control computer system. The heterogeneity of contextual units is fundamentally different from the hierarchical decomposition seen in the mainstream of engineering literature.

Consider the granularity of goals and motives

A specific alteration of the technical arrangement may appear as a transformation of the basic condition for one activity, while it from the perspective of another activity reflects maintenance of stability. Thus, introducing a new polymer into the wastewater cleaning process, as we saw at the plant, meant some of the workers had to extent their daily work routines to include new tasks. The introduction of the polymer changed their work practice. From the point of view of the city wastewater office, or the plant manager, however, the new polymer was perceived more as an adjustment than as a transformation. Such differences are related to the granularity of goals and motives. In dealing with this granularity we need an understanding of the historical development of the setting, its background and motivation (Markussen 1993).

Identifying processes

As discussed above process can be understood as mere movement in time and space. This notion of process is needed in understanding the technical arrangement of a wastewater treatment plant and in understanding the purification process as such; water flowing, phases oscillating, etc. Human work is another kind of process, possibly highly routinised, like the daily test sample collection round, but always motivated at some level. The question to ask for every process is whether it is causal, according to laws of nature or if it is intentional, dialectically directed by motives. In both cases, the technical structuring of the process, e.g. timing of sample taking determined by phases in the purification process, can be taken into account.

Linking processes with the contextual units

In linking processes to the structuring of contextual units we consider processes structured by the contextual units as well as processes changing or moving the structures of these units. The test sample collection round is structured by the distribution of test sample points around the plant. The arrangement of test points at the plant is changed by the development of new ways of testing, such as automatic sensors, and by new insights and requirements from the society. The process-structure diagrams described by Mathiassen (1981) supports this step, although it doesn't fully acknowledge the heterogeneous nature of the contextual resulting from variability of purpose, and the non-hierarchical features of the technical structure.

Identifying modes of formalisation

The identification of modes of formalisation is primarily related to the work going on in the considered domain, and can be treated in the terminology of constraints and possibilities (Mogensen 1994). In the study of wastewater treatment, it was particularly useful to analyse the modes of formalisation in terms sequentially, enforced or emerged, as well as dynamics or flexibility of routines. Large parts of the work of the unskilled workers at the wastewater treatment plant are formalised by daily rounds at the plant, by forms that have to be filled out. Most of the sequential formalisation at the plant could be rearranged, implying that these sequences serve more as well-structured checklists than scripts. The formalisation in relation to work at the laboratory is less flexible in that the formalisation here is embedded in the tools. Thus, the test tubes must be shaken, heated for 15 minutes, etc. in order to work at all.

Identifying types of technical structuring

The technical structuring is the structuring around the physical, chemical and biological processes as well as the structuring of the process control and automation system. This structuring can be analysed from the perspective of the present paper, limited to the basic considerations of the type of process, as well as from the expert perspectives of the relevant engineering disciplines. As an example, automation theory yields a distinction between the process (water flowing) and the control system, which is particularly useful. A feature of the particular technical structuring of the wastewater treatment plant was the number of false alarms that routinely had to be unset.

Dynamics in Wastewater treatment

The analysis of the case study can be summarised in two issues concerning dynamics. First we propose a five level model of dynamics, secondly we discuss the contradiction between maintenance and optimisation as an instance of the general contradiction between motives of different praxes.

Levels of dynamics

We have chosen the perspective of wastewater treatment work as a (dialectic) correlation between elements of structure and process that on the one hand shapes and delimits but also, and more importantly, has within it the ability to transform and transcend. We chose this view because it supports the understanding we have obtained of the work during the field study, namely as constantly adapting and changing to reflect several levels of other dynamic systems that affect different aspects of the wastewater treatment process. We now try to substantiate this perspective by mapping out the different kinds of dynamics and structures we see present in the wastewater treatment process, and we do this aided by the checklist.

The technical process

The most basic level of dynamics in wastewater treatment, its *sine qua non*, is the movement of water through pipes and tanks and the alternation between phases, of e.g. nitrification and de-nitrification, in the purification process. In the same way movements of people working at the plant is a basic, and obvious, form of dynamics.

People moving around

Large parts of the work at the plant is associated with walking around, often moving through the same, remote parts of the plant several times a day. This is done to collect test samples, but more often just to monitor the condition of the plant and the process, as a vital part of preventing breakdowns and verifying system information.

Technical re-arrangement

During the period of our visits at the wastewater treatment plant, the technical structure of the plant changed. On our second visit, we saw a tank located in a driveway. The tank contained a polymer, an oil-based substance that separates water and sludge, decreasing the percentage of water in the sludge before it is processed in the bio gas generator. This was one of many experiments to increase the wastewater treatment capacity. When we visited the plant three weeks later, a shed had been build around the polymer tank. Thus, the experiment had attained a more permanent status. This example has two implications for the study of dynamics. First, that the technical structure is moving, and that the change may begin as experimental fluctuations and end as sustained change of the technical structure. Second, that movement in the technical the structure, e.g. the appearance of the polymer shed, for the chief biologist at the central wastewater office may be a case of mere adjustment of the established mode of operation. For the men at the plant, however, the shed and the new equipment in it was an alteration of the working environment, introducing new tasks in the day to day work, calling for adjustment of established practice, and the building of it was an object in itself.

Flexible routines

One worker, while checking the area around the sludge tanks, noticed that the surface water in the tanks was brownish. He immediately proceeded to the building the water would have come from to check a filter he suspected to be the cause of the water being discoloured, and which turned out to be in dire need of a rinse. He explained that if the water hadn't been discoloured, he would have gone down to check the filter anyway because that building is part of his area of responsibility, but that he would not have done so until much later. This situation may seem too simple to be of interest; one man works alone, going on a well-defined round. However, even though the contextual unit, namely the part of the plant associated with the tasks on the round, both physically and process-wise, and the goals, namely checking up on a number of things on the plant, are well-defined, we see that this situation reveals some interesting points with regards to the identification of modes of formalisation and the process.

Because he encounters the brown water, which we may call a causal process outside of but interfering with his actual work, his motive changes with regards to what needs to be done when and he initiates a change in his routine. Even though the daily round is well defined in terms of which tasks should be done and checkpoints visited, the routine still leaves plenty of flexibility for the reorganisation of the order of tasks. The alternative, which would be to perform the related tasks in a strict sequence, perhaps related to the physical layout of the plant would contradict an overall motive of work at the plant, namely to keep the purification process running continuously. The lack of response to warnings such as the brown water would seriously increase the risk of an actual machine breakdown. Going exclusively by the physical layout also renders the process-look at the purification process invalid, because it becomes impossible to look at connections between the components that are related in the process but not physically standing side by side. Most importantly, though, is that these reservations holds double for cooperative situations. If the workers have to leave their routines to collectively recover from a machinery breakdown, the flexibility is even more crucial.

After arguing that a high degree of flexibility is important in the everyday routines, we would like to emphasise that this is not the case for all aspects of wastewater treatment processes. It would be absurd to claim that flexibility is necessary in the physical flow of the water through the plant, thereby making it possible to send the water out into the bay before the chemical or mechanical cleaning process. This is also why we argue that the technical structure of the wastewater treatment process needs to be identified and juxtaposed with the continuously changing processes.

Transformation of the domain

Some of the most profound changes in wastewater treatment have come from the development of environmental legislation. The water quality plan passed by the Danish parliament in the late 80'es introduced new norms for pollution of water resources. One motive for this legislation was instances of severe extirpation of the fauna in several lakes, rivers and sea areas caused by too many nutrients in the outlet of water from houses, industry, and the primary production. Thus it was no longer acceptable to let 'black' water from the wastewater treatment plant out in the bay, neither legally nor according to public opinion. Depending on the degree of effort necessary for the wastewater treatment plant to reach the new legal level of nutrients, the technical process and the work routines changed in accordance to this; small changes on existing technology would not affect the purification process noticeably whereas the implementation of new technology and a radical change in the tasks performed or the staff involved would more or less completely change the process on a contextual or non-technical level. In the former case we wouldn't talk about the contextual unit of the plant being changed whereas the latter situation would call for a redefinition of several levels of contextual units, possibly including the wastewater treatment system for all of the city. From this example it becomes apparent that we must deal with a whole range of external influences that may affect the wastewater treatment process, possibly quite profoundly. Similar influences could be the consequence of the development of new technology making the purification process more efficient and economically attractive, even though the means for effective purification and economic gain rarely go hand in hand.

Maintenance vs. optimisation

In the following we discuss the tension between maintenance and optimisation as an instance of conflicting motives in wastewater treatment. Throughout our field study we have seen several examples of how the contextual units or work horizons may differ, especially between management and workers. Management and workers share the goal of making the plant run smoothly. Management also has the goal of improving how the plant runs, both economically and in terms of cleaner water. In specific situations, such as when experiments of adding a new polymer to improve the quality of the sludge (work horizon for management) causes the sludge to stick to the canvas in the press thus making it harder to empty it, this disrupts the work of maintaining the sludge press process (which is the work horizon for the workers in the sludge press). These types of disruptions, if not identified and handled, may in the last instance cause collaborative efforts to break down. To aid us in this identification and handling process we find it fruitful to consider two different work perspectives: maintenance and optimisation.

Maintenance focuses on keeping the wastewater treatment system (or parts of it) stable and running without breakdowns. The motive for optimisation is to change one or more processes to obtain a better end-result in terms of cleaner water. So managers may consciously introduce disturbances to optimise the running of the plant, whereas maintenance workers will try to eliminate disturbances and preserve the status quo. When the goal changes over time, the maintenance work changes to reflect this, so stability in this context does not equal a completely fixed state but rather a space defined by the levels of dynamics affecting the wastewater treatment process within which maintenance work operates. Similarly, optimisation work is delimited by the structures within the different levels of dynamics and thus not free to make arbitrary changes. Consequently, the two perspectives contain many identical elements, which makes it hard tell them apart. However, they differ on a few but significant counts, namely with regards to the motive and possibly the contextual unit in a given situation. The proposed framework offers methods for analysing work in relation to motivation and thus helps us assess which perspective is driving the different actors in a collaborative activity.

Conclusion

In line with the mainstream of CSCW research following Suchman's (1986) questioning of formal constructs, our study of the wastewater treatment plant establishes yet another case where deviations and situated action is a hindrance to complete formalisations. Further, we have questioned the applicability of formal constructs in relation to the technical arrangement based on the analysis of the various types of dynamics observed in the wastewater treatment plant, according to their degree of permanent change, motivatedness, and transformative feature.

It can be expected that the general technological development will bring the cost of relevant computer hardware down to a level where it will be feasible to introduce a higher degree of fine masked control technology, sensors, on-line meters, etc. in wastewater treatment plants. Our study points to the likely difficulties in implementing such formal constructs, not just in relation to the flexibility of work at the plant, but also in relation to the process system as such. Because of the dynamics of the technical arrangement, fine-grained control systems will need to be updated at a rate where it is not likely to pay off. For every modification of the plant, for every new polymer tank, the control system may need to be modified. Design approaches enabling technical tailoring based on strong modularisation and encapsulation, or approaches locating parts of the control system in the components, may help; however not when it comes to the more home brewed changes in the process system, and clearly not in relation to the flexibility of work routines.

The proposed five levels of dynamics, as well as the framework for identifying the dynamics, have helped us understand the domain of wastewater treatment. These conceptual tools may also be helpful in the design of CSCW-systems for complex technical settings, especially in handling formalisation and the design of formal constructs. In future activities in the wastewater project the reported analyses of levels of dynamics will be used and evaluated as a basis for design.

Acknowledgements

We will like to thank the people at the wastewater treatment plant, and our colleagues in the wastewater project. Also, thanks to the anonymous reviewers for constructive criticism. Finally, we owe a special thank to Wendy Mackay for being extraordinarily helpful. Our work on the wastewater project has been supported by The Danish Basic Research Foundation, Centre for Human-Machine Interaction and The Danish National Centre for IT-Research, project no. 23 (Usability Work in the Danish Industry).

References

Andersen, N. E., F. Kensing, J. Lundin, L. Mathiassen, A. Munk-Madsen, M. Rasbech and P. Sørgaard (1990). *Professional systems development*. New York: Prentice Hall.

Bardram, J. E. (1998). *Collaboration, Coordination, and Computer Support. An Activity Theoretical Approach to the Design of Computer Supported Cooperative Work*. Ph.D. Thesis, Aarhus: Computer Science Department DAIMI PB - 533

Blackburn, S. (1994). *The Oxford Dictionary of Philosophy*. Oxford: Oxford University Press.

Bowers, J., G. Button, and W. Sharrock (1995). Workflow From Within and Without: Technology and Cooperative Work on the Print industry shopfloor. Proceedings of ECSCW95

Droste, R. L. (1997). *Theory and Practice of Waster and Wastewater Treatment*. NY: John Wiley & Sons, Inc.

Engeström, Y. (1987). *Learning by Expanding: An activity-theoretical approach to developmental research*, Helsinki: Orienta-Konsultit Oy.

Engeström, Y., K. Brown, L. C Christopher and J. Gregory (1991). Coordination, Cooperation and Communication in the Courts: Expansive Transitions in legal Work. In *The Quarterly Newsletter of the Laboratory of Comparative Human Cognition*, Vol 13, Number 4.

Heath, C.C. and P. Luff (1992). Collaboration and control: Crisis Management and multimedia technology in London Underground line control rooms. *CSCW Journal*, 1 (1 - 2), pp. 69-94.

Israel, J. (1979). *The Language of Dialectics and the Dialectics of Language*. Copenhagen: Munksgård Humanities Press.

Markussen, R. (1993). A Historical Perspective on Work Practice and Technology: The Case of National Labour Inspection Service. In Andersen P. B., Holmqvist, B. and Jensen, J. F. *The Computer as a Medium*. Cambridge: Cambridge University Press, 1993. pp.457-477.

Mathiassen, L. (1981). Systemudvikling og Systemudviklingsmetode [English: System development and system development method]. Aarhus: Computer Science Department DAIMI PB-136 .

Robinson, M. (1989). Double Level Languages and Co-operative Working, *Conference on Support, Society and Culture. Mutual uses of Cybernetics and Science - Proceedings. Amsterdam 1989*. pp. 79-114.

Raeithel, A. (1996) From coordinatedness to Coordination via Cooperation and Co-construction. Paper presented ad *Workshop on Work and Learning in Transition*, San Diego, January 1996.

Schmidt (1997) Of maps and scripts: The status of formal constructs in cooperative work. In S. C. Hayne and W. Prinz (eds.): *GROUP'97, Proceedings of the ACM SIGGROUP Conference on Supporting Group Work, Phoenix, Arizona, 16-19 November 1997*. ACM Press, New York, N.Y., 1997, pp. 138-147.

Star, S. L. (1989). The Structure of Ill-Structured Solutions: Boundary Objects and Heterogeneous Distributed Problem Solving. In L. Gasser and M. N. Huhns *Distributed Artificial intelligence, volume II*. London: Pitman Publishers, pp. 37-54.

Suchman, L. and E. Wynn (1984) Procedures and Problems in the Office. In *Office: Technology and People,* vol. 2, 1984, pp. 133-154.

Suchman, L. (1986). *Plans and Situated Actions*. Cambridge MA: Cambridge University Press.

S. Bødker, M. Kyng, and K. Schmidt (eds.). *Proceedings of the Sixth European Conference on Computer-Supported Cooperative Work, 12-16 September 1999, Copenhagen, Denmark*
©1999 Kluwer Academic Publishers. Printed in the Netherlands

WebDAV

A network protocol for remote collaborative authoring on the Web

E. James Whitehead, Jr.[†] & Yaron Y. Goland[‡]
[†]Dept. of Info. and Computer Science, U.C. Irvine, USA, *ejw@ics.uci.edu*
[‡]Microsoft Corporation, Redmond, WA, USA, *yarong@microsoft.com*

Abstract. Collaborative authoring tools generate network effects, where each tool's value depends not just on the tool itself, but on the number of other people who also have compatible tools. We hypothesize that the best way to generate network effects and to add collaborative authoring capability to existing tools is to focus on the network protocol. This paper explores a protocol-centric approach to collaborative authoring by examining the requirements and functionality of the WebDAV protocol. Key features of the protocol are non-connection-oriented concurrency control, providing an upward migration path for existing non-collaborative applications, support for remote manipulation of the namespace of documents, and simultaneous satisfaction of a wide range of functional requirements.

Introduction

Despite many compelling research examples of collaborative authoring, so far their impact on actual authoring practice has been limited. While BSCW (Bentley et al., 1997) and HYPER-G (Maurer, 1996) have developed communities of use, electronic mail remains the dominant technology used for collaborative authoring, mainly due to its ubiquity.

In order to perform collaborative authoring, all collaborators need to use compatible authoring tools—typically all collaborators use the *same* tools, tailor-made to support collaboration. To collaborate using PREP (Neuwirth et al., 1994), all collaborators need to use PREP, likewise for GROVE (Ellis et al., 1989) and

292

DUPLEX (Pacull et al., 1994).

The economics of compatibility drive network effects (Rohlfs, 1974), where the utility of each tool depends not just on the tool itself, but on the number of other people who also own compatible tools. If there were just one telephone in the world, its utility would be small, with two or three not much more useful. But when millions, or hundreds of millions of people own telephones, their utility is immense. Like the telephone, one collaborative authoring tool by itself has limited collaborative value, but when millions have compatible collaboration technology, the utility of each tool is great. When a common network protocol ensures interoperability between collaborative authoring tools and authoring servers, as each tool adopts the protocol, the value of servers that support the collaboration protocol increases, since *without any further investment in the server*, they can now support an additional tool. The reverse is true as well. As more servers become available, the value of the authoring tools increases without any further investment in the tools, since there are now more individuals and organizations capable of collaboration. By creating a network protocol with a focus on interoperability, it is possible to generate network effects among compatible collaborative authoring technologies.

Users of existing applications have invested significant time in gaining expertise in the applications they frequently use, hence the cost to users of switching to another tool is high. Yet users must switch tools to gain the advantages of existing collaborative authoring systems. Exceptions to this rule are BSCW and MESSIE (Sasse and Handley, 1993), which leverage standard network protocols to allow the use of existing non-collaborative tools with the system; the Hypertext Transfer Protocol, HTTP, (Fielding et al., 1997) is employed this way by BSCW, while MESSIE piggybacks on the Simple Mail Transfer Protocol (Postel, 1982). CONTACT (Kirby and Rodden, 1995) also supports collaborative authoring while remaining compatible with the heterogeneous non-collaborative tools in the user's environment. Like BSCW, CONTACT provides a Web forms interface to a collaboration support system, but does not provide BSCW's HTTP upload/download support. BSCW, MESSIE, and CONTACT share our view that collaborative authoring capability is not, by itself, sufficient to overcome the costs of switching authoring tools. Unlike these systems, we go further and assert that collaborative authoring capability must be added to existing tools.

Our hypothesis is *the best way to generate network effects and to add collaborative authoring capability to existing tools is to focus on the network protocol*, the mechanism by which collaborative tools communicate. There are many reasons for focusing attention on the network protocol that underlies a remote collaborative authoring system. From a technical viewpoint, focusing on the network protocol elevates the protocol's behavior across the Internet to a first-class concern. This ensures that thorny issues are addressed up-front, such as how to ensure efficient behavior under high-latency conditions, the provision of adequate security and authentication, and giving the protocol good scalability and extensibility characteristics. If addressed poorly, these factors can cripple the widespread adoption of a remote authoring technology.

The Web Distributed Authoring and Versioning (WEBDAV) working group of the Internet Engineering Task Force (IETF) has adopted this protocol-centric approach, and developed a novel network protocol, the WEBDAV DISTRIBUTED AUTHORING PROTOCOL (hereafter called the WEBDAV protocol), which supports interoperable remote, asynchronous, collaborative authoring. The WEBDAV protocol, a detailed specification of which can be found in Goland et al. (1999), is a set of extensions to HTTP which provide facilities for concurrency control, namespace operations, and property management. The protocol allows users to collaboratively author their content *directly* to an HTTP server, allowing the Web to be viewed not just as a read-only way to download information, but as a *writeable, collaborative medium.*

IETF protocol specifications foster interoperability by providing a concrete specification used to develop multiple applications. Indeed, for a specification to advance along the standards track within the IETF, it must demonstrate two interoperable implementations of every protocol feature. This requirement, combined with the group review process within the IETF, works to ensure that the semantics of the protocol are precise. Furthermore, the focus on interoperability across many applications helps limit the likelihood that the concerns of any one program will bias the protocol's design.

Since IETF specifications can be retrieved free of charge, and there are no licensing fees for using IETF technology, IETF network protocols are very attractive to both corporate and open-source developers. This freedom of the intellectual property rights aids in the adoption of the protocol by a wide variety of tools.

One use scenario for the WEBDAV protocol is collaborative authoring of an academic paper by a geographically dispersed authoring team. When the project begins, one member of the project uses server-specific mechanisms to create username/password pairs for each collaborator, and then creates the shared document with a WEBDAV-enabled word processor by saving it to a URL. After giving each collaborator write access, they communicate the URL of the document to the rest of the team using email, or perhaps in a teleconference. The authors take turns working on the document, using email, telephone conversations, and other out-of-band communications to negotiate editing slots. During each editing pass, an author loads the document from the URL, causing it to be locked. They then work within the editor, saving directly back to the URL. When done, they perform a final save to the URL, then unlock the document. At all times, other authors can load the document directly from the URL using either their word processor (it will be read-only if locked) or their Web browser (if it can view the word processor format), to see its current status. When done, they can give the URL to colleagues interested in the paper, and create hyperlinks to the paper in other Web pages.

This paper reports on the WEBDAV protocol, presenting the requirements it satisfies, and how these requirements, combined with the constraints of operating in the Internet environment, guided its design. Key contributions of the WEBDAV protocol include:

Protocol focus: The focus of this work is a network protocol, the abstractions and semantics which inform the syntax of octets transmitted during a TCP/IP connection. This contrasts with existing work on remote collaborative authoring which focus on user interface, awareness, and other concerns.

Providing an upward migration path for existing non-collaborative applications: There are many applications that have no support for remote collaborative authoring. The WEBDAV protocol provides these applications a way to add remote authoring support without dramatically modifying the input processing of the application, as would be necessary if the application were modified to support fine-grain synchronous authoring. Furthermore, its grain size for concurrency control is compatible with most existing file-oriented tools.

Non-connection-oriented protocol for concurrency control: The WEBDAV protocol provides long-duration exclusive and shared write locks, a well-known concurrency control technique. To achieve robust Internet-scale collaboration, where network connections may be disconnected arbitrarily, and for scalability, since each open connection consumes server resources, the duration of WEBDAV locks is independent of any individual network connection.

Support for remotely manipulating the namespace of documents: The WEBDAV protocol provides copy and move operations, and provides support for listing the members of Web collections, similar to a directory listing in a file system. Though these operations have appeared before in numerous systems, their appearance in remote collaborative authoring systems is unusual, reflecting the awareness that these systems need to provide mechanisms for navigating to the document which will be authored, and for maintaining logical groupings of documents in collections.

Simultaneous satisfaction of requirements: The WEBDAV protocol simultaneously satisfies a wide range of difficult requirements, a non-trivial engineering activity in which tradeoffs amongst goals impacted the protocol. WEBDAV addressed several concerns which are critical to adoption of a remote collaboration technology, but which are either not mentioned, or not addressed in the collaborative authoring literature, including connection security, strong authentication, internationalization, and independence from authoring environment. While WEBDAV benefited by adopting existing technologies such as Transport Layer Security (TLS) (Dierks and Allen, 1999), Digest Authentication (Franks et al., 1997), and XML (Bray et al., 1998), the identification of the requirements, and the integration of these technologies to satisfy those requirements is unique.

Extensibility: The WEBDAV protocol recognized that it would not be able to address all features that an authoring system would need. Thus extensibility became a critical feature. The protocol has been designed with well defined feature namespaces that allow for new features to be added later on. Existing systems will always be able to recognize new commands and have sufficient information to determine if they should ignore the unknown command or fail.

The remainder of this paper presents requirements for remote collaborative authoring of Web content, then describes the WEBDAV protocol and how it meets these requirements. The key attributes of the WEBDAV protocol, discussed in the Introduction above, will be expanded in this section. Following sections will briefly describe the existing servers and clients that implement the WEBDAV protocol, and discuss the WEBDAV protocol in relation to other existing work.

Requirements in support of collaboration

Requirements given below are an abridged version of those found in Slein et al. (1998), the consensus requirements document of the WEBDAV working group.

Equal support for all content types

The Web is composed of documents, images, and objects of many content, or Internet media types (Freed et al., 1996). *A Web authoring protocol must treat all content types equally.*

A Web authoring protocol which only provides operations for resources of one preferred content type, such as HTML, or which requires authoring-specific extensions to support features such as versioning, would have limited applicability due to its lack of support for the wide variety of other content types. Furthermore, since many common content types are in constant evolution, in order to ensure stability of the protocol a strict separation between the protocol, and the format of the objects operated upon by the protocol, must be maintained. For example, during the development of the WEBDAV protocol itself, new standards for HTML 3.2, 4.0, and XML were issued, highlighting how quickly these document formats can develop and evolve. Tailoring an authoring protocol too closely to any one content type would rapidly make the protocol obsolete.

Concurrency control support

Since the Web is inherently multi-user, *a Web authoring protocol must mediate concurrent access by multiple authors.*

Early Web authoring tools encountered the "lost update problem" which occurs when two or more simultaneous authors of a Web page clobber each other's work with successive saves to the same URL, without first merging changes by other authors. Although HTTP 1.1 added support for *detecting* lost updates through the use of unique identifiers associated with the document state, no support was provided for *preventing* lost updates in the first place.

Early on, WEBDAV decided to use long duration, whole resource locking as its concurrency control mechanism (the rationale for this choice is discussed in the section on Locking). This then allowed the WEBDAV requirements to focus on desired properties of locks:

Lock independence: the lock operation must be independent of other operations. For example, it should not be necessary to retrieve the resource to lock it (e.g., as would be the case with a GET with lock operation). The primary motivation for this requirement is to maintain a separation of concerns between locking and other HTTP operations.

Multi-resource locking: the protocol must support an atomic operation to lock multiple resources on the same server. Documents often consist of many separate files. For example, Web pages are composed of text, images, and executable content stored as separate Web resources. Hence an authoring tool needs the ability to prevent lost updates on all the components of these multi-part documents, so the document can be authored as a unit. A multi-resource lock guarantees this. The atomicity restriction ensures that if two people are trying to lock the same group of resources, only one will be granted a lock.

Write locks: the protocol is only required to support a write lock, and no read lock is necessary (or provided by the WEBDAV protocol). On the Web, by default a resource is readable, although it may be protected by access control. Therefore, HTTP does not require that a Web browser obtain a lock in order to read a resource, as is the case with traditional database locking, and retrofitting the Web with this capability was not feasible, or desirable.

Lock discovery: it must be possible to discover whether a resource is locked. This allows a user interface to be constructed which indicates whether a resource is locked.

Support for properties (metadata)

Since there is a significant amount of information about Web resources which is not directly stored in the contents of the resource, *a Web authoring protocol must provide facilities to create, modify, read, and delete arbitrary properties (metadata) on all Web resources, irrespective of content type.*

Most Web resources have associated descriptive information, such as its author, title, publisher, keywords, copyright status, content rating, etc. While HTML, with its META tags provides a way to embed this information within HTML documents, many Web resource types have no capability for storing metadata in their data formats. For those that do, their capabilities and storage locations vary by content type, making them awkward to use. Properties, essentially *name, value* pairs, are useful for recording bibliographic information, which can later be used in searches on property values, a capability currently being developed by the DAV Searching and Locating (DASL) working group within the IETF (DASL, 1999).

Properties can be viewed as an assertion about a resource. For example, an author property asserts that the author of the resource is given in the value of the property. In a distributed system, the issue of consistency maintenance for properties is important—if a new author starts editing a resource, the author property must be updated, or it will be inconsistent. A Web server can automatically maintain the consistency of property values that it can compute, such as a property that records the length of the resource. Other properties, such as copyright status, can only be maintained by the client. WEBDAV terms properties whose syntax and semantics are enforced by the server as "live properties", and properties which are stored without processing, and without automatic consistency maintenance, as "dead properties." This leads to the requirement that *a Web authoring protocol must support both live and dead properties.*

Support for content-type independent links

As Web resources have a wide variety of relationships between them, and since existing Web links are unidirectional, and are supported by only a few content types, *a Web authoring protocol must provide operations to create, modify, read, and delete typed links (relationships) between Web resources of any content type.* Links can be used to capture a wide variety of relationships, such as the print ordering of a set of HTML documents, or related documents such as a table of contents, an index, or a glossary.

Retrieval of unprocessed source for editing

When a Web resource is retrieved using HTTP, the transmitted octets (known as the response entity body) are a *representation* of the state of the resource, and there is no guarantee that the actual state of the resource is being returned. Many Web resources exploit this, providing a representation that differs greatly from the underlying state of the resource. Examples include HTML with server-side-include directives and active server pages, which are both processed by the server before creating the response entity body, as well as CGI scripts, where the response entity body typically has no correlation with the persistent state of the resource, the code of the CGI script itself. Since HTTP GET always returns a response entity body *after* the server has performed its processing, *a Web authoring protocol must provide support to retrieve an authoring-suitable representation of the source of a Web resource.*

Namespace manipulation

Since resources may need to be copied, or moved as a Web site evolves, *a Web authoring protocol must provide support for copying and moving Web resources.*

There are ramifications beyond mere renaming—the behavior of a server's namespace may not be uniform, and policies such as freedom from automatic download by robot, or different cache expiration dates may vary across the namespace. This requirement also follows from our user metaphor of saving to a Web site just like any other filesystem, since most "Save As" dialog boxes provide the ability to list directories and manipulate names.

The key insight is that focusing on facilities for authoring a single resource is insufficient. Web resources exist within a space of URL names, and a Web authoring protocol needs to provide support for manipulating this environment.

Support for collections

A Web authoring protocol must provide support for creating and deleting a collection, adding and removing members to/from a collection, and for listing the members of a collection.

Collections are resources which act as containers of other resources, including other collections. They provide an abstraction that can group resources, and thus reduce the burden of authoring within a large corpus of documents. Collections are also used for navigation within large document spaces, as evidenced by the ubiquitous file navigation windows within the "Save As" and "Open" dialog boxes of current tools. Web authoring protocols need to support this navigation style. With DASL, collections will support navigation-by-query as well.

The WebDAV protocol

This section describes in detail the major features of the WEBDAV protocol—properties, locking, and namespace management—that were designed to satisfy the Web collaborative authoring requirements given in the previous section.

Properties

WEBDAV properties are *name, value* pairs. A property name is a Uniform Resource Identifier (URI), as defined in Berners-Lee et al. (1998). Property values are expressed as XML elements. Two methods are provided to manipulate properties, PROPFIND and PROPPATCH.

The PROPFIND method is used to retrieve properties, and supports three operations: retrieve all property names and values, retrieve selected names and values, or retrieve only the property names. When applied to a collection resource PROPFIND can be instructed to act recursively against the collection resource and its members. By recursively we mean that if any of the members of the collection are themselves collections then PROPFIND will be executed against the members of the sub-collections, and so on. Note that even when used recursively, only a single request is sent, and only a single response, with property information for all affected resources, is returned.

The PROPPATCH method can set or remove multiple properties on a resource in an atomic operation. That is, all the set and remove commands in the PROPPATCH will either be successfully applied in the order submitted, or none will. To support dead properties, WEBDAV servers are capable of supporting arbitrary properties, as client-maintained "dead" values. Like PROPFIND, PROPPATCH can also be applied recursively against collection resources.

For example, *DAV:source* is one normative property defined in the WEBDAV protocol. If present, it provides a link from a resource to a URL where a representation suitable for authoring can be retrieved.

Design rationale for properties

Several different designs were considered for properties. The first design used typed links: a set of URLs that expressed a relationship between two or more resources. To express the relationship "is-author-of", a link would be defined from the document being authored to a separate resource that contained the name of the author. Though powerful, this link-based design was rejected for performance reasons, since it resulted in many network requests, and because consistency maintenance of linked metadata is difficult.

The approach which was finally adopted flowed from the notion of allowing "links" to record metadata strings directly. Thus small properties could be recorded directly inside of the property's value, while large values could be accessed indirectly through a URL. This design better suits the preponderance of metadata which consists of "small" data items, such as an author's name.

The PROPFIND method allows multiple property values to be retrieved at once, thus satisfying performance requirements. XML is used for the default property syntax as a simple, yet structured format for property values. In addition, WEBDAV's additional rule that any XML elements not understood must be ignored allows property values to be extended while retaining backward compatibility. XML also allows properties to contain arbitrary data with less complexity than the dual method design.

The ultimate argument in favor of this design for PROPPATCH is the interdependence of property values and resource state. For example, if properties

A & B have mutually dependent values and a client crashes between updating A and B, the resource would be left in an inconsistent state. This led to the inclusion of both set and delete commands in the PROPPATCH method, in conjunction with the atomicity requirement.

URIs are used to name WEBDAV properties, because many different groups and applications will create new properties. URIs form a controlled namespace that provides support for both centralized and decentralized extensions yet guarantees uniqueness. Registering a new URI scheme gains the benefits of a centrally controlled namespace, while using URLs allows any organization with a domain name to create new property names.

Locking

Concurrency control within the WEBDAV protocol is provided by write locks. The LOCK method supports two types of locks: "exclusive write locks" and "shared write locks". Since any kind of principal—human or Web robot—could write to a Web resource, a write lock prevents any principal other than the lock owner, from writing to a locked resource. An exclusive write lock prevents *all* principals other than the single lock owner from writing to the resource, while a shared write lock can be owned simultaneously by several users. This terminology differs from the typical database use, where a shared lock is typically taken out prior to reading a database cell.

The lock compatibility table for write locks is given in Table I.

CURRENT LOCK STATE	SHARED LOCK REQUEST	EXCLUSIVE LOCK REQUEST
None	Granted	Granted
Shared Lock	Granted	Not Granted
Exclusive Lock	Not Granted	Not Granted

Table I: Lock compatibility table. The current lock state of the resource is given in the leftmost column, and lock requests are listed in the first row. The intersection of row and column gives the results of a lock request, where "granted" means the lock was granted, and "not granted" means the lock was not granted.

Principals are identified using Digest Authentication, an extension to HTTP specified in Franks et al. (1997). This scheme, which uses multiple one-way hashes to encrypt a username, password pair, is substantially better than authentication schemes in existing remote authoring tools. For example, MESSIE (Sasse et al., 1993) only transmits an unencrypted username before granting write access to a repository. HYPER-G, whose Client-Server Protocol is described in

Kappe and Pani (1996), has a much-stronger DES-encrypted username, password pair to authenticate users. Unfortunately, most remote authoring system papers do not describe how they authenticate their users, making it impossible to determine how secure they are—raising questions on how easily their concurrency control and access control schemes can be spoofed.

The WEBDAV locking mechanism is non-connection-oriented. When a lock is granted, the server returns a lock token, a globally unique identifier, to the client. So long as it stores the lock token, the client need not remain connected. When the client subsequently wants to perform write operations on the locked resource, it recreates the network connection, then passes authentication credentials and the lock token to the server along with the write request. The authentication credentials ensure the requesting principal is who they claim to be, and the lock token ensures the requesting principal's client software is aware of the lock. This eliminates cases where the same principal could have multiple applications running at the same time, only a subset of which are aware of a given lock.

Since any client can discover the lock token for an active lock by examining the *DAV:lockdiscovery* property, lock tokens are public knowledge. Thus, possession of a lock token does not, by itself, grant a client permission to write a locked resource. It is the combination of having correct authentication credentials and demonstrating knowledge of the lock, by passing the lock token, that grants the ability to write a locked resource.

Multiple resources can be locked with a single lock request by performing a recursive lock upon a collection and its children, receiving a single lock token in the response to represent the entire lock.

Design rationale for locking

Internet connections are inherently unreliable: an application should be prepared for a connection to go down at any time. To achieve robust behavior, a protocol must be designed to gracefully handle broken connections. For robustness as well as efficiency, HTTP was designed as a "stateless" protocol, where no state is associated with a network connection. This is more robust than approaches which associate state with a network connection, since a dropped connection only affects a single request, and is more efficient, since it does not require connection state to be established every time a connection is created. It also eliminates the need for a "resynchronization" operation in the protocol to recover connection state after an interruption.

Concurrency control within the WEBDAV protocol was designed to satisfy the goals of keeping the protocol independent of content type, allowing merges to be avoided, providing robust, even disconnected, operation in the Internet environment, and offering an easy adoption path for existing non-collaborative applications like spreadsheets, word processors, and text editors.

Synchronous collaborative authoring applications such as GROVE (Ellis & Gibbs, 1989) and PREP (Neuwirth et al., 1994) willingly forgo content type independence to provide fine-grain merging down to the keystroke level. DUPLEX (Pacull et al., 1994) and ALLIANCE (Salcedo and Decouchant, 1997) both exploit special knowledge about the internal hierarchical structure of their documents to provide concurrency control on document subtrees.

While these approaches mitigate the major drawback of locking, the lack of availability of a locked document, the cost is too high: adding content-type specific knowledge to the protocol. The major problem with adding content-type knowledge to the protocol is the number, and variation among content types. There are currently 19 text/* and over 150 application/* Internet media types. Some of these are word processing formats where operations like "insert a character" and "delete a character" make sense, others are image formats with different editing semantics, such as "change pixel's color", and "draw a line". Furthermore, some content types are revised incompatibly, requiring the protocol to distinguish between—and provide support for—multiple versions of these content types.

The approach in GROVE and PREP of sending fine-grain update notifications requires a constant network connection to be held open between collaborating applications. This requires such systems to be fully network connected throughout collaborative authoring sessions, and easily reconnect accidentally disconnected authors. In contrast, WEBDAV locking does not require a constant network connection, even allowing collaborators to completely disconnect from the network once a resource has been locked and downloaded to a local machine.

As Grinter (1996) noted in her study of configuration management system use, merging can be a complex activity, requiring coordination between authors to resolve overlapping changes, discussing the rationale behind the changes, and how the changes work together. The WEBDAV exclusive write lock is a tradeoff between preventing the need for merges and document unavailability during the lock.

Finally, WEBDAV locks have a granularity of an entire Web resource, which maps easily onto concepts like a spreadsheet, a word processing document, or an image. Since many existing applications work on files, these applications can more easily be converted to using WEBDAV than if they had adopted a locking model with finer granularity. Grain size smaller than an entire file would increase availability, but would require significant reworking of how the application accepts input, since it would now need to listen to update notifications from other collaborators. While it is conceivable that applications will eventually be restructured to provide fine-grain concurrency control for application-specific media types, the WEBDAV protocol initially aims to provide a stable intermediate level which allows applications to become collaboration-aware without a significant reengineering burden.

Namespace Management

WEBDAV provides five methods for manipulating the namespace, DELETE, MKCOL, COPY, MOVE and PROPFIND. The DELETE method, first defined in Fielding et al., (1997), takes a single argument, the name of a resource to be deleted. The WEBDAV protocol extends the DELETE method so it can be applied recursively against collection resources. The MKCOL method takes a single argument, the URL where a new collection resource is created.

The most basic form of the COPY method takes two arguments, the URL of a source resource and a destination URL. A successful COPY results in the source resource being copied and made available at the destination. A COPY method may also applied recursively against a collection resource, with best-effort (not atomic) semantics. By default any properties on the source are copied onto the destination. Live properties that cannot be supported as live properties on the destination are copied across as dead properties. For example, if the source had an iso:time_of_day property which returned the current time of day and the destination is on a different server that doesn't have the code to support iso:time_of_day as a live property then a dead property called iso:time_of_day will be created on the destination and set to the value of the property at the time of the copy. The COPY method can be set to fail if all live properties are not copied as live or if a specified list of live properties are not copied across as live. A looser restriction is also available which specifies that the COPY should not fail for any property related reasons such as the inability to copy any properties across.

The MOVE method is defined as the *logical equivalent* of a COPY followed by a DELETE, performed as an atomic operation. Like COPY, MOVE may be recursively applied to a collection, again with best-effort semantics. Properties are handled in the same manner and with the same options as for the COPY method.

The PROPFIND method is relevant to namespace management since it is used to retrieve a listing of a collection's members. To retrieve a collection's membership list, either a recursive or single level PROPFIND is executed on the collection resource. By asking for one or more properties to be returned, the result lists every member of the collection, even if the result just states the property isn't defined on the member resource.

Design rationale for namespace operations

WEBDAV's namespace design was strongly motivated by the needs of existing authoring clients and servers, specifically ones who expect a strictly hierarchical namespace. A strictly hierarchical namespace is one in which if resource "a" and "a/b" both exist then "a" must be a collection and must contain "a/b" as a member. The "/" character specifies containment. Many systems, especially more advanced versioning environments, do not require a strictly hierarchical namespace. Their namespace is usually flat with versioning relationships used to express containment. However clients and servers who require a strictly hierarchical namespace, including all file system based programs, cannot operate properly if the hierarchical namespace requirements are not met.

For example, in a fully generic containment system, resource "a" and "a/b" could both be non-collection resources and both be contained by "a/b/c". In other words, in a generic containment system the "/" character has no special meaning. It is possible to layer a generic containment system on top of a strictly hierarchical namespace through the use of sufficient mapping information. For example, a WEBDAV server built on top of a strictly hierarchical namespace could store all files in a single container and then map WEBDAV names to those files.

The compromise solution was WEBDAV collections would enforce a strictly hierarchical namespace while a later specification (Slein et al., 1999) would provide for linking facilities that allow WEBDAV collections to refer to resources outside of their hierarchical namespace.

Example implementations

Several WEBDAV client and server applications have been implemented, providing valuable feedback during the development of the protocol and its extensions. Interoperability testing is ongoing, and while some implementations are not yet entirely compliant (normal for the early stages of deployment of a protocol), the existence of interoperable client/server pairs has demonstrated that the WEBDAV protocol is a firm basis for interoperable collaborative authoring on the Web. Current WEBDAV applications are briefly described below.

WebDAV Servers

PyDAV - The PYDAV server, by Jim Davis while at Xerox PARC, is a fully compliant WEBDAV server (Davis, 1999). It is written in PYTHON, (a scripting language created by Guido van Rossum, described in Lutz (1996)) and runs on UNIX and WINDOWS. Persistent storage for resources is the filesystem, while storage and retrieval of properties is handled by a DBM database.

The architecture of the server maintains a clean separation between the code that handles the WEBDAV Protocol, and the code that manages the repository of resources and properties. This architecture allows handlers for other protocols to access the same repository, and for the WEBDAV protocol to access the content of other repositories, such as a document management system, or a relational database. This architecture shows the promise of the WEBDAV protocol as an object integration technology, providing a standard, network-accessible front-end to a wide variety of persistent stores.

Internet Information Services 5™ (IIS 5) - IIS 5 is Microsoft™'s HTTP & Application Web Server for WINDOWS 2000™. IIS 5 is fully WEBDAV compliant and leverages the file management, property storage and locking features of the WINDOWS 2000 file system to provide WEBDAV storage, property management and locking. This integration ensures that a user cannot get around a WEBDAV lock by going directly to the file system, or lose WEBDAV properties just by copying a file somewhere else in the system. Thus users who access the server's file system directly or who go through WEBDAV will enjoy the same experience.

MOD_DAV - A module for the APACHE Web server (Fielding et al., 1997) which currently implements the Class 1 features of the WEBDAV Protocol (it does not support locking, an area of ongoing development). MOD_DAV (Stein, 1999) is an open source project led by Greg Stein that is written in C for the LINUX operating system, and handles resource and property persistence similar to PYDAV, with resources stored in the filesystem, and properties stored in GDBM.

WebDAV Clients

POSTIES - This application provides collaborative, shared notes, similar to POST-IT™ notes. Written in Java, POSTIES stores each note as a separate Web resource within a collection. A user modifies a note by clicking within a note, then starting to type. This causes a background thread to request an exclusive lock on the note. If the lock is granted, the note is locked without the user being aware of the activity. If the note is already locked, an error dialog appears, and modifications to the note are lost. Since HTTP, and hence the WEBDAV protocol, is not currently suitable for sending notification messages (a deficiency noted by many, including Trevor et al., 1997, and Dix, 1997), the DAV POSTIES application polls for changes to notes on a regular interval.

SITECOPY - Written in C by Joe Orton, this program uses the WEBDAV protocol to update a remote Web site from a local directory (Orton, 1999). SITECOPY synchronizes a remote site from a local directory, uploading, deleting and moving files on the server as necessary. Changes on the server are not reflected in the local directory; the synchronization is only one-way (two-way synchronization is an area of future work). SITECOPY demonstrates the flexibility of a protocol-based approach, since it is a type of application which was not originally considered when developing the protocol.

Internet Explorer 5™ (IE 5) – IE 5 provides support for WEBDAV through a namespace extension which allows a WEBDAV server to be displayed using the same WINDOWS EXPLORER™ interface provided for browsing the local file system. This interface provides for copy, move, delete, rename, create new file, create new collection and drag/drop functionality. Users can activate the namespace extension through the WINDOWS™ shell using a special wizard, through pre-defined shell shortcuts, through the file-open dialog or through scripting in an HTML page. In addition, the namespace extension provides access to a WEBDAV compliant off-line synchronization manager which can handle automatically downloading and synchronizing the off-line store with the server.

Office 2000™ – OFFICE 2000 fully integrates IE 5 and so supports all the WEBDAV features that IE 5 supports. In addition OFFICE 2000 also provides for rich resource management directly in its File-Open and File-Save dialogs. Thus all the WEBDAV functionality provided in the WINDOWS EXPLORER is now available directly through OFFICE 2000's File-Open/Save dialogs. This allows users to treat a WEBDAV server the same way they would treat any file system. OFFICE 2000 makes full use of WEBDAV exclusive write locks in order to enforce single access to edited files. While OFFICE 2000 supports merging, in general OFFICE users strongly prefer to avoid merges whenever possible.

Related Work

Similar network protocols to WEBDAV can be characterized as either an extension to HTTP, a non-HTTP hypertext authoring protocol, or a file transfer protocol.

To date, extensions to HTTP for remote authoring have been proprietary, implemented by just a single vendor, and have scant documentation. For example, the FRONTPAGE™ web authoring tool uses a set of remote procedure calls implemented using the HTTP POST method to perform remote authoring operations, and only work with Web servers which support them. WEBDAV differs from the FRONTPAGE extensions by using separate HTTP methods for each operation, an approach that has advantages for access control. When the name of an operation is specified both in the HTTP request line, and in the message body of an HTTP POST method request, a server implementing access control must look in two places for the name of the operation.

AOLPRESS/AOLSERVER (some details of the protocol can be found in America Online, 1998) and the Netscape Enterprise Server (Cunningham and Faizi, 1997) both extended HTTP by defining new HTTP methods. Since both of these efforts fed ideas and contributors to the WEBDAV effort, there are many similarities in approach. Both add locking, and namespace operations (copy, move, make directory, list directory) in separate HTTP methods. The Netscape extensions also have methods for properties, providing operations to set and remove name/value pairs, and for versioning, providing check-out, check-in, list history, destroy, and set default version methods. But, despite the similarities, the WEBDAV protocol differs from these extensions in many ways. The semantics of locking are well defined in the WEBDAV protocol, and are insufficiently specified in these other extensions. Furthermore, WEBDAV locks return a lock token, allowing multiple clients operated by the same principal to work within the same portion of the namespace free from overwrite conflicts caused by unexpected tool interactions. The WEBDAV lock, copy, and move operations can apply to an entire hierarchy of resources, providing support for Web pages composed of multiple resources. Unlike the Netscape extension's properties, which are simple ASCII strings, WEBDAV property values accommodate contents in multiple character sets, providing internationalization support. Since WEBDAV property values are XML, they offer better extensibility characteristics than strings. An important differentiator for WEBDAV is that it is a non-proprietary protocol, and hence more likely to be broadly adopted than any of these proprietary extensions.

Several systems have employed a non-HTTP network protocol to provide remote collaborative authoring. Open hypermedia systems, as discussed in the survey by Østerbye and Wiil (1996), employ protocols for authoring hypertext links and for transmitting link traversal events, and often also have a protocol for authoring and retrieving hypermedia objects. Protocols in open hypermedia systems have many differences in their marshalling strategies, varying from the ASCII linearization of Lisp and Scheme data structures in HYPERDISCO (Wiil and Leggett, 1996), the use of XDR and RPC by CHIMERA (Anderson et al., 1994), to a different use of ASCII by the Open Hypermedia Protocol for Navigation (OHP-Nav), developed as a community effort by open hypermedia researchers (Davis et al., 1998). Although it does not label itself as such, the HYPER-G Client-Server Protocol (Kappe and Pani, 1996) can also be considered an open hypermedia protocol. Despite many differences, open hypermedia protocols do share some similarities in approach. All are client-server protocols, where a hypermedia-aware application is a client, and the open hypermedia system is the server. Unlike HTTP, open hypermedia protocols allow server-initiated asynchronous notification messages to be transferred to the client, where they signal a link traversal, or give collaboration awareness information. As a result, these protocols maintain a stateful, open connection during use sessions. The WEBDAV protocol differs from open hypermedia protocols by providing a stateless, non-connection-oriented protocol. The WEBDAV protocol does not treat hypertext links as first-class objects, instead modeling them as properties. This avoids the scalability bottleneck in open hypermedia systems of having a single point of control for links, and link consistency. An in-depth discussion of the control tradeoffs in the architectures of open hypermedia systems and the Web is presented in Whitehead (1999).

Finally, the WEBDAV protocol differs from the ubiquitous File Transfer Protocol (Postel and Reynolds, 1985) in several respects. Each FTP session opens two network connections, a control channel, used to send commands from client to server, and a data channel, used for transferring files from machine to machine. This differs from HTTP, which combines control and data information into a single channel, permitting even more simple client implementations. While FTP provides namespace operations equivalent to those of WEBDAV, it does not provide any form of overwrite prevention, thus making it unsuitable for authoring, and has no metadata facilities. Furthermore, an FTP session is stateful, which would lead to robustness problems for long-duration collaborative sessions.

Conclusions

This paper has explored a protocol-centric approach to collaborative authoring by examining the requirements and functionality of the WEBDAV protocol. Providing an upward migration path for existing applications has proven crucial. We have shown that freedom from licensing restrictions, large-grain locking, and namespace management operations reduce reengineering barriers for collaborative authoring with existing applications. Several WEBDAV applications now exist, promising to generate network effects, accelerating widespread adoption of collaborative authoring.

Since compatibility among collaborative authoring tools is essential for the generation of network effects, our protocol-centric approach focused design attention on issues of interoperability, security, internationalization, extensibility, and protocol scalability. The resulting design separated several concerns: the behavior of locks from the behavior of network connections (and from other protocol operations); and the semantics of the protocol from the content types authored using the protocol. Simultaneously addressing these issues has yielded a well-engineered protocol adapted to the Internet environment.

Finally, our experience has validated the importance of designing collaborative authoring applications from the user down, and from the protocol up. Both approaches focus on important issues, different facets of the same design space.

Acknowledgements

Since the WEBDAV protocol is the consensus output of the WEBDAV working group, the authors wish to explicitly note that they are not the sole creators of the WEBDAV protocol, and gratefully acknowledge the numerous, substantial contributions made by the members of the WEBDAV working group. While a complete list of contributors to the WEBDAV protocol can be found in the acknowledgements section of Goland et al., 1999, we would like to specially thank the other authors of the WEBDAV protocol, Asad Faizi, Steve Carter, and Del Jensen, as well as working group members Larry Masinter, Jim Davis, Jim Amsden, and Judy Slein for their contributions. Similarly, the WEBDAV requirements document, Slein et al. (1998) is a consensus document of the working group and we would like to specially acknowledge the editors of this document, Judy Slein, Fabio Vitali, and David Durand for their contributions.

Finally, we would like to thank David McDonald, Rohit Khare. and David Norris for their thoughtful reviews.

Jim Whitehead's work on this project was sponsored by the Defense Advanced Research Projects Agency, and Air Force Research Laboratory, Air Force Materiel Command, USAF, under agreement number F30602-97-2-0021. The views and conclusions contained herein are those of the authors and should not be interpreted as necessarily representing the official policies or endorsements, either expressed or implied, of the Defense Advanced Research Projects Agency, Air Force Research Laboratory or the U.S. Government.

References

America Online (1998): "AOL Server Administrator's Guide", America Online, 1998. http://www.aolserver.com/server/docs/2.3/html/admin.html

Anderson, K. M., Taylor, R. N., and Whitehead, Jr. E. J. (1994): "Chimera: Hypertext for Heterogeneous Software Environments", in *Proc. 1994 European Conference on Hypermedia Technology (ECHT'94)*, Edinburgh, Scotland, Sept. 18-23, 1994, pp. 94-107.

Bentley, R., Horstmann, T., and Trevor, J. (1997): "The World Wide Web as enabling technology for CSCW: The case of BSCW", in *Computer Supported Cooperative Work: The Journal of Collaborative Computing*, vol. 6, nos. 2-3, 1997, pp. 111-134.

Berners-Lee, T., Fielding, R., and Masinter, L. (1998): "Uniform Resource Identifiers (URI): Generic Syntax", MIT/LCS, U.C. Irvine, Xerox. RFC 2396, August, 1996.

Bray, T., Paoli, J., and Sperberg-McQueen, C. M. (1998): "Extensible Markup Language (XML)", World Wide Web Consortium Recommendation REC-xml-19980210, February, 1998.

Cunningham, J. and Faizi, A. (1997): "Distributed Authoring and Versioning Protocol", Unpublished manuscript, 1997. http://www.ics.uci.edu/pub/ietf/webdav/ns_dav.html

DASL (1999): "DAV Searching and Locating Home Page", http://www.ics.uci.edu/pub/ietf/dasl/

Davis, H., Reich, S., and Millard, D. (1998): "A Proposal for a Common Navigational Hypertext Protocol", Open Hypermedia Systems Working Group draft, http://www.ecs.soton.ac.uk/~hcd/ohp/ohp35.htm

Davis, J. (1999): "PyDAV WebDAV Server", http://sandbox.xerox.com/webdav/, 1999.

Dierks, T. and Allen, C. (1999): "The TLS Protocol Version 1.0" Certicom. RFC 2246, Jan., 1999.

Dix, A. (1997): "Challenges for Cooperative Work on the Web: An Analytical Approach", in *CSCW: The Journal of Collaborative Computing*, vol. 6, nos. 2-3, 1997, pp. 135-156.

Ellis, C.A., and Gibbs, S. J. (1989): "Concurrency control in groupware systems", in *Proc. ACM SIGMOD '89 Conference on the Management of Data,* Seattle, WA, May 2-4, 1989.

Fielding, R., Gettys, J., Mogul, J., Frystyk, H., and Berners-Lee, T. (1997): "Hypertext Transfer Protocol -- HTTP/1.1", U.C. Irvine, DEC, MIT/LCS. RFC 2068, January, 1997.

Fielding, R., Kaiser, G. (1997): "The Apache HTTP Server Project", *IEEE Internet Computing*, 1(4), July/August, 1997.

Franks, J., Hallam-Baker, P., Hostetler, J., Leach, P., Luotonen, A., Sink, E., and Stewart, L. (1997): "An Extension to HTTP: Digest Access Authentication", Northwestern Univ., CERN, Spyglass, Microsoft, Netscape, Spyglass, Open Market. RFC 2069, January, 1997.

Freed, N., Borenstein, N. (1996): "Multipurpose Internet Mail Extensions (MIME) Part One: Format of Internet Message Bodies", Innosoft, First Virtual. RFC 2045, November, 1996.

Goland, Y. Y., Whitehead, Jr., E. J., Faizi, A., S. R. Carter, and D. Jensen (1999): "HTTP Extensions for Distributed Authoring -- WEBDAV", Microsoft, U.C. Irvine, Netscape, Novell. RFC 2518, February, 1999.

Grinter, R. (1996): "Supporting Articulation Work Using Software Configuration Management Systems", in *CSCW: The Journal of Collaborative Computing*, vol. 5, 1996, pp. 447-465.

Kappe, F., and Pani, G. (1996): "Hyper-G Client-Server Protocol (HG-CSP)", in Maurer, H. (ed.) 1996, pp. 550-591.

Kirby, A. and Rodden, T. (1995): "Contact: Support for Distributed Cooperative Writing", in *Proc. Fourth European Conference on Computer Supported Cooperative Work (ECSCW'95)*, Stockholm, Sweden, September 10-14, 1995, pp. 101-116.

Lutz, M. (1996): *Programming Python*, O'Reilly & Associates, Cambridge, MA.

Maurer, H. ed. (1996): *Hyper-G, now Hyperwave: The next generation Web solution*, Addison-Wesley, Harlow, England.

Neuwirth, C. M., Kaufer, D. S., Chandhok, R., and Morris, J. H. (1994): "Computer Support for Distributed Collaborative Writing: Defining Parameters of Interaction", in *Proc. ACM 1994 Conference on Computer Supported Cooperative Work (CSCW'94)*, Chapel Hill, NC, October 22-26, 1994, pp. 145-152.

Orton, J. (1999): "sitecopy Home Page", http://www.lyra.org/sitecopy/

Østerbye, K., and Wiil, U. (1996): "The Flag Taxonomy of Open Hypermedia Systems", in *Proc. Hypertext'96*, Washington, DC, March 16-20, 1996, pp. 129-139.

Pacull, F., Sandoz, A., and Schiper, A. (1994): "Duplex: A Distributed Collaborative Editing Environment in Large Scale", in *Proc. ACM 1994 Conference on Computer Supported Cooperative Work (CSCW'94)*, Chapel Hill, NC, October 22-26, 1994, pp. 165-173.

Postel, J. (1982): "Simple Mail Transfer Protocol", ISI. RFC 821, Standard 10, August, 1982.

Postel, J. and Reynolds, J. (1985): "File Transfer Protocol (FTP)", ISI. RFC 959, October, 1985.

Rohlfs (1974): "A theory of interdependent demand for a communications service", *Bell Journal of Economics*, vol. 5, no. 1, 1974, pp. 16-37.

Sasse, M. A., Handley, M. J. (1993): "Support for Collaborative Authoring via Email: The MESSIE Environment", in *Proc. Third European Conference on Computer-Supported Cooperative Work (ECSCW'93)*, Milan, Italy, September 13-17, 1993, pp. 249-264.

Salcedo, M. R. & Decouchant, D. (1997): "Structured Cooperative Authoring for the World Wide Web", in *Computer Supported Cooperative Work: The Journal of Collaborative Computing*, vol. 6, nos. 2-3, 1997, pp. 157-174.

Slein, J. A., Vitali, F., Whitehead, Jr., E. J., and Durand, D. (1998): "Requirements for a Distributed Authoring and Versioning Protocol for the World Wide Web", Xerox, Univ. of Bologna, U.C. Irvine, Boston Univ. Informational RFC 2291, Feb., 1998.

Slein, J., Davis, J., Babich, A., Whitehead, Jr., E. J. (1999): "WebDAV Advanced Collections Protocol", Internet-Draft, work-in-progress, draft-ietf-webdav-collection-protocol-03, Feb. 26, 1999.

Stein, G. (1999): "mod_dav: A DAV module for Apache", http://www.webdav.org/mod_dav/

Trevor, J., Koch, T., and Woetzel, G. (1997): "MetaWeb: Bringing synchronous groupware to the World Wide Web", in *Proc. of the Fifth European Conference on Computer Supported Cooperative Work (ECSCW'97)*, Lancaster, UK, September 7-11, 1997, pp. 65-80.

Whitehead, Jr., E. J. (1999): "Control Choices and Network Effects in Hypertext Systems", in *Proc. Hypertext '99*, Darmstadt, Germany, February 21-25, 1999, pp. 75-82.

Wiil, U., and Leggett, J. (1996): "The HyperDisco Approach to Open Hypermedia Systems", in *Proc. Hypertext'96*, Washington, DC, March 16-20, 1996, pp. 140-148.

S. Bødker, M. Kyng, and K. Schmidt (eds.). *Proceedings of the Sixth European Conference on Computer-Supported Cooperative Work, 12-16 September 1999, Copenhagen, Denmark*
©1999 Kluwer Academic Publishers. Printed in the Netherlands

Informing Collaborative Information Visualisation Through an Ethnography of Ambulance Control

John Bowers
Centre for User-Oriented IT-Design (CiD), Department of Numerical Analysis and Computer Science (NADA), Royal Institute of Technology (KTH), Stockholm, Sweden

David Martin
Psychology and Computer Science Departments, University of Manchester, UK

Abstract. An ethnographic analysis of an ambulance control centre is presented, specifically investigating the design of information displays and their practical use in this setting. The spatial distribution of the displays around the control room is described and its consequences for cooperative work drawn out. From these analyses, we make several suggestions for information visualisations in virtual environments, including a design concept of multiple displays coexisting within a 3D environment as an alternative to the notion of 'immersive' information visualisation more commonly encountered. The paper closes with a reflection on the relationship between ethnographic analysis and system development that our work here exemplifies.

Introduction

This paper presents an analysis of field work conducted at an ambulance control centre in a large metropolitan region in the North of England. The purpose of this analysis is to inform the development of Collaborative Virtual Environments (CVEs), and in particular, CVEs which are designed to support collaborative information visualisation. In recent years in the research field of Computer

312

Supported Cooperative Work (CSCW), there has been much interest in CVEs, where distributed virtual reality technology is deployed to support cooperative working activities. While a number of general CVE platforms and development environments exist, (e.g. DIVE, Carlsson and Hagsand, 1993, and MASSIVE, Greenhalgh and Benford, 1995) and have been presented within CSCW, three areas have been the principal focus of application development and usage. *Virtual conferences*, where a CVE is deployed to provide some form of meeting environment as an arena for social interaction, have been discussed by Greenhalgh and Benford (1995) amongst others. *Inhabited television* explores strategies for combining CVEs with broadcast media (McGrath et al., 1998, Benford et al., 1999). *Collaborative information visualisation* has been the subject of applications such as VR-VIBE (Benford et al., 1995) and Q-PIT (Mariani et al., 1995). Here a (typically 3D) visualisation is embedded within a CVE so that, in a sense, users are embodied within the database itself. This might enable them to be aware not only of information but also of other users and the interactions with information and each other that they are engaged in.

An overarching concern in our work is how understandings of virtual reality, and in particular CVEs, might be informed by empirical social scientific analysis. Specifically, we are concerned to deploy ethnographic research methods (which emphasise protracted contact with a research setting and the deep descriptive documentation of the social organisation of activity) alongside video analysis work (concerned with the detailed study of how social interaction is coordinated on a moment-by-moment basis). Throughout, we prefer the study of real-world settings which have an existence independent of our interest in them. There are two strands to our research agenda with respect to CVEs. On the one hand, we conduct studies in real-world settings to inform CVE development—settings which, though often automated, do not typically involve the usage of virtual reality technology. For example, Pycock and Bowers (1996) report a study of work in the fashion industry so as to investigate the plausibility of introducing CVEs to support 3D design and information visualisation in this setting. On the other hand, we conduct studies of the usage of CVEs to explore whether the arguments for their utility are borne out in practice. For example, Bowers, O'Brien and Pycock (1996) and Bowers, Pycock and O'Brien (1996) address questions such as: do (and in what sense) CVEs enable users to deploy their everyday interactional competencies in the 'natural' way that is often hoped for? Do (and in what sense) users achieve a sense of 'place', 'presence' or 'immersion' in a CVE? Do users obtain an awareness of the conduct of others in a CVE which enables a sense of mutuality to come into existence? If so, how?

The present paper is of the first sort—a study of an existing setting: ambulance control. However, it is important that we are clear at the outset of the purposes of our study and exactly how we intend it to inform CVE research. We are *not* proposing the use of CVEs to support real world ambulance control, nor are we here concerned with making suggestions for other forms of cooperative technology in this setting. These are matters more prominently covered in Martin, Bowers and Wastell (1997). Our preeminent concerns in the current paper concern more basic issues in research on CVEs for collaborative information visualisation.

In particular, we wish to inform the design of collaborative information visualisations by offering a social scientific perspective on how databases are used in a complex, time and safety-critical setting. In existing work, the design of 3D information visualisations in the research literature has largely been considered from a computing, indeed algorithmic, standpoint. The distribution of virtual objects, signifying database entries, around a 3D space has been governed by algorithms based on, for example, cluster analysis, physical spring models of attractions and repulsions, or a weighted summing of overlaps between database entries and queries (see Benford et al., 1995; Chalmers, 1994). From time to time, considerations of human perception enter into the design of 3D visualisations. For example, Chalmers (1994) discusses the importance of 'landmarks' and 'regions' for making an information visualisation more easily perceptible and navigable. However, rarely have the actual principles by means of which representations of data are constructed been discussed from a social scientific viewpoint. Largely, an algorithm is selected on the basis of computational (e.g. efficiency) or aesthetic (e.g. the visual elegance of the virtual forms produced) criteria. This means that, ironically, existing CVEs for collaborative information visualisation tend to employ algorithms for constructing information displays *without explicit regard* for how differently designed displays might or might not afford the social interaction and mutual awareness their designers hope for. It is our belief that exactly how objects are distributed in virtual space will matter critically to whether a CVE for information visualisation will effectively support cooperative work. We suggest that designers of CVEs can learn from real-world settings in this regard and that (maybe) even the selection of the algorithms used for the construction of information visualisations might be influenced by empirical social scientific work. The following study is an exploration of this possibility.

Field Study

The ambulance control room is located above one of the 35 ambulance stations that serve the region (population around 2.5 million), centrally, in its main city. The control room operates by answering calls from the public (on the 999 emergency line), medical services and other emergency services. These calls are received by Call Operators (1-6 working depending on time of day/week) who enter basic details onto a computer-based form, their central task being to gain a geographical fix on the incident and some details of the nature of the problem.

As soon as a geographical fix is made and 'enter' is pressed these details are passed directly over to the Dispatchers (4 working at all times), whose job it is to assign each incident to an ambulance in the region (30-70 operational at any one moment). Dispatchers are constantly overseen by two Supervisors who sit behind them. This group work to ensure that, with a finite number of ambulances, incidents can be assigned to them such that adequate cover is maintained throughout the region (at least one ambulance covering every station) and ambulances are dispatched and reach incidents within UK government guidelines.

In order to manage incidents for the whole region it is divided up into four areas known as 'boards' with each dispatcher assigned one of these as their central dispatch area. Supervisors on the other hand have responsibility for the whole region. Dispatchers are presented with the geographically relevant incidents to their board as soon as they are entered. Their job is then to select a proximal, free ambulance for that incident while ensuring that adequate cover will be left consequent upon that selection. Once a selection is made, Dispatchers send abridged details electronically to an alphanumeric display and keypad on the relevant ambulance's dashboard. Supervisors, while not being assigned a particular set of dispatch jobs are constantly involved in monitoring and overseeing work, suggesting and even making dispatches (relieving Dispatchers' workloads) and preparing and planning with a special eye to maintaining adequate cover. The final staff member of importance to our study is the Control Manager, who for the majority of the time has a less hands-on presence dealing instead with general morale, quality of work, contacts with other organisations, and so forth. However, even the Control Manager might actually assign incidents to ambulances at times of extreme workload in the control room.

The central technological resource utilised by control room workers is a computer system containing a series of DOS-based applications (accessible via sequences of keystrokes) for the purpose of collating ambulance information in various ways so operations can be performed on it and distributed to relevant parties. The system is networked to over 20 terminals within the room and has a radio link to the display panels in the ambulances. A Global Positioning System (GPS) links to the database providing near real-time information on, for example, positions of ambulances relative to incidents. We now discuss the three most used applications and their relevance for dispatch.

The Incident Stack

As fixes are made on incidents they are visible through an application that lists them. This is known as the Incident Stack. It is split into two halves. The top displays 'WAITING' incidents (those still to be assigned to ambulances), the bottom 'ACTIVE' incidents (assigned). In each line, a variety of information is displayed including the time the call was received and, for incidents in the 'ACTIVE' category, the call signs of ambulances attending the incidents and their as-the-crow-flies distance (computed by the GPS). At the top of the 'WAITING' list is the oldest unassigned emergency incident while at the top of the lower half is the most recently assigned incident. Each Dispatcher has an Incident Stack for their 'board' accessible via their terminal (indeed this is their default screen setting), while the stack for the whole region is displayed on a large screen on the left hand side of the wall in front of the Dispatchers (see Figures 1 and 2).

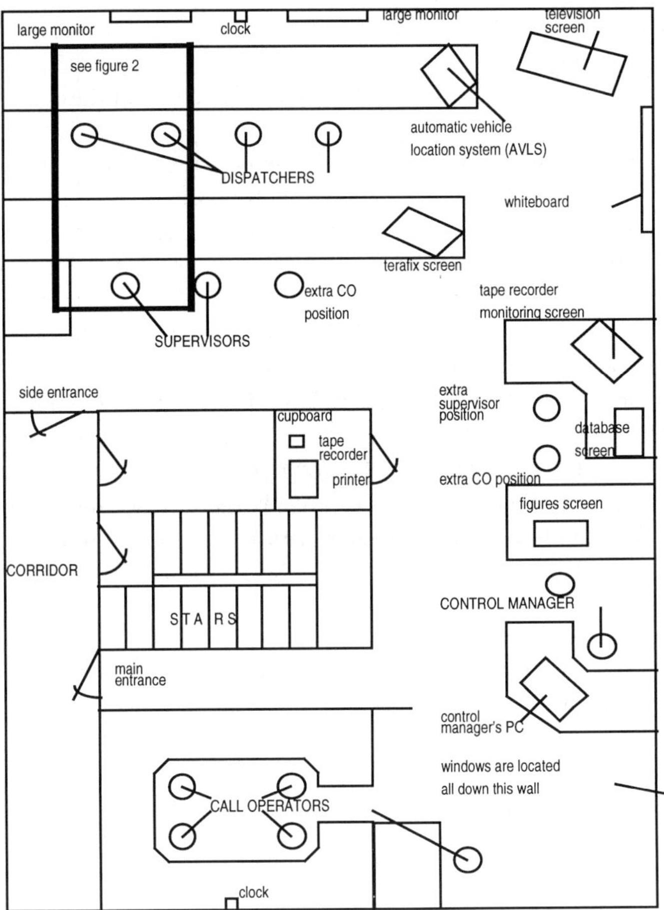

Figure 1: Plan of the ambulance control room.

The Dispatch Selection Screen

When a new incident appears highlighted at the top of the Dispatcher's Incident Stack it is selected simply by pressing the enter key. The screen then refreshes to show the basic details of the incident (e.g. its type and location) in the top half of the screen and a list of the nearest as-the-crow-flies ambulances in the bottom half. This list does not take into account the status of these ambulances (whether active or free), however the nearest free ambulance is flagged in blue as a guide to allocation. The Dispatcher then selects an ambulance (often the flagged one), which again leads to the screen refreshing, this time showing the full incident details. These are then checked and abridged by the Dispatcher and transmitted to the ambulance. On receipt the crew press the first button on their keypad which leads to an automatic updating of the Incident Stack (the incident moves to the top of the 'ACTIVE' list) and the Vehicle Availability Map.

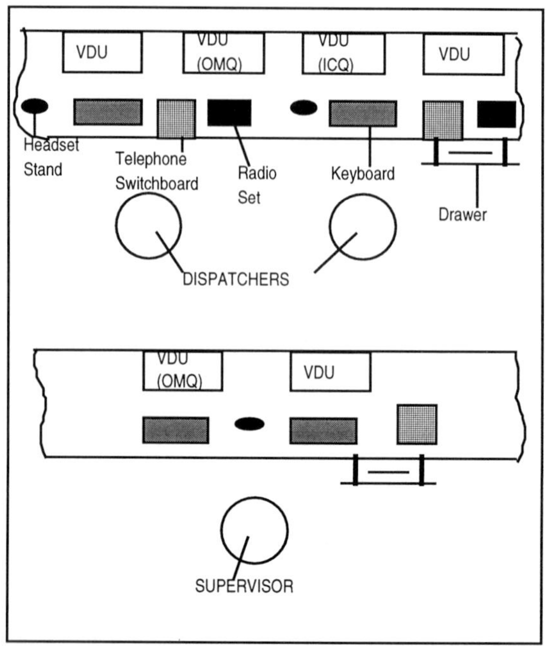

Figure 2: Dispatchers' and Supervisors' local environment.

The Vehicle Availability Map (VAM)

As mentioned before, a key role of the Dispatchers and Supervisors is ensuring that adequate cover for the region is maintained. The VAM, which is displayed on the right hand large monitor on the front wall (Figure 1), is the central resource for this purpose. The VAM (see Figure 3) is a set of 15 lists each headed by a three letter abbreviation of the area covered, and comprising the call signs of ambulances from 2-3 proximal stations. The lists are arranged to correspond roughly to the actual geographical distribution of stations in the region (e.g. stations close to each other tend to be part of the same list, adjoining areas are listed proximally on the VAM). The important features of ambulance statuses are displayed by colour coding. Ambulances actively attending emergency incidents are shown in red. Those attending urgent incidents (transporting patients under doctor's orders) are flagged in green. Those placed at standby locations (a designated place to provide cover between two stations) have flashing call signs and those that are free are unflagged. Through examining the VAM, Dispatchers and Supervisors can glean a variety of important information for dealing with cover issues, as we shall shortly describe in more depth.

WIG	ATH	BOL	HIG	BUR	ROC	ECC	ALT
7345	5578	5661	3346	4110	2120	9786	2336
7563	4242	5563	3217	4243	2115	9866	3114
7224	4455	6245	2354	3447	2332	9786	3122
6224	4411	6562	3737	3388	2112		2255
7797	4116	4113			2889		
8761							
7556							

BEL	CEN	SAL	OLD	DUK	STO	GLO
4466	5778	6536	6684	8843	4426	3557
4117	5331	6868	7553	8854	4473	3749
4119	5462	6565	7776	9982	4335	2561
4421	5567	6769	7787	8822	4333	2239
4434	5579	7652	8114			
5337	5882					
	6577					

Figure 3: The Vehicle Availability Map (VAM) which lists ambulances by regions and is approximated here in greyscale. Ambulances active on emergencies are here shown with their IDs against a black background. Ambulances on urgent calls are shown against a grey background. Ambulances on standby are shown 'flashing'. Available ambulances are just depicted by their ID. See main text for further explanation.

Display Design

We now wish to analytically draw out some features of the work of ambulance control and its relationship to the design of the displays we have just discussed. Focusing on displays is justified both by our interest in information visualisation and because there is a strong sense in which *ambulance control work is display-inspection-and-manipulation-work*. That is, much of the work of ambulance control precisely consists in the inspection and manipulation of displays and it is through such activities that ambulance dispatch and cover maintenance are achieved. Dispatch could, of course, be accomplished by other means and, before the introduction of the system we have discussed, the extensive use of radio for voice communication with crews would have been essential. However, comparatively rarely now is there the need for direct communication with crews in order to accomplish dispatch. Such interactions are now occasioned by 'non-routine' occurrences such as if the crew cannot find the incident or if they are being asked to attend an incident when they are due a meal break or as a back up check to make sure the electronically delivered dispatches have been noticed (as crews can be in a station's staff room when a message is sent to their cab). However, routine dispatch work is accomplished by and monitored through the inspection and manipulation of displays. This centrality of the displays to control room work prompts us to analyse out various features of significance to them.

Distribution of Functionality

A first observation: different screens are used for different purposes. It is *not* the case that any screen in the control room can display any view on incident data from any application. There are dedicated screens for displaying incoming and outgoing message packets (the ICQ and OCQ) to monitor the effectiveness of radio transmission and to troubleshoot possible technical failures. For example, a message which has been transmitted but which does not appear in an ambulance's own display suggests that the latter may be at fault. There is a dedicated screen for the VAM. There is a dedicated, though not routinely used, screen for the display of ambulance locations on a map-like representation of the region (the AVLS display which presents the GPS information in cartographic form, see below). Furthermore, a password system controls access to applications so that, for example, the screens in front of the Dispatchers tend to display only dispatch-related information for the Dispatcher's region. That is, a number, but not all, of the applications making use of incident data will display to these screens. Equally, there are applications available to a Supervisor which allow for incident data from a number of areas to be compared on the one screen. The Control Manager can, in addition, inspect the results of applications which compute running statistics on the performance of the service in getting ambulances to incidents. The overall inspection of such statistics and the monitoring of control room performance is an important feature of the Control Manager's work. Hence, displays of such information are ready-to-hand for him on his screen and not on the screens of Supervisors and Dispatchers. Supervisors and Dispatchers will become aware of such matters through interaction with the Control Manager and not direct from the system to their screens.

This distribution of functionality across displays facilitates workers in that the information they need for their job is at hand, and readily so—it does not have to be found amongst a range of job-irrelevant displays. It also ensures that if workers need become aware, for whatever reason, of information *not* accessible from their own screen that they engage in embodied activity which makes the fact that they are so doing available to others in the control room. For example, if a Dispatcher needs to check on the activity in an adjacent board in order to ensure adequate cover for the service, they may lean over to glance at their neighbour's screen. The fact that they are so checking is thereby available to the Supervisor behind them. This may, in turn, alert the Supervisor to issues concerned with the relationship between ambulance deployments across the two boards—a matter of relevance to the Supervisor's job. In short, *constraining* accessibility and systematically *distributing* the displays and the functionality of the system across the control room *enables* opportunities for work-relevant communication and awareness.

Text

The vast majority of the information displays on view in the ambulance control room is textual in nature. We tend not see graphical objects being used to depict incidents or ambulances. This is *not* because control room personnel are tolerating antiquated non-graphical DOS systems. Rather, it is because the appropriate way of delivering information to control room personnel is in textual form. For example, the primary means for individuating one ambulance from another is by means of its call signal ID—a four number string. If ambulance-specific information needs to be displayed, attaching it to a four letter string seems most effective—especially if any anomalies about its status or whatever may well be resolved through spoken interaction with the crew which will be initiated by keying in the call sign on the radio (this opens a channel to the ambulance). Denoting ambulances with their ID in this fashion compactly individuates them, while giving exactly what is required to initiate interaction if problems occur. A graphical representation (e.g. a little ambulance icon coloured distinctively) might require personnel to *remember* which ambulance is which, how colour is used and so forth. Simple textual displays often give the information required *here and now* (memory not required).

Numerical and compact letter IDs are used ubiquitously in the control room (for incidents, areas within the region and ambulance stations, as well as a key for different types of incident: e.g. RTA for road traffic accident) in ways which are well and commonly understood. This gives text a priority in making displays of information work-relevant. It also makes means of organising text on screen around 'lines' and 'fields' essential. This is not to say that other means of organising text at the interface are not worth exploring. It is not even to say that iconic or symbolic means for representation might not also on occasion have a role. Rather, it is to emphasise that DOS-based textual displays have a lot going for them with a considerable work-relevant rationale behind them.

Colour

Colour is used sparsely in display design and for little other than highlighting purposes. Colour is not used for representational purposes, at least not alone. Colour is always attached to text. Colours do not appear attached to an iconic graphical object or to an abstract symbolic form. The colour 'palette' is restricted to red, blue, green and yellow. Again, this is not merely because control room personnel are being tolerant of or held back by DOS restrictions. In the VAM, for example, red versus green, flashing versus non-flashing, coloured versus plain, are used to indicate primary distinctions of relevance to the work of ambulance dispatch and cover maintenance. It is questionable whether more needs to be shown without introducing confusions which might be caused by reducing perceptual clarity (this restricted colour set allows the same discriminations to be made under different viewing conditions) or difficulties remembering a more complex coding scheme. The restricted colour palette also enables all the greens (say) to be seen as instances of the same class. In other words, at-a-glance perceptual categorisation is possible, something which might be militated against if more varied shadings were used. Again, we do not deny that it might be possible to creatively use colour in displays. Rather, we note that simple distinctions, made with a limited colour palette, seem appropriate for supporting the cooperative work of ambulance controlling practiced in the fashion we have observed.

Dimensionality

We have remarked that, for the purposes of the cooperative work of ambulance controlling, textual representations and displays seem most effective. If text has a kind of priority in display design, then so will lines and lists and fields (for input). Familiar reading practices can then be capitalised upon so that there will arise an expectation that a sense will be found reading a line from left to right and a screen from top to bottom. In the Incident Stack, for example, to the top are the incidents which are yet to be assigned and at the very top are the oldest, the most overdue. To the left of each line, one will find information to individuate the event (e.g. its time, its geographical fix in an abbreviated form), to the right information about what has been done (the ID of an ambulance mobilised, its distance from the event). In other words, while the screen can be considered a flat 2D display, this surface becomes enriched not just with text, colour, lines, fields, lists but also with incidents, locations, times, and a sense of urgency. Skills of normal reading practice give the user of such a display much. A working practical knowledge of ambulance controlling enables yet more to be read in. It is questionable whether other uses of the screen (for example as a graphically ornate representation of information) would give any more. Indeed, again the question arises as to whether such displays might distract through over-elaboration.

Let us give an example to illustrate this last point. Perhaps the most aesthetically interesting screen within the control room is also the least used. The Automatic Vehicle Location System (AVLS) is a map-like display of the region containing representations of ambulances positioned by means of GPS data. This, while situated on the desk near the Dispatchers and Supervisors, is seldom consulted for a number of reasons. First, it only displays a part of the region at one time meaning that it needs to be scrolled through. In contrast, the VAM shows *all* the ambulances *there* and *then*. Second, estimating distances becomes a task of spatial judgement on the AVLS rather than simply reading figures or noticing blue highlighting on the Dispatch Selection Screen. Finally, ambulances which are close to one another geographically tend to appear on top of each other on the AVLS (e.g. if several are together at a station). The VAM, by contrast, separates out different ambulances and gives a clearer picture of the relative workload in different areas.

The VAM shows ambulances with a geographical sensitivity that is *appropriately approximate* for dispatch decisions. The areas in the region are given a quasi-geographical distribution around the VAM screen. This enables comparisons to be made between, say, the commitment levels of adjacent areas, without, for the time being, being distracted by exactly how far apart those areas and the stations within them are. It is this that is important for making judgements about whether to move an ambulance to a standby location. One might well miss opportunities for flexibly deploying ambulances to standby locations if, say, one could not see that one area could help another out because their relative level of commitment had to be discerned from a display rather than seen at-a-glance. Equally, a more literal geographical representation might hide from ready-view *which* comparisons of commitment should be made. Two stations which seem near each other but which are separated by a motorway with entry and exit restrictions may not have a convenient standby location between them. The grouping of stations into areas and the spacing of area-lists around the VAM has been done precisely so that such confusions tend not occur. The VAM captures the 'logic of the region' with respect to ambulance cover maintenance—a very different matter from the logics of more geographically oriented maps or spaces defined by separation distance alone.

This is not to say that geographically oriented maps are irrelevant to ambulance controlling. Copies of the local street atlas (the so-called A-Z) are ubiquitous in the control room and on board ambulances and the page numbering and grid reference system of one publisher have even been adopted to give a representation of the location of incidents internally within the database system. However, the use of such maps themselves is occasioned. They might be consulted if an incident location cannot be found by a crew or if the Call Operator cannot get a fix. Similarly, the (rare) occasions we have seen the AVLS used within ambulance controlling are confined to helping out an ambulance crew who report being lost.

The summary point to make out of these observations is that there is no sense in which any form of display (textual, 2D, 3D) is *inherently* superior to any other. What is important is designing displays so that the information required for the job is ready-to-hand *and no more*. To accomplish this may point to the (principled) selection of textual, list-oriented displays on a 2D screen and may point away from graphical, map-like or 3D projections if those would just confuse the work.

Layers of Seeing

Consider again the VAM containing its lists of ambulance IDs colour-flagged to indicate their current status. To the experienced worker, this shows at-a-glance how busy the service is. Swathes of red across the VAM screen (as is typical on a Friday night) reveals a service whose resources are stretched. While such summary impressions are available at-a-glance, both the VAM and the Incident Stacks can be engaged with further to find out exactly which individual

322

ambulances are deployed and exactly which incidents are being attended to. While the displays afford the pick-up of both sorts of information, what exactly a Dispatcher or a Supervisor will get from the screen depends upon the kind of engagement they have with it. Indeed, we have observed personnel dramatising the form of engagement they have with a screen so as to ensure that any other personnel who might be attending can pick up on what they are picking up from the screen. For example, a Supervisor might lean forward over their desk conspicuously peering into the VAM. In so doing they are displaying to all who might see that they are engaged in careful scrutiny and, in all likelihood, are focusing on a problematic deployment rather than the status of the service as a whole. Naturally, such understandings of the screen and the activities of persons in relation to it is essentially contextual. The point is that the fact that such variable understandings are possible is in part afforded by the coexistence on the VAM of (quite gross) visual features which enable different kinds of seeing.

We might say then that the VAM and similar displays afford 'layers of seeing' varying from an at-a-glance perception of the load on the service to a more detailed picture of the activities of individual ambulances with more careful scrutiny. This layering is accomplished through the careful and sparing use of the simple interface techniques we have discussed. Indeed, this further testifies to the subtlety of list-based representational formats in this setting. More complex displays may well not permit such readily distinguishable forms of seeing. A complex display may always require extensive engagement, thereby making it hard for others to fathom just what someone is doing or is concerned with.

No End-User Configurability

Above, we noted that the distribution of function across displays in the control room enables personnel to become aware of the status of each other's work in just such a way as to help them with their own. This can, for example, be sustained by juxtaposing different views of the state of the service. For example, a Supervisor might compare the Incident Stack of one Dispatcher with that of another to gain an impression of the relative stress being placed on different regions within the service. This might enable the Supervisor to judge that an ambulance should be moved to a standby location between the regions. Part of what makes views on the service juxtaposable is that the displays are *not* end-user configurable. Use of mouseless, keyboard-driven, window-free interfaces helps ensure that one Incident Stack has the same basic appearance as any other. Thus, visible differences between them will be work-related affairs and not arising from preferences of different users or from any work-unrelated layering of windows. Supervisory activities could well be disrupted by seemingly more sophisticated techniques and principles of user-choice (cf. Bentley et al., 1992).

Display Combination

So far we have been pointing to various features of the information displays employed in the ambulance control setting we have studied. There are good, work-oriented reasons why the displays are predominately textual, use colour sparingly, have standard non-tailorable formats, are often structured around lists presented on a flat screen (rather than graphical objects in any higher-dimensional space), are many in kind (each devoted to some particular purpose or related purposes), and are distributed around the screens of the control room, rather than each being available on every screen. We have already hinted that the *juxtaposition* of multiple displays is important to ambulance control. This and other related features of the work will be further emphasised in this section.

Different Loci and Spatialising What is Variable and What is Not

The different displays of information have specific loci on screens distributed through the ambulance control room. This spatial distribution is not haphazard. Indeed, it was carefully designed and considered by control room staff at the same time as requirements were put together for the current information system. In other words, the information system and its physical, ecological realisation were designed together, the new system requiring new furniture and some rebuilding of the control room itself.

Figures 1 and 2 depict this spatial distribution of information displays. The far wall is the site for the merged Incident Stack, the VAM, and a clock. The ICQ and OCQ sit between the Dispatchers just in front of this wall. The displays are all large (20" plus) monitors and are spaced out evenly. This gives them a clear boundedness and facilitates picking up on which display a control room worker might be glancing at. These displays are not variable under normal operation. The monitor showing the ICQ always shows the ICQ, the monitor showing the VAM always the VAM, and so forth.

The monitors on individual control room worker's desks, by contrast, are variable in what can be displayed upon them. The Dispatchers can access a number of different information displays, the Supervisors yet more, the Control Manager more still. That these displays are located before designated workers gives them the information they need ready-to-hand as we have emphasised. It also enables workers, who may need to know something not normally provided for on their own displays, to know where to look. A Supervisor concerned with performance statistics knows that this information can be accessed from the Control Manager's terminal. The spatialisation of different displays to specific loci enables routine information to be ready-to-hand without interfering confusion from what is needed only occasionally, while the locus of information required only on occasion is nevertheless commonly known.

The seating of control room personnel 'in rows' with Dispatchers nearer the far wall than Supervisors facilitates supervisory activities while minimising the distractions Dispatchers might otherwise be exposed to. There is a similar 'layering' of displays as one follows a trajectory from the far wall of the control room past the Dispatchers, past the Supervisors, and then to the Control Manager. We move from displays which are invariable, larger, generally available and show 'merged' features of the service through displays which are variable and manipulable, smaller, designated for individuals and concerned with area-specific reckoning through again to displays which are still individual, variable and manipulable but add in summaries of the whole service. In short, the disposition of displays and persons in the room comprise a structured working ecology.

Displays and Inspectable Embodied Conduct

We have given examples already of how the distribution of several, separate displays, each with their own specific locus, enables workers' embodied conduct to be intelligible to others. If a Dispatcher leans over to scrutinise another Dispatcher's display, this can enable a Supervisor to pick up on a matter of potential cross-board significance. If a Supervisor stares long and hard at the VAM, this may alert the Control Manager to a problem in maintaining cover in a part of the region. The variety of different displays, each with their own distinct spatial locus, supports discriminability in the understandings that can be obtained through inspecting the embodied conduct of others. The existence of potential issues to do with message transmission, providing cover, a difficult dispatch decision, a particularly feisty crew and so forth can all be distinguished *in part* because relevant displays are in turn distinguished. Naturally, there is no one-to-one mapping going on here which could be captured in crude 'rules' like 'if a Supervisor glances to display D, this means X'. This is why we emphasised *in part*. The variety of coexisting displays in the one space affords such opportunities, it doesn't mandate the attributions made in any mechanical fashion.

The Personal and the Public

In Martin et al. (1997), we emphasise in depth how control room personnel maintain a 'working division of labour' so as to help each other out when the service is stressed and to collectively manage the contingencies which arise in control room work, while nevertheless maintaining a sense of 'my job'. In the terms of Hughes et al. (1992), personnel simultaneously maintain an *egological* orientation to the division of labour (what is there for *me* to do? what's on *my* board?), and an *alteriological* orientation (what can I do to make the work of *others* easier? how can I help with *their* overdue dispatches?). The distribution of information displays in the control room is apt for the management of a working division of labour. There are to be sure 'personal' machines and displays. Personnel have a sense of 'my computer'. However, viewing information displayed on 'my computer' doesn't rule it out being inspected by some other who may be looking over my shoulder or who inserts themselves into a side-by-side view to momentarily share the screen. Equally, there are the public displays towards the far wall. But their being public doesn't necessarily rule out their accessibility from a personal terminal. This distribution of information displays allows routine work to be carried on without disruption from others while not disabling the possibility of making a problem public if needs be. For example, a particularly desperate Dispatcher can draw the attention of the entire control room to the paucity of available ambulances in their board by gesturing towards the VAM and pointing out on the merged Incident Stack an incident which is hard to deal with. Between the extremes of routine work and pleas for help, personnel have a range of displays and other persons they can call upon so as to appropriately make their own difficulties public or attune to the conduct of others.

Conclusions

We now rejoin our initial discussions of information visualisation in collaborative virtual environments (CVEs). This will be structured around our development of *multiple information displays coexisting within a shared virtual space* as a design concept for consideration. We offer this image as an alternative to notions of 'immersion in information' more commonly explored in CVEs for information visualisation.

Coexistence of Multiple Embedded Displays

Scrutiny of our ambulance control study suggests the utility of having multiple displays coexisting and embedded within a shared environment. Multiple displays enable the information required at each 'station of work' to be made readily available there and so be ready-to-hand when required by persons working at that station. This enables some division and distribution of function and work activity. However, the coexistence of multiple displays in a shared environment enables the in-principle accessibility of other information if needs be.

The principles governing the distribution of displays in the control room are subtle. Manipulable displays have different loci from non-manipulable displays. Monitors for variable displays have different loci from those with fixed displays. Displays which are public to all control room workers have different loci from those which are personal. This variation and distribution supports a working division of labour between personnel, a collective sense of the state of the service coupled with personal duties.

The possibility of multiple coexisting displays all embedded in a shared space has not been directly explored in work on CVEs for information visualisation. Most existing systems focus on producing a single information visualisation within a 3D space. Much attention has been paid to different visualisation and manipulation techniques but typically only a single visualisation at a time is computed. We would suggest that this ignores a critical feature of information sharing in a setting like ambulance control and, perhaps, more generally: *information is typically visualised (and acted on) in the context of other visualisations systematically distributed in the same space.*

Recent, yet to be published, work by Taylor (in prep.) is a partial exception to this as he experiments with various techniques by means of which multiple simultaneous displays can be computed, manipulated and distributed within a common virtual space. However, Taylor's systems are for single users and are not yet integrated within a CVE. This means that several features his work (e.g. choice of algorithms for computing displays and their distribution) have not yet been explicitly responsive to the requirement to support cooperative work. What we are attempting here are some first steps at using ethnographic work to inform the design of shared information visualisations of this sort.

Interactional Affordances and Freeing Up Space

We have been at pains to argue that distributing functionally and spatially distinct displays enables the gestures and talk of personnel to be richly yet readily understood by others. Some aspects of this can be captured in the notion of 'interactional affordance' (cf. Martin et al., 1997). Information displays afford interaction in the dual sense that (i) they enable a user to interact with the information displayed, and (ii) such human-computer interaction can be publicly available to 'third parties' and afford them with opportunities for interaction with either of the first two 'parties' (user or display). Information displays can be designed not merely to make them readily intelligible by their users but also to make their users' activities with them be intelligible to others. For example, the VAM not only affords different forms of seeing, it also enables people viewing it to make their forms of seeing public to others. In our ambulance control setting *human computer interaction is a public phenomenon.* Let us give some further elaboration to see how understanding this notion of interactional affordance might shape the development of design ideas for collaborative information visualisation.

For interactional affordances to exist, for the actions of persons with artifacts to be coherently available visually to third parties, *space must be left free.* For example, the disposition of the displays towards the far wall of the control room leaves a great deal of the wall space free. As we have argued above, this separates out the displays one from another to make gesture and gaze to one clearly discriminable by third parties from gesture and gaze to another. There would be no clear advantage in having a very large (and very expensive) monitor across the whole of this wall displaying many information sources when keeping those sources distinct is important to the intelligibility of them and of gesture and gaze with respect to them... and this is most readily accomplished by having a number of cheaper, more conventional monitors!

Just as a 'plane' (like the control room's wall) need not be completely filled with displays, a three dimensional space (like a control room or, we would suggest, a VE for information visualisation) needn't be densely filled either. More densely packing our control room with displays would not merely make for a claustrophobic working environment, it would also make it harder to interpret the actions of others. Perhaps we can say: in a shared space containing multiple displays, the local intensities/densities of information need to be sparsely distributed for interactional affordances to be possible. Put less grandly, if the whole space is cluttered with information sources not only will you have difficulty making sense of it all, you'll also have trouble picking up on what others are doing and making sense of that.

These considerations also have, we believe, novel implications for research on shared information visualisations using virtual reality technology. First, they give us good reasons for exploring visualisation techniques which yield geometrical forms with a dimensionality less than three, even if such forms are embedded within a 3D CVE. The discipline of confining oneself to 2D forms (for example) can encourage us to thin out data to show just what is relevant for the purposes of the display. 2D forms allow 'side-by-side' or 'face-to-face' views between two or more embodied users who have lines of sight (more or less) perpendicular to the 2D plane. This can facilitate the mutual intelligibility of activity, as our gestures and lines of sight can become 'aligned' more readily. There is also a lesson in the ClearBoard system (Ishii and Kobayishi, 1992) which combines two video streams and a shared 2D drawing surface with participants having 'face-to-face' views on either side of the surface—an arrangement which also can support mutually intelligible gesturing. Here, not only are the shared forms confined to a 2D plane, most of the drawing plane is unfilled, indeed is 'clear' (hence the name of the system). This further testifies to the importance of *leaving space free for interactional purposes*. Finally, Chalmers (1994) argues that 2.nD (n small) displays, having a dimensionality suggestive of a 'landscape' enable us more readily as earthbound, perambulatory creatures to utilise everyday perceptual and naming practices (e.g. 'up' and 'down' can have a ready significance). In summary, then, there are good reasons, based on questions of what forms of perception and interaction are afforded by different geometrical forms for (1) exploring forms with a dimensionality less than three even (especially) if they are to be embedded in 3-space and (2) preferring external viewpoints which allow 'side-by-side' or 'face-to-face' mutual orientations towards displays rather than 'immersed' viewpoints which not only militate against obtaining an overview but also might cause problems for the mutual intelligibility of gaze and gesture.

Considered in this way, there are strong practical reasons for flat, more or less two dimensional information displays in VEs. Yet more arguments for flatness accumulate for settings where text is to be visualised, as argued above. These arguments intensify still further, we would suggest, when multiple displays coexist embedded within a shared VE. Flat displays sparsely distributed in separate loci minimise the occasions when one display (or visual forms from it) might occlude another (or forms from it). When they do occur, such occlusion problems can be rectified by (in the real world) leaning around, standing up or 'craning the neck', or (in the virtual world) by a small levitation of the user-embodiment. But this is possible principally only if the displays are themselves laid out so that they do not fill three dimensions evenly. Space has to be left free so that such adjustments of viewpoint counteract occlusions systematically. If 3D space is, in principle, always everywhere equally filled, then an occlusion problem might be remedied this time by a shift up, this time by a shift down, on yet another occasion by a movement to the side. A flatter 'landscape' or other 2.nD (n small) structure will encourage occlusion problems to be resolved and overviews to be sought by means of displacements in the direction of the 'fractional dimension' ('up' in the case where displays gravitate towards the groundplane).

This systematicity lays the ground for an interactional affordance. In the case of a 'landscape' of displays close to the groundplane, displacements up can become intelligible to others as attempts to get a view of a distant display rather than a 'pure' navigational movement. If, as in the control room, displays can be different from each other functionally and not just spatially, then rich inferences can potentially be drawn about the exact significance of a simple move up. An embodiment moving up can be supposed to be one trying to find out about just those things that the distal display depicts. Systematically distributed displays help enable *actions* to be perceived, not just behaviour noted.

When the visualisation of complex dynamically changing data from multiple perspectives is at issue, then, we are developing an argument for exploring CVEs comprised of displays which:

- are multiple, localised, discrete, functionally distinct and embedded within the VE
- have a distribution in the VE which fills out its three dimensions unequally and sparsely
- each have a dimensionality less than the VE itself (i.e. tend to be relatively flat)
- are designed for 'external viewing' primarily (i.e. while user-embodiments and information displays are to be 'immersed' in the VE, the further immersion of users within the displays themselves may not always be called for or desirable).

It is algorithms which generate spatial distributions of this sort that we would commend for exploration for collaborative information visualisation.

Naturally, VEs for particular applications will have to be developed in ways which are sensitive to application-specific requirements. We are not suggesting that CVEs along these lines above will always satisfy all needs. Any one of the features we note could be relaxed in a particular case. What we are suggesting is that the above is a particularly interesting constellation of features for CVEs which is motivated by our ethnographic consideration of ambulance control and is under-investigated in the literature on CVEs for information visualisation to date.

Ethnographic Practice in CSCW

We are aware that this has been an ambitious paper in that we have tried to present ethnographic analyses in some detail while also engaging with technical design issues in CVE application development. Some readers may feel uneasy about this, believing that we are overstepping what can be legitimately concluded from empirical social scientific research. To allay these fears, let us try and be clear again about what we are offering and the limits of our argument.

We are putting forward for consideration a *design image*, a set of concepts which could be instantiated in actual systems. Our design image (of multiple coexisting information displays embedded within a shared virtual space) is proposed as something to *add* to the stock-in-trade of CSCW researchers concerned with shared environments for information visualisation. It is an alternative to an idea of 'immersion within information' and, under some circumstances, may turn out to be more useful, under others, less. As is standardly the case with ethnographic practice in CSCW, we want to add to developers'/designers' resources, not take anything away (cf. Randall, Hughes and Shapiro, 1992). What we are offering is not any abstract theory of information display and manipulation but a design image of potential practical use inspired by our ethnographic description. And like many 'design recommendations' arising from social scientific work, it is *inspired by* field study, not *deduced from* it. The proper evaluation of this would be by reference to particular applications of our design image in plausible contexts of use. It would be too much, we believe, to ask of this now in the current paper but, naturally, this is the subject of our ongoing work.

To be willing to offer up such 'design images' when they present themselves is, for us, *a* response (we have others!) to Plowman, Rogers and Ramage's (1995) question, posed at ECSCW95, *what are workplace studies for?*

Final Word

Gibson (William) once defined cyberspace as "the mind turned inside out". We prefer an altogether more mundane conceptualisation. Virtual environments comprise another arena for social interaction and cooperative work alongside others. Under these auspices, we have argued that virtual environments are to be apprehended in terms of how they display information so that it can be practically acted upon and so that one person's engagement with information can be picked up by others. This is why we emphasise Gibson's (J.J.'s, 1979) conception of affordance. It is also why we grant that there can be good reasons for displays which are textual, list-oriented, non-user-configurable, not very subtly coloured and flat. We do not believe that this is conservatism or lack of imagination on our parts when confronted with the 'new frontier' of virtual reality. Rather it is sensitivity when confronted with the details of lived work practice and a desire to take those seriously as a source of inspiration for technical design.

Acknowledgements

The authors acknowledge support from the eSCAPE (Electronic Landscapes) and eRENA (Electronic Arenas for Culture, Performance, Art and Entertainment) projects of the European Communities' ESPRIT Long Term Research Programme.

References

Benford, S., Greenhalgh, C., Craven, M., Walker, G., Regan, T., Morphett, J., Wyver, J. and Bowers, J. (1999): "Broadcasting on-line social interaction as inhabited television", *Proc. ECSCW99.* (in this volume)

Benford, S., Snowdon, D., Greenhalgh, C., Ingram, R., Knox, I. & Brown, C. (1995): "VR-VIBE: A virtual environment for co-operative information retrieval", *Proc. Eurographics'95.*

Bentley, R., Hughes, J., Randall, D., Rodden, T., Sawyer, P., Shapiro, D. & Sommerville, I. (1992): "Ethnographically-informed systems design for air traffic control", *Proc. CSCW'92.*

Bowers, J., O'Brien, J. & Pycock, J. (1996): "Practically accomplishing immersion", *Proc. CSCW'96.*

Bowers, J., Pycock, J. & O'Brien, J. (1996): "Talk and embodiment in collaborative virtual environments", *Proc. CHI'96.*

Carlsson, C. & Hagsand, O. (1993): "*DIVE*", *Computer & Graphics*, vol. 17, pp.663–669.

Chalmers, M. (1994): "Information environments", in L. MacDonald & J. Vince (eds), *Interacting with virtual environments*, Wiley, Chichester.

Gibson, J. J. (1979): *The Ecological Approach to Visual Perception*, Bantam, New York.

Greenhalgh, C. and Benford, S. (1995): "MASSIVE: A virtual reality system for tele-conferencing", *ACM: TOCHI,* vol. 2, no. 3, pp. 239-261.

Hughes, J., Randall, D. & Shapiro, D. (1992): "Faltering from ethnography to design", *Proc. CSCW'92.*

Ishii, H. & Kobayishi, M. (1992): "Integration of inter-personal space and shared workspace", *Proc. CSCW'92.*

McGrath, A., Oldroyd, A. and Walker, G. (1998): "The Mirror: reflections on inhabited TV", *Proc. CSCW'98 Video programme.*

Mariani, J., Rodden, T., Colebourne, A., Palfreyman, K. & Smith, G. (1995): "Q-PIT: a populated information terrain", *IS&T/SPIE Symposium on Electronic Imaging: Science and Technology.*

Martin, D., Bowers, J. & Wastell, D. (1997): "The interactional affordances of technology: an ethnography of human-computer interaction in an ambulance control centre", *Proc. HCI'97.*

Pycock, J. and Bowers, J. (1996): "Getting others to get it right", *Proc. CSCW'96.*

Plowman, L., Rogers, Y. and Ramage, M. (1995): "What are workplace studies for? ", *Proc. ECSCW'95.*

Randall, D., Hughes, J. and Shapiro, D. (1992): "Using ethnography to inform system design", *Journal of Intelligent Systems*, vol. 4, pp. 1-2.

S. Bødker, M. Kyng, and K. Schmidt (eds.). *Proceedings of the Sixth European Conference on Computer-Supported Cooperative Work, 12-16 September 1999, Copenhagen, Denmark*
©1999 Kluwer Academic Publishers. Printed in the Netherlands

Moving document collections online: The evolution of a shared repository

Randall H. Trigg, Jeanette Blomberg, Lucy Suchman
Xerox Palo Alto Research Center
{trigg, blomberg, suchman}@parc.xerox.com

Abstract. This paper reports on a work-oriented design project concerned with the question of how to migrate shared, workgroup document collections currently kept on paper online. Based in a civil engineering work group, the focus of our project is a document collection called the "project files," a heterogeneous mix of documents that serve as an ongoing resource for the group during a project's course as well as an archival record at its completion. We describe the dynamics of the standardized classification scheme in use for the project files, existing practices of document filing including routine troubles, and the prototype developed to move the project files online. The latter includes a configuration of hardware and software along with associated practices of document scanning, coding and search. We conclude with some reflections on the difficulties of maintaining alignment across paper and digital media in the migration to online document collections, and with a summary of the questions posed and answers provided by our project.

Introduction

The organization and management of documents is viewed as a persistent problem for office workers of all kinds. Researchers have noted that people's offices and work areas frequently appear (to them and to their colleagues as well as to researchers) cluttered with documents. These documents often claim most of a work area's horizontal surfaces, and are typically arranged in more and less meaningful piles (Malone, 1983, Nardi & Barreau, 1997). While the potential of computational technologies to ease the burden of office filing and facilitate later document retrieval seems obvious, it largely remains to be realized (Celentano et al., 1991). In this paper we report on a project to explore the requirements for creating online repositories of scanned documents within a workgroup.

Our project is focused on what we call *working document collections* that are maintained jointly within a project team and serve as shared resources for the group's work (see also Blomberg et al., 1996). Working collections occupy a niche between active documents currently in use at any given time and those stored in an archive, with the file cabinet being the typical example. Some have suggested that the documents stored in file cabinets or scattered throughout offices have limited value as they are seldom retrieved for later use (see for example Kidd, 1994). The argument goes that once a document's immediate use has passed (e.g. to convey information, to denote that an action has occurred, etc.), its value is significantly reduced. In such cases the retention of the document is motivated more by difficulty in deciding to discard it or by the archival requirements of the organization than by the anticipated value of the document in some future transaction. Our research suggests, however, that in many organizations collections of documents are deliberately retained for their potential value in the day-to-day operations of the organization. Far from losing their value over time, these documents are critical to the effectiveness of workers and work groups. In such organizations the problem that confronts workers is how to organize document collections so that on those occasions when a document is needed, it can be found.

Our current project is part of a larger research program in *work-oriented design* (Ehn, 1988; Greenbaum and Kyng, 1991; Kyng & Mathiassen, 1997). Our approach comprises workplace studies closely integrated with the cooperative development of prototype systems, meant to exemplify new and useful work practice and technology configurations. We combine in situ interviewing, workplace observations and video analysis with design interventions that engage a range of representational artifacts (from paper mock-ups to working prototypes). Throughout the course of a project we move back and forth between our field studies and our design activities looking for opportunities to introduce design ideas and artifacts into the work environment.

At present we are engaged in a collaborative research project with a team of engineers employed by a state Department of Transportation in the U.S. (called here "the Department").[1] The team is involved in a bridge replacement project undertaken as part of a larger effort to bring the area's existing roads and bridges up to earthquake safety standards. Although our research has looked at various aspects of the work of these engineers (Suchman, 1998; Suchman, 1999; Suchman et al., 1998), our design efforts have focused on the work of filing and retrieving a collection of workgroup documents referred to as the *project files.*

Our prototype system for the engineering design team had its genesis in an earlier case-based prototyping project at a Silicon Valley law firm (Blomberg et al 1996).

---

[1] The engineering team was initially composed of six civil engineers but has grown to more than 20. The prototype system we developed is intended to support the work of the entire team.

The previous prototype also acted as an online, scanned repository for a working document collection, and we learned several lessons from that experience that have informed our current design:

- *The problems in requiring extensive coding as a prerequisite for the addition of a document to the collection.* The only classification information that we had about the attorneys' documents was the name of the file folder in which the physical document would be placed. Attorneys made it clear that they had no time to input additional metadata.
- *The value of page images for document browsing and retrieval.* We learned from the users of our earlier prototype that a range of scaled reductions of page images were valuable for different purposes: thumbnails for browsing the results of a search, intermediate reductions for browsing the pages of a document, and larger, readable reductions for viewing single pages.
- *The importance of hybrid search.* Though our searches were primarily restricted to the OCR text of the scanned documents, we saw the potential value in providing multiple, alternative search strategies in a single interface.
- *The need to reproduce the current physical organization of the document collection in the online interface.* As one view among others, a representation of the filing scheme used in the paper collection serves both as a familiar, transitional rendering from paper to digital media, and as a useful option for filing and search in its own right.

Our focus at the law firm was on document search and browsing, rather than on practicalities of document scanning and coding. In addition, the prototype that we developed was never fully integrated with the firm's infrastructure, making it impossible to access the collection from multiple workstations. Our primary goals in redesigning and reimplementing the law firm prototype in our current project were to move to a WWW-based interface that would allow workgroup access from diverse platforms, and to develop fully the practices and infrastructure necessary for scanning and printing as well as search. Indeed, we think of the current prototype as more than a document repository with an online interface; it is a collection of artifacts (workstation, scanner, in-box, etc.) and associated practices of scanning, coding, browsing, retrieval, and printing (see Figure 1).

The creation and maintenance of project files is a basic requirement for every engineering project at the Department. The *Project Development Procedure Manual* explains that these documents represent a partial record of the activities of the group, "... that document project decisions, and that would be useful (or required) to develop a subsequent project." Project engineers make reference to these documents throughout the project's life. Initiated by the design team, when a project moves from design to construction some number of the documents are copied and made available to the construction team. At the conclusion of all stages of a project, a select group of documents from the project files are assembled for the Department's permanent archives.

Figure 1: Project file binders and prototype scanning station.

Project file documents are a heterogeneous collection of letters, memos, reports, minutes of meetings, working design plans, and the like that originate both from inside the Department and from outside sources such as citizen groups, consulting firms, and other governmental agencies. The project file acts as a shared resource for team members and on occasion is referenced by other groups within the Department needing access to project file documents.

All project file documents are currently kept in hardcopy and stored in three-ring binders within the project team's work area. Our collaborative project with the bridge replacement team is to develop an online project file, accessible through the World Wide Web.

The basic design goals for the prototype are threefold:

- To require minimal overhead for entering documents into the online repository.
- To provide for incremental, modifiable coding of documents at any time.
- To provide multiple resources for document search and viewing.

In the remainder of the paper we describe the project and the lessons learned to date. We begin with a discussion of the work of document coding, including the dynamics of document classification and current practices of document filing. With that background we describe the development of an online project files prototype, including the design of working practices for scanning, document coding and document search as well as the configuration and development of associated hardware and software. We conclude with some reflections on the difficulties of maintaining alignment across paper and digital media in the migration to online document collections. Finally, we offer a summary of the questions posed and answers provided by our project.

The Uniform File System

Engineering teams are responsible for the maintenance of project files and are instructed to file documents according to a standard, organization-wide filing system called the Uniform File System or UFS:

> The Uniform File System is to be used by all Caltrans projects – regardless of size or type of project. The originating unit should start the file system as soon as preliminary studies can identify the project (*Project Development Procedure Manual*).

The UFS is a three-level hierarchical classification system in which an exclusive numerical code is assigned to each document, which is then placed in the corresponding location in the binders. This apparently clear structure masks, however, what is in fact a diverse, cross-cutting and sometimes conflicting set of interests in the documents to be filed. The latter include the type of document (correspondence, reports, maps and the like), the source of the document, to whom it was sent, the project stage to which the document relates (e.g. project approval, design, construction), and the main subject matter covered by the document. To address this problem the Department's procedure manual states that the source of the document should be the primary determiner of its UFS code, on the argument that "[m]any letters and reports cover more than one project issue. Consequently, items will be classified and filed according to the source that generated them, rather than by subject." The standard UFS framework has been relatively stable, with organization-wide changes occurring on the order of every five years. It is recognized, however, that minor modifications and elaborations to the UFS will be required by project teams in response to the particular requirements of a given engineering project.

The Project Development Procedure Manual suggests that "[t]he PE (Project Engineer) should use personal discretion when creating sub-categories for filing purposes." The changes to the UFS framework that we have observed include elaborating existing categories by naming particular entities, creating subcategories where none existed, and adding new, high order categories.

Elaborating existing categories: As an example, the UFS sets aside the 300 category for General Correspondence. Within that category, code 330 denotes Correspondence with Federal Agencies. The bridge replacement team has elaborated the UFS scheme by specifically naming the six federal agencies with whom they correspond, first as hand annotations and later as typed entries in a revised version of the UFS for their project. Similarly code 351, Correspondence with Cities, has been specified to include the five cities within or adjacent to the project area.

Creating new subcategories: The UFS may also be modified to reflect changes in the situation of an ongoing engineering project. For example, when the bridge replacement project first began, the Bay Area Transportation Authority (BATA) did not have jurisdiction over this particular project. BATA's authority was later extended to include oversight of funds set aside for the bridge replacement project. The engineering team then found it useful to add a new category, 134, specifically for

BATA resolutions. At the same time they elaborated code 353, Correspondence with Areawide Agencies, to include correspondence with BATA (but not resolutions).

Adding high order categories: Perhaps the biggest change that we have observed is the addition of a new category where none existed before. The 700 category was thought to be necessary because much of the project work in this case was being done by outside consultants. This level of contracting-out is a relatively new phenomenon at the Department, and the organization-wide UFS has not yet reflected this change. The bridge project team initially added the 700 category for all documents relating to their work with consultants. Later in the project, however, the 700 category was redesigned to cover only task order agreements with the consultants. All other correspondence with consultants was moved to a new category, 314, under the General Correspondence category.

Each of these changes to the UFS has had implications both for current filing practices and for the design of our prototype.

Filing practices using the Uniform File System

Our interest in understanding what would be required to move the project files online has led us to look closely at the bridge team's current filing practices. On one occasion we arranged to sit with Dave, the Senior Project Engineer, while he assigned UFS codes to documents destined for the project files. In the course of filing documents Dave commented to us about particular difficulties he was having in deciding which UFS code to assign to particular documents:

> D: One thing I'm noticing as I'm picking out where I want to store these things you know like for instance this one right here, it's our letter to the FHWA [Federal Highway Administration] regarding consultation for the endangered species act. So there's a permit involved, environmental is involved, the federal, FHWA is involved, external agencies. So there's all these categories it could conceivably go under and I have to pick one. Then I have to go back and maybe search for, because maybe I wasn't thinking, the next time when I'm looking back. So that's why it would be really cool if you could enter these things like you said, you could have a date, or a title, or a subject or keyword or whatever. So that's why I think it would be really handy, because I'm sitting here and I'm going, well, correspondence to federal agencies, yea, that's the one I think it is. But it could easily be thrown underneath permit, and certainly my assessment may be different than the guy next aisle over.

Dave here is experiencing common troubles of filing, involved in deciding to which of several possible categories a document should be assigned. Several alternative UFS codes seem equally plausible, but insofar as the document in hand will go in only one location in the binders, he must pick only one code. He also recognizes that his choice will have consequences for his ability to find the document later on. Finally Dave is concerned that his choice of UFS may differ from "the guy the next aisle over," adding to the uncertainty that he or others in the workgroup will be able to find documents once they have been filed.

Dave also struggles in assigning codes with the conflicting logics of the Uniform File System. As we mentioned earlier, the UFS orders documents variously according to, among other things, the stage of a project and the topic covered in the document:

> D: (looking through UFS documentation) OK now I don't see what I thought I was looking for. So uhm, I guess I would stick it under uh Floodplain Evaluations. What was the other spot? Drainage is usually done during the design phase and we're not there yet. So that's why I would pick uhm, but see 231 is Draft Environmental Document which is pretty vague. So I'll never find it. It's just not going to happen. I'd probably be more inclined to stick it under Drainage even though that's not where it belongs? So that's what I'm going to do. I'm probably not doing it right but that's what I would do. So this is why your system would be nice.

In this case Dave finds it difficult simply to locate the UFS category he is looking for within the scheme itself, as he has to flip back and forth through the pages of the UFS documentation to find the appropriate code. Dave is also confronted with the problem of a misalignment between the normative chronological order of engineering projects and the topical concerns of the document in hand. While the bridge project is still in the environmental assessment stage at this point, the document is about "drainage." As Dave explains, the UFS code that deals specifically with drainage is found later on in the scheme, under a category that concerns the design stage of a project. As a result he is faced with the question of filing the document "where it belongs," or alternatively where he is most likely to look for it later on.

Extending the options for document coding

At this point in our project we could see clearly that putting the project files on line would ease the bridge replacement team's reliance on the UFS classification scheme as their primary means of document retrieval. Our observations and discussions with members of the team convinced us as well of the potential value of a system that would allow them to assign multiple, heterogeneous property values to project file documents. We first explored the possibility and practicality of assigning new metadata classes to project file documents by mocking-up a paper coding form with fields for UFS code, date, keywords, and document type.[2] We again sat with Dave as he used our coding form to code project file documents, asking him to add keywords and document types as he saw fit. This provided us with a tentative set of keywords and document type categories to include in an online coding form.

To explore the feasibility of using our online coding form, we asked Andrea, an engineer working on the bridge project to code documents using the form. As with our original paper coding form, we allowed new keywords and document types to be added as needed. Andrea's experience using the coding form led us to rethink the

---

[2] We originally hoped to support the automatic processing of the paper coding form but so far have not been able to do so with the technologies available to us.

form's design. In particular, we observed that Andrea had difficulty in locating relevant keywords for a given document. She would peruse the list of keywords, and failing to find what she was looking for she would instead add a new keyword. This despite the fact that the keyword for which she was looking, or at least a reasonable synonym, might on closer inspection already be on the list. We realized that the list of keywords would soon grow to be unmanageable (if it was not already) without some way of further structuring it.

Our approach was twofold. First, we added structure to the list of keywords by creating separate properties for the source and recipient of a document. Many of the keywords in the original list had been the names of organizations and groups with whom the bridge team corresponded. We pulled these names out of the keyword list and grouped them by type of entity (e.g. federal, state, local, other). It was now much easier to find the source/recipient values and the remaining list of keywords, now called topics, became much smaller.

An added benefit of creating a source/recipient property is that people with little knowledge of engineering practice or of a specific engineering project are able to assign source/recipient values for a large percentage of the documents in the project files. This information is often directly available from letterhead, memo fields, or in the text of the document. In the case of the bridge replacement team, a student intern has been hired to help with project file management. He has now assumed the responsibility for scanning documents and adding them to the online repository. He is able to assign sources and recipients, as well as dates, topics and document types to many of the documents. In keeping with the design goals mentioned earlier, there is no requirement that property values be assigned to documents at the time that they are added to the online repository. The intern does as much as he can as he scans, and engineers can assign additional topic values to documents, or modify those already assigned, at any time.

Along with adding further structure to the property lists, we addressed the problem of the proliferation of keywords by adding a free text field on the coding form, in which useful information about a document that was not easily indicated by the assignment of values from the existing list could be noted. This free text field could later be searched when attempting to retrieve a document. At the same time, we wanted to support users in adding new items to the coding form as needed. Relevant topics and associated organizations change over the course of an engineering project (which can last upwards of ten years), particularly as it moves from project approval through to design and construction. To provide for modifications we added a link to another online form where new property values can be entered. Our reasoning was that the separation of document coding from property value modification, combined with the possibility of keying relevant information into the free text field, would reduce the frequency with which new values would be added to the metadata fields.

At the suggestion of the engineers we also added two new binary-valued properties; "RE doc" for documents to be made available to the Resident Engineer on the construction team, and "Project History" for documents to be included in the permanent archives of the Department. The existing paper-based practice requires that engineers go through the project files pulling relevant documents when the project moves to construction and again at the completion of the project. Because this is a time consuming task, the engineers thought that it would be useful to mark such documents in the online repository in advance. It has turned out to be difficult to know at the time that the repository is created, however, which documents should become part of the resident engineer's file and which should go to the archives. As a consequence, these properties are now thought of as potentially useful when the engineers are actually faced with the task of pulling RE and project history documents. Engineers could first go through the online repository and mark the documents. They could then more easily be assembled either for printing or for access within another online repository.

As we were developing the online coding form, one of the engineers asked if we could provide a hardcopy version of the form, that he and other engineers could fill out in advance of scanning documents. His question opened up further discussion about divisions of labor across the work of scanning and coding project file documents. The paper coding forms meant that those with engineering expertise can code documents without having to become directly involved in scanning. They can simply drop a document with code sheet attached into a project files in-box. It is then scanned by the intern assigned to the project files, who uses the online coding form to enter the codes designated by the engineer. This practice has now been added to that of simply writing UFS designations on the upper right hand corner of the document, again placing it in the in-box for scanning and coding by the intern. The separation of document coding from scanning, both in time and space, provides flexibility in the working division of labor that accommodates differences in the responsibilities and expertise of the project team.

Organization of the prototype interface

In contrast to the binders for the paper project files, the Project Files home page is the user's entry into the online repository. From there one can add new documents to the repository, view the existing collection along various dimensions, search the repository, and perform various miscellaneous ("administrative") tasks.

Figure 2 shows how the different operations are ordered and interconnected in the interface. Each box in the diagram corresponds to a single interactive web page. As indicated schematically, there are separate web pages for each of the repository views depending on the form of metadata chosen.

Altogether, the interface comprises sixteen pages all of which, apart from the home page and the third-party pdf viewer used to print, are generated dynamically by cgi scripts. (Not shown are various help pages containing textual documentation.)

As there is not sufficient space to describe each of these interfaces in detail, we will briefly describe those that are the most frequently used.

Our efforts to date have focussed on building the online repository, which as of this writing includes approximately 1600 documents or five times that number of pages. The online coding interface is used both to upload a scanned document in the form of a multi-page tiff file, and to upload metadata, usually a subset of the properties available on the coding form. The repository is currently maintained at PARC, where PARC technologies are used to process the image file, creating scaled gif images, ascii text from the OCR, and pdf files suitable for printing. After indexing the text and metadata, we add the new documents to the repository. At that point, they are available for browsing and retrieval from the Department.[3]

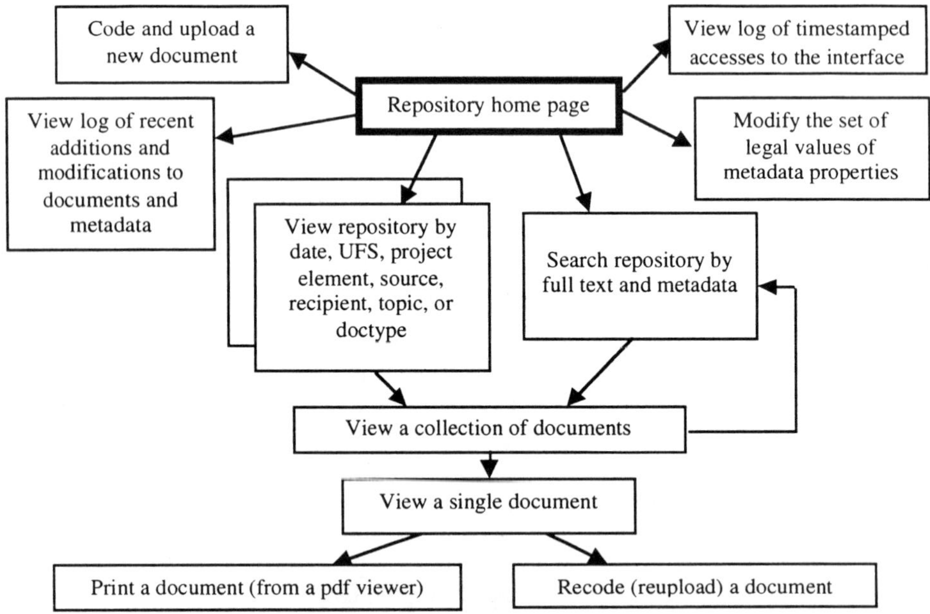

Figure 2: Primary flow of control through the prototype's web interface. Boxes represent interactive web pages each generated and controlled by a CGI script. To reduce complexity, the links that connect pages to each other apart from the main flow are not shown.

Documents in the repository are browsed using a variety of *views*. Each repository view offers an overview of the entire corpus with links to subcollections along the given dimension. Figure 3 shows two of these views: by UFS, and by date. There are also viewers for several of the other metadata properties. For example, the view by Source provides a listing of all legal Source entities and the numbers of documents coded as having that entity as source. Following the link from a given Source entity

---

[3] We expect to move the management of the repository onto the Department's intranet in the near future.

brings up a collection browser over the documents having that source.

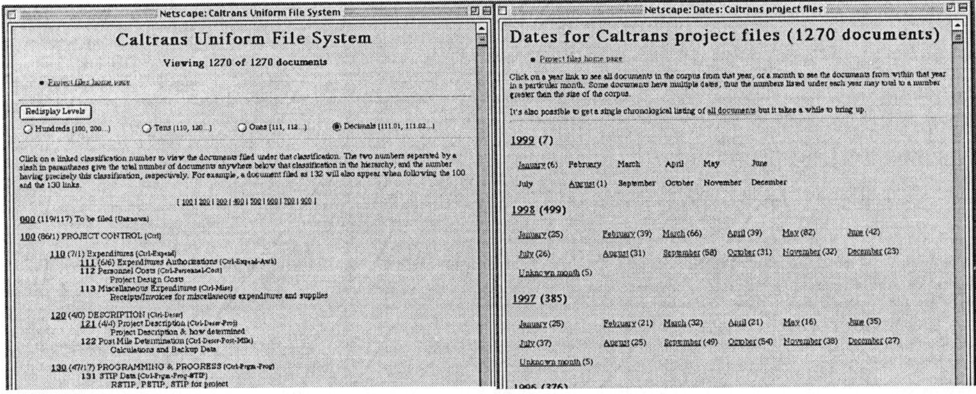

Figure 3: Two views over all the documents in the corpus, one organized hierarchically by UFS category, and one chronologically by date. A link from a non-empty category or a year or a month, brings up a browser over the documents having that category, or having dates in the given year or month.

The search interface retrieves documents by means of queries that combine multiple criteria. For example, Figure 4 shows a search for documents that have the word "resolution" in the full text, were dated sometime in the latter half of 1998, and for which the acronym "BATA" appears in any metadata property. Below the query fields is a button panel that lets the current search be combined with the results of a previous search.[4]

The results are displayed in a separate interface shown to the right in Figure 4. The search query can be refined by clicking on the "Revise search" button. This returns to the search interface retaining the current settings of all parameters. The "Revise search" functionality is especially handy after following a link from one of the repository views. For example, following the 1997 link from the Dates view brings up the results interface showing the 385 documents coded as having a date in 1997. Clicking on "Revise search" moves to the search query interface with the start and end date set to the beginning and end dates of 1997. This date range could be limited to portions of 1997, or other query fields could be combined with date to narrow the search. In this way, browsing from repository views can smoothly segue into more refined searches.

We also offer an expanded search interface that lets the user specify particular values of properties from pull-down menus as search terms. The expanded search interface includes fields for text search across the document title and notes properties.

---

[4] The Chabot system (Ogle and Stonebraker, 1995) uses multiple means of retrieval including text, metadata and image attributes for a corpus of photographic images. To date, we have seen less work on hybrid search across scanned document collections.

Below the "Revise search" button is a textual description of the search query as it currently stands, including any previous searches that were combined. Beneath that is a panel for controlling the display of search results. Each result is displayed either using a thumbnail image, or as a row in a table. In either case the metadata properties, dates, categories, and titles are always shown. Other properties can be included by clicking on the appropriate checkboxes. Because of the time required to download a large number of images, we default the display to thumbnails only if there are fewer than 50 results. This threshold can be adjusted by the user.[5]

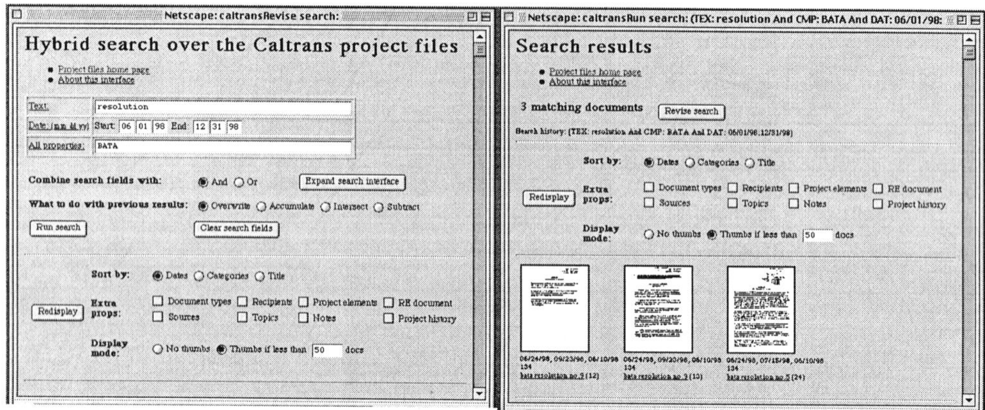

Figure 4: A search form with three query fields specified, and the web page showing the three matching documents; namely, those containing the word "resolution", dated in the latter half of 1998, and coded with "BATA" in one or more metadata properties.

Each result, whether thumbnail or title, is linked to the document displayer interface, shown in Figure 5. Here, one can browse the pages of the document at various sizes, view the OCR text, and print the pdf rendition. The metadata is displayed along with a link that leads to a coding form with which to modify the metadata values. This coding form is automatically filled in with the current values, and allows the document image file to be re-uploaded in case the paper document has been re-scanned.

Other parts of the interface include an access log that lists anonymous timestamped entries for each time any of the web page cgi scripts is invoked, and an interface that allows users to change the names of property values and add new ones. More significant reorganizations of the metadata scheme cannot be formulated in this "Modify Props" interface. To date users have tended not to use this interface for even simple additions, preferring to convey their requests to us either directly or through the intern.

---

[5] Our use of thumbnails to represent the results of a search and to display document pages derives from the Protofoil project (Rao et al, 1994) and is motivated in Blomberg et al (1996).

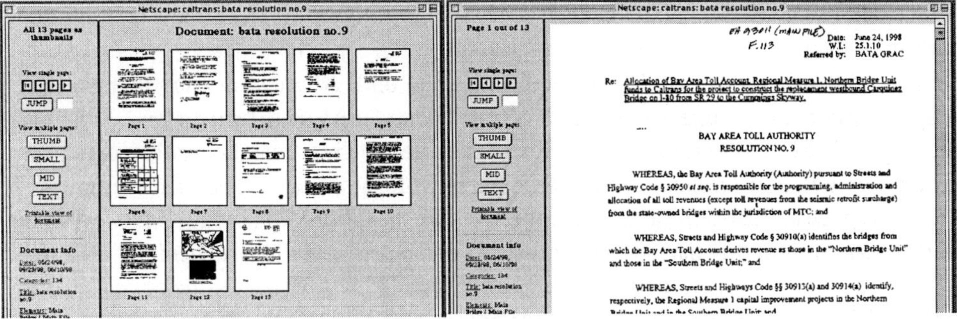

Figure 5: The document displayer interface is used to browse the pages of a document either as thumbnails as shown on the left, or in larger reductions up to a readable size for a single page as shown on the right. The ascii text from OCR can also be displayed. The metadata settings are shown on the left of the interface. The interface includes links to display and print the pdf rendition of the document as well as to modify the document's metadata.

Relations between online and paper documents

Keeping the renderings of online documents aligned with the paper files is crucial to the success of our project.[6] In this section, we describe some of the practices of maintaining this alignment and discuss issues relevant to repository design. We first, however, describe a significant event in the life of the project files that had implications for the alignment problem.

Grouping the project files by subproject

As the bridge replacement project has moved out of the environmental impact phase and into design, it has also grown in size and scope. Recently the project was split into a dozen or so subprojects comprising independent budget centers, named according to "Expenditure Authorization" (EA) number. Because each subproject (and its project files) moves into construction according to its own time schedule, the engineering team decided to subdivide the project files according to EA number. The result is a collection of mini-project files, each named by EA number and sorted by UFS and date.

In response to this reorganization of the project files, we added an "EA" property to our metadata. Assigning an EA number was mainly an issue for more recent documents, as documents created before the split were given the original EA number. Engineers were encouraged to pencil in an EA number along with a UFS code on the

---

[6] The paper project files continue to be maintained in binders alongside the online collection, because of the experimental status of the prototype and the fact that some documents will always be kept in hardcopy.

top corner of the document's first page, to help the intern in doing the scanning and coding.

The new scheme seemed to be working well until it became clear that the EA numbers were not a stable category. New ones were being formed and old ones merged and even reassigned uncomfortably often. This posed a problem for the binders, which were relabeled to reflect the new designations. One of the engineers then proposed abstracting from specific EA numbers to a short designation corresponding to the part of the project (e.g. MAIN for main bridge, INT for interchange, etc.). Each of these "project elements" was expected to cover several possibly shifting EA numbers, while remaining relatively stable over the remainder of the project. Again the binders were relabeled to reflect the new designations, and our metadata scheme was changed as well.

The problem of alignment

For the work of aligning the online and physical files, three of the metadata fields are most significant: project elements, UFS categories, and dates.[7] These are grouped uppermost on our coding form. They are also the three values that govern where in the binders a document is filed: first by subproject, then UFS, and finally by date. For subprojects with few documents, some levels of the UFS hierarchy (say, below the tens digit) are not allocated separate sections, but rather are simply sorted by date.

Of the three properties, the date is most easily read off of the document, whereas project element and UFS are harder to code. For this reason, the engineers pencil in those values on the document. The three properties are thus represented in three ways in the overall filing system:

- On the paper document itself: Dates appear in the document text, while project element and UFS code are penciled onto the first page.
- In the document's location: Binders are organized according to project element and UFS code; within these, documents are filed in chronological order, most recent first.
- In the online metadata: For each document, our system stores up to three dates, three UFS codes, and any number of project elements.[8]

We should note that there are good reasons for the redundancy in coding. The value of the codes for document filing and for online search are perhaps obvious. But what about the penciled values on the physical document? Here, the primary goal is mobility; the document should carry its codes when it is found out of the binders. This happens before the document is scanned, when the penciled codes serve as

---

[7] Though each of these fields can have multiple values, the paper documents are filed and ordered according to the first project element, the first UFS, and the first date.

[8] As described above, our system stores many more metadata properties than these three, but the others raise no alignment problems, since they are neither used in organizing the paper files, nor written in a modifiable way on the document itself.

instructions to the intern, as well as after filing, if the document is pulled from the binders for inspection or copying.

Ideally, a change to one of the three representations should lead to immediate updates of the other two. But this is not always easy. For example, an engineer changing the values of codes at her workstation might be reluctant to take the time to walk over to the project files, find the binder, move the documents to their new home, and change the penciled in codes. Likewise, someone working with the binders might choose a more appropriate UFS code for a document. In such a situation, refiling the physical document and writing down its new code is likely to be much easier than getting onto the system and searching for the document. At present we see engineers pulling documents from the binders, crossing out their current UFS codes and writing in new ones. They then place these documents in a stack for the intern to revise on the system and refile in the binders.

There is a further complication to the three-way redundant coding of documents. As we mentioned, at scan time most of the documents have penciled on them a project element value and UFS code. These penciled values are legible on the system when browsing the page images online. Though we can perhaps expect the workgroup to maintain the alignment of the three representations described above, it is certainly too much to expect them to rescan the first page and upload it into the system after changing the penciled marks. We could address this misalignment by giving precedence to the online metadata over any codes visible on the online page images. Unfortunately, this misses the problem of printing. One of the advantages of retaining a printable rendition of the scanned document online is that users can obtain hardcopy without having to recover the document from the binders (say, if they are working remotely). Once this rendition is printed, however, its out of date codes may lead to subsequent confusion.

Techniques for maintaining alignment

At any given time the shelves near the project files include stacks of documents in need of coding or recoding, recoded documents whose metadata needs modification online, scanned documents in need of filing, and the like. Sometimes these stacks are labeled as to their status, sometimes not. Amidst the confusion of piles of paper near the project files, it can help to have at least one record of the history of the processing of the document easily readable. In particular, when encountering a physical document a question arises as to whether it has been scanned and is thus findable online. The work of scanning a document now includes, therefore, the practice of affixing a self-sticking blue dot to the document's upper right corner.

Another aid to recording the status of the document's processing history is the engineers' choice to cross out rather than erase the penciled UFS codes when changing them. This can help with the task of aligning online metadata with the codes on the physical document. If the online code matches the one crossed out on paper, one can usually assume that the new code on the paper reflects the most recent change.

Technological possibilities

Online metadata include "standard" filing classifications relevant to the bureaucracy of project management (Marshall, 1998) or to schemes like the UFS maintained across the enterprise. In some future world perhaps all relevant workgroups (e.g. design, construction, archives, legal) could be assured access to the online project files, which they could assume held the "truth" - the trusted values. But in a transitional world like the one we encounter at the Department, where some of the players depend on having versions on paper or where paper is saved for legal signatures and the like, the problems of paper and digital alignment will persist.

One simple improvement to the technology of alignment could involve the automatic maintenance of a comprehensive version history. In particular, one could obtain the time of any change to any property value in the repository. This record of changes could be matched against the penciled values on the physical document to resolve cases of misalignment between online and offline codes (Dourish et.al., 1998).

A more radical change to both technology and practice would involve inscribing machine-readable codes on each project file document (Bloomberg, 1997; Barrett & Maglio, 1998). Ideally, the code would be human-readable as well as machine-readable so as to allow changes to be marked up on the physical document. To input these changes to the system, one could "swipe" the bar code or rescan that portion of the image to prompt the system to bring up the online rendition for recoding. If desired, the document could then be reprinted with a new machine-readable code.

Toward flexible document management

Several issues, we believe, should be considered by those who contemplate putting document collections online in support of group work. We present the issues here as a set of informed questions that together can be thought of as a kind of "due diligence" for analyzing and enabling flexibility in workgroup document handling both online and off.[9]

Who scans; who codes; who searches?:

Allowing flexibility with respect to who scans and who codes documents permits

---

[9] Drawing on an ethnographic study, Marshall (1998) analyzes metadata along several dimensions that include location, source, access, scope and temporality. We see our analysis as complementing hers, focusing on the day-to-day practical and technological contingencies that enable and constrain the emergence of document coding practices.

reconfigurable divisions of labor within workgroups. In our project, scanning has been done almost exclusively by a part-time student intern, but we imagine that other groups within the Department and elsewhere might make other choices. Coding on the other hand requires the involvement of engineers on the project. While the intern is able to assign date, source and recipient codes, project element and UFS codes require engineering expertise and familiarity with the project's history.

Our web interface supports distributed access to the project files from individual desktops. Nonetheless, most of the online searches to date have been done by the intern on behalf of the engineers. The intern has become familiar with both the coding and search interfaces through his experience in scanning documents, and therefore is viewed as an expert when it comes to the particulars of our prototype. We believe, however, that others will begin to conduct searches on their own as they gain familiarity with the interface.

When are documents coded?

The experiences of the bridge replacement team in developing a working practice around document coding suggest that the ability to code documents at various times is desirable. Specifically, document coding in this case occurred at three different times: before the document is scanned, usually by an engineer penciling in codes on the first page or filling out a coding form; at the time the document is uploaded just after scanning; or later upon encountering the document after a search.

Allowing coding and recoding at any of these times means that the system is able to meet the organizational contingencies of filing and search. These can include the need or desire to rush hardcopy documents into the system without taking the time required for coding, or the need to recode documents following changes to the metadata scheme or on discovering errors or omissions in a document's current coding.

How much coding is necessary/appropriate?

An initial goal of our prototyping work was to allow documents to be added to the system with a minimum of required coding. Early on, documents were entered into the system with little more than a date. In order to enable physical filing, however, documents must be coded with at least a UFS and a project element. Other codes may be added at scan time or following a search.

The question of how much to code is an issue that is under debate within the workgroup itself with some engineers taking the position that only minimal coding is required, relying on full-text search and UFS codes, while others support the idea of coding as much information as possible. Our approach has been to build a technology that accommodates either view, not casting any single perspective into stone through our design.

How to keep online and hardcopy documents aligned?

A continuing concern for us has been the relation between online and hardcopy documents. Here we see difficult tradeoffs between flexibility and alignment. In the case described here we attempt to align three representations of metadata codes: location in the physical files, codes inscribed on the document pages, and online representations of metadata. While these may well generalize across a variety of cases of working document collections, significant variation is also possible.

For example, in some cases alignment may not be that important. An organization might be willing to tolerate the occasional inconsistency if it was always clear which rendition of the coding to trust. In other cases keeping some record of changes to metadata, both online and on the document's pages, could address some alignment problems. But even such lightweight versioning might not be worth the trouble for still other organizations. In part the degree of investment placed on maintaining alignment may be a function of an organization's need to move quickly from paper to online and vice versa.

How does a metadata scheme evolve?

Our project has made visible some of the effort required to support evolving metadata, both for locally customizable, enterprise-wide standards like the UFS, and for locally designed and implemented schemes like a list of source and recipient entities. Our commitment to flexibility requires that the online and physical filing system keep up with changing agendas as projects progress from stage to stage.

At the same time, changing metadata schemes incur costs (Bentley & Dourish, 1995; Trigg & Bodker 1994). While some changes expand a scheme without affecting the coding of existing documents, other changes can cause a collection of documents to become "legacy"; that is, out of synchronization with newly scanned and coded documents. At times the change to a scheme comes with instructions on how to handle affe ted documents. On occasion, these instructions can even be automated with scripts ("Recode all documents in category 710 as 314"). In other cases, the documents may have to be visited one at a time by someone who is an expert in the content matter.

Conclusion

The activities reported in this paper make visible once again the dynamic character of the CSCW domain, where the latter encompasses both our own work as system builders and the work of those we aim to support. Our design project on working document collections is positioned within the larger project of cooperative design with users, as an approach to the creation of more useful and useable computer artifacts. It is the combination of envisioning, building and use that affords the power of cooperative design, as we work our way through successive rounds of trial and discovery regarding all of the ways in which the world is different than we had imagined it to be. We hope here to have provided a view onto the practicalities involved in moving working document collections online, as well as the interesting research questions that such a project poses for us and how we have attempted to answer them. This unfolding horizon of design questions and at least tentative answers is one sense of what we mean by the shared repository's evolution.

Another, less obvious aspect of CSCW as an evolving practice emerges from our experience as well. This aspect is tied to the fact that our prototyping project runs alongside and in relation to the bridge replacement project itself. Far from a situation in which we as designers enter a stable arena engaged only in maintaining itself, we find ourselves joining in with ongoing processes of development and change. In particular, systems of classification like that used in the management of critical documents mediate the interests of organization-wide consistency, manifest here in the basic template of the Uniform File System, with the requirements of specification and customization evident in the elaborations, modifications and re-workings of that scheme by the local workgroup. More generally, the project of designing a bridge itself constitutes a trajectory of shifting concerns, accountabilities and actors. All of this makes up the dynamic field of action both for us and for our collaborators. In this sense, co-development of CSCW technologies like a shared document repository means more than engaging prospective users in the design of new computer systems to support their work. It requires that we as designers engage in the unfolding performance of their work as well, co-developing a complex alignment among organizational concerns, unfolding trajectories of action, and new technological possibilities.

Acknowledgments

We would like to thank the members of the bridge engineering team for the time they graciously devoted to this project and for their insights on just what is required to design really useful online document repositories. Without their willing participation this project would not have been possible. We are also grateful to four anonymous reviewers for helpful comments.

References

Blomberg, J., Suchman, L., & Trigg, R. (1996). Reflections on a Work-Oriented Design Project. *Human-Computer Interaction, 11*(3), 237-265.

Barrett, R. and Maglio, P. P. (1988) "Informative Things: How to attach Information to the Real World", *Proceedings of the 11th Annual ACM Symposium on User Interface Software and Technology*, pp. 81-88.

Bloomberg, D. (1997) "Embedding digital data on paper in iconic text.", In *Proceedings of IS&T/SPIE EI'97, Conference 3027: Document Recognition IV*. San Jose, CA, Feb 12-13, pp. 67-81.

Bentley, R. and Dourish, P. (1995) "Medium versus Mechanishm: Supporting Collaboration through Customization", *Proceedings of the Fourth European Conference on Computer-Supported Cooperative Work ECSCW'95* (Stockholm, Sweden). Dordrecht: Kluwer.

Celentano, A., Fugini, M. G.,. Pozzi. S. (1991) "Classification and Retrieval of Documents Using Office Organization Knowledge", *Proceedings of the Conference on Organizational Computing Systems*s, pp. 159-164.

Dourish, P., Edwards, K., LaMarca, A. and Salisbury, M. (1998) "Presto: An Experimental Architecture for Fluid Interactive Document Spaces." Xerox PSRC report (submitted to ACM Transactions on Computer-Human Interaction) Palo Alto: Xerox Corporation.

Ehn, P. (1988). *Work-Oriented Design of Computer Artifacts*. Stockholm: Arbetslivscentrum.

Greenbaum, J. & Kyng, M. (Eds.), (1991) Design at Work: Cooperative Design of Computer Systems. Hillsdale, New Jersey: Lawrence Erlbaum Associates.

Kidd, A. (1994) "The Marks are on the Knowledge Worker Accessing and Using Stored Documents", *Proceedings of ACM CHI'94 Conference on Human Factors in Computing Systems* , vol. 1 pp.186-191.

Kyng, M., & Mathiassen, L. (Eds.). (1997). Computers and Design in Context. Cambridge, MA: MIT Press.

Malone, T. W. (1983) "How Do People Organized Their Desks? Implications for the Design of Office Information Systems", *ACM Transactions on Office Information Systems*, vol. 1, no. 1, 1983, pp. 99-112.

Marshall, C. C. (1998). Making Metadata: A study of metadata creation for a mixed physical-digital collection. In I. Witten, R. Akscyn, & I. Frank M. Shipman (Eds.), *Proceedings of Digital Libraries '98*. Pittsburgh, PA, June 23-26. ACM Press, 162-171.

Nardi, B., Barreau, D. (1997) Finding and Reminding" Revisited: Appropriate Metaphors for File Organization at the Desktop / ACM SIGCHI Bulletin v.29 n.1 p.76-78.

Ogle, V. E., & Stonebraker, M. (1995). Chabot: Retrieval from a Relational Database of Images. *IEEE Computer, 28*(9).

Rao, R., Card, S. K., Johnson, W., Klotz, L., & Trigg, R. (1994). Protofoil: Storing and Finding the Information Worker's Paper Documents in an Electronic File Cabinet. In B. Adelson, S. Dumais, & J. Olson (Eds.), *Proceedings of ACM CHI '94 Conference on Human Factors in Computing Systems*. Boston, Massachusetts, April 24-28. ACM Press, 180-185.

Rose, D. E., Mander, R., Oren, T., Ponceleon, D. B., Salomon, G., Wong, Y. Y. (1993) "Content Awareness in a File System Interface: Implementing the 'Pile' Metaphor for Organizing Information", *Proceedings of the Sixteenth Annual International ACM SIGIR Conference on Research and Development in Information Retrieval* , pp. .260-269.

Suchman, L. (1998) Organizing Alignment: The case of bridge building", Symposium on Situated Learning, Local Knowledge and Action: Social Approaches to the Study of Knowing in Organizations, Academy of Management Meeting, August 9, 1998 SanDiego, CA.

Suchman, L. (1999) "Embodied Practices of Engineering Work", To appear in Mind, Culture and Activity.

Suchman, L., Trigg, R. and Blomberg, J. (1998) "Working Artifacts: Ethnomethods of the prototype", Presented at the 1988 American Sociological Association Meetings, August 22, San Francisco.

Trigg, R. H., & Bødker, S. (1994). From implementation to design: Tailoring and the emergence of systematization in CSCW. In R. Furuta & C. Neuwirth (Eds.), *Proceedings of the Conference on Computer Supported Cooperative Work (CSCW'94)*. New York: ACM Press, 45-54.

S. Bødker, M. Kyng, and K. Schmidt (eds.). *Proceedings of the Sixth European Conference on Computer-Supported Cooperative Work, 12-16 September 1999, Copenhagen, Denmark*
©1999 Kluwer Academic Publishers. Printed in the Netherlands

PSI: A Platform for Shared Interaction

Kevin Palfreyman[1], Tom Rodden & Jonathan Trevor

Computing Department, Lancaster University, UK

{kev, tom, jonathan}@comp.lancs.ac.uk

This paper presents an infrastructure to support the dynamic sharing of information across a range of cooperative environments. The infrastructure builds upon the use of shared common spaces by using a distributed tuple space to provide information sharing at its base level. The platform extends existing considerations of tuple spaces by adding mechanisms to provide active support for sharing data elements. The use of a tuple space moves away from previous models of distribution in cooperative systems that focus on the propagation of events to focus on active data sharing. The use of data tuples allows the sharing of information to be independent of the information model allowing a wide range of applications and environments to be supported. The paper presents the infrastructure and shows how it can be used to support information sharing across a number of different forms of cooperative system and application.

1. Introduction

The CSCW research community has seen the development of a variety of systems that support real time cooperation through some sense of shared interaction. Initial systems focused on the development of shared interface techniques such as WYSWIS (Foster, 1986), interface coupling (Dewan, 1991) and the tailoring mechanisms (Greenberg, 1991). Underpinning the development of these interface techniques was a growing acceptance of a common model of shared interaction. The general strategy agreed was to consider multi user interfaces in terms of

---

[1] Now at: Xerox Research Centre Europe, Cambridge Laboratory, 61 Regent Street, Cambridge, UK,
           kevin.palfreyman@xrce.xerox.com

different views on a shared data model (Bentley, 1992; Dewan, 1991; Hill, 1993; Lee, 1996; Mansfield, 1997). This separation allowed the interaction to be shared by sharing the underlying model while allowing its effects to be presented in a variety of different ways.

In addition to these technical developments, a number of researchers began to consider the development of "Common Information Spaces" (Bannon, 1997) and suggest that one way to support cooperation was to consider the cooperation in terms of users interaction with a pool of shared information. It is clear that both technical and conceptual agreement on the development of applications to support cooperative interaction have started to emerge. The core of this agreement is an exploitation of the concept of some form of shared space that provides a focus for interaction. These shared spaces allow resources associated with the cooperative interaction to be gathered together and presented to a community of users. These spaces all provide a number of features to promote shared interaction.

- Information and resources can be shared between users by placing them in shared spaces with the effects of interaction propagated to other users.
- Users have an awareness of others in these shared spaces as user actions are reflected through their effects on shared resources in the space.
- Some agreed model is used to manage and structure access to the shared information in the space. Essentially, two main models are used to manage interaction.

  Space based models where the space is partitioned to manage the interaction. (For example, room based systems (Roseman, 1996))

  Time based session models where the access to the space is managed by providing a series of different sessions (Edwards, 1994)

The majority of these information spaces agree on the need to allow resources and information to be shared, the provision of techniques to structure this sharing and the need to allow users to be aware of the activities of others. However, despite this broad agreement the majority of systems do not provide any mechanism for interaction with other cooperative systems. In essence, each of these cooperative systems each still behaves as closed environments with limited access to other forms of cooperative systems.

In this paper we present the development of a platform to support sharing across a heterogeneous collection of applications. The platform allows interaction to be shared between cooperative applications by providing support for the active sharing of information. This allows cooperative applications exploiting a pool of common shared information to extend this model beyond their traditional application boundaries.

Within the Platfrom for Shared Interaction (PSI) sharing is provided through an active sharing infrastructure that combines a simple data model with active sharing mechanisms. The platform is realised as an active layer on top of an extended tuple space that allows *information tuples* to be shared across a number of distributed applications. The development of the platform required both the construction of the platform itself and the augment of an existing tuple space with notification mechanisms to make it an active tuple space. The representation of information as tuples in the active tuple space allows us to support a number of different forms of presentation and interaction of the shared information.

In the remainder of this paper we present an overview of the need to provide support for active sharing that moves beyond existing event based awareness models. We outline an overall architecture for the platform and then consider the development of the platform itself. The developed platform combines extensions to the existing model of tuple spaces to make them active and the development of a set of services to provide access to this tuple space. We outline and describe these extensions before considering how the platform is used in practices and how it may be used by existing applications.

2. The Development of Supporting Services

One reason for the lack of cooperation across cooperative systems is that a mismatch exists between the need for sharing within these systems and the provision of supporting infrastructures. The current generation of infrastructures provided to cooperative applications are motivated by the need to support awareness and focuses on the propagation of user actions. While the notion of awareness is important we feel that this focus has led to an imbalance in the provision of supporting services and we need to consider the development of active sharing services that allow interaction with different forms of heterogeneous information to be shared between cooperative systems.

The majority of supporting services and protocols have tended to focus on the propagation of awareness information in the form of events. This has included the development of protocols to augment the World Wide Web (Palfreyman, 1996) and a number of general event and awareness protocols. Although they focus on propagation of awareness some of these protocols already incorporate some model of sharing and information spaces. For example, the Corona communication service incorporates a model of shared spaces (Hall,. 1996). The use of a shared information space is also mirrored in the development of the NSTP protocol that uses "places" and "things" (Patterson, 1996).

The use of places and the move to state based services is also manifest at in applications in the way in which the shared interaction is managed. As we have said previously, two models for managing shared interaction have emerged.

1)   Event based supporting services have tended to be based on the notion of *application sessions* as an abstraction to represent the set of destinations to which application events are delivered.

2)   State based applications have seen the introduction of space based or *room based* approaches for managing shared interaction where updates

are clustered around a set of collected resources.

We wish to develop a shared interaction platform that exploits the active sharing of state. This allows us to marry both these approaches and our platform provides mechanisms to support both paradigms. Additionally the focus on state as a means of conveying interaction allows us to provide a bridge between real time and more asynchronous forms of interaction.

Existing systems also offer some form of structuring model to manage shared interaction. Often these models exploit some concept of space or a spatial model. For example, the supporting services in Teamwave are articulated in terms of rooms (Roseman 1996), while Corona offers shared spaces (Hall, 1996) and ORBIT offers locales (Mansfield, 1997). Similarly, Collaborative Virtual Environments (CVEs) such as DIVE (Carlsson, 1993) and Massive (Greenhalgh, 1995) exploit 3D models of spatial arrangements as a means of structuring the shared information space.

In developing our supporting platform we wish to recognise the need for providing some form of structure and the need to provide support that allows a diverse set of structuring models to coexist. It is important that we do not impose an external structure but that we recognise the situated nature of these cooperative applications and the emergent properties of the structure used to manage interaction in shared information spaces. *Thus rather than develop another model of shared information spaces and support for this model we wish to provide support to bring these different spaces together.*

In order to allow a range of models to coexist we focus on the provision of very lightweight data model for shared state that allows users to make information available to others and to allow linkages between different forms of shared state. The service we have developed provides a number of key features

- Λ lightweight data model that allows support for a number of different forms of shared space
- Extensible support for sharing allowing the addition of different persistence mechanisms.
- Support for a wide variety of forms of data by providing a clear canonical representation of information
- Support for flexible forms of sharing with varied patterns of use.

In order to provide these features we have chosen to move away from more traditional communication based model of distribution. This move reflects a response to the emerging demands cooperative applications place on the supporting infrastructure. However, as we build upon these alternative distribution techniques we in turn place new requirements upon them requiring changes to these underlying platforms. In the following section we show how we formed an overall architecture by building a supporting platform on top of an amended tuple based distribution platform.

3. The PSI Architecture

The PSI architecture provides an active distributed real-time sharing platform. The central approach is the cooperative sharing of arbitrary data among a heterogeneous set of distributed applications. The platform allows cooperative applications to make application information externally available by sharing it with the environment. The arrangement of the platform is shown in figure 1:

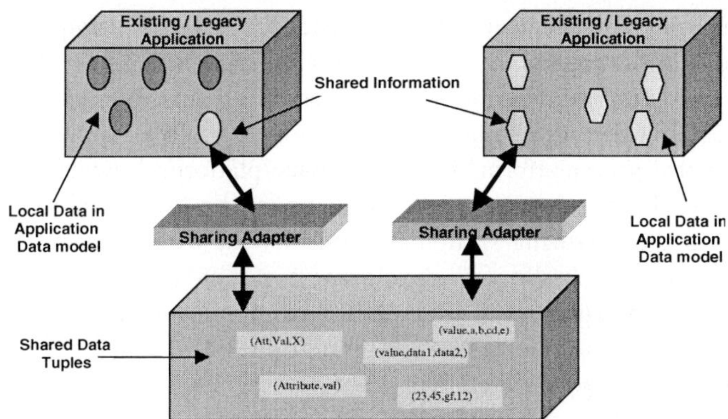

Figure 1: The general view of the Platform for Shared Interaction

To share information an application makes it available to the platform through a simple sharing adapter that provides a mapping between internal representations and the facilities provided by the PSI sharing mechanisms. Once internal application data has been made available to the platform its state information is held as a set of shared data tuples with updates and alterations to these tuples propagated to all applications sharing this information. Other applications can access this state information through *local proxies* that reconstruct the information. The platform manages alterations to the state by propagating updates through the tuples in the active tuple space.

The platform provides flexible sharing by extending current work on tuple spaces to provide an active tuple infrastructure. Traditionally tuple spaces have provided distributed access to simple data tuples and managed the issues of distribution to ensure that changes to these tuples are made available across a community of users. The platform for shared interaction extends these facilities to provide a set of cooperative shared interaction services by augmenting the existing tuple model in two ways.

- Extending the existing passive state based model of sharing to provide active support for sharing where applications are informed of alterations to shared tuples.
- Providing a simple and lightweight data model and API that supports the structuring information between cooperative applications.

What makes the PSI approach novel and advantageous over previous approaches is that the shared information space metaphor is being supported at the underlying distributed system level in a completely semantic-less manner. This is important for several reasons. First, it enables the programmer to reflect changes in the applications model of cooperation within the underlying communications structure of the distributed system (Bentley, 1995). Secondly, by moving the data sharing into the distributed system, the natural boundaries of sharing between applications can be transcended, allowing the data to be accessed and shared across applications, operating system and network.

In the following section we consider both the extensions to the underlying tuple space and the development an application interface that exploits this extended tuple space platform. The tuple space platform provides the advantage of offering a simple state representation that can be used to model a range of structures. In the following section we consider the extensions we made to the tuple space paradigm to allow the development of more active shared spaces. This is then build upon to provide the shared platform application interface.

4. Extending Tuple Spaces

A *tuple space* is a well known distributed systems mechanism originating from the work on the Linda project (Gelernter, 1985). Tuple spaces have their roots in the development of parallel processing applications and are traditionally used for (and best suited to) supporting systems that have well identified producer-consumer flows of data - where one part of the system is responsible for providing data that another part processes.

A tuple space contains zero or more *tuples*, as well as references to other tuple spaces. Each tuple consists of an ordered list of typed fields. For example, a tuple that would hold a name-value pair would be (*<String>*, *<Data>*), where <> identifies the type of the field. Note that fields are not named, making the ordering of the fields within a tuple important. Each field within a tuple is also said to be an "*actual*" or a "*formal*". An "actual" field is one that contains real data, whereas a "formal" field is a placeholder used in matching (see below). Traditional tuple spaces support three key operations, shown in Table I.

Op	Params	Description
RD	Tuple	Read any tuple from the tuple space that matches certain fields in the query tuple. There is no guarantee as to which tuple will be consumed if more than one would match the query tuple. Matching is performed by checking the "actual" fields have the same types and values as the tuple in the space. Once all the fields have been matched, the remaining (if any) formal fields in the tuple are filled with the matching tuple's corresponding values.
IN	Tuple	This operation is similar to RD but removes the matched tuple from the space. Again there is no guarantee as to which tuple will be consumed if more than one would match the query tuple.
OUT	Tuple	Write the tuple from this application out to the tuple space. Once the tuple has been written it becomes available to all applications connected to the space. All the fields in a tuple being OUTed must be "actuals".

Table I Standard tuple space operations

The PSI exploits and extends a distributed tuple space called L^2imbo that is described in detail elsewhere (Davies, 1997). The design and implementation of L^2imbo is such that it is more suited than other systems for use in distributed and mobile applications; it makes extensive use of IP multicast and supports interaction across a range of heterogeneous platforms (Davies, 1998). These characteristics differ from previous systems, which generally had more of a focus on performance for parallel processing within homogeneous networks and dedicated parallel processing environments. L^2imbo is also fully distributed, rather than being based on a client-server architecture. The system uses application-level framing techniques from the Scalable Reliable Multicast protocol, as used in a number of the MBone tools, and models each distributed tuple space as a multicast group.

The use of the L^2imbo tuple space provides us with two distinct advantages in terms of an infrastructure for real-time cooperative applications.

i. The mechanism is based on fast access to *decentralised* shared state and the infrastructure is optimised to support this arrangement. Applications sharing data with the space do not have to worry about how changes to their shared state are propagated to other applications.

ii. The use of tuples as a representation of information does not impose a particular data model and applications can externalise diverse forms of structured information across heterogeneous applications.

The L^2imbo tuple space is a passive entity which ensures that state information is available to all those who access the platform. It is the applications responsibility to continually monitor for changes to a given fixed set of tuples and act upon the changes to these tuples. This is done by making the RD operation blocking so that the execution of the application making the RD call stops until a tuple successfully matches the RD

4.1 Augmenting distributed tuple spaces for CSCW

Although the tuple space metaphor inherently supports the notion of a shared space the traditional view of a tuple space is limited to a fixed producer-consumer model of information flow. This model is problematic because the consumers are *expecting* the information to be produced. No facilities are provided for actively notifying applications of events occurring in a tuple space (such as a new tuple arriving) and only very limited facilities are available for querying, rather than consuming or extracting, the current contents of the tuple space.

To allow the more dynamic arrangements involved in cooperative settings we have extended the existing view of tuple spaces by augmenting the L^2imbo tuple space with an awareness facility offering additional operations that extend the standard set of tuple operations. These are summarised in Table II.

Operation	Params	Description
Register	Callback OUT/IN type	Register a callback in the application executed whenever a particular type (or subtypes) of tuple is added/arrives (OUTed), or removed/deleted (INed) from the tuple space. The callback receives the identifier of the tuple space where the operation occurred and a copy of the actual tuple the operation occurred on.
Unregister	reg-id	Remove previously registered callback

Table II Extended tuple space access operations

The core of this extension is a simple registration based notification facility that allows applications to register an interest in particular tuples and be informed via a callback mechanism when a tuple matching the given pattern is added or removed from the tuple space. The development of this callback mechanism means that applications reading the tuple space need no longer block and are free to handle other events while waiting for particular changes to the tuple space. Other useful facilities in this particular tuple space implementation include *collect / copy_collect*, which *in / rd* all matching tuples into a new tuple space. There are also non-blocking versions of *in* and *rd*, named *inp* and *rdp*.

These extensions assist in transforming the traditional tuple space to make it an active distributed shared space. The platform is realised on top of this active tuple space and provides an interface that can be used by a range of applications. The following section provides an overview of the application interface.

5. The PSI application interface

The platform for shared interaction (PSI) basically views applications as isolated "data spaces" populated with local data in their particular information model. These applications may choose to share some or all of this data so that other applications may access this information. The platform provides support for applications to insert and extract information from the platform and allows applications to interact with this shared information. The PSI architecture is divided into three separate layers, as shown in Figure 2.

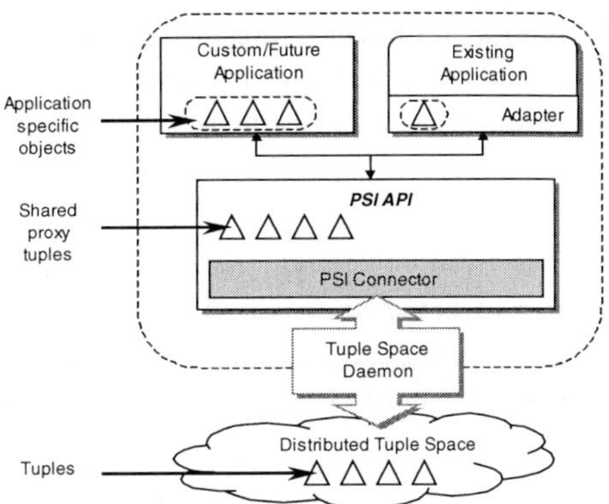

Figure 2 Architecture of the Platform for Shared Interaction

The core features of the architecture can be best described in four separate pieces. The *application layer* contains the applications themselves (or adapters for legacy applications). The application contains *application specific objects* that are native to that application. The application decides which of these objects are exported to the shared information space. The application communicates with the platform through the PSI API.

The *PSI API* maintains and decomposes the application specific data into *shared proxy tuples*. These are objects that reflect the contents of tuples in the underlying *tuple space*. They change as their tuple-space counterparts change and visa-versa.

The *PSI connector* provides the main coordination point for applications and the API, facilitating access to information in the shared spaces. This includes tasks such as adding and removing shared state from the tuple space and monitoring the tuple space for changes.

The *tuple space daemon* provides access to the tuple space and allows applications (such as the PSI connector) to add, query and remove data from the tuple space, as well as maintaining the same tuple spaces in a replicated fashion across any number of machines.

5.1 The PSI API

The API for the platform provides a simple common interface to allow applications to share and manipulate data through the tuple space. The API is currently realised in Java to provide as much cross-platform support and integration as possible. The API defines two types of tuple that are exported into the shared tuple space and carry application data: *data tuples* and *relation tuples*. These tuples are realised locally as proxies with corresponding tuples created in the shared tuple space.

In the following sections we consider the structure of the data tuples and relation tuples that provide the application interface for the platform. A dedicated connector object that manages the connection between the proxy tuples and the tuples in the underlying tuple space supports these two tuples.

Data tuples

The Data tuple represents a single atomic piece of shared data. A Data tuple consists of the fields shown in Table III.

Field	Type	Description
Tuple ID	String	Some unique identifier that identifies this particular tuple in the tuple space. It contains a tuple sequence identifier.
Application	String	Identifier of the application sharing the object (typically its mime-type)
Session ID	String	Some unique identifier for this session.
Object ID	String	Some unique identifier for the shared object to which this data belongs.
Data Name	String	The name of the data value
Data Type	String	The type of the data value
Data Value	Data	The data itself

Table III Fields in a Data tuple

To extract tuples relevant to a particular application from the shared space, it must be possible to identify distinct pieces of application shared data. Aside from the *TupleID* field which is used for state update (see later), an application may uniquely identify a particular piece of data using the following quad:

```
{Application, SessionID, Object ID, Data name}
```

The uniqueness or scope of each identifying field in the quad is the responsibility of the previous field. Thus each application with a given application identifier is responsible for maintaining and allocating the different *Session-ID*'s in that application. Each session allocates the *Object-ID*'s for objects in that session and so on.

The platform is policy free with the *Application* field and the *Session-ID* field being given equal weighting. This means that the platform supports a number of alternative arrangements allowing both session-based and space-based views of the data, even simultaneously. If an application were to query the tuple space using a specified *Application* class (resource), then it would be possible to present to the user a view of current application sessions and the data associated with them. In contrast, the *Session-ID* can be associated with a particular space (for example a room in Teamrooms(Roseman, 1996) or a region of a CVE (Greenhaulgh, 1995) and if the tuple space is queried using a specified *Session-ID* it would present a view of all of the applications available in that particular space.

Consider a particular collaborative application based on the rooms metaphor which needs to obtain all of the data for all of the resources (chat, whiteboards, shared documents, reference to audio channel, etc.) in a given room, then it simply queries the space using the session identifier for the required room. Alternatively, if a particular type of resource (application) is being used in many different sessions, then querying with the application class will produce a list of the session identifiers all of the instances where it is used.

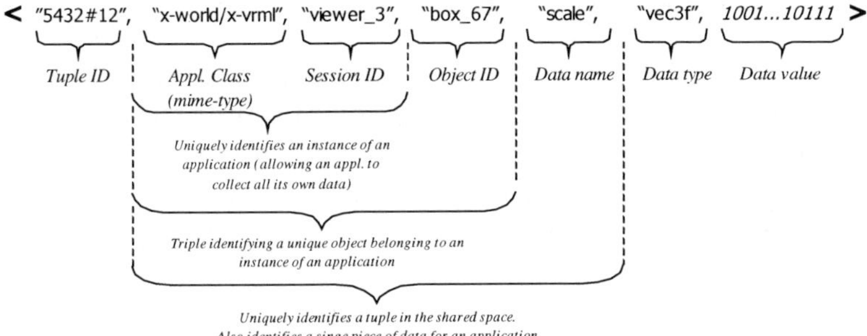

Figure 3 Composition of an example Data tuple

The value for the *Application* field of a data tuple is specific for each class of application and would normally be compiled into the application code (or its external interface). For any given application class, there are a number of *Object-ID* (and their nested arbitrary *Data-name*) values reserved for management functions. This enables an application to display standard properties for each item in a list of sessions or resources.

Once data is made available in the tuple space, it can be retrieved using the normal tuple space operations. By combining different actual and formal values in a data tuple, applications can execute template queries for different data. Some useful combinations are shown in Figure 3, above. For example, by providing an application class of "x-world/x-vrml" and leaving all other fields as formals in a data tuple, the application can obtain a list of all *Session-ID*'s for that type of application in the shared space.

Relation tuples

Arbitrary M-N relations can also be shared within the platform by using multiple 1-1 relationship tuples, whose definition is shown in Table IV.

Field	Type	Description
Application	String	Identifier of the application defining this relationship (typically its mime-type)
Session ID	String	Some unique identifier for this session.
Object ID	String	Unique identifier for the shared object which this relationship concerns.
Relation	String	Name of the relationship to which this 1-1 mapping belongs.
Left	String	The LHS of the relationship
Right	String	The RHS of the relationship

Table IV Fields in a Relation tuple

This allows us to reflect and share the core connections central to the information models and data structures used internally by cooperative

362

applications by making the relations linking information objects externally available through the shared interface platform. Particular instances of given relations are therefore defined by the quad:

```
{Application, Session ID, Object ID, Relation}
```

An entire M-N relationship is broken down by the API into 'M x N' 1-1 tuples, to allow queries to be executed on the platform over the shared relationships. To extract an entire shared relationship, the API need only perform a single "collect" operation on the tuple space with a complete quad.

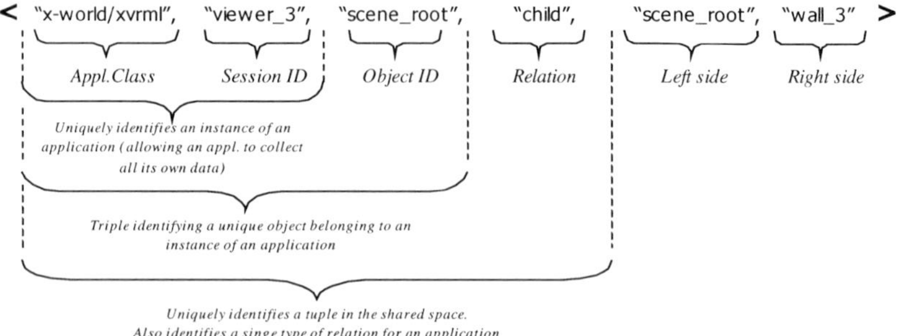

Figure 4 Composition of an example Relation tuple

Relation tuples can be used to store hierarchy, such as those used in information and organisation models. Equally they can be used to share the hierarchy in 3D geometry. In this case the geometry would typically be broken into several smaller simple parts and grouping nodes used to tie them together. To share this state across the space we need data tuples for each part of the geometry and a data tuple for the group node. We then need to create a relation tuple to link the parent to each of its children. An example of this style 1-N use of relation tuples can be seen in Figure 4 above.

The PSI Connector Object

The Connector object provides the point of communication between the PSI API and the underlying tuple space daemon, manifesting changes to the local shared data proxies as the actual values are modified in the tuple space, and visa versa. The connector provides methods that can be invoked through the API to query and manipulate the shared spaces in the platform.

The two methods *shareData( )* and *shareRelation( )* instruct the connector to share some application-defined data tuple or a MxN relationship with the space. If the shared space already contains a matching data tuple (i.e. it has the same unique quad fields) or set of 1x1 relation tuples (for the MxN relationship) then the connector makes local proxies for these existing tuples and returns their values to the application. If no such data or relation exists then new tuples are put into the shared space and local proxies are created. These API methods provide a very simple interface for an application to either share new data with the platform or to get existing shared values back.

5.2 State update and propagation

Propagation of state and notification of state changes between the underlying tuple space and the application is performed in two distinct ways depending on the nature of the update and the demands of the cooperative application. Consider a telepointer object whose position is shared in the tuple space. Another application is displaying the co-ordinates of the point in a simple text field. If the pointer moves quickly from point A to point B several hundred potential state changes may occur. However, the most important changes are the starting position of the pointer and the final resting position of the pointer. Those in the middle tend to be less important. In essence we categorise state updates to data tuples as either *transient* (if we miss an update it doesn't matter) or *persistent* (everyone sharing this state should see the same value). A data tuple can be updated using either mechanism at any time. Which update mechanism is used for a particular data tuple is left to the actual application(s) changing the data value (which can exploit semantic knowledge about what the data *is* to decide on the most appropriate method).

Persistent updates

Because persistent events change the fundamental state of the data in the shared space, no explicit event tuple is created for these updates. Rather, the sender (the source) of the event (typically the local tuple proxy) IN's the state to be changed, modifies it, and then re-OUTs it back to the space. Two fields of the tuple are modified: the new state value containing the new data value and the tuple ID, which has its sequence component incremented.

From the tuple space perspective one tuple has been removed and a new one added. Therefore these changes to the tuple space are then distributed to the other clients of the tuple space, where the daemon will trigger all the registered callbacks in the PSI connector for the newly OUTed tuple. The connector then extracts the new state from the tuple and updates the local proxy for the data in question. Any objects, such as the applications, which have registered callbacks on the shared proxy tuple are subsequently called. Note there are two levels of callback, first from the tuple space daemon to the proxies via the connector, and secondly from those proxies to any interested applications.

Transient events

Transient events are carried by special event tuples in an event tuple space. The format is shown in Table V.

Field	Type	Description
Tuple ID	String	Identifies the data tuple containing the same Tuple ID to which this transient event applies.
Event Sequence#	Int	Current sequence number for this transient update
Data name	String	The name of the data value
Data value	Data	The data itself

Table V Fields in a Transient Event tuple

The tuple ID identifies the data tuple over which this transient update is occurring, while the event sequence number provides ordering between each transient event. This sequence number is maintained by each PSI connector, which updates its last known value whenever a new transient event is added to the event tuple space or arrives through a callback.

To generate a new transient event, the source of the event (typically the proxy of the shared data tuple) creates a new transient event tuple (incrementing the local sequence number and using the last known tuple ID of the state being changed) and adds it to the tuple space. This tuple is propagated by the underlying tuple space system to all connected machines, which may issue callbacks to connected applications via the PSI connector. Each connector receiving this callback forwards the change in state (carried in the transient tuple) to the relevant PSI object and records the last event sequence number of the tuple.

Transient events are never IN'ed by the platform API, only RD. Consequently no negotiation has to occur in the distributed system for the ownership of this tuple, which allows transient events to send information is very fast. However, because they are never IN'ed transient events are never explicitly removed from the tuple space by the platform API or applications. Therefore each transient event has an *expires* field to enable the tuple space to remove old events during garbage collection.

Update Consistency

Consistency between the persistent events and transient events on the same data tuple is guaranteed because of the incremented tuple ID sequence value on the shared state whenever a persistent change is OUTed to the space. This means if the "tuple ID" of a transient event refers to a data tuple with a tuple ID which no longer exists, or whose sequence number is less than the last known one, these events can be safely discarded as they are "behind" some other part of the system (and are transient anyway).

Consistency between the transient events themselves is fairly loose as the sequence ordering is only guaranteed on each machine rather than across the whole tuple space. This is because no IN's are ever needed for transient events and consequently no serialisation is ever performed at the tuple space level. The advantage of doing RD's rather than IN's is a vast improvement in performance (no checking of ownership exchange needs to occur across the distributed replicas of the tuple space). Consequently, the sequence numbering of two contradicting "actions" in a distributed application could coincide since the sequence number is added by the local PSI connector. This could cause the object to get wildly different transient state updates in quick succession. However the first machine to commit a persistent value for the data tuple to the tuple space will "win" as it will change the actual tuple ID to which these transient events apply - and persistent updates *are* serialised because they rely on IN's.

6. Using the platform

To demonstrate some of the features and operation of the platform consider the following example where two applications (in these case two different CVE systems) are modified to allow them to export and share an object through the PSI. Note these applications do not have to be the same application (one could be VRML and one could be DIVE), nor do they need to be on the same machine but are connected through the distributed tuple space under the PSI.

The first step in sharing the object between the applications is the construction of two shared adapters, one for each application. For the purpose of this example, the adapters share a common application class identifier within the PSI, "x-application/x-shared-vr".

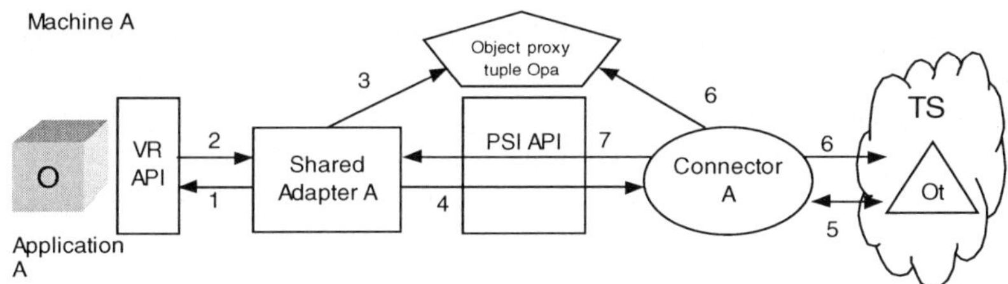

Figure 5 Exporting a VR object to the universe

The second part of making the object commonly available and shared between the applications is to export the state of the object held by the application to a common shared space in the PSI. Figure 5 illustrates this process. First, the adapter requests the object data through the applications API (such as the EAI) (1,2). The adapter proceeds to create a local "data" proxy tuple to contain this data (3), defining the various fields as appropriate - the application class "x-application/x-shared-vr", a session identifier "session1", and the name of the object "Opa" as well as value of the data just extracted from the application. The adapter performs a "shareData" call on the connector using this proxy tuple. The connector tries to locate any tuple in the tuple space that may match this (5) by making the data type and value fields in the tuple formals rather than actuals (see section 4). This will fail to match any existing tuple so the connector OUTs a new data tuple to the tuple space (Ot) (6). The original "shareData" calls returns and a reference to the local proxy Opa is passed to the adapter by the connector (7).

During (6) the connector also registers itself and the shared adapter making the shareData call as objects to be notified whenever the proxy (Op) changes. Whenever the local proxy is updated by either the connector (in response to a change in the tuple space data tuple) or the adapter (in response to a change in the application) the adapter and connector will receive notification of the change. The change in data value can be propagated down to the tuple space or up to the application depending where that change originated from.

Now that the object O is being shared in the PSI tuple space other applications may also share it by connecting to the PSI. This is accomplished in a similar manner to the initial exporting of the object, and is shown in Figure 6.

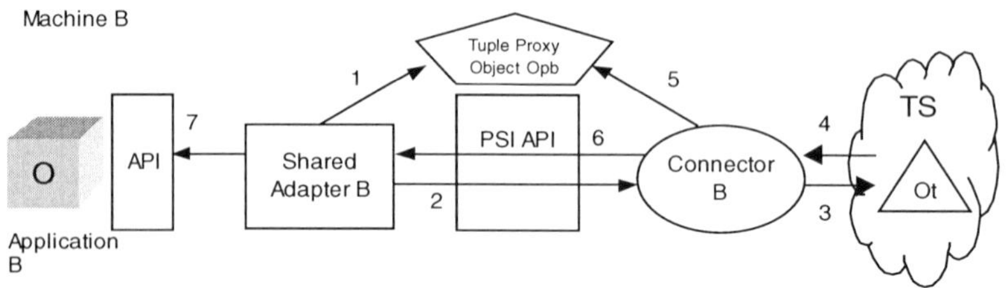

Figure 6 Importing a VR object from the universe

The adapter creates a local proxy tuple (Opb) the same application class, session ID, and object ID as was previously shared above, placing dummy values in the data value field (1). As before, the adapter performs a "shareData" request on the connector (2) that queries the tuple space for data tuples with a matching application, session, object and data name (3). However unlike before, the query succeeds and a matching tuple is RD in (4). The connector fills in the missing fields in the local proxy (Opb) (5) before registering itself and the adapter to be notified whenever the data in the proxy object is modified (5). A reference to the proxy object is returned to the shared adapter (6) and the adapter uses the VR API to add the shared object (Opb) into the applications VR world (7).

Now that each adapter and connector are registered to receive updates from Op and Opb, and each connector is monitoring changes to the data tuple being shared in the tuple space Ot, updates to O are automatically propagated throughout the system. For example if the second application modifies the object adapter B only needs to change the data value in the proxy tuple Opb. The connector is notified of this change which updates the data tuple Ot in the tuple space. The distributed tuple space updates all of its replicas including the one on machine A. The tuple space daemon notifies connector A of the change to the tuple which updates the local proxy tuple Opa. The tuple notifies adapter A about the change to its state that then uses the application API to send the update to the application.

If both applications A and B had been running on the same machine and had contacted the same connector then the shareData call issued by adapter B would have been matched within the current tuples being proxied by the connector. A reference to *that* proxy would have been returned to the adapter rather than the same proxy it passed initially.

Finally, even if both applications and adapters quit, the shared object Ot remains in the active tuple space. Therefore when either of the adapters reconnected to the PSI at a later time and try to share the same data value again they will receive the current, last known, value from the tuple space.

7. Additional supporting services

In addition to providing a series of supporting mechanisms we have also realised a number of supporting services on top of PSI. These services illustrate how the semantically neutral nature of the platform has allowed us to build upon it to provide an additional layer of abstraction. In particular we present an abstraction that supports the sharing on different media and the use of existing components.

7.1. Sharing multimedia data

The original L^2imbo tuple space was initially designed to support streamed media, such as audio and video, across networks with variable performance and capabilities (e.g. between a wireless connection and a local area network). Consequently, the PSI architecture is not limited to facilitating the sharing of persistent (and fairly static) pieces of data.

Sharing streamed multimedia data, such as an MPEG stream, between applications is accomplished by creating a virtual buffer in the tuple space using one or more Data tuples; these are updated through a combination of persistent and transient changes. The source of the stream keeps updating the Data tuple in the tuple space while any number of recipients consume the updated "buffer" and play the media.

Although this method works reasonably well in practice the main advatange is the flexibility of the platform rather than performance. The flexibility of the platform allows different mechanisms for performing media streaming to improve performance. For example, the tuple space could be used to setup and establish a well-known but separate multicast group for the broadcast of the media between the various platform clients using protocols like RTP.

7.2. Shared JavaBeans

Building on top of the platform and API, another level of abstraction has been added to the platform that provides the ability share public properties of arbitrary JavaBean components[2]. This functionality enables the extremely simple

---

[2]   Considerable thanks are due to John Lamping at Xerox PARC for the initial development of a JavaBeans platform that greatly influenced the development of the shared beans layer in PSI.

368

construction of collaborative applications from existing standard components. For example, it becomes relatively simple to construct shared graphical user interfaces, or indeed to share an underlying model that may then be represented in a number of ways in different user applications.

This mechanism works by using the reflection facilities of the Java platform and dynamically constructing listeners for all bound properties of a bean. As the value of a bound property of a bean changes, the property change events are reflected as changes to tuples in the shared tuple space. Since PSI architecture builds upon our active notification extensions to the tuple space concept, these property changes are in turn passed on to any other application that uses the same shared instance of the component.

The functionality provided means that a developer may treat PSI as a simple way of sharing Java components between applications that may either reside of the same host machine, or be spread across a distributed set of heterogeneous hosts on a network. The basic pattern of interaction for applications wishing to use the mechanism follows two simple steps.

> Attempt to connect to a shared instance of the component.
> IF instance_found THEN use that instance
> > ELSE create new instance and share that with the platform

To provide this functionality we provide two basic methods, namely *connect()* and *share()*. The *connect()* method is overloaded to enable an application to retrieve particular instances of a component, for example by specifying property values. The *share()* method provides all of the functionality required to persist a component (recursively through all of its properties) into the shared space.

This application of PSI has been used to create a number of applications. For example, it was straightforward to take an existing 3rd-party compiled bean that provided a 3D geometry viewer and create a distributed shared viewing application (without being able to access any of the source).

The open design of the PSI API and tuple spaces makes it easy to add additional services and functionality to the platform – an application or service needs only to connect to the tuple space and can then query, add or remove the tuples within it. One of the most common types of service is the persistence service. The service simply registers a callback for all tuples being added or removed from a particular tuple space. This callback then copies or removes tuples it receives from a local database. If the tuple space crashes or fails for some reason the backup application can restore the lost information by retrieving the original persistent data and relationship tuples from the database and merging them with the current state of the tuple space.

8. Conclusions

In this paper we have presented the development of a platform that allows the active sharing of information across cooperative applications. The platform has extended an existing tuple space platform to allow applications to actively share cooperative information between heterogeneous applications. The developed PSI platform extends existing event based awareness models by promoting active sharing of a state using a lightweight data model.

The developed platform needed to augment an existing tuple space by adding mechanisms to support notification in order to allow better support for the dynamic arrangement central to cooperative work. This active tuple space allowed the development of an API centred on a set of defined tuples. These tuples provided an interface that allowed object to be placed in the platform by creating locally proxies. The platform managed the connection between these local proxies and the tuples in the active tuple space to propagate updates to state across and between applications.

A number of areas are being considered for future work. One option is the possibility of migrating some of the functionality described down into the underlying tuple space implementation, thereby providing a more active platform at the level of the networking service. We are also investigating a number of other tuple space implementations, e.g. IBM's Tspaces and Sun's JavaSpaces. This is in order to determine if may be possible to provide our abstractions over these alternative base platforms, thereby providing a flexible sharing mechanism across completing platforms.

Another area of continued research that needs be addressed in the future is the area surrounding access control and authentication. Current the platform places information in a shared tuple space with little or no consideration of access control and security management. We are currently considering the investigation of private tuple spaces and encrypted tuples as a means of providing this form of access management. Our final consideration is to extend our existing set of higher level services by adding even more a range of CSCW tools and management utilities as standard services.

9 . Acknowledgements

This work was supported in part by the eSCAPE long term research project. Thanks are due to Adrian Friday and Nigel Davis at Lancaster University for their considerable work in the development of the original L^2imbo tuple space. Thanks are also due to John Lamping for the inspiration, structure and motivation for the development of the shared Beans facility.

10. References

Bannon, L. and Bodker, S. (1997) "Constructing Common Information Spaces", *In Proc. ECSCW'97*, Lancaster, UK, Sept. 1997, pp 81-96, Kluwer.

Bentley, R., Dourish, P. (1995) "Medium versus Mechanism: Supporting Collaboration through Customisation" *In Proc. ECSCW'95*, Stockholm, Sweden, Sept. 1995, pp 133-148, Kluwer.

Bentley, R., Rodden, T., Sawyer, P., Sommerville, I. (1992) "An architecture for tailoring cooperative multi-user displays", *In Proc. CSCW'92*, Toronto, Canada, Oct. 1992, pp 187-194, ACM Press.

Carlsson, C., Hagsand, O. (1993) "DIVE: A Multi User Virtual Reality System". *In Proc. IEEE VRAIS*, Sept. 1993, pp394-400

Davies, N., Friday, A., et al. (1998). "An Asynchronous Distributed Systems Platform for Heterogeneous Environments". *Proc. 8th ACM SIGOPS European Workshop: Support for Composing Distributed Applications*, Sintra, Portugal, 1998, ACM Press.

Davies, N., Wade, S. P., et al. (1997). "Limbo: A Tuple Space Based Platform for Adaptive Mobile Applications". *International Conference on Open Distributed Processing / Distributed Platforms (ICODP/ICDP'97)*, Toronto, Canada, May 1997, pp291-302.

Dewan, P., Choudhary, R. (1991) "Flexible User Interface Coupling in a Collaborative System", *In Proc. CHI'91*, New Orleans, LA, April 1991, pp 41-48, ACM Press.

Edwards, K.W. (1994) "Session management for collaborative applications" *In Proc. CSCW '94*, Chapel Hill, NC, Oct. 1994, pp 323-330, ACM Press.

Foster, G., Stefik, M. (1986) "Cognoter: Theory and practice of a Colab-orative tool", *In Proc. CSCW'86*, Austin, TX, Dec. 1986, pp 7-15, ACM Press.

Gelernter, D. (1985) "Generative Communication in Linda." *ACM Transactions on Programming Languages and Systems*, 7(1), 1985, pp80-112, ACM Press.

Greenberg, S. (1991) "Personalizable groupware: accommodating individual roles and group differences", *In Proc. ECSCW'91*, Amsterdam, September 1991, pp 17-31.

Greenhalgh, C. M., & Benford, S. D. (1995) "MASSIVE: A Virtual Reality System for Tele-conferencing", *ACM Transactions on Computer Human Interfaces (TOCHI)*, 2 (3), Sept. 1995, pp. 239-261, ACM Press.

Hall, R.W., Mathur, A., Jahanian, F., Prakash, A. Rasmussen, C., (1996) "Corona: A Communication Service for Scalable, Reliable Group Collaboration Systems", *In Proc. CSCW'96*, Boston, MA, Nov. 1996, pp140-149, ACM Press.

Hill, R. D., Brinck, T., Patterson, J. F., Rohall S. L., Wilner, W. T. (1993) "The Rendezvous language and architecture", In *CACM*, 36(1), Jan.1993, pp 62-67.

Lee, J. H., Prakash, A., Jaeger, T. (1996) "A Software Architecture to Support Open Distributed Collaboratories", *In Proc. CSCW'96*, Boston, MA, Nov. 1996, pp 344-353, ACM Press.

Mansfield, T., Kaplan, S., Fitzpatrick, G., Phelps, T., Fitzpatrick, M., Taylor, R. (1997) "Evolving Orbit: a progress report on building locales". *In Proc. Group'97*, Phoenix, Arizona, Nov. 1997, pp241-250, ACM Press.

Palfreyman K. A. Rodden T. (1996) "A Protocol for User Awareness on the World Wide Web". *In Proc. CSCW'96*, Boston, MS, USA, Nov. 1996, ACM Press.

Patterson, J. F., Day, M. Kucan, J., (1996) "Notification Servers for Synchronous Groupware", *In Proc. CSCW'96*, Boston, MA, Nov. 1996, pp 122-129, ACM Press.

Roseman, M., Greenberg, S, (1996) "TeamRooms: Network Places for Collaboration". *In Proc. CSCW'96*, Boston, MA, Nov. 1996, pp 325-333, ACM Press.

S. Bødker, M. Kyng, and K. Schmidt (eds.). *Proceedings of the Sixth European Conference on Computer-Supported Cooperative Work, 12-16 September 1999, Copenhagen, Denmark*
©1999 Kluwer Academic Publishers. Printed in the Netherlands

An Experiment in Interoperating Heterogeneous Collaborative Systems

Prasun Dewan

University of North Carolina, USA

Anshu Sharma

Oracle Corp., USA

Abstract: Currently, collaborative systems manipulating the same artifact but implementing different policies and architectures cannot interoperate or "collaborate" with each other. Therefore, it is not possible for users to use different collaborative systems to work on a single shared artifact. As an initial step towards such interoperation, we have carried out an experiment involving the interoperation of two heterogeneous collaborative spreadsheets. The experiment has resulted in some general protocols, techniques, and lessons applicable to the interoperation of systems offering different concurrency-control policies, couplings, and architectures. The paper surveys different approaches along these three dimensions, motivates the rationale for inter-operating them, identifies issues in their interoperation, and presents and evaluates solutions for a small number of interoperation scenarios in the surveyed design space.

Introduction

The promise of computer supported cooperative work has resulted in a proliferation of collaborative systems supporting the same task. For instance, almost every infrastructure developer provides a shared whiteboard, and several custom-ones have been developed as both research and commercial products.

These systems tend to be heterogeneous, that is, offer different policies and architectures for supporting collaboration. As the usage of these systems gains popularity, it will become important for them to be able to interoperate with each other so that collaborators can use different systems to manipulate the same artifact. Such interoperation is useful for two related reasons:

- *User Preferences:* Systems tend to be heterogeneous because they make different tradeoffs, each offering a unique set of benefits. Collaborators may wish to use different policies because different features are important to them. This is true in single-user interaction. For instance, users tend to seldom agree on a particular word-processor or word-processor settings. It is not likely to change when they collaborate with others.

- *User Constraints and Training:* Users in different organizations may be trained in and constrained to use different systems. They may not have the time, desire, or ability to learn a new, common system in order to collaborate with each other.

In general, formation of work groups is dynamic, usually in response to an identified need, and brings together people with different training, skills, and work habits. Thus, members of these groups are likely to use different systems.

It can be argued that standardization of collaboration systems will eliminate the need for interoperation. Even if standardization is successful in this area, we believe the standardized collaborative tools, like single-user tools of today, will offer a range of parameters. Not all collaborators are likely to prefer the same configuration, thereby requiring interoperation at the policy and architecture (but not system) levels. It is these levels that the paper mainly focuses on.

The general concept of interoperation is not new - this is the classical problem of heterogeneous software systems. Specific instances of this problem have been addressed in programming languages, operating systems, and database systems. These solutions are applicable to the collaboration domain, since collaborative systems tend to use different underlying software. However, they are not sufficient for the collaboration domain since they do not address differences in policies and architectures invented in this area.

Because of the newness of this field, researchers and developers have so far concentrated on building new kinds of collaborative systems, disregarding how their tools would work with those offering alternative solutions. The main exception is the work on DistEdit (Knister 90), which explored the use of heterogeneous single-user editors in a single collaborative session. However, we know of no previous work on interoperation of two complete collaboration systems.

In order to understand some of the basic issues and solutions involved in such interoperation, we carried out an experiment involving interoperation of two different collaborative systems. The experiment has resulted in some general protocols, techniques, and lessons applicable to the interoperation of systems offering different concurrency-control policies, couplings, and architectures. We have found that existing mechanisms for supporting latecomers in a session support interoperation along the coupling dimension. We have also devised general protocols and policies for supporting interoperation along the concurrency-control dimension. We have found that the choice of the policies being interoperated influences the fairness of the interoperation, and that tickle-locks and queue-based floor control offer better fairness than regular locks and floor control, respectively.

The rest of the paper is organized as follows. We first survey the dimensions of coupling, concurrency control, and architecture, identifying and evaluating some of the popular solutions along each of these dimensions. The purpose of this section is to give the reader background in some of the concepts needed to understand our work in interoperation, and to show the need for allowing alternative solutions along each of these dimensions to coexist in a collaborative session. Next we outline some of the basic issues in interoperation. We then describe the two systems we interoperated, abstracting out details not relevant for the interoperation experiment. The next section is the bulk of the paper, describing and evaluating our approach to interoperation of the two systems. Finally, we present conclusions and directions for future work.

Background

Collaboration systems differ along a variety of dimensions. We consider here the dimensions along which our two systems differed: coupling, concurrency control, and architecture. We survey some of the popular solutions along each of these dimensions and enumerate their advantages and disadvantages to show that none of these solutions is preferable over all others.

Coupling

Coupling [Dewan 95] determines how the displays of different users are linked to each other. One of the popular policies for coupling, termed WYSIWIS (Stefik 87) (What You See Is What I See), ensures that all users' displays are identical. This policy is ideal for meetings in which all users share a common focus. However, it has two main problems. First, experience has shown that users get involved in "window wars" and "scroll wars" as they try to place their windows and scrollbars at different positions (Stefik 87). In general, we can expect a war whenever users are forced to share something they do not want to share. Second, broadcasting each event to all workstations creates performance problems, which are particularly unfortunate when users to do not wish to share all events.

Therefore, there has been considerable work in identifying non-WYSIWIS coupling by exploring dimensions along which coupling can be relaxed (Stefik 87, Hill 94, Dewan 95). Many systems allow collaborators to see different views of a common model. Others also allow them to determine which of the user-interface objects such as cursor positions and scrollbars are coupled. Some support asynchronous coupling, allowing users to determine when changes are transmitted to/received from others. Transmission/receipt of changes can occur explicitly because of execution of special commands or implicitly as a side effect of other commands (such as moving the cursor out of the object changed) or passage of time (e.g. coupling every hour). While these non-WYSIWIS schemes give collaborators better performance and flexibility, they have the disadvantage that users do not have "referential transparency", that is, cannot refer to objects based on their screen appearance and location. For instance, "the red square on the upper left corner", may not be meaningful to all users if they can color and scroll their displays independently. Another important disadvantage is that non-WYSIWIS coupling modes cannot be implemented by systems such as Microsoft NetMeeting that allow sharing of existing single-user programs.

Thus, each of these coupling schemes has its advantages and disadvantages, and which policy is chosen may depend not only on the collaboration task but also the individual users. For instance, some users may prefer reuse and referential transparency offered by WYSIWIS systems, while others may prefer the performance and flexibility of an asynchronous non-WYSWIS interaction. Interoperation of the heterogeneous coupling schemes would allow the individual user rather than the whole group to make the choice.

Coupling Architecture

There is also considerable variation in the architecture used for coupling users. In general, users' actions are processed by multiple application layers such as the kernel, window system, toolkit, and application semantics. Different architectures differ in the way in which they replicate these layers. Some systems completely replicate the application, some completely centralize it, while others centralize the top-level (semantics) layer but replicate the layers below it. These architectures can be described using the generalized zipper model [Dewan 98]. The model assumes that if a layer is replicated, all layers below it are also replicated. Differences in architectures can result from differences in the top-most layer that is replicated. The higher this layer, the more the replication degree of the architecture. This degree is thus increased by "opening the zipper" until we reach the fully replicated architecture. Figure 1 shows the zipper opened to different degrees for the same set of layers.

Replicating a layer has two main advantages. First, it allows objects defined in the layer to be uncoupled, since multiple instances of these objects are created for different users. Second, all processing in that layer is done on the local workstation, thereby giving better performance. The disadvantages are that replicas are difficult to synchronize, not all workstations may have the software and hardware to run a replica, and performing the same operation multiple times in different replicas can be expensive, cause bottlenecks if a centralized resource is accessed by the operation, and result in undesired semantics if the operation has a side effect (such as printing a check or sending a mail message.)

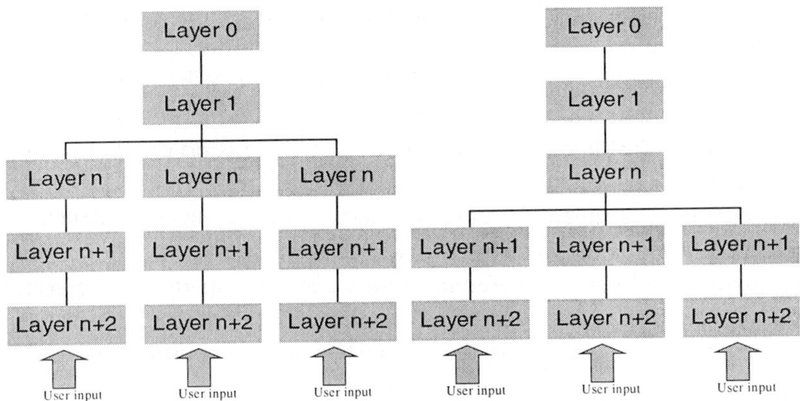

Figure 1: Different Instances of the Zipper Architecture

Thus, in some cases, the architecture of an application depends on its layers. In others, it depends on the workstations and couplings of the individual users. In these cases, it is important to interoperate architectures suitable for different sets of collaborators.

Concurrency Control

Since collaborative applications allow multiple users to alter the state of the system, certain inter-leavings of user actions can lead to inconsistent state. Most collaborative systems either provide mechanisms to prevent any inconsistencies to appear in the system, or resolve them at a later (suitable) stage. These mechanisms may or may not involve active user involvement. The term concurrency control is used to describe these mechanisms.

The aim of concurrency control mechanisms is to allow for maximum concurrency while trying to restrict the system from becoming inconsistent or irrecoverable. Different systems differ in the degrees to which they satisfy these two competing goals.

The simplest form of concurrency control is floor control. In this scheme, only one user is allowed to give input to the system at any given time. Any user that wishes to become active has to request the *floor*. If the floor is free, the request succeeds and the user gets the floor. If some other user has the floor, the result of the request can be one of many possible options. The simplest scheme is to discard the request. Otherwise, the request may be en-queued, and all the users who have requested the floor may get it on a first-come-first-served basis.

Another option is to have priorities associated with each user or request, and use priority queues. In some variations of this scheme a moderator may decide whom to relinquish the floor to. All these schemes are minor variations of what can be collectively called turn-taking protocols (Ellis 91).

These protocols are easy to implement, and in some cases (e.g. mediated meetings) very suitable. However, they limit parallelism since only one user is active at any instant. Even if two users' actions do not conflict, they are not allowed to perform them concurrently. For example, two users will not be allowed to edit different cells of a spreadsheet even if there is no conflict. This is overly restrictive for many interactive groupware applications. Moreover, some of the discussed floor control schemes can lead to starvation (e.g. priority queues).

These problems are addressed by lock-based concurrency control, which allows users to obtain locks on different objects constituting the collaboration artifact such as cells in a spreadsheet. Two or more users can obtain locks and thus work concurrently as long as they do not wish to work (acquire locks) on the same objects. Locking is a popular concurrency control scheme and has been implemented in several systems such as (Newman-Wolfe 92, Greenberg 94).

Several variations of this basic scheme have been implemented to optimize performance, user-effort, and concurrency. It is usually cumbersome for a user to explicitly request and release locks. In many cases, it is possible for the system to implicitly issue lock requests as a side effect of other operations such as selecting an object (Newman-Wolfe 92, Greenberg 94). At the same time, the user should be allowed to explicitly request locks on several objects to perform atomic operations.

A problem in distributed systems is high latency and, thus, response time. A simple-minded implementation of locking scheme would be to maintain the state of the locks on a single host. In this case, for each lock request, the remote users' host would have to communicate with the centralized process resulting in high latency for remote users. Noting that there is locality of reference in the user's lock requests, some systems cache locks (Prakash 94). When a user no longer needs a lock, instead of releasing the lock to the central lock manager, the lock is locally held until some other user requests the same lock. The requests made by a new user would take more time now because the request has to go to the central manager and then relayed to the host that currently holds the lock. But as long as there is locality of reference and different users work on different subsets of objects, this scheme results in faster response on the average.

If one user holds the lock for a long time, other users may have to wait indefinitely. This problem can be solved to some extent by using the concept of tickle-locks (Greif 86). These locks have an associated time-to-live value associated with them. If the user does not perform any operation during this time, the locks are released automatically. Depending on the application semantics, the value of the object that the user is editing may or may not be committed before releasing the locks. (In some cases, it may be more appropriate to perform an *undo* operation before releasing the locks).

Locking schemes fall into the category of pessimistic concurrency control. A slightly optimistic locking scheme (Greenberg 94) can be implemented as follows to improve the performance. Whenever a user requests a lock, the control returns to the application immediately and the user can modify the state of the object while the request is being processed, possibly at a remote site. If the lock request is denied, an undo operation is performed on the object.

Fully optimistic concurrency control (not addressed by our experiment) is offered by systems such as COAST (Schuckman 96) that support transactions. A transaction is a sequence of instructions that executes atomically, that is, either all or none of its steps complete execution. Serializability and recoverability are two important properties of transactions. Serializability means that the concurrent execution of a set of actions is equivalent to some serial execution of the same actions. Recoverability means that each action appears to be all-or-nothing: either it executes successfully to completion (*commits*), or it has no effect at all (*aborts*).

Both locking and transactions offer more concurrency control than floor control. An important disadvantage of locking is that it can lead to deadlocks. An important disadvantage of transactions is that they may abort, undoing possibly hours or days of user work. Merging can be used as an alternative to abort (Munson 97), but it cannot automatically resolve all conflicts.

Thus, as with coupling and architecture, the choice of the concurrency control may depend on the individual user.

Interoperation Issues

Interoperability is not a new concept. The advent of the internet, which is an interconnection of heterogeneous systems, forced systems designers to create tools such as ftp and mail that would allow users on different systems to work together on shared artifacts. For instance, two users can use ftp to share files that may be stored in a different format on their respective file systems (e.g. AFS and Windows). More recently, CORBA (Vinoski 97) allows objects created on different platforms using different programming languages to interoperate. Java RMI (Remote Method Invocation) allows interoperation among objects executing on different platforms. However, none of the previous systems addresses interoperability along the three dimensions discussed above. Such interoperation requires us to address three kinds of problems.

Semantics

It is not always clear as to what the semantics of two different heterogeneous schemes are when they are integrated. In other words, a consistent state according to one scheme may be inconsistent according to another. For example, in

WYSIWIS coupling, all users see the same state at all times, while in a non-WYSIWIS interaction, this is not the case. We will see later how we address this and other forms of inconsistencies that appear in our experiment. To better understand the nature of this problem, consider below a more complicated inconsistency scenario that does not manifest itself in our experiment.

Suppose Jim is using a lock-based system, which means that any changes that Jim makes will be accepted. If Jane wants to use a transaction-based concurrency control scheme, then it is not clear as to what should happen in case of conflicts. Suppose Jim acquires a lock on cell A with value "Apple". Now, Jane reads the value of the cell A ("Apple") and wants to change it to "Orange". Since, Jane read a correct value and changed it to another correct value, according to transaction semantics, the change will be committed. But this is wrong according to the lock-based system's consistency criterion, since as long as a user has a lock on an object, no other user can change the value. Now, if Jim writes a new value ("Banana") into cell A, his changes should be aborted by transaction semantics. But there is no concept of abort in lock-based systems.

A solution to this problem would be to deny any transaction operation as long as any user has a lock on the object. However, in a collaborative application it is not very clear as to what constitutes a read operation, since users may not explicitly execute this operation. Typically, the system responds to the commitment of a change by one user by updating the displays of the remote users without knowing if a remote user has actually read the value. A conservative approach would be to assume that all values displayed to the user are considered as read, but this would unduly limit the concurrency.

Implementation

In general, groupware applications and infrastructures are built on different platforms and do not adhere to any standard. For instance, Habanero (Chabert 98) is a Java-based system while Suite (Dewan 95) uses C and has its own RPC-based communication mechanisms. In order to interoperate the systems, both the semantic and syntactic gaps have to be bridged. A language- independent system such as CORBA can be used to allow objects on different systems to communicate with each other. Thus, the problem is reduced from providing many-to-many translations to providing a translation between every system and a standard such as CORBA. These problems have been studied and solutions suggested and implemented elsewhere. In our solutions, we assume that the systems are implemented in Java or have proxy objects written in Java. The proxy objects may communicate with the existing systems through any suitable mechanism such as CORBA.

Deadlock, Fairness

These two issues arise in interoperation of concurrency control schemes. Apart from being correct, these schemes should also be fair and not susceptible to deadlocks. As we saw earlier, different schemes fare differently on these criteria. Floor control with queuing is fair and precludes deadlocks. On the other hand, lock-based concurrency control can lead to starvation and deadlocks. When interoperating schemes with different behaviors with respect to fairness and deadlocks, it is difficult to ensure that the resulting system does not introduce new forms of unfairness and deadlocks that were not present in the original systems. The design of interoperability mechanisms should take these factors into consideration.

Case Studies

Before we discuss how we addressed these issues in our interoperability experiment, we describe the two systems we interoperated.

Habanero Spreadsheet

Habanero (Chabert 98) is a system developed at NCSA that provides a toolkit for building collaborative applications. It supports full replication by running a copy of the application at each user's machine. It receives events from each replica and broadcasts them to all other replicas. It also supports latecomers by dynamically creating a new replica for the new user. Finally, it provides flexible mechanisms for implementing coupling and concurrency control. It provides a central module for sequencing the coupled events received from different replicas.

We used Habanero to implement a simple spreadsheet offering fixed synchronous, near-WYSIWIS coupling (that allows users to scroll independently) and ordinary and queue-based based floor control.

UNC Spreadsheet

We also implemented, using libraries developed at UNC, another version of the spreadsheet that differed from the Habanero spreadsheet in the architecture, coupling, and concurrency-control dimensions. It is built using the model-view-controller paradigm (Krasner 88), with the controller combined with the view. Instead of replicating the whole application, it replicates the view but not the model. It offers flexible non-WYSIWIS coupling, allowing users to choose whether they wish to send values incrementally (as they type in a cell), or when they move the cursor away from the cell. It offers a large range of locking policies including centralized, cached, optimistic, and tickle locks. Like the Habanero spreadsheet, this spreadsheet supports latecomers by dynamically creating a view for the new user, and allows independent scrolling.

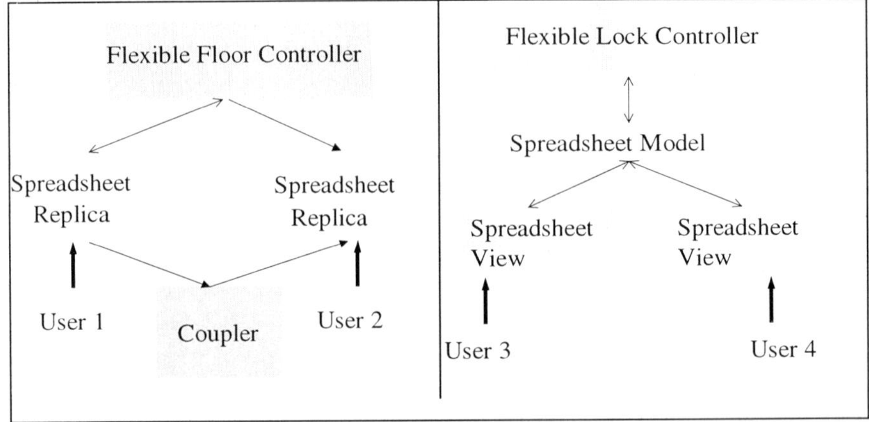

Figure 2 Habanero Spreadsheet (left) and UNC Spreadsheet (right)

Interoperation Policies and Mechanisms

Given two systems used by two different sets of users, we must consider two aspects of the behavior of the interoperating system:

- Local Behavior: The behavior of each system with respect to its users. Thus, in our experiment, it defines the architecture formed for each set of users, and the semantics of coupling and concurrency control for each set of users.

- Interoperation Behavior: The behavior of the system with respect to users of different systems. Thus, in our example, it defines how the architecture of each system is changed to accommodate the other users, and the semantics of the coupling and concurrency control between users of the two different systems.

Ideally, the local behavior of the original system should not change in the interoperating system. Otherwise, the added flexibility of collaborating with the other set of users comes at the cost of changes to the preferred mode of collaboration among users of each set. Therefore, in our interoperation experiment, we ensure that the local behaviors along each dimension are preserved.

Ideally, also, the interoperation behavior should be the same as the local behavior of each system to allow each set of users to use the preferred mode of collaboration with the other set. Of course, this is not possible when the two behaviors are different. Thus, an interoperation behavior must be defined for each dimension of heterogeneity that is consistent with both local behaviors (by being an abstraction of them) and as close to them as possible.

Coupling

Let us first consider the dimension of coupling. The coupling semantics of the two systems to be interoperated are:

- Habanero Spreadsheet: Each user sees the same values as the other user. Each change to a value is immediately sent to other users.
- UNC Spreadsheet: Users changes to shared objects can be buffered, and these changes are seen by other users when they are committed (implicitly or explicitly). Coupling settings determine whether changes are committed on each keystroke or when the user moves the input cursor away from a cell.

The interoperating semantics cannot be the same as both of the local semantics, which are different. Therefore, we define the following compromise semantics for interoperation: Changes made by one user to an object are seen by other users sharing the object when these changes are committed (implicitly or explicitly).

These semantics meets our requirement of being an abstraction of the two local semantics. In fact, they seem identical to the coupling semantics of the UNC spreadsheet. However, there is a subtle difference. In the case of the UNC spreadsheet, each user knows that others can buffer changes, and thus hide intermediate results that are not to be discussed. Thus, they may think it rude if they receive such results. However, in the interoperating spreadsheet, this assumption cannot be made regarding users of the Habanero spreadsheet. Thus, users of the UNC spreadsheet must treat local and remote users differently. Users of the Habanero spreadsheet must, of course, treat local and remote users differently, since they are guaranteed synchronous coupling with the former but not the other. These semantics are realized in our example by keeping the model of the UNC spreadsheet consistent with replicas of the Habanero spreadsheet.

Coupling Architecture

Figure 3 shows the interoperation architecture for implementing these coupling semantics. We extended the Habanero spreadsheet so that it appears to the model of the UNC spreadsheet as a view. When users of the two systems need to join each other in a collaborative session, we dynamically add this modified spreadsheet as a new user to both systems. Since it does not interact with an actual user, we refer to its "user" as "dummy user".

The modified spreadsheet translates between the events received from the two systems to ensure that the UNC model is kept consistent with the Habanero replicas. The UNC model and the Spreadsheet replicas expect to receive new cell values (from view and other Habanero replicas, respectively) as strings and CellValue objects, respectively. A CellValue object is basically a wrapper of the cell string entered by the user; therefore, the translation between these two kinds of values is straightforward and simply involves wrapping and unwrapping a string. However, the architecture of the system remains the same even for more complex translation logic. For instance, if the Habanero spreadsheet had implemented full WYSIWIS interaction by coupling the scrollbars, the translator would simply ignore these events. Similarly, if the UNC spreadsheet had stored cell values as integers, the translator would be responsible for parsing and unparsing the string and integer representations, respectively.

The modifications to the Habanero spreadsheet were minor and consisted of about 100 lines of code. The modified spreadsheet implements only those aspects of the view of the UNC spreadsheet that are relevant to the model. It does not implement other aspects (such as changing the coupling policy) that are seen by the user but not the model. As it turns out, it implements the full functionality of the Habanero spreadsheet. This is because we did not find a convenient way to execute different programs for the different replicas of the Habanero spreadsheet. This means each Habanero replica must implement the union of the functionality needed by both the real users and the dummy user. The UNC spreadsheet allows the views of a model to execute different programs. Otherwise, the program executed by the dummy user would have had to implement the union of the functionality of the two systems and the translation function.

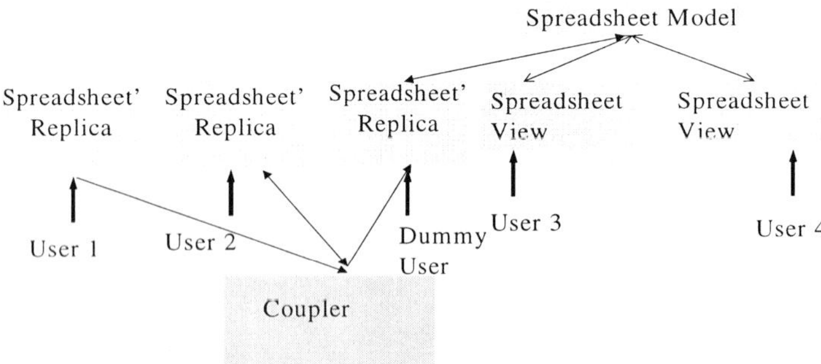

Figure 3 Architecture for Interoperating Coupling

We can describe the approach used in our interoperation architecture in terms of the abstract zipper model described before (Figure 4). Two different architectures can be made to interoperate by creating a module that appears to be a branch of both architectures and translates between the events received from the two architectures according to the coupling interoperation semantics.

If both systems support latecomers, then the new branch can be created dynamically to allow the two groups of users to join each other after they have done some intra-group collaboration. If the two systems also allow the branches to execute different programs, then the individual systems do not have to be changed. The users of each system appear to the users of the other system as a single user.

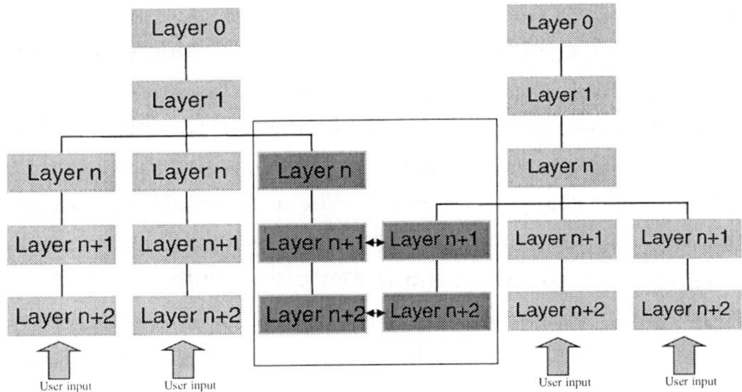

Figure 4 Interoperation in Terms of the Zipper Model

Concurrency Control Semantics

Let us now consider the dimension of concurrency control. Its semantics in the two systems are:

- Habanero Spreadsheet: The default is ordinary floor control. Users can change it to queue-based floor control.
- UNC Spreadsheet: The default is ordinary (implicit and explicit) centralized locks. Users can change it to tickle, optimistic, or cached locks.

We use the following interoperation semantics: If the user has reserved an object (through floor control or fine-grained locking), then no other user can manipulate the object.

As in the case of coupling, the interoperation semantics are a weaker form of the semantics of the two systems. As we shall see later, they are weaker than we might desire, since they make no promises about fairness. For certain concurrency control modes (queue-based floor control and tickle locks), we will be able to offer stronger semantics with better fairness properties.

Concurrency-Control Architectures

We implemented two different architectures for interoperating the concurrency control of the two systems. In one, the floor-controller is the master or server, and the lock-controller is the slave or client (Figure 5); while in the other, the reverse is true. The server system is the one that keeps global information about which objects are reserved (through locking or floor control). The client system must check with it before granting a reservation request to its users. The client system makes this check in addition to the check it makes for local conflicts. All users of the client system appear to the server system as a single "dummy user".

There is a third architecture possible in which both systems are considered equal and replicate the reservation information. However, we did not consider this alternative.

Unlike coupling, our schemes for interoperating concurrency-control require the two systems to follow certain protocols that collaboration systems currently do not. As we will argue later, these protocols also support extendibility, and are thus useful even if interoperability is not a goal. Nonetheless, since current systems must be changed to implement these protocols, we may be constrained by what kind of changes can be made easily to a system. The architecture determines the protocol – thus, which architecture is chosen depends on what kind of changes can be easily made to a system. It is for this reason we defined both architectures and associated protocols to give the interoperator some flexibility.

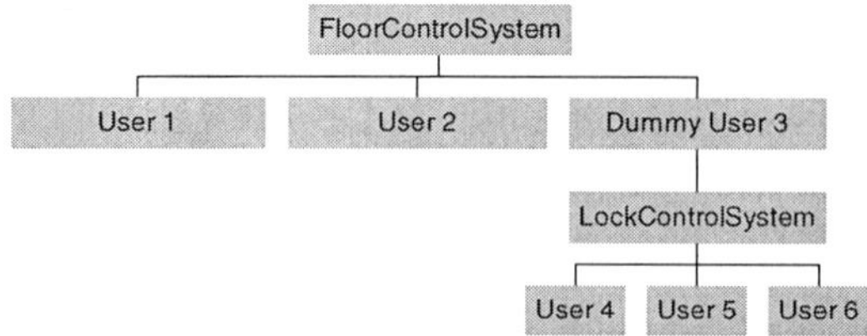

Figure 5 Floor Controller as Master

General Protocol

We first present a general protocol that is sufficient to implement both architectures, and later, under the discussion of each architecture, identify which aspects of this protocol are necessary for it.

We assume that the floor-control system generates the following events:

- *FloorRequestedEvent*: This event is generated whenever a request for the floor is made by the user. This is a *vetoable* event, which means that any of the event listeners can veto the event, and the object that generated the event gets notified of the veto. We assume that whenever the *FloorRequestedEvent* is vetoed, the floor-control system denies the request. The event also contains reference to a *principal* object that identifies the user.
- *FloorAcquiredEvent*: This event is generated by the floor-controller when a user successfully acquires the floor. This event also contains reference to the principal. This event is necessary because one of the (possibly) several event listeners may have vetoed the request for the floor.
- *FloorReleasedEvent*: This event is generated when the floor is released by a user and also contains a reference to the principal.

We also assume that the floor-controller acts as a server for the operations, *AcquireFloor* and *ReleaseFloor*, which take a principal as an argument.

Similarly, we assume that the lock-based concurrency control system generates the events *LockRequestedEvent, LockAcquiredEvent, LockReleasedEvent,* and serves the requests, *AcquireLock* and *ReleaseLock,* which are like the corresponding floor-control events/requests except that they take an extra *lockable* argument.

Though this protocol has been defined for supporting interoperability, it also supports extendibility, since it allows user-supplied modules to veto events and make requests.

This protocol does not take into account differences in the various forms of the locking and floor-control policies implemented in the system, abstracting out these differences. Thus, the interoperation code we give below will work for all variations of these two policies implemented in the two systems, though, as we will see below, the fairness of the implementation will depend on the exact variation.

Neither of our two systems originally implemented this protocol. Implementing the complete protocol required about 10 lines of additional code in each spreadsheet.

Floor Controller as Master: Policy 1

Figure 6 illustrate the run-time architecture of the interoperability mechanism of this policy. The LockToFloorProxy is the representative of the Lock-Controller to the Floor-Controller, translating between the lock events and the floor requests.

The proxy executes the following pseudo algorithm:

```
LockToFloorProxy

//Lock system wants a lock
On  (LockRequestedEvent(Lockable item, Principal user)) do
        // check with floor controller if dummy user can get lock
        If ( ¬ floorControllerObject.acquireFloor( LockUser ) )
             Veto
// Keep track of which items are locked so that floor can be released
On  (LockAcquiredEvent(Lockable item, Principal user)) do
        Lock-status[item.id]=LOCKED;
//When all locks are released, release floor
On  (LockReleasedEvent (Lockable item, Principal user)) do
        Lock-status[item]=FREE;
        For all lockables item do
                If (Lock-status[item]==LOCKED) Return;
        floorControllerObject.releaseFloor( LockUser )
```

It implements the interoperation semantics discussed earlier. When a lock user requests a lock, the lock-system first checks for local conflicts and then asks the proxy to acquire the floor from the server as the dummy user, *LockUser.* Thus, locks are denied as long as the floor is not with *LockUser.* Conversely, when any user has a lock on an item, the floor is with *LockUser* and thus only the users of the lock-based system are active. And since the lock-based and floor-control systems are (assumed to be) correct, the resulting system also correctly implements the interoperation semantics. In order to release the floor when all locks are released, the proxy must duplicate the semantics of the lock controller by keeping track of which items are locked.

In this policy, the lock-based system would have an unfair advantage, as even if one item were locked by any user, the floor would stay with the lock-based system. So, the floor-control users may be easily starved. It is important to note here that even though the floor-control and lock-based systems may be free of starvation, the interoperation scheme introduces starvation into the system. The starvation is due to the fact that *LockUser* can hold the floor for infinite time even if the users of the lock-based system acquire the locks for finite intervals.

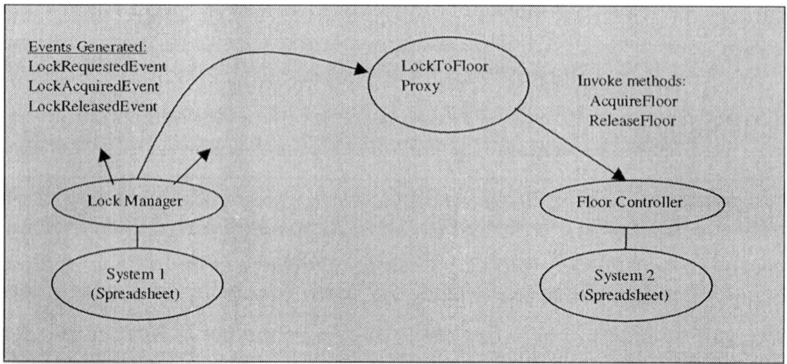

Figure 6 Proxy-based Runtime Architecture

Such starvation is particularly unfortunate when the floor-control system enqueues requests, since if the floor is with the lock-based system, the users of this system can continue to lock new items even after a user of the floor-control system makes a request for the floor.

Floor Controller as Master: Policy 2

This policy fixes the problem above and assumes queue-based floor control. We add two additional objects to the runtime architecture – a *FloorListener* object, and a *State* object. The FloorListener listens for events from the floor controller in order to determine if there is a pending request for the floor. This information is now used by LockToFloorProxy to determine if future lock requests should be denied. It is stored in the State object, which is shared by FloorListener and LockToFloorProxy. The code below describes the behavior of the three objects.

This code differs from the previous one in that whenever a user requests the floor, a flag is set, and any subsequent lock requests are denied. The flag is reset whenever a user of the floor-controller gets the floor. We could instead use a count of the number of users in the floor queue, but that could starve the users of the locking system, since the count may never go to zero.

    State

    Boolean floorRequested initially false

    LockToFloorProxy

```
On  (LockRequestedEvent(Lockable item, Principal user)) do
            // floor system has requested floor, disallow further locks
            If( floorRequested ) Veto;
            If ( NOT floorControllerObject.acquireFloor( LockUser ) )
            Veto

On  (LockAcquiredEvent(Lockable item, Principal user)) do
        Lock-status[item.id]=LOCKED

On  (LockReleasedEvent (Lockable item, Principal user)) do
        Lock-status[item.id]=FREE;
        For all lockables item do
                If (Lock-status[item.id]==LOCKED);
                    Return;
        floorControllerObject.releaseFloor( LockUser )
```

    FloorListener
```
// keep track of whether floor-control system has a pending request
On  (FloorRequestedEvent(Lockable item, Principal user)) do
        floorRequested=true;

On (FloorAcquiredEvent(Lockable item, Principal user)) do
        floorRequested=false;
```

In comparison to the previous policy, this is fairer to the users of the floor-control system. Assuming that users of either system reserve the floor/object for finite times, users will be able to get their reservations in finite time. This time can be further decreased (for both systems) if tickle locks are used.

Lock Manager as Master

Finally, we consider the implementation of the second policy under the dual architecture that assumes the lock-manager as the master. The LockToFloorProxy and FloorListener objects are now replaced by their duals, a FloorToLockProxy and a LockListener object. A floor request from the slave is mapped by the proxy to a reservation of all the locks in the master. The floor release event asks the lock system to release all locks.

As before, a shared state object keeps track of a pending request from the floor-control system to prevent new locks from being acquired by users of the lock system. Policy 1 can be implemented for this architecture by ignoring such a request. As can be seen by the code, the two architectures and associated policies require different aspects of the general protocol to be implemented. The first architecture requires the floor-control system to implement the server operations for acquiring and releasing the floor, while the second architecture requires the lock control system to implement the server operations for acquiring and releasing locks. The first policy, which ignores queued floor requests, does not require the server system to broadcast events, while the second policy does.

```
State
Boolean floorRequested initially false


FloorToLockProxy

//Get all locks or none to prevent deadlocks
On  (FloorRequestedEvent(Principal user)) do
        For all lockables item do
                If( NOT acquireLock(item, FloorUser) Veto;
                        For all lockables item do
                                ReleaseLock(item, FloorUser);
                        floorRequested = TRUE;

On (FloorAcquiredEvent(Lockable item, Principal user)) do
        FloorRequested = FALSE;

On(FloorReleasedEvent(Lockable item, Principal user)) do
        For all lockables item do
                ReleaseLock(item, FloorUser)


LockListener

// Disallow further  lock requests if there is a pending floor request
On  (LockRequestedEvent(Lockable item, Principal user)) do
        If (floorRequested) Veto;
```

It is important to ensure that the interoperating system not only not introduce inter-system unfairness but also deadlocks. In all of our policies, the two systems cannot simultaneously reserve shared items. When the floor-control system is the master, this is easy to ensure, since either the lock-system or the floor-system has the floor. When the lock-control system is the master, we make sure that if a floor request cannot get all locks, it releases all locks it does manage to acquire.

In our implementations, as mentioned before, the entire concurrency control protocol has been implemented by both systems. This has allowed us to dynamically change the architecture and policy at runtime.

The proxy and state code required to implement all of the policies above is about 800 lines. Recall that this code resides outside the individual systems, and interacts with these systems using the concurrency-control protocol.

Conclusions and Future Work

The surprising result from this work is that it is possible to interoperate a synchronously-coupled, fully replicated, floor-control system with a flexibly-coupled, partially centralized, lock system; that it is possible to reason about the semantics of the interoperating system; that it is possible to devise clean architectures for interoperation; and that such few changes are required in the two systems to interoperate.

In this paper, we have motivated the need for interoperating the two systems by showing that the features they implement are found in a large number of existing systems and that each set of features has important advantages that the other set does not have. We have identified interoperation semantics that are abstractions of and close to the local semantics of the individual systems.

We have shown that existing latecomer support can be used to implement the interoperation semantics for coupling, and that if the existing systems allow different branches in the zipper architecture to execute different programs, then interoperating the coupling does not require changes to the two systems.

We have identified two different proxy-based architectures for interoperating the concurrency-control components of the two systems. In one, the floor-control system keeps global reservation information, acting as a server to the lock system; while in the other, the reverse is true. For each architecture, we identified two interoperation policies. The first policy applies to both ordinary and queue-based floor control, but can result in starvation even if the original systems are free of starvation. The second policy is fairer but applies only to queue-based floor control.

These architectures and policies require the interoperating systems to follow a certain concurrency-control protocol that current collaborative systems do not. The exact protocol depends on the architecture and policy used. We have identified a general protocol that applies to both architectures and policies. It does not take much code to implement and is also useful for extendibility.

The question that this paper does not answer is whether users would be satisfied with interoperation semantics that are different from their preferred semantics. Given that the alternative is either not collaborating with users with different preferences or conforming to a standard system and policies, we believe the answer is yes. A firm answer to this question requires modifications to production software systems and extensive user-studies, which are beyond the scope of this work.

Future work is also required to address interoperation policies for concurrency control with better fairness properties. Moreover, it will be useful to tackle interoperation issues not addressed by this work such as interoperation of more than two systems; and interoperation of other points in the large design space of collaboration systems. In particular, it will be useful to study how popular awareness policies can be interoperated. The approach used in our work of reducing all users of a foreign system to one user is not likely to give the desired awareness interoperation-semantics, and adaptations/extensions to it will be required. Finally, it is important to determine the limits of interoperability – when are two competing approaches so inconsistent that no useful interoperation semantics can be defined. This paper provides a framework for attacking some of these unresolved issues.

Acknowledgments

This work was supported in part by a UNC fellowship, U.S. National Science Foundation Grant Nos. IRI-9508514, IRI-9627619, and CDA-9624662, and U.S. DARPA/ONR Grant No. 6601-96-C-8507. The insightful comments of the referees helped improve the presentation of the paper.

References

Chabert, E. Grossman, L. Jackson, S. Pietrowicz, and C. Seguin, "Java Object-Sharing in Habanero," Communications of the ACM 41:6 (June 1998). pp. 69-76.

Dewan, P. and Choudhary, R. "Coupling the User Interfaces of a Multiuser Program," ACM Transactions on Computer Human Interaction 2:1 (March 1995), pp. 1-39.

Dewan, P. "Architectures for Collaborative Applications," Trends in Software: Computer Supported Co-operative Work 7, Wiley (1998), pp. 165-194.

Ellis C.A., Gibbs S.J., and Rein G.L. *Groupware- some issues and experiences.* Communications of the ACM, January 1991, Vol.34, No.1, pp. 9-28.

Greenberg, S., and Marwood, D. Real Time Groupware as a Distributed System: Concurrency Control and its Effect on the Interface. CSCW Conference (Oct., 1994), ACM, pp. 207-217.

Greif I., Seliger, R., and Weihl, W. Atomic Data Abstractions in a Distributed Collaborative Editing System (Extended Abstract). ACM, pp. 160-171.

Hill, R. Brinck, T., Rohall, S., Patterson, J.and Wilner, W. "The Rendezvous Architecture and Language for Constructing Multiuser Applications," ACM Transactions on Computer Human Interaction 1:2 (June 1994).

Knister, M.l J. and Prakash, A. "DistEdit: A Distributed Toolkit for Supporting Multiple Group Editors," Proceedings of ACM Conference on Computer Supported Cooperative Work, October 1990, pp. 343-356.

Krasner, G.E. and Pope, S. T. "A Cookbook for Using the Model-View-Controller User Interface Paradigm in Smalltalk-80," Journal of Objcct-Oriented Programming 1:3 (August/September 1988), pp. 26-49.

Munson, J.P., and Dewan, P. *Sync: a Java framework for mobile collaborative applications.* Computer, Vol. 30, No.6 (June 1997), pp. 59-66.

Prakash A., and Hyong, S.S. DistView: Support for Building Efficient Collaborative Applications using Replicated Objects. CSCW Conference (Oct., 1994), ACM, pp. 153-164.

Newman-Wolfe, R.E., Webb, M.L., and Montes, M. *Implicit Locking in the Ensemble Concurrent object-oriented graphics editor.* Proceedings CSCW 92 Conference on Computer Supported Cooperative Work (Nov.1992), ACM, pp. 265-272.

Schuckmann C., Kirchner L., Schummer J., and Haake J.M. *Designing object-oriented synchronous groupware with COAST.* CSCW 1996, ACM, pp. 30-38.

Stefik, M., Bobrow, D. G., Foster, G., Lanning, S., and Tatar, D. "WYSIWIS Revised: Early Experiences with Multiuser Interfaces," ACM Transactions on Office Information Systems 5:2 (April 1987), pp. 147-167.

Vinoski S., CORBA: Integrating Diverse Applications within Distributed Heterogeneous Environments. IEEE Communications Magazine, Vol.14, No.2, February 1997.

S. Bødker, M. Kyng, and K. Schmidt (eds.). *Proceedings of the Sixth European Conference on Computer-Supported Cooperative Work, 12-16 September 1999, Copenhagen, Denmark*
©1999 Kluwer Academic Publishers. Printed in the Netherlands

NESSIE: An Awareness Environment for Cooperative Settings

Wolfgang Prinz
GMD-FIT, Germany

This paper describes NESSIE[1], an awareness environment for cooperative settings. Key elements of NESSIE are an application independent generic infrastructure, an open and extendable protocol including dynamic event types, and a set of sensors and configurable indicators, both for discrete and contextual event notifications. Special aspects of the NESSIE server are the support access control, reciprocity, event transformation, the provision of different interaction methods, the implementation of a subscription method that is based on interest profiles, as well as the possibility of sharing profiles among groups. With the integration of real-world sensors and tangible interfaces for the presentation of awareness information, NESSIE enables new ways to foster task-oriented and social awareness.

Introduction

The importance of awareness for a successful application of groupware has been pinpointed by many studies and much interesting research has been undertaken in this CSCW research area. This yielded a number of models and applications that provide awareness about the activity and actions of others in a cooperative environment. Examining the current approaches for the support of awareness in cooperative systems we can identify two types of awareness that these systems

---

[1]   This project is part of the Social Web Research Programme (Hoschka, 1998). NESSIE stands for awareNESS envIronmEnt. However, the notion of awareness has many similarities with the "real" Nessie of Loch Ness in Scotland – nobody has seen it yet ...

address: social awareness and task-oriented awareness.

We consider *task-oriented awareness* as the awareness that is focussed on activities performed to achieve a specific shared task. This kind of awareness can be promoted by change notifications or information about the state of a certain document or a shared workspace. It allows users to coordinate their activities on the shared object. This might happen either in a synchronous or asynchronous way. Notifications that contribute to the task-oriented awareness, embody information on who does or did which actions on which shared task or task-related object.

Social awareness includes information about the presence and activities of people in a shared environment. Systems focussing on social awareness provide notifications similar to the information received when walking along an office floor. Notifications that contribute to the social awareness embodies information on who is present and in which state in a shared environment.

The difference between task-oriented and social awareness is primarily determined by the shared context. For task-oriented awareness the shared context is established by an object that is part of a cooperative process, for social awareness it is the environment that is inhabited by the users. We believe that it is essential for a cooperation support environment to support both types of awareness. However, looking at the different systems it appears that most are concentrating on the support of either of these types. Gutwin et al. (Gutwin, et al., 1996) distinguish additional forms of awareness, but for the following considerations a concentration on these two forms is more appropriate.

GroupDesk (Fuchs, et al., 1995) or Interlocus (Nomura, et al., 1998) are examples for systems that provide task-oriented awareness. They supply a shared workspace for the support of asynchronous cooperative work. Changes to shared objects are indicated to users by visual notifications. All notifications are closely associated to the shared objects.

Video based systems such as Portholes (Dourish, Bly, 1992, Lee, et al., 1997) increase the social awareness of people in a shared environment, e.g. an office building. Systems like Social Awareness@work (Tollmar, et al., 1996) provide social awareness by an indication of the presence and state of people.

For the Internet and the World-wide web many systems are being developed that supply information on the presence of other users in the Internet or on a currently visited web-page. Probably the most successful application is ICQ, a tool that informs users about the Internet-presence of other people. More sophisticated applications such as CoBrow (Siedler, et al., 1997) present the list of users who are currently visiting a web pages and offer additional communication channels. All these systems belong to the group of social awareness systems. They display information on the presence of others in a shared environment.

Room based systems represent an approach to integrate social and task-oriented awareness. Examples are: Diva (Sohlenkamp, Chwelos, 1994) or TeamRooms (Roseman, Greenberg, 1996). In these systems virtual rooms provide a shared location for the organisation and collection of task-oriented objects. For users who cooperate on a task and thus share a room, the information that somebody is working on a document, contributes to the task-oriented awareness. Social awareness is increased by supplying general information about the presence of people in virtual rooms or buildings. Another approach for the integration of social awareness into a task-oriented system, i.e. the BSCW (Bentley, et al., 1995), is the MetaWeb (Trevor, et al., 1997) application.

Most of these applications either augment a single application, such as a shared application tool (Dourish, Bellotti, 1992), with additional awareness features, or they provide a new cooperation environment that embeds other applications and incorporates notification mechanisms to inform users about relevant cooperative activities. Common to the second group of applications is, that they provide a new desktop interface and that users who want to benefit from the awareness functionality need to perform all their cooperative work using these desktops, e.g. as in DIVA, GroupDesk or TeamRooms. Since most users are very reluctant to change from one working environment to another, just for the benefit of a single new feature, such awareness augmented platforms are very valuable for the evaluation of specific awareness features, but they seldom have the potential to become a general purpose working environment.

Further characteristic of these systems is that they primarily focus on the support of a specific application and that they do not interweave mechanisms for the support of social and task-oriented awareness. Moreover, most are designed as closed solutions which can not be extended in a simple way

We believe that a more promising approach is the provision of a generic extendable awareness infrastructure including simple and lightweight mechanisms for the generation and user configurable presentation of notifications at the standard desktop interface. This is the motivation for the NESSIE awareness environment that is described this paper. First we give an overview of the conceptual model and the architecture, followed by a description of different sensors for the reception and generation of events. Then we describe different methods for the presentation of awareness information. Two scenarios illustrate the applicability of the environment. The paper concludes with a discussion of related work.

Conceptual Model

It is essential for a general purpose awareness environment to provide its services application independent. Experiences with PoliAwaC (Sohlenkamp, 1998), show that a presentation of awareness information just within an application is not sufficient. It is necessary that relevant events about user activities can be externalised from one application and promoted to other applications. Thus users can stay aware about important events and activities even if they are not actually using or running a particular groupware system. Principle for NESSIE is therefore that it supplies its services application independent as an awareness bridge for different applications and settings. This should also allow for a mixture of events from real world and electronic settings.

The conceptual model of NESSIE is based on the approach that information about cooperative actions that are relevant for the awareness of the state of a co-operative setting can be captured through the generation of events. Events are generated by sensors that are associated with actors, shared material, or any other objects that constitute or influence a cooperative environment. They contain identifiers of the originator, the action, the time, and the context in which the action took place (e.g. shared workspaces, cooperative process, workflow).

The reception and generation of activity events is enabled through the realisation of lightweight *sensors*. Different sensors should be provided by the infrastructure for the integration into other applications, such as document change notifications, presence sensors, or information monitoring agents. Additional sensors should be realisable without a large effort, i.e. the environment should supply simple protocols for the interaction with sensors. Sensors are not restricted to the reception and generation of events in electronic environments. In the near future, sensory environments will emerge and will become integral part of our working and living environments (Saffo, 1998). Thus the infrastructure should integrate real world sensors to recognise activities and states of places in the "real world" and to promote this information to other real or virtual places.

After creation, an event is transmitted to an awareness server. An important task of this server is the propagation, transformation, and notification of events. Several models exist for the computation of that task. In (Mariani, Prinz, 1993) a model based on the water-ripple metaphor is presented, that interprets the relationships between shared objects as a transport media for events. Following that approach in (Fuchs, Pankoke-Babatz, et al., 1995) and later in (Fuchs, 1998), the notion of interest profiles is introduced as a method to specify the awareness information someone is interested in. Empircial studies of that concept in the PoliAwaC groupware client show, that this is a suitable specification method (Sohlenkamp, et al., 1999). Thus we have adopted that notion and concept for the event distribution and notification method of the NESSIE environment.

Alternative approaches are suggested by the spatial model presented in (Benford, Fahlén, 1993) and its generalisations and extensions in (Rodden, 1996) and (Sandor, et al., 1997). We believe, that CSCW research is still lacking enough experiences to decide which model is the most appropriate for a specific setting. Therefore we propose implementations of these models as plug-ins to the awareness server. This will allow a setting based selection of the appropriate model.

The presentation of awareness information is performed by configurable *indicators*. Tools are offered that allow an easy mapping of activity events to suitable indicators. Analogue to real world sensors it is also possible to integrate real world indicators such as the artefacts proposed in (Wisneski, et al., 1998) with the NESSIE environment to foster awareness of virtual presence and remote activities beyond the limitations of a computer monitor.

The NESSIE environment is not intended to support highly synchronous applications such as application sharing systems that rely on a high frequency of technical synchronisation events, e.g. mouse-clicks or scroll events. The NSTP (Patterson, et al., 1996) platform provides a suitable support for such applications. We aim at the support for action relevant events that increase the social and task-oriented awareness of the cooperation status, not of the technical application status. Such kinds of events occur in a lower frequency, allow for other architectures and demand new ways of information presentation.

Architectural Overview

An awareness environment should be integrated with and based upon current Internet technologies. Beyond the advantage of an easy distribution of the environment, the interoperability of the environment with other applications can be more easily achieved. Many applications offer communication interfaces to Internet services. In addition to that baseline, the following requirements, derived from the considerations of the conceptual model, guided the design of the NESSIE awareness environment:

- application independent infrastructure;
- open, extensible protocols for the interaction with the environment;
- lightweight sensors and means for an easy realisation of new sensors;
- configurable set of indicators and means for integrating new indicators;
- integration with web-technology to provide a high level of interoperability.

The following sections first give an overview of the systems architecture, then specific aspects such as access control and reciprocity are discussed in more detail.

Architecture

Figure 1 illustrates the architecture of the NESSIE awareness environment. Central components are the NESSIE server in combination with the event database and the NESSIE client. The server supports two methods for the production and provision of events: asynchronous (pull) server interaction by a cgi-interface or synchronous (push) notifications based on registered interest profiles by the NESSIE client. Both methods are described in the following two subsections.

396

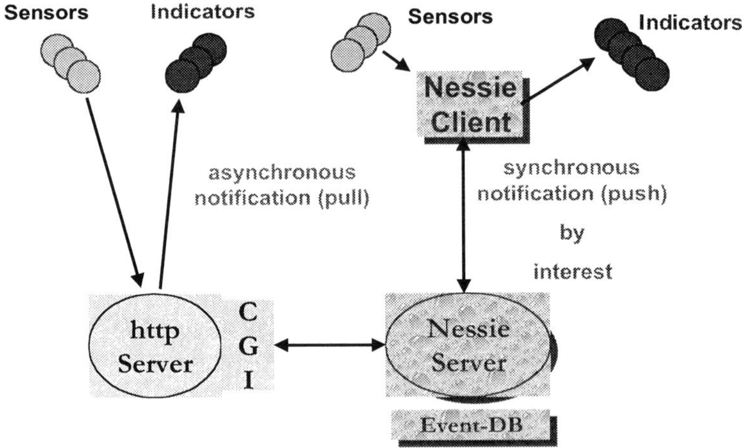

Figure 1: The NESSIE Architecture

Server Interaction via http

A very simple technique is provided for the interacting with the server using cgi scripts (left hand side of Fig.1). This interface allows the submission of events via http-calls of a cgi script. The script interprets the call parameters that consists of attribute-name/value pairs, as a event descriptions.

The event protocol is open and can be easily extended. The server requires only the provision of the two parameters: sensor-type and event-type. All other parameters can be dynamically defined. The creation of a new, or the extension and modification of an existing event-type requires no server-side modifications. Optionally, for common reference, event-type specifications can by documented in the event-type registry (an HTML-document). This registry provides a set of well-defined core-events and is furthermore used by the NESSIE client to create user interface templates for the specification of event-queries in interest profiles. The expiration date of an event can be specified by a special attribute. After the expiration date this event is no longer returned to any event-query and will be transferred with next event garbage collection into a history database.

The cgi interface offers a showevent-operation for event-queries. Regular expressions can be used as parameter values to describe generic event-patterns. The format (lists, HTML-documents) and content (number and types of returned attributes) of the return-result can be controlled using additional control attributes.

By the provision of this cgi-interface it is possible for a wide range of applications to report events to the NESSIE server. Through this externalisation, information becomes available for users outside of a specific application domain. For example, the integration with the MS-Office suite was easily realised by the implementation of simple macros. These macros signalise document modifications to the NESSIE environment and they indicate the document history or other relevant events, e.g. modifications on related documents or the presence of co-authors of that documents, by retrieving event information from the server.

With the cgi-interface for event generation and retrieval the NESSIE environment can be easily integrated as an application independent awareness bridge into legacy infrastructures. Dynamic event types are a key factor for scalability and enable the application of NESSIE in different organisational boundaries. However, the http solution embodies the disadvantage that applications must explicitly pull the NESSIE server for new events. Accordingly, this mode of operation can not be used for settings where events must be immediately processed or indicated, but provides appropriate means when loosely coupled interactions are sufficient. The following subsection describes an alternative mode.

The NESSIE Client – Support for Interest Profiles

The right hand side of Figure 1 illustrates the interaction of the NESSIE client with the NESSIE server. The client is user specific and represents a user within the environment. It realises the following functions:

- indication of the currently online NESSIE users and provision of ad hoc communication tools;
- a user interface for the specification of interest profiles;
- a communication interface to the server for the registration of interest profiles and receipt of events that have been submitted by sensors;
- interfaces to configure and communicate with awareness indicators.

When users log into the NESSIE client their presence is indicated to other users. On demand they will receive events that have been submitted since their last presence, that match their interest profiles and that have not yet expired.

In this section, we concentrate on the concept and support for the specification of interest profiles. Users describe their interest in events by the specification of interest profiles. An interest profiles contains the specification of:

- an event-query describing the events that are relevant for that profile,
- the indicator that is used to present that event,
- and a specification of the actual event information that shall be presented by the indicator.

Figure 2 shows the user interface of the client for a profile description. First, the user has to specify the indicator and indicator-type that shall be used to present the event. For that purpose the NESSIE client provides a number of pre-registered indicators (see section below). It is possible to indicate different events by a single indicator. In this case a single indicator can by used as unique place for the presentation of events that originate in the same context. For example, all events produced by the modifications of a certain document set or by the presence of people that belong to the same organisational context, e.g. a project can be presented by a single indicator.

In the second step, an event-pattern is specified applying the same language that is used for the cgi-interface. An event-pattern is registered at the NESSIE server by the client. Whenever the server receives an event that matches the registered event-pattern, it immediately forwards all event attributes to the client. Users can select the event-pattern either from existing profiles or they can create new patterns. If the event-type specification is documented in the event-type registry, then the NESSIE client dynamically creates user interface templates that support the specification of event-patterns.

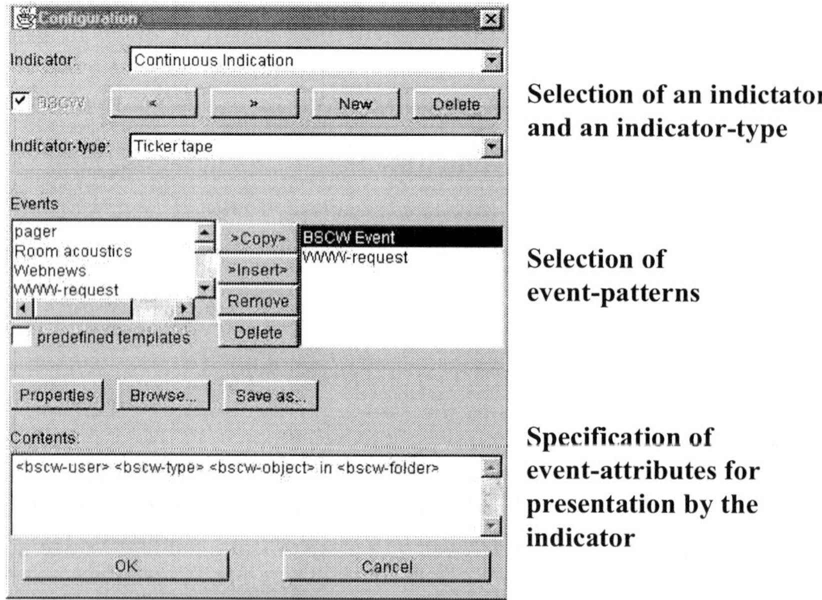

Figure 2: The configuration window of the NESSIE client user interface

In the third step, users specify the event attributes that shall be presented by the selected indicator. Explanatory text can be added to the selected attributes if the indicator supports a textual presentation. In addition to the list of pre-registered indicators, it is also possible to launch external applications such as media players and to forward event attributes as parameters to these applications. This allows for an easy integration of new indicators into the awareness environment.

Initially the NESSIE client stored the whole user configuration at the users computer. The application of the client quickly indicated that users wanted to exchange their interest profiles. This led to a redesign that allows the storage of single interest profiles as single objects in a BSCW shared workspace. The sharing of profiles between different users offers new opportunities for the configuration of awareness information within a group. It is for example possible to use a shared workspace for the administration of group-wide interest profiles, i.e. profiles that each member of the group should use. Individual profiles can be added by retrieving profiles from additional workspaces. When a user launches the client, the user profiles are read from the workspaces and registered at the NESSIE server.

The provision of two interfaces (cgi and NESSIE client) by the NESSIE server enables different modes of interaction between client applications and the server. Ramduny et al. propose a taxonomy for the classification of notification servers (Ramduny, et al., 1998). The sensor-server interaction fits into the category A2 ("client tells server"). Category A4 ("server bound to data") is supported too, because of the close association of the event database with the server. This enables the server to provide notifications of past events which is important for the support of asynchronous working modes. The indicator-server interaction covers B2 ("server tells client") and B3 ("client polls server").

Access Control and Reciprocity

An often discussed awareness issue is the danger of misusing awareness information for control purposes. We address that problem by the introduction of event access rights and the disclosure of interest that others have registered in events that a user generates by interacting with shared objects.

An event that is submitted to the NESSIE server can be protected against unauthorised access by the inclusion of an access control attribute. This attribute lists the ids of users or a group of users who are allowed to receive that event. For simplicity the usage of the cgi-interface to the NESSIE server requires no authentication. Therefore access protected events can not be retrieved through that interface. However, the client requires a login on start-up for user identification and for the retrieval of the users interest profiles from the BSCW workspaces. The user identification is presented to the server together with the registration of the interest profiles. This enables the server to perform an access validation on protected events. If the identified user is member of the access control list, a protected event is forwarded to the respective NESSIE client. With the introduction of access control for events the awareness environment ensures that activity information can be made visible to a restricted group only.

Although access rights are a suitable method to restrict access to awareness information, it can not guarantee to exclude misuse. An approach towards that problem is the provision of reciprocity. This is achieved by disclosing those users who have registered interest in event to those users who produce the event – "when you see me I see you". Whenever an event is submitted to the NESSIE server this information can be requested by inclusion of a special "observer" attribute into the parameter list. The return information lists those users who will receive that event instantly and those who are potential recipients. Potential users are those who have registered interest in that kind of event, but who are not currently running a NESSIE client. If the event is not already expired, they will be informed the next time they start NESSIE client.

This information is useful not only for the support of reciprocity. It further informs a user about the list of people who will become aware of the activity that is indicated by the event. This is important when a certain reaction is expected on the activity that raised the event. Users who participated in the field study of the PoliAwaC client considered that functionality as very important. Borning and Travers (Borning, Travers, 1991) experienced a different user behaviour in their evaluation of Polyscope. The symmetry functionality offered by Polyscope was not considered as useful. We assume that the reason for the different receptions of this functionality is grounded in the fact that Polyscope provides synchronous awareness, while both PoliAwaC and NESSIE aim at the provision of asynchronous awareness. In the asynchronous case events are not that volatile, i.e. it is more important to know who is able to receive events later in time. Another fact is that in video-based systems reciprocity can easily cause disruptions (Hudson, Smith, 1996), while NESSIE allows for the configuration of less intrusive indicators. Borning, et al. report that users actually preferred less intrusive bitmap images over full video and NYNEX portholes users required the indication of the audience in the main display (Lee, Girgensohn, et al., 1997, pg. 391).

Event transformation

An event transformation module of the NESSIE server allows the transformation of submitted events. This functionality is useful for two purposes. First, it allows the mapping of events into other event-types to transform the event semantic. It is used for example to map noise and move events that are submitted from room sensors into more general events that indicate activity in a room. Second, it enables forwarding events from one NESSIE server to another one at another location. This contributes to the scalability of the environment and provides in addition a bridging function for the exchange of selected events between two settings that both use a local NESSIE server.

Sensoring Activities

This section gives a brief overview of the sensors that have been developed for the NESSIE environment. Sensors are used to create and submit events to the NESSIE server. Sensors are not necessarily software based. We have also integrated real-world sensors as we will see in the following.

Presence sensors are used to detect the presence of people in a certain place or at a certain location. We understand places or locations as real places or as locations in an information space. Therefore we have developed software sensors, that can be integrated into web-pages, BSCW workspaces, or a computer desktop to sensor the presence of a person at a certain location. In addition, sensors based on video image motion recognition, infrared-motion detection, and photoelectric barriers have been realised to sensor the physical presence of people in a room. The event information and precision differs between these sensors. Some are able to identify the event originator because they are located at a location where users need to identify themselves, others forward anonymous events only. The utilisation of that information differs, too. Presence sensors in information spaces are primarily used to indicate the presence to people at the same location in the information space. This promotes the social awareness of others and turns information objects into places and encounters where others can be met. The application domain for real world sensors are public rooms, e.g. coffee rooms. Presence information about these places is primarily used by people at other locations who want to stay aware of the social activities in order to decide if they want to join in.

The cgi interface enables the introduction of presence sensors into closed environments, such as Active Worlds, a multi-user virtual world that allows users the creation of their own places and buildings. People spend an enormous effort into the design of their houses, but it happens rarely that someone meets somebody else at the own house (Fuchs, et al., 1998). It would be a helpful feature being able to detect if somebody is approaching a place, even if one is not currently running the Active Worlds client. An externalisation of presence information can solve that problem. The Active Worlds system provides a function to combine a collision event with a call of a web page. This is often used to pop up web pages when users enter certain places. We are using that function to create a presence event through the cgi interface. By registering an interest profile for that event it is possible to become aware of the presence of others at a particular place in Active Worlds and to join in immediately.

Task and activity sensors are used in combination with shared material to indicate modifications to shared documents. Simple macros have been developed as sensors for MS-Office documents. Embodied in a document they create events whenever a document is modified. These macros are also used as indicators. They report about past actions on that or related documents and the current presence of co-authors. The integration of sensors with the BSCW systems allows the externalisation of user activities in shared workspaces.

Real world activity sensors include acoustic sensors that measure the noise level and map that onto a discrete set of activity levels, i.e. silence, smalltalk, discussion, or even party using the servers event transformation module. The installation of such a sensor in a coffee room allows the perception of the activities without being able to observe and control in detail what's going in. This distinguishes these kind of low-fidelity sensors from a web-cam which obviously provides a clearer view of the activities in a room but also more sophisticated means for control which may violate privacy.

Content watcher sensors are realised to observe the content of web pages for the occurrence of special keywords. These sensors are used to observe web pages that report traffic news, weather reports and news. For example, users can configure a sensor that creates events about traffic jams on the way home observing of a traffic report web page. Other content watcher sensors are used to create events based on an extraction of news from newspaper pages. By configuring an appropriate indicator for such events, e.g. a tickertape, users can create private push channels with the NESSIE environment.

The sensors introduced so far are sensors that automatically create events based on the occurrence of a specific situation. Additionally, NESSIE provides web pages for the manual creation of events. This is used to announce meetings, internal news, or visitors to our research group.

Early experiences show that these sensors provide a good starting point for the generation of events that foster awareness about the task-oriented and social activities in a cooperative environment. We believe that the ubiquity of internet tools and the extensibility of event-types makes it easy to develop and integrate new sensors into the NESSIE environment.

Presentation of Information

Gutwin et al. discuss a number of awareness widgets in (Gutwin, et al., 1996). Their work is focussing primarily on presentation methods for awareness information in synchronous work on shared material. The various awareness widgets are tightly bound to the shared objects and workspaces. Furthermore the presentations are internal to the shared application, i.e. the awareness information is available only for users who are currently using the application. PoliAwaC is an example for a user interface supporting asynchronous work that also uses awareness widgets (coloured icon overlays, icon enlargements, etc.). These are closely bound to the shared objects, too. The association of an awareness widget with the shared object has the advantage that the awareness information is presented in the context of its origin, i.e. the associated object.

NESSIE aims at the presentation of awareness information for more loosely coupled modes of cooperation that are not restricted to the simultaneous use of shared material. Additionally NESSIE aims at the externalisation of awareness information from applications to promote this information also to users who are not currently working with the system. Therefore we need to consider presentation methods that are not tightly coupled with the objects of origin.

This section presents examples of presentation tools for discrete event notification, for the indication of virtual presence through real world indicators, and for the presentation of awareness information in a cooperative context.

Discrete Event Information

The NESSIE client provides a number of indicators for the discrete presentation of events. These include simple windows for the listing of event information, different background images, or sounds. Applet indicators have been developed to show the presence of others on a currently browsed or on related web-pages.

For the presentation of news, activities in shared workspaces, and visitors to web pages of our research group, the tickertape has proven useful (Fitzpatrick, et al., 1998). The actual appearance of an event in the tickertape can be specified individually using the NESSIE client.

Event indicators such as the tickertape are suitable for the presentation of single events that require a textual representation for being understood. In the following sections we discuss the transfer of events to a presentation by real world indicators and in a contextual presentation of a cooperative setting.

Virtual Presence Through Real World Indicators

The limited screen real estate raises a problem for all monitor based indicators. Users prefer a full screen mode of their applications. Consequently, awareness indicators are always in danger of being quickly overlaid by other windows. One solution to that problem is the use of additional screens in the periphery of the main monitor or projections onto the background of the users computing screen (see Fig. 3). Another solution is the utilisation of tangible interfaces (Ishii, Ullmer, 1997) to foster awareness through ambient indicators.

We are particularly interested in the design of real world indicators that promote a sense of virtual presence. An example for such an indicator is the activity balloon. This indicator consists of a tube that contains a fan. Within the tube resides a balloon that is blown out and that circulates above the tube when the fan is activated. The fan itself is connected to a computer by an interface card that can be controlled by the NESSIE client. Thus it is possible to use the activity balloon as an indictor for any incoming event. We found the activity balloon in particular useful for the indication of visitors to a web-cam. The faint noise of the fan and the dancing balloon produce an ambient feeling for the presence of a virtual visitor who is accessing the web-cam. It supports peripheral awareness and reciprocity of seeing and being seen. Because it is an indicator that is rather overheard it avoids disturbance of the actual work.

The activity balloon operates also as an actuator. If a user removes the balloon from the tube the web-cam is switched of by a switch that is integrated into the tube. This combination of an indictor with an actuator turns the activity balloon to a tangible interface for virtual presence.

An extension of this indicator is the balloon theatre that combines several tubes into a single indicator. Each balloon can be controlled individually, i.e. different balloons can be bound to different incoming events. Examples are the presence of visitors at a set of web pages, in different virtual rooms of a VR environment, or in rooms of a real building. Mixing the indication of presence events with activity events, this indicator can be used to indicate bustle activity of an environment.

Information in Context

The indicators presented so far are suitable for the discrete presentation of events. For other settings, awareness of the activities in a cooperative environment can be better achieved when awareness information is presented either in the context of work or in a social context. This section presents approaches for each of these alternatives.

A BSCW shared workspaces represents a context for a group of people who manage and share their working documents by that workspace. The BSCW user interface uses a number of different awareness icons to indicate actions on shared documents. This presentation is helpful to find out about the activities on a single object in detail, but it is difficult to become aware of the current and past activities within the group or on the particular activities of a group member. The new monitor tool (Trevor, Koch, et al., 1997) provides a better synchronous awareness of the current activities, but it still concentrates on the actions at a single object level. Especially after a temporal absence, it is difficult to find out what has happened. In such situations it is more likely to ask "What did people do?" than "Which operations have been performed on which objects?".

NESSIE provides that awareness information by the presentation of pictorial activity indicators for the members of a group as part of the shared workspace user interface. User activities in a shared workspace are received by the BSCW sensors and submitted to the NESSIE server. These object specific events are collected, interpreted and transferred by the event transfer module into an activity description for the members of a workspace. We distinguish between the activities: reading, contributing, absence. A mixture of activities is possible. Special indicators are included into the workspace user interface that retrieve this information from the NESSIE server and map it onto a comic-like, animated pictorial presentations (using "animated GIFs"), that display the activities of the group member since the last visit. This gives a user a first overview on the past activities in this specific work context.

Additionally, we investigate the presentation of awareness information using the 3D multi-user environment SmallView (Broll, 1998). The 3D environment is used to build different rooms, each room representing a different context (Figure 3). A context can be either an organisational context, e.g. a project, or a spatial context, e.g. a coffee room. A project context for example, combines different visualisation methods for the display of presence or activity events. These events originate from presence and activity sensors that are located in shared documents, workspaces, and other project related material. Events produced by real world sensors that are located for example in a coffee room are used to drive the presentations of the virtual rooms.

The 3D indicators are not intended for navigational purposes, i.e. we do not intend that users navigate between rooms using the 3D interface. Instead they perform their work using their normal office- and groupware-applications. Sensors recognise when a users work affects the state of the cooperative environment or when a user changes the working context, e.g. by switching between different shared workspaces or folders, or by processing documents that belong to different contexts. The events that result from these actions are interpreted and the avatar that represents the user is moved to the appropriate room in the 3D environment. McGraths pertinent phrase for that technique is "let the system do the walking" (McGrath, 1998, p. 22). In addition to moving a users avatar around, the state of a user is also mapped onto the animation of the avatar. At the moment we distinguish between the states: idle, reading, and writing.

Figure 3: Ambient display of a 3D world that indicates the activities of users in several BSCW workspaces as well as in a public coffee room.

Using the 3D indicators, users are able to the get an immediate overview of the task-oriented, but also of the social activities in their environment. With the integration of instant communication media new social encounters emerge through the 3D indicators. Users can see who else is currently working in the same context, they can immediately communicate with these people, or they may decide to stroll to the coffee room because the corresponding 3D indicator shows activity.

One might ask why we do not use video based media spaces. The difference is that video based systems do not allow the creation of artificial rooms as we do with the organisational context based rooms. From a video image it also difficult to guess what type of operations a user is currently performing on shared material. By the visualisation of a users action through symbolic animations of the users avatar this kind information is much easier to present. For the perception of real rooms video is a very useful approach. However, the advantage of symbolic representations based on acoustic sensors and motion sensors is the provision of a higher grade of inaccuracy, thus protecting more privacy. Observers can see a level of activity, but they can't see who is actually acting. Video images can be blurred to reduce the accuracy of the original, but we believe that a sharp 3D visualisation is more attractive than a blurred video image.

The problem with 3D indicators is that the amount of required monitor space is higher than the space that is normally left when users run their everyday applications. For the use of these indicators we therefore envisage an office scenario with peripheral monitor screens or projections onto the background of the users monitor.

Related Work

A protocol for presence awareness for web users is presented in (Palfreyman, Rodden, 1996). The proposed architecture includes also an awareness server and client. However, both the architecture and the protocol are intended for the provision of presence awareness on web pages. The authors do not consider the provision of a generic awareness infrastructure.

The Notification Service Transfer Protocol (NSTP) (Patterson, Day, et al., 1996) presents a more comprehensive approach. In contrast to NESSIE the NSTP infrastructure is developed for the support of synchronous groupware applications. NSTP supports event exchange for the synchronisation of shared applications, while NESSIE supports the exchange and externalisation of activity relevant awareness information.

"Buddy Lists" application such as ICQ or AOL messenger are widespread presence information tools. Since recently an IETF working group is developing an instant messaging and presence activity proposal (Saraswat, 1998) which results in PIP, a "Presence Information Protocol" (Mohr, et al., 1999). These proposals are focussing on presence awareness only, other forms of awareness are not investigated. The scope of NESSIE goes beyond presence awareness, but we observe the standardisation initiatives and plan to incorporate the PIP protocol in future versions of the NESSIE server.

In summary, non of these approaches considers the provision of a generic awareness infrastructure including a set of application independent sensors and indicators. They are either infrastructures for the support of mainly synchronous applications, e.g. NSTP, or they require the use of new applications. A configurable mapping of awareness information on configurable indicators is also out of their scope.

More related to NESSIE are the internet notification service Elvin (Segall, Arnold, 1997) and Khronika (Lövstrand, 1991). Elvin is a publish-subscribe notification service where consumers use content-based addressing to select notifications of interest. The developers consider the application domain for Elvin in area of network management, legacy application integration and as an infrastructure for computer-supported cooperative work. Khronika is an event browsing and notification system that addresses the problems of information overload and information distribution. Key elements are events, daemons, and notifications. Initial motivation for Khronika was the information overload caused by the massive distribution of undirected event-information, e.g. through email list. The system provides a central service for the management of such events. Users can express their interest in events by constraints that are observed by daemons. Instead of being swamped with email announcement users can select the information they want to be aware of.

The NESSIE infrastructure provides a generic and open platform for the submission, transformation, and notification of events that are relevant for the promotion of task-oriented and social awareness in a cooperative setting. The provision of event access control, the support for reciprocity, the event transformation functionality, the sharing of interest profiles among groups, and integration of real-world sensors and indicators as well as the transformation of discrete events into a contextual presentation are unique characteristics of the NESSIE environment.

Conclusion

In this paper we have introduced the awareness environment NESSIE. Key elements of NESSIE are an application independent generic infrastructure, an open and extendable protocol including dynamic event types, and a set of sensors and configurable indicators, both for discrete and contextual event notifications. The NESSIE server supports access control, reciprocity, different interaction methods, and implements a subscription method that is based on interest profiles. With the integration of real-world sensors and tangible interfaces for the presentation of awareness information, NESSIE enables new ways for the provision of task-oriented and social awareness.

NESSIE supports distributed team members in providing and receiving awareness information on the task-oriented progress, but also on the social activities at the local and remote sites. The various discrete event notification mechanisms are suitable for the indication of task-oriented activities, in particular on time critical work items. For example users can register interest on documents or shared workspaces so that they are immediately notified about all activities on these document spaces. In addition, the 3D indicators can be used to become aware of the activities of remote team members. The real world indicators can be applied to create a cooperative ambience by indicators for virtual presence between remote sites. Another aspect of the NESSIE environment for virtual teams is the support of the team building process: By the provision of mutual awareness on the actual and past presence of others within an Intranet information space it is possible to create chance encounters. These encounters support people in finding coworkers with similar interests and thus can facilitate a team building process.

Future development work concentrates in the realisation and integration of alternative awareness models such as the spatial model into the NESSIE server. The current NESSIE environment is in use by our research group. Initial experiences indicate that the approach of an application independent awareness service is promising. The open protocol and the flexible configuration of the NESSIE client and indicators supported the ad-hoc integration of new sensors and the rapid realisation of new ideas for the presentation of awareness information.

I wish to thank all members of the NESSIE project for their contribution to the developments of the NESSIE environment. Special thanks to Wolfgang Gräther, Tom Gross, Uta Pankoke-Babatz, and the anonymous reviewers for their valuable comments on this paper.

Literature

Benford, S. and L. Fahlén, "A Spatial Model of Interaction in Large Virtual Environments", in *Proc. of Third European Conference on Computer Supported Cooperative Work - ECSCW '93*, G.d. Michelis, C. Simone, and K. Schmidt eds., Milan, Kluwer, 1993, pp. 109-124.

Bentley, R., T. Horstmann, K. Sikkel and J. Trevor, *Supporting Collaborative Information Sharing with the WWW: The BSCW Shared Workspace System, The World Wide Web Journal* 1995, pp. 63-73.

Borning, A. and M. Travers, "Two Approaches to Casual Interaction Over Computer and Video Networks", in *Proc. of Proceedings of the Conference on Human Factors in Computing Systems - CHI'91*, New Orleans, LO, ACM, 1991, pp. 13-20.

Broll, W., "SmallTool - A Toolkit for Realizing Shared Virtual Environments on the Internet," *Distributed Systems Engeneering - Special Issue on Distributed Virtual Environments*, 1998, Vol. No. 5, pp. 118-128.

Dourish, P. and V. Bellotti, "Awareness and Coordination in Shared Workspaces", in *Proc. of CSCW '92 - Sharing Perspectives*, J. Turner and R. Kraut eds., Toronto, Canada, ACM Press, 1992, pp. 107-114.

Dourish, P. and S. Bly, "Portholes: Supporting Awareness in a Distributed Work Group", in *Proc. of Proceedings of the Conference on Human Factors in Computing Systems - CHI'92*, Monterey, CA, ACM, 1992, pp. 541-547.

Fitzpatrick, G., S. Parsowith, B. Segall and S. Kaplan, "Tickertape: Awareness in a Single Line", in *Proc. of CHI'98: ACM SIGCHI Conference on Human Factors in Computing*, Los Angeles, CA, ACM Press, 1998,

Fuchs, L., *Situationsorientierte Unterstützung von Gruppenwahrnehmung in CSCW-Systemen*, in GMD-Research Series, GMD, 176 pages, 1998. http://www.gmd.de/publications/-research/1998/003/

Fuchs, L., U. Pankoke-Babatz and W. Prinz, "Supporting Cooperative Awareness with Local Event Mechanisms: The GroupDesk System", in *Proc. of Fourth European Conference on Computer-Supported Cooperative Work: ECSCW '95*, H. Marmolin, Y. Sundblad, and K. Schmidt eds., Stockholm, Kluwer Academic Publishers, 1995, pp. 247-262.

Fuchs, L., S. Poltrock and R. Wojcik, "Business Value of 3D Virtual Environments," *ACM SIGGROUP Bulletin*, 1998, Vol. 19, No. 3, pp. 25-29.

Gutwin, C., S. Greenberg and M. Roseman, "Workspace Awareness in Real-Time Distributed Groupware: Framework, Widgets, and Evaluation", in *Proc. of HCI'96: Conference on Computer Human Interaction: People and Computers*, London, UK, Springer-Verlag, Heidelberg, 1996, pp. 281-298.

Gutwin, C., M. Roseman and S. Greenberg, "A Usability Study of Awareness Widgets in a Shared Workspace Groupware System", in *Proc. of CSCW'96: Conference on Computer Supported Cooperative Work*, M.S. Ackermann eds., Boston, MA., ACM Press, 1996, pp. 258-267.

Hoschka, P., *The Social Web*, 1998, GMD-FIT, http://orgwis.gmd.de/projects/SocialWeb/

Hudson, S.E. and I. Smith, "Techniques for Addressing Fundamental Privacy and Disruption Tradeoffs in Awareness Support Systems", in *Proc. of Conference on Computer Supported Cooperative Work (CSCW'96)*, M.S. Ackermann eds., Boston, MA., ACM, 1996, pp. 248-257.

Ishii, H. and B. Ullmer, "Tangible Bits: Towards Seamless Interfaces between People, Bits and Atoms", in *Proc. of CHI'97: Conference on Human Factors in Computing Systems*, Altanta, GA, ACM Press, 1997,

Lee, A., A. Girgensohn and K. Schlueter, "NYNEX Portholes: Initial User Reactions and Redesign Implications", in *Proc. of Group'97 Conference*, S. Hayne and W. Prinz eds., Phoenix, AZ, ACM Press, 1997, pp. 385-394.

Lövstrand, L., "Being selectively aware with the Khronika System", in *Proc. of 2nd European Conference on Computer Supported Cooperative Work*, L. Bannon, M. Robinson, and K. Schmidt eds., Amsterdam, Kluwer Academic Publishers, 1991, pp. 265-277.

Mariani, J. and W. Prinz, "From Multi-User to Shared Object Systems: Awareness about Co-Workers in Cooperation Support Object Databases", in *Informatik - Wirtschaft - Gesellschaft*, H. Reichel (eds.), Springer, Berlin Heidelberg, 1993, pp. 476-481. http://orgwis.gmd.de/~prinz/pub/gi93-awareness.html

McGrath, A., "The Forum," *ACM SIGGROUP Bulletin*, 1998, Vol. 19, No. 3, pp. 21-24.

Mohr, G., S. Aggarwal, M. Day, A. Houri, Y. Kohda and D. Marvit, *PIP-DEMO: An Interoperable Presence Information Protocol*, 1999, http://www.ietf.org/internet-draft/draft-mohr-pip-pipdemo-00.txt

Nomura, T., K. Hayashi, T. Hazama and S. Gudmundson, "Interlocus: Workspace Configuration Mechanisms for Activity Awareness", in *Proc. of CSCW '98: ACM Conference on Computer Supported Cooperative Work*, Seattle, ACM Press, 1998, pp. 19-28.

Palfreyman, K. and T. Rodden, "A Protocol for User Awareness on the World Wide Web", in *Proc. of Conference on Computer Supported Cooperative Work (CSCW'96)*, M.S. Ackermann eds., Boston, MA., ACM Press, 1996, pp. 130-139.

Patterson, J.F., M. Day and J. Kucan, "Notification Servers for Synchronous Groupware", in *Proc. of Conference on Computer Supported Cooperative Work (CSCW'96)*, M.S. Ackermann eds., Boston, MA., ACM Press, 1996, pp. 122-129. http://www.lotus.com/home.nsf/-welcome/research

Ramduny, D., A. Dix and T. Rodden, "Exploring the Design Space for Notification Servers", in *Proc. of CSCW '98: ACM Conference on Computer Supported Cooperative Work*, Seattle, ACM Press, 1998, pp. 227-236.

Rodden, T., "Populating the Application: A Model of Awareness for Cooperative Applications", in *Proc. of Conference on Computer Supported Cooperative Work (CSCW'96)*, M.S. Ackermann eds., Boston, MA., ACM, 1996, pp. 87-96.

Roseman, M. and S. Greenberg, "TeamRooms: Network Places for Collaboration", in *Proc. of Conference on Computer Supported Cooperative Work (CSCW'96)*, M.S. Ackermann eds., Boston, MA., ACM Press, 1996, pp. 325-333.

Saffo, P., *Sensors: The Next Wave of Infotech Innovation*, Institute for the Future, 1998, http://www.iftf.org/sensors/sensors.html

Sandor, O., C. Bogdan and J. Bowers, "Aether: An Awareness Engine for CSCW", in *Proc. of ECSCW'97: Fifth European Conference on Computer Supported Cooperative Work*, H. Hughes, W. Prinz, *et al.* eds., Lancaster, UK, Kluwer, 1997, pp. 221-236.

Saraswat, V., *Instand Messaging and Presence Activity in the IETF*, 1. Nov., 1998, http://www.research.att.com/~vj/imp.html

Segall, B. and D. Arnold, "Elvin has left the building: A publish/subscribe notification service with quenching", in *Proc. of AUUG*, Brisbane, AU, http://www.dstc.edu.au/Elvin/, 1997,

Siedler, G., A. Scott and H. Wolf, "Collaborative Browsing in the World Wide Web", in *Proc. of JENC8: 8th Joint European Networking Conference*, Edinburgh, 1997,

Sohlenkamp, M., *Supporting Group Awareness in Multi-User Environments through Perceptualization*, PhD, Universität Paderborn, Fachbereich Mathematik-Informatik, 1998, 160 pages.

Sohlenkamp, M. and G. Chwelos, "Integrating Communication, Cooperation and Awareness: The DIVA Virtual Office Environment", in *Proc. of Conference on Computer Supported Cooperative Work*, R. Furuta and C. Neuwirth eds., Chapel Hill, NC, USA, ACM Press, 1994, pp. 331-344.

Sohlenkamp, M., W. Prinz and L. Fuchs, "PoliAwac - Design and Evaluation of an Awareness Enhanced Groupware Client," *AI and Society - Special Issue on CSCW*, 1999, to appear.

Tollmar, K., O. Sandor and A. Schömer, "Supporting Social Awareness @ Work, Design and Experience", in *Proc. of Conference on Computer Supported Cooperative Work (CSCW'96)*, M.S. Ackermann eds., Boston, MA., ACM, 1996, pp. 298-307.

Trevor, J., T. Koch and G. Woetzel, "MetaWeb: Bringing synchronous groupware to the World Wide Web", in *Proc. of ECSCW'97: Fifth European Conference on Computer Supported Cooperative Work*, J. Hughes, W. Prinz, *et al.* eds., Lancaster, UK, Kluwer, 1997, pp. 65-80. http://bscw.gmd.de/bscw_help/english/sec-53.html

Wisneski, C., H. Ishii, A. Dahley, M. Gorbet, S. Brave, B. Ullmer, and P. Yarin, "Ambient Displays: Turning Architectural Space into an Interface between People and Digital Information", in *Cooperative Buildings - Integrating Information, Organization,and Architecture,* N.A. Streitz, S. Konomi, and H.-J. Burkhardt (eds.), Springer - LNCS, 1998, pp. 22-32.

S. Bødker, M. Kyng, and K. Schmidt (eds.). *Proceedings of the Sixth European Conference on Computer-Supported Cooperative Work, 12-16 September 1999, Copenhagen, Denmark*
©1999 Kluwer Academic Publishers. Printed in the Netherlands

411

Meaning-Making Across Remote Sites: How Delays in Transmission Affect Interaction

Karen Ruhleder
University of Illinois, USA, *ruhleder@uiuc.edu*

Brigitte Jordan
Xerox Palo Alto Research Center, USA, *jordan@parc.xerox.com*

Abstract: Distributed organizations increasingly rely on new video-supported communication technologies that may be subject to transmission delays. These delays systematically misalign the feedback one side receives from the other. Through micro-analysis of video data from a video-supported meeting in a geographically distributed company, we examine the impact of delay in such communication systems. We specify some ways in which they may subliminally affect communication between remote parties. We illustrate typical kinds of breakdown and conclude with observations about the impact of delays on distributed interaction and the ways in which these impacts can be mediated.

Remote Communication

Defining the Problem

Companies, government agencies and academic institutions increasingly rely on remote communication to carry out their daily work. Audio, video and data communication between remote teams are become increasingly common, and their use in certain settings is already almost unremarkable. Yet, in spite of the fact that significant sums are being spent on the acquisition of technologies to support distributed work, we are only beginning to understand the intricacies of these interactions. This paper identifies and analyzes one particular limitation of video-based teleconferencing integral to an on-going dialogue within the CSCW community, that is, the impact of an audio and video delay on distributed communication. Our aim is to map out this obstacle through our analysis and to suggest ways in which designers and users can establish a synergy between new technologies and new work practices.

We are engaged in long-term research to investigate how communication technologies affect interaction and collaboration across distributed sites. Our approach for the current phase of our research focuses both on the *types of interactions* carried out over remote links and on the *characteristics of the technologies* which support (or hinder) those exchanges. Specifically, we are interested in what interactions may be best suited for different kinds of remote communication and what work practices are required to support them.

The body of our paper is concerned with a detailed micro-analysis of some of the interactions the new video-, audio- and data-sharing technologies support. In particular, we explore in detail the impact which technology-generated delays may have on shared meaning-making between remote participants. In the final section, we draw conclusions about the significance of our findings for understanding talk, interaction and collaboration across remote links and provide a potential set of recommendations for both designers, users and implementors who seek to integrate these new technologies into their worklife.

Delay

One feature of some remote communication technologies is that they generate transmission delays. Whenever this is the case, what is said and heard by users on each side of the communications link is different, but in such a way that neither side is aware of the discrepancy. To put it another way, communicants are not co-present to the communication in the same way. Consider a conversation between two remote collaborators. One person asks her collaborator a question, which he answers as he hears it. She, however, hears the response as coming after a gap determined by the length of the delay inherent in the technology. He thinks he has answered promptly, she thinks his response was delayed. This has, as we shall see, far-reaching consequences.

Some of the computer conferencing systems in current use generate a delay of one second or more. Earlier work has identified certain effects of video-based communication which may be related to this delay phenomenon (O'Conaill, et al., 1993; Sellen, 1995). This includes a lower frequency of backchannels, speaker feedback, and interruptions, as well as an increase in formal hand-overs. While Sellen finds no effect on turn frequency, duration, and distribution, O'Conaill, et al., noted that longer turns with deliberate hand-offs and trouble switching speakers characterized interactions via technologies with an inherent delay.

Our findings offer further evidence for and additional illustration of these observations. In our analysis, we see that the interaction of the delay with the conversation on either side leads to unusual phenomena, such as words getting swapped around or comments occurring out of place because of the delay. The causes and consequences of these phenomena are often invisible to participants. Only by detailed review of transcripts, based on a painstaking micro-analysis of the interaction, can one see the lack of alignment occasioned by the delay, and the ways in which the delay contributes if not to breakdown at least to potentially serious shifts in meaning. While our setting did not enable us to compare our results to face-to-face meeting situations between the same group of people, a subsequent meeting with an audio-plus-shared workspace set-up was not characterized by any of the problems we observed in the audio-plus-video meeting situation.

The work of O'Conaill, et al. (1993) and Sellen (1995) as well as our own may offer insight into why research across multiple environments has found greater discomfort, lower levels of trust and greater skepticism about others' competence in remote interaction (c.f., Isaacs, et al., 1995; Olson, et al., 1995; Storck and Sproull, 1995; c.f. also early work on delay and telephony, i.e., Riesz and Klemmer, 1963). The phenomenon we describe here, technology-generated delays, may play a role in these dynamics within the context of teleconferencing. We hypothesize that the mechanisms through which transmission delay affects trust and confidence between communicants is *turntaking,* a key element in demonstrating social and subject matter competence.

Understanding the impact of delay is particularly important in light of Sellen's (1995) and Whittaker's (1995) findings that audio forms the essential component in distributed interaction, and Heath and Luff's (1993) complementary finding that video mediated communication makes the performative impact of nonverbal behavior problematic. These findings are set against the significant positive contributions which video can make to collaborative interactions, especially in its ability to support the coordination of distributed collaboration by providing cues about availability, current state, and awareness (Sellen, 1995; Whittaker, 1995; Heath and Luff, 1993; Dourish & Bellotti, 1992). Furthermore, the availability of a synchronous, video-based medium as part of a broader suite of technologies facilitates interaction and improved communication, and long-term users of video-conferencing evolve both visual and verbal strategies to address certain kinds of interactional problems and strengthen certain benefits (Dourish, et al., 1996; Tang and Isaacs, 1993).

This paper is driven by these findings. It identifies particular classes of interactional problems, some of which may have no easy counter-strategy as they are not available to the user in real-time. We draw on these observations in our concluding section, in which we suggest design issues, implementation strategies, and work practices which may ameliorate the impact of delay and enable the realization of the powerful benefits video-conferencing offers.

Turntaking

Taking turns at talk is the basic mechanism for interaction, and is supported by both verbal and non-verbal cues (Kendon, 1967; Sacks, et al., 1974). It forms a hidden, underlying foundation for order in human interaction. Conversational turntaking is as critical in informal interaction between individuals as it is in corporate negotiations. Communicants have the expectation that other participants in an interaction will appropriately enact the rules which govern social intercourse. Situation-appropriate turntaking is the foundation for ascribing competence to others in face-to-face interaction. When disrupted, it can lead to frustration and misunderstanding (Jordan and Fuller, 1975; Schegloff, et al., 1977).

To be social means to take appropriate turns. This is true on the conversational level, within systems of etiquette, and in social norms about gift exchanges, favors, and reciprocal invitations. Explicit and tacit turntaking systems have shaped human discourse throughout history, between generations, on conscious and unconscious levels. Turntaking is part of what it means to be human, and being able to enact a particular turntaking system is part of what it means to be a competent member of a particular social group.

In verbal exchanges, speakers signal the end of a turn in a number of ways. They may do this by pitch of voice, by body language, by asking a question, or by verbally letting people know that their story is done ("and that was that!"). Who gets to speak next is governed by a basic set of rules for turntaking, here paraphrased from a seminal paper by Sacks, Schegloff and Jefferson (1974):

(1) When the current speaker reaches a point at which they may be done taking a turn, one of three things happen:

(a) The current speaker can pass along the turn to another person by gaze or recipient design (e.g., finishing in a way that suggests a next speaker).

(b) If no particular person is indicated through linguistic or non-verbal cues, the first person who starts speaking gets the next turn.

(c) If no one else takes a turn, the original speaker can resume, often building on or adding to the prior turn.

(2) These rules hold sway throughout the conversation.

Applying rules of this sort is something speakers are competent to do as members of a particular social system. Their application is invisible, and requires split second timing. This timing is finely coordinated between speakers and listeners. A disruption of this system leads to anywhere from discomfort to breakdown or open rupture.

For current purposes we are interested in the turntaking that happens in conversations between groups of people whose talk is mediated by technologies subject to transmission delay, and in the ways in which that differs from what would happen if the parties were physically co-present. Current understanding of conversational rules derives largely from face-to-face settings. Yet we can predict that the circumstances under which people "talk" to each other will become increasingly electronic in the society of the future.

In face-to-face conversation and other speech exchange systems such as lectures or court proceedings, when trouble occurs (if, for example, somebody answers in a way that the hearer finds inappropriate) a repair is promptly initiated and carried out (Jordan and Fuller, 1975; Schegloff, et al., 1977; Schegloff, 1979b). People ask, "huh?" or look confused, or don't take their turn when they should. The original speaker immediately repairs the problem by repeating or rephrasing the utterance. The repair is initiated by a "trouble flag"— the "huh?" or confused look that tells the speaker that something is not right. Key here is that the trouble flag serves as a *shared resource* for multiple participants in an exchange: both parties present understand that something has gone wrong and must be fixed.

In technology-mediated remote communication there may be no trouble flag comparable to that of face-to-face communication. The origin of a problem may not be available to either speaker or hearer, as a conversation will be heard differently on each side of the link. As a consequence, no specific repair can be initiated. This leaves participants with a vague but pervasive feeling that something is "not quite right." In "normal" conversation, hitches in the sequencing of turns are routinely seen and treated as evidence for trouble in the interaction and are remedied by repairs of various sorts. The disturbances in turntaking generated by transmission delays are particularly insidious because they raise no easily identifiable trouble flags.

Data and Methods

The Data

Our data are derived from a broader ethnographic study of a now-defunct holding company which used cutting-edge groupware and communication technologies to support a distributed work environment (Ruhleder and Jordan, 1997; Ruhleder, et al., 1996). Company headquarters managed several business units distributed across the United States. Lotus Notes® and remote meeting technologies such as LiveBoard® and PictureTel® were widely disseminated in order to facilitate interactions between headquarters and these geographically distributed holdings.

We carried out fieldwork over a period of four months, collecting data at headquarters and several business units through participant observation, unstructured interviews, and review of on-line and paper materials. The resulting data set includes a number of video tapes capturing both sides of various small- and large-group remote interactions using both audio-plus-shared workspace and audio-plus-video technologies, from which we derive the data for this paper.

In this paper, we draw on a 19-minute video segment including pre-meeting and meeting activities between three East Coast software developers and three West Coast accountants. The meeting was conducted using PictureTel, a video-conferencing technology, and was organized as a preliminary discussion for a software prototype demonstration set up for the following day. Ann is one of the three accountants, and Bill is one of the three developers. Neither the genders nor the names necessarily correspond to those of the original participants, and the excerpts we are presenting were all drawn from interactions between the most senior members of each group. Neither the developers nor the accountants have had extensive experience with video-conferencing. Though all three accountants and the most senior member of the developers' group have vicarious knowledge of the technology through attendance at large, formal video-conference meetings, this is only the second meeting which they themselves initiated.

Our analysis in this paper focuses on the audio component of the transmission. Because of the delay of approximately one second, we noticed that what one side heard was different from what the other side heard. Silences were of different duration, cues came at the wrong times. We identified 32 episodes within the 19 minute interaction which exhibited these characteristics and in which these characteristics were identified by multiple analysts without the aid of any special technological manipulation or assistance (slowing the sounds down, using a metronome, etc.).

Methods: Interaction Analysis

If turntaking is foundational to ordered human interaction and forms the basis for social life, then people or groups having two fundamentally different conversations with each other raises serious questions about what it means to "share" a conversation in a distributed setting. It challenges our notion of a mutually-constructed reality.

In order to examine this phenomenon, we analyzed videotapes of participants' activities on both sides of a remote communications link using video-based Interaction Analysis, as outlined in Jordan and Henderson (1995). This technique consists of an in-depth micro-analysis of how people interact with one another, their physical environment with its documents and artifacts, and their "virtual" or "distributed" environment with its remote participants and shared electronic artifacts. Like ethnography in general, Interaction Analysis looks for orderliness and patterns in people's routine interactions, but operates at a finer level of detail than conventional ethnographic observation. The roots of this technique lie in ethnography, sociolinguistics, kinesics, proxemics, and ethology. However, it has been shaped most significantly by conversation analysis and ethnomethodology. Having emerged over the past 20 years as a distinct form of analysis, it has been extended to a wide variety of organizational settings, and can serve as one source of insight for designers and practitioners (Button and Dourish, 1996).

Interaction Analysis involves several different types of activities on the part of the ethnographer or ethnographic team. Extensive ethnographic fieldwork enables the researcher to identify specific interactions for video taping and furnishes a background against which the video taping is carried out. Video tape content logs provide an overview of the data corpus for locating sequences for further analysis.

Collaborative tape analysis is carried out within a multi-disciplinary research group. Analytic categories are allowed to emerge out of a deepening understanding of the taped participants' interaction. Emerging patterns are checked against other tape sequences and against other forms of ethnographic observations.

These activities are iterative, and frequently overlap. Content logs generate potential tape sequences for analysis; tape analysis suggests further content logging and transcribing according to emergent categories. This, in turn, identifies new sequences for analysis, or suggests new venues for video taping. The application of Interaction Analysis to this particular project is outlined in more detail in (Ruhleder and Jordan, 1997).

Turntaking and Technology

Turning now to the analysis of videotaped remote interaction, we note that according to the rules of conversational interaction mentioned above, a current speaker may pass along a turn, or simply indicate that they are done with their turn, at which point another person present can take a turn. We are interested in what happens when turntaking is disrupted because of a delay in transmission. Consider the *hypothetical* conversation in Figure 1, in which no transmission delay occurs.[1]

what Ann says	what Ann hears	time in sec	what Bill hears	what Bill says
Ann says: Did you get the report I sent you?		1.00	**Bill hears:** *Did you get the report I sent you?*	
	Ann hears: *Yes, thanks.*	2.00		**Bill says:** Yes, thanks.

Figure 1: Face-to-face, no transmission delay

Ann and Bill are in the same room, speaking face-to-face. When Ann (far left column) asks a question, Bill hears it right away as she speaks it (second column from the right). When Bill replies (far right column), Ann hears the response as it is being produced (second column from the left). Bill has access to multiple cues that suggest that a response is called for, including not only the tone of the speaker's voice, but also the speaker's gaze, body orientation, and gesture. Ann asks a question and Bill offers a response that is prompt and appropriate to the

---

[1] This fragment is derived from a video-mediated interaction. We use a hypothetical example to illustrate how the same utterance may be experienced differently under different circumstances.

situation. It may be worth noting here that the speed with which an answer is delivered is implicative. Face-to-face and on the phone a negative response to a question is routinely foreshadowed by a brief pause, often followed by "uh," "well..." or "yes, but...," or something of that sort. In other words, a pause in this spot potentially indicates an upcoming disagreement.

What happens if Ann and Bill are in different locations, and the medium they are using generates a one second transmission delay? Let's now consider the same hypothetical conversation and the subtle differences engendered by the delay, outlined in Figure 2.

what Ann says	what Ann hears	time in sec	what Bill hears	what Bill says
Ann says: Did you get the report I sent you?		1.00		
	(Ann hears silence)	2.00	***Bill hears:*** *Did you get the report I sent you?*	
	(Ann hears silence)	3.00		**Bill says:** Yes, thanks.
	Ann hears: *Yes, thanks.*	4.00		

Figure 2: Technology mediated, one second delay

Ann and Bill are not in the same room, but are speaking via a teleconferencing set-up. When Ann speaks (far left column), Bill hears the question about a second later. Ann, meanwhile, hears no response at all. When Bill replies (far right column), Ann still hears no response for a full second. Bill perceives his answer as having been given promptly, but Ann perceives a delay in the response. Additionally, due to the generally low quality of video as implemented in today's teleconferencing systems, both parties have only limited access to interactional cues such as a speaker's gaze, body orientation, and gesture. Ann asks a question and, while there may still be a shared perception about the appropriateness of the answer, there is no longer a shared perception about its promptness.

If from Bill's perspective, this particular exchange is essentially the same as above— Bill heard Ann's question and responded— from Ann's perspective the delayed response opens up multiple new interpretations. She may recognize it as a phenomenon of the technology. Human delay, however, may also signal hesitancy or doubt, subconsciously triggering a set of questions. Why isn't Bill responding? Does he know what report she is talking about? Is he trying to remember whether the report was in yesterday's mail? Is he angry about the contents of the report and doesn't know how to say this? Within this turntaking system, waiting for the response to a simple question raises a trouble flag in the interaction, but in this setting, it would be a flag operational only for one party.

In this hypothetical example, Ann waited and Bill's response eventually reached her. All sorts of other variations are possible: Ann could have rephrased the question during the delay, she could have decided to drop the topic altogether and move on, or she could have given further justification for why she asked her question. Depending on her choice, Bill might have come to believe that she is not all that competent or that she is uninterested in the issue on the table.

Some of Ann's choices would have led to crossovers and collisions in terms of her conversation with Bill. In all cases, however, what happened on her side of the link would have been *different* from what happens on the Bill's side in terms of the words they heard and the conversation in which they think they are participating.

Below, we look at these crossovers and collisions and the meanings they may generate on each side of the link from the perspective of the rules that govern turntaking in conversation. We do that by examining the data described above, drawing from 32 episodes in which we see the rules of normal turntaking undermined, and in which cues used to follow the rules are not accessible as they are in face-to-face settings. Our examples constitute discrete, identifiable instances in which the transmission delay inherent in the technology did not allow for the successful application of the conversational rules outlined in (Sacks, et al., 1974).

Collisions and Swaps

Unless the previous speaker selected a specific next speaker at the end of a turn (e.g., "How about you, Gitti?"), another person can start or the first speaker can resume (Sachs, et al., 1974:704). In settings where the audio signal is significantly delayed and visual cues are not helpful, the effectiveness of this turntaking system breaks down in subtle ways for the simple reason that what one side hears and responds to is not what the other side hears and responds to. In Figure 3, we see what happens when speakers are unable to perceive the cues for applying the rules.

what Ann says	what Ann hears	time in sec	what Bill hears	what Bill says
Ann says: Will Omega Group join us?		1.00		
		2.00	*Bill hears: Will Omega Group join us?*	
Ann says: They're not being involved?		3.00		Bill says: No.
	Ann hears: No.	4.00	*Bill hears: They're not being involved?*	
Ann says: OK		5.00		
		6.00	*Bill hears: OK.*	

Figure 3: "Will Omega Group join us?"

In this example, Ann and Bill are talking about an upcoming meeting. They are in the process of working out which groups will take part in the discussion. Note that in the excerpt, Bill's answer, "no," to Ann's question, "Will Omega group join us?," is heard by Ann as the answer to her *second* question, "they're not being involved?"

Let's consider this exchange from Ann's perspective. Ann, in asking, "Will Omega Group join us?" has completed a turn, designating Bill as the next speaker. She waits for his answer, but receives no indication that he has heard the question or that he needs to think about the answer ("Gee, I might have to check with so-and-so on that."). After a second has passed, Ann rephrases the question, "They're not involved?" She now hears what seems to be a prompt answer to her question, "No," which she acknowledges with equal promptness, "OK."

Let's consider this now from Bill's perspective. Bill hears the question and answers it promptly, "No." With this answer, Bill has completed a turn and, according to the rules for turntaking, it is quite appropriate for Ann to take the next turn with a response or another question. But Ann's response is not meaningful in context. Bill has already told her that Omega group is not involved. Her "OK" is too late and out of sequence if it is to serve as an acknowledgment of his answer to the original question.

On each side, the rules for conversation and the orderly interchange of words have been met, yet they have not facilitated the orderly creation of shared meaning. On both sides an awkward moment arises: Ann repeats a question she thinks Bill hadn't addressed, leading Bill to hear a question he thought he had already answered. Without an understanding of the delay phenomenon, and working in real-time, each instance could be interpreted negatively. Delayed or inappropriate responses could indicate the other party is not paying attention ("is Bill listening?"), doesn't have necessary information ("but he works with Omega group"), or challenges someone's statement ("I already told Ann 'no'").

It would be difficult if not impossible for individuals on either side of the link to identify the source of trouble— the technology delay— within their real-time experience, as the other's conversation appears to be occurring naturally and spontaneously. Multiple instances of this kind open up the possibility of rising confusion or discomfort across the link.

Unnecessary Rephrasings

The rules for turntaking imply that when one person is done, another person may pick up the conversational ball. If a speaker comes to the end of a turn without indicating who should go next, and finds that there are no self-selecting next speakers, he or she may resume with several options. One of these options is to rephrase the previous utterance. This rephrasing might elaborate on part of the previous utterance, and may also serve to specifically select or narrow down the choice of next speaker.

We have identified 12 instances in our 32 episodes where this orderly progression is disturbed in some way. The cases fall into one of two categories. In some instances, the speaker on one side of the link had selected the next speaker, but restated or rephrased their question when they perceived a lack of response due to the delay (see Figure 3, above). On the other side of the link, however, the speaker had responded appropriately. In other cases, the speaker on one side of the link acted in accordance with a perception that no self-selection of next speaker had taken place. On the other side of the link, however, the next speaker had self-selected. The result in both cases was somewhere between confusion and collision.

Figure 4 illustrates one form of collision resulting from unnecessary rephrasing. In this excerpt, Bill is just finishing up an answer to a previous question about the status of a particular component of the software being developed.

What Ann Says	What Ann Hears	time in .5 sec	What Bill Hears	What Bill says
		1.00		Bill says: ....through the report screens.
		1.50	(Bill hears silence)	
	Ann hears: ...through the report screens.	2.00		Bill says: Maybe I
Ann says: So you're		2.50		Bill says: didn't communicate
	Ann hears: Maybe I didn't communicate	3.00	*Bill hears: So you're*	Bill says: that clearly.
	Ann hears: that clearly.	3.50		
Ann says: Yeah.		4.00		
Ann says: You're farther along		4.50	*Bill hears: Yeah.*	
Ann says: than we expected...		5.00	*Bill hears: You're farther along...*	

Figure 4: Communicating Clearly?

Ann hears Bill finish an explanation about the report screens. He has completed a turn, and she attempts to take the next turn. Just as she begins to speak, she hears Bill break in with a statement about not having communicated the status clearly. She responds to him, "Yeah," then returns to her original statement commenting on the status of the project.

Bill, on the other hand, experiences the episode differently. He finishes his explanation, but receives no acknowledgment or comment. He adds a statement about half a second later, suggesting that his explanation wasn't clear enough, thereby downgrading his own competence ever so slightly. Towards the end, Bill hears the start of Ann's next turn overlap with the completion of his own. Then there is a second's worth of silence, an affirmative, and Ann's continuation.

Note what happens here and how this interaction may be interpreted as a lack of competence on multiple levels. From a turntaking perspective, both speakers have behaved inappropriately, Bill cutting Ann off at 3.00 (from her perspective), and Ann not waiting until Bill is finished at 3.00 (from his perspective).

The ordering of utterances and duration of silences here also causes problems in terms of each side's ability to judge the competence or understanding of the other. Bill's comment at 2.00 about not having communicated clearly, which comes in reaction to a lack of response from Ann, implies that he thinks she didn't understand his explanation. But she did, and her attempt at introducing a follow-on to his explanation at 2.50 shows that she has understood it and knows what it means within the context of the project. That acknowledgment, which would have signaled successful communication, gets cut off by Bill's comment about a lack of communication. After her "yeah" she continues her original statement about how far along the project is.

In these small ways, competence is repeatedly called into question on multiple levels. People appear to behave incompetently as turn takers in a conversation, even as they themselves work hard to play by the rules. And people make statements that appear inappropriate within their local context because that context is not shared by both parties. What is the impact of these kinds of situations where trouble is apparent to only one side of the link? And what happens when multiple exchanges pile trouble upon trouble on both sides of the link?

Misapplied Feedback

In face-to-face conversation, participants who do not currently have the floor communicate with the speaker through various types of feedback (c.f., Jefferson, 1984; Yngve, 1970; but esp. Schegloff, 1981). Feedback to the speaker can provide acknowledgment or confirm understanding on the listener's part through expressions such as "mm, hm" and "yeah"; sentence completion; requests for clarification ("such as?"); brief restatements ("in Omega" following "we'll ask everyone in Omega group"); and head nods and shakes. They offer an opportunity for shared meaning-making, giving both speaker and audience confidence that they are on the same wavelength (Jordan and Fuller, 1975).

The sequencing of these kinds of messages is systematically related to signals from the speaker. They occur when the speaker has been looking away and turns towards the listener or completes a grammatical clause. They may also be a response to the speaker's elicitation of confirmation or acknowledgment (Schegloff, 1981). At these points, it is appropriate for the listener to signal that they are still paying attention and that they continue to understand (c.f., Goodwin, 1981; Kendon, 1967).

In video-supported remote conversation, the medium may fail to support these mechanisms (Dourish and Bellotti, 1992; Sellen and Harper, 1997). In fact, feedback may actually disrupt the discourse it was intended to support because participants provide feedback or indicate understanding at what is an appropriate point from their point of view, but is heard at a moment when it does not produce the intended meaning. Figure 5 illustrates how intended supportive feedback can induce a noticeable, unintended pause or hesitation in the speaker's utterance.

<table>
<tr><td colspan="2">Ann's perspective</td></tr>
<tr><td>Bill: ...we could all sit around the table and look at it. But in the future, I think that's (pause) why...</td></tr>
<tr><td>Ann: I see</td></tr>
<tr><td colspan="2">Bill's perspective</td></tr>
<tr><td>Bill: ...we could all sit around the table and look at it. But in the future, I think that's (pause) why...</td></tr>
<tr><td>Ann: I see</td></tr>
</table>

Figure 5: "But in the future..."

Ann is listening to Bill's plan for the demo. Her comment, "I see," is spoken directly after Bill has delivered a key point, appropriately indicating comprehension on her part. Ann hears Bill continue, then pause for no reason apparent to her before going on. Bill hears the dialogue differently. On his side of the link, Ann's, "I see," is heard at a conversationally inappropriate place. Instead of being placed at the end of a sentence or after a grammatical clause, and instead of reflecting back understanding, it comes in the middle of a new utterance.

From Ann's perspective, she has behaved helpfully by confirming an understanding of Bill's arrangements for an upcoming meeting. She has no access to the reason why Bill might hesitate or pause in the middle of a sentence. From his perspective, however, her utterance formed an interruption. It broke his stride, leading him to pause a moment before continuing.

Conclusions and Implications

Talk is not just about the exchange of information, but about shared meaning-making on multiple levels. The examples above illustrate how delay impacts the ability of conversational participants to create shared meaning through talk via remote communication technologies. In each case:

- some kind of trouble arises,
- this trouble disrupts the turntaking system, and
- the trouble source *cannot be identified* by participants.

Participants may sense that something might be "wrong"— in several examples above, for instance, one person appears to violate the rules of the turntaking system by interrupting or saying something contextually inappropriate. The nature of the distributed technology, however, may preclude people from identifying the trouble and making repairs. Even when people know about the delay as a technical specification of the system, they may have difficulty recognizing and adjusting their meaning construction *in real-time* in the course of producing talk over the link as part of a broader set of work activities.

The potential consequence is a pervasive sense of uneasiness similar to that described in Jordan and Fuller (1975) where non-native speakers using Spanish as their *lingua franca* were unable to repair trouble in conversation. They knew something was wrong, but they were unable to locate the source of the trouble. We find significant potential for troublesome miscommunication and interpretation in our own data. Here, too, people were unable to identify and repair trouble as it occurred because its origin was obscured.

The point here is not that people break conversational rules. Rather, it is that by seeming to behave in ways that violate the expectations of their conversational partner, multiple explanations for those violations may be generated. Explanations may be generated for seemingly aberrant behavior. In conversations repeatedly punctuated by episodes such as the ones above, these explanations may be overwhelmingly negative when judged within the cultural expectations for turntaking in face-to-face settings.

Implications for Design and Training

Technological systems that support distributed communications are already challenging us to rethink the notion of interaction and to revisit our current understanding of exchange systems. Our paper contributes to this dialogue by examining in close detail one particular kind of twist on "ordinary" conversation: the impact of a delay on the workings of a turntaking system developed within a co-located, face-to-face context. We would like to consider this impact in the following terms:

What people can learn to compensate for. As noted earlier, there is already evidence that people pick up on the delay phenomenon and learn to moderate their manner of speaking (O'Conaill, et al., 1993). As people become more accustomed to these technologies, they will become more facile at adapting their manner of communication to the medium.[2] For years to come, however, corporations and other organizations will have to deal with a continuing stream of novices or people whose very sporadic use of these technologies mitigates against any long-term development of effective delay-compensating work practices.

What people must learn to reinterpret. What people cannot pick up are the more serious class of problems, those where the trouble that is generated by the delay is apparent to only one side *or to neither side* of the interaction. This kind of trouble may be recognizable only through retrospective analysis, while generating

---

[2] Early research in conversation analysis includes the study of telephone conversations, in which greetings, leave-takings and turntaking differ from face-to-face interactions and require participants to draw on different resources in managing turntaking and repair (Schegloff, 1979a).

real-time reactions among participants. As such, people may need to learn to develop a kind of "meta narrative" which analyzes and challenges negative assumptions about one's conversational partners, in the way that people must occasionally remind themselves that the abrupt or angry tone of an email message may be a product of the medium, and not the intention of the other party.

How these findings can guide meeting strategies. If certain forms of conversational patterns are difficult to sustain in interactions characterized by delay, then the use of delay-generating technologies can be focused on those interactions in which trouble is less likely to arise. For instance, interactions with explicitly laid-out rules for turntaking, such as structured events and formal meetings, are less likely to suffer from the kinds of trouble illustrated above. Broader participation in these events through the use of video-conferencing technologies can additionally help draw junior members of the organization more deeply into a distributed community of practice (Ruhleder, et al., 1996; Ruhleder, forthcoming). Brainstorming or design sessions, however, may be more feasible using non-delayed audio-only channels and some form of shared electronic workspace. By understanding the impact of particular technologies on real-time interactions, users and implementors can more effectively chose an appropriate technology set.

How these findings contribute to development efforts. Current development efforts are concerned with ways of indicating presence and attention in remote meetings, such as through gaze. An extension of these efforts may yield a variety of ways of signaling the current state of a conversation, the readiness of a workgroup to move on to the next topic, the nature of feedback to the speaker given by different workgroup members, etc. These development efforts will continue to improve the ability of a workgroup on one side of the link to judge the state or readiness of members on the other side of the link. This may contributed to their ability to manage the impact of the delay. When systems development is driven by inaccurate or incomplete assumptions about conversation, the system itself will fail to effectively support the communication process (Tatar, et al., 1991).

The increased integration of audio-only and video-plus-audio channels into applications for collaborative work also requires the development of technological components and workplace strategies for determining awareness and calling attention to specific activities and elements in the shared workspace. The content of a conversation can be used to maintain awareness (i.e., Dourish and Bellotti, 1992; Hindmarsh, et al., 1998; Hindus, et al., 1996); more importantly from our perspective, the *structure* of an utterance can be used to generate attention (Goodwin 1980). Delays disrupt this fundamental function. While we do not explicitly address this issue in our current paper, our data suggest this as an important consideration in further analyses.

Finally, we suggest that the turntaking system itself be considered with respect to the development and implementation of new communication technologies. In

426

normal, face-to-face conversation, the sequencing of turns forms a basis for meaningful interaction. Hitches, problems and false starts are treated as trouble in interaction which can be repaired. Yet in the interactions we have examined, the affordances of the technology prevented identification of the problem; hence, no repair was possible in real-time. Further research and development in technology-mediated communication must account for the ways in which affordances interact with and affect the turntaking system.

Acknowledgments

Our work has benefited immensely from collaborative working sessions with Manny Schegloff. Valuable input was provided by participants in Xerox Palo Alto Research Center and University of Illinois Interaction Analysis Laboratories.

This research was supported by NSF Grant #9712421, Xerox Palo Alto Research Center, the Institute for Research on Learning, the Graduate School of Library and Information Science, and the University of Illinois Research Board.

References

Button, G., and Dourish, P. (1996): "Technomethodology: Paradoxes and Possibilities," *Proceedings of the Conference on Human Factors in Computing Systems,* pp. 19–26.

Dourish, P., Adler, A., Bellotti, V. and Henderson, A. (1996): "Your Place or Mine? Learning from Long-Term Use of Video Communication," *Computer Supported Cooperative Work: The Journal of Collaborative Computing,* vol. 5, no. 1, pp. 33–62.

Dourish, P., and Bellotti, V. (1992): "Awareness and Coordination in Shared Workspaces," *Proceedings of the Conference on Computer Supported Cooperative Work ,* pp. 107-114.

Garfinkel, H. (1967): *Studies in Ethnomethodology,* Cambridge, MA: Blackwell Publishers.

Goodwin, C. (1980): "Restarts, Pauses, and the Achievement of a State of Mutual Gaze at Turn-Beginnings," *Sociological Inquiry,* vol. 50, nos. 3–4, pp. 272–302.

Goodwin, C. (1981): *Conversational Organization: Interaction between Speakers and Hearers,* New York: Academic Press.

Heath, C. and Luff, P. (1993): "Disembodied conduct: Interactional asymmetries in video-mediated communication," in Button, G., *Technology in Working Order: Studies of Work, Interaction, and Technology,* Routledge, London, pp. 35–54.

Isaacs, E. A., Morris, T., Rodriguez, T. K., and Tang, J. C. (1995): "Comparison of Face-to-face and Distributed Presentations," *Proceedings of the Conference on Human Factors in Computing Systems,* pp. 354–361.

Jefferson, G. (1984): "Notes on a Systematic Deployment of the Acknowledgment Tokens 'Yeah' and 'Mm hm,'" *Papers in Linguistics,* vol. 17, no. 1–4, pp. 197–216.

Jordan, B. and Fuller, N. (1975): "On the Non-Fatal Nature of Trouble: Sense-Making and Trouble-Managing in Lingua Franca Talk," *Semiotica,* vol. 13, no. 1, pp. 1–16.

Jordan, B. and Henderson, A. (1995): "Interaction Analysis: Foundations and Practice," *The Journal of the Learning Sciences,* vol. 4, no. 1, pp. 39–103.

Kendon, A. (1967): Some Functions of Gaze-Direction in Social Interaction. *Acta Psychologica,* vol. 26, pp. 22–63.

O'Conaill, B., Whittaker, S., and Wilbur, S. (1993): "Conversations over video conferences: An evaluation of the spoken aspects of video-mediated communication," *Human-Computer Interaction,* vol. 8, pp. 389–428.

Olson, J. S., Olson, G. M. and Meader D. K. (1995): "What Mix of Video and Audio is Useful for Small Groups Doing Remote Real-time Design Work?" *Proceedings of the Conference on Human Factors in Computing Systems,* pp. 362–367.

Riesz, R. R., and Klemmer, E. T. (1963): "Subjective Evaluation of Delay and Echo Suppressors in Telephone Communications," *The Bell System Technical Journal.* November, pp. 2919–2933.

Ruhleder, K., and Jordan, B. (1997): "Capturing Complex, Distributed Activities." in Lee, A. S., Liebenau, J. and De Gross, J. I. *Information Systems and Qualitative Research,* Chapman and Hall, London, UK, pp. 246–257.

428

Ruhleder, K., Jordan, B., and Elmes, M. (1996): "Wiring the 'New Organization': Integrating Collaborative Technologies and Team-Based Work," *Annual Meeting of the Academy of Management,* http://alexia.lis.uiuc.edu/~ruhleder/publications/96.academy.html.

Sacks, H., Schegloff, E. and Jefferson, G. (1974): "A Simplest Systematics for the Organization of Turntaking for Conversation," *Language,* vol. 50, pp. 696–735.

Schegloff, E., Jefferson, G., and Sacks, H. (1977): The preference for self-correction in the organization of repair in conversation.," *Language,* vol. 53, pp. 361-382.

Schegloff, E. (1979a): "Identification and Recognition in Telephone Openings." In Psathas, G., *Everyday Language: Studies in Ethnomethodology,* pp. 23–78.

Schegloff, E. (1979b): "The relevance of repair to syntax-for-conversation," in Givon, T., *Syntax and Semantics 12: Discourse and Syntax,* Academic Press, New York, pp. 261–288.

Schegloff, E. (1981): "Discourse as an Interactional Achievement: Some Uses of 'Uh huh' and Other Things that Come Between Sentences," in Tannen, D., *Analyzing Discourse: Text and Talk,* Georgetown University Roundtable on Languages and Linguistics, pp. 71–93.

Sellen, A. J., (1995): "Remote conversations: The effects of mediating talk with technology," *Human-Computer Interaction,* vol. 10, pp. 401–444.

Sellen, A. J., and Harper, R. (1997): "Video in Support of Organisational Talk," in Finn, K., Sellen, A. and Wilbur, S., *Video-Mediated Communication.* Lawrence Erlbaum Associates, Mahwah, New Jersey, pp. 225–244.

Storck, J. and Sproull, L. (1995): "Through a Glass Darkly: What Do People Learn in Videoconferences?" *Human-Computer Research,* vol. 22, no. 2, pp. 197-219.

Tang, J. C., and Isaacs, E. (1993): "Why do users like video?" *Computer Supported Cooperative Work: Journal of Collaborative Computing,* vol. 1, no. 3, pp. 163–196.

Tatar, D. G., Foster, G., and Bobrow, D. G. (1991): "Design for conversation: lessons from Cognoter," *International Journal of Man-Machine Studies,* vol. 34, no. 2, pp. 185–209.

Whittaker, S. (1995): "Rethinking video as a technology for interpersonal communications: theory and design implications." *International Journal of Human-Computer Studies,* vol. 42, no. 5, pp. 501–29.

Yngve, V. (1970) On Getting a Word in Edgewise. *Papers of the 6th Regional Meeting of the Linguistic Society of Chicago,* pp. 564–577.

S. Bødker, M. Kyng, and K. Schmidt (eds.). *Proceedings of the Sixth European Conference on Computer-Supported Cooperative Work, 12-16 September 1999, Copenhagen, Denmark*
©1999 Kluwer Academic Publishers. Printed in the Netherlands

Augmenting the Workaday World with Elvin

Geraldine Fitzpatrick, Tim Mansfield, Simon Kaplan, David Arnold, Ted Phelps, Bill Segall
CRC for Distributed Systems Technology, The University of Queensland, Australia 4072. Ph: +61-7-33654310. Fax: +61-7-33654311.
Email: {g.fitzpatrick,t.mansfield,s.kaplan,arnold,phelps,bill}@dstc.edu.au.

This paper addresses the problem of providing effective, computer-based support for awareness and interaction in the distributed workaday world. We report the story of how our content-based pure notification service, called Elvin, became widely adopted in our organisation and elsewhere, augmenting the virtual work environment, and providing perceptual resources for awareness. Examples of its uses include: support for interaction via bi-directional chat-like facilities as well as support for uni-directional notifications, for example push-based information from services such as WWW and email, and notifications of the activities of others through rooms bookings, version control changes, and so on. These uses have had a significant impact on the way people interact with information sources and on social cohesion within the organisation. The attraction of Elvin lies in its conceptual simplicity, absence of built-in policy, expressive power and multilingual range of simple APIs. Its uptake is largely a result of the Tickertape Elvin client, which provides a simple, compelling interface usable in numerous different situations. We contend that even though it does not try to be a collaboration-friendly notification service, Elvin is paradoxically very useful for collaborative awareness and interaction support.

Introduction

Events, such as people arriving or leaving, phones ringing, sighs of frustration, the grind of the coffee machine, the hum of the printer, provide us with the perceptual resources we need to maintain awareness of our environment and of the possibilities we have for interaction with others. We use relevant events to coordinate our work or play: arranging our activities to take account of the exigencies of the moment and work toward our goals, while at the same time filtering out irrelevant events. Frequently this contingent arrangement takes place with little or no conscious effort (Heath and Luff (1992) and Robertson (1997) give more detailed discussions of these phenomena).

In the virtual world, events that would keep us informed of what's going on 'around us' and of who we could interact with become imperceptible. We don't know a file has changed, a colleague has arrived at work or a new directory has been created, and so on, unless we explicitly think (or know) to check. Thus the low-effort mechanisms through which we coordinate our activities in the real world are unavailable to us. That is, there are no inherent mechanisms in the virtual realm by which these actions or events can be made available as a perceptual resource (Robertson 1997) for awareness.

With the growing appreciation for the importance of awareness in promoting a sense of shared place and shared work, there has been an increasing emphasis in the CSCW community on how to provide effective computer-based support for awareness in distributed environments. This has typically taken the form of event-based notification services (Ramduny et al. 1998). However, most tend to be designed to support synchronous collaborative applications, either as an application-specific service (Fuchs et al. 1995) or as a generic service to a single class of applications, for example (Hall et al. 1996; Patterson et al. 1996).

Rather than simply trying to build targeted collaborative environments, our focus is on how we might go about making the workaday world (Moran and Anderson 1990) more 'inherently' collaborative. When much of that workaday world happens within a distributed virtual and physical environment, as it does in our organisation, the DSTC[1], the question becomes one of how can we instrument and augment everyday working tools to give events a virtual presence and to support social interaction.

This paper concerns the design, uses and possibilities for presence and awareness support of a notification service called *Elvin* (Segall and Arnold 1997). Elvin is a generic service middleware designed for distributed systems. Rather than designing it to be domain-specific; Elvin's designers attempted to design a *general-purpose notification service.*

After its construction, it began to be spontaneously used for new purposes by different research and prototyping groups within our organisation, including our own Orbit project (Mansfield et al. 1997). The technical attraction of Elvin lies in its conceptual simplicity, its absence of built-in policy, its expressive power and its multilingual range of simple APIs making it usable by both users and pro-

---

[1] Distributed Systems Technology Centre

grammers of many different biases and skill levels. Its uptake is largely a result of the Tickertape Elvin client, which provided a simple, compelling interface usable in numerous different situations.

We contend that even though it does not try to be collaboration friendly, Elvin (and other pure notification services (Ramduny et al. 1998) like it) is paradoxically very useful for collaborative awareness and interaction support. We will show that this is because it allows us to *augment* the workaday world to provide the perceptual resources for awareness. Its design makes it easy to produce information about events in the virtual (and even, in some cases, the physical) and to select relevant information.

The discussion is structured as follows. First, we outline the design of Elvin, its features and conceptual model. Secondly, we summarise related work. Thirdly, we describe some user and programmer experiences with Elvin gathered by interview from around our organisation. Fourthly, we discuss how the design of Elvin facilitates those experiences and we argue why we think that pure notification services are particularly effective for CSCW. Finally, we discuss future work.

The Elvin Event Notification Service

The function of a notification service is to act as a distributor for *notifications* which we define as descriptions of *events*. We define an event as any significant change in the state of an observed object. *Producers* detect events (and are responsible for determining that the status change is significant), and send descriptions to the notification service for dissemination to interested *consumers*, as shown in Figure 1.

Elvin is a 'pure' notification service (Ramduny et al. 1998): producers send notifications to the service, which in turn sends them to consumers. The notifications describe events using a set of named attributes of simple data types and consumers subscribe to a events using a boolean subscription expression. When a

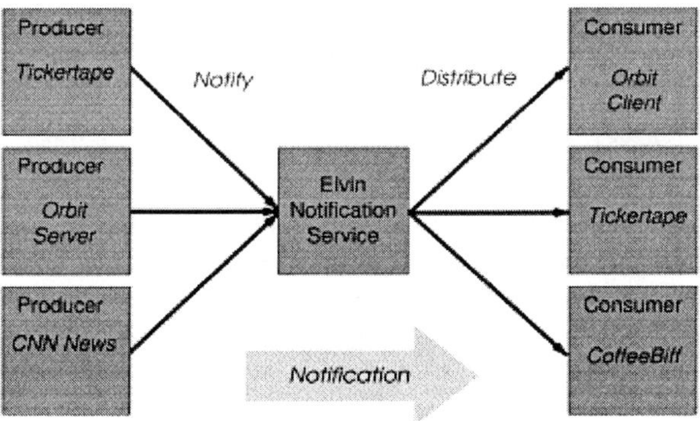

Figure 1. Elvin Architecture Overview.

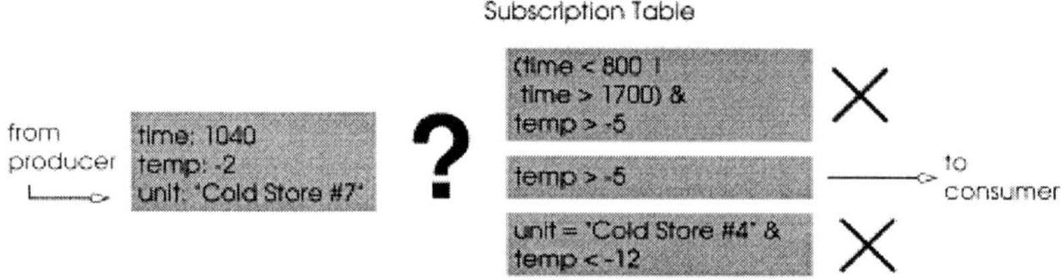

Figure 2. Subscription examples for an environmental monitoring system.

notification is received at the service from a producer, it is compared to the consumers' registered subscription expressions and forwarded to those whose expressions it satisfies. An example of this is given in Figure 2.

This *content-based* selection of notifications is often sacrificed by other notification services in favour of less flexible mechanisms because it is difficult to implement efficiently. A common alternative uses named 'channels' or 'topics' that must be specified by both the producer and consumers. A key benefit of content-based notification is the absence of this 'coupling' between producers and consumers, promoting system evolution and integration.

Once producers are freed of the responsibility to direct notifications, the determination of the significance of a state change becomes less important: they can promiscuously notify any potentially interesting information, and rely on the notification service to discard notifications of no (current) interest to consumers.

While large volumes of unused notifications may be useful from a user's perspective, they consume network bandwidth. To overcome this problem, Elvin includes a *quenching mechanism* which allows producers to discard unneeded notifications without sending them to the server (see Segall and Arnold 1997 for more detailed discussion).

In order to support organisation-wide notification, the implementation of the notification service must cater for many client applications. A single Elvin server can effectively service thousands of clients (producers or consumers) and evaluate tens of thousands of notifications per second on moderate hardware platforms. Further, additional servers can be configured in a *federation*, sharing the load of notification delivery, providing wide-area scalability (allowing Elvin to work across multiple LANs) and ensuring fault-tolerance in the face of individual server failures.

Like other pure notification services, Elvin does not store the notifications it sends – it provides no persistence for notifications.

The Elvin server is implemented in C for Unix platforms, and client-side libraries are available for C, TCL, Smalltalk, Python, Lisp and Java. The basic Elvin services are implemented via several simple library calls that support session setup and termination, producer notification, consumer subscription and callback registration, polling (where required) and quenching.

Producer and consumer commands make the service accessible from a command line shell and from shell scripts. Non-programming users can use graphical tools like Tickertape (see below) to produce and consume certain kinds of notifications.

Related Work

Numerous workplace studies (for example, Heath and Luff 1992) have identified awareness as being crucial for the dynamic coordination of ongoing work. The approaches to computer-based support for awareness are many and varied. Dourish and Bellotti (1992), for example, identify three mechanisms: explicit informational awareness mechanisms (such as those provided by version control system annotation); role-restrictive mechanisms (such as those used in some group editing systems and later in many workflow systems); and shared feedback mechanisms (where information about actions or events is collected and presented as background information in a shared workspace). More recent research has, as observed by Sandor et al (1997) evidenced an overwhelming concern with such event-based shared feedback approaches to awareness, which are more flexible than role-restrictive approaches.

Sandor et al provide a critique of event-based approaches which only permit subscription based on event types, arguing that the need to define event types *a priori* make such systems inflexible. By using content-based subscription, Elvin avoids this problem.

Previous work on notification services for awareness within the CSCW community has tended to focus on the support of synchronous collaborative work. The term is used to refer to a variety of systems with very different behaviors and which may provide notifications directly to users or only to applications or both.

Ramduny et al (1998) introduce a taxonomy for characterizing notification services based on their communication behavior and the level at which they operate (system or user). The authors distinguish between services primarily on how they enable a client that effects a change in some piece of data (the active client) to communicate information about that change (the notification) to a client that wants to know (the passive client). They also discuss the possibilities of differences in pace and volume between system level services and corresponding user level services.

In the terms offered by Ramduny et al, Elvin is a pure notification service (active client tells notification service, notification service tells passive client) which remains completely separate from the observed data. Elvin primarily serves the system level, offering support for applications to exchange notifications but little explicit support for user notification and volume or impedance matching.

Perhaps the best known CSCW notification service is Lotus PlaceHolder, which is based on Notification Service Transfer Protocol or NSTP (Patterson et al. 1996). Rather than providing a pure notification service, the designers of NSTP opted to focus on facilities for synchronous collaborative applications. They therefore conflate a notification service with a centralized data store for shared data. The work primarily focuses on providing a protocol (based loosely on HTTP) for interoperation between notification services. PlaceHolder is a sample implementation of such a service. The notification service includes a number of design notions such as, Things (roughly, application objects) in Places (generalization of application session), with Facades (which moderate access to Things). The service is also envisioned as providing some system and some user level services ("place browsing" allows users to move between Places).

The design of NSTP means that PlaceHolder will primarily be useful for the construction of bespoke synchronous collaborative applications. The explicit centralization of shared data makes it difficult to integrate PlaceHolder with existing applications. The complexity of the required implementation also makes it difficult to produce competing servers for PlaceHolder to interoperate with. In contrast with Elvin, the service is also essentially channel-based and no concessions to scalability appear to have been made.

Hall et al (1996) also focus on the design of a shared data communication service for synchronous groupware with CORONA. The designers of CORONA however, partition the system into a number of services and maintain the 'publish-subscribe service' as a pure notification service using a channel-based approach. Optimized for wide-area use, the publish-subscribe service multicasts published notifications to distributor nodes which in turn multicast to other distributors which then send on to local subscribers. This enhances scalability by "minimizing system-wide awareness and change". This use of multicasting is not available to systems such as Elvin which do not rely on channel-based subscription.

Lövstrand (1991) describes the Khronika system, which for several years was in use at Rank Xerox EuroPARC (Now Xerox Research Centre Europe, Cambridge). Khronika was fundamentally an event database that stored user-level events (meetings, brown-bag lunches, etc). Users could discover events by browsing the database or by assigning 'event daemons' to issue notifications when certain kinds of events triggered. The system is very relevant to our discussion because it had a constraint language allowing users to specify quite complex subscriptions to events in which they were interested. We can consider Khronika's constraint language analogous to Elvin's subscription language.

Khronika is also interesting because it was primarily a user-level notification service not a system-level service. Despite its intended domain, its design was quite similar to Elvin.

Using Elvin for the Workaday World

As indicated above, Elvin quickly began to be used by a number of different research and prototyping groups within our organisation. A key trigger in facilitating this usage was an application called Tickertape (Fitzpatrick et al. 1998; Parsowith et al. 1998) (to be discussed below) that developers initially created to give a visual display of event traffic. Tickertape enabled people to quickly understand what Elvin was, how it worked, and how it could be used for their own purposes.

The usage examples that we discuss here were thought of and/or developed by a wide variety of people most of whom were not directly involved in the Elvin project, most of whom were technical developers and some users. Some of the systems, applications or tools take advantage of the Tickertape interface. Others use Elvin directly, plugging it into some other piece of software. Some are primarily to support 'individual' tasks. Others are to support collaborative aspects of work. Some started out to support an individual and were soon found to be useful as a way of providing others with the information they needed to better coordinate their work. The authors are also active users or developers of Elvin and/or its many associated tools.

In the following section, we briefly discuss the methodology for this study. We then separate the following discussion into *bi-directional* uses (where users themselves can generate messages as notifications as well as receive notifications, supporting awareness through interaction) and *uni-directional* uses (where notifications are generated from some external source, supporting awareness via information flow) (Parsowith et al. 1998).

Methodology

The following usage comments are an aggregate of a Tickertape usage study reported in (Parsowith et al. 1998) (relying on semi-structured interviews and some conversational analysis based on 20,000 element log-files) and a further survey and semi-structured interviews conducted at the time of writing. In our initial study, Tickertape had roughly 20 users, usage has risen slowly in the last year to roughly 40 users.

The analysis of that data has been informal, without reference to a theoretical framework.

Bi-Directional Uses of Elvin

Three key tools give users access to Elvin for bi-directional use: Tickertape, Tickerchat and CoffeeBiff.

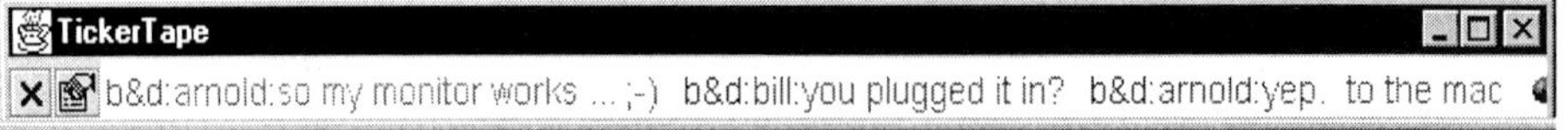

Figure 3 The Tickertape interface showing exemplary scrolling messages

Tickertape

Tickertape is a highly tailorable tool that uses Elvin. It is both a producer and a consumer of notifications. It displays notifications that the user subscribes to and it can be used to construct chat-style messages that are sent as notifications.

The Tickertape interface, as shown in Figure 3, consists of a single resizable, rectangular window, showing small, colour-coded messages that scroll from right to left. Each message corresponds to an Elvin notification of a specific format that has been received by the Tickertape application. For example, the left-most message in the figure is from user 'arnold', has been sent to the group 'b&d', and has the text 'so my monitor works'. The Tickertape is designed to take up minimal space – the active area is a single line, and borders, etc can be removed to make the Tickertape 'fade into the background'. Most users position their Tickertape(s)[2] on the edges of their screens, where they provide a simple kind of peripheral access to the information that scrolls by.

Tickertape users subscribe to messages at two levels: they indicate the 'groups' they are interested in, where group is an attribute contained in the content of all messages to which Tickertape can subscribe, and they indicate some filters over the contents of messages which have the appropriate group attribute values. A simple set of dialog and menu list boxes is used to allow non-programmers to perform this customisation. If events have a MIME attachment, associated graphics on the scrolling marquee indicate this, and the user can trigger the attachment with a mouse click.

Individual notifications have a lifetime over which their appearance fades from colour to grey, thus providing an indication of how timely the information is. The lifetime is user-defined for each group. Users can also choose to delete or save a scrolling message by clicking on the message itself. Tickertape therefore provides users with a mechanism for controlling the transience of information.

Tickertape provides no persistent storage of notifications, once a message fades away – it is lost.

One of the most popular uses for Tickertape is as a lightweight channel-based *semi-synchronous chat tool*. Users can define new chat groups by agreement with their peers. Messages can be sent as Elvin notifications by clicking on the Tickertape and using the resulting pop-up dialogue shown in Figure 4. Messages are

---

[2] One of the authors of this paper runs three tickers at all times, each customised to different types of information and running at different speeds.

received as text on the Tickertape (Figure 3 shows an example conversation).

Examples of interactive groups are: the 'Chat' group for all the people in the organisation (used as a general discussion forum and for user-generated announcements), the 'lunch' group (used by regular lunch-goers to organise lunch times and venues), the 'b&d' group (for Bill and David who are working closely together on a project) and the Elvin group (for the developers of Elvin).

Such chat groups are used extensively within the organisation by both technical and non-technical staff, especially as people are distributed across different offices on different floors and, for a time, in different buildings. Tickertape is also used by people working from home to interact with colleagues in the office. In fact, the authors of this paper used it to discuss the paper while one was located in another country. It supports work-related discussions – a recent newcomer used the Chat group to ask for help in setting up his new environment and finding out what services were available. It is also used for social chitchat, and for broadcast announcements, such as "paging Dr Tim" (acting as a silent public announcement or paging system).

Interactions over these bi-directional groups tend to be spontaneous, short, informal, often irreverent, and 'bursty', similar in nature to face-to-face conversation. They incorporate the synchronicity and immediacy of the telephone with the asynchronous style of email and are especially suited for temporally relevant information, such as "there are cakes in the kitchen".

Very quickly, Tickertape has become embedded into the normal working environment of the organisation as yet another means for communication and interaction along with the telephone, email, face-to-face discussions, and porthole video images. Each of these has particular uses for which they excel and Tickertape has found its niche amongst them. It is not uncommon to see a discussion over Tickertape that ends with a comment such as "uh oh, see email…" or "wait a minute … I'm coming down" when the content of the discussion becomes more detailed than can be usefully handled in short chat messages.

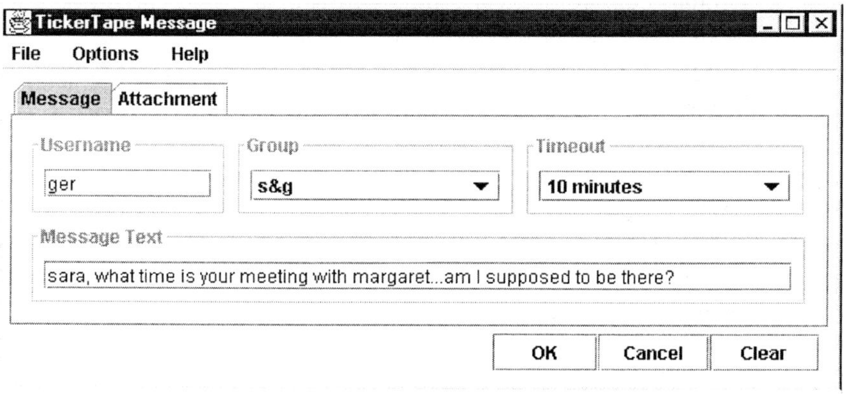

Figure 4 Sending a chat message via the Tickertape Dialog

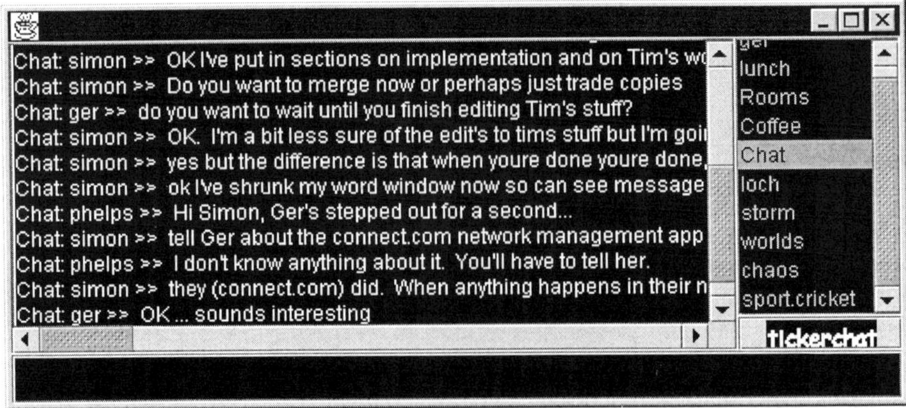

Figure 5 A Tickerchat discussion. One person was at home, the others are in the office.

Tickerchat

For various reasons, three separate programmers developed a chat-tool-style interface to Tickertape. All of these *Tickerchat* implementations provide the same basic interface, shown in Figure 5: a large window in which previous messages are shown, a line at the bottom in which one may enter new messages, and some way of selecting the group to which one's messages should be directed. Messages shown in Tickerchat do not fade, they simply scroll up the transcript window. Users can choose to clear the buffer or save the buffer when they no longer want to see the message stream.

The Tickerchat tool extends the transience of the information in Tickertape making it more convenient for discussion as opposed to notification. This persistent quality allows users greater discretion about when they attend to discussions because they know they won't miss anything through time-out. One developer was motivated to build a Tickerchat by his frustration at regularly finding, upon returning to his desk after an absence, a raging debate on the Tickertape in which the original issues had long since faded out.

Many users now choose to run both a Tickertape and a Tickerchat, using the Tickerchat when they enter a discussion and reserving the tape for observation of the flow of information.

Churchill and Bly (1999) study the use of a MUD for informal communication and coordination in a laboratory quite similar to our own. While Tickertape and Tickerchat provide affordances similar to those of the MUD, with similar positive experiences to those reported by Churchill and Bly. We have avoided some of the pitfalls that they describe, notably the problems with participating in multiple ongoing chats simultaneously, and the disconnection between the MUD and the user's real-world tools. Our tools avoid problems with multiple channels by simply providing access to multiple channels of conversation on different ticker channels. By designing Tickertape in particular as a peripheral application that typically sits on the top or bottom edge of the screen, we obviate the need to always switch context between the chat tool and other tools.

CoffeeBiff

A different example of a bi-directional use of Elvin is *CoffeeBiff*. When people go to the kitchen for a coffee break, they can click on the CoffeeBiff icon to indicate their intention to colleagues, as shown in Figure 6. If a person knows when her friends from other parts of the building are taking a break it can help her to coordinate her break times, or to identify when a colleague will be in the kitchen and possibly free for a casual chat. A background application subscribes to CoffeeBiff notifications and sends a *second-level* notification to the Tickertape "Coffee" group when more than five people are drinking coffee, indicating that some kind of party is clearly in progress.

Figure 6. CoffeeBiff icon with number and scrolling names.

Uni-Directional Uses of Elvin

Another significant use of Tickertape has been for uni-directional events where pre-existing external event streams are instrumented to produce Tickertape notifications. This supports awareness through notification, providing content-based information filtering. Event streams in regular use include: postings to Usenet news groups, commercial news sources on the World Wide Web (WWW), personal email, and other sources such as a schedule system. Various developers around the organisation have written programs to translate an event source into an Elvin notification.

Content Filtering

Users can subscribe to these event sources by content. This means, for example, that a user can essentially say "show me all the postings to comp.groupware that mention 'shared drawing tool'" or "show me all the ABC headline news postings except for sport". Whenever a corresponding posting is detected, a Tickertape message will display the subject header with the text of the new article attached in a MIME attachment. The attached article can be viewed with a mouse click.

Users have also used the content-based subscription feature to implement a form of social filtering of information. For example, several people have subscriptions of which mean "if this person from our organisation posts to the (newsgroup), tell me about it". This is making use of what they know about others' shared interests and areas of expertise – it is highly likely that if that person is contributing to a thread, then it will be of interest to them as well.

Users who take advantage of Usenet, WWW and email filtering in this way uniformly report that the way in which they interact with external information sources has been radically altered. Many users stated in interviews that the only time they go to a Usenet newsgroup now is when a Tickertape notification indicates there might be a thread of interest to them. Others never go to the source but read postings via Tickertape only.

Email Notification

There are now several ways for users to be alerted via Tickertape that they have received e-mail. Users can add a script to their mail processing (`.forward`) file which is run whenever they receive an email. This script generates a notification with appropriate summary information (sender, subject, and MIME information to access the message), and sends it to a private Tickertape group. More sophisticated versions of the script can be used in conjunction with automated mail filtering and sorting programs such as PROCMAIL. A user can access the email message directly by using the MIME attachment to open the appropriate folder and message. By enriching the messages generated by the mail script so that it contains more of, or all of, the mail message users can then use the content filtering capabilities of the subscription language to filter the mail-related notifications they see on the Tickertape.

Many users report that email is now far less of a distraction since they can see immediately who an email is from, and what its subject is, and thus make a quick judgment about whether it is important enough to stop what they are doing to go read it.

Advance Schedule Warning

We have already noted that Tickertape is particularly useful for presenting temporally relevant information of transient importance. This feature has been exploited in the instrumentation of the DSTC Rooms Booking calendar. At ten minutes prior to the booked time, a Tickertape notification is generated stating the time, room, and meeting description. Most obviously, this serves as a useful reminder to people. More importantly though, it serves as a general mechanism for making activities within the organisation more visible, and giving people a way of 'keeping an eye' on activities that they might not otherwise have known about.

Making Actions Visible

There are many examples of users writing code to generate events that reflect their activities in the virtual computing environment. One user, for example, has written scripts to generate a notification whenever he logs into or out of his workstation. In this way, others know when he has arrived at or leaves from work.

There are also 'file-watcher' and 'web-watcher' event generators that monitor changes to the network file stores and local web pages respectively and send out notifications via the relevant Tickertape groups. These serve as an important information source for people who rely on system files, maintain sections of the company Web, etc.

Analogous information is available via notifications generated from CVS. CVS is a revision control package used extensively within the DSTC to manage source code. Typically, a programmer will have a copy of the source tree of a project 'checked out'. She keeps the copy synchronised with the copies of other programmers by occasionally updating her copy in order to incorporate their changes and commit her own changes. As part of the 'commit' process, the user is prompted to log a comment as to what has changed and why. These comments play an important role in the coordination and articulation of software development by teams because others can go to the log file and read about what changes have happened (see Grinter 1997).

To enhance out-of-band communication among developers, and facilitate early identification of conflicts, we have extended CVS to generate a Tickertape notification that includes the commit comments whenever a commit is performed. In addition to providing warnings about various kinds of commit problems, such as a race condition, this informs the other programmers who subscribe to the 'CVS' group of what changes other users are making. In effect this makes visible the previously invisible activities of the user's colleagues. This allows the group of developers to contingently rearrange their work, negotiate to resolve problems, offer warnings and suggestions, and so on, all in a more timely manner than previously possible.

Other Elvin Applications

Other applications have been developed using Elvin as the underlying event notification structure. We will mention two here:

ORBIT: Although we described Elvin as generic notifications service rather than a service for a bespoke collaborative system, it can still be used in collaboration-specific environments as we have done with Orbit (Mansfield et al. 1997).

Orbit is a collaborative desktop environment that has a client-server architecture. When a client initiates interaction with the server, it uses a remote procedure call (RPC) mechanism (CORBA) to send a request to, and receive the reply, from the server. If the server initiates communication, it is because the server's state has changed and clients might need to be notified. In this case, it sends a notification of the state change via Elvin. This offloads the responsibility from the server to Elvin for keeping track of which client is interested in what information.

Tickertape has also been extended so that bi-directional groups can be created that correspond to a group zone, thus providing Orbit users with a low-bandwidth communications tool that is specific to their work context. By adding additional information to the notifications that the Orbit server sends to its clients, we were able to display these notifications in Tickertape as well. For example, when the membership of a group zone changes, the same notification that is sent to update the state of the client can also be displayed on the Tickertapes of the members of that zone to tell them of the new (or lost) member.

Network Management: An Internet service provider runs status on each of its servers which then forward information via Elvin to diagnostic correlation engines. When problems with the status of a server are identified (or diagnostic messages fail to arrive), events are sent via an Elvin-to-pager gateway to the pagers worn by the sysadmins on duty.

Summary

In this section, we have shown a variety of ways in which Elvin has been used within the organisation. The chat-based tools and Coffee Biff tool that use Elvin for both production and consumption of events (we called this 'bi-directional') have been significant additions to existing communication resources for supporting interactions, both for work and fun, in a distributed workplace. Not only have information and expertise been shared, but social cohesion and relationships have also been strengthened.

The uni-directional uses where Elvin, mostly via Tickertape, has been used to push information to users from externally produced event streams has radically changed the ways in which people go about accessing and using many of these external sources (such as email, WWW, Usenet news etc). Other uni-directional uses, for example, where CVS or the Room Booking systems have been instrumented, have facilitated opportunities for far greater awareness of activities and events both within the virtual realm and the social/organisational realm than has otherwise been possible. This is because Elvin and Tickertape give a way to make the information available or 'present' as a perceptual resource for awareness.

Why Does Elvin Work?

Many of the cases given above are not intentionally CSCW-related, and this is precisely what makes them interesting to us. They are all examples of ever more powerful facilities being evolved through the incremental instrumentation or augmentation of workaday tools.

Moreover, the user community were prepared to put in this development effort because they believed, and indeed found, that the facilities would be useful for their for their everyday work (thus avoiding Grudin's (1994) work-benefit disparity problem). Perhaps one of the most surprising facts about the uptake of Elvin-based services around DSTC (and beyond) is that there has hardly been any effort to promote the use of the system; its uptake has been entirely spontaneous, as our users came to recognise and take advantages of the benefits.

The essence of Elvin's success is that it fulfilled a key need: providing a way to gather and redistribute collaboration-focussed information produced during the everyday work of our users. Another key element of its success was that it did not detract from or inhibit the use of existing tool sets, yet provided the ability to flexibly, spontaneously and incrementally construct a suitable workaday environment that afforded substantially improved awareness and interaction.

Gutwin and Greenberg (1996) define a taxonomy of information that users need to be aware of in a synchronous collaborative application. When the target domain is the larger context of all of the user's computer-based work, gathering this information is even more challenging. We cannot provide a collaboration toolkit and request that programmers use it, since they are not usually constructing applications which they would think of as collaborative. Indeed we cannot provide a collaboration environment and request that users use it, either; users are going to use the tools that they need to accomplish their work, and shy away from tools that inhibit this accomplishment.

Using Gutwin and Greenberg's taxonomy, Elvin has been used to inform about participant, location, activity level, actions, changes and objects. In so doing, Elvin helped to make perceptible a significant portion of the 'event-based' cues which we use as perceptual resources for awareness to shape our workaday lives, and which have been missing in virtual (ie., computer-based) activities. It also facilitated lightweight informal interactions in a distributed environment.

Elvin Design Characteristics

We believe there are four *design characteristics* of Elvin that have contributed to its widespread use, specifically: simplicity; genericity; performance; and informality. These characteristics make the use of Elvin popular with authors of new software and straightforward to add to existing software. Tools constructed with Elvin also tend to exhibit these characteristics, which makes them popular with the broader user community. We will discuss these characteristics in turn.

Simplicity

The key design feature of Elvin is the simplicity of its API. Because the Elvin API is available for several programming languages, authors can usually use Elvin from their choice of development language. Because the API is simple (usually involving in the order of five method or procedure calls) and at a high-level of abstraction, it is an appealing choice for busy developers. Developers often try to use Elvin for tasks outside of its design criteria (such as mimicking RPC behaviour) for this reason alone. The designers often find themselves in the enviable position of explaining to hopeful Elvin users why they should **not** use it for their proposed task!

The service is also accessible from the command-line making it feasible to use the service without extensive programming. Technically-aware users can easily write shell scripts to issue or subscribe to notifications. The log in/log out notification mentioned previously is implemented using shell scripts, for example. For the even less technically aware, GUI applications such as Tickertape provide an indirect way to use Elvin.

A secondary and related reason is that Elvin programming is fun. The various Tickertape and Tickerchats, CVS, mail handlers, etc are all examples of developers building simple applications for sheer enjoyment, and then propagating into the wider community. This sense of fun and adventure soon passed from the narrower developer community to the larger community, including computer-phobic staff members (among them authors of this paper).

Genericity

Ramduny et al (1998) characterise notification services like Elvin (in which an active client tells the service about a change in some data and then the service tells a passive client about the change) as a "pure" notification service. Elvin lacks any inbuilt policies about information distribution and it stores none of the information it transmits. Its only purpose is the notification of events.

This means that Elvin can be used in any application that requires distributed notification, not just synchronous collaborative applications. It also means that it is not typically onerous to add Elvin code to (or 'elvinize') existing applications. Its lack of policy means that it is more likely to 'fit' into the target application.

The process of elvinizing an application is simply that of adding notifications wherever significant status changes occur in the application. Status change notifications allow any interested parties elsewhere in the network stay informed about the state of the application. This can be used to provide feedthrough (in Ramduny's terms) to other users or to share status with other applications or both.

Because Elvin is generic, programmers often add notification code to an application for reasons other than providing awareness. Some applications, for example Orbit, use Elvin as a means of implementing change notifications for a distributed Model-View-Controller architecture. Those notifications can still be used to gather awareness information even though that was not the programmer's intent.

Performance

The design of Elvin emphasizes efficient performance. The quench feature is designed specifically to minimize unnecessary network traffic. The consequence of quench (particularly when quenching is performed automatically by the producer API) is that developers can add notifications wherever status changes occur without regard to who might receive them now or in the future.

Quenching suggests potential applications such as using Elvin to generate debugging trace from immature applications. Rather than requiring the author to explicitly place conditional statements around trace generating code, they could simply use Elvin notification code which would produce no trace unless some consumer (a transcript window perhaps) subscribed to it.

Quenching allows an application author to know that unnecessary notifications will not be sent. Combining quenching with other design characteristics such as genericity and simplicity means that it costs little more to include notifications of significant status changes. This low cost encourages programmers to include such notifications just in case the notifications become useful later.

Informality

Elvin notifications are not explicitly typed. Every notification is simply a tuple of attribute-value pairs. Elvin does not require that any semantics (other than base type) be formally associated with any of these attributes or the tuple as a whole. Consumers subscribe to notifications based on content and typically select only what information they need from any notification they receive. This means that application authors can add more information to the tuple as the application evolves.

For example, the notification format for Tickertape initially included only attributes for the group, user, message text and timeout. Later, attributes were added to the notifications to encode MIME attachments. These additions had no effect on older Tickertape clients, which simply ignored the new attributes. As new requirements were determined additional attributes were unproblematically included.

As this example illustrates, this property of *informality* makes piecemeal growth and evolution of a large-scale event infrastructure feasible. All potential consumers will subscribe to the notification in the same way: using the Elvin subscription language. No *a priori* typing system – of message contents or structure – needs to be imposed on the set of notifications an application can send. The informality also means that awareness clients can gather awareness information based on any information in any notifications, not just based on what types of events the original authors thought might be interesting or useful. In this way awareness clients based on Elvin avoid problems associated with having to pre-specify all message types (Sandor et al. 1997).

The Tickertape GUI

Without the Tickertape interface, however, it is doubtful whether these design features alone would have made Elvin so popular among the user community. A significant effort in making any notification service more accessible for user-level awareness is the effort involved in building an appropriate GUI. With Tickertape, that effort has already been expended.

Despite some obvious shortcomings of Tickertape both as an application and an interface, its main feature is that it exists. This makes Elvin accessible, understandable and usable by the broader user community. Once the user invests the initial effort to install and configure Tickertape, the subsequent barrier to usage for a whole variety of purposes (possible because of its tailorability) is very low.

It also promotes less than optimal strategies. For example, in our translation of commercial WWW news pages into Tickertape notifications, in many cases more specialised interfaces would probably be more suitable. In the room booking notifications example, it would be useful to have an interface that would allow one to cancel a booking. Our online notifications from the weather station could probably be better represented graphically than in a scrolling text line. On the other hand because of the difficulty of producing special-purpose graphical interfaces, it is unlikely that any of these interfaces would ever have been built. Because Tickertape was there, it was easy to add additional information sources and the interface via Tickertape was good enough, so the solutions worked well enough.

Summary

Elvin provides a simple way for application authors to provide information about significant status changes to other parties in the network. The potential ubiquity of the information and its lack of explicit semantics mean that gathering information about user presence, location, activity level, actions, the changes they are making and the objects they are acting on is feasible even from applications that are not designed for collaboration. This point is extremely important.

Conclusions & Future Work

The thesis of this paper has been that a generic notification service can be used to both enable users to maintain awareness of the activities or status of others and support interaction between users. It does this by providing users with a stream of information about events in the virtual and physical world and providing powerful tools for selecting relevant information. We have illustrated how a number of different event sources (for example, Web news, CVS, email delivery, information stores) can be instrumented to produce meaningful events, and how clients can be used to feed this information to users in a relatively unobtrusive fashion. Gluing this all together through content-based message subscription provides a high degree of flexibility, since new consumers or producers can be added independently of one another. Potentially any state-based information source or event stream could be instrumented in this fashion, and many different kinds of clients could consume these events. The limiting factor, as always, is whether the effort one must expend to get the notifications generated in the first place is worth the resulting benefits.

In our case we focused on information that was clearly 'out there' and reduced the effort required by users to access it (by pushing it through notifications). A number of immediate benefits resulted. These include timely access to information and an ongoing perception of what individuals around the organisation are doing. The examples given clearly demonstrate that Elvin helps to do this, precisely because it augments people's real, workaday environment and allows them to share (or make visible) the resulting information with their peers.

Future work on Elvin will focus on infrastructure issues concerned with scaling and quench propagation, secure notifications and event correlation – the generation of higher-order events from patterns of simpler events. We also plan to continue to augment the working environment, on one hand through further instrumentation of applications and utilities. Much of this work we expect will continue the tradition of work of this kind in projects such as Keryx (Low 1997). We also plan to begin instrumenting the physical world, through the development of sensors and actuators that can transmit and respond to Elvin events. We hope this approach can begin to more effectively integrate the virtual and physical worlds.

Acknowledgments

Bill Segall and David Arnold are the key designers and developers of Elvin. Julian Boot has also contributed to the design and development of Elvin. We acknowledge Sara Parsowith for her work on earlier evaluations of Tickertape usage. We also thank the user community at the DSTC who contributed to the evolution of Elvin applications and appropriated it into their daily lives. More information about Elvin can be found http://www.dstc.edu.au/Elvin.

The work reported in this paper has been funded in part by the Co-operative Research Centre Program through the Department of Industry, Science & Resources of the Commonwealth Government of Australia.

This work has also been supported in part by the United States Defence Advanced Research Projects Agency under grants F30602-96-2-0264 and F30603-94-C-0161 (both administered by the US Air Force through Rome Laboratories). The views and conclusions contained in this document are those of the authors and should not be interpreted as representing the official policies, expressed or implied, of the Defence Advanced Projects Research Agency or the U.S. Government.

References

Benford, S., and Fahlen, L. (1993). "A Spatial Model of Interaction in Large Virtual Environments." *Third European Conference on Computer-Supported Cooperative Work (ECSCW '93)*, Milan, Italy, 109-124.

Churchill, E., and Bly, S. (1999). "Virtual Environments at Work: ongoing use of MUDs in the Workplace." *International Joint Conference on Work Activities Coordination and Collaboration*, San Francisco.

Dourish, P., and Bellotti, V. (1992). "Awareness and Coordination in Shared Workspaces." *CSCW'92*, 107-114.

Fitzpatrick, G. (1998). "The Locales Framework: Understanding and Designing for Cooperative Work," , The University of Queensland, Brisbane.

Fitzpatrick, G., Parsowith, S., Segall, B., and Kaplan, S. (1998). "Tickertape: Awareness in a single line." *CHI'98 Summary*, Los Angeles, CA, 281-282.

Fuchs, L., Pankoke-Babatz, U., and Prinz, W. (1995). "Supporting Cooperative Awareness with Local Even Mechanisms: the GroupDesk System." *Fourth European Conference on Computer-Supported Cooperative Work*, Stockholm, Sweden, 247-262.

Grinter, R. E. (1997). "Doing Software Development: Occasions for Automation and Formalisation." *Fifth European Conference on Computer Supported Cooperative Work (ECSCW97)*, Lancaster, UK, 173-188.

Grudin, J. (1994). "Groupware and Social Dynamics: Eight Challenges for Developers." *Communications of the ACM*, 37, 93-105.

Gutwin, C., and Greenberg, S. (1996). "Workspace Awareness for Groupware." *Common ground: CHI'96 Conference Companion*, Vancouver, Canada, 208-209.

Hall, R. W., Mathur, A., Jahanian, F., Prakash, A., and Rassmussen, C. (1996). "Corona: A Communication Service for Scalable, Reliable Group Collaboration Systems." *CSCW'96*, Boston, MA, 140-149.

Heath, C., and Luff, P. (1992). "Collaboration and control; crisis management and multimedia technology in London Underground line control rooms." *Computer Supported Cooperative Work*, 1(1-2), 69-94.

Lovstrand, L. (1991). "Being Selectively Aware with the Khronika System." *ECSCW'91*, Amsterdam, 265-277.

Low, C. (1997). "Integrating Communication Services" IEEE Communications, v35 n6, June 1997.

Mansfield, T., Kaplan, S., Fitzpatrick, G., Phelps, T., Fitzpatrick, M., and Taylor, R. (1997). "Evolving Orbit: A Progress Report on Building Locales." *Conference on Supporting Group Work (Group '97)*, Phoenix, Arizona, 241-250.

Moran, T. P., and Anderson, R. J. (1990). "The Workaday World as a Paradigm for CSCW Design." *CSCW'90*, 381-393.

Parsowith, S., Fitzpatrick, G., Kaplan, S., Segall, B., and Boot, J. (1998). "Tickertape; Notification and Communication in a Single Line." *APCHI'98*, Japan, 139-144.

Patterson, J. F., Day, M., and Kucan, J. (1996). "Notification Servers for Synchronous Groupware." *CSCW'96*, Boston, MA, 122-129.

Ramduny, D., Dix, A., and Rodden, T. (1998). "Exploring the Design Space for Notification Servers." *CSCW'98*, Seattle, WA, 227-235.

Robertson, T. (1997). "Cooperative Work and Lived Cognition: A Taxonomy of Embodied Actions." *Fifth European Conference on Computer Supported Cooperative Work (ECSCW97)*, Lancaster, UK, 205-220.

Sandor, O., Bogdan, C., and Bowers, J. (1997). "Aether: An Awareness Engine for CSCW." *Fifth European Conference on Computer Supported Cooperative Work (ECSCW97)*, Lancaster, UK, 221-236.

Segall, B., and Arnold, D. (1997). "Elvin has left the building: A publish/subscribe notification service with quenching." *Queensland AUUG Summer Technical Conference*, Brisbane, Australia.

S. Bødker, M. Kyng, and K. Schmidt (eds.). *Proceedings of the Sixth European Conference on Computer-Supported Cooperative Work, 12-16 September 1999, Copenhagen, Denmark*
©1999 Kluwer Academic Publishers. Printed in the Netherlands

Index of Authors